THE LETTERS OF
ST BERNARD
OF CLAIRVAUX

THE LETTERS OF
ST BERNARD
OF CLAIRVAUX

TRANSLATED BY
BRUNO SCOTT JAMES
INTRODUCTION BY
BEVERLY MAYNE KIENZLE

CISTERCIAN PUBLICATIONS

First published in 1953 by Burns and Oates

First published in this edition in the United Kingdom in 1998 by
Sutton Publishing Limited, Stroud, Gloucestershire, GL5 2BU

First published in the United States in 1998 by
CISTERCIAN PUBLICATIONS

Distribution: Saint Joseph's Abbey
167 North Spencer Road
Spencer MA 01562-1233

Editorial: Institute of Cistercian Studies
Western Michigan University
Kalamazoo, MI 49008

ISBN 0 87907 162 1

Cover illustration: the earliest known image of St Bernard and the only one from his
lifetime. Sitting before an open book within the opening initial of his first treatise, *The
Steps of Humility*, St Bernard's right hand is raised in blessing, his left hand holds a knife
From the Benedictine abbey of St Augustine, Canterbury.

The work of Cistercian Publications is made possible in part by support fr
Michigan University to The Institute of Cistercian Studies

Printed in Great Britain by
Biddles Limited, Guildford, Surrey.

NEW INTRODUCTION

The need for reprinting Bruno Scott James's English translation of
Saint Bernard of Clairvaux's letters demonstrates both the enduring
importance of the letters for students of medieval Christianity and the
high quality and vitality of James's translation. The letters, gems of
literary art and mirrors of monastic culture and society in the twelfth
century, still provide engaging and entertaining reading as well as
fruitful material for scholarly endeavours. They both edify and delight,
calling to mind Horace's recommendation that poets should write to
benefit and amuse the reader, to make their words at the same time
pleasing and instructive for life: 'Aut prodesse volunt aut delectare
poetae/aut simul et iucunda et idonea dicere vitae' (De arte poetica, 333).
In that sense, Bernard's letters are truly classics of literature, and like
other classic works, they are read with fresh insights by each new
generation of readers. Understanding the culture to which they belong
enriches the reader's appreciation of single letters and of the entire
corpus. Each of the texts constitutes a small, integral masterpiece, like
an intricate section of a tapestry, that benefits and delights the beholder.
The entire collection instructs and pleases the reader with the harmony
of scenes forming a panorama of twelfth-century monasticism. To
enhance the reader's appreciation of the letters, this new introduction
first looks rapidly at recent studies on Bernard of Clairvaux's life and
character, then views the role letters generally played in monastic
culture and the insights on monastic spirituality and twelfth-century
society offered specifically by Bernard's letters. The final section
examines briefly the differences between the Latin editions of the
letters used by James and the more recent edition by J. Leclercq and
H.-M. Rochais which James was awaiting with great anticipation at the
time his translation went to press. A comprehensive comparison of the
new edition with James's translation and the necessary reworking of the
translation awaits another reprinting of the letters.

BERNARD OF CLAIRVAUX: RECENT STUDIES
In 1990, the nine-hundredth anniversary of Bernard's birth stimulated a
body of new research on the man whom Giles Constable assesses as 'the
great master of late medieval and early modern piety' (Constable, 326)
and Brian Patrick McGuire calls 'the difficult saint' (McGuire, 17). The
scope of scholarly studies on Bernard indicates the widespread interest

his works hold for students and specialists in history, theology, spirituality, liturgy, art, rhetoric, and other fields. A selection of the vast research on Bernard published since 1990 appears in the back matter of the present volume.

The events of Bernard's life and the traditional stories related about him are contained in James's introduction and will not be repeated here. From the letters James traces a brief, psychological portrait of Bernard, a man of 'tempestuous temperament'. Recent studies tend to strive for an understanding of the man behind the hagiographical legends and for an explanation of how Bernard maintained a balance between the contemplative monastic life and his intense involvement in affairs of the world.

THE LETTER IN MONASTIC CULTURE

In an electronic age when e-mail is replacing the carefully penned letter, readers may not grasp how letters can be such valuable historical and biographical documents. It will be beneficial to consider the importance of letter writing in the twelfth century and particularly in monastic culture.

All medieval monastic literature issued from life in the monastery, its permeation with the Scriptures, and its integration of the oral, aural, and written word through recitation (speaking out loud), listening, and reading. Reciting, listening, and reading were key elements of the monastic day, all involving the Scriptures or texts permeated by them. Monks recited the divine office that incorporated much of the Scriptures, intoning the whole of the Psalter, for example, each week. They listened to talks on the *Rule of Benedict* with its strong scriptural base. They also heard sermons that commented on the Scriptures, and letters, sermons, and saints' lives read aloud. Those texts proclaimed *in alta voce* were generally composed for public reading in imitation of an oral style. The *Rule* provided for private silent reading as well as reading aloud to the community. The silent reader voiced the words either with a slight murmuring sound or without uttering them aloud at all.

Since the monastic composition and use of texts intertwined oral, aural, and written elements, scholars encounter difficulty in separating the oral from the written in the extant texts. Specialists generally search for indications of orality, such as plural direct address or exhortations, to identify sermons, while the hallmarks of a letter are the features of its standard form: the salutation (*salutatio*), securing of good will (*benevolentiae captatio*), narration (*narratio*), petition (*petitio*), and conclusion (*conclusio*). These elements of letter form were codified in manuals known as *artes dictaminis*, guides to correct style in letter writing.[1] A talented writer such as Bernard of Clairvaux knew these formulas well and varied them deliberately to make a special impact on his reader.

The letter and the sermon are two of the literary genres represented in medieval monastic writing. Other genres included exegetical commentaries, *florilegia* (collections of sayings and stories), and histories including saints' lives and chronicles.[2] In form and function, letters, sermons, exegetical commentaries, and shorter treatises overlapped: their boundaries were so fluid that the function of one could substitute for another. Of these literary forms, letters and sermons perhaps have the closest similarities. Both could substitute for conversations, and a letter could stand in the place of a sermon. When received, letters were often read aloud either by individual readers or by a lector to a congregation. After praising the superiority of the living word over the spoken, Bernard himself explains that a letter serves as a substitute for a conversation: '. . . being absent from you, . . . I must satisfy myself with the second best alternative of a letter' (L 424, p. 494). In Letter 392 Bernard describes how his letter substitutes for a sermon: 'This zeal of mine impels me to write in a letter what I would far sooner inscribe upon your hearts with my voice, if I had the power to follow my will in the matter' (p. 463). Both genres, letter and sermon, were solidly grounded on the Bible and could have persuasive power over their audiences, whether congregations or individual readers.

The eleventh and twelfth centuries represented a sort of Golden Age of letter-writing, followed by a decline in the thirteenth century.[3] When sent over long distances from one monastery to another, letters linked distant communities. Monastic correspondence involved messages of friendship, advice, consolation, or inspiration. They often provided encouragement to persevere in the monastic vocation or persuaded new recruits to undertake it. Letters of recommendation, business letters, and discussions of doctrine also were exchanged. Saint Benedict must have anticipated some problems arising from the transmittal of letters, for the *Rule* stipulates that letters be sent to the addressee through the abbot: 'On no account shall a monk be allowed to receive letters, tokens or any little gift whatsoever from his parents or anyone else, or from his brethren, or to give the same, without the Abbot's permission' (*RB* 54). The reference to letters exchanged among the brothers implies that, in the silence of the monastery, letters between members of the same community sometimes provided a means of communication.

People in high positions enlisted special messengers to deliver letters. A few examples from Bernard's correspondence clarify the process of letter transmission. Bernard's Letter 389 recommends the noted scholar John of Salisbury who carried the recommendation himself to the recipient. Other letters such as 264 and 424 indicate that the messenger conveyed a confidential message aloud in addition to the written text. Some describe the letter-bearer as one dear to Bernard (L 268, 269) and commend him to the recipient (L 290). The seal carrying Bernard's personal stamp authenticated the letter's authorship. Seals were susceptible to forgery, however, and Bernard states in Letter 354 that he had to have a new seal made because his had been forged. The new seal also was stolen by Bernard's infamous secretary Nicholas (L 363).

Besides the correspondence relayed by personal messengers, communication between monasteries was made possible by regular courier service that circulated the announcements of deaths from one religious house to another in the form of a mortuary roll commonly called the 'Book of the Dead.' The messenger arrived at a monastery, where bell-ringing announced his visit and summoned the monks to gather for a communal reading of the message. At the end of the mortuary roll, a blank space was left for acknowledgements, condolences, or news to be written; additional vellum was added when needed. The rolls could become very lengthy; one from the abbey of St Bavo measures almost 100 feet. The couriers transporting mortuary rolls delivered other correspondence as well and thereby allowed the sending of letters from one monastery to another.[4]

The Cistercian administrative structure, with its network of mother and daughter houses, and its annual meeting called 'general chapter', required abbots to travel and thereby generated the exchange of letters and ensured their conveyance. Abbots made regular visitations to their monastery's mother house and also to their own daughter house(s). They also attended the general chapter, and from there, they conveyed messages home to their abbeys. Some abbots were appointed to deliver penances to the absent abbots whose excuses for non-attendance had not been accepted. All these journeys of abbots within the order required and facilitated the exchange of letters.[5]

Communities also received letters from a bishop or an abbot in response to their questions about the Scriptures or concerning thorny theological problems. The letter substituted for the abbot's physical presence among them and for his speaking to them on certain issues. Its arrival could be the occasion for great excitement in the monastery. The Cistercian Hugh of Francigena, monk at Silvanès in southern France, described how the monks of that abbey received a letter from Gaucelin, bishop of Lodève (1161-87).[6] They read silently but mouthed the words: 'It was snatched, stolen, and taken by everyone, and whoever was able to get it would read and reread it, sitting motionless, hidden from others in a corner of the cloister, opening his mouth like a pauper eating in secret.'[7]

Letters of an influential figure such as Bernard of Clairvaux had great potential for persuasion and his recommendations were in high demand.[8] Consequently, letters of recommendation from the abbot of Clairvaux appear throughout the collection (L 36, 38, 44, 284, 287, 337).

In Letter 339 Bernard expresses his anger that someone obtained letters of recommendation written in his name without his knowledge. Persuasive letters on matters of widespread interest were often addressed to a whole community or to the people of a region, where they were read aloud in the churches and served as sermons. Bernard's letters on the Crusades were proclaimed to many congregations.[9] Letter 394 alludes to the process for public proclamation of such a letter, a decree that '. . . a copy of this letter should be carried everywhere and that the bishops and priests should proclaim it to the people of God' (p. 467).

A MIRROR OF MONASTIC SPIRITUALITY AND MEDIEVAL SOCIETY

Bruno Scott James wrote eloquently about Bernard's literary style and the strength of the abbot's spirit and personality as it radiates from his letters. The present introduction will briefly touch upon some of the many aspects of monastic spirituality, ecclesiastical affairs, and medieval society reflected in the letters. Many letters are not confined to one theme or issue but weave together several. The numbers of a few letters dealing with the topic specified appear in parentheses below, but limitations on space do not allow for complete listings here.

Bernard turned his attention so frequently to matters outside the monastery that he described himself as a chimaera: 'neither cleric or layman' who 'kept the habit of a monk' but 'long ago abandoned the life' (L 326, p. 402).[10] He intervened in numerous conflicts involving ecclesiastical politics. Letters 127 to 149 treat the 1130 schism and Bernard's effort to rally support for Innocent II; those range from appeals for support addressed to the cities of Genoa and Pisa to expressions of homesickness sent back to Clairvaux. Innocent II later heard Bernard's reproaches on behalf of Albero, archbishop of Trèves, who felt he lacked the pope's support (L 218, 220–222). Numerous letters sent advice to Pope Eugene III, whose election to the Holy See is hailed in Letters 314 and 315. Bernard did not hesitate to admonish Eugene III that he had been deceived (L 340), for example, or to warn him against the bishop elect of Rodez, whom he called a monster (L 381). Bernard also reprimanded the people of Rome for their rebellion against Eugene III (L 319). Several letters concern the Second Crusade, which Bernard preached at Eugene's request. Number 391 exemplifies this sort of letter intended for public reading aloud. An appeal for the crusade, it urges Christian men to take up the cross to reconquer the Holy Land, and it admonishes against persecution of the Jews, the subject of number 393 also. Letter 396 orders excommunication for any monk or lay brother who leaves the monastery to join the expedition. Bernard's refusal to transgress the bounds of his monastic profession and lead the Third Crusade resounds from Letter 399. Royal affairs also prompted the abbot's intervention. A quarrel between King Louis VI and the bishop of Paris drew Bernard's intervention (L 49ff), and King Louis incited the abbot's anger for his heedless violence and reprisals in a controversy over the count of Vermandois' attempt to divorce his wife (L 297). Bernard also intervened in disputes over the elections for the archbishop of York in 1141–3 (L 187ff) and for the see of Auxerre in 1152 (L 345–8). Many bishops benefited from the abbot of Clairvaux's advice, consulting him on whether to accept election (L 9), or on decisions to be made in office (L 10, 11, 26–30, 62–5). He reproached them when necessary. A letter to the clergy at Sens after the death of their archbishop serves as exemplary advice on choosing a new leader (L 260).

Several letters revolve around vocation to the religious life: persuasion to undertake or resume its discipline, rejoicing over such a decision when made, and lamenting over vows broken (L 92, 104, 105, 110, 111, 443). Debates over the best form of religious life surface in Letter 1, from Bernard to his cousin Robert (known as his nephew), who was entrusted to Cluny as a child. Bernard apologizes for his severity toward the young man, who came for a time to Clairvaux, and the abbot persuades him to return. In retelling Robert's story in the third person, Bernard criticizes Cluniac practices such as the reception of child oblates. The Cistercians insisted on receiving young men who were old enough to themselves decide to enter the monastery. Bernard also reprehends the fine food and clothing of the Benedictines and praises a simple diet and hard work.

Negotiations between abbots often involved fugitives who fled one monastery for another, or monks who were seeking to live under a different style of observance (L 67, 68, 86, 234, 428). The latter discussions sometimes revolved around preferences for the Cistercian, Cluniac, or another order's way of life, but often they merely explain simple details of transfer from one place to another. A quarrel between the Cistercians and the Premonstratensians underlies Bernard's arguments in Letter 328.

Rivalries between Cistercians, Cluniacs, and other orders have been exaggerated, and friendly cooperation seems to have been the usual *modus operandi*, as seen in Bernard's Letter 440, when he commends a cleric to the Canons Regular at Troyes, fearing that the Cistercian life would be too harsh for him; or Letter 450 granting a forge built by Cistercians to the Benedictines at Celles. Nonetheless, rivalry escalated into violence when the Benedictines at Gigny, engaged in a prolonged conflict over the white monks' exemption from tithes, attacked the Cistercian abbey of Miroir (L 353).

The letters commemorate important events in Cistercian history, for example: the founding of Rievaulx abbey in 1132 (L 95); around 1140, the establishment of a sister house of Clairvaux in Sicily (L 276–8); and the election of Bernard Paganelli in 1145 as Pope Eugene III (L 314, 315). Letters of consolation mark the passing of important figures such as Malachy, archbishop of Ireland in 1148 (L 386). Expressions of gratitude for benefactors' donations (L 32) are found, as are requests for aid to monasteries in need, not only Cistercian houses such as Maison-Dieu in Bourges (L 406), but also those of other orders such as the Benedictine houses of Liessies (L 233) and Molesme (L 232), the monastery that a group of monks left in 1098 in order to found the 'new monastery' at Cîteaux.

One of the abbot's chief responsibilities was the proper correction of the monks entrusted to his charge. Letter 103 deals with the correction and discipline of a brother, and several letters offer advice to abbots, Cistercians and others, facing troublesome situations (L 73, 76–9, 81–5, 380). The duty to reproach was often extended to those who needed correction but who did not ask for advice. Bernard chastizes an abbot who deserted his flock to journey to the Holy Land (L 4). His desertion also moved Bernard to compose a treatise on obedience (L 8). Bernard also reprimands his friend, Atto, bishop of Troyes, for appointing a child as an archdeacon (L 263). One letter hails the decision by Abbot Suger to reform the abbey of Saint Denis, not sparing him reprimands for the earlier excesses under his leadership (L 80). Some correspondence addresses the problems of opposition to reform (L 85, 286), and in one case, letters lament the murders of two reformers (L 164–7).

Images of monastic spirituality, themes, and subjects appropriate for meditation and study intertwine throughout the letters. Letter 67 contains the well-known description of the monastery of Clairvaux as the nearest earthly approximation to the heavenly Jerusalem, object of monastic contemplation and the desired end for the monk's life of spiritual discipline. Letter 107 praises the lessons learned from nature, superior for Bernard to those the schools offered. The strength and high value of friendship in twelfth-century monasticism is evident in letters such as 87 and 88 to William of St Thierry, and 119 to Ermengarde, a female friend. Letters 90 and 217 reflect on humility. Letter 423 constitutes a discourse on spiritual progress in the monastic life, and Letter 116 expounds on virginity and contempt for the world.

A few letters reflect views on the liturgy. Bernard wrote Letter 430 to send along with sermons, a hymn, and responsories that he composed for the Office of St Victor. Responding to a request for these liturgical compositions, he sets forth his views on the proper qualities of liturgical music. A liturgical dilemma surfaces in Letter 72, where Bernard advises an abbot who seeks counsel after finding that during a mass he celebrated, there was no wine in the chalice at the moment of consecration.

The letters address numerous exegetical and theological subjects, including famous controversies. In Letter 215 Bernard objects to the feast of the Conception of the Blessed Virgin instituted by the canons of Lyons. He expounds his views on the Virgin Mary's conception, asserting that she was sanctified in the womb and not at the moment of her conception. Letter 98 constitutes a discourse on the story of the Macchabees and on martyrdom. Bernard comments on baptism in Letter 435, responding to an inquiry about the baptism of an infant by a layman who used a formula that did not correspond word for word to the liturgical norm. Letters 236 to 249 reflect Bernard's famous controversy with Peter Abelard. The abbot of Clairvaux, using formulas common to writing against heresy, repeatedly compares his learned adversary to the heretics Arius, Pelagius, and Nestorius. With similarly vehement language, Bernard also targets Arnold of Brescia (L 250, 251) and Henry of Lausanne (L 317, 318), whose heresy prompted his journey to southern France in 1145.

Several letters shed light on Bernard's other works, proving useful in establishing dates for them and providing a fascinating glimpse into the abbot's process of composition. In Letter 19, Bernard cites *On Humility* and the homilies on *Missus* est, the *Apologia* (also referred to in L 87 and 91), as well as unidentified letters and discourses. Letters 159 and 160 refer to the sermons *On the Song of Songs*. Aelred of Rievaulx's treatise, the *Speculum charitatis*, is the subject of Letter 177, where Bernard urges his fellow Cistercian to write the text. Once it was completed, Bernard's letter served as the preface.

The busy abbot was pressed for time to write even to his friends. In letter 91 he complains that he received a second letter from canon Oger before he had had time to answer the first. The long working days of summer curtailed the time available for writing: 'I scarcely had time to read [your second letter] when it came during my dinner. And now by getting up early I am just able to scribble, on the quiet, this brief reply' (p. 135). In another letter to Oger, Bernard asks that the pace of their letter exchange be slowed down:

> We wear ourselves out in scribbling to each other and we exhaust our messengers in sending them backwards and forwards between us. Let us give our heads a respite from dictating, our tongues from chattering, our hands from writing, our messengers from running to and fro, and apply ourselves to meditating day and night on the law of the Lord, which is the law of charity (p. 139).

Letter 92 describes the energy and agitation unleashed when Bernard wrote:

> How can the mind be quiet when composing a letter and a turmoil of expressions are clamoring and every sort of phrase and diversity

of senses are jostling each other? when words spring into the mind, but just the word one wants escapes one; when literary effect, sense, and how to convey a meaning clearly, and what should be said, and in what order it should be said, has to be carefully considered; all the things which those who understand these matters scrutinize carefully? . . . Can you call this silence even if the lips are not moving? (pp. 137–8)

These statements about composition testify to the painstaking scrutiny that Bernard applied to the writing process. May the readers of these English letters appreciate the scope of James's contribution in translating the complex and sonorous Latin of Saint Bernard and also aspire to read the Latin originals produced so carefully by the master.

JAMES'S SOURCES AND THE LECLERCQ-ROCHAIS EDITION

While Bruno Scott James was keenly aware that a new edition of Bernard's letters was imminent, it did not appear in time for his translation to take it into account. The definitive edition of Bernard's complete works includes two volumes of letters, edited by Jean Leclercq and Henri-Marie Rochais. A summary of the introduction to that edition will provide necessary background information to appreciate the importance of the letters and the complexity of their manuscript tradition.

The first matter to consider is the number of letters in the two Latin editions and in James's translation. While Leclercq and Rochais respected the Mabillon edition as closely as possible, they added Letters 496–547 to their edition. James knew and translated forty of those, indicated in the chart found in the back matter of this volume.[11] Readers should be advised that the total number of authentic letters in Leclercq-Rochais is 500; the numbering reaches 547 because many of the letters that Mabillon included have since been judged as inauthentic and five were found to be duplicates.

J. Leclercq and H.-M. Rochais based their edition on five hundred letters thought authentic, extant in almost 400 manuscripts. The editors found 'extreme' variations in the letters' series; the copying of numerous, often short texts produced many scribal errors. Nonetheless, three groups of manuscripts were distinguished by historical references to the letters and by evidence in the manuscripts themselves: (1) a first and oldest collection, in which no letters appear from the last years of Bernard's life; (2) a second collection, which probably corresponds to the corpus mentioned by Geoffrey of Auxerre in 1145 and which does not contain letter 310 (James L 469), supposedly written by Bernard shortly before his death;[12] (3) a more extensive and complex collection, apparently an amplification of the 1145 grouping. Establishment of group one is achieved in two ways: (1) evidence for a small collection of letters existing in the summer of 1126, when Bernard in Letter 18 (James L 19) refers to a 'few letters that he has dictated;' and (2) a highly complex study of the manuscripts pointing to the existence of a series of letters later than 1126 but earlier than 1145. For group two, references from Geoffrey of Auxerre, probably dating from May of 1145, and from William of Saint-Thierry, sometime before his own death in September of 1148, signal the existence of a corpus of letters, called *corpus epistolarum* and *codex epistolarum* respectively. Group two contains revisions of several letters in group one, and no manuscript from Clairvaux appears in group two. Group three was probably constituted after Bernard's death on 20 August 1153 and Geoffrey of Auxerre doubtless played a role in establishing the register. Many manuscripts from Clairvaux and its daughter-houses are found in this group, pointing to the role of the Clairvaux scriptorium in disseminating Bernard's writings after his death.

The Leclercq-Rochais edition maintained the order of letters 1–495 established in the Mabillon edition and reproduced by J.-P. Migne in the *Patrologia latina*. That traditional order corresponds more or less to the sequence of the letters in group three of the manuscripts. Overall, differences between the Mabillon edition and that of Leclercq-Rochais are too complex to describe here. However, the dating of the letters deserves attention. Leclercq and Rochais established dates for the letters using not only Mabillon but also the findings of other scholars. The more recent edition of the letters by F. Gastaldelli proposes modifications to the dating Leclercq-Rochais suggested for some letters. Those findings are indicated in the table to be found in the back matter of this volume. An asterisk next to the date given designates a change, even a slight one; most modifications involve the assignment of a more specific date, such as the choice of months within a given year. More information can be found in the notes of the Gastaldelli and Leclercq-Rochais volumes.

BEVERLY MAYNE KIENZLE
The Divinity School, Harvard University

NOTES

[1] On the *ars dictaminis*, see James J. Murphy, *Rhetoric in the Middle Ages. A History of Rhetorical Theory from St. Augustine to the Renaissance*, (Berkeley, Los Angeles, London: University of California Press, 1974), pp. 194–268.

[2] J. Leclercq reviews genres of monastic literature in *The Love of Learning and the Desire for God*, trans Catharine Misrahi, (New York: Fordham University Press, 1988), pp. 153–72.

[3] Giles Constable, *Letters and Letter Collections*, Typologie des sources du moyen âge occidental 17, (Turnhout, 1976), pp. 31–9. Constable associates the later decline of letter writing with its condemnation by monastic and canonical reformers who must

have thought that it threatened monastic seclusion. Constable (p. 37) cites the testimony of Robert of Bridlington from around 1150, who deplored the 'great evils' brought about by the exchange of secret letters and concluded that St Augustine, whose rule was used by medieval canons, was justified in banning secret letters originating either inside or outside the monastery.

⁴ See J. Leclercq, *Love of Learning*, pp. 176–7.

⁵ I am grateful to Christopher Holdsworth for the suggestions in this paragraph. On the Cistercian administrative structure, see Martha G. Newman, *The Boundaries of Charity. Cistercian Culture and Ecclesiastical Reform, 1098–1180* (Stanford, Calif.: Stanford University Press, 1996), pp. 48–53.

⁶ Those two letters and a reply to the first are extant in Dijon, Bibliothèque Municipale Ms. 611, edited by Beverly Mayne Kienzle, 'The Works of Hugo Francigena: *Tractatus de conversione Pontii de Laracio et exordii Salvaniensis monasterii vera narratio; epistolae* (Dijon, Bibliothèque Municipale MS 611)', *Sacris erudiri* 34 (1994): 273–311.

⁷ 'De epistola quam misistis nobis quo gaudio, quanta laeticia, quanta devotione, et exultacione mentis a fratribus suscepta fuerit; possibilitatis meae non est edicere nec ... memorare valebo, quo legendi studio, quo videndi desiderio rapiebatur ab omnibus, furabatur, tollebatur, et quicumque eam habere poterat in angulum claustri secedens remotus a ceteris legebat atque relegebat adaperiens os suum quasi pauper edens in occulto.' B. Kienzle, 'The Works of Hugo Francigena,' *Sacris erudiri* 34 (1994): 309, ll.26–33.

⁸ Giles Constable underscores the persuasive power of the letter in: 'Papal, Imperial and Monastic Propaganda in the Eleventh and Twelfth Centuries', in *Preaching and Propaganda in the Middle Ages: Islam, Byzantium, Latin West*. Penn-Paris-Dumbarton Oaks Colloquia III, Session of October 20–25. 1980, ed. George Makdisi, Dominique Sourdel, Janine Sourdel-Thoumine, (Paris, 1980), pp. 181–2.

⁹ Giles Constable, 'The Second Crusade as Seen by Contemporaries', *Traditio* 9 (1953): 245.

¹⁰ On this well-known passage, see the articles of Christopher Holdsworth, 'Bernard chimera of his age?', in Robert G. Benson and Eric W. Naylor, ed., *Essays in Honor of Edward B. King* (Sewanee, Tenn., 1991) and Adriaan Bredero, 'St Bernard and the Historians,' in M. Basil Pennington, ed., *Saint Bernard of Clairvaux*, CS 28 (Kalamazoo: Cistercian Publications, 1977), pp. 27–62.

¹¹ The list of letters not in Mabillon but translated by James, found on page 526 of James, omits letter 233 (C 513), published by Hüffer. The F. Gastaldelli edition, *Opere di san Bernardo: Lettere* (Milan: Scriptorium Claravellense, 1986–7), the source for the dates of the letters, includes an additional letter, number 548; and two more letters were published in 1987, numbers 549 and 550, by F. Heinzer, 'Zwei unbekannte Briefe Bernhards von Clairvaux in einer Handschrift der Zisterzienserinnenabtei Lichtental', *Scriptorium* 41 (1987): 97–105.

¹² Articles examining Letter 469 that were published after the 1987 Italian edition of the letters include: Adriaan Bredero, 'Der Brief des heiligen Bernhards auf dem Sterbebett; ein authentische Fälschung', in *Fälschungen im mittelalter*, MGH Schriften B 33 V, V, 201–24; and D. Farkasfalvy, 'The Authenticity of Saint Bernard's Letter from his Deathbed', *Analecta Cisterciensia* 34 (1987): 263–8.

ACKNOWLEDGEMENTS

I wish to express my gratitude to several people who contributed in different ways to the writing of the new introduction. Roger Thorp helped to shape the content and focus. AnneMarie Luijendijk prepared the selected bibliography and designed the table in the back matter with painstaking scrutiny. Readers of James's translation will be able for the first time to start from James's numbering system to find the corresponding Latin letters in the Leclercq-Rochais edition and to learn what dates are assigned to them in the Gastaldelli edition. Tammy Zambo greatly expanded and improved the index, also making the volume much more usable for scholars. Brian McGuire made helpful suggestions on the content, as did Christopher Holdsworth, who provided several references for specific letters and proposed other valuable clarifications to the text. My father Lewis, his wife Bette, and her daughter Jane encouraged and supported my finding the periods of quiet and concentration needed for completing the new introduction during a time of great stress for us all. I wish to dedicate the new introduction to them. Finally, my daughter Kathleen read and commented on the new introduction with the very helpful perspective of an undergraduate student.

INTRODUCTION

1. Salient Facts in the Life of St. Bernard

St. Bernard was born at Fontaines-lès-Dijon in the year 1090 and died at Clairvaux on August 20th, 1153. Tescelin, his father, was of the ancient stock of Chevaliers de Châtillon who held feudal lordship over territory in Burgundy and Champagne. He was said to have been a religious man of unblemished character. His mother, Aleth, was related to the Dukes of Burgundy. There is reason to suppose that her father was Bernard of Montbard. Bernard was one of seven children all dedicated to God at birth by their mother. If we are to believe the pious traditions of hagiographers his birth was presaged and accompanied by signs of his future greatness and sanctity. Whether these are the shadows which coming events are supposed to cast before them, or whether they are the prophecies of coming greatness imagined after the event, we have no means of ascertaining.

All the usual legends surround his early childhood. Although he was believed to have been mature in virtues from earliest infancy we are assured that he was a child in worldly affairs—a not surprising quality in a child. If the lineaments of the child may be divined from the character of the grown man, it may be supposed that there was little of the prig in young Bernard. He received the education usual for children of his position and age. As a youth he is said to have been highly intelligent, good looking, and distinguished for his urbanity. All of which we can well believe. He did not escape the usual difficulties and temptations of adolescence, nor is there any reason why he should have done. But we can believe that he passed the crisis unscathed. Berengarius of Poitiers, a disciple of Abelard, asserted that in his youth Bernard had written ribald rhymes. This was hotly denied by his disciples and afterwards withdrawn by the author. But there does not seem to have been any *a priori* reason why it should not have been true.

For such a young man as Bernard any distinguished career would have been open in either Church or State. For a time he seemed to hesitate, but in the year 1111 he finally decided to enter the monastic way of life, not in any great monastery but in the poor and obscure house of Cîteaux. This house had been founded some years previously by Robert of Molesme in order to follow in all simplicity the Rule of St. Benedict without any of the elaborations which had been accumulated down the centuries by contemporary monasticism. For some years it had been languishing for want of recruits until its future was assured by the arrival of Bernard, and thirty companions whom he had induced to follow him, in the year 1112. When they entered, St. Stephen Harding, the Englishman, was abbot. In the way that Bernard induced so many of his noble companions to undertake with him such a hard and rough manner of life we encounter for the first time an indication of that extraordinary power of moving others which was to be characteristic of him all through his life. On the other hand we must not exaggerate the contrast between the manner of life to which these young noblemen would have been accustomed and the rough living they found at Cîteaux. The life of even the nobility in those days would seem rough by modern standards.

Three years after his entering at Cîteaux Bernard was sent by Stephen to make a new foundation at Clairvaux. He was formally installed in his office as abbot of the new foundation by the Bishop of Châlons-sur-Marne, William of Champeaux, who immediately became one of Bernard's firmest friends. This is significant for it was undoubtedly William who first spread the fame of Bernard throughout France, while his influence on Bernard's intellectual outlook may well have been responsible for the strong line he took in combating Abelard in after years. From this moment Bernard began reluctantly to enter the field of great affairs. Bishops and great ecclesiastics began to insist on having his advice and help in their troubles. His decision was required and followed in all difficulties. We begin to find letters from him addressed to the King of France and the Pope. From the first he was fearless in his condemnations of the folly and vice of those in high positions. No one, no matter how exalted, was exempt from the sometimes very scathing rebukes of the young Abbot of Clairvaux. Times have changed. Such freedom of language is not permitted nowadays. In St. Bernard's time it was permitted but naturally it gave rise to ill feeling and jealousy. It was not long before men were asking themselves who this truculent young abbot could be, and why he did not stay in his monastery. There is a letter of his to Cardinal Haimeric in which he answers just this accusation. There is little about it of conventional humility. Of course he will stay in his monastery, he says. There is nothing he would like better. But the cardinal must not think that the troubles of the Church will cease just because he has ceased to give them tongue. In fact there will be no improvement until the Roman Curia ceases to heed tales told behind people's backs. But in view of these accusations which were levelled against the saint, at any rate at the beginning of his career, and which may raise a question in the minds of modern readers, it were well to remember that although Bernard seems to have been torn between love for the solitude of his monastery, a sense also of responsibility to his monks, and a burning desire to reform the current abuses in the Church, yet he never concerned himself with public affairs save under the compulsion of a strong sense of duty to

the Church and under obedience to his superiors.   His letters are full
of complaints that he is always being torn away from his monastery
by the commands of his superiors, and we find him repeatedly begging
to be left in peace.   On one occasion he firmly refuses the request of
the Pope himself that he should come to Rome.

When in the year 1130 the Roman cardinals surpassed themselves
by electing two popes on the same day and within a few hours of each
other, St. Bernard entered for the first time on the field of world
affairs.   He could not hesitate.   The whole Church was in danger.
Without delay he threw his weight on the side of Innocent II against
Peter Leonis who had been elected anti-pope under the name of
Anacletus, a few hours after Innocent.   Anacletus seems to have been
a Jew by birth and to have obtained his election by intimidation and
bribery.   Even Peter the Venerable has no good word to say for him.
For a time the fate of the two popes swung in the balance, but it was
Bernard who turned the scales in favour of Innocent.   He stormed
through Europe persuading, encouraging, and threatening.   It was
he who alone had the courage to withstand the Emperor Lothair
when he attempted to make his support of Innocent conditional on
being granted the right of investiture.   He fearlessly rebuked the
Emperor before all the assembled bishops, whereupon the Emperor
quailed, and gave way.

When he was not actually on the road, letters to every person of
note or influence in the West were pouring from his pen.   And not
only was he writing letters, he was also receiving them.   Almost
anyone in difficulties seemed to think that he could appeal to the
Abbot of Clairvaux.   Sandwiched between letters to popes and kings
one finds other letters to poor and insignificant people consoling them
in their small troubles.   He himself tells us that he made a point of
answering every letter, even those from the most insignificant people.
He kept more than one secretary at work, and he is said to have been
able to dictate more than one letter at a time.   At the same time there
was his responsibility to his own community.   Every day Clairvaux
was growing with fresh recruits, and almost every year it was sending
out fresh foundations.   During the troubled years of the schism nearly
twenty foundations were made from Clairvaux alone, carrying everywhere with them the influence of their abbot and monastery, and
providing Bernard with an army of supporters for his tasks of reform.
All the world was becoming Cistercian.   Undoubtedly he had the
gift of delegating his authority, yet when we consider that besides the
care he had for his monks, besides his concern in great affairs, besides
his vast correspondence, and his many theological and mystical writings,
he was tortured by ill-health, some distressing gastric malady which
made it difficult for him to retain his food, his vitality and energy seem
to surpass human strength, as undoubtedly they did.   No one could

have achieved all that Bernard did, under the conditions that he did it, with only his unaided human strength.

The final entry of Bernard on to the stage of world affairs was his preaching of the Second Crusade. This was a task imposed upon him by the Cistercian Pope, Eugenius III. As everyone knows, the Crusade ended in disaster. This was not Bernard's fault but of course everyone blamed him: ' *iniquissima haec bellorum conditio est: prospera omnes sibi vindicant, adversa uni imputantur,*' as Tacitus has observed. And so like many other great and holy men Bernard died under a cloud of disappointment and failure.

2. ST. BERNARD IN HIS LETTERS

Every age has its great men, but seldom does any age have a man great enough to transcend all the limitations of his age. Beyond any doubt St. Bernard was such a man. His doctrine, his writings, his example are as fresh and valid today as they were eight hundred years ago. During his life he bestrode the world like a colossus, the counsellor and mentor of kings, popes, philosophers, and ordinary men and women; and he has not ceased in our time to dominate the consciousness of Christians. His massive figure still looms across our horizons, his winning personality still enchants the hearts of men. With all his old persuasiveness he still moves men to follow the hard and narrow way he trod himself, still attracts men to the Order which he so powerfully propagated in his lifetime. Nothing that we can learn about such a man, no small detail, is too trivial to be without significance and interest. For this purpose we have the early biographies of his friends and disciples, and a knowledge of them is indispensable for anyone who would study his life. But their value is limited just because they were so near to their subject, too near to him fully to understand his significance. Great men like great mountains need to be seen from a distance. Furthermore these biographies were submitted for revision to the authorities of the Order, and we can be sure that anything considered to be not tending to edification would have been excluded. Fortunately the saint has provided us in his letters with a living picture of himself. The letters of St. Bernard far exceed in number the letters of any of his contemporaries, and they are addressed to men and women of all classes in every quarter of the West. For this very reason they are a recognized source for the history of his time.

But valuable historical documents as the letters of St. Bernard are, they are no less valuable for the picture they give us of the man, and such a man! A painting, did we have one, would be less significant than they are, for it would portray only, as it were frozen and in still life, the external expression of a passing moment. But here, in these letters, we have an animated and moving picture, reflecting without pose or self-consciousness every passing mood and feeling of the writer. But, it must be admitted, this picture does not easily reveal itself. It is buried in a mass of four hundred and more letters, some of them dull, all of them in an idiom not easily understood or appreciated by the modern mind. Yet even the most desiccated theologian and historian would find himself amply repaid for a close study of these letters, for the doctrine as well as the actions of St. Bernard are so highly coloured by his personality that they may hardly be understood without some knowledge of his character. And when at last we have broken through the crust of antique phraseology and out-of-date idiom, how living and how lovable is the picture we see, the friend we meet! Bernard has lost none of his old power of making friends. Here is no plaster saint, here no disembodied spirit, but a man who, like ourselves, knew what it was to contend with ill-health, moods of depression, irritation with fools, awkward situations, and the petty persecutions of mean men with narrow horizons. Perhaps we have here one reason why the letters of St. Bernard have not received all the attention they deserve, even in quarters where one might most expect it. We have all become so used to conventionalized cameo pictures of child-saints that we are apt to be a little shocked and, perhaps, a little scared when suddenly confronted with the gaunt figure of one who was a little over life size, of one who was a whole man just because he was a holy man. Perhaps, such a thing would not be impossible, our taste has become a little vitiated by a too soft and sugary presentation of sanctity, in which nothing is allowed to offend our sense of propriety, or by traits too human to suggest that we too, were we generous, might be saints. Perhaps we have forgotten that to be a man of God it is first necessary to be a man. Certainly this is true of a monk, for no one, unless he be a man, could persevere for long in seeking God within the stark cloisters of a monastery, where the poetry and romance in which we try to shroud the life soon wear away to nothing at all.

In estimating the character of St. Bernard from his letters, we are at once confronted with a man of tempestuous emotions. Of a man who in one and the same letter will pass rapidly from expressions of white hot indignation to phrases indicating all the affection and anxiety of a friend. Sometimes we find him very terrible indeed, as when he asks Henry, Archbishop of Sens, whether he imagines everyone to be as lacking in all sense of justice as he appears to be; or just irritated, as when a certain Canon Oger complained because he did not receive a prompt reply to a rather tiresome letter; or as when the Bishop of Rochester was objecting because Bernard had advised one of his men to make his studies in Paris. At another time we see him worried and anxious, as when he writes to console one of his sons who had been sent out on a new foundation and was finding the difficulties too much for him and feeling homesick for Clairvaux; or as when he writes to comfort a poor mother whose only son has left her. Quite often we find him in a playful and joking mood, as when he wrote to the Bishop of Noyon to say that he was sending him a youngster to eat his bread, so that he might find out how mean he was and added that, as he had lost his seal, the good bishop would have to recognize that the letter was from him by its style. But sometimes his tempestuous temperament would land him in difficulties. There is a letter to Peter the Venerable in which he excuses himself for the strong and bitter language he had used in a former letter on the grounds that his secretaries had misunderstood his meaning. Most of us have found ourselves in similar situations, but not all of us have had secretaries to blame. There is no doubt too that Bernard was apt to over-state his case at times, and he is not always free from *parti pris*. Undoubtedly he was too severe on William of York. He was too prone to listen to what other people said of third persons, especially if his informants were his dear Cistercian sons. One feels that all his geese were swans and all his enemies the vilest of men. They often were, but not always. Yet all through these purely human frailties there shines his overpowering singleness of purpose, his absorbing love of God, and his often disconcerting and always disarming humility. He never ceases to love, even when he is lashing hardest. If his opponent, if the victim of his wrath, shows the slightest indication of sorrow for his misdeeds, the merest shadow of right purpose, then at once all his anger melts into tender affection, like hoar-frost in the sun.

It is interesting to compare St. Bernard with another contemporary character, no less distinguished by birth, no less highly endowed by nature, Henry de Blois, Bishop of Winchester. Like Bernard, Henry was cut on the grand scale. Like him too there was nothing petty about Henry. And he too was a counsellor of kings and moved in great affairs. But Henry de Blois, for all his real greatness, is dead. A figure of great interest and not unattractive, yet a figure of only historical significance. A man of his times whose influence has passed with his times. The difference between the two, between Bernard of Clairvaux and Henry de Blois, is the difference between a man of God who fought valiantly and sometimes unwisely, but never for himself, and an ambitious, highly endowed statesman, who might perhaps have been great in any epoch, who was perhaps even a saintly man, but never a saint.

3. LITERARY STYLE OF ST. BERNARD IN HIS LETTERS

Much has been written about the style of St. Bernard. Undoubtedly he was an artist in words and sensitive to their value. In one of his

letters we find him describing the care he took in all his literary compositions. Yet his style is not without blemish and in his letters the
blemishes are more apparent than in his more considered literary work.
Largely it was the taste of the times which was at fault, but no useful
purpose is served by allowing our admiration for the man to blind us
to the faults of his style. The most obvious characteristic of all his
literary work is his constant quotation from the sacred Scriptures.
It is said that he knew them all by heart, and we can well believe it.
Quotation from the Scriptures is a characteristic of all the ecclesiastical
literature of the time. It was as fashionable to quote the Scriptures
then as it was to quote the classics in the eighteenth century. But
Bernard carries it further than any of his contemporaries. His
quotations and allusions are both more spontaneous and more happy.
Many of his letters are little else than a brilliant and pointed pastiche
of the Old and New Testaments. But happy though most of his
quotations and allusions are, there are occasions when they appear
forced and in fact obscure the sense of what he is trying to say.
Alliteration is another literary foible of the age, and again Bernard
carries it further than most. Often he achieves striking effects by it,
but sometimes he uses it at the cost of clarity. Nor is he able to resist
inverting his sentences. A typical example is when he refers to his
humble profession and then, immediately, to his professions of
humility. It would be quite impossible for him to speak of patient
zeal without promptly mentioning zealous patience. As soon as we
meet a substantive with an adjective we know what to expect. After
a time this becomes rather wearisome. It is a mistake to say, as has
been said repeatedly, that Bernard was an artist in words and never
wasted a word. Certainly he was an artist in words, but equally
certain is it that he wasted words. In his letters, at any rate, he shows
not the vaguest conception of classical economy, and sometimes his
sense becomes obscured by mere verbiage. But, when all is said, the
literary faults of Bernard were the faults of contemporary taste, and
in spite of them he remains an accomplished artist in words, head and
shoulders, in this respect as in every other, above his contemporaries.
His turns of phrase are often exceedingly happy and defy translation:
he can be colourful and vivid in a manner all his own. He is at his
best when he is angry. Then words flow from his pen like thunder-
bolts and their effect, even at this distance of time, is very striking and
moving. Often when he is writing to the Pope or some high ecclesiastic
about the misbehaviour of some unfortunate cleric, he will suddenly
break off the sentence and address himself to the culprit in person.
This is apt to be a disconcerting habit, but it is certainly effective.
Throughout all his letters, indeed all his writings, there is a wonderful
sense of ease and spontaneity. The art is always there, but nearly
always it is well concealed.

4. The Methods and Principles followed in Translating the Letters

It is admittedly an almost impossible task to translate poetry into a foreign language so as to lose nothing of the original. ' Poesie ', writes Sir John Denham, ' is of so subtle a spirit, that in pouring out of one language into another, it will all evaporate.' With prose the difficulty is not so great, but even here great prose must suffer something in the process of translation, except perhaps in the hands of a genius. Only bishops, it has been said, profit from translation! Unfortunately the prose of St. Bernard has a lyrical quality which has certainly defied the best endeavours of the present translator. It was, I believe, Mr. Belloc who said that a translator should ask himself not only what his author says, but also how a man living at the same time and writing in the same language as himself, would say it. I have tried to carry this principle a step further by asking myself not only how a man would say this or that were he living now, but how St. Bernard would say it were he still alive. But in doing this I have at once been faced with the difficulty that St. Bernard could not be living now. As well ask oneself how a man from another planet would behave in the streets of Paris or London. The answer would be that he could not live because the climate would kill him. The mentality of the age of St. Bernard is wholly different from that of our own, almost a different dimension. Many of the saint's ideas cannot be translated into modern idiom because there is no modern idiom capable of expressing them. Our modern age could no more produce a man with the mentality and outlook of St. Bernard then the counting house could produce a poet, or the laboratory a metaphysician. It might be done, but it would be a freak case, and the man in question would have to forge himself an idiom other than that of the counting house or laboratory. So in asking myself the question how St. Bernard would say this or that were he living now, I have sometimes been forced to the conclusion not only that he would not say it, but even that he could not say it so as to be understood. Fortunately it has only been very rarely that I have been faced with this total *impasse*, and when I have, all that I have been able to do is to give a rendering as near as possible to the original while remaining comprehensible to the average reader. On every such occasion I have given the original Latin in a footnote. But there have been many border-line cases when anything like a literal translation could only have been achieved at the cost of all the life and bloom of the original. In such cases I have cast aside all attempt at being literal and aimed only at giving the sense of the original in a way that would read easily. With regard to the many alliterations, because they are so characteristic of Bernard's style I have tried to keep them when it could be done without impairing the sense. The constant quotations from the sacred

Scriptures have proved another difficulty. On the very rare occasions when they have seemed forced and to impair the sense, I have not hesitated to discard them. But for far the larger part of them I have made use of Mgr. Knox's translation. There have, however, been occasions when the more literal version of the Douay has seemed preferable. There have also been times when Bernard's verbal interpretation of some passage from the Scriptures has made the use of any accepted version impossible. An obvious and all too frequent example is that vexed verse from the Vulgate Psalm: '*Funes ceciderunt mihi in præclaris*'. Mgr. Knox gives an excellent interpretation of this difficult verse, but as it bears little obvious relation to the original it is always useless for the purpose of translating St. Bernard's use of the text. The Douay gives another interpretation that approximates the original only in being equally unintelligible. In this case, and in other similar ones, I have been forced to give a rendering of my own which, while it may not always approximate the original very closely, at any rate suits the interpretation put on each word by Bernard. On yet other occasions I have used both the translation of Mgr. Knox and of the Douay with modifications which are not necessarily improvements but which serve to bring the quotation into line with the text. Scriptural passages are enclosed within quotation marks in the letters.

Finally there is the very thorny problem of language. There is something to be said for translating into a completely modern idiom and there is also something to be said for an archaic phraseology. I have tried to avoid all risk of inappropriateness on the one hand and on the other anything that might savour of sham gothic, by steering a middle course. I have tried to retain something of the atmosphere of the original by a slight archaism, while at the same time remaining perfectly intelligible to the modern reader. I have also tried to avoid the rather turgid and lifeless effect of a too literal interpretation of the original. Whether or not in trying to preserve a middle course between an inappropriate modernity on the one hand and an artificial archaism on the other, I have merely succeeded in retaining the disadvantages of both with the advantages of neither, it is for the reader to judge.

5. THE ARRANGEMENT OF ST. BERNARD'S LETTERS

About the year 1145, Bernard's secretary, Geoffrey, published a collection containing between two and three hundred of his letters. Since then the researches of Mabillon, Martène, Durand, Migne, Kervyn de Lettenhove, Hüffer, Leclercq, and Talbot have considerably augmented their number. Even so there can be no doubt that we are far from possessing all the letters written by Bernard. Hüffer estimates the total number of letters written and received by Bernard at not less than a thousand. A very moderate estimate in our opinion.

After Mabillon had published his first edition containing four hundred and forty-four letters, Martène and Durand published another thirty-five, of which five had already been published by Mabillon, and eight were of doubtful authenticity. Hüffer added to the total by discovering another twenty, and Kervyn de Lettenhove augmented it yet further by the letters he discovered and published in the *Bulletin de l'Académie royale de Belgique*. The discoveries of other scholars have already been mentioned and are all noted in their separate places in the body of this work.[1]

As a general principle I have not translated the spurious or doubtful letters attributed to the saint. Thus the letter numbered 460 in Migne, a long letter concerning the religious life, is clearly unauthentic and has not been translated. Neither the style nor the matter is St. Bernard's. Of the letters addressed to the saint, I have contented myself with giving a digest, except in certain cases of outstanding interest, and I have not, as a rule, translated the letters supposed to have been written by the saint, but under the names of others. On the other hand I have been able to include some which have never before been translated and a few very recent discoveries which have not yet been published.

The order of the letters has proved a difficulty. The early compilers of the letters paid no regard to chronological sequence, and the many attempts of more modern scholars to correct this have not met with any great success. I have not attempted the task but, for the convenience of readers, I have grouped the letters in a rough chronological order according to the chief subjects but within the framework of the traditional order. Thus all the letters concerning the schism, the foundation of Fountains Abbey, the disputed election of the Archbishop of York, and other outstanding events, have been grouped together roughly according to their dates. But for the sake of reference an index has been added by means of which letters in the traditional enumeration can be found.

6. ACKNOWLEDGEMENTS

To a greater or less extent every translator must be indebted to the work of his predecessors, and I do not claim to be any exception in this. I most gratefully acknowledge the help I have received from the translation of St. Bernard's Letters made by the Rev. Samuel Eales towards the end of the last century. The work of Dr. Eales will remain a monument of industry and scholarship however much the

[1] All the world is waiting with eager anticipation and gratitude the definitive edition of St. Bernard's works which is now being prepared by the well-known scholar Dom Jean Leclercq. But as it may be some years yet before the fruit of Dom Leclercq's labours is ready for the public, I have used as my basic text for this translation the edition of Dom Mabillon, whenever possible checking obscure passages by having recourse to the manuscripts themselves and to the advice of better scholars than myself.

fashions in translation may change. If I have not very often been able to agree with his interpretation of some of the more obscure passages in the text of St. Bernard, it has only been with the greatest diffidence that I have ventured to dissent from him.

No Englishman who works on St. Bernard can ignore the labours of the Rev. Watkin Williams. His works on St. Bernard remain the only modern studies in English of the saint's life. I have found his biography useful on many occasions, but it is a book that needs to be read with care. There is also a life of the saint by Fr. Ailbe Luddy, Cistercian monk of Mount Melleray Abbey in Ireland. It is a valuable work for those who seek edification and it has been compiled with great love and devotion. We still await a modern and critical life of the saint in English.

The researches of Dr. David Knowles in mediæval history are too well known to need recommendation. It is from his work on the subject published in the *Cambridge Historical Journal* that I have derived much of my information concerning the vexed question of the York election. I am also deeply indebted to Dr. Hugh Talbot whose researches have brought to light a score of new letters from the saint concerning the same subject which I have been able to embody in this work. I express my gratitude both to Dr. Talbot and to the *Cambridge Historical Journal* for permission to use the text of these letters.

The work of modern scholars has enabled me to augment this book with several letters hitherto unknown and untranslated, all of which have been noted in their separate places. In particular I must express my gratitude and thanks to Dom Jean Leclercq, O.S.B.; Fr. Maurice Dumontier, and Fr. Grill, all of whom have most generously permitted me to cull the fruit of their learned researches. I am also indebted to the *Bulletin de l'Académie royale de Belgique* for the new letters of the saint which it published in 1861.

No one who would seriously study the writings of the early Cistercian Fathers can afford to ignore the learning and scholarship of the monks of Chimay Abbey in Belgium. I am indebted to many of them for their kind help and encouragement as well as for their boundless hospitality, but especially to the learned editor of the Cistercian chapters, Fr. Joseph Canivez. I must also express my appreciation of the kindly enthusiasm with which my modest labours have been greeted by the Cistercian Historical Commission at Aiguebelle.

It would be impossible for me even to estimate the help I have received from the monks of Caldey Abbey. Certainly, if any credit at all attaches to this work, it is due to them. Where all have been so helpful, it would be invidious to mention particular names. I will simply say that the work was undertaken at the suggestion of their superior, but without the help and encouragement of both him and the monks of his community it would never have been completed. It was they who provided me with the most powerful of all possible incentives.

My thanks are due also to the well-known scholar Mr. Archdale King for having taken immense pains to read through the typescript and correct the innumerable slips of spelling.

Finally, I want to express my very deep appreciation of the endless patience of my publishers. Without their help this work could never have seen the light of day, and would never have been undertaken.

LETTER 1

TO ROBERT, HIS NEPHEW

(About the year 1119)

*Robert of Châtillon was the son of Otho of Châtillon and, probably, Diana,
the younger daughter of Robert of Montbard. He would thus be Bernard's
first cousin although, because of the great disparity in their ages, he was
always known as his nephew.*

*When he was still a child his parents promised him to Cluny. But later,
when old enough to act on his own account, he joined the Cistercians, attracted,
no doubt, by the fame of his kinsman. After some delay owing to his extreme
youth, Robert was admitted into the novitiate at Cîteaux and, after the
regular year of probation, made his vows as a Cistercian monk.*

*Whether he was professed at Cîteaux and then followed St. Bernard to
Clairvaux, or whether he went with Bernard when he made the foundation,
is not certain. But he was not long at Clairvaux before he began to find the
austerities irksome and to compare the life there with the easier ways of Cluny.
To support his unsettled state came the insidious doubt as to whether he was
not bound to Cluny by the promise of his parents.*

*This is one of the most characteristic of Bernard's letters and it is interesting
from an historical point of view as the first shot fired in the great controversy
between the congregation of Cluny and the Cistercian reform. It is also
interesting for the circumstances under which it was written. The monk
William, Bernard's secretary at this time, tells us that while Bernard was
dictating in a secluded corner out of doors, where he could not be overheard,
heavy rain began to fall. But when he tried to protect the letter Bernard
told him to write on for it was God's work and yet, although rain fell all
round, the letter remained dry ' in imbre sine imbre '.*

LONG enough, perhaps too long, have I waited, dearest Robert, for
the Lord that he might deign to touch your soul and mine through
yours, moving you to salutary regrets for your error and me to joy
for your deliverance. But seeing myself still disappointed of my hope,
I can no longer hide my sorrow, restrain my anxiety, or dissemble my
grief. And so, against all the laws of justice, I who have been wounded
am forced to recall him who wounded me; who have been spurned,
him who spurned me; who have been smitten, him who struck the
blow. In short I must cast myself at the feet of him who should cast
himself at mine. Sorrow is not careful to count the cost: is not
ashamed; does not nicely weigh the pros and cons; is not fearful for
its dignity; respects no rules; it cares only that it has what it would
be without, or lacks what it would have. ' But ', you will say, ' I
have hurt no one, spurned no one. Rather have I, spurned and

repeatedly hurt, sought only to fly my oppressor. Who can I have hurt, if I have only avoided being hurt? Is it not wiser to yield to the persecutor than to resist him? To avoid him who strikes than to strike back?' Quite so; I agree. I am not writing to dispute with you, but to remove the grounds for dispute. To fly persecution implies no fault in him who flees but in him who persecutes. I do not deny this. I shall overlook the past. I shall not ask why or how the present state of affairs came about. I shall forget old injuries. To act other-wise were better calculated to open than to heal wounds. I am concerned with what lies closer to my heart. Unhappy man that I am who have not you by me, who cannot see you, who am obliged to live without you for whom to die would be to live, and to live without whom is no better than death! So I do not ask why you left me, I only grieve that you do not return; I do not blame your going away, I only blame your not coming back. Only come and there will be peace; return and there will be satisfaction. Return, I say, return, and I shall sing in my heart, ' My brother who was dead has come to life again; was lost and is found '.

2. No doubt it may have been my fault that you left. I was too severe with a sensitive youth, I was too hard on a tender stripling. Hence your grumbles against me (as I remember) while you were here; hence your ceaseless complaints about me even now that I am absent. The fault of this will not be laid at your door. I might, perhaps, excuse myself by saying that only in this way could the passions of youth have been curbed and that, at first, a strict way of life must be hard on a raw youth. I could quote Scripture to support me saying, ' Smite thy son with a rod and thou shalt deliver his soul from hell ', and ' It is where he loves that the Lord bestows correction ', and ' The wounds of a friend are better than the deceitful kisses of an enemy '. It may have been my fault that you left, as I have said. We will not let arguments about who is to blame delay correction of what is blameworthy. But it will surely begin to be your fault as well if you do not spare me now that I am sorry, if you do not forgive me now that I acknowledge myself to blame because, although I have been unwise in my treatment of you, I was certainly not malicious. And if you in future distrust my wisdom, you must know that I am not the same man I was, because I do not think you are what you used to be. Having changed yourself, you will find me changed too. You may now embrace me without hesitation as a companion whom you used to fear as a master. And so if you left through my fault, as you believe and I do not deny, or through your own fault, as many believe but I do not affirm, or, as I think more probable, through the fault of both of us, from now on you alone will be to blame if you do not return. If you would be free of all blame in the matter you must return. If you acknowledge your share of the blame, I forgive you.

But you too must forgive me what I acknowledge as my share. Else if you acknowledge your share and at the same time dissemble it you will be too lenient with yourself, or if you refuse to forgive me even when I declare myself ready to make satisfaction, you will be too hard on me.

3. If you still refuse to come back you must seek another pretext to quiet your conscience because there will no longer be anything to fear from me. You need not fear that in future you will have any reason to fear me because even while you are not with me I have cast myself with my whole heart at your feet, moved thereto with all my affection. I humble myself before you, I assure you of my love: can you still be afraid? Be bold and come where humility beckons you and love draws you. Forearmed by my assurances, approach without fear. Now that I am become gentle, return to me from whom you fled when fierce. My severity frightened you away; let my tenderness draw you back. See, my son, how I long to lead you now not any more in the spirit of slavery to govern you in fear, but in the spirit of adoption whereby we cry ' Abba, Father '; you who have been the cause of so much grief to me, I shall lead not with threats but with encouragements, not by menacing but by entreating. Perhaps anyone else would try another method. And indeed who would not rather insist on your guilt and inspire you with fear; face you with your vow and propose judgement. Who else would not scold your disobedience and be angry at your desertion, that you should have left the coarse habit for soft raiment, a fare of roots for delicacies, in fine poverty for riches. But I know your heart. I know that you can be lead more easily by love than driven by fear. And what need is there to goad you again who have not kicked against the goad, why make you more fearful who are already timid enough, abase you more who are by nature bashful, you who are schooled by your own reason, whose own conscience is a rod, and whose natural shyness is a discipline. And if it seems wonderful to anyone that a shy and timid boy should dare to desert both his vow and his monastery against the will of his brethren, the authority of his superior, the injunctions of the rule, let him wonder also that the sanctity of David was defrauded, the wisdom of Solomon deceived, the strength of Samson destroyed. What wonder if the Evil One should have been able to deceive a youth in a place of horror and a great wilderness who could deceive the first man when he was in the paradise of Eden. And this youth was not deceived by physical beauty like the old men of Babylon, nor by money like Giezi, nor by ambition like Julian the Apostate, but he was duped by sanctity, misled by religion, allured by the authority of age. Do you ask how?

4. First there came a certain Grand Prior sent by the chief of all the priors himself. Outwardly he came in sheep's clothing, but within he was a ravening wolf. Alas! The shepherds were deceived by his

semblance to a sheep and admitted him alone into the fold. The smallest sheep in the fold did not fly from this wolf, he too was deceived and thought he was a sheep. What happened then? This wolf in sheep's clothing fascinated, allured, and flattered. He preached a new Gospel. He commended feasting and condemned fasting. He called voluntary poverty wretched and poured scorn upon fasts, vigils, silence, and manual labour. On the other hand he called sloth contemplation, gluttony, talkativeness, curiosity and all intemperance he commended as discretion. 'When', he asked, ' was God pleased with our sufferings; where do the Scriptures say that we should kill ourselves; what sort of religion is it to dig the soil, clear forests, and cart muck?' Does not Truth itself say, ' It is mercy that wins favour with me and not sacrifice'; and 'I do not wish for the death of a sinner but rather that he should turn from his ways and live'; and ' Blessed are the merciful for they shall obtain mercy'? Why did God make food if we may not eat it? Why did he give us bodies if we may not look after them? In fact ' Whose friend is he, that is his own enemy, and leaves his own cheer untasted ?' 'What healthy and sane man has ever hated his own flesh?'

5. By such sophistries the too credulous boy was talked round, led astray and led off by his deceiver. He was brought to Cluny and trimmed, shaved, and washed. He was taken out of his rough, threadbare, and soiled habit, and clothed with a neat and new one. Then with what honour, triumph, and respect was he received into the community! He was favoured beyond his contemporaries; a sinner in the desires of his heart, he was praised as if he were a conquering hero returned from battle. He was set up on high and, although a mere youth, was allocated to a position above many who were his seniors. He was befriended, flattered, and congratulated by the whole fraternity. Everyone made merry over him as though they were victors dividing the booty. O good Jesu, what a lot of trouble was taken for the ruin of one poor little soul! Who would be so hard-hearted as not to soften at the sight of it! Whose soul, be it never so detached, would not be troubled by it! And who in the midst of all this would care to consult his conscience? And how could anyone amidst such vanities recognize the truth and achieve humility?

6. In the meantime representations were made at Rome. The authority of the Holy See was cajoled. And to make sure that the Pope would not refuse his assent, it was suggested to him that this youth while still a child had been oblated at Cluny by his parents.[1] There was no one present to refute this nor was it anticipated that there

---

[1] An oblate was a young child formally offered to a monastery by his parents. St. Benedict lays down the conditions under which the offering must be made in the 59th chapter of his Rule. The hand of the child is to be wrapped in the altar cloth together with the petition of the parents. If the parents are rich they can offer land for the support of the child and retain, if they wish, the income of it for their lifetime. Poor parents simply offered their child without any gifts.

would be. Judgement was pronounced on the case in the absence of the judged. Those who had done the injury were upheld, the plaintiffs lost their suit, the defendant was absolved without making satisfaction. And this far too indulgent sentence of absolution was confirmed by a cruel ordinance whereby the hesitating and doubtful youth was confirmed in an ill-advised stability and security. The gist of the rescript, the sum of the judgement, the whole significance of the suit was nothing more than that the robbers could keep their spoils and that those who lost thereby must keep silent. And withal a soul for whom Christ died must be lost to please Cluny. So another profession is made, what will not be kept is vowed, what will not be performed is proposed: and since the first sin has been made void, in the second transgression is doubled, and sinning there is sin beyond measure.

7. But he will come, he will come who will judge again the misjudgements of men, who will confute what has been unlawfully vowed, who will execute judgement for them that suffer wrong, who will judge the poor with justice and reprove with equity on behalf of the meek of the earth. He will surely come who has warned us by the Prophet in the psalm, 'When I shall choose a time, I will judge righteousness'. What will he do about unjust judgements who will judge even righteousness? It will come, I say, the day of judgement will come and then a clean heart will avail more than crafty words, and a good conscience more than a full purse. He will then be judge who can neither deceive nor be deceived by words and who cannot be bribed by gifts. To your judgement seat, Lord Jesu, I appeal; I reserve my defence for your court. To you I commit my suit, Lord God of Sabaoth, who judges justly and searches the reins and the heart, who can neither deceive nor be deceived. You know who they are that seek their own ends and who they are that seek your glory. You know with what agony of heart I waited upon the youth in his trials, how I beat upon your loving ears with my prayers for him, how for his anxieties, troubles, and vexations, I was on fire, and torn, and afflicted. And now, I fear, it has all been in vain. I believe that, so far as I know, for a youth already hot-blooded and insolent enough such foments were of little use to the body and such trials of glory of

Footnote continued from page 4

But whether rich or poor the child might not under any circumstances receive anything or have the prospect of receiving anything either from the parents or from a third person. The child thus formally offered became a member of the Community and might not return to the world.

The dangers of this system were fully realized. Two successive popes, Clement III and Celestine III, granted a general permission for all oblates to return to the world if they wished. Guigo, Prior of the Chartreuse, forbade in his statutes the reception of oblates because of the dangers involved by the system.

St. Bernard contends in this letter that Robert was only promised and not formally oblated to Cluny. And in any case, he maintains, a vow made by parents on behalf of their child before he was old enough to know anything about it, could not weigh against a vow, especially for a higher perfection, made by the child when he was old enough to be responsible for his own actions.

little avail to the mind.   And so, Lord Jesu, be you my arbiter, let my judgement come forth from your countenance.

8. Let them see and judge which has the most force: the vow a father makes on behalf of his son, or the vow a son makes on his own behalf, especially when it is a vow of something better.   Let your servant and our law-giver, Benedict, judge which is the more in order: a vow made for a child when it is too young to know any-thing about it, or the vow he afterwards makes for himself when he realizes and understands what he is doing, when he is of an age to speak for himself.   However there is no doubt that the boy was only promised to Cluny without any formal oblation, for the petition prescribed by the Rule was not made by his parents, nor was his hand bound in the altar cloth, and the offering made before witnesses.[1] They point out the land which, they say, was made with the child and for him.   But if they received him with the land how was it they kept the land and not the child?   Can it be that they prized the land more than the child?   If he had been oblated what was he doing in the world?   A nursling of God, why was he exposed to the maw of the wolf?   You yourself, Robert, are a witness that you entered our Order from the world and not from Cluny.   You implored to be admitted, you begged and besought, but, much against your will, your entrance was put off for two years on account of your tender age. When this time had been allowed patiently to pass and without evasion, at last with prayers and (as you will remember) with many tears you besought the long awaited mercy, and were granted the admission you had sought for so long.   You were tried in all patience for a year according to the Rule, living perseveringly and without complaint. After the year had passed you, of your own free will, made your profession and then, for the first time, you put off the attire of the world and were clothed in the habit of Religion.

9. You foolish boy!   Who has bewitched you to break the vows which adorned your lips?   Will you not be justified or condemned out of your own mouth?   Why then are you so anxious about the vow your parents made and yet so regardless of your own?   It is out of your own mouth and not out of the mouth of your parents that you will be judged.   Of your own vow, not of theirs, will you be called to render an account.   Why does anyone try to bamboozle you with an Apostolic absolution, you whose own conscience is bound by a divine sentence, ' No one putting their hand to the plough and looking back is fit for the kingdom of God '?   Would they persuade you that you have not looked back who say to you, ' Well done! '   My son, if sinners shall entice you, consent not to them. Believe not every spirit.   Be at peace with many, but let one in a thousand be your counsellor.   Gird yourself, cast off your seducers,

[1] See note, p. 4.

shut your ears to flatterers, search your own heart, for you know yourself best. Listen to your conscience, examine your intentions, consider the facts. Let your conscience tell you why you left your monastery, your brethren, your own place, and myself who am related to you by blood, but even more closely by spirit. If you left so as to lead a harder, higher, and more perfect life, fear not, you have not looked back, rather you can glory with the Apostle, saying, ' Forgetting what I have left behind, intent on what lies ahead, I press on with the goal in view '. But if it be otherwise, be not high minded but fearful because (you must pardon my saying this) whatever you permit yourself in food, unnecessary clothes, idle words, vain and curious travel in excess of what you promised when you were with us, is without any doubt to look back, to equivocate, to apostatize.

10. And I have said this, my son, not to put you to shame, but to help you as a loving father because if you have many masters in Christ, yet you have few fathers. For, if you will allow me to say so, I begot you in Religion by word and by example. I nourished you with milk when, while yet a child, it was all you could take. And I would have given you bread if you had waited until you grew up. But alas! how soon and how early were you weaned. Now I fear that all I had cherished with kindness, strengthened with encouragement, confirmed with prayers, is even now fading and wasting away. Sadly I weep, not for my lost labour, but for the unhappy state of my lost child. Do you prefer that another should rejoice in you who has not laboured for you? My case is the same as that of the harlot Solomon judged, whose child was stealthily taken by another who had overlain and killed her own. You too were taken from my side, cut from me. My heart cannot forget you, half of it went with you, and what remains cannot but suffer.

11. But our friends who have tried to do this thing, whose sword has pierced my side, whose teeth are spears and arrows and whose tongue is a sharp sword, for what advantage of yours have they done it, for what necessity? If I have in any way offended them (and I am not conscious of having done so) they have certainly paid me back in full. I would not wonder if I have received more than my share of retaliation, if indeed they have suffered anything like what I suffer now from them. It is not a bone of my bones, flesh of my flesh that they have taken, but it is the joy out of my heart, the fruit of my spirit, the crown of my hopes, and (so it seems to me) the half of my soul. Why have they done this thing? Perhaps they were sorry for you? Perhaps they feared that because I was like a blind man leading the blind, we would both fall into the ditch. So they took you under their leadership. Hard necessity! Grievous charity! So careful of your good that it must strike at mine. Is it not possible that you should be saved except at my cost? Ah! would that these men might save you apart

from me. Would that if I die you, at least, may live! But how can
this be? Does salvation rest rather in soft raiment and high living
than in frugal fare and moderate clothing? If warm and comfortable
furs, if fine and precious cloth, if long sleeves and ample hoods, if
dainty coverlets and soft woollen shirts make a saint, why do I delay
and not follow you at once? But these things are comforts for the
weak, not the arms of fighting men. They who wear soft raiment are
in kings' houses. Wine and white bread, honey-wine and pittances,
benefit the body not the soul. The soul is not fattened out of frying
pans! Many monks in Egypt served God for a long time without
fish. Pepper, ginger, cummin, sage, and all the thousand other spices
may please the palate, but they inflame lust. And would you make my
safety depend on such things? Will you spend your youth safely
among them? Salt with hunger is seasoning enough for a man living
soberly and wisely. If we eat before we are hungry, then we must
concoct mixtures with more and more I know not what far-fetched
flavours to arouse our greed and stimulate our flagging appetites.

12. But what, you say, is to be done if one cannot live otherwise?
Good. I know you are not strong, that you would now find it difficult
to support a harder way of life. But what if you can act so as to make
yourself able to do so? I will tell you how it could be done. Arouse
yourself, gird your loins, put aside idleness, grasp the nettle, and do some
hard work. If you act thus you will soon find that you only need to
eat what will satisfy your hunger, not what will make your mouth
water. Hard exercise will restore the flavour to food that idleness
has taken away. Much that you would refuse to eat when you had
nothing to do, you will be glad of after hard work. Idleness makes
one dainty, hard work makes one hungry. It is wonderful how work
can make food taste sweet which idleness finds insipid. Vegetables,
beans, roots, and bread and water may be poor fare for one living at
his ease, but hard work soon makes them taste delicious. You have
become unaccustomed to our clothes and now you dread them as too
cold in winter and too hot in summer. But have you not read, ' They
that fear the frost, the snow shall fall upon them'? You fear our
vigils, fasts, and manual labour, but they seem nothing to anyone who
considers the flames of hell. The thought of the outer darkness will
soon reconcile anyone to wild solitudes. Silence does not displease
when it is considered how we shall have to give an account of every
idle word. With the picture before our eyes of that weeping and
gnashing of teeth the difference between a rush mat and a feather bed
seems small enough. If we spend well all the night enjoined by the
Rule in psalmody, it will be a hard bed on which we cannot sleep. If
we labour with our hands as much during the day as we are professed to do, rough indeed will be the fare we cannot eat.

13. Arise, soldier of Christ, I say arise! Shake off the dust and

return to the battle. You will fight more valiantly after your flight, and you will conquer more gloriously. There are many soldiers of Christ who have begun valiantly, stood their ground well, and finished by conquering, but few who have returned to the battle after they had fled, thrown themselves once more into the thick of the danger from which they had escaped, and put to flight the foe from whom they had run. A thing is the more precious for being rare, so I rejoice that you can be one of those who are the more glorious for being so scarce. But if you are still fearful, I ask you why you should be afraid where there is no cause for fear, instead of where you have every reason to tremble. Do you think that because you have forsaken the front line the enemy has forsaken you? Far from it. He will follow you in flight more readily than he would fight you when striking back. He attacks you more willingly from behind than he would strive with you face to face. Can you sleep unarmed without anxiety in the morning hours when it was at that time that Christ rose from the dead? Do you not know that unarmed you are both more fearful and less to be feared? A multitude of armed men surround the house, and can you still sleep? Already they are scaling the ramparts, swarming over the barriers, pouring in at the rear. Would you be safer alone or with others? Naked in bed or armed in camp? Get up, arm yourself, and fly to your fellow soldiers whom you have forsaken by running away. Let the fear that drove you away also bring you back. Is it the weight and discomfort of arms that you shun, feeble soldier? Believe me when an enemy is at hand and darts begin flying a shield seems none too heavy, and a helmet and corselet are not noticed. Everything seems hard at first to someone coming suddenly from darkness into light, from leisure to labour. But when you have got away from your former habits you will soon get used to the labour. Practice soon makes perfect. What seemed difficult at first presently becomes quite easy. Even the bravest soldiers are apt to tremble when they first hear the bugle summon to battle, but after they have closed with the enemy hope of victory and fear of defeat soon inspires courage. Surrounded by a company of single-hearted brethren, what have you to fear? What have you to fear at whose side angels stand and whom Christ leads into battle encouraging his friends with the words, ' Fear not, I have overcome the world '. If Christ is with us, who is against us? You can fight with confidence where you are sure of victory. With Christ and for Christ victory is certain. Not wounds, nor falls, nor bruises, nor (were it possible) can a thousand deaths rob us of victory, if only we do not forsake the fight. Only by desertion can we be defeated. We can lose the victory by flight but not by death. Happy are you if you die in battle for after death you will be crowned. But woe to you if, by forsaking the battle, you forfeit at once both the victory and the crown. May Christ save you from this, dear son, for at the last judgement you will incur a greater penalty on account of this letter of mine if, when you have read it, you do not take its lesson to heart.

LETTER 2

TO FULK, A YOUNG MAN WHO LATER BECAME ARCHDEACON OF LANGRES

Little seems to be known about Fulk beyond what can be gathered from this letter. Evidently he was a young man who, after he had been professed as a Canon Regular of St. Augustine, was persuaded by his rich uncle to return to the world. As he later became Archdeacon of Langres we may assume that he did not follow the advice of St. Bernard and return to his Order.

To the youth of great promise, Fulk, from Brother Bernard, a sinner, that he may so rejoice in his youth as to have no regrets in his old age.

I DO not wonder if you are surprised that I a rustic and a monk should address myself to you, a citizen of towns and a student, with no excuse or clear reason that can occur to you. I should wonder if you were not surprised. But you will perhaps understand how better motives than presumption dictate my letter to you if you consider those words of Scripture, ' I have the same duty to all, learned and simple ', and ' Charity does not seek its own '. I am indeed bound in charity to exhort you who are in charity to be grieved for although you do not grieve; to be sorrowed for, although you are not sorrowful. And all the more so for the very reason that, an object of grief, yet you do not grieve; of sorrow, yet you are not sorrowful. But perhaps my pity for you will not be wasted if you will only listen while I tell you why you are to be pitied. Charity would have you feel sorrow that then you may begin to have less cause to be sorry; she would have you know yourself to be shameful so you may then have less cause for shame. Our good mother Charity loves us all and shows herself differently to each one of us, cherishing the weak, scolding the restive, exhorting the advanced. But when she scolds she is meek, when she consoles she is sincere. She rages lovingly, her caresses are without guile. She knows how to be angry without losing patience, how to be indignant without being proud. It is she, the mother of angels and men, who brings peace not only on earth, but even in heaven. It is she who brings God to men and reconciles men with God. It is she, my dear Fulk, who makes those brethren with whom you once ' broke sweet bread ' to live together in concert. And it is this mother whom you have wounded, whom you have affronted. Yet although you have affronted her, she does not contend with you. Spurned by you she calls you back, showing by this how truly it has been written of her 'Charity is patient; charity is kind '. Although wounded and affronted by you yet, should you return to her, she will meet you as an honoured mother. She will forget how you repudiated her and throw herself into your arms, rejoicing that her son who was lost is found; who was dead has come to life again.

2. But, you will ask, how have I wounded and affronted charity. Listen. You have done so by tearing yourself from her when she was feeding you with the milk of her breasts; when suddenly and frivolously you spewed her sweet nourishment from your mouth, the sweet milk of charity on which you might have grown strong in virtue. Foolish child ! A child more by reason of your folly than your years. Who has bewitched you that you should have left the good work you had begun? You say it was your uncle. Thus Adam blamed Eve and Eve blamed the serpent, making excuses in sin. Yet their excuses did not save either of them from a punishment they deserved. I would not have you accuse the Dean; I would not have you blame him for your folly. His sin does not excuse yours. There is no excuse for you. What has he done? Has he carried you off by force? He asked you, but he did not compel you. He enticed by flattery, but he did not drag you with violence. Was there any obligation to believe his flattery, to give in to his enticements? He was not bound by any vow of poverty, so that what wonder if he should want you with him whom he regards as his own? If a man loses a sheep or a calf he may seek it and no one complains. Why then should not your uncle seek you who are more precious to him than many sheep and calves? He is not obliged to that state of perfection for which it has been laid down that ' If any man take what is thine, do not ask him to restore it '. He was only seeking his own when he was entitled to do so. But were you obliged to follow a career in the world when you had renounced the world? The trembling sheep flies when the wolf comes, the timid dove hides when it sees the hawk, the hungry mouse dare not leave its hole when the cat is about, and yet you when you see the thief must you run with him? What else but a thief is he who would steal your soul, the precious pearl of Christ?

3. I was hoping, had it been possible, to draw a veil over the fault of your uncle for fear that I should receive no thanks but hatred for telling the truth. But I confess that I cannot let his conduct pass without mention. For he who does not what he may to restrain his hand from evil, even though that evil may sometimes be frustrated, the purpose is not less blameworthy. He certainly tried to damp my novice's ardour but, thanks to God, he was not able. He also resisted strongly the good intentions of Guarike, his other nephew and your kinsman. But he did no harm, in fact he rendered a service, for at length the old man grudgingly gave way and Guarike came through

all the more glorious for having surmounted the trial. How then was he able to win you over who could not win Guarike? How did it happen that he was able to overcome you who was overcome by him? Is Guarike stronger or more prudent than you? Certainly anyone who had formerly known you both would have put Fulk first. But when it came to the fight the result proved the judgement of men wrong. He who had been thought the stronger flies—for shame! and he who had been considered the weaker conquers.

4. But what shall I say of the malice of this uncle of yours who draws his nephews from the army of Christ that he may drag them with him to hell? Is this the way he rewards those he loves? Whom Christ calls to share with him his heavenly kingdom, this uncle invites to burn forever with him in hell. I should not wonder if Christ were not already angry and saying to him, ' How often have I not been ready to gather thy nephews together, and thou didst refuse it. Behold your house is left desolate to you.' Christ says, ' Let little children be, do not keep them back from me, the kingdom of heaven belongs to such as these '. But your uncle says, ' Leave my nephews to me that they may burn with me '. ' They are mine ', says Christ, ' and must serve me.' ' They shall perish with me ', replies your uncle. ' I redeemed them, they are mine ', says Christ. ' But I fed them ', says your uncle. ' The bread you fed them with was mine not yours, but my blood not yours redeemed them ', says Christ. Thus their uncle after the flesh fights with their heavenly father for his nephews in order to disinherit them of heavenly joys and burden them with earthly gifts. Yet Christ thinks it no robbery to gather together his elect, who were created by him, and whom he redeemed with his blood, according to his promise, ' Him who comes to me I will never cast out '. He opened the door gladly to Fulk as soon as he knocked and with joy he embraced him. What more? He put off the old man and was clothed in the new and the ideals of a Canon, which had existed only in name, he professed in his life and conduct. The fame of it took wings, a sweet savour before Christ: the novelty of the thing was noised abroad and came to the ears of his uncle.

5. What would his guardian in the flesh do about this? He had lost the comfort of his nephew's presence whom he had loved too much according to the flesh. Although for others this event had been as a sweet savour of life eternal, it was not so to him. Why? ' Because the sensual man perceiveth not the things that are of God for it is foolishness to him.' Had the spirit of Christ been in him he would not have grieved so much in the flesh as he would have rejoiced in the spirit. Because he was wise rather according to the world than according to heaven, disturbed and put out he mused with himself something like this: What is this I hear? I am undone! I have been deprived of my great hope. But come! this thing cannot be done

without me, without my consent.   What right, what justice, what
reason is there in it?   My hair is already white and shall I spend the
rest of my days in grief because I have lost the staff of my old age?
Were my soul to be required of me this night, who would have
what I have put by?   ' My store-houses are full, overflowing on this
side and that, my sheep are bearing fruitfully and throng the pasture-
land' and to whom will all this belong?   Farms, meadows, houses,
gold and silver vessels, for whose benefit have I amassed them all?
I had acquired for myself certain richer and more sought-after honours
in my Church: the rest, although it was not lawful for me to have them,
yet I held on to them for the sake of Fulk.   What can I do now?
Must I lose all these things just because of him?   For whatever I have
without him to inherit, I might as well not have at all.   It were better
to keep everything and recall him if I could.   But how can this be
done?   Fulk is a professed Canon Regular.   This is an accomplished
fact.   It is known by everyone.   What has been done cannot be
undone.   What is known cannot be hushed up.   If he returns to the
world now it will be known and ill spoken of.   But it were better to
hear this of him than to live without him.   On this occasion what is
right must give place to what is useful;   propriety to what is necessary.
I would rather sacrifice the good name of the boy than subject myself
to misery.

6. And so consenting unto these counsels of the flesh the uncle
forgot all law and reason.   Fearing nothing sacred he raged and
roared like a lion prepared for its prey or a lioness robbed of its cub.
He burst into the dwelling of these holy men where Christ had hidden
his raw recruit to protect him from the strife of tongues that he might
afterwards consort with angels.   He begged and implored that his
nephew be given back to him.   He shouted and cried that he had been
unjustly left.   Christ called back: ' Unhappy man, what are you
doing?   Why are you raving like this?   Why are you persecuting me?
Is it not enough for you that you should have robbed me of your own
soul and, by your example, the souls of many others, so that you must
also lay sacrilegious hands on this one?   Have you no fear of the judgement?   Do you care nothing for my anger?   To whom are you doing
this thing, against whom have you declared war?   " Against him who
is terrible, even him who taketh away the spirit of princes."   Madman!
put your own house in order.   Remember your last hour and tremble.
And you, boy,' he says, ' if you give way and consent to your uncle,
you shall die the death.   Think of Lot's wife.   She was saved from
Sodom because she believed in God.   But she was turned to a pillar
of salt on the way because she looked back.   Learn from the Gospels
that no one who has put his hand to the plough may look back.   Your
uncle has lost his own soul and wants yours; " The words of his
mouth are iniquity and guile ".   Do not be one of those who will not

2

understand lest they do well.   Pay no attention to vanity and deceitful folly.   Lo!   On the path you tread the fowler has laid his snare and spread his nets.   His words are as smooth as oil, but they are very darts.   Take care, my son, that you are not deceived by the lips that speak guile and the deceitful tongue.   Let the love of God quicken your heart lest carnal affection deceive you.   He flatters you but under his tongue lurks labour and tears, and he lieth in ambush that he may catch the innocent.   I tell you, my son, take heed lest you consent to flesh and blood for my sword is sharp and shall devour all flesh. Despise his flattery, spurn his promises.   He promises great things, I promise greater.   He offers many things, I offer more.   Will you throw away heaven for earth, eternity for time?   If not you must keep the vows that have adorned your lips.   You are justly bound to honour your vows since you were not bound to vow.   Although I opened to you when you knocked, yet I did not force you to come in. It is therefore not permitted you to cast aside what you have promised; it is not lawful for you to seek again what you have freely put away. I warn both you and your uncle.   I have salutary advice to offer you. To you, the uncle, I say do not take back to the world one who is bound to a rule or you will take him with you to hell.   And to you, my son, I say do not follow after your uncle; if you do so you follow against me whom you injure.   To you, the uncle, I say if you lead astray a soul for whom I have died you set yourself up as an enemy of the cross.   " He that gathereth not with me, scatters ", and how much more so if he scatters what has been already gathered!   And you, my son, if you consent unto your uncle you dissent from me, because he who is not with me is against me.   And how much more will you be against me if you desert me after having once been with me.   But you, the uncle, if you offend one of these little ones who come to me, you shall be judged a seducer and a sacrilegist.   Whereas you, the nephew, if you pull down again what you have built up, you will make yourself an apostate.   Both of you must appear before my judgement seat, both must appear before my tribunal, the nephew to be judged for his own apostasy, the uncle for the apostasy of his nephew.   And if one die in his iniquity his blood shall be required at the hands of the other.'   These and the like, thou, O Christ, didst thunder unseen to the consciences of both the nephew and the uncle, with these warnings thou didst lovingly besiege the hearts of both. Who would not tremble at these words of thine and look to it with fear lest he become like unto the deaf asp who stoppeth her ears that she hear not the voice of the charmer charming wisely and either not hear or feign to have not heard.

7. But I have already written enough, even perhaps too much, of what it were better to keep silent.   But why, fearful of revealing the whole shameful affair, have I approached the truth by ways so round

about? I will explain, although I do so with shame. I would rather say nothing but what is already known I could not hide even if I would. And indeed why should I be ashamed? Why should I be ashamed to write of what they were not ashamed to do? If it should shame them to hear what they have shamelessly done; at least let them not be ashamed to correct what they do not willingly hear. Ah the pity of it! Neither of them could be kept from his evil ways; not the one from seducing by fear or reason nor the other from apostasy by shame or his vow. What more? The crafty tongue devises words of guile: it has brought forth grief and persuaded iniquity. It perverted the converted, and the dog returned to its vomit. Their Church has taken back its alumnate whom it were better for it to have lost. It was the same thing at Lyons. By a like zeal and industry of their Dean, they disgracefully took back his nephew, one of their Canons, whom they had lost to a good purpose. Just as the one filched Fulk from St. Augustine, so the other filched Osbert from St. Benedict. How much better would it have been for these young men to have become saintly under the rule of a saint rather than to have been perverted by a pervert! How much more beautiful if the religious boy had persuaded the worldly man so that both should conquer, than that the worldly man should have led astray the religious boy so that both were overcome! Unhappy old man! Cruel uncle! Already you are infirm, soon to die, but first you must kill the soul of your nephew! You have deprived your nephew of the heritage of Christ so that you may have an heir to your sins! But ' whose friend is he that is his own enemy?' So he preferred to have an heir to his goods than an intercessor for his sins.

8. But what have I to do with deans? They are our instructors and they hold a high place in the Church. They hold the key of know-ledge and take the first seat in the synagogues. Let them see to it how they judge their subordinates; how they call back their fugitives, and pack them off again if they so wish; how they gather together whom they have scattered and scatter again whom they have gathered to-gether. I must confess that it was on account of my affection for you, my dear Fulk, that I have rather overstepped the bounds of my humble state. I tried at their expense to spare your own shame and to mitigate your fault. I will now pass them over in case they become more angry with me than with their fault and think more of abusing me than of correcting themselves. I am not concerned with those in high places but with an ingenuous youth who does not know how to be indignant and angry! Unless indeed a child more in good sense than in malice you should throw this very thing in my teeth and say: What have you to do with me? What concern of yours are my sins? Am I a monk? And to this, I confess, I have no answer except that I believed in the gentleness of your nature and trusted in the love of God to which, you

may remember, I appealed at the beginning of this letter. It was my zeal for the love of God that moved me to pity for your error, to compassion for your unhappy state, so that I interfered beyond my accustomed measure and manner in order to save you, although you are not a monk of mine. Your sad lapse and miserable fall spurred me on to presume this thing. For whom else of your contemporaries have you seen me rebuke or write even the shortest letter? Not that I think they are saints or can find nothing to blame in their lives!

9. Then why, you will say, do you single me out for rebuke? I reply that I do so on account of the singular gravity of your fault, on account of the enormity of your sin. Although many of your contemporaries may lead bad lives, although they may be irregular and undisciplined, yet they have not been professed in any Order nor have they vowed to keep any rule. They may indeed be sinners, but they are not apostates. Your case is different. No matter how quietly and honourably you may live, no matter how chastely, soberly, and even piously you may conduct yourself, yet would God be less pleased with this than he would be angered at your breaking your vows. Therefore, beloved, you must not compare yourself with these men of the world for you are separated from them by your religious profession. They are not, as you are, bound by vows. Nor must you flatter yourself on account of your, perhaps, stricter self-control, for the Lord says to you, ' Would that I had found you either hot or cold '. By this he clearly means that you please him less being luke-warm than you would if you were stone cold even as these are. God waits for these that they may at last turn from coldness to the heat of fervour, but he sees with anger that you have become lukewarm after being fervently hot. ' And because I have found you ', he says, ' neither hot nor cold, I will spew you out of my mouth ', and deservedly, because you have rejected his grace and returned to your vomit.

10. Alas! How soon you tired of Christ, of whom it is written, ' Honey and milk are under thy tongue '. I wonder that you should have turned against the taste of this sweet nourishment unless perhaps you have never tasted and seen how sweet is the Lord. Either you have never tasted the sweetness of Christ and so do not miss what you have never known or else, if you have tasted and yet not found sweet, your palate is sick. Wisdom itself says, ' They that eat me shall yet hunger; and they that drink me shall thirst again '. But how can anyone hunger and thirst for Christ who is filled every day with the husks of swine? You cannot drink from both the cup of Christ and the cup of devils. The cup of devils is pride; the cup of devils is slander and envy; the cup of devils is debauchery and drunkenness; and when these fill the mind and body there is no room for Christ. You must not wonder at what I am going to say. In the house of your uncle you cannot taste the plenty of the house of God. You ask why?

I answer because the house of your uncle is a house of delicate living and as water cannot mix with fire, so the delights of the flesh and the joys of the spirit cannot go together. Christ does not deign to pour out his wine, sweeter than honey and the honeycomb, for one whom he sees debauched in his cups. The bread of heaven is not tasted amid a delicate variety of foods and napery of every colour, so that both eyes and belly are filled. 'Rejoice, therefore, O young man in your youth.' When the joy of life fades endless remorse will devour you. Far be this from our Fulk; may God forefend his child from such a fate! Let him rather scatter those who with lips of guile give you such counsels, who say to you, 'Well done! Well done!!' but who seek your soul that they may devour it. These are they whose evil counsels corrupt good manners.

11. But how long is it already, and you are still among them. What business have you in towns who have chosen the cloister? What do you in the world who have renounced the world? 'The Lord is your portion in pleasant places' and yet you still gape after worldly riches. If you wish to have both you will receive the short answer, 'Son, thou didst receive thy good fortune in thy lifetime'. It says 'received' not 'robbed', so you cannot flatter yourself even on the grounds that you are content with what you have and do not rob other people. What, in fact, are the things you have? Benefices of the Church? Quite right, they are. And if you rise from your bed for the Vigils, if you attend Masses, if you frequent choir for the day and night offices, you do well. In this case you have not received your prebend from the Church for nothing. It is fitting that he who serves the altar should live by the altar. And I grant you that if you serve the altar well, you can live by the altar, but not in luxury, not in pride. You cannot provide yourself from the altar with golden trappings for your horse, inlaid chairs, silvered spurs, and every sort of multicoloured furs for your gloves and collars. In fact what you take from the altar in excess of your bare needs is not yours, and it is sacrilege and robbery. Wisdom prays to be given only what is necessary for life, not what is superfluous, and the Apostle says that he is content with food and clothing, not with food and ornaments. And another saint has said, 'If God shall give me bread to eat and raiment wherewith to be covered'. Note you, he says 'raiment wherewith to be covered' not 'wherewith to be adorned'. So let us then be content just with clothes for covering ourselves, not for wantonness, not for effeminacy, not for pleasing lewd women. But, you say, those with whom I live do this, and if I should behave otherwise I would make myself singular. Just so, and it is for this reason that I say to you, Come out from their midst, so that you need not live in a manner to cause remark in towns or lose your soul by following the example of others.

12. What business have you in towns, fancy soldier? Your brother soldiers, whom you have deserted by running away, are fighting and conquering, they are knocking on the gates of heaven and it is being opened unto them, they take the kingdom of heaven by force and are kings, while you trot around the streets and market places on your horse, clothed in scarlet and fine linen. But these are not the accoutrements of war! Or are you one of those who say, ' Peace, peace and there is no peace'? Sumptuous clothes are no protection against lust and pride, they do not keep avarice at bay, nor quench any other fiery darts of the enemy. Nor do they help against the fever you fear even more and they cannot keep death away. Where, then, are your arms of war? Where is your shield of faith, your helmet of salvation, your corselet of patience? What do you fear? There are more with us than against us. Take up arms and act the man while the fight is still in progress. We have angels for witnesses and allies. The Lord himself is at hand to sustain us, to teach our hands to make war and the fingers of our hands to fight. Let us set out to help our brothers, lest they should fight and conquer, and enter the kingdom without us. It will be too late to knock when the doors are closed, we would then receive the answer, ' Verily I know you not'. Make yourself known, I pray you, first in the battle, show yourself in the fight, lest on that last day you be known only to the devils in hell and not to Christ in glory. If Christ recognizes you in battle, he will recognize you then, and as he promised, reveal himself to you. But only if you recover your senses and repent so that you may be able to say with confidence, ' Then I shall know even as I am known'. And now I have besieged enough for the present the heart of a shy youth with my invectives, it remains to besiege the ears of divine mercy on his behalf, so that if the Lord should find it to have softened but a little under my blows I shall, without doubt, be able to rejoice in him with great joy.

LETTER 3

TO THE CANONS OF EAUCOURT[1]

It is not known who these Canons were.

To the superior of the holy body of clergy and their disciples now gathered together at the place called Eaucourt, from the little flock of Clairvaux and their humble servant Brother Bernard, that they may walk in the ways of the spirit and in the spirit search all things.

---

[1] D. Mabillon, on the authority of a MS. at Corbei, entitled this letter to the Canons Regular of Horricourt (*Aildicurte*), but there are no records of any Canons Regular having been at Horricourt. Lately the well-known Trappist scholar, Fr. Anselm Dimier of Scourmont, has established beyond doubt that the correct reading is Eaucourt, not Horricourt.

I HAVE wondered at and admired the great learning and charity evident from the most helpful and comprehensive exhortation in the letter you addressed to me. But the praise you bestow upon myself is better evidence of your devotion than your knowledge of me; although, as an example of your humility, I can learn from it not a little, yet, knowing myself to be far beneath what you imagine, it cannot but fill me with fear. For who, with any knowledge of himself, could accept such praise without either great fear or great danger? It is not safe for anyone to commit himself to a judgement of this kind even from another. Our judge is the Lord. As for those brothers for whose well-being I know you to be so charitably anxious, that you may set your mind at rest about them I must tell you that on the advice and encouragement of many illustrious persons and especially of that very distinguished man William, Bishop of Châlons-sur-Marne,[1] they have begged us with many prayers and supplications to receive them at Clairvaux. For the sake of a stricter way of life they wish to transfer themselves, with the help of God, from the rule of St. Augustine to the rule of St. Benedict, yet they depart not by so doing from the teaching of him who is the only Master of us all, nor do they render void by their action the first faith they received amongst you, yea at the Baptismal Font, but rather do they preserve it safe and whole. If perchance within the year of probation, laid down by the Rule, they should falter in their new purpose and wish to return to you, I shall not keep them here against their will. Being then such men and received in such wise, may it be far from me to believe that you are hurt by us receiving them or will be hurt by us keeping them. And so, most holy brothers, it would but ill become you vainly to attempt to hamper the liberty of spirit which is theirs by any ill-considered anathema, unless perhaps (which God forbid) it is your own interests and not the glory of Jesus Christ you are trying to promote.

LETTER 4

TO ARNOLD, ABBOT OF MORIMOND

Arnold was the first Abbot of Morimond, an abbey founded from Cîteaux in the year 1115. He was the brother of Frederick, Archbishop of Cologne, and Henry, later Abbot of Riddagshausen, a Cistercian house in Brunswick.

This letter belongs to the year 1124[2] and was occasioned by a sad moral disaster to the Order. Arnold, tiring of the difficulties of his charge (apparently

---

[1] This is William of Champeaux, the great friend of St. Bernard. He had been Archdeacon of Paris and, at his feet, when he presided over the Cathedral school of Notre Dame, Abelard had sat. In 1108 he founded the abbey of Canons Regular of St. Victor and entered it himself as a canon. In 1113 he became Bishop of Châlons-sur-Marne and there ordained St. Bernard and consecrated him as abbot. Henceforth Clairvaux is said to have become a second home for the bishop and the entire city of Châlons-sur-Marne as a home for the monks of Clairvaux. He died in the habit of a Cistercian monk and was buried at Clairvaux in the year 1121.

[2] See *Statuta Capitulorum Generalium Ordinis Cisterciensis*, Ed. D. Josephus Canivez.

his lay-brothers were lazy, his monks disobedient, and his neighbours hostile), suddenly, and without consulting anyone, left his charge and with a handful of monks set out for the Holy Land ' where ', says Bernard in another letter concerning the same subject, ' it is well known that soldiers to fight and not monks to sing are what is wanted '. But he died suddenly in Belgium the next year without having either accomplished his purpose or corrected his error.

As soon as the news of Arnold's death reached Bernard he set about trying to mitigate the ill-effects of his behaviour. He immediately wrote letters to persuade the fugitive monks to return and had his own prior, Walter, appointed to succeed him.

From the dates, as well as from the evidence of the following letter, it is clear that Arnold and Bernard had been at Cîteaux together and were well known to each other. As Bernard knew the headstrong character of Arnold, so Arnold must have been fully aware of the persuasiveness of Bernard for, unwilling to be turned from his purpose, he was careful to keep out of Bernard's way.

Of some passages in this letter the late Watkin Williams has said: ' They are some of the few that have come down to us revealing the tumultuous emotionalism of the Saint, an emotionalism which with him is never the master, but always the servant, deliberately controlled, disciplined to a purpose, directed to an end as the keenest of instruments in the hands of the kindest of surgeons. And real! . . . Bernard could safely be severe because he loved so tenderly; and the more tenderly, the more robust ' (Journal of Theological Studies, Oct., 1939).

To the Lord Abbot Arnold, the spirit of compunction and counsel, from Brother Bernard of Chairvaux.

I WANT you to know first of all that our lord of Cîteaux had not returned from Flanders where he had lately gone, passing by here, when your messenger arrived. So he has not received the letters you instructed to be given him and is still ignorant of this novel venture you have taken upon yourself. He is happy, even if it be for only a short time, to know nothing of the sad rumours that are going round. And by forbidding me to attempt your recall, saying it would be useless for me to try to dissuade you by letter from what you have, as it were, firmly settled with yourself, you have reduced me to despair. In this matter I probably ought not in reason to obey you and, I confess, in any case, for the very grief I feel I could not do so; although, were I to know how to find you, I would come in person rather than write to you, perhaps to achieve more by my presence than I could by letter. Confident in your own obstinacy and sure that no force, no prayers, no efforts whatsoever can turn you from your purpose, you probably smile at what you will consider my futile assurance. But I trust in the power of him who has said, ' To him who believes all things are possible ', and I do not hesitate to apply to myself the words

'Nothing is beyond my power thanks to the strength God gives me'. Although I know something of the obstinacy of your stony heart, yet I wish I were by your side to persuade you even if I could achieve nothing. Whether it would be of any avail I do not know, but I would lay before you the great reasons that compel me to oppose you, I would plead with you not only by my words but also by my tears and sorrow. I would throw myself at your feet, embrace your knees, hang upon your neck and kiss your dear head, that head which has been bowed with mine in a like purpose under the sweet yoke of Christ for so many years. I would beg and implore you with tears, with all my might, in the name of the Lord Jesus first that you should spare his cross, the cross which redeemed those whom you are doing your utmost to destroy, the cross which gathered together those whom you are scattering. I say advisedly destroy and scatter, for, whether they be those you are taking with you or those you are leaving behind, they are both in danger of an equal though different fate. And then that you should spare us your friends for whom, quite undeservedly, you have left only tears and sorrow. Were it only permitted me I would bend you by affection, if I could not convince you by reason! That steely heart of yours, so far proof even against the fear of Christ, I would soften with the touch of brotherly affection! But alas! even this opportunity you have taken from me.

2. Great support of our Order! listen, I beg you, even to an absent friend wholly opposed to your venture, yet sympathizing wholly with your difficulties and dangers. Great support of our Order, have you no fear at all that with your fall the collapse of the whole structure will soon follow? But, you say, I have not fallen. I know quite well what I am doing. My conscience is clear. Be it so; I believe what you tell me of yourself. But what about us who already groan under the heavy burden of scandal caused by your departure and who fear more to come? Can it be that you know all this and yet pretend not to? How can you suppose yourself to stand when you are causing the fall of so many? You were placed in a position of authority not for your own sake, but for the sake of others; not to promote your own interests, but to promote the interests of Jesus Christ. How, I ask, can you possibly set forth with security when by so doing you deprive of all security the flock which has been entrusted to your care? Who will be there to keep away the prowling wolves? Who will be there to console the afflicted and counsel the tempted? Who will hold at bay the raging and roaring lion that goes about seeking whom it may devour? They will all be exposed, without any doubt, to the teeth of the evildoer who devours the children of God as if they were bread for the eating. Alas! what will happen to those new plantations[1] of

---

[1] The foundations of Morimond referred to here are: Bellevaux in Haute-Saône on March 22nd, 1120; La Creste, near Chaumont, on June 30th, 1121; Vieux-Camp, near Dusseldorf, on January 31st, 1123.

Christ set by your own hand in ' the wilderness and fearful desert places'? Who will be there to dig them about and dung them? Who will build a hedge round about them and prune away their untoward growth? Either these still tender saplings will be easily uprooted by the first storms of trouble, or else for lack of anyone to clean the ground about them they will be choked by the weeds that grow up with them, so that they will bear no fruit.

3. Judge therefore for yourself what sort of good this can be which you are seeking, or whether, involving as it does so many evils, it can be a good at all. However great the fruit of repentance you hope to bring forth, will it not be choked for certain by these thistles? In fact, as the Scripture says, ' Even if you offer rightly, will you not sin if you divide not rightly'. What of this? Perhaps you will say that you have divided rightly because you have consulted the good of your own soul. But can you say this while knowing that you have deprived of a father's care those sons whom you have left behind and left orphans? Unhappy and wretched are they, and all the more so for being deprived of their father while he is still alive! You should have some doubts, to be sure, whether it is the good of your soul that you have consulted, seeing that you have presumed such an unheard-of thing without the advice of your brethren and brother abbots and without the licence of your father and master. What upsets many is that you should have taken with you only weak boys and inexperienced youths. Either they are strong and experienced men, in which case, they would be necessary for their orphaned house; or else they are, as I have said, weak and inexperienced, and therefore not fit for the long and tedious journey. But I do not think you can still wish to rule over them as their superior, since I know you to be minded to lay down your pastoral charge and henceforth to care only for your own soul. And indeed it would be most unfitting were you to presume to undertake, without being asked, in one place what in another with equal audacity you have given up against the will of your superiors. But you know all this and so I conclude by promising you in all good faith that if you but give me the chance of speaking with you, I for my part will do what I can so that this venture you have undertaken against orders and therefore with great danger to your soul, you may be able to finish with permission and without disobeying your superiors.

LETTER 5

TO POPE CALIXTUS

This letter, concerning the vagaries of the Abbot of Morimond, is addressed to the ' Chief Pontiff C . . .' and in the Benedictine edition by Mabillon is attributed to the year 1143, the initial C being understood as referring to

Pope Celestine II (1143-1144) and the contents as concerning Abbot Raynald, the fourth Abbot of Morimond.

As the letter would seem clearly concerned with the vagaries of Abbot Arnold, after some hesitation (for D. Mabillon is not lightly to be suspected of error) we include it here. In this case the Pope would be Calixtus II and not Celestine II. See concerning this: ' Arnold of Morimond' by Watkin Williams, Journal of Theological Studies, *October,* 1939.

To the Supreme Pontiff Calixtus, the devoted obedience due from subjects, and all that the prayers of sinners can effect, from the little flock at Clairvaux.

WE are happy that you should hold the place of him who said that his daily burden was the care of all the Churches, because, although you are occupied with greater affairs, we have no fear that your Holiness will consider our insignificance beneath your notice; and indeed we are urged by the greatest necessity. Nor can you listen with no concern to us, of whom you will one day hear, ' Inasmuch as you did it to one of these the least of my brethren, you did it unto me '. Our cause concerns not us alone, but the whole of our Order. Your son, the father of us all, the Abbot of Cîteaux, had he been at home, would either have come to your Majesty in person or he would have written under his own name concerning this wretched and deplorable affair. So as not to keep your anxiety in any longer suspense we must tell you that one of our brother abbots, styled of Morimond, has ill-advisedly enough left the monastery over which he ruled and, impelled by a spirit of frivolity, has determined to set out for Jerusalem. But first, they say, he will try whether he can, in any way, wring a licence from you for his blunder. If you were to countenance him at all in this matter (which God forbid), consider, we implore you, how great an occasion of harm it would be to our Order. With such an example before him any abbot would believe himself at liberty to throw over the burden of his office as soon as it became irksome, and especially would this be the case with us where the burden seems great and the honour small. And for the even greater desolation of the monastery committed to his charge, as if he had not done enough harm already, this abbot has taken with him, as companions in his vagaries, certain of the best and most perfect of those who were under him. Nor is this all, for among those he has taken with him is that noble youth whom, as you will surely remember, he carried off from Cologne some time ago not without scandal and whom, with even greater scandal, he has presumed to take off with him again. And if he says that he wishes to keep the observances of our Order in that land and for this reason has taken with him a crowd of brethren, who would not be able to see that what is wanted there is soldiers to fight not monks to sing and pray! And from this too our Order will take great mischief, since it may easily occur to anyone wanting to wander that he might set off there without danger to find the same way of life observed as he had professed at home. But it is now for your discretion to decide and not for me to dictate how it shall please you to act in this matter, how it shall become your authority to judge it.

LETTER 6

TO THE MONK ADAM

Little seems to be known about the monk Adam beyond what may be learned from the following letters. There is reason to believe that he mended his ways and died in the odour of sanctity.

BOTH the humility which I know to be yours as well as the circumstances of danger in which you are placed lend me courage to address you more sharply and rebuke you more freely than I would otherwise do. Who has beguiled you, senseless one, to depart so soon from the salutary resolutions on which you and I, with God our only witness, lately agreed? Do not be foolish, but see that you direct your steps in the way of God's law. Have you forgotten how at Marmoutier you dedicated the first-fruits of your conversion; then how at Foigny you commended yourself to my care, such as it is; how at Morimond you confirmed your stability and then, again on my advice, how you frankly renounced the pilgrimage, or rather vagabondage, suggested by Abbot Arnold, deciding that if he could not lawfully set off, you could not lawfully accompany him? What then? Do you now say that he set off lawfully after all when he went without even waiting for the permission of his superior and left behind such a deplorable scandal among those committed to his care?

2. What is the point, you will ask, of going over all this? The point is to show you your manifest levity, to show you clearly that you say yes and no to the same thing; that I may oblige you to learn from the Apostle, even late in the day, not to believe every spirit, from Solomon to have many friends but only one in a thousand as counsellor, from the Lord's precursor not to wear soft raiment nor to be blown about by every doctrine like a reed in the wind; from the Gospel not to build your house upon sand, and with the disciples to combine the prudence of the serpent with the simplicity of the dove. From these as well as from very many other texts of Scripture you should understand in how many different ways the tempter has deluded you and how, when he was unable to obstruct the beginnings of your conversion, he envied your perseverance and judged that if he could but rob you of this the one virtue that could assure you of the crown, his malice would be satisfied. I implore you by the mercy of Christ

that you go not away at all, or at least that you first come to speak with me at a place convenient to us both that we may see what can be done to remedy all the evils I feel to have come from your departure or fear will soon come.

LETTER 7

TO BRUNO OF COLOGNE

This Bruno, a friend of Bernard, subsequently became Archbishop of Cologne.

To the Lord Bruno, a man eminent and beloved, health, and whatever good the prayers of a sinner can bring, from Brother Bernard, styled Abbot of Clairvaux.

EVER since we lately met, with mutual pleasure, at Rheims, I do not think I have ceased to hold a small place in your memory. So I write to you whatever I want to say with complete confidence as to an old friend, not timidly as if to a stranger. Arnold, the Abbot of Morimond, has deserted his monastery unlawfully and to the great scandal of our Order. He left without waiting to consult his brother abbots on the thorny matter or even for the permission of the Abbot of Cîteaux to whom he is especially bound by obedience. A man under authority having under himself soldiers, he has become impatient of his allegiance and has proudly thrown off his neck the yoke of his superior, while even more proudly retaining his own on the necks of his subjects. Of the great crowd of monks which, by encompassing sea and land, he had gathered together not for Christ's sake but for his own, he has taken with him, as companions in his error, the better and more perfect, and abandoned the more simple and least fervent. Among these, there are three whose abduction especially troubles me; he has dared to lead off and lead astray Everard your brother,[1] Adam whom you know well, and the noble youth Conrad who lately, and not without scandal, he carried off from Cologne. I am fully confident that, should you endeavour to do so, you could by exerting yourself recall these men.

2. I would not have you waste any time over Arnold, I know too well the obstinacy of his character. But I have heard that Adam and Everard, with some other brethren of the same company, are in your parts. If this is the case, it behoves you, should you so deign, to visit them and persuade them by entreaty, and convince them by reason, instructing their dove-like simplicity with something of the serpent's prudence that they may understand they are not bound by obedience to one who is himself disobedient or by the Rule to one who is wandering abroad against the Rule, so as to abandon the Order of their profession for the sake of one who is disordered. They should learn

---

[1] Another text reads 'Our brother'.

on apostolic authority, to hold anathema without hesitation, even an angel from heaven should he preach another gospel, and on the same authority to have nothing to do with any brother who leads a vagabond life. And you too, the same Apostle teaches, ' not to be high minded ' nor to put your hope in uncertain riches until Christ shall claim his true disciple, proved by the renunciation of all things for his sake.

LETTER 8

TO THE MONK ADAM

Abbot Arnold had just died when this letter was written. Evidently the leadership of the party had devolved on Brother Adam, the same Brother Adam to whom Letter 6 is addressed. The implications of monastic obedience are discussed in it at great length, so that it is more a small treatise on the subject than a letter. In a manuscript referred to by D. Mabillon it is, indeed, entitled De discretione Obedientiæ.

WERE you still abiding in the charity which at one time I knew or thought abided in you, you could not but feel the condemnation of charity for the scandal you have caused to the weak. Charity would not offend charity nor scorn when she is offended; she cannot be divided against herself, nor deny her own nature. Rather is it her nature to unite again what has been divided. If, as I have said, she abided in you and you in her, she would not be keeping silent, she would not be resting, or feigning ignorance, but she would be groaning, she would be on fire within you and clamouring, ' Who is scandalized and I am not on fire ', for she is kind, and loves peace, and rejoices in unity. It is she alone who begets unity, confirms it, binds it up, and preserves it in the bonds of peace. Wherever charity is, there too is peace. So, I ask you, how can you, when you have thus wounded the mother of unity and peace, dare to hope that your offering will be acceptable to God? The Apostle himself believes that even martyrdom without charity ' availeth nothing '. How can you believe that you have not offended her whose very bowels and dear pledges you have lacerated by your brutal treatment of her? You have not spared her in the past, nor do you spare her now, but you rend unity and break the bonds of peace. Lay down your offering by the altar and go first to be reconciled, not with just one brother, but with the whole multitude of brethren who have this against you and those few who are with you, that, as with a sword, you have wounded their peace and unity by your desertion. They lament with the bride in the Canticle crying, ' The sons of my mother have fought against me ', and rightly so, because being no longer joined in unity with them you are against them. And do you think that charity, their loving mother, can hear without grief this just complaint of her children? She joins her tears with theirs and says of you: ' My own sons, that I have reared and brought to manhood, think to defy me '. Charity is God himself. Our peace is Christ, ' who hath made two nations one '. In the Trinity itself, unity is honoured. What share, therefore, can the enemy of charity, peace and unity have in the kingdom of Christ and God?

2. But perhaps you will say, ' My abbot commanded me to follow him. Would you have me disobedient? ' But you surely have not forgotten the decision we reached together when you first told me of the scandalous project which you were even then considering. If only you had remained firm to that it might have been said of you not inaptly, ' Blessed is the man who hath not walked in the counsel of the ungodly '. But be it so, as you say. Let us grant that as you were his sons and disciples you ought to have followed your abbot; that an abbot may lead his sons where it shall please him and teach them what he wishes—but surely not now that he is dead? Now that he is dead whose teaching you were bound to hear and in whose footsteps you were bound to follow when he was alive, why do you delay in setting right the great scandal you have caused? Who is now to prevent you hearing, I do not say myself, but God sweetly calling to you through the mouth of Jeremias: ' Shall not he that falleth rise again? And he that is turned away, shall he not turn again? ' Does he intrude even from the grave to prevent you rising again or daring to think that you should turn again? Now that he is dead is it necessary for you to obey him against charity and at the peril of your soul? You would allow, surely, that the bond which links abbots with their disciples is not stronger than the bond which God has tied with an inviolable sacrament between husband and wife, according to the words of our Saviour himself: ' What God has joined together let no man put asunder '? Yet on the authority of the Apostle a woman is no longer tied to her husband when he is dead. Do you then believe yourself still bound by the command of your abbot now that he is dead, against an even holier law, the law of charity?

3. I have not said this because I think you ought to have obeyed your abbot in this matter, even when he was alive; or that such yielding to him could even be called obedience. That sentence from Scripture applies to all obedience of this kind: ' Feet that stray into the snare the Lord will punish as he punishes wrong doers '. And so that no one should contend that this does not apply to obedience, even when it is in something evil, it says more clearly in another place: ' The son shall not bear the iniquity of the father, and the father shall not bear the iniquity of the son '. From this it is clearly apparent that no one is to be obeyed when he commands evil, especially as, although we may seem to be obeying a man when we do so, yet really we are disobeying God who has forbidden all evil. It is extremely perverse to profess to be obedient by disobeying the higher for the sake of the lower, or

in other words by disobeying the commandments of God for the sake of the commands of a man. What then? Am I to turn a deaf ear to God when a man commands what he forbids? Not so the Apostle who cried out: ' It is better to obey God than man '. For this the Lord rebukes the Pharisees in the Gospels saying: ' Why do you transgress the commandments of God for the sake of your own traditions? ' and by the prophet Isaias he says: ' In vain they worship me teaching the commandments and doctrine of men '; and again to the first man: ' Because thou hast harkened to the voice of thy wife rather than to mine, the earth is accursed in thy work '. Therefore to do evil, command it who may, is to disobey rather than to obey.

4. Now so that you may understand me you must know that there are some things wholly good and others wholly evil, and in these latter there can be no obedience due to any man. No one may forbid the former; no one may command the latter. And between these two extremes there are middling things; things neither good nor evil, but indifferent. And these things derive their character of goodness or badness from the circumstances of manner, place, and time. It is in this sphere that the law of obedience obtains as in the tree of the knowledge of good and evil which was in the midst of Paradise. In these things we may in no wise follow our own will so as to ignore the commands of our superiors. Let us see now whether it is a thing such as this that I have rebuked in you, when, perhaps, on this account I should not have done so. This will be all the clearer if I give some examples of the foregoing distinctions. Faith, hope, charity, and the like are wholly good and it can never be wrong to enjoin them and never right to forbid or neglect them. Wholly evil are theft, sacrilege, adultery, and the rest, which it can never be right to enjoin or to do and never wrong to forbid or not to do. The law of obedience is not concerned with these, since no prohibition is valid against what has been laid down, and what has been forbidden cannot be recommended by the commands of anyone. Then there are the middling things, neither good nor evil, and these can be indifferently, either well or ill, commanded or forbidden. In these things obedience is never wrong. As examples of them I give fasting, vigils, reading, and the like. But you must know that some middle things can often become either wholly good or wholly evil. Thus marriage is neither enjoined nor forbidden; but once contracted it cannot be dissolved. What, therefore, before the nuptials was clearly a middling thing, after them becomes, for the persons married, a thing wholly good. Likewise, whether a secular person should hold property or not is a matter of indifference; but for a monk it is wholly evil, for he is not permitted to hold any property at all.

5. Do you see now, brother, to which of my foregoing divisions your leaving the monastery belongs? If it can be classed as wholly good, it

is praiseworthy; if as wholly bad, it is blameworthy. But if it is to be classed between the two extremes as being neither good nor evil, then the going forth might be excused on the grounds of obedience, but not the delay in returning. From what has been said already it should be quite clear to you that if your abbot commanded anything he ought not to have done, now that he is dead he is no longer to be obeyed. This should be clear enough, but, for the sake of those who unreasonably seek opportunities to object, I will try to make it still more clear, so that there can be no shadow of doubt that it was not an indifferent matter, neither good nor evil, but wholly evil that you should have obeyed and left your monastery in the way you did. But so that God shall not say of me with righteous anger, ' Men have taken away my judgement ', I shall not mention your abbot. He now has God for his only judge and before his Lord he either stands or falls. I will discuss not what he did, but what he ordered, so that we may see whether his orders had force to bind his subjects even in the teeth of the scandal they have given. But first I will say this, if there be some, as I could well believe there are, who, although they did wrong to leave their monastery, yet did it in good faith, supposing their abbot to have had the permission of the Bishop of Langres and the Abbot of Cîteaux, to both of whom he was subject, my rebuke does not touch them, providing they return to their monastery so soon as they learn the true facts of the case.

6. I speak only against those, or rather for the sake of those, who knowingly and deliberately have put their hands into the fire; who, though conscious of their audacity, yet followed the audacious one, heedless of the Apostle warning them to have nothing to do with a vagabond brother, and of the Lord himself saying: ' Who does not gather with me, scatters '. You, brothers, you, I say, take particular heed of that taunt of Jeremias which I remember with grief: ' This is a people which hath not harkened to the voice of the Lord their God '. For this is the voice of God authoritatively pointing out his enemy, as with a finger, to deter the simple from his ungodly example: ' Who is not with me ', he says, ' scatters ', as if to say, if you follow him when he scatters abroad what I have gathered together, you can know that you are not with me. When God himself cries out, ' Who does not gather with me, scatters ', must you follow the scatterer? When God, I say, invites you to gather, ought you to obey in preference a man so as to scatter? He ignores his superiors, he betrays his subjects, he troubles his brethren, and yet you on seeing the thief ran with him! I had intended to keep silent about the dead but I am obliged, I confess, to overstep a little my limit, because the obedience cannot be blamed without showing up the command as blameworthy. Further, as both the command and the deed were united in the same man, it would appear impossible to blame the one

without reflecting blame on the other. Yet it is clear that this sort of command cannot be obeyed for to do so were to disobey God. Also the ordinances of our fathers are to be preferred to those of lesser persons, and there can be no doubt that personal commands must not be obeyed if they conflict with the common observance, for all this is in the Rule of St. Benedict.

7. I might indeed bring forward the Abbot of Cîteaux as complaining that you have ignored him in favour of your own abbot. And he would have every right to complain for he is as much the superior of your abbot as a father is of his son, or the master of his disciple, or in fact an abbot of his monks. I might also cite the Bishop of Langres for whom he showed inexcusable contempt by not awaiting his permission before setting out, even when the Lord has said: ' He who despises you despises me '. But because the authority of the Roman Pontiff could be opposed and preferred to these as being more weighty, since they say that you have not omitted to fortify yourselves with his licence (this matter of licences I will deal with later), I will cite one whose authority no man may gainsay, the High Priest who, by his own blood, alone and once and for all entered into the sanctuary having obtained eternal redemption, and I will cite him crying with a great voice that no one shall dare scandalize one of his little ones. But the scandalizing of one might be forgiven you if the evil rested there, for pardon comes speedily to the fault from which no great evil arises. But now that, beyond doubt, many have been scandalized, who cannot clearly see how churlish you have been in obeying man rather than God? Who, unless he were mad, would dare to call such an action as yours good or even middling, neither good nor bad, however great the dignity of the man who commanded it? But what is not good nor ever able to be good is, without doubt, wholly evil. Consequently your journey forth from your monastery because it gave rise to the scandal of so many was, for this reason, against the command of God, and so it was not either wholly good or indifferent, but wholly evil. For what is wholly good can never be anything but good, and what is between the two, neither good nor evil, can be good.

8. Since, as it has been shown, what is wholly evil can never be justly commanded or lawfully done, how, I ask you, can the command of an abbot or the permission of the Pope render it lawful? When violation of God's law is involved the excuse of human obedience is futile. Nor do I fear your taking refuge behind that answer the Lord gave when they told him of the scandal he had given to the Pharisees, ' Let them be, they are blind leaders of the blind ', as if on that account you need not worry about the scandal you have given us. There is no comparison either between the persons or the causes. Our Lord is speaking there of the scandal caused to the proud Pharisees, whereas you have given scandal to the humble poor of Christ. And in his

case it was truth that caused the scandal, in yours it is frivolity. Also, to repeat what has been said already, you have preferred not only human authority to divine, but private judgement to the common life. But it should be proof enough for you that not only the whole of our Order, but also the usages and customs of every monastery cry out against your strange novelty and insolent audacity.

9. 'We have sought and obtained', you say, 'an apostolic licence.' I reply that this is just an indication that you were not easy in your mind or satisfied in your conscience. What a futile expedient! It is like the first man trying to cloak his shame with fig leaves, as if they were a remedy and not just a cover. It would have been better had you sought the counsel rather than the consent of the Pope. But why did you obtain this licence? In order that you might lawfully do what it was not lawful for you to do? But what is unlawful is evil. Therefore the intention which inclined to evil, was evil. Unless indeed you say that it was lawful for you to do with a licence what would not have been lawful otherwise. But that argument has been utterly demolished further back. When God said, 'See to it that you do not treat one of these little ones with contempt', he did not add, 'unless you have permission of the Pope'; nor did he say, 'Whoever scandalizes one of these little ones without an apostolic licence . . .'! It is clear that, except in the interests of truth, and there is no question of that in your case, it is never lawful for anyone to give scandal or to command what would give scandal. You think it necessary to obtain a licence from the Pope in order to commit this sort of evil. So that, I suppose, you may sin more impudently and therefore more perilously! What wonderful caution! What astonishing foresight! The evil you conceived in your heart you were careful not to bring forth until you had secured a licence! You conceived sorrow, but you did not bring forth iniquity until the Pope had given his consent. But what have you gained? How is the evil lessened? Does it, on account of the Pope's consent, cease to be evil or become a lesser evil? As if anyone would think it was not evil to consent unto evil! I refuse to believe the Pope did this unless you got round him by lies or overwhelmed him by importunity. How else could he have been induced to permit the sowing of scandal, the stirring up of schism, the upsetting of friends, the disturbing of peace, the disruption of unity, and the contempt of the bishop? And all this for what purpose? There is no purpose in my saying for the results are a clear enough indication. I bewailed your progression, but I have yet to see any progress.

10. You tell me that to assent to such great evils, to yield to them, to assist them, is to be obedient, modest, and meek. I tell you that you are simply cloaking the worst vices under the names of the virtues. You call the most deceitful presumption, obedience; the most outrageous frivolity, modesty; the most cruel discord, meekness.

By doing this you merely foul the holy names of the virtues. This is not the sort of obedience I would want for myself; such modesty, I should say molestation, would not be for me; may such meekness be far from me! Such obedience is worse than any haughtiness; such modesty exceeds all mode. Shall I say it is beyond measure or not up to measure? It would be perhaps more true and more pertinent to say that it is completely outside any measure. What sort of meekness is this of which the very mention exasperates everyone? Nevertheless I wish you would show a little meekness to me. As you are so patient that you allow yourself to be dragged without complaining even where you ought not to go, permit me, I beg you, to be a little more bold with you, or else, if I alone am singled out for the object of your wrath, I have indeed deserved ill of you.

11. I invoke your conscience. Did you set out from your monastery because you wanted to or unwillingly? If because you wanted to, then it was not from obedience. If unwillingly, then it would seem that you were doubtful about the order to which compliance was such a burden. But when an order is in doubt, there should be inquiry. Yet so that you might put your patience to the proof, or give a proof of your patience, without any inquiry whatsoever, you suffered yourself to be dragged off not only unwillingly, but even against your conscience. Who would not be impatient with such patience! I cannot help, I confess, being angry with such headstrong patience. You saw your abbot scattering the flock and you followed with him; you saw him ordering scandal, and you obeyed him. It is the nature of true patience to suffer and act against self-will, but not in excess of what is lawful. I wonder how you heard the whispers of a man when you were deaf to the voice of God proclaiming in tones of thunder: 'Woe to the man through whom scandals come!' Not only the voice of the Lord, but also his blood cries aloud with a terrible voice for even the deaf to hear. The pouring of it forth is its cry. It was poured forth for the scattered children of God that they might be gathered together in one fold, and justly it raises its voice against the man who would scatter again. Concerned only to gather together, it abhors the man who scatters. With a great and mighty cry it awakes the dead in their tombs and summons souls from below. It is the voice of a trumpet calling heaven and earth together to give peace to both. The sound of it has gone out to the ends of the earth, but it has not pierced your deafness. That voice of power, that voice of glory, was powerless to pierce your deafness! And what does it say? 'Let God arise, and let his enemies be scattered'; and again: 'Scatter them by thy power; and bring them down, O Lord, my protector'. It is the blood of Christ, Brother Adam, it is the blood of Christ which raises its voice for the faithful gathered to-gether, against the impious one who would scatter them abroad. The

blood which was poured forth to gather together those who had been scattered, threatens to scatter the men who would scatter what it has gathered together. If you do not hear its voice, he hears it from whose side it flowed. And how could he not hear the voice of his own blood, who heard the voice of the blood of Abel?

12. ' But what is all this to me? ' you say. ' He should have looked to it who gave me the order. It was not for me to contradict my abbot. The disciple is not above his master. I clove to him in order to be taught, not to teach. I was the disciple and it was for me to follow, not to lead, my master.' So you are another simple Paul![1] If only your abbot had been another Anthony, so that there would have been no need for you to inquire into anything he said, but simply to obey without question the slightest word that fell from his lips! What an obedient monk you are, you do not suffer one jot or one tittle of your senior's words to escape you: it is enough for you that a thing should be commanded that without pausing to question the command . . .[2] And this is the true obedience without delay. But if this sort of obedience were proper, then it would be useless to read in Church: ' Prove all things; hold fast that which is good '. Were this sort of obedience becoming, then we should delete the words of Scripture, ' You must be prudent as serpents ', for it would be enough to have said ' . . . as simple as doves '. I do not say that subjects should question the orders of their superiors when it is clear that they do not conflict with the divine ordinances, but I say that prudence is necessary in order to understand whether they do conflict, and freedom too in order candidly to ignore them if they do. But you reply that it does not concern you to question the orders of your superiors; that they are responsible for their orders. Tell me then, I beg you, were your abbot to place a sword in your hand and command you to cut his throat, or were he to tell you to push him headlong into the fire, would you obey? Would you not say that it would be murder even not to hinder such a thing? Come then and see to it that you have not co-operated in an even graver matter, under pretext of obedience. You know who said (in case you do not believe me), ' If anyone scandalizes one of these little ones that believe in me, he had better be drowned in the depths of the sea '. Why did he say this if not to indicate that torments so great beyond the grave await those who give such scandal that in comparison temporal death seems a blessing rather than a punishment? Why then did you co-operate in the scandal by obeying and following your abbot? Would it not have been better for him that he should have been drowned in the depths of the sea with a millstone about his neck? What then?

[1] The Paul here mentioned was the disciple of St. Anthony in Egypt about the year 300. St. Anthony was called by St. Athanasius, who wrote his life, the model for monks and the founder of asceticism. His disciple Paul was well known for his docility and childlike simplicity.
[2] The MS. is here defective.

O most obedient monk, so obedient that rather than part with your abbot for one second or by a palm's breadth, you followed him into the pit, not blindly but, like Balaam, with your eyes fully open; do you believe that you were acting for his good by showing such obedience, an obedience that was for him more grievous than death? Now indeed I understand the truth of those words: ' A man's enemies are of his own household '. If you see and understand this, do you not groan and tremble for what you have done? According to the judgement, not of myself, but of Truth, your obedience has been worse than murder.

13. If you know this, how can you not fear? And if you are afraid, how is it you do not mend your ways? Otherwise what sort of conscience will you bring before the dire judgement of God? Then the judge will not want for a witness, then truth itself will search the intentions, then the scrutiny of faults will reach into the most hidden places of the heart, then the eye of God will search the most remote secrets of the mind. Then the corners of the heart will expand under the sudden brightness of the sun of Justice and pour forth the good and bad which they were hiding. Then, Brother Adam, those who have done evil and those who have consented to evil will receive a like penalty. Then both thieves and their partners in guilt will await the same punishment. Then both those who entice to sin and those who have allowed themselves to be enticed will receive a like judgement. Go ahead then, Brother Adam, and say: I have touched pitch and yet I am not black, I have held fire to my bosom, and yet I am not burned. Say that you have taken your portion with adulterers, and yet it is no business of yours. Isaias thought differently. He blamed himself not only for being unclean, but for keeping company with the unclean, saying: ' Woe is me because I am a man of unclean lips and I dwell in the midst of a people with unclean lips '. He blamed himself, I should have said, not because he lived with evil men, but because he did not blame the evils, for he says: ' Woe is me because I have held my peace '. But where do we hear that he yielded to the evil which he blamed himself for not blaming in others? And what about David? Did he not believe that he could be infected with the sins of others when he said: ' Not mine to take part with wrong doers, not mine to mingle with the company they keep '? And then he prays: ' From my secret sins cleanse me, O Lord, and from those of others spare thy servant '. It is also clear that he declined the company of those whose evil he did not wish to share, for he says: ' I have not sat with the council of vanity, neither will I go in with the doers of iniquity '; and to this verse he adds: ' I have hated the assembly of the malignant, and with the wicked I will not sit '. Finally Wisdom counsels us: ' If sinners entice thee, consent not to them '.

14. Did you really think that you ought to have obeyed anyone in the face of these and many other testimonies of truth? What hateful perversity! Obedience which has hitherto always been the ally of truth, you have armed against it. I should call happy the disobedience of Brother Henry. He soon repented of his error and returned to his monastery without experiencing such obedience as yours. How much more sweet and desirable is the fruit that he plucks of his disobedience and even now is tasting with a good conscience because, while his other companions are breaking the hearts of their brethren with the scandal they are causing, he is living peacefully among his brothers faithful to his Order and profession. Had I to choose I would rather have his inactive disobedience with his good conscience than the zealous obedience of the others with the scandal. I consider he does better thus preserving unity in the bonds of peace, disobedient to his abbot yet not to charity, than those others who for the sake of obedience to one man endanger the unity of all. I would add with all assurance that it is better to endanger obedience, than to jeopardize all the benefits of piety and the vows of our profession.

15. Not to mention anything else there are two things handed down to us who dwell in monasteries for especial observance. One is submission to the abbot, the other is stability in our monastery. And these two are so to be observed that there is no conflict between them. That is to say, we should not be led by our stability to disdain subjection to the abbot, or by our subjection to the abbot, to lose stability. Further, if you abominate one who although persevering in stability yet ignores the commands of his abbot, can you wonder if I censure the obedience you adduce as the cause or occasion of your losing stability by leaving your monastery? Especially as in our regular profession while stability is explicitly promised there is no mention at all of it being subject to the abbot.

16. But perhaps you will ask how I reconcile the stability I confirmed at Cîteaux with living elsewhere. I answer that while it is true I was professed a monk of Cîteaux in that place and was sent by the abbot to live where I do, yet I was sent in peace, without any scandal or discord, according to the customs and common observance of our Order. Therefore so long as I persevere in the same peace and concord wherein I was sent, so long as I stand fast in unity, I am not preferring my private judgement to the common observance. I am remaining quietly and obediently where I was put. I say my conscience is at peace because I have not broken the bond of unity, because I have not left the firm ground of peace. And if under obedience I am absent in body from Cîteaux, yet by a fellow devotion, by a life in all things the same, I am always there in spirit. But the day on which I begin to live by other rules (which may God forbid!) and other habits, to keep other observances, to introduce new things and follow different

customs, on that day I shall no longer believe I keep my promise of stability. I say, therefore, that the abbot is to be obeyed in all things, but according to the tenor of our profession. You, who were professed according to the Rule of St. Benedict, when you promised obedience, you promised as well stability. So if you should be obedient, but not stable, by offending in one, you offend in all, and if in all, then also in obedience.

17. Do you now see the force of your vow of obedience? That it cannot, in fact, suffice to excuse the transgression of stability, not even having the force to support itself. We make our professions solemnly and according to Rule in the presence of the abbot, but only in his presence, not at his pleasure. The abbot witnesses, but does not dictate the profession. He is there to help, not to hinder, its fulfilment. He is there to punish, not instigate, infringement. What then? Do I leave in his hands what I have confirmed by my mouth and hand before God and his saints, knowing from the Rule if I ever act otherwise I will be condemned by him whom I mock? If my abbot, or even an angel from heaven, should command what is contrary to this, I shall boldly excuse myself from an obedience that I know would render me a transgressor of my vow and a perjurer before God. I know from Scripture that out of my own mouth I shall be justified or condemned because ' the mouth that lies killeth the soul ' and because we chant before God, ' Thou wilt destroy all that speak a lie ', and because ' Everyone shall bear his own burden ' and ' Everyone of us shall render an account of himself to God '. Were it otherwise how could I dare to sing before God: ' I will render unto thee the vows my lips have uttered '? It is the duty of my abbot to consider how he may best follow the explicit direction of the Rule that ' he should maintain the present rule in every particular '. In the same way it is also laid down in the Rule as a general principle from which no one may be excused: ' Let all follow the Rule as their guide, and from it let no man rashly turn aside '. And I have so determined to follow my abbot always and everywhere providing that he never by his teaching departs from the Rule which, in his presence, I have vowed and determined to keep.

18. Let me now meet another question that might be raised, but briefly so as to bring this letter, which is already too long, to a close. It seems at first that by receiving and keeping monks that come to me from other monasteries I act contrary to my own teaching. It could be asked why I receive monks who break their vow of stability and ignore the commands of their seniors by coming to me when I condemn those who leave their monasteries not only with permission of their abbot but even by his order. To this there is a short answer, but a perilous one. I fear that what I am to say will displease some people. But I think I would have more to fear for myself if, by not telling the

truth, I could no longer sing from my heart: 'I have not hid my righteousness within my heart: my talk has been of thy truth and thy salvation'. Therefore I will say that I received them for the reason that I did not think they were wrong in leaving their monasteries, if they could not observe there the vows their lips have uttered, and coming to where they may be better able to render them to God who is everywhere, repairing the harm they have done by breaking their vow of stability by an exact observance of the others. If there is anyone whom this does not please, and who murmurs against a man for seeking his own salvation, the author of all salvation shall answer him with the words: 'Is thine eye evil because his is good?' O whoever you are who envies another his salvation, spare at least your own. Have you not read: 'By the envy of the devil, death entered the world'? Take heed for yourself. If death and envy go together, you cannot envy and live. Why trouble your brother if he tries to honour the vows his lips have uttered? What do you lose by a man seeking how and where he may best fulfil what he has promised to God? Perhaps if he owed you a little money you would oblige him to encompass sea and land until the whole debt had been repaid even to the last farthing. What then has your God deserved of you that you should not wish him too to receive his due? In fact by envying one you have offended two. While you deprive the Lord of his servant's service, you also deprive the servant of the grace of his Lord. Why do you not imitate him by also paying what you owe? Do you think that your debt too will not be required of you? In fact you impiously anger God even more by saying: 'He will not require it of me'.

19. 'What', you say, 'do you condemn all those who do not follow these monks into your Order?' No, I do nothing of the sort. But listen to what I have to say of them and do not make futile accusations. Why do you try to make me hateful in the eyes of many thousands of holy men, who live under the same vows as I but not in the same manner, yet who live holy lives and make holy deaths? I know quite well that God has left to himself seven thousand men who have not bowed the knee to Baal. Listen and attend to what I have to say, envious and calumnious man. I have already told you why I believe that those who come to us from other monasteries are to be received. Does it follow that I condemn those who do not come? I have excused those who do come but I have not accused those who do not. I only do not excuse the envious, for I cannot. Leaving aside these, if there should be any who wish to change to the purity of the Rule but dare not for fear of scandal, or cannot on account of some bodily weakness, I think they do not sin providing they live where they are soberly, honestly, and piously. If by the customs of their monastery they cannot live so strictly as the Rule would seem to require, they will

probably be excused either on account of their charity which holds them back from hastening to something better for fear of giving scandal, according to the words of Scripture, ' Charity covers a multitude of sins ', or else on account of their humility by which they are conscious of their own infirmity and deem themselves imperfect on that account, and of such it has been written: ' God gives grace to the humble '.

20. I have said much to you, beloved, without there being any need for many words in your case, for I know well how quick you are to understand and how prompt you are to follow good advice. But although I have addressed myself to you especially, I have not written at such great length especially for you, but for those who need it. But I do warn you, as one who has been now for long well known to me, with few words and the fullest confidence, not to keep the souls who need you in any longer suspense, to the fearful peril of your own soul. You hold in your hand the fates of yourself and, unless I am deceived, of those who are with you. I believe they will follow you in whatever you do or wish to be done. Otherwise do not hesitate to proclaim to them the sentence of excommunication, which none can ignore, passed on them by all the abbots in Chapter: ' Who return shall live, who refuse shall die '.[1]

LETTER 9

TO BRUNO, ARCHBISHOP-ELECT OF COLOGNE

The same Bruno as Letter 7 is addressed to. In spite of the doubts of St. Bernard he accepted the Archbishopric of Cologne. He was consecrated in the year 1132 and died in Italy four years later. He left a reputation for great learning.

YOU ask my advice, most illustrious Bruno, whether you should yield to those who would raise you to the episcopate. But what mortal would venture to decide such a matter? Perhaps God calls you, and then who would dare to dissuade you? Perhaps he does not call you, and then who would dare to persuade you? But whether or not he does call you, who can tell save the Spirit, who can search even the hidden things of God, or one to whom God himself might perhaps reveal it? The humble but terrible confession you make in your letter, accusing your past life so gravely yet not, I believe, untruly, renders advice on the matter even more doubtful. It cannot be denied that the sort of life of which you accuse yourself is not worthy of the sacred ministry. But again you are afraid, and not without reason, for I also fear the same thing, that you might do wrong if you did not trade with the talent of knowledge which has been committed to you,

---

[1] This was the Chapter held in 1124, when St. Bernard was instructed to recall the fugitives. See *Statuta Capitulorum Generalium Ordinis Cisterciensis*, ed. D. Josephus Canivez, Louvain, a work of superb erudition and interest.

because you feel unworthy; unless there is some other sphere in which you could use it, less fruitfully perhaps, but also with less peril. I confess (for I must tell you what I feel in the matter) that I tremble for you when I consider from what depths you are being called to such heights, especially as there is no time for you to prepare yourself by penance for the perilous transition. And indeed right order requires that you should learn to look after yourself before you undertake the care of others. It is written that the first step in piety is to ' have pity on your own soul, pleasing God '. And from this an orderly charity proceeds on right lines to the pity of others, inasmuch as it is laid down that we should love others as we love ourselves. But were you to love others as you have hitherto loved yourself, I for one would not wish to be committed to your care. Learn first to love yourself, and then you can love me.

2. But what if God were to hasten his graces and multiply his mercies so that your innocence is restored to you more effectively by his prompt compassion than it would be by years of penance, according to the words: ' Blessed is the man to whom the Lord hath not imputed his sin '. Who shall indict the elect of God? Who is he that condemns if God justifies? The good thief took this short way to salvation. On one and the same day he confessed his sin and was brought to glory, satisfied to use the cross as a short bridge from the state of otherness[1] into the land of the living, from the filth of this life to the paradise of delights. And the sinful Magdalen was also blessed with this same prompt remedy of piety, when grace began immediately to abound in her soul where iniquity had superabounded. Without any great labour of penance many sins were forgiven her because she had loved much, and in a short time she deserved to receive the abundance of charity which covers a multitude of sins. And the paralytic in the Gospels immediately experienced the double favour of being cured first in his soul and then in his body.

3. But it is one thing to obtain immediate forgiveness of sins and quite another to step immediately from enormities into the bishop's throne. I see Matthew raised immediately from the seat of custom to the dignity of an Apostle, but what disturbs me here is that he did not immediately hear with the other Apostles: ' Go ye into the whole world and preach the Gospel to every creature '. Before hearing this he had first to do penance by enduring with the Lord in his trials and by following him for a long time and with great labour whithersoever he went. If Ambrose occurs as an example of one who was raised immediately from the secular tribunals to the dignity of

---

[1] *De regione dissimilitudinis.* This is almost a technical phrase with St. Bernard. Created by God in his own likeness, man has become disfigured by sin and so exiled from the land of Likeness to God to the land of Unlikeness . . . *Regio dissimilitudinis.* Actually the phrase is taken from St. Augustine (*Confessions,* Book vii, ch. 10), but St. Bernard makes a very personal use of the expression. See St. Bernard, *Sermo ' de diversis ',* XLII.

the priesthood, it is no comfort because from boyhood he had lived in the world but not of the world and, deeming himself unworthy of the dignity, he tried to avoid it by flight, by hiding himself, and by other ruses. If Saul becoming immediately Paul the vessel of election and Doctor of the Gentiles is cited, the example lacks force because although he sinned, he did so, as he himself tells us, in ignorance and firm incredulity. Although there may be other good and excellent instances of what the Scriptures call ' the change of the right hand of the Most High ', they are to be regarded more as miracles of grace than examples to be followed.

4. For the time being you must be satisfied with this provisional answer. I cannot give you a certain answer because I am myself uncertain about the matter. And unless a Prophet is consulted this must always be the case. Clear water cannot be drawn from a muddy pond. But there is one thing we can always do for a friend without any danger and with great advantage, and that is to offer him such help as our prayers to God can achieve. Leaving therefore to God his hidden counsels, of which I am ignorant, I pray him with humble devotion and devout humility to bring to pass in you and for you what most becomes his glory and your good. You have Father Norbert[1] to consult quite near you. As he lives closer to God he would be better able to know his hidden mysteries.

LETTER 10

TO THE SAME, NOW ARCHBISHOP OF COLOGNE

I HAVE received with devotion the letter of your Grace and I have been careful to do what you asked. It will be for your Grace to judge how far I have been successful. But enough of this. I am writing what follows in the same spirit of charity. If it is certain that all who are called to the ministry are also called to the Kingdom of heaven, then the Archbishop of Cologne has nothing to fear. But if it is true that Saul was called to the kingship and Judas to the priest-hood by no other than God himself; and the evidence of Scripture cannot be gainsaid; then the Archbishop of Cologne has every reason to fear. And if, as is indeed true, the sentence of Scripture still holds good for to-day, that not many noble, not many mighty, not many wise according to the flesh are chosen, has not the Archbishop of Cologne a threefold cause to fear? Let us in high places have a care that we become not high minded, but walk with the humble, and fear. ' Have they made you ruler? ' says Scripture. ' Be among them as one of them '. And again: ' The greater thou art, humble thyself the more in all things '. Very wise is this counsel and not other than the words of Wisdom himself saying: ' He that is greater among you,

---

[1] This is St. Norbert, the founder of the Premonstratensian Order.

let him become as the younger'. Otherwise 'a most severe judgement shall be for them that rule', so let the powerful fear. And the
servant who knows the will of the Lord but does it not, shall be
beaten with many stripes; so let the man of letters fear. And let the
noble also fear, for the judge of all is no respecter of persons. This
three-strand rope of necessary fear is difficult to break. Does it seem
hard that I do not flatter you, but incite you to fear, that for my friend
I wish the beginning of wisdom? It is my wont ever thus to favour
my friends, inciting them with wholesome fear rather than with
deceitful flattery, and to this I am urged by the words, 'Blessed is the
man that is always fearful', and I am recalled to it by him who says:
'O my people, they that call thee blessed, the same deceive thee'.

LETTER 11

TO THE SAME

ALTHOUGH by reason both of the office you hold and of the Apostolic
injunction, your Grace is bound to punish so shocking an infamy
yet, in such a grave matter, I do not think that the admonition of a
friend would come amiss. In such a matter as this I would wish one
who is both a father and a friend to be advised that he should punish
with the zeal that the occasion demands, so that not only this present
outrage may be penalized, but that any malicious person hearing of it
may be restrained from a like rashness.

LETTER 12

TO THE PRIOR GUY AND OTHER RELIGIOUS OF THE GRANDE CHARTREUSE

*Guy was the fifth Prior of the Chartreuse (1109–1136) and became the
organizer of the Order. He codified the observances of his House in a book
of customs for the benefit of other foundations. The Scale of the Cloisters
and a book of Meditations are also attributed to him. He died in 1137,
leaving a reputation for great sanctity.*

To the most reverend of fathers and most dear of friends, Guy, Prior
of the Grande Chartreuse, and the other saints who are with him,
eternal life, from Brother Bernard of Clairvaux.

I RECEIVED the letters of your Holiness with a delight equalled only by
my longing eagerness for them. I have read them and mused upon
them and they have fired my heart like so many sparks from the fire
which the Lord came to spread over the earth. How great must have
been the fire burning in your meditations to have sent out such sparks
as these! Your burning and kindling greeting seemed to me, I
confess, to have come, not from man, but from him who 'sent word

to Jacob'. It was no ordinary greeting such as one gives in passing on the road, or from habit; I could feel it came from the heart, a welcome and unexpected benison. May the Lord bless you for troubling to meet me, your child, with such a blessing in your letter to me that you have given me the courage to write back to you, after I had for so long wanted to, but not dared. For I was loath to harass your holy peace in the Lord, to disturb even for one moment your unbroken silence from the world, the whispers of your heavenly converse, by my uncalled-for scribbling; or to distract with my own affairs your ears absorbed in celestial praises. I feared lest by so doing I should be as one disturbing Moses on the mountain, or Elias in the desert, or Samuel watching in the temple. When Samuel cries, ' Speak, Lord, for thy servant heareth', should I dare to push myself forward? I feared lest I should be as one troubling David when he was taking to himself the wings of a dove to fly away far off, and hear the angry words: ' Let me be. I cannot hear you. I would sooner listen to what I can hear with greater pleasure : " I will hear what the Lord will speak in me; for he will speak peace unto his people and unto those whose hearts are turned towards him ". Or even: " Depart from me, ye malignant; and I will search the commandments of my God " '. What? Should I be rash enough to wake the bride sleeping gently in the embraces of the Bridegroom for so long as she wishes? I think I would thereupon hear from her the words, ' Do not trouble me. " My beloved to me and I to him who feedeth among the lilies." '

2. But what I do not dare, charity does. She knocks confidently on the door of a friend, knowing that she is the mother of friendships and will not be repulsed. Sweet as your leisure is, she does not fear to disturb it a little on her business. She it is who, whenever she wishes, can draw you away from your contemplation of God for her own sake; and it was she who, when she wished, made you attentive to me, so that you have not thought it at all beneath you, not only to bear with me when I am speaking, but moreover kindly to encourage me to speak when I am silent. I embrace your goodness, I admire your condescension, I praise and venerate the purity of your intention which leads you to rejoice in the Lord for what you consider my progress. I glory in the testimony you have given me of your good will, in your spontaneous friendliness. It is now my joy, my glory, and the delight of my heart that I have not lifted my eyes in vain to the hills from which I have already received so much help. From these hills a sweet dew has come down: may it still come until our valleys are filled with corn. It will ever be for me a day of joy and a day worthy of lasting remembrance on which I was honoured to see and welcome that worthy man through whom I was received into your affections. Although it is clear from your letters that you had received me into

your affections even before this, yet now I understand it will be with an even closer and more intimate affection, since he has told you certain favourable things about me which he doubtless believed, although without sufficient cause.   Far be it from such a religious and good man to have said anything but what he believed to be true. So I have now found out for myself the truth of those words of our Saviour: ' He who gives a just man the welcome due to a just man, shall receive the reward due to a just man '.   The reward due to a just man is to be thought just, for no other reason that than he has received a just man.   If he has said anything else about me then he was judging me, not according to the facts, but according to his own goodness. You have listened to him, you have believed him, you have rejoiced in what he said, you have written to me, and thereby you have gladdened me not a little, not only because I have won a place and no small place in your affections, but also because you have shown me something of the purity of your own soul.   In a few words you have shown me for certain of what spirit you are.

3. I rejoice on my own account and on yours; I congratulate you on your charity, and myself on the profit my soul has derived from it.   For that is a true and sincere charity to be attributed entirely to a pure heart and unfeigned faith which leads us to love our neighbours' good as well as our own.   The man who loves his own good in preference to his neighbours' good or who loves only his own good proves, by the very fact that his love is not disinterested, that he does not love the good with a chaste love.   Such a one could not obey the Prophet when he says: ' Praise the Lord because he is good '. He may praise the Lord because he is good to himself, but not because he is Goodness itself.   And he should know that the same Prophet is casting a reproach at him for this when he says: ' He will praise thee when thou do well to him '.   There are those who praise the Lord because he is powerful, and these are slaves and fearful for themselves; there are those who praise him because he is good to them, and these are hirelings seeking themselves; and there are those who praise him because he is Goodness itself, and these are sons doing homage to their father.   Both those who fear for themselves and those who seek themselves are acting only for themselves; only the love of a son seeks not itself.   On this account, I think that the words ' The Law of God is unspotted ' refer to charity, because it alone can turn the heart from love of self and the world, and direct it to God alone.   Neither fear nor love of self can turn the soul to God; they may sometimes change the aspect or influence the actions of a man, but they will never change his heart.   Even the slave sometimes does God's work, but because he does not do it willingly he proves that his heart is still hard.   And the hireling too will sometimes do God's work, but because he only does it for reward, he is known to be attracted only by his greed.   Where

there is self-seeking, there too is self-esteem; where there is self-esteem, there too is private interest; and where private interest makes a corner for itself there rust and filth will collect.[1] Let fear itself be the law of a slave, by it he is bound; let greed be for the hireling his law, by it he also is confined when by it he is led off and enticed away. Neither of these two laws is unspotted, neither can turn the soul to God; only charity can do this, because she alone can render a soul disinterested.

4. I would call his charity unspotted who never keeps anything of his own for himself. When a man keeps nothing of his own for himself, everything he has is God's, and what is God's cannot be unclean. Therefore the unspotted law of God is charity, which seeks not what may benefit itself, but what may benefit many. Charity is called the law of the Lord, either because the Lord himself lives by it or else because none may have it except by his gift. Let it not seem absurd that I should have said even God lives by law, for I have also said that the law is nothing else but charity. What else but charity preserves that supreme and unspeakable unity in the blessed Trinity? Charity is therefore a law, and it is the law of the Lord holding together, as it were, the Trinity and binding it in the bonds of peace. Yet let no one think that I speak of charity here as if it were a quality or something accidental to the Godhead, as if I were saying (may it be far from me to say any such thing!) that there was something in God which is not God; but I say that charity is the divine substance itself. And there is nothing new or strange about this, for St. John himself has said, ' God is charity '. It follows that charity can be correctly said to be both God and the gift of God; that charity gives charity; the substance of charity, the quality of charity. When we speak of the giver we mean the substance; when we speak of the gift we mean the quality. This is the eternal law, the creator and ruler of the Universe, since through it all things were made in weight, measure, and number. Nothing is left without law, since even the law of all things is not without a law, yet a law not other than itself for, although it did not create itself, it nevertheless rules itself.

5. The slave and the hireling also have a law, a law not from God, but which they make for themselves; the one by not loving God and the other by loving something more than God. They have, I say, a law, but a law of their own, not of God, yet a law which is, nevertheless, subject to the law of God. Anyone can make a law for himself, but he cannot withdraw it from the immutable order of the eternal law. But anyone who thus makes a law for himself is perversely trying to imitate his Creator by ruling himself, and making his own self-will a law for himself, just as God is his own law and subject only

---

[1] *Porro ubi proprietas, ibi singularitas; ubi autem singularitas, ibi angulus; ubi vero angulus, ibi sine dubio sordes sive rubigo.* Literally: ' Where there is proprietorship, there is singularity; where there is singularity, there is a corner; where there is a corner, there without doubt is filth or rust '.

to himself.   Alas! what a heavy and insupportable burden is this on the children of Adam; we are bowed down and bent under it, so that our lives are dragged down nigh to hell.   'Unhappy man that I am, who will deliver me from the body of this death', by which I am so oppressed that unless the Lord had helped me, I would almost have dwelt in hell.   He too was groaning under this burden who said: 'Why hast thou set me opposite to thee, and I am become burdensome to myself'.   When he says, 'I am become burdensome to myself', he shows that he has been a law unto himself, and that no other than he himself had done this.   But when, speaking of God, he says, 'Why hast thou set me opposite to thee', he shows that he has not escaped from the law of God.   It is the property of the eternal law of God that he who will not be ruled sweetly by him, shall be ruled as a punishment by himself; that he who, of his own will, throws off the sweet and light yoke of charity shall unwillingly suffer the insupportable burden of his own self-will.

6. And so in a wonderful way the eternal law keeps the renegade both 'opposite itself' and yet subject to itself, so that he is neither able to evade the law of justice nor to rest in the peace and light of God. He remains subject to the power of God and yet far removed from happiness.   O Lord, my God, why dost thou not take away my sin, why dost thou not remove my iniquity, so that I may cast off the burden of my self-will, and breathe again under the light yoke of charity, no longer forced by servile fear nor enticed by the hireling's lust for gain?   Why am I not led by thy spirit, the spirit of liberty, the spirit which leads thy sons, and which bears witness to my spirit that while thy law is also mine, I too am one of thy sons; and as thou art, so also may I be in this world.   For it is certain that those who fulfil the words of the Apostle and 'owe no man anything except to love him' are in this world even as God; not hirelings nor yet slaves but sons.   Therefore neither are the sons of God free from law, unless anyone should think differently on account of the words, 'The law is not made for the just'.   But it should be understood that the law promulgated in fear by the spirit of slavery is one thing, and the law given graciously by the spirit of liberty is quite another.   Sons are not bound by the former, but neither are they suffered to live without the latter.   Listen to why the law is not made for the just, 'because', says Scripture, 'you have not received the spirit of bondage again in fear'.   Listen also to why the just are under the law of charity: 'You have received the spirit of the adoption of sons'.   And now hear the just man admitting that he is at once not under the law and not without law: 'I became to those that are under the law, as if I were under the law (whereas myself I am not under the law), that I might gain them that were under the law.   To them that are without the law, I became as if I were without the law, whereas I was not without the

3

law, but was in the law of Christ.'   Hence, ' The law is not made for
the just' does not mean that the just are without law, but that the law
is freely and lovingly accepted by them from him who graciously
inspired it and not imposed on them against their wills.   Wherefore
the Lord has beautifully said, ' Take my yoke upon you', meaning
that he does not impose it on us against our will, but that we can take
it on ourselves if we wish, and if we do not we shall find labour and
not peace for our souls.

7. Good and sweet is the law of charity, not only light to bear, but
also an easement of the law of slaves and hirelings.   For it does not
destroy these laws, it brings them to perfection, according to Our
Lord's words: ' I have not come to set aside the law, but to bring it to
perfection '.   Tempering the one and controlling the other, it eases
both.   Charity will never be without fear, but a chaste fear;   nor
ever without self-interest, but an ordered self-interest.   It brings the
law of the slave to perfection by inspiring it with devotion;   and also
the law of the hireling, by controlling self-interest.   When devotion
is mixed with fear it does not nullify it, but amends it;   it takes from it
the anguish which it never lacks when it is servile, and renders it
chaste and filial.   The words ' Perfect charity casteth out fear ' must
be understood as meaning that it removes the anguish which, as I
have said, is never lacking to fear so long as it is servile.   It is a common
mode of speech, putting the cause for the effect.   And the self-interest
inherent in the law of the hireling is controlled by charity, so that it
entirely rejects what is evil, prefers what is better to what is good, and
what is good only for the sake of what is better.   And, when this is
fully effected in the soul by the grace of God, the body and all
created good are only loved for the sake of the soul, and the soul only
for the sake of God, and God for his own sake.

8. Because we are flesh and blood born of the desire of the flesh,
our desire or love must start in the flesh, and it will then, if properly
directed, progress under grace by certain stages until it is fulfilled in
the spirit, for ' that was not first which is spiritual, but that which is
natural; afterwards that which is spiritual ', and we must first bear the
image which is earthly and afterwards that which is heavenly.   At first
a man loves himself for his own sake.   He is flesh and is able only to
know himself.   But when he sees that he cannot subsist of himself,
then he begins by faith to seek and love God as necessary for himself.
And so in the second stage he loves God, not yet for God's sake, but
for his own sake.   However when, on account of his own necessity,
he begins to meditate, read, pray, and obey, he becomes accustomed
little by little to know God and consequently to delight in him.   When
he has tasted and found how sweet is the Lord he passes to the third
stage wherein he loves God for God's sake and not for his own.   And
here he remains, for I doubt whether the fourth stage has ever been

fully reached in this life by any man, the stage, that is, wherein a man loves himself only for God's sake. Let those say who have experienced it; I confess that to me it seems impossible. It will come about, doubtless, when the good and faithful servant shall have been brought into the joy of his Lord and become inebriated with the fulness of the house of God. For he will then be wholly lost in God as one inebriated and henceforth cleave to him as if one in spirit with him, forgetful, in a wonderful manner, of himself and, as it were, completely out of himself.

9. I consider the prophet to have felt this when he said: 'I will enter into the powers of the Lord; O Lord, I will be mindful of thy justice alone'. He certainly knew that when he would enter the spiritual powers of the Lord, he would leave behind him all the frailties of the flesh, so that he would no longer have to think any more of them but would be wholly occupied with the justice of God. Then each of Christ's members will be able to say for himself what St. Paul said of their head: 'We have known Christ according to the flesh, but now we know him so no longer'. For no one will know himself there according to the flesh because 'flesh and blood cannot possess the kingdom of God'. I do not say that the substance of the flesh will not be there, but that every carnal need will be absent, that the love of the flesh will be absorbed in the love of the spirit, and that what are now weak human affections will be transformed into divine powers. When charity shall pull up on to the shore of eternity the net which she is now drawing through this vast and great sea so as to bring in without ceasing every sort of fish, she will then cast aside the bad and keep only the good. For in this life her net keeps every sort of fish within its ample folds and she accommodates herself to all making, in a sense, her own all the good and evil fortunes of everyone, not only so as to rejoice with the glad but also to weep with the afflicted. When she shall have come to shore everything that she has hitherto borne with sorrow she will cast aside as evil fish, retaining only what gives her pleasure and happiness. Will St. Paul, for example, then become weak with the weak or on fire for the scandalized, when all scandals and all weaknesses are done away? Or will he weep for those who have not repented where it is certain that as there will be no one who sins, so there will be no one to repent? Far be it from him to mourn for those who are condemned to eternal flames with the devil and his angels, in the city of God 'which the stream of the river maketh glad' and the 'gates of which God loves above all the tents of Jacob'. Because, although there may sometimes be rejoicing over victory in tents, yet there is also the labour of battle and often danger to life. But in that home-land no adversity or sorrow is admitted according to those words which are sung of it: 'All the world rejoicing finds its dwelling place in thee' and 'Everlasting joy shall be unto them'.

And then how can there be any recollection of mercy where only the justice of God is remembered? Where there will be no place for misery or time for mercy, there can be no feeling of compassion.

10. I feel myself driven to compose a long discourse by my insatiable desire to speak to you, my most dear brothers, but there are three things which indicate that it is time for me to finish. The first is that I fear more than anything to become a burden to you. The second is that I am ashamed of my wordiness. The third is that I am hard pressed by the cares of my household. Finally I beg you to have pity on me. If you have rejoiced over the good you have only heard about me, have compassion on the evils that are real. Perhaps the good man who told you such favourable things about me saw certain small things and made of them something great. And you, in the goodness of your heart, found no difficulty in believing what you were so glad to hear. I give thanks for your charity which ' believeth all things '; but I am abased to the dust for the truth which knows all things. I want you to believe what I, rather than another, who sees only the surface, say of myself: ' No man knoweth the things of a man, but the spirit of a man that is in him '. I tell you, therefore, who speak of myself from experience and not from conjecture, that I am not as I am believed or said to be. I say this with an assurance supported by the proof of experience, so that I would prefer to obtain nothing more by your special prayers than to be such as your letters make me out to be.

LETTER 13

TO THE SAME

It is impossible to say when precisely this letter was written, but internal evidence would seem to indicate some time during the Papal Schism (1130–1138).

To the most dear Lord and reverend Father Guy, Prior of the Chartreuse, and to the holy brothers who abide with him, the humble duty of Brother Bernard of Clairvaux.

FIRST let me tell you that it was the troubles and evils with which I had to contend that kept me from coming to see you when I was in your neighbourhood. Although you may be satisfied with this, I confess that I am very far from being so. I am vexed with the affairs that rendered my visit to you not unsought, but impossible, but this often happens and so I am often vexed. Would that I were deserving of the pity of holy men for without it, a pitiful object undeserving of pity, I am doubly pitiful. I feel that I hold a place in your brotherly affections, but that I do not deserve it. Have pity on me, I beg not because I deserve it, but because I am poor and needy. Justice seeks out the merits of the case, but pity only regards the need.   True pity does not judge, it gives; it does not deliberate, it solaces; it does not seek for reasons, it is moved by affections.   When Samuel mourned for Saul, he was moved not by reason but by pity.   When David shed tears for his parricide son, they were fruitless, but they were loving. Therefore do you have pity on me, not because I deserve it, but because I need it.   Have mercy on me as those who have already received mercy from the Lord, so that, far from the upheavals of the world, you may serve him peacefully and without fear.   Ah! Happy are those who during evil times are hidden in the house of the Lord, who under the shadow of his wings are able to await in hope their passing. As for me, unhappy man, naked and poor, it is my lot of labour.   An unfledged nestling, I am obliged to spend most of my time out of my nest exposed to the tempests and troubles of the world.   I am shaken and upset like unto a drunken man, and cares devour my conscience. So once more I say have pity on me who certainly need it, even if I do not deserve it.

LETTER 14

TO POPE HONORIUS

The Alberic mentioned in this letter was a master at the Cathedral School of Rheims, and famous for his learning and prudence.   He was nominated to the bishopric of Châlons in the year 1126, but was never consecrated.   Later he became Archbishop of Bourges, in the year 1139, and died in 1141.

To the Supreme Pontiff Honorius, from a certain brother, by profession a monk, in life a sinner, his humble duty.

IT is said that the prayers of the poor are of more avail with your Holiness than the presence of the powerful.   Taking courage from this holy report I have no fear in addressing myself to your Highness, especially on a matter prompted by charity.   I write, my Lord, of the Church of Châlons, for I cannot and ought not to conceal the peril which threatens it.   We who are in the neighbourhood see and feel that the peace of this renowned Church is already threatened and will be soon grievously disturbed if the confirmation of your holiness for the election of that excellent man Master Alberic, who is supported by the suffrages of both the clergy and the town, cannot be obtained. I believe, if my own opinion in the matter is of any value, Master Alberic to be a man of irreproachable faith and doctrine, prudent alike in divine and human affairs, and I have every hope that, should he be chosen by God, he will be a vessel of honour in his house, and a credit to the whole Church in France.   It is for your Holiness to determine whether it is becoming to entreat a dispensation from you in favour of one from whom so much can be expected.

LETTER 15

TO THE SAME

This letter concerns the affairs of the monastery of St. Benignus, where St. Bernard's mother was buried before her body was removed to Clairvaux. St. Bernard and other writers of his time often refer to a monastery as the 'church' of its district. Here the Monastery of St. Benignus is called the church of Dijon because it was the first church of the town.

The quarrel referred to concerned the churches of Clermont and Vignory.

To the Supreme Pontiff Honorius, health and all that the prayers of a sinner can avail, from Brother Bernard, styled Abbot of Clairvaux.

OUR Blessed Lord, whom I fear in you, knows with how great a fear I write to you. But the Lady Charity gives me courage for she it is who commands us both. I have undertaken to petition your Holiness on behalf of the church of Dijon, but I am rather doubtful what precisely I should ask. Just as it is iniquitous to attempt anything against justice by purse or prayer, so it is superfluous to exert oneself on behalf of justice before a lover of justice. But, although I do not know exactly what it would be best for me to ask, I am yet sure that your own good will, especially towards religious, will not suffer you to remain idle in this matter. What would be revealed by the prudent and careful examination of the facts by your Holiness, I cannot say; but I have heard and still hear it said that it is a long-standing and unshaken tenor of the church of Dijon which the people of Luxueil are contesting, and that their unfounded claim is causing great surprise and indignation among the oldest inhabitants of the neighbourhood.

LETTER 16

TO CARDINAL HAIMERIC

To the most illustrious Lord Haimeric, Chancellor of the Apostolic See, that he may forget the things that lie behind and with the Apostle look forward to those which are before, from Bernard of Clairvaux.

YOUR affection for me is not hidden from our friends and, were I to keep the fruit of so great a happiness to myself, they would be envious of me. The monks of Dijon are very dear to me, because theirs is so venerable a foundation. May they learn, if it please you, that neither your love for me nor my love for them is fruitless, saving in all things justice, against which it would not be right to invoke the help even of a friend.

LETTER 17

TO PETER, CARDINAL PRIEST IN CURIA

To his very dear Lord Peter, Cardinal Priest, eternal life, from Brother Bernard, Abbot of Clairvaux.

I<small>T</small> is not my cause that I plead before your Eminence, but the cause of the monks of Dijon, which I have made my own because they are religious men. Take it up, I beg you, as if it were my own; and as much mine as it is the cause of justice. I am sure it is, and so also is almost everyone else.

LETTER 18

TO PETER, CARDINAL DEACON

This is not Peter Leonis, who was also a Legate, but a Cardinal Priest. It is probably the Peter whom Pope Honorius sent as legatus a latere *to France.*

To his venerable Lord Peter, Cardinal Deacon and Legate of the Roman Church, his entire devotion, from Brother Bernard of Clairvaux.

I<small>T</small> was not laziness but a very much better reason that prevented me from coming when you sent for me. The truth is, saving your reverence and the reverence due to all good men, I have determined never to leave my monastery except for certain reasons none of which could be invoked on this occasion, as a pretext for satisfying your wishes and, indeed, my own. But what are you doing about the promise you gave in your first letter to come here? As for those writings of mine, which you say you have asked to be sent to you, I can only tell you I know nothing about them, and so I have prepared nothing. In fact I do not remember ever having written anything on morals which I would consider worthy of the attention of your Excellency. But you have by you Gebuin, the Precentor and Archdeacon of Troyes, who was one of those who noted down what I said when I was speaking on the subject in public, so you can easily get the notes from him if you think it worth while. When you pay us the visit we are all expecting, should you think it worth the trouble or if you are ever sufficiently free from troubles to come, then, if I have anything on my hands or if I can prepare anything that seems likely to please you, I shall try as far as I can not to disappoint you. It would give me great pleasure if, mere rustic though I be, I could satisfy your wishes, for I am much in love with all I hear of you, and I have a great respect for your care and zeal in the things of God.

LETTER 19

TO THE SAME[1]

EVEN were I able to give myself wholly to you, it would seem to me a little enough return for even a small part of the favour with which, I am told, you regard me.   Of course I am very pleased to be so honoured by you but, I must confess, my pleasure is tempered by the thought that I have won your favour not by my merits but by my reputation.   I am ashamed to take any pride in your favour, because I am conscious that what you honour and respect in me is not what I am, but what I am believed to be.   It is not me you love when you love me in the way you do, but something, I know not what, which is in me but not of me.   To be honest, I do know what it is you love in me, it is nothing at all; for what does not exist, even though we may think it does, is without any doubt nothing at all.   When we love what we think is there but which is not there, it is not the love or the lover that is defaulting, but the thing which is loved.   It is more a matter for sorrow than for wonder that it should be possible to love what does not exist.   We can learn from this whence we come and whither we go, what we have lost and what we find.   In other words, we learn that when we cleave to him who always is and is always happy, we too live for ever and are always happy.   When we cleave, I should say, with the heart, not just with the mind.   When we love him, not just when we think of him.   For certain children of Adam 'because, when they knew God, have not glorified him as God, or given thanks, have become fantastic in their notions'.   They deserved to have their stupid hearts darkened, and they were rightly punished by having their knowledge of the truth taken from them; because when they did see it, they ignored it.   Alas! by allowing his heart to draw his mind away from truth, or in other words by loving vanity instead of truth, 'man has become like unto the vanity' he loves.   And what could be more fitting than that the knowledge of truth should be taken away from those who did not take advantage of it when they had it.   I say, what could be more right than that they should lose their knowledge, so that they can no longer pride themselves on it who, when they had it, flattered themselves on having it rather than glorifying the truth they knew by it.   To desire vanity is the same thing as to ignore the truth, and this ignoring of the truth is the cause of our blindness: 'and because they scorned to keep God in their view, God has abandoned them to a frame of mind worthy of all scorn.'

2. It is from this ignoring of the truth that the blindness comes

---

[1] According to some MSS. this letter is addressed to Haimeric, in others it is inscribed to Peter the Cardinal Deacon, which Mabillon believes to be the correct address.

whereby we are led to love and approve what does not exist as if it did, because ' while we are in this body we are exiles from him who is ', from God who is the plenitude of being. 'And what is man, O God, that thou art made known to him?' By ignorance of God man is reduced to nothing, for the reason of his existence is to know him. But God has pity on those who are reduced to nothing by their ignorance of him, and treats them as though they were already his creatures. Because we cannot yet contemplate the reality nor fully embrace him by love, he feeds us on that hidden manna of which the Apostle says: ' Your life is hid with Christ in God ', allowing us to taste him by faith and to seek him by desire. By these two, faith in him and desire for him, we are brought a second time from a state of nothingness to a state of being, and we begin once more to be, after a fashion, creatures of God, to pass at last into the perfect man, ' into the measure of the age of the fulness of Christ '. And this will come about when ' justice shall be turned into judgement ', that is to say when faith will be turned into understanding or when the justice which arises from faith is transformed into the judgement that comes from full knowledge, and the desire experienced in exile is changed into fulness of love. If faith in God and desire for him start the exile off on the way, they culminate in understanding and love when he is there. As faith leads to full knowledge, so desire leads to perfect love. Just as it is said, ' If you will not believe, you shall not understand ', so it can be equally well said, ' If you do not desire God ardently, you will not love him perfectly '. Understanding is therefore the fruit of faith, and perfect love of desire. In the meantime, ' The just man lives by faith ', but the blessed in heaven by understanding. Even as ' the hart pants after the fountains of living water ', so does the just man thirst for God, but the blessed in heaven ' draw waters of joy out of the Saviour's fountains ', which is to say that they delight in the fulness of charity.

3. With these two, understanding and love, which are knowledge of and delight in the truth, as with two arms of the soul, the length and breadth, the height and depth, which are eternity, love, power and wisdom, are comprehended and embraced. And what are these but Christ himself? He is eternity because ' This is eternal life, to know thee the only true God and Jesus Christ whom thou hast sent '; he is love because he is God and ' God is love '; he is also ' the power and wisdom of God '. But when will all this be? When shall we see him as he is? When shall we be able to love him as he deserves? For ' the expectation of the creature waiteth for the revelation of the sons of God. For the creature was made subject to vanity.' It is the nature of this universal vanity which is in us to wish for praise when we deserve blame, and to be loath to praise others when we know them to be praiseworthy. And this also is a vain thing: in our ignorance we often commend what does not exist, and are silent about

what does. What can we say of this but that ' the sons of men are vain, the sons of men are liars, so that by vanity they deceive each other '. We praise deceitfully and are foolishly delighted when we are praised, so that they become vain who are praised and they are liars who praise. Some flatter and are deceitful; others praise what they think worthy of praise and are mistaken; both preen themselves on the praises of each other, and are vain. He alone is wise who says with the Apostle: ' I forbear lest any man should think of me above that which he seeth in me, or anything he heareth of me '.

4. I have jotted down rather than dictated all this hastily and therefore carelessly, and I may have been too long-winded. But I have said what I felt to be true and I cannot do more than that. Now to end at the point where I began: I do not want you to trust too much to my reputation. As you know full well reputations are apt to err on one side or the other, either by blaming too much or by praising too highly. Judge for yourself, I beg you, and consider how far your love and favour are deserved. I assure you that they will be more pleasing to me, your friend, if they are in proportion to my merits. The praise that comes from mature consideration may be less lavish than when it is based on idle gossip, but it is less embarrassing. What renders me, such as I am, especially devoted to you is that I hear you concern yourself vigorously and sincerely with the things of God. May you always do this, so that it may continue to be said of you truthfully.

5. You have the book you asked for in order to copy. Those booklets you want are not very many, and I do not think them at all worthy of your attention. Yet as I would rather be blamed for poor understanding than for lack of good will, and that my relations with you should be endangered by ignorance rather than by disobedience, you have only to indicate in a note by this messenger which of the booklets you want and where you would like them sent and I, if I do not have them by me, will get them from those who have them and send them on to wherever you want. So that you may know what to ask for, I must tell you that I have written one booklet entitled *On Humility*, another in praise of the Virgin Mother which bears this name, and is based on that text from the Gospel of St. Luke which begins ' The Angel Gabriel was sent '. I have also written for the benefit of a friend[1] an *Apologia* which is concerned with the observances of Cluny and ourselves, the Cistercians. I have written a few letters to various friends and there are some discourses which certain of the brothers have taken down in their own style while I was talking, and have kept by them. I could wish, but hardly dare to hope, that these efforts of my simplicity may be of some use to you.

[1] William of St. Thierry, a great friend of St. Bernard and the author of the well-known *Golden Epistle to the Carthusians of Mont Dieu*.

LETTER 20

TO THE SAME

IT is time for me to keep you to your promise, so that I can discover whether or no the trust I have always placed in you since I was honoured with your notice and friendship is justified. You can rest assured that any help you afford the deputies from Rheims[1] I shall regard as given to myself. I do not venture to write this because I think myself of any importance whatsoever, but because you have given me your promise; whether justifiably or not is your affair.

LETTER 21

TO HAIMERIC, CARDINAL DEACON AND CHANCELLOR OF THE HOLY SEE

This letter concerns the same affair as the above. Haimeric was Chancellor of the Holy See and very much in the confidence of St. Bernard.

To that illustrious man, the Lord Haimeric, Chancellor of the Holy Roman See, health and prayers from Brother Bernard of Clairvaux.

BECAUSE I have once begun let me speak again and speak to you. I will be importunate, but it will be the importunity of charity, of truth, and of justice. Although I am not so important as to have affairs at Rome, yet nothing that concerns the glory of God is a matter of indifference to me.[2] If popular report does not lie when it says that I stand high in your favour, then, I beg you, let the delegates of my Lord of Rheims know it by helping them in their present business. I am quite sure that they are not trying to do or to obtain anything but what is right.

LETTER 22

TO MATTHEW, THE LEGATE

The following letter is addressed to Matthew du Remois, Cardinal Bishop of Albano. It was evidently written in reply to a summons from the Legate to attend the Council of Troyes over which Matthew presided in the year 1128. In this letter Bernard tries to excuse himself from attendance on the grounds of ill health, but at the end he indicates that he is willing to obey the summons in spite of his illness. In fact he was present, and it was under his influence that the Knights Templar received the formal sanction of the Church at the Council.

---

[1] It is not known for certain what this deputation from Rheims was about. Mabillon thinks it may have been to obtain the pallium for Raynald de Martini, who had been transferred from the see of Angers to that of Rheims in 1124.

[2] *Humani nihil a me alienum puto*: ' No human concern is a matter of indifference to me ' (Terence, *Heaut.* 1.1.23).

MY heart was ready to obey your summons, but not so my body. My weak flesh, parched by the heat of a raging fever and exhausted by constant sweating, was not able to satisfy the demands of my willing spirit. And so, although I wanted to come, my weakling body impeded my ready will. Whether or not this is a sufficient reason for not coming, those friends of mine must judge who, regardless of my protests, are always trying to drag me, enmeshed in the net of obedience, from the cloister to the cities. They must know that this is not a mere pretext, but a grievous affliction, and so they will learn that there is no evading the will of God. They would certainly have been indignant with me if I had said to them: ' I have put off my garment, how shall I put it on? I have washed my feet, how shall I soil them?' But now they must either be angry with the providence of God or submit to it, for it is not my fault that I cannot come when I am ready to do so.

2. They tell me that the matter is important and the necessity grave. If this is so then they must find someone suitable. If they think I am he, then I assure them not only that I believe they are mistaken, but that I am quite certain they are. Be the matters weighty or trivial which they press upon me, they are no concern of mine. If these matters in which you try so hard to involve your friend at the cost of his peace and silence are simple, then they can be settled without me; if they are difficult then they cannot be settled by me. Unless of course I am considered a person of such consequence that great and difficult matters must be reserved for me because there is no one else to settle them. If this is so then only in my case have the designs of God been frustrated. Why has he put me under a bushel when I could give light from a candlestick or, to speak more clearly, why, if I am necessary to the world, a man without whose aid the bishops cannot settle their own affairs, has God called me to be a monk and ' hidden me in his tabernacle in the day of evil things '? As it is, all that my friends have done for me is to make me feel troubled when I speak to one whom, hitherto, I have never thought of without serenity and joy. But you know, and it is to you I speak, my father, that ' I am ready and not troubled that I may keep your commands '. But I beg you, of your kindness, to spare me whenever you can.

LETTER 23

TO HUMBOLD, ARCHBISHOP OF LYONS AND LEGATE

From being Archdeacon of Autun, Humbold became Archbishop of Lyons. Early in the pontificate of Honorius II he was legate with Cardinal Peter de Fontaines. Mabillon believes that the Bishop of Meaux referred to in this letter was Burchard and not his successor, Manasses II. It would appear that this letter was written not long after 1125 and certainly before 1129 when

Rainald, the successor of Humbold, died after occupying the see of Lyons for only a few days.

His Lordship the Bishop of Meaux was, it so happened, on his way to see me when he received your letter. He wanted to answer it before leaving here so that with his letter he could enclose one from myself in the hopes that as I am friendly with you, it might forward his business. As I could not deny his request I have thought it well to make known to your Reverence in a few friendly words that it would ill become your dignity and your office were you to pay any attention to the complaints of those who love themselves and seek their own interests against a bishop who is concerned only with the things of Christ.

LETTER 24

TO ATTO, BISHOP OF TROYES

The good Atto was in a great way because in a moment of panic, when he thought he was dying, he had distributed all his possessions to the poor. St. Bernard writes the following letter to comfort him.

The greeting of a poor abbot to a poor bishop that he may gain the reward of poverty which is the Kingdom of Heaven.

I would praise you, and rightly, were it not for that verse of Scripture which says: 'Praise not any man in his life'. You have done a thing worthy of all praise, but the praise is due to God who gave you the good will to conceive what was praiseworthy and the strength to carry it out. So it is God working through you and in you whom I glorify. And only for this does he deign to manifest his glory in you, that he may render you also glorious. Although he is wonderful in his own majesty, yet he deigns to appear glorious in his saints, so that he may not keep all his glory for himself. Although he is glorious enough in his own magnificence and needs not the glory of any man, yet he seeks to be glorified in his saints, not to increase his glory but to share it. He knows who are his own, but they are not so easily known to us unless he is pleased to reveal them. Certainly we know those of whom it is written: 'They are not in the labour of men, neither shall they be scourged like other men'. But these words hardly apply to you. Yet nevertheless we know it is also written: 'Whom the Lord loveth, he chastiseth; he scourgeth every son he receiveth'. So when I see someone scourged and corrected, can I doubt that he is one of his sons? I see in your present poverty a clear enough sign of correction. The title of poverty is a noble one, which God himself is pleased to commend through the mouth of his

Prophet when he says: 'I am the man that sees my poverty'. Poverty is a surer title to nobility than all the purple and pearls of a king.

2. I am aware that I have just quoted Scripture, saying that a man should not be praised in his life, but how can I refrain from praising one who has ceased to pursue gold and who now scorns to put his trust in money and treasures? Of such a man Scripture itself says: 'Who is he and we shall praise him?' Perhaps it means that we are not to praise a man during his life, because life on earth is a trial which is not over so long as life remains. But shall we not praise a man when he is dead to sin and living only for God? The praise given to a sinner in the desires of his heart is certainly vain and deceptive. Anyone who calls me blessed leads me into error if I believe him. But we are not for that reason to refrain from praising one who can say: 'Now not I live, but Christ lives in me'. When we praise such a man who lives not his own life, but the life of Christ, we do not praise him 'in his life' but in the life of Christ, and so we do not act contrary to Scripture when it forbids us to praise a man 'in his life'.

3. And why should he not deserve my praise whom God has honoured with the praises of his name, according to the words: 'The poor and needy shall praise my name'? Shall I not praise a bishop who has freely parted with his goods and generously distributed them, when Job is praised for bearing with patience the loss of them? He did not wait until he was dead and no longer able to give or keep his goods, as many do whose will is not executed until they are dead. No, while still living and able to do what he would with his goods, 'he distributed and gave to the poor, so that his justice remaineth for ever and ever'. Would money last for ever like this? Surely justice is a good return for money, when that which cannot endure is replaced by that which lasts for ever? Certainly it is incomparably better, for while money enriches only our treasure chest, justice enriches our soul. 'The priests of God are clothed with justice', and much more becomingly and richly than with gold and silk.

4. Give thanks to God who, by smiting you with a healthy fear for the state of your soul, has wrought in you a glorious scorn for the passing glory of the world. How great has been his goodness to you! He threatened you with death so as to save your life; he allowed you to fear so that you should have nothing to fear. He did this to cure you of loving your goods more than your good. Your bones were aching with a raging fever. The pains got daily worse because you could not sweat the fever out. The grievous heat withdrew from your chilling limbs to collect itself within and consume your bowels already weakened by long days of illness. Then the sad spectre of pale death haunted you. And lo! as if from on high a voice came and said unto you: 'I am, I am he who blots out', not you but 'your iniquities'. Then presently, when the priest of God has distributed

all his goods to the poor that he may die in poverty, the health-giving sweats, despaired of and unexpected, break forth, and health returns to soul and body alike. Thereby were fulfilled the words of God speaking through his Scriptures and saying: ' I will kill, and I will make to live: I will strike, and I will heal '. He smote your flesh so that your spirit might live: he killed your avarice so that you might live for justice. Now that you are restored to life and health what more is there to hope for except that none may snatch you from the hand of God. And this will not happen if you are mindful of that warning in the Gospel: ' Sin no more lest a worse thing befall thee '. Our loving Father only forewarns you of this because he does not wish it to happen. He does not wish for the death of a sinner, but rather that he should be converted and live. And rightly. For what advantage is there in the death of a sinner? Hell shall not confess God nor shall death praise him, but do you who live, bless the Lord and say, ' I shall not die but live: and I shall declare the works of the Lord '; and again, ' I reeled under the blow, and had well-nigh fallen, but still the Lord was there to aid me '.

LETTER 25

TO THE UNIVERSAL DOCTOR, GILBERT, BISHOP OF LONDON

Gilbert was Bishop of London from 1128 to 1135. It is therefore probable that this letter was written about the year 1130. He was called the ' Universal Doctor ' because he excelled in all branches of learning. St. Bernard congratulates him in his letter for overcoming avarice by living as a poor man while Bishop of London. Henry of Huntingdon, however, attributes the spartan life of the bishop to miserliness.

THE fame of your life has spread far and wide, and it has been as a most sweet odour for all unto whom it has come. Your avarice has been stifled: who would not delight in this? Charity rules in its stead: who does not relish this? All men know you to be wise because you have crushed the chief enemy of wisdom. This is something worthy of your priesthood and your great name. The witness of your life well becomes your philosophy; it is a fitting crown of your studies. Yours has been the true wisdom which scorns filthy lucre and refuses to consort with the service of idols. For you it was no great thing to be a bishop, but to be a bishop of London and yet to live as a poor man, this is something clearly magnificent. The dignity of high office could have added little to the lustre of your fame, but the humility of your poverty has added much. To bear poverty with resignation argues great patience; to seek it of one's own free will is the highest wisdom. The Scriptures acclaim and praise the man who does not set his heart on riches, but you have deserved even higher praise by scorning them.   Unless cold reason can see nothing wonderful in a wise man acting wisely.   And without any doubt you are a wise man, taking your pleasure in all the books and studies of the wise men of the world, and studying all the divine Scriptures so as to give life to their meaning and apply it to the present day.   For have you not ' dispersed and given to the poor '?   But it is money you have given.   And what is money in comparison with the justice for which you have exchanged it?   ' His justice remaineth for ever and ever.'   Can the same be said of money?   It is certainly a desirable and worthy sort of commerce to exchange what passes for what lasts for ever.   O admirable and praiseworthy Master, may you always be able to do business in this way !   It only remains for you to finish the good work you have begun, so that the tail of the victim may be joined to the head.[1]   I gladly accept your blessing, especially as it comes recommended by the joy I take in your high perfection.   Although the bearer of this letter is a most worthy person in himself, yet I wish him to be acceptable to you for my sake as well, because he is very dear to me by reason of his integrity and piety.

LETTER 26

TO HUGH, ARCHBISHOP OF ROUEN

Hugh was elected Archbishop of Rouen in the year 1130.   Before his election he had been a monk of Cluny and then Abbot of Reading.

THE evils of our time may grow worse every day, but they cannot prevail.   They may disturb us, but they should not dismay us. ' Wonderful is the surging of the waves ', but more wonderful is the Lord on high.   If you are frank with yourself you must admit that God has been very good to you.   The care of Providence has seen to it that you were not put in charge of sinners before you had associated with good people, so that in their company and by their example you might become good enough to lead a good life among evil people. We save our souls by living a good life amongst good people, but we deserve praise as well by living a good life amongst evil people. The first is safe and easy, the second all the more virtuous for being more difficult.   It is as difficult to do this as it is to touch pitch without being sullied, to put one's hand into the fire without being burned, to live in darkness without losing the light.   There was once darkness over the land of Egypt so thick that it might be felt, but ' wheresoever the children of Israel dwelt there was light '.   David was a true Israelite and therefore he was careful to say that he did not live in Cedar, but ' with the inhabitants of Cedar ', as if to imply that although the dwelling place of his body was with the people of Cedar, yet he dwelt always in the light.   And he rebuked some who were not

[1] This is a favourite metaphor of St. Bernard, taken from *Lev.* 3.7, to signify perseverance.

true Israelites because 'they mingled with the heathen and were a stumbling-block to them'.

2. So I say to you that according to the words, 'With the innocent man thou wilt be innocent', it was enough for you when you were at Cluny to have kept yourself innocent, but now that you live amongst the people of Rouen you must also have patience according to the words of the Apostle: 'The servant of God must not wrangle, he must be mild to all men, ready to teach them, and be patient'. And you must not only be patient so as not to be overcome by evil, you must also be peaceable so as to overcome evil by good. By being patient you will bear with evil people, by being peaceable you will heal them of their evil. In your patience you will possess your soul, but you must also be peaceable so as to possess the souls committed to your care. What is more glorious than to be able to say: 'With them that hated peace, I was peaceable'? So be patient because you are with evil people; and be peaceable too because you have to rule over them. By all means let your charity be zealous, but for the time moderate your severity. You must never condone evil, but sometimes it is well to defer rebuking it. Justice should always be eager, but never hasty. All that pleases is not lawful, so all that is lawful is not always expedient at the moment. But you know all this better than I, so I will forbear from saying any more. Pray for me without ceasing, for I am ceaselessly sinning.

LETTER 27

TO GUY, BISHOP OF LAUSANNE

You have put your hand to great things, therefore you need great strength. You have become a watchman on the housetops of Israel, therefore you must be prudent. You have the same duty to all, learned and simple, therefore you must be just. But above all you must rule yourself, lest having preached to others, you yourself become a castaway.

LETTER 28

TO ARDUTIO, BISHOP-ELECT OF GENEVA

It is difficult to say whether this is a letter of congratulation or a warning.

I HAVE heard that your election was greeted unanimously by the clergy and people, and I believe it to have been of God. I give thanks for the grace of God, not to mention your merits; and so as not to flatter you more than is fitting, I say you owe your election to his mercy rather than to your good works. If you should think otherwise, and may it be far from you to think any such thing, you will only be setting yourself up in order to be thrown down. But if you acknowledge God's grace, you must see to it that you have not received it in vain. Set your ways right, keep your life good, and your ministry holy. If holiness has not preceded your election, at least see that it follows after it. Then I shall be able to admit with truth that 'you have been met in the way with abundant blessing', and hope that from this may come even greater things. I shall rejoice and be glad that a good and wise servant has been placed over the household of the Lord; a happy and strong son of his father worthy to be set in charge of all his goods. But if, on the other hand, you take pleasure in being more haughty than holy, I shall expect not your reward but your fall. I hope and pray that this may never be, yet I shall stand by to hold out my hand to catch you, and to do the little I can to help you towards what is suitable and becoming.

LETTER 29

TO THE SAME, AFTER HE HAD BEEN CONSECRATED BISHOP

CHARITY gives me the courage to speak to you with confidence. The bishop's throne for which you, my dear friend, were lately chosen, demands many virtues, none of which, I grieve to say, could be discerned in you, at any rate in any strength, before your consecration. Neither your actions nor your pleasures seemed at all to befit the office of a bishop. But what of this? God can raise up a child of Abraham even from this stone. He can bring it about that the virtues which should have gone before consecration, follow afterwards. When I hear of this happening I am always pleased. I do not know why, but this sudden 'change of the right hand of the Most High' in you will be more gratifying than if you had a long life of virtue to recommend you. Certainly I will say: 'This is the Lord's doing and it is wonderful in our eyes'. In this way Paul, after persecuting the Church, became suddenly the Doctor of the Gentiles. And it was in this way that Matthew was called from the customs' house and Ambrose was taken from a palace, the former to become an Apostle, the latter a bishop. So have I known many others called from a worldly life to do good work for the Church. And then it often happens that where sins have abounded greatly, grace abounds in like measure.

2. And so, my dear friend, I pray that you may be inspired by these and other examples to gird yourself like a man and set your ways right and your occupations too, so that your new habits may put to sleep your old ones and in the evening of your life you may mend the follies of your youth. Try like Paul to be an honour to your ministry, by the gravity of your manners, by the maturity of your counsel, by the integrity of your actions. It is these qualities that especially adorn and ennoble the episcopal office. Take counsel in all things, but only of

the good, not of everybody and anybody.[1]   Have good men in council, good men in your service, and good men under your roof; these will be the guardians both of your life and your integrity, and the witnesses of it.   By the witness of good men you will be proved to be good.   I commend to your care my poor brethren who are near to you, both those of Bonnemont in the Alps and those at Hautecombe.   May I experience in their persons how much you care for me.

LETTER 30

TO STEPHEN, BISHOP OF METZ

The appendix to the History of the Bishops of Metz *tells us that Stephen was 'illustrious for birth and still more illustrious for his virtue'.   He succeeded to his see in the year 1120.   Although St. Bernard praises him in this letter, later on in Letter 218 to Pope Innocent he refers to him as being more of a tyrant than a bishop.   It is possible that he displeased St. Bernard by adopting too violent measures in order to recover the goods of the Church, in fact by being too active an administrator of the Church.*

To Stephen, by the grace of God an active administrator of the Church of Metz, health and prayers from his humble brothers in Christ at Clairvaux.

IT is only lately, if you remember, that you deigned to be associated with our community and humbly commended yourself to our prayers.   Ever since then, as was only right, we have been anxious to know how you were.   We have been zealous in making frequent enquiries about how you fared from all whom we could, and we have not ceased to desire and pray God to prosper you in the work you have been raised up to do for him, and to direct your steps in the way of his commandments.   And now we can say: 'Blessed be God who has not rejected our prayer nor withheld his mercy from us'!   For our hearts have been filled with joy by the venerable Brother William whose account of your health and success, and of how you have restored peace to the Church, we believe as well as if we saw it with our own eyes.   We all congratulate you, but we give glory to God because we know that it is to him and not to yourself that you owe what you are and what you are able to do.   And in a friendly way we admonish you that you never forget this, but keep it always before your eyes, for, if you should think otherwise and attribute to your own merits or prowess any good that you do, the time would come when you would cease to be able either to be anything good or to do anything good.   May such a thing be far from you!   Otherwise it is much to be feared that your peace would be turned to trouble and your prosperity into

---

[1] Cf. *Rule of St. Benedict*, Ch. 3, *ad fin.*

adversity, by God, who, acting ever justly, withstands the proud and gives his grace to the humble. For the Psalmist says of him, ' Lovingly thou dost treat them who love thee, and from the man who turns against thee thou dost turn away ', and the Prophet Isaias calls him ' the maker of peace, the author of calamity '.

LETTER 31

TO ALBERO, PROVOST OF METZ

Mabillon writes of Albero: ' I find three persons called Albero who bore this title in succession at this time. I believe that the following letter was written to the second of them, who afterwards became Archbishop of Trèves.' St. Bernard was very friendly with him and wrote on his behalf several letters—Letters 218-222.

To the most estimable Albero, by the grace of God Provost[1] of the church of Metz, health and prayers from the brothers who try to serve God at Clairvaux.

WE now know from personal experience what we had already seen and heard of your zeal for the things of God. Although you are so favourable to the suggestions made by the brothers who were sent on your advice, and although the bishop has given his ready assent, yet above all and before all it behoves us to seek and observe the pleasure of God in everything, and especially in what directly concerns him. And therefore, so as to know his will more surely, we have decided not indeed to abandon but to postpone, until after the harvest, the matter as it had been agreed between the monks and the bishop, with the assistance of yourself, who were arranging how everything should be done, urging us to do it quickly, and helping us to do it honourably. We hope that this will be more convenient for yourself and more opportune. Then, if you and the bishop are still in the same mind, we shall be more confident that it is God's will and hope to satisfy the devotion of you both according to our arrangement. We believe that if the project is to be acceptable to God we should be as careful as we can be not to burden anyone lest it should seem that we are seeking not so much his glory as our own profit, and may it be far from us to do this ! We believe very strongly that it would be wrong and quite out of keeping with our custom were we to make this an occasion for troubling and importuning you without need when you are busy with affairs more important and of greater moment.[2]

---

[1] *Primicerius Mettensis Ecclesiæ.* This title was used for the chiefs of various departments. In the church of Metz it was always given to the senior canon of the chapter whose position corresponded to our provosts.

[2] Unlike many of St. Bernard's letters this one consists almost entirely of one long and very involved sentence. For the purpose of translation it has been rearranged with as little distortion to the general sense as possible.

LETTER 32

TO HUGH, COUNT OF CHAMPAGNE, WHO HAD BECOME A KNIGHT
OF THE TEMPLE

He was the son of Theobald III. He was extremely generous to religious houses, and gave to St. Bernard and his monks the site of Clairvaux. He became a Knight of the Temple in 1125.

IF it is for God's sake that you from being a count have become a simple soldier, from being a rich man have become poor, then it is right that I should congratulate you, and glorify God in you, seeing in this a ' change of the right hand of the Most High '. But that your joyous presence which, were it possible, I would never be without, should be removed from me by an inscrutable judgement of God, this is something I find hard to bear with equanimity. How can I forget your long-standing affection and generosity to this house? May God, for the love of whom you did it, be ever mindful of you! I am as grateful as I can be to you and keep the memory of your great goodness ever before my eyes and, if I might, I would prove my gratitude by deeds. How willingly would I provide for your soul and body were it but granted to us to live in the company of each other! But because this is not to be, because I may not have you ever present as I should like, it only remains for me always to pray for you absent.

LETTER 33

TO JORANNUS, ABBOT OF SAINT NICASIUS OF RHEIMS

This letter is written to comfort Abbot Jorannus on the loss of one of his monks, a certain Brother Drogo, to the Cistercians. If it is read with the two following letters which are also concerned with the same brother, St. Bernard is shown in a very human light.

Apparently Drogo did not persevere with the Cistercians, but returned to St. Nicasius before his profession.

Later on Abbot Jorannus himself left the Benedictines to become a Carthusian.

Mabillon ascribes this letter to the year 1120.

HE who bore in his body all our griefs knows how deeply I sympathize with you. I would willingly counsel you if I knew what to say, and help you if I knew what to do, even as I hope for the counsel and help of him who knows all things and to whom all things are possible. I would certainly never have advised Brother Drogo to leave you, if he had consulted me on the matter; I would certainly never have received him here, if he had come to me after leaving you![1]

---

[1] Cf. the following two letters.

But, as you know, I have done what I could by immediately writing to the abbot who received him. What, my father, can I do more than this now? As regards yourself, you know as well as I do that perfect men are 'confident not only in their hope of attaining glory as sons of God, but are confident even over their afflictions', being consoled by those sayings from the Scriptures: 'Pottery is tested in the furnace, man in the crucible of suffering. Though a hundred trials beset the innocent, the Lord will bring them safely through them all. We cannot enter the kingdom of heaven without many trials. All those who are resolved to lead a holy life in Jesus Christ will meet with persecution.' But this is not to say that we are not to commiserate with our friends when they are in trouble, for we do not know what the outcome of it will be, and there is the chance that they may fall away. With the saints and elect trouble makes for endurance, endurance gives proof of their faith, and a proved faith gives ground for hope. But with the damned and reprobate on the contrary trouble makes for faint-heartedness, faint-heartedness for worry, worry for despair, and that is the finish.

2. So that you may not be drowned in this horrid storm, so that you may not be swallowed up in the depths, so that the mouth of the insatiable pit may not close over you, do you in humble prudence take care that you are not overcome by evil, but rather overcome evil by good. And overcome you will if you put your hope in God and patiently await the issue. If Brother Drogo[1] should be brought to his senses either by his fear of you or by the difficulty of what he has undertaken, well and good; but if not, then for your own good you must 'bow down under the strong hand of God' and not kick against the ruling of heaven, because what is of God cannot be undone. You should try to control your stirrings of anger, however justified they may be, by remembering that saying of one of the saints who, when some of the brethren were provoking and reproaching him for not recalling a brother who had gone to another monastery in defiance of him, replied: 'Not at all. Wherever he is, if he is good, he is still mine.'

3. My advice to you would not be sincere if I did not follow it myself. When one of my own monks, not only a professed religious but also a relation of mine, was received and kept at Cluny against my will, I was sorry certainly, but I held my peace and prayed to God for those who had taken him away that they might return him, and for him too that he might come back of his own free will. But I left my vengeance to God 'who redresses wrongs' and 'who rights the wrongs of the defenceless'.[2] Through your mouth my spirit warns Brother Hugh of Lausanne 'not to believe every spirit' nor hastily to leave a certain good for one that is uncertain. Let him understand that

[1] Apparently this brother was sometimes known as 'Hugo-Drogo', because he was held in such high esteem by Hugo, Abbot of Pontigny.
[2] See Letter 1.

the devil always attacks perseverance because he knows that it is the only virtue which wins the crown. I warn him that it would be safer for him to persevere with simplicity in the vocation to which he has been called, than under the pretext of seeking supposedly higher good to abandon what he has begun only perhaps to find that he is not equal to what he has presumed to undertake.

LETTER 34

TO HUGH, ABBOT OF PONTIGNY

To his most beloved Lord, Abbot Hugh, all that he could wish for himself, from Brother Bernard of Clairvaux.

As far as I can gather from your letter it appears that either I have worded myself less clearly than I had wished or else that you have not understood me in the way I had intended you to do. The warning I gave you of the consequences of receiving that monk was quite genuine, I really did fear them and I still do, even as I wrote to you. But I had no intention of trying to persuade or advise you, still less did I mean, as you said I did, that the monk ought to be returned to his monastery. As I have known his wish to join us for a long time, I ought rather to congratulate him than urge his return. But when I was implored by his abbot,[1] with whom I am very intimate, and by the Archbishop of Rheims, to write to you and ask for his return, I tried so far as I could both to clear myself of any suspicion of complicity in the affair and to warn you of the abuse you might incur by your action, while at the same time satisfying them. Knowing your shrewdness I thought you would read between the lines and see this, or that at any rate you would gather what I meant from what I put at the end of the letter, if you read it in the spirit in which it was written. For when I had warned you of the consequences which I feared, and not without cause, might come of your receiving this monk, I added, if I remember right: ' Should you prefer to endure all this rather than lose the man, that is your affair and you must see to it '. These, or very nearly these, were my words. I had intended by saying this at the end of the letter to give you a covert hint that I had written what I did under pressure to satisfy, not to say hood-wink, others.

2. What you say about my insinuating to this monk by means of the messenger, that if he came to me I would obtain secretly a dispensation from Rome is, I assure you by the very Truth, quite untrue. Is it likely that I would boast or even hope that I could receive a monk from a monastery which is well known to me, whom I do not think even you can keep without giving great offence? But even were this

[1] See previous letter.

so, even if I did envy you the monk and try to attract him to myself, hoping or pretending I could engineer his dispensation from Rome, is it likely that I would reveal to the messenger of all people that I was plotting against his own monastery? I must tell you, so that you may not think the affection you have had for me hitherto has been misplaced, that I shall consider it my duty to continue to work for your interests as I see them as hard as I do for my own, or even harder, and this, not so that the harmony between us may be further strengthened, as I have done hitherto, but that it may not now be altogether broken. What more can I say? Only that I could never have believed you capable of such an action as you, on the sole grounds of mere suspicion, attribute to me.

It remains for me to tell you that Count Theobald has now received the letter I wrote on behalf of Humbert, but has not yet replied to it. What more you can do about it your own pity will suggest if you consider the misery of a man who has been exiled unjustly.

LETTER 35

TO THE MONK DROGO

This letter should be read with the two preceding. It is to the monk with whom those letters are concerned.

IT is now quite clear, my dearest Drogo, that my affection for you has not been misplaced. Even before this I saw that you were a very lovable person, and I perceived that there was something about you, I know not what, apart from what I saw and heard of you, entitling you to respect as well as to affection. Perhaps even then you had heard the voice of the Bridegroom, in whose pure arms you are now closely held, whispering to your soul, as to a shy dove: ' Fair in every part, my true love, no fault at all in thy fashioning '. Who would have believed what you have done! The whole city was talking of your holiness and exact observance, so that it was hard to believe that there could be any improvement possible in you. And now you have left your monastery, as a secular would leave the world, and, although already bent under the burden of Christ, you have not considered it beneath you to submit yourself again to the observances of a new discipline. In you, brother, the truth of that saying of Scripture is proved once more: ' Reach thou to the end of thy reckoning, thou must needs begin again '. That you should have now begun again, is an indication that you had reached the end of your reckoning; that you should have considered you had not yet finished, indicates that you had already done so. No one is perfect who does not wish to be still more perfect; the more perfect a man is, the more he reaches out to an even higher perfection.

2. But, dearest friend, he whose envy brought death into the world is not asleep, even now ' his bow is bent in readiness '. He has no power within you because you have turned him out of your heart, but outside he rages as much as he can. To speak more clearly: do you not know that the Pharisees are scandalized at what you have done? But remember that there are some scandals that we do not need greatly to trouble about, according to the answer our Blessed Lord gave under similar circumstances: ' Let them be, they are blind leaders of the blind '. It is better that there should be scandal than that the truth should be denied. Remember who it was who was born for the rise and fall of many and do not wonder that for some you should be ' a life giving perfume ' and for others ' a deadly fume '. If they should threaten you with curses, if they should hurl the darts of their anathemas at you, harken to Isaac answering them for you: ' A curse on those who curse, a blessing on those who bless thee '. And do you, protected by the impregnable wall of your conscience, answer them from within: ' Though a whole host were arrayed against me, my heart would be undaunted; though an armed onset should threaten me, still I would not lose confidence '. You will not be overcome if you answer them thus at the door. I am confident in the Lord that if you stand up firmly to the first blows and do not give way either to threats or to blandishments, you will quickly crush satan under your feet, and ' honest men will rejoice to witness it, and malice will stand dumb with confusion '.

LETTER 36

TO HUGH FARSIT

There were several Hugh Farsits at this time, and it is not certain to which of them this letter was addressed.

To his dearest brother and co-abbot, the due of a sincere affection, from Brother Bernard.

CONFIDING in your charity I commend to your protection this poor man Humbert who, they say, has been unjustly disinherited. For the love of God I took up his cause with your count, and I have every hope that through your intervention and with the help of the Lord of Heaven he may be reconciled with his temporal Lord and restored to his home, family, and friends. By undertaking this you will deliver the needy from the hand of the sinner and none the less benefit the soul of his oppressor. You will also be rendering me a great service as well as proving yourself one of the sons of God by fulfilling the rôle of peacemaker.

2. If they told you I threw your letter into the fire, it is quite untrue.

I still have it by me. It would have been an act of sheer envy, even of madness, to pass such a hasty condemnation on a good and useful work in which I see nothing but what makes for sound faith, salutary doctrine, and spiritual edification. But I must except one passage, for timid dissimulation among friends is dangerous as well as deceitful. What I confess troubled me and still does trouble me is the opinion you defended in our recent conversation on the Sacraments, and which you restate and defend at the beginning of your letter. If you remember what you said on the matter then you will see whether it conforms with the mind of the Church. It is a mark of your innate humility not to mind correction, if sometimes you are in error.

LETTER 37

TO THE SAME

To his friend, now as ever very dear, Hugh, by the grace of God a holy abbot, the sincere assurance of an unfaltering affection from Brother Bernard of Clairvaux.

ALTHOUGH your letter was shorter than I could have wished, it was longer than I deserved, and I would like and ought to answer it at length, but the messenger is impatient to start back. So that he should take back something in return for so much from you, I am replying with this hasty scribble, and even this is almost more than he can wait for. First of all, I must briefly and truthfully tell you that from the bottom of my heart I accept you as a Catholic and as a holy man and embrace as most dear to me, my beloved and loving old friend. As evidence of the integrity of your faith, I believe your confession; of your holiness, the renown and esteem in which you are held; of the affection which I have professed for you, my own heart. As regards that opinion of yours which troubled my simple heart with scruples (quite rightly, as I believe), I gladly accept your statement that you have put it out of your mind. I accept it all the more gladly for having read with great pleasure, in your last letter, your brief assertion of the most orthodox faith. In fact I would almost sooner believe that I mistook the sense of your words than that you supposed anything that was not right.

2. Lastly I advise you with the audacity of a brother to cease molesting now that he is dead the holy and learned bishop[1] against whom you had nothing to say when he was alive. Otherwise, since he is unable to answer for himself, you may hear the whole Church answering for him that you are inspired more by lack of charity than zeal for truth. I ask you again, as I have asked you before, not to fail Humbert in such advice and protection as you are able to afford him.

[1] This may have been William of Champeaux.

LETTER 38

TO THE COUNT DE BLOIS

To his dear friend in Christ the Count de Blois, prosperity and peace, from Bernard, Abbot of Clairvaux.

I COMMEND unto your Excellency this priest, Eberhard, as one most faithful to myself, whom you may trust without fear to bring, as if he were myself, anything from me to you or from you to me.

LETTER 39

TO THEOBALD, COUNT OF CHAMPAGNE

A contemporary writer says of Count Theobald that he was distinguished among all the princes of France for his scrupulous justice. He had a reputation for great piety and was a staunch friend of St. Bernard.

To the most praiseworthy Prince Theobald, prosperity and peace, from Bernard, the worthless servant of the servants of God at Clairvaux.

IT pleased me more than a little to hear of your anxiety about the state of my health. And while I see in this a proof of your kindness towards myself I cannot doubt that it is also a clear indication that you love God. Why else should a great man like yourself care about an insignificant person like me? Therefore, since it is clear that you love God, and myself for the sake of God, it is all the more extraordinary that you should refuse a small petition of mine which is neither unreasonable nor unjust. If I had asked for gold or silver or anything of that sort, I know you well enough to be sure that I should have received it. I say 'if I had asked you' but in fact you have loaded me with generous kindness without my having even asked you. Why then do you deny me this thing that I ask of you, not for my own sake but for God's sake and your own sake? Do you consider it unbecoming that I should ask you to have pity on a fellow Christian, of however great a crime he is accused, after he has cleared himself? Even if you do not consider that he has fully cleared himself, because he has not done so in your courts, at least you should admit him to your presence, and let him obtain your pardon by making satisfaction.

2. Do you not know who it is that threatens: 'When the time is ripe I will judge strictly'? Do you think that he who will 'judge strictly' will overlook our unjust judgements? Do you not fear that 'as you have judged, so you will be judged'? Do you not realize that God can disinherit Count Theobald quite as easily as Count Theobald has disinherited Humbert? Even when the fault is open and inexcusable, so that mercy cannot be granted except at the jeopardy

of justice, you should punish with fear and sorrow, compelled more by the duty of your office than by personal rancour. But when, as in this case, the crime is uncertain or excusable, you ought not to avoid, but willingly to embrace, the opportunity provided for being merciful without sacrificing justice. This is the second time I have implored your Highness to have mercy on Humbert even as you yourself hope for the mercy of God, and begged you to harken to the promise of the Lord, ' Blessed are the merciful for they shall obtain mercy ' or fear his warning, ' The merciless shall be judged mercilessly '. Farewell.

LETTER 40

TO THE SAME, ON THE SAME SUBJECT

To the most merciful Prince Theobald, health and prayers from Bernard of Clairvaux.

I VERY much fear that I may become a nuisance by daring to besiege your already distracted ears with my repeated petitions. But what else can I do? If I fear to offend you with my many letters, how much more ought I not to fear offending God, to whom still greater fear is due, by ignoring the plight of an unfortunate like Humbert? But in any case I beg you to pardon me for being unable not to pity the pitiful state of this man, all the more to be pitied for having been reduced from great riches to poverty and begging his bread; and his widow and orphans who are all the more wretched for being deprived of their father while he is still alive. And so I return to vex you once more with my pleas on his behalf. I am indeed most grateful to you for the favour I have found in your eyes over this matter, and for having deigned to hear the true facts of his case from Humbert himself, and for having put aside the false accusations against him. But your crowning act of charity, the arrangement you made for restoring Humbert's heritage to his wife and children, what has hindered its execution? This is a matter of great surprise to me.

2. If other princes speak lightly or even falsely, no one considers it something new or wonderful. But with Count Theobald it is a different matter. We are by no means accustomed to hear ' Yea and Nay ' from him. His lightest word has always been as good as another man's promise, a small untruth from him as serious as a perjury from anyone else. Among the many virtues which ennoble your dignity and render your name famous throughout the world, your constant truthfulness has always been especially appreciated. Who then has by encouragement or counsel undermined your great strength of purpose? Who has tried by guile to uproot from your heart that steadfastness in truth which is so holy, so excellent, and such an example for other princes? Deceitfully and not sincerely does he

love you, falsely and not faithfully does he counsel you, whoever tries through his own greed to cast a cloud over your glorious reputation for truthfulness and through I know not what hidden malice to bring to naught, to the injury of an unhappy man, the command your lips have uttered, a command pleasing to God, worthy of yourself, most mercifully just, most justly merciful. I implore you, as you yourself hope for God's mercy, to beware lest ' the wicked man is triumphant and the heart of the poor man whom he has ensnared burn within him '. Do you see to it, then, that you honour the promise you made first to Dom Norbert and then to myself, that you would restore their possessions to Humbert and his wife and children. Farewell.

LETTER 41

TO THE SAME

AMONG the many marks you have given of your affection for me, what especially attracts me to you is that, although I have dared to importune you on behalf of many people, I never remember an occasion when you have turned me away. And so it is not surprising that I have become more confident and do not hesitate to come to you once more, this time on behalf of the Canons of Larzicourt.[1] I do not plead with you for their rights because such is my confidence in your sense of justice and law that I do not think even your greatest enemy would have any cause to fear when pleading his rights at your court. But this is the favour which, though absent, I ask with them and for them, knowing it to be most important, namely that you shall grant them ready admittance to your august presence with greater promptness and favour than is usual, so that their neighbours, hearing you are well disposed towards them, may have due respect for their way of life; and that if by chance any of your ministers or soldiers should unjustly lay hands on their property or harass the peace in God which is theirs, they may know that by so doing they incur your displeasure.

2. There is still another thing I would ask you. When I was passing through Bar the other day I met a woman in a pitiful condition, for her heart was full of bitterness. She implored me with tears and prayers to intercede with you for her, and my heart was moved to pity for her troubles. She is the wife of that man of yours Balin on whom you have lately visited many great penalties for the evil he has done. Be merciful to her that you may obtain mercy.

3. And now that I have begun I shall continue to speak to my Lord. In a duel that was lately fought in the presence of the Prefect[2]

---

[1] These were Canons Regular of St. Augustine. Larzicourt is in the diocese of Châlons-sur-Marne and, in the time of Mabillon, the Jesuits had a house there.

[2] *Præpositus.* The natural translation is Provost, but as this word now has a purely ecclesiastical significance, and in this case he was a secular official, Prefect seems the best translation.

of Bar, the defeated party immediately had his eyes put out under your orders.[1]　And, as if to have been vanquished and to have lost his eyes were a mere nothing, your ministers, so he complains, have taken away his goods.　It is only right, if you will be so pleased, that enough of his goods should be returned for him at least to support his miserable life.　And the sin of the father ought not to be visited on his innocent sons, so that they cannot inherit the family property, if there is any.

4. Finally I hope that you will show all honour to the bishops that have met in your capital to discuss matters that concern God.　May you devoutly and obediently assist the Legate who has decided to honour both you and your city by celebrating there so great a Council, and take pains to confirm and support all that he commands and institutes for the glory of God.　And may you receive with especial deference the Bishop of Langres who is my bishop as well as yours, and render him reverently and humbly the homage you owe for the fief you hold from him.　Farewell.

LETTER 42

TO THE SAME

THERE are two things I commend to you in this man whom you see: his poverty and his holy way of life.　If you do not pity the former, at any rate reverence the latter, and do not deny him what he has come so far and with such difficulty to ask you.　Help him, if not for his sake at any rate for your own, because, if his poverty makes you necessary to him, his holy way of life makes him just as necessary, if not more so, to you.　Of all those whom I have sent to you, I can think of none whom you would please God more by helping.

LETTER 43

TO THE SAME

I AM afraid of bothering you with my constant scribbling.　But in this case the compelling motive is the love of Christ as well as the need of friends.　This man I commend to you is old, as you see, he has also been sent from a good religious house, as I know, and I beg you not to send him empty away.　Moreover I beg you to furnish him with a letter to your uncle the King of England,[2] whom he is

---

[1] In spite of the testimony of Mabillon and others it is hard to escape the impression that the brutal penalty referred to here was not for duelling, but for having been defeated in a duel. Although clean contrary to the laws of the Church duelling was in fact very common at this epoch.　Apparently monasteries and great churchmen had lay champions to fight their duels for them.

[2] Henry I of England was uncle of Theobald by Adela, daughter of William the Conqueror, sister of Henry I, and mother of Theobald.

on his way to see. I would wish, were it possible, for all the servants of God to be your debtors, so that in return for what you give them of your goods they might one day receive you into the everlasting mansions.

LETTER 44

TO THE SAME

To the praiseworthy Prince Theobald, greetings and prayers from Bernard, Abbot of Clairvaux.

I FEAR to tire you with my constant letters when you are busy. But because it is charity, which is God, that compels me, I would have more reason to fear her if I did not obey. If I have found any favour in your eyes, if you are still as just and kind as I have hitherto believed you to be, I beg you by the Lord Jesus, and by that bond of brotherhood that was conferred on you in our Chapter,[1] I throw myself at your feet and beg you with my whole heart, that you show mercy to Anseric who is prepared to submit to your dominion in all things, saving his faith and the law. You may count the favour you show him as shown to me. It was by my advice that his castle came into your hands and, so great is my confidence in your trustworthiness, I have not yet regretted it.

LETTER 45

TO A FRIEND WHO WILL HAND THE PREVIOUS LETTER TO THEOBALD

To his friend greetings in the Lord from Bernard, Abbot of Clairvaux.

As I, although a sinner, eagerly and faithfully pour forth my prayers to God for your sins, so I beg you, beloved, carefully to explain and faithfully to commend this sealed letter to the Count. Speak to your lord for me, so that I may pray for you to the Lord of all.

LETTER 46[2]

TO COUNT THEOBALD

To Count Theobald whom he believes to be a faithful minister of God, all that the prayers of a sinner can avail, from Bernard, Abbot of Clairvaux.

---

[1] This is interesting as indicating that some sort of oblateship was conferred on benefactors in St. Bernard's day.

[2] This is one of the letters first published in the *Bulletin de l'Académie royale* at Brussels in the year 1861.

I BEG you to lend an ear to this religious and to help him. To his petition I add my own because I know his necessity since his abbot, by whom he was sent, is a friend of mine and very well known to me for his sanctity.[1] It would take too long to tell you all about this man, who he is, where he comes from, and what necessity has brought him to where he is now. But I can briefly and truthfully say that whatever it may please you of your liberality to confer on him as a true servant of Christ, you may be sure you have conferred on Christ himself.

NOTE

A letter to Henry, Archbishop of Sens (Benedictine Edition, 42), is not included in collections of St. Bernard's letters but in his treatises, under the title, *De Moribus et Officio Episcoporum Tractatus*, or ' A Treatise on the Life and Duties of a Bishop '.

LETTER 47

TO HENRY, ARCHBISHOP OF SENS

YOUR kind reception of my last request gives me grounds for hoping that you will not deny me a further one. I thank you from the bottom of my heart for the kindness I have formerly experienced from you, and I am bold to ask you for a favour which will place me still further in your debt. Permit the monks of Molesme, I beg you, to possess the church, which they are painfully aware has caused them to lose something of your favour, with the same liberty wherewith it is certain that they held it in the time of your predecessors.

LETTER 48

TO THE SAME

As soon as I have been satisfied by the concession of one request, I boldly return with another—so you see how much I count on your kindness ! It is great presumption on my part, but you must not be angry, for it has its source in charity, not temerity. Your Paternity will remember, unless I am mistaken, that at Troyes you gave up all the claims you had against the monks of Molesme for the church at Senan. And now the monks complain that you are making all sorts of new claims to which, so they say, you have no title. I beg you to remit these claims of yours and I am confident you will not refuse me this request. You have already granted me so many great favours that I am sure you will not deny me this trifle. Farewell.

THE QUARREL BETWEEN LOUIS VI AND THE BISHOP OF PARIS

THE letter which follows refers to an unfortunate quarrel between Stephen of Senlis, Bishop of Paris, and Louis VI, surnamed ' The Fat ', King of France. The

---

[1] ' . . . *propter religionem suam* '.

origins of the crisis are obscure and the threads of the story become very entangled. It appears that the bishop tried to introduce certain much needed reforms into his diocese.   The king supported him in this until the reforms touched the vested interests of the bishop's chapter.   The dean and the archdeacons, who seem to have been prime movers in the trouble, appealed to the king for protection.   Louis supported them and forbade the bishop to change any of the established customs.   The bishop, very conscious of his strong canonical position, regarded this as unwarrantable interference, and seems in some way to have irritated the king who confiscated his ' regalia '.   Whereupon the bishop put the diocese under an interdict.   This vigorous measure led to violence, and the bishop had to fly for his life.   The king then confiscated all his goods and all the goods of his supporters.   It is probably at this juncture that the letter to Louis from ' Stephen, Abbot of Cîteaux, and the whole assembly of Cistercian abbots and brethren' printed in the Benedictine Edition (No. 45) was written.   Mabillon dates it for the year 1127, but more probably it was not written until 1129.

Apparently the king did meet certain bishops and abbots, among whom were the Archbishop of Sens, St. Bernard, and Hugh of Mâcon, Abbot of Pontigny. But little good seems to have come of the meeting.   The bishops and abbots were received rudely and dismissed summarily.   The threat of an appeal to Rome made matters worse, for the king got in first and persuaded Honorius II to lift the interdict. Then the king became more high handed and overbearing than ever.   Precisely how the affair ended is not known.   But there was a meeting between the bishop and the king at which some sort of peace was patched up.   In Paris the ill feeling died hard.

LETTER 49

TO POPE HONORIUS II

To the Sovereign Pontiff Honorius, whatever the prayer of sinners can avail from the abbots of the Poor of Christ, Hugh of Pontigny, and Bernard of Clairvaux.

THE tears and lamentations of the bishops and indeed of the whole Church cannot be ignored by us who, however unworthy, are her children.   We speak of what we have seen.   A great crisis has drawn us from our cloister into public life, and we speak of what we have seen there.   We have seen with sorrow, and sorrowfully we record the great wound that has been inflicted upon the honour of the Church in the reign of Honorius.   The wrath of the king had already begun to bend before the humility, or rather the firmness of the bishops, when lo! the supreme authority of the Supreme Pontiff intervenes to overthrow their firmness and to confirm his pride.   We certainly know, it is indeed clear from your rescript, that the command to lift this just and necessary interdict was sneaked from you by a lie. But should not malice, when at last the lie has been detected, be made to feel that it has over-reached itself and not the majesty of the Supreme Pontiff?   What does astonish us is that judgement should have been given on the hearing of only one of the parties, and that it should have been passed against the absent party.   We do not rashly presume to censure this, but we do mention with filial love to your fatherly heart

4

that the wicked man derives great triumph from this, and the heart of the poor man burns within him. But how long you should allow the former to triumph or how much compassion you should show to the latter, it is not for us to dictate to you, but for you, Holy Father, to consult your own heart. Farewell.

LETTER 50

TO THE SAME, IN THE NAME OF GEOFFREY, BISHOP OF CHARTRES

Concerning the same affair as the former letters. It is difficult not to be favourably impressed, as so often with the letters of St. Bernard, with the courteous but very robust attitude of this letter to Pope Honorius.

THERE is no need to unfold to you, Holy Father, the whole sad story of the quarrel with the king or to go into its causes again, for I do not doubt that you have been moved to the depths of your heart by what you have heard from the holy Bishop of Paris. But so that the support of my own testimony shall not be lacking to my brother bishop, I think it necessary to inform your Holiness of what I myself have seen and heard. When we received the very moderate complaint of the bishop, all the bishops of the archdiocese of Sens, together with our venerable metropolitan and certain other religious persons whom we had summoned, represented to the king with becoming humility the evil thing he had done. We asked him to return to the bishop his goods which he had quite unjustly seized. But we received no satisfaction at all. However, believing that we would have recourse to ecclesiastical penalties in defence of the Church, he at length became afraid and declared he would make full restitution. But almost at the same hour that he did this your rescript arrived lifting the interdict from his domains. Whereupon most unfortunately, fortified in his evil purposes, he refused to honour the promises he had made. Nevertheless the day upon which he again promised that he would fulfil his undertaking, we presented ourselves to him, but we looked for peace and it did not come, we expected better times and found confusion. The effect of your rescript has been that what he has unjustly seized he is still more unjustly keeping and that day by day, in all places, he is seizing the property of the bishop with all the more confidence now that it can be held with impunity. The most just (so it seems to me) interdict of our bishop has been lifted by your command, what we were ready to do with the hope of obtaining peace has been suspended for fear of offending you, and in consequence we have become the laughing stock of our neighbours. How long will it seem good to your Holiness that this state of affairs should continue?

LETTER 51

TO CARDINAL HAIMERIC, CHANCELLOR OF THE HOLY SEE

It is clear from this very instructive letter that someone had been making mischief in Rome about St. Bernard. There is nothing new or surprising in this. It was indeed inevitable that a man like St. Bernard should have been the victim of petty jealousy and even the quite sincere distrust of men with narrow horizons. It is not always wicked people who stone the prophets, more often it is the perfectly sincere formalists.

To the illustrious Haimeric, Chancellor of the Holy Roman See, salvation in eternity, from Brother Bernard, styled Abbot of Clairvaux.

CANNOT wretchedness escape envy? Must truth breed hatred even for the poor and needy? Should I be glad or should I deplore that I am treated as an enemy? Is it because I spoke the truth or because I did right? This is for your brothers in Curia to decide who ' speak evil of the deaf ' against the law and who, regardless of the Prophet's curse, ' call evil good and good evil '. What have I done that displeases them? Is it because at Châlons a man discredited on all sides was removed from his stewardship for squandering the goods of the Lord in the Church of Verdun over which he had been placed?[1] Or because at Cambrai Fulbert, who was manifestly wrecking his monastery, was forced to withdraw in favour of Parvin whom everyone considered a wise and prudent servant? Or because at Laon his sanctuary was restored to the Lord after being a brothel of Venus?[2] For which of these things do you, I do not say stone me, for I would not set myself in the place of my Lord, but tear me to pieces? This is what I might have answered you rightly and with pride if I could have claimed for myself any credit for these things. But why am I blamed for the actions of others? Or supposing they were mine, why am I blamed for them as though they were evil? No one could be so imprudent as to doubt or so impudent as to deny that these things were well and justly done. You can choose between either denying or admitting that I am the author of them. If I am, then I am wrongfully rebuked and deserve praise for doing what was praiseworthy. If I am not, then I am no more worthy of blame than I am of praise.

[1] Henry, Bishop of Verdun, was suspected of corrupt administration of the funds of the Church. He consulted St. Bernard on the matter and St. Bernard advised him to resign, so as to avoid public scandal. His resignation was accepted by the Pope's Legate, Matthew, Bishop of Albano, at a Council held at Châlons-sur-Marne in 1129.

[2] The Abbey of St. John at Laon is referred to here. The lax and scandalous life of the nuns there had for long been a cause of grave anxiety to the bishop, Bartholomew le Vir. A council was held at Arras in 1128, attended by the king (for the abbey was a royal foundation), the Archbishop of Rheims, the Bishops of Laon, Arras, and Soissons, as well as several abbots, including St. Bernard. The reform of the abbey was decreed and confirmed by the Pope through his Legate, Matthew, Bishop of Albano. This time the king made no objections, probably, as Williams in his *Life of St. Bernard* says, because the state of affairs was too scandalous to admit of any doubt as to the correct procedure.

This is a new sort of detraction, not dissimilar to what Balaam did who covered the people with blessings when he had been summoned to curse them. For what could be more just and pleasing than that while intending to rebuke me you should have only commended me the more, so as to have used all unknowingly praises instead of insults; than that while intending to disparage me, you should have praised me unwittingly? It is as if your brothers in Curia were reproaching me or rather crediting me with other people's good deeds, because they could not find any evil that I had done.

2. I am not disturbed by undeserved blame nor do I accept unmerited praise. I am not greatly concerned about things for which I am not responsible. Let them praise, if they wish, or blame, if they dare, for the first my lord of Albano, for the second my lord of Rheims, and for the third the same archbishop together with the bishop of Laon, the king, and many other reverend persons. None of them will deny responsibility for these affairs or that they were the chief persons concerned. If they have done well it does not concern me any more than if they have done ill. Is it my whole and only fault that I was present on those occasions, I who am only fit to live hidden away, I who am my own judge, accuser, and witness of my life, to see that my actions become my profession and that the name I bear of monk is justified by my solitary existence? I was present, I do not deny it. But I was summoned and dragged there. If this does not please my friends in Curia, it pleases me just as little. I wish that I had not gone there, I wish that I need never go on similar occasions. I wish that I had not lately been where I saw with shame a violent tyrant armed against the Church by the Apostolic authority, as if he were not raging enough without such help.[1] When a sudden load was placed upon my shoulders by the indisputable authority of the Apostolic rescript, then I felt, in the words of the Prophet, my tongue cleave to the roof of my mouth. 'I was dumb and patient so that I would not speak even to good purpose', when I saw the innocent suddenly covered with ignominy by that rescript and wicked men rejoice the more in their wickedness and delight exceedingly in their vile deeds, and my sorrow was renewed within me. The ungodly was shown mercy so that, according to the words of the Prophet, he should not learn his lesson. He who in the land of the righteous worked iniquity was freed of the most just interdict under which his domains were held.

3. For reasons of this sort, even were there no others, I am vexed at having been embroiled in these disputes, especially as I knew that I was not concerned personally in them. I am vexed, but I am dragged into them none the less. But by whom can I better hope to be relieved of all this than by you, the best of men? You do not lack

---

[1] See Letters 49 and 50.

the power to do this, and I see that you do not lack the will. I am delighted to know that you are displeased that I should have been concerned in these affairs. It is most just and friendly of you. May it please you to bestir yourself in the matter, and because you understand that it is expedient for your friend and becoming for a monk, see that what we both want is speedily effected for the sake of justice and for the salvation of my soul. May it please you to bid the noisy and importunate frogs to keep their holes and remain contented with their ponds. See that they are heard no more in the councils of the mighty or seen in the palaces of the great, that no necessity and no authority may have the power to drag them into public affairs and embroil them in disputes. In this way perhaps your friend can avoid the stigma of presumption. Indeed I do not know how I was able to incur it, for I know that it was my purpose and determination never, except on the business of my Order, to leave my monastery unless the Legate of the Apostolic See or my own bishop bade me do so. As you know very well, a person in my humble state may not refuse the command of such authorities, except by the privilege of some higher authority. So if I can ever achieve this through your good offices, then without any doubt I shall have peace at home and leave others at peace. But I do not think that because I am hidden away and keeping silent the troubles of the Church will cease so long as the Roman Curia continues to pass judgements to the prejudice of the absent in order to please those who are at hand. Farewell.

LETTER 52

TO POPE HONORIUS

This letter is written by St. Bernard in the name of the Abbots of Cîteaux and Pontigny, on behalf of Henry, Archbishop of Sens. Henry, surnamed the Wild Boar, was converted from a worldly life by St. Bernard. He ceased to be a courtier and began to take the work of his diocese seriously. When the Bishop of Paris got into trouble with the king (see Letters 49, 50 and 51) Henry came to his support and drew the guns on to himself.

To the Sovereign Pontiff, Honorius, what is due to their most reverend Lord and loving Father from his servants and, if they are deemed worthy, sons, from Stephen of Cîteaux, Hugh of Pontigny, and Bernard of Clairvaux.

WE who are compelled, by reason of our sins, to shelter in monasteries, pray without ceasing for you and for the Church committed to your care, rejoicing with the bride over such a faithful guardian, and with the friend of the Bridegroom over such fruitful labour. And so with confidence and loyalty we advise your Paternity that we are seeing with sorrow our mother, the Church, assailed in our kingdom. As far as we who are on the spot can understand, it is more zeal for righteousness, piety of life, and religion itself in the persons of the bishops than the bishops themselves that the king is persecuting. Your Holiness will easily see this if you understand that it is only now, when they are living in a manner becoming their priesthood and creditable to their sacred calling, that they are treated as enemies: before this, when they were living worldly lives, they were treated as intimate friends and shown every honour. For this reason the king attacked the Bishop of Paris, when he was innocent, with grave insults and injuries. He was shaken, but he did not fall, for the Lord upheld him with his hand, when yours was against him.[1] And now for the same reason, he has turned against my lord of Sens and is trying to shake and overthrow his constancy, so that when the archbishop has been cast down, he can set about the suffragan bishops as he likes. No one can dispute that it is really religion which the king is assailing. He openly proclaims that it is the destruction of his kingdom and the enemy of his crown. Another Herod, he is not troubled about Christ in the manger now, but envies Christ reigning in the churches. We do not believe that he has anything at all against the Archbishop of Sens except his spirit of zeal: it is this that he is trying to extinguish in him, as he has tried to do in others. If we are thought to be deceived or to be deceiving in this matter, your own prompt examination will reveal the facts so that, as we hope and pray, 'judgement may come forth from thy countenance' 'to protect innocence and keep right before thy eyes'. If on the other hand, the matter is again submitted to the presence and power of the king, it is clear that the just man will be delivered into the hands of his enemies.

LETTER 53

TO THE SAME

IF it should seem good to your Holiness, it would be desirable that the cause of my lord of Sens should be judged in your presence. For if he has to answer his adversaries in the presence and power of the king, who hates him, he would be like a man delivered into the hands of his enemies. Whatever your Holiness decrees must be final, so it is much to be hoped that your decision may result in what will be unquestionably good. The only thing we, and all the religious who stand with us, beg with all humility is that if by any chance he should feel himself oppressed in the presence of the mighty, as is wont to happen, he may have recourse to the paternal heart of his Father, which we have

---

[1] . . . *pulsata est, sed non quassata; quia Dominus supposuit manum suam, cum vestram opposuit.* Eales translates: '. . . yet he has not been crushed, because the Lord arrested the king's hand when he opposed yours'.

never heard that you denied to anyone in trouble. Otherwise Joseph, the just man, must take care for the child and his mother, because even now Herod is seeking to destroy Christ in the diocese of Sens. To speak the truth openly, it is quite manifest that what the king is persecuting in the archbishop is his new religious fervour, for, when he was living his old worldly life, his interests were furthered in every way and he was sent into his diocese completely secure from all attack.

LETTER 54

TO CARDINAL HAIMERIC

This letter concerns the same matter as the above.

To the illustrious Haimeric, Chancellor of the Holy Roman See, health and whatever the prayers of a sinner can avail, from Brother Bernard, styled Abbot of Clairvaux.

FOR how long will it be true that ' all those who are resolved to lead a holy life in Jesus Christ will meet with persecution '? For how long will ' godless men bear rule in the domain of the just '? Who will grant that the just may begin to withstand ' those who thwart all their striving '? Who can now endure the conflict which rages between heaven and earth so fiercely, that while angels delight over the correction of a sinner, the sons of Adam gnash their teeth with rage and pine away? As if Jesus had not suffered to bring peace to heaven and earth with his blood; as if God in his person had not reconciled the world with himself. Formerly, when the archbishop was ruled by the desires of his heart, he was praised; when his life was worldly, he was esteemed. But now they are looking for simony under the swaddling clothes of the child Jesus, and their spiteful curiosity is probing for the corpse of dead vice under new born virtue. You see that even now Jesus is a sign to be denied for these men. By him I implore you, for his sake I pray you. He has claims upon your reverence, and upon your pity. Stand up for him now in the person of the archbishop, and you will have him to stand by you in the hour of your judgement.

LETTER 55

TO THE SAME

YOUR friend and mine, the Lord Bishop of Chartres, desires me to assure you that it is quite untrue that he wished for permission to set out for Jerusalem, as certain people have tried to persuade the Pope. He has neither the intention nor the inclination to do so. Although he had greatly wished to set out, yet he was not able to do so without giving grave scandal to all of our good people, who feared that his absence would do more harm to his own flock than his presence would do good to strangers. So much for the bishop. Now let me speak a little for myself according to the words of Scripture: 'Thy own self befriend, doing God's will'. Do you wish me to be burdened and occupied by public affairs and to gain nothing by being relieved from my own responsibilities, because I am immersed in other people's business? If I have found any favour in your eyes, see that I am released from these burdens, so that I may have time to pray for my own sins and yours. Certainly I consider it is safer for myself to obey the Lord Pope, but only if he would but deign to note my limitations, only if he would understand that I am not able to do these things, or at least only with great difficulty. And now I have said enough to a wise man. The aforesaid bishop has asked for one of my booklets to send to you. But I had not anything by me at the time which I could believe worthy of your attention. However I have lately brought out a little work on Grace and Free Will. I will gladly send you this, if you wish it.

LETTER 56

TO THE SAME

I HAVE sent you letters by many people on behalf of many people, but now 'behold, I am here; I myself that spoke'. In these two people, you see three; because where they are, there also am I. In their hearts I always dwell, more safely and more gratefully than in my own. This will only seem incredible to one who does not know the strength of friendship, and the power of love, or who does not believe that there was 'one heart and one soul in all the company of believers'. Therefore he who sees these two, sees also myself; although not in the body. And what they say, I also say; but through their lips. I grant that I am absent in the body, but that is the least part of me. Should anyone see only my face, he could say, quite truthfully and without error, that he has seen me and not just a part of me; yet it would only have been a part of me that he had seen, and a small part. I can therefore say with far greater truth that I am present wherever I feel my will, spirit, and affection to be, which are indeed the better and more effective part of me, even though in body I am not there. You must know therefore that we are one person in three bodies, united not indeed in equal sanctity, in which I feel myself far inferior to both of them, but in equality of will and great concord of spirit. And why should not the bond of charity effect this unity of spirit among different people when we know that the union of the body can unite 'two in one flesh'? I would wish to unite yourself as a fourth, if you should deem it fitting and concur in the same unity of love. You can easily achieve this if you do not consider it beneath you, and I only beg that you should let them know that you do not.

LETTER 57

TO THE SAME

I DESIRE and beg for the love you owe to God and myself that the bearer of this letter, the venerable Abbot Vivian of Hautecombe, with whom I am on terms of intimate friendship because of his piety, may find you ready to help him. So much for the abbot, and now with regard to yourself. 'What', I ask, 'doth it profit a man, if he gain the whole world, and suffer the loss of his own soul? Or what exchange shall a man give for his soul?' Not the whole world would be enough. How precious is the soul redeemed by the blood of Christ! Grievous the loss of a soul which could only be repaired by the cross of Christ! If it fall again into sin, sin even unto death, who shall now restore it? Is there another Christ, or shall he be crucified for it again? Upon this matter I would have you always mindful of that counsel of the Wise Man: 'Remember at all times what thou must come to at last, and thou shalt never do amiss'.

LETTER 58

TO GEOFFREY, BISHOP OF CHARTRES

To the most faithful and wise servant of God, Geoffrey, Bishop of Chartres, that he may be enlightened with the glory of the everlasting hills, from Bernard, servant of the Poor of Christ at Clairvaux.

THE more fame and honour your worthy life brings you, the greater the burden it lays upon you. This letter is written on behalf of the bearer. Like many others, of whom you know not a few, he has been drawn from afar by the fragrance of your virtues to seek with confidence the pity that is open to all, hoping to find not only advice as to what he ought to do, but also help to do it. His case is this. He was enclosed in a cell with the intention of living as a recluse for the love of God. He himself will tell you why he transgressed by coming out. Now he intends to return to the life to which he was dedicated and he proposes to do this with your favour, if he can obtain it by my mediation with which he has taken care to fortify himself. Therefore act with your accustomed generosity and help the poor wretch; or rather, as you recognize that you have the same duty to all, learned and simple, make haste to snatch this wandering sheep of Christ from the jaws of the wolf, lead him back to his former pastures, and see that he is enclosed in some cell near one of your sheepfolds . . . unless something else more expedient occurs to your mind that you judge permissible and are able to persuade him to do.

LETTER 59

TO THE SAME

I DO not know whether Dom Norbert is going to Jerusalem or not. When I last saw him a few days ago and was deemed worthy to drink in his heavenly wisdom, he never mentioned the matter to me. He spoke of the coming of Antichrist and, on my asking him when he thought this would be, he declared himself quite certain that it would be during this present generation. But when I heard the reasons he had for his certainty, I did not feel compelled to agree with him. He concluded by saying that he would live to see a general persecution of the Church.

2. May I remind you of that poor and exiled man, Humbert? He twice begged you, when you were at Troyes, to intercede for him with Count Theobald who has dispossessed him. And now I join my prayers with his to implore your aid in the matter. I myself have written to the Count but, not finding favour, I achieved nothing.

3. And now I must tell you something which you will be very glad to hear. Your Stephen is ' not running his course like a man in doubt of his goal; or fighting his battle like a man who wastes his blows upon the air '. Pray that he may so run as to reach the goal, so fight as to conquer.

LETTER 60

TO THE SAME

Dom Mabillon believes that this letter concerns the same person as Letter 58.

I AM told by this man that you are still hesitating to satisfy his desire and petition, because you believe that it conflicts with his first vow to go to Jerusalem. Should you wish for my opinion on the matter, I would say that lesser vows ought not to hinder greater ones, and that God does not exact fulfilment of a promise if something better has been done in its stead. Would you, for instance, be justly angry with a man who, on the day allotted for the payment of his debt, paid you more than he owed you? But if you are afraid of offending his bishop, I can set your mind at rest on that score, because I happen to know that so far from offending him you will please him very much by helping this man.

LETTER 61

TO EBAL, BISHOP OF CHÀLONS

To the Lord Ebal, by the grace of God Bishop of Châlons, whatever the prayers of a sinner can obtain, from Brother Bernard, Abbot of Clairvaux.

IT is not well for you to ignore the danger which threatens that small ship. I refer to the church of All Saints which, under your own eyes, is drifting without a helmsman.[1] The matter is your responsibility, and I cannot but wonder with what reason and what sort of conscience you can desist from requiring acceptance of the post from that ecclesiastic himself, a religious man, they say, who has been elected by religious persons, even if the supineness and indolence of certain people do not deserve it. I have heard that these people object to the man for no other reason than that he is religious, and that they have presumed to force your hand in the matter of electing someone else on the pretext that someone who was not a stranger would be more agreeable and friendly, better known and more acceptable to the townspeople, more familiar with local customs, and better able to administer the affairs of the church. But what they really mean is that they want someone who will not rebuke their vices, who will wink at, or at any rate not dare to oppose their wretched habits. But do not listen to them. Whether they like it or not, you should do all you can to install this man who is of good repute, to care for that church. If he is the sort of man that report says he is, God will undoubtedly be with him and pour out his grace upon him, so as to render him pleasing to all, and successful in all his works.

2. And if it should happen that this man can in no wise be had for the post, perhaps because those persons I have referred to are not worthy of him; then let some other suitable person be procured from another religious house. But let him not be such a man as they want, one, that is, who would encourage their carnal tastes, but someone who would so arrange the affairs of the Church as to put the care of souls before all else. When the two monasteries of St. Peter and St. Urban were deprived of their pastors' care in a similar manner, your predecessor of holy memory, the Lord William, quite regardless of the labour of the long journey and the sharpness of the winter, went in person twice (unless I am mistaken) to Cluny and once to Dijon. But only with the greatest difficulty by his prayers and supplications was he able to bring that good man Dom Hugh, who has since died, from Dijon, and the venerable Dom Radulf, who is yet with us, from Cluny, so as to put one of them over each of the monasteries, and all because he did not think that he could safely commit these monasteries to the care of one of their own monks. I have cited this example so that you may see how in the matter on hand it behoves you to be not less cautious and careful.

[1] The Abbey of Canons Regular at Châlons-sur-Marne.

LETTER 62

TO GUILENCUS, BISHOP OF LANGRES

To his Lord and Father Guilencus, by the grace of God Bishop of Langres, the complete devotion of Brother Bernard, Abbot of Clairvaux.

As soon as I heard of the death of Archdeacon Garnier[1] I felt that I must at once approach you to plead with you, and even to advise you, if you should think that advice from a person like myself would be worth listening to, to the end that you may generously exalt mercy over justice with regard to the property held by the church of St. Stephen at Dijon, by renouncing the rights which you have over it. I am fully aware that the property should return to you according to the arrangement agreed upon and confirmed in writing at the chapter of Langres when your son Hubert was constituted first abbot of the house. But I know too that it would be an occasion of grave scandal to the canons and a great reproach to the abbot if you should, under any pretext whatsoever, lay your hands upon the property which that church has held for so long, because they would immediately accuse the abbot of establishing a bad precedent, since as soon as he entered office the church had suffered on his account so great a loss. I therefore beg you of your great mercy, and in begging I also advise you, to spare so many of Christ's weaker servants such a scandal and at the same time to release his representative of any reproach by conceding to that church what it has held by right for so long.[2]

LETTER 63

TO THE SAME

I COME to you as a suppliant and not, I hope, as an importunate busy-body, on behalf of the church of Molesme. There are several reasons which encourage me to believe that there is no fear of your rejecting my petition. First, it is not for a strange church that I am petitioning you, but for one of your own. Second, I understand that the church is not claiming anything that does not belong to it, but only its own rights. Third, there is one associating himself with me who on his own account is of sufficient consequence to ask and obtain far greater things; he is the Count Theobald. And if I add my own prayers as a fourth reason I do not think I should be merely rashly presuming. Even I have not so little faith in myself as to hesitate, if needs be, to rely boldly on your well-tried kindness and to approach you for anything that seems reasonable. Farewell.

[1] He had been abbot at the church before Canons Regular were introduced in 1113.
[2] This was in fact done by Guilencus in the year 1129.

LETTER 64

TO RICUIN, BISHOP OF TOUL

To the Reverend Father Lord Ricuin, by the grace of God Bishop of Toul, health and prayers from Brother Bernard, styled Abbot of Clairvaux.

THIS poor sinner tells me that you have sent him to me, who am also a sinner, for spiritual counsel. For the present I have no better advice to offer him than that he should return to the bosom of your fatherly love and 'seek guidance from the lips of the priest'. In view of my own insignificance and the limits of my office I am always most careful not to overreach myself by presuming to lay penances on people especially in criminal cases, except when the persons are under my own jurisdiction. It would be exceedingly rash of me to undertake the functions of a bishop, being myself no more than a sinner like other men and quite unskilled in all such matters. When any serious question arises which either I do not know how to settle, or cannot settle, or do not dare to settle, like everyone else I refer it, as is only fitting, to the decision of the bishop, and am not easy about it until I have been fortified by his judgement or advice. And so let this sick sheep be cared for by his own shepherd, a shepherd who knows the canons and is able to administer the medicine of suitable penance. May God forbid that this soul for whom Christ died should die in his sins, and that the chief Shepherd should require his blood of your hands. As God has inspired him to leave the world, I have persuaded him to do so, if by your intervention an old and poor man like him can gain admission into some convent of holy men within your diocese. Full of days may you, at length, holy and venerable father, be received into the courts of the Lord where one day is better than a thousand.

LETTER 65

TO HENRY, BISHOP OF VERDUN

Of this bishop, see Letter 51.

To the Lord Henry, by the grace of God Bishop of Verdun, health and prayers from Brother Bernard, styled Abbot of Clairvaux.

THIS poor woman whom for many years Satan has bound in tangled knots of sin has asked my advice on the state of her soul. She has taken what I said to her so much to heart that now, after much wandering for many years, the poor stray is prepared to return with confidence to the care of her shepherd. And he will help her all the more readily and eagerly for knowing that he will have to give a strict account of his charge to the Lamb of God who died for her. It was my duty to correct her when she was wandering; it is now yours, not to despise her as a sinner, but to welcome her back as a penitent. If the unhappy story which she has told me of herself be true, she must either be reconciled to her former husband, or else they must both live single lives.

LETTER 66

TO THE SAME

CONCERNING those matters which it has pleased your Excellency to enquire of me, I can only say that either I am deceived or else that your informant is deceiving. But experience has taught me to distrust my feeble memory and I am loath to suspect in a brother such grave falsehood, so if there is anything in what he has said I am nevertheless quite certain, and wish you to believe without any doubt, that I have never accused you or reproached you with anything, in any way, to anyone.[1] It would be the sheerest presumption for one in my insignificant position to blame bishops and those who are not present to answer for themselves, for things that do not concern me and of which I have no proof.

2. I am most touched by what you say of your desire to meet me and certainly nothing would please me more than to know you better and to be better known to you. With a like confidence I venture to petition your highness and recommend to your benevolence the monastery which under your auspices and, so I hear, with your encouragement, my reverend brother and co-abbot, Guy of Trois-Fontaines, has undertaken to build.[2] Regard as done for myself whatever you do for him and let him see how much you care for me. Farewell.

LETTER 67

TO ALEXANDER, BISHOP OF LINCOLN

This letter concerns a young canon named Philip who, on his way to Jerusalem, turned aside to pause at Clairvaux, and was blessed to find there his vocation, even as St. Stephen Harding on his way to Rome found it at Molesme. Alexander was Bishop of Lincoln from 1123-1147, and was known as Alexander the Magnificent.

To the honourable Lord Alexander, by the grace of God Bishop of Lincoln, that he may desire honour in Christ rather than in the world, from Bernard, Abbot of Clairvaux.

[1] See note 1, Letter 51, p. 79.
[2] La Chalade in the diocese of Verdun.

I WRITE to tell you that your Philip has found a short cut to Jerusalem and has arrived there very quickly. He crossed 'the vast ocean stretching wide on every hand' with a favourable wind in a very short time, and he has now cast anchor on the shores for which he was making. Even now he stands in the courts of Jerusalem and 'whom he had heard tidings of in Ephrata he has found in the woodland plains, and gladly reverences in the place where he has halted in his journey'. He has entered the holy city and has chosen his heritage with them of whom it has been deservedly said: 'You are no longer exiles or aliens; the saints are your fellow citizens, you belong to God's household'. His going and coming is in their company and he has become one of them, glorifying God and saying with them: 'We find our true home in heaven'. He is no longer an inquisitive onlooker, but a devout inhabitant and an enrolled citizen of Jerusalem; but not of that earthly Jerusalem to which Mount Sinai in Arabia is joined, and which is in bondage with her children, but of that free Jerusalem which is above and the mother of us all.

2. And this, if you want to know, is Clairvaux. She is the Jerusalem united to the one in heaven by whole-hearted devotion, by conformity of life, and by a certain spiritual affinity. Here, so Philip promises himself, will be his rest for ever and ever. He has chosen to dwell here because he has found, not yet to be sure the fulness of vision, but certainly the hope of that true peace, 'the peace of God which surpasses all our thinking'. But this blessing, although he has received it from on high, he wishes to have, and is indeed quite sure that he does have, with your good will, because 'a wise son maketh the father glad'. He begs you of your fatherly love, and I unite my prayers with his, that the arrangement he has made for his creditors to have his prebend, may be allowed to stand, so that he may not become (God forbid) a defaulter and breaker of his covenant, and his daily sacrifice of a contrite heart be unacceptable because a brother has something against him. He also begs that the house which he has built for his mother on Church lands with the ground which he has assigned to it, may remain hers so long as she lives. So much for Philip.

3. And now I turn to yourself. I feel impelled and even inspired by the Charity of God to exhort you not to regard the passing glory of the world as if it would never pass away, and so lose the glory that endures for ever; not to love your possessions more than your self or only for your own sake, and so lose both your possessions and your self; not to allow the flattery of present prosperity to hide from you the inevitable end, so that when it comes it will bring endless adversity; not to allow the pleasures of this world to beget for you and conceal from you the endless woe which they beget by concealing, so that when you think death is far off, it may come upon you unawares,

and while you are counting on a long life, life itself may suddenly leave you ill prepared, according to what has been written: 'It is just when men are saying, All quiet, all safe, that doom will fall upon them suddenly, like the pangs that come to a woman in travail, and there will be no escape from it'.

LETTER 68

TO ALVISUS, ABBOT OF ANCHIN IN THE DIOCESE OF ARRAS

A monk named Godwin had left his abbey to join the Cistercians, and soon after died. His former abbot appears to have been angry at losing one of his best religious but, on hearing of his death, immediately put aside his anger and, perhaps, attended his funeral. In this letter St. Bernard congratulates the abbot on his forbearance and apologizes most abjectly for having offended him by accepting his monk. Alvisus later became Bishop of Arras.

To Alvisus, Abbot of Anchin monastery, cordial greetings from Bernard.

MAY God reward you with his mercy for the mercy you have shown to your holy son Godwin. For I heard that as soon as you received news of his death you forgot old differences and not only satisfied but reaffirmed your friendship.[1] Most appropriately you behaved as a father rather than a judge and tried, as a true father should, to satisfy the claims of charity and pity. You could not have acted better or in a way more excellent and worthy of yourself. But who would have believed it possible! Truly ' who else can know man's thoughts except man's spirit that is within him'. All the sternness and severity which you formerly showed him, all the anger which was evident in your words and looks, left you. At the first mention of your son's death your fatherly heart was touched and all those signs of your anger were immediately put aside, as if they had been mere masks put on for the time to hide the true goodness and kindness of your nature. And so mercy and truth met in you and, because mercy prevailed over judgement, justice and peace have embraced. I think I can infer what happened in your soul when in the interests of truth you were aroused with zeal for justice and girded yourself to avenge the injury you believed had been done. Like Joseph you prudently hid your mercy until you could no longer endure to do so when, also as in the case of Joseph, it broke forth from the hidden fount of pity in you and meeting with truth it soothed anger, tempered zeal, and made peace with justice.

2. Then from the fountain of your pure heart flowed like streams of crystal water such thoughts as these. Why should I be angry?

---

[1] . . . *non amicitiæ, consolatorem potius quam ultorem vos exhibuistis.* Eales translates: '. . . remembering only your friendship for him, you behaved with kindness, not resentment'.

Surely it is better to have mercy according to those words of Scripture,
'It is mercy not sacrifice that wins favour with me', better to preserve
the unity of the spirit in the bond of peace, and to await the mercy
that has been promised to the merciful.   After all was he not my son?
Who can be angry for long with his son?   Or did he cease to be my
son as soon as he left me?   But was he no longer with me in spirit
when he left me in the body?   Could even death have taken him from
me?   Is the liberty of the hearts of those who love each other restricted
by the necessities of body and place?   Surely neither distance of place
nor the absence or death of the body can separate those whom one
spirit quickens and one love unites?   And if 'the souls of the just are
in God's hands' surely those who have put off the flesh and rest in
him are not separated from us who are still struggling on in the flesh,
but not according to the flesh.   Therefore he was mine when he was
alive and is still mine now he is dead, and I shall know him again when
I reach the heavenly home.   He could only be separated from me if
he could be torn from the hand of God.

3. And so your very affection for your son excuses him, but what
reasons can you have, my father, for excusing me?   What adequate
satisfaction can I make to you?   What satisfaction can you ask of me
for the great injury I have done you in receiving your son when he
left you?   What can I say?   If I tell you that I did not take him in
(and would that I could say this without sin), it would be an obvious
lie.   If I admit that I received him, but maintain that it was right
for me to have done so, I would seem to be excusing myself.   If I
take the safer course and admit that I have done wrong, there is a
question of how far I have done wrong.   I do not say in self-defence,
'Who would not have taken him in?'   I say, 'Who would have
turned that holy man away when he was knocking on the door or
would have sent him off when he had been received?'   Who can
tell whether God was not satisfying my need from your abundance
by sending me one out of your many good religious to be at the same
time a comfort to me and a credit to you, for the Scriptures tell us
that a wise son is a credit to his father.   I did not try to anticipate his
wishes by inviting him to come, I did not attempt to lure him away
from you.   God knows that, on the contrary, when he was imploring
me to take him in I would not do so before I had first tried to persuade
him to return to you.   Only when he refused to return, and then only
grudgingly, did I give way to his importunity.   If I am at fault for
receiving a good man, a stranger,[1] and alone, and for receiving him
in the way that I did, it is the only time I have offended you by such

---

[1] *caveat Abbas, ne aliquando de alio noto monasterio monachum ad habitandum suscipiat sine consensu
Abbatis ejus aut litteris commendatitiis, quia scriptum est* 'Quod tibi non vis fieri, alii ne feceris' (*Rule
of St. Benedict*, Ch. 61).   'Let the Abbot take care never to receive permanently a monk from
any known monastery without his own Abbot's consent and letters of recommendation; because
it is written: "What thou wouldst not have done to thyself, do not thou to another".'

a fault and it would therefore not be unbecoming in you to forgive it, seeing that it is not lawful for you to refuse pardon even to one who has fallen seventy times seven.

4. I want you to know that I do not regard it as a small matter to have offended you in any way, that on the contrary it is causing me much sorrow. I often call upon God to witness that I come to you as a suppliant in my imagination as I cannot come in body, and see myself before you making humble satisfaction on bended knees. Would that the Holy Spirit, who perhaps it is that inspires me to do this, would make you feel how sadly and unhappily I throw myself in spirit at your knees. How often with naked shoulders and scourge ready in my hands, prepared as if at your command to punish myself, I implore your forgiveness, and anxiously await your pardon. If it is no trouble to you I beg you to let me know as soon as you can whether you have forgiven me, so that if you are satisfied I can feel confident of your pardon, but if not I can humble myself yet more and demand something yet more of myself, if I can, so as to make worthy amends.

LETTER 69

TO GEOFFREY, ABBOT OF ST. MÉDARD

To Dom Geoffrey of St. Médard good health, but of the soul, from Brother Bernard, the ill-conditioned ruler of Clairvaux.

I BEG that you may be so good as to forward the enclosed letter to the Abbot of Anchin and that, when an opportunity presents itself, you will do what you can for an absent friend in the matter with which the letter is concerned. For whether it be just or unjust I ought not to ignore resentment against me especially when it is of such a father as the Abbot of Anchin. I could have better appeased his anger by word of mouth than by letter for, in matters like this, the living word is better than the written word and the tongue than the pen. The pen cannot so well express a meaning as the expression of the face; the look in the eyes attests the sincerity of the speaker. And so because I cannot go to him in person to apologize, I am trying to do what I can through you. I beg you again and again to do what you can while you may to remove this offence from the Kingdom of God which is within us. I very much fear that either one or both may be taken if this ill feeling between us should last until the angels come who will be charged at the end of the world to remove all scandals. With regard to the complaints you make in your letter about your troubles, you must know that ' the Lord is nigh unto those whose hearts are troubled '. Have confidence in him for he has conquered the world and his eyes are upon those who trouble you. He knows the people you live amongst. He will hear you when you cry out to him in your misery, he will give you audience under a canopy of cloud, who tests your loyalty at the Waters of Rebellion.   Farewell.

LETTER 70

TO THE MONKS OF FLAY

The Cistercian life and the dynamic character of St. Bernard were constantly attracting monks from other houses, especially from the Black Benedictines. It was the main source of rancour between the two Orders.   The Rule of St. Benedict is quite explicit on the point[1]: a monk coming from an unknown monastery may be received and, if he seems a desirable acquisition, he may even be persuaded to stay, but a monk from a monastery which is known may on no account be accepted.

This letter concerns yet another trouble occasioned by a monk leaving his monastery to live at Clairvaux.

To Dom H.,[2] superior of the church of Flay, and to the brothers who are with him, greetings from the brothers who are at Clairvaux.

WE understand from your letters that you are upset by our having received one of your monks here.   We are sorry that you should be sad about this for we are not sure that your sadness is that ' sadness according to God ' or supernatural sadness, spoken of by the Apostle Paul.   If it were this sort of sadness we do not think you would have reproached us so bitterly without knowing anything about us although, indeed, we are your brothers and could be, if you wished it, your friends; or without ever having met us or held any communication with us either by letter or word of mouth.   You say that you are amazed that we should have received Brother Benedict and you threaten us with the consequences if we do not return him to you at once.   Taking it for granted that your monastery is well known, you cite the Rule[3] forbidding the reception of monks from a known monastery.   Your monastery may be well known, but not to us. Even though the fame of your religious observance may have reached Rome, as you say it has, it does not follow it has reached us who are, in fact, some way from Rome!   It may seem to you surprising, but it is none the less a fact, that we have not the slightest knowledge of any one of you, abbot or monks, or even of your neighbourhood, and we have never heard of your religious observance or way of life. And this is nothing to be wondered at seeing that we are separated by great distances, different provinces, and another language.   We have not the same bishop nor even the same archbishop.   So we do

[1] *Rule of St. Benedict*, Chap. 61; *vide* note, p. 93.
[2] This appears to be Abbot Hildegard.
[3] *Vide* note, p. 93.

not consider that the passage you quote from the Holy Rule to the effect that a monk may not be received from a known monastery is particularly relevant to the case in dispute, for if it meant that a monk could not be received from any monastery that was known to anyone then, as there is no monastery that is not known to someone, there would be no monastery left from which we could lawfully receive anyone. And how could one reconcile this with that other injunction of Blessed Benedict which lays it down or at any rate allows that a stranger monk should be received not only into the guest house for as long as he likes, but that, if he is suitable, he should even be persuaded to join the community.

2. However, we acted very differently in the case of Brother Benedict. When he came and begged us to receive him we turned him away and advised him to go back to his monastery. He would not listen to us and betook himself to a hermitage near by and lived there quite quietly, without any trouble, for nearly seven months. But he did not think it safe for himself to live alone any longer and so he was not ashamed to ask again for what had already been refused him once. We again advised him to return to his own monastery and asked him why he had ever left it. Then he told us that his abbot used him not as a monk but as a doctor[1]; that he forced him to serve or rather used him to serve not God but the world; that in order to curry favour with the princes of this world he was made to attend tyrants, robbers, and excommunicated persons. And he told us that when he suggested to his abbot both in private and publicly that all this was a source of danger to his soul, no attention was paid to him, so that finally, with the advice of experienced men, he left, not so much his monastery as the occasions of sin, not so much his holy religion as his unholy way of life. When he had told us all this he once more begged us to open to his knocking and admit him for the safety of his soul. And when we saw his constancy and heard the reasons for his leaving the monastery and could discover nothing against him, we granted him admission, proved and approved him, admitted him to profession, and now regard him as one of ourselves. We did not compel him to enter and we will not force him to leave. He says that if we should drive him out he would not come back to you but would go still farther away. So stop, we beg you, reviling us with unmerited abuse for we have done you no harm, and cease troubling us with your useless letters. Even your accumulated insults cannot force us to reply to you save as respect demands, nor can your threats scare us for we are quite confident that we have acted lawfully in receiving your monk.

---

[1] It was the custom in those days for monks to work as doctors. It was eventually forbidden by Canon Law.

LETTER 71

TO THE SAME, AND CONCERNING THE SAME SUBJECT

THE greetings of Brother Bernard to the reverend brothers of Flay, to the Abbot H(ildegard) and all the other brothers.

IT would have been more becoming, dear brothers, if you had been content with my last reply to your complaints and ceased from your uncalled-for invectives. But as to your former charges you have now added worse ones and tried once more to give me grounds for quarrelling with you (may the grounds you have given be no more fertile than formerly). I shall truthfully answer a second time the accusations you impudently throw at my head, lest if I say nothing my silence may be interpreted as an acknowledgement of guilt. As far as I can make out, the great injury I have done you, my whole fault, amounts to nothing more than this, that I have opened the doors of my monastery to a lonely, strange, poor, and unhappy monk who, fleeing from danger to his soul and seeking his salvation, knocked and implored to be admitted; and that I refuse to turn out again without sufficient reason the man I have received under these circumstances, ' to put myself in the wrong by pulling down what I have built up '. On these grounds alone you accuse me of breaking the Rule, of transgressing the Canons, of violating the natural law. You angrily reproach me for doing to others what I would not tolerate others doing to myself, by receiving into my monastery one of your own monks whom you have excommunicated. What can I say about this excommunication when you yourselves know the answer, namely that he was not excommunicated by you before he was received by me. And, as he had been already received and lawfully received by me, it follows that you excommunicated, not one of your own subjects, but one of mine. Whether this is as it should be is your affair!

2. The only grounds for enquiry between us, the only thing that remains to be discovered, is whether he was rightly received by me. You for your part, as you cannot deny that a monk may be lawfully received from an unknown monastery,[1] contend that you are not unknown to me. I deny this, but you will not believe me. And so, as you will not believe my simple word, I affirm it again by oath. By the very Truth, which is God, I assure you that I have not known you and do not know you. Your letters are from persons quite unknown to me, and my letters to you are to unknown persons. I have experienced vexation and worry from you, but I have had no experience of you who vex and worry me. So as to prove me guilty of feigned ignorance you bring forward the irrefutable argument that

---

[1] *Vide Holy Rule*, Chap. 61, and note, p. 93 above.

I must know you because I have inscribed the name of your abbot and monastery upon my letters,[1] as if to know the name of a thing were the same as to know the thing itself. By this reasoning it would be a great thing for me to know the names of the angels Michael, Gabriel, and Raphael because by the very sound of the words I would be blessed with a knowledge of the blessed spirits. By this reasoning I must have profited not a little by hearing the names of Paradise and the third heaven from the Apostle, because, although I have not been rapt there with him, from the very names themselves I should be able to know the secrets of heaven, and words unspeakable which it is not lawful for men to utter. And how foolish I must be, for although I know the name of God yet I continue to groan and sigh with the Prophet, saying, ' I long, Lord, for thy presence ', and, ' When shall I come and stand in the presence of my God? ' and ' Smile upon us, O God, and we shall find deliverance '.

3. And what is it that I have done to you which I would not tolerate others doing to myself? You believe it is that I would not want a monk who had left my monastery to be received into another. I can only say that I wish all those committed to my care could be received by you and saved without me ! If one of my monks should come to you for the sake of greater perfection or a stricter way of life, not only would I not complain if you were to minister to his desire, but I should beg you to do so. And so far from considering myself offended I would admit that I had been greatly helped by you. Finally you deny the truth of what I have heard of you, namely that by your command or consent Brother B was obliged to turn his medical skill to secular uses while he was with you, and you accuse him of falsehood who has said this. Whether he has lied or not I do not know, that is his affair, but this much I do know: whether he did this of his own will, as you say, or of your will, as he says, he nevertheless did it at great risk to his soul. And who would be so inhuman as not to help, if he could, a soul in such peril, or who would not at least advise him if he could not help him? But if, as you say, he was drawn by his cupidity and curiosity to run around here and there selling his art, what was his reason for leaving you? Was it because a stricter application of pastoral discipline made such wandering no longer possible? If so why when he had already come to us did you try to entice him back by promising that he would be left in peace in the cloister, if you did not know that he wanted this and did not remember that he had asked for it? But now that he has found among strangers the peace and seclusion he could not find among his own, he is not willing to leave what is certain for the sake of what is doubtful. He

---

[1] Clearly the difference between knowing something and knowing of something. The Monks of Flay must have thought that the relevant passage in the Rule referred to monasteries the abbot knew *of*, but did not necessarily know.

holds on to what he has and scorns to accept what is offered too late.

4. Cease therefore, brothers, cease worrying your brother about whom you have no cause to worry, unless indeed (and may such a thing be very far from you!) it is your own interests and not the glory of God you are seeking, your own satisfaction in your brother's return and not the salvation of his soul. As you say he was always a rolling stone with you and, contrary to his state and the commands of his abbot, spending the money he made from the practice of his art upon himself, if you love him you ought to rejoice now that by the mercy of God he is cured. For I bear witness that never now does he wander abroad but, peacefully persevering in the monastery, he lives without complaint among poor men the life of a poor man. So far from having betrayed the faith he first pledged with you, he has now ratified it; together with obedience and conversion of manners,[1] without which he is deceived who trusts in his stability, he now keeps that faith whole and entire. So I beg you, brothers, calm your anger and stop worrying me. But if you will not, then do what you like, write what you like, abuse me as much as you like, charity suffers all things, beareth all things. And for my part, I am determined that from henceforth I shall love you with a pure love, treat you reverently, and regard you as friends.

LETTER 72

TO GUY, ABBOT OF TROIS-FONTAINES

A letter of advice and consolation to Guy who is in great distress because when he came to the Communion at Mass, he discovered that through an oversight of the server there was no wine in the chalice. In the twelfth century the chalice was prepared by the servers before Mass. It has been suggested that water instead of wine had been put into the chalice. This is a mistake that can be very easily made by the half light of candles in the early dawn when a white wine is used. It is true that there is nothing in the letter to suggest that this is how the mistake happened, but it would explain what would otherwise be a very extraordinary carelessness of the server who prepared the chalice, and also why Guy did not notice the mistake at the fraction of the Host.

The Guy to whom this letter is addressed is the same person as the Guy mentioned in Letter 66. He succeeded Roger as Abbot of Trois-Fontaines in 1129, and was elected Abbot of Cîteaux in 1134, but was deposed some months later by the General Chapter. The abbey of Trois-Fontaines was founded from Clairvaux in the year 1118 and is to be distinguished from the other abbey near Rome called Tre Fontane and dedicated to SS. Vincent and Anastasius.

---

[1] Monks, as distinct from Friars and Clerks Regular and post-Tridentine Orders, explicitly vow only obedience, stability, and conversion of manners.

I SYMPATHIZE with your sorrow, my dear friend, because I know the cause of it; but only if it is not excessive. Unless I am mistaken it is that supernatural sorrow or sorrow 'according to God' spoken of by the Apostle. There can be no doubt at all that such sorrow will be one day turned to joy. And so, dear friend, 'do not let anger betray you into sin', as the Psalmist says. On an occasion like this you would sin just as much by being too angry with yourself as by not being angry at all. Not to be angry with oneself when one should be is complacency, but to be more angry than one should be is to add sin unto sin. If complacency in sin is wrong, how could it not be wrong to accumulate one sin on the top of another? If guilt is made to depend on the matter of our actions, your sorrow, even were it immense, would not be to blame, because it would be sorrow for an immense fault. For the fault would be great in proportion as the matter concerned was sacred. But now in judging what you have done you should, according to my opinion, consider rather your own intention than the dignity of the sacred matter because the motive not the matter, the intention and not the results of the action constitute its moral character, according to those words of our Blessed Lord: 'If thy eye is clear, the whole of thy body will be full of light; if thy eye is diseased, the whole of thy body will be in darkness'. My prior and I after having thought a great deal about it by ourselves and discussed it at length between ourselves, can see in it ignorance on your part and carelessness on the part of the servers, but certainly no malice. You surely know very well that as there is no good but what springs from the will, so there can hardly be any great evil in a matter which is clearly involuntary. Otherwise were involuntary good actions to merit no reward and involuntary evil actions to deserve heavy punishment, for one and the same cause evil would be reckoned but good not recognized. Let him who believes this say if he wish, not that 'wisdom has overcome evil', but that evil has overcome wisdom.

2. But so as to ease your unquiet conscience and in case what has happened should be a warning of some more grave evil lurking in the monastery, I give you as penance the seven penitential psalms to be said with seven prostrations every day until Easter and seven disciplines. And let him who served your Mass make similar satisfaction. As for him who prepared the chalice before Mass and forgot to pour in the wine, he seems to me to be the one most at fault so, if you agree, I leave him to your judgement. And if word of this thing should have got out among the brethren let each of them receive the discipline once so that it shall be fulfilled what is written: 'Bear ye one another's burdens'. And now as regards your action when you had discovered what had happened, in pouring wine on to the particle of the sacred Host in the chalice; I commend it and in such a difficulty I do not

think you could have done better. Although of course the wine would not have been turned into the blood of Christ by its proper consecration, yet it would have become holy from contact with the sacred body.[1] They say that some writer or other has thought differently, namely that the presence together of all three elements, bread, wine, and water, is necessary for the Sacrifice, so that the lack of one would invalidate the whole. But this is a matter on which each one must believe as seems best to himself.

3. If the same thing had happened to myself, in my own poor opinion there is one of two things I should have done to remedy the situation: either I should have acted as you did, or else I should have repeated the consecration prayer from the words *Simili modo postquam cœnatum est* . . . [2] and so have completed the Sacrifice. I would have no doubts in this case about the validity of the consecration of the bread, for by her very rites the Church teaches me what she has herself received from the Lord, namely that although bread and wine are both consecrated together, they are not both consecrated together at the same time. Therefore since first the bread is consecrated, so as to become Christ's body and then the wine so as to become his blood, if through forgetfulness the wine is presented later, I cannot see that the delay would annul the preceding consecration of the bread. And I think that if it had pleased the Lord to have postponed a little the consecration of the wine or to have omitted it completely after the bread had been consecrated, so as to have become his body, his body would have nevertheless remained and what had not yet been done would have in no way affected what had already been accomplished. I do not deny that bread and wine mixed with water ought to be presented together, on the contrary I maintain that this ought to be done; but I say it is one thing to blame negligence if this is not done, and quite another to deny the validity of the sacrament. It is one thing to discuss whether a thing was well done, and quite another to deny that it was done at all. This is all I have to say on the matter at present, and I have said it without any prejudice to what you or others wiser than myself may think.

LETTER 73

TO THE SAME

To the Lord Abbot Guy, a spirit of knowledge and of pity, from Brother Bernard.

---

[1] During the Canon of the Mass the priest breaks the sacred Host into three pieces . . . two large and one very small piece. The small piece he drops into the chalice. Therefore if the chalice was empty, Guy would have found at the Communion that only the particle of the sacred Host was there. If there was water in the chalice, as some think, the particle would have been in the water.

[2] ' In like manner after he had supped . . . .'.

I AM certainly moved to pity when I consider the pitiful condition of this poor wretch, but I rather fear it will be in vain. And yet my pity does not seem to me to be wasted, even though it benefit only myself without helping the wretched object of it. Yet I was not moved to it by any thought of self-interest, it was the sight of a neighbour's wretchedness, a brother's misery, which smote my breast. Pity is an emotion that moves tender hearts irresistibly to compassion for suffering, but it cannot be induced by the will and it is not subject to the reason. Reason and will, although they can prevent emotion from having any effect on a man's actions, yet they cannot stifle it. And so as long as he for whom I pour forth my prayer remains unconverted let them keep away from me who would console me by saying that ' my prayer shall return to my own bosom '. As long as the wicked man remains in his wickedness, I will not listen to those who would flatter me by saying: ' Good will befall the good '. I will not, I say, be consoled, while I witness my brother's misery. So if, dearest son, your kind heart is moved to pity or, I should say, because it cannot be otherwise moved but by pity, although the poor man seems to you to have made a habit of his wretched comings and goings from the monastery, yet because he thinks he has a grievance, you should listen to what he has to say, not only patiently, but even willingly. I think we ought to take every reasonable opportunity to save a man in such desperate circumstances, a thing which (as we both know from experience) will be difficult enough in the Order, but far more so outside. So I advise you to call all the brethren together in council and not to be ashamed to withdraw any previous sentences you may have given against him, so that his obstinate pride may be healed by your humility and some means be found for receiving him back without violating the Rule. Do not fear that by so doing, by thus preferring mercy to justice, you will displease the merciful and just God.

2. I will tell you, for an example, of a similar thing that I remember happening to myself. One day I commanded, with angry voice and threatening looks, a brother who had upset me to leave the monastery. He immediately betook himself to one of our granges and remained there. When I found out where he was I wanted to recall him, but he said that he would not come back unless he was first reinstated in his old position, and not put in the last place as if he had been a runaway; for he had been turned out of the monastery, so he said, without consideration and without his case being heard, and that as he had not been given a fair trial when he was turned out, he ought not to be made to submit to judgement when he came back. As I could not trust my own judgement in the matter owing to my natural feelings about it, I submitted it to the consideration of the brethren. And they, when I was absent, ruled that the brother should not be subjected to the discipline of the Rule on being received back, as his

expulsion had not been according to the Rule. If therefore such kindly consideration was shown to a monk who had only once left the monastery, how much more ought it not to be shown to a monk in such desperate circumstances as yours. Farewell.[1]

LETTER 74

TO A MONK OF THE SAME MONASTERY

D o not think that because I have not come to see you I do not care. I care for you as if you were one of my own sons, and I could no more be suspected of neglecting you than a mother could be suspected of neglecting her child. I have in fact been waiting and hoping for an opportunity of visiting you, so that when I did come it might not be without profit. In the meantime do not let your heart be troubled by the death of your abbot,[2] God, we hope, will provide him with a worthy successor. You have not lost him, for, although he has passed away, he has not left you. Only now he who was your own special father in God, belongs to us all. Until I come ' play the man and keep your courage high ', doing all your actions for the love of God. Farewell.

LETTER 75

TO RAINALD, ABBOT OF FOIGNY

Foigny was in the diocese of Laon and was founded from Clairvaux in 1121, soon after which year this letter must have been written, for Rainald was the first Abbot, and it is clear from the context that he was still home-sick for Clairvaux and St. Bernard.

To his dearest Rainald, all that one devoted brother and faithful fellow-servant could wish for another, from Bernard, his brother and fellow-servant, not his father and lord.

D o not be surprised if I am frightened at the titles of honour you give me when I do not feel worthy of the honours themselves. It may indeed be becoming that you should give them to me, but it is not fitting that I should agree to them. If you think you are bound by those words of the Apostle, ' Be eager to give one another precedence ', and, ' As you stand in awe of Christ, submit to each other's rights ',

---

[1] The candour with which St. Bernard tells this story seems to us wholly in keeping with his saintly character. But others have thought differently and from early times, through a mistaken idea of the nature of sanctity and a greater zeal for edification than for truth, on purely *a priori* grounds suspicion has been cast on the authenticity of this passage. Even Mabillon relegated it to the notes of his edition of the letters averring that it was out of keeping with the character of the saint, and found in only five out of the eight MSS. But now a recent discovery in the library of the Abbey of Runa of a manuscript of the thirteenth century (No. 13) containing the complete text establishes the authenticity of the passage beyond all possibility of cavil.

[2] This was Abbot Roger, the immediate predecessor of Abbot Guy, to whom the two preceding letters are addressed.

I reply that in both cases the respect mentioned is supposed to be mutual, so unless this means nothing they apply equally to myself. And if you believe that you must observe that command of the Rule which bids juniors honour their seniors,[1] there immediately occur to me certain other sayings from the rule of Truth: ' They shall be first who were last, and they shall be last who were first '; ' No difference is to be made, among you, between the greatest and youngest of all, between him who commands and him who serves '; ' The greater thou art, the more in all things abase thyself'; ' Not that we would domineer over your faith; rather, we would help you to achieve happiness '; ' You are not to claim the title of *Rabbi* . . . nor are you to call any man on earth your father '. And so the more you extol me by your praises, the more I am weighed down by these texts and have cause to lament and not sing with the Psalmist, ' I have been lifted up only to be cast down and left bewildered ' and, ' So low hast thou brought me who didst lift me up so high '. But perhaps I would be describing more truthfully what I feel were I to say that he who extols me, humiliates me; he who humiliates me, extols me. You by vaunting me on high, let me down; by making too much of me, belittle me. But although you humble me by your praises you do not altogether crush me for these and the like words of Truth do comfort and, in a wonderful way, exalt me even while they abase me; instruct me, even while they humiliate me, so that by the very same words that I am abashed I am also ' lifted up joyfully singing with my whole heart ': ' It was in mercy that thou didst humble me, schooling me to thy obedience. Is not the law thou hast given dearer to me than rich store of gold and silver '. This wonder is done by ' the living and effectual word of God ' working sweetly and powerfully, that very word by which all things were made; in fine, it is the work of Christ's sweet yoke, of his light burden.

2. It is pleasant to admire the lightness of the burden of Truth. And it is indeed really light, for not only is it no burden for the man who carries it, but it even carries him! And what can be lighter than a burden which not only does not burden, but even carries him on whom it is laid? This is the burden which the Virgin bore and by which she was borne and not burdened.[2] This is the burden which supported the very arms of the old Simeon who bore it in his arms. And this is what snatched Paul up to the third heaven, even when he was weighed down by the corruptible body. When I look for an example among created things to illustrate this disburdening burden, nothing occurs to me more apt than the wings of a bird, for they, in

---

[1] *Rule of St. Benedict*, Chap. 63.

[2] *Hoc onus potuit uterum gravidare Virgineum, gravare non potuit.* During the whole of this section, St. Bernard is playing upon words in a graceful, but almost untranslatable, manner. Eales translates this sentence: ' This weight was able to render fruitful the Virgin's womb, but not to burden it '.

an extraordinary way, render the body both greater and yet more nimble. What a wonderful achievement of nature that a body should be rendered lighter by its very increase in size, so that the more it increases in bulk the more it decreases in weight. Here certainly we have a clear illustration of the sweet burden of Christ which carries those who carry it. And a chariot occurs to me too, for this also increases a burden which could not be carried by a horse alone, while at the same time rendering it more portable. One burden is added to another with the result that the whole is less burdensome! Thus when the four-in-hand chariot of the Gospels is yoked to the heavy burden of the law, it at once increases the perfection of it and reduces its difficulty. 'How swiftly runs his word', says the Psalm, and his word which at first could not extend beyond the confines of Judea, because it was so oppressive that it weighed down even the hands of Moses, when lightened by the touch of grace and yoked to the four-wheeled chariot of the Gospels swiftly went out into the whole world, and was quickly carried to the ends of the earth. But I am wandering from the point.

3. And so do you, dearest friend, stop smothering rather than applauding me with undeserved titles, otherwise you will be siding with my enemies, although with the best of intentions. Of them I am in the habit of complaining to God alone in the words of the Psalmist: 'And they that flattered me did curse me'. And to this complaint of mine I soon hear the answering words of God, 'And they that called you blessed have led you into error', to which I again reply, 'Let them therefore go their way baffled, they that rejoice over my misfortune; slink away in confusion that crowed over me so loud'. But lest it should be thought that I ever launch curses and imprecations against my enemies, I ought to explain how I understand these words. I pray, then, that those who believe me to be better than they see or hear me to be, may go their way baffled, that is to say withdraw from ignorantly praising me whom they do not know, and go on their way. How will this happen? It will happen when they know better the man they have excessively praised, so that they go their way baffled by their own error and by the discovery they have made of their friend's futility. In this manner both kinds of those people who injure me go their way baffled: the first kind who bear ill-will towards me, and flatter me with adulation; the others who are indeed quite sincere, yet injure me just as much by their well-meaning but extravagant praises. And so against both these kinds of people who praise me I am in the habit of protecting myself with these two verses as with two shields. Against the first sort who praise me malevolently, I say: 'Baffled let them go their way that rejoice in my misfortune'; and against the second sort: 'May they slink away in confusion that crowed over me so loud'.

4. But to return to yourself. As I ought, after the example of the Apostle, not to dominate over you, but only to rejoice with you, and as, according to the words of our Lord, we are all brothers having one father in heaven, it is not improper for me to turn off from myself with the shield of truth the high names of lord and father with which you think to honour and not burden me, and more appropriately call myself brother and fellow-servant as we share the same Father and the same condition. Were I to arrogate to myself what belongs to God, I might hear the words: 'If I am your master, where is the reverence due to me; and if your father, where the honour?' That I have a father's affection for you, I do not deny, but I refuse the authority of a father; nor, I think, is the affection with which I embrace you less than the affection of a father for a son. Now enough on the matter of titles.

5. To answer the rest of your letter. I could make just as well the same complaint about your absence as you do about mine, unless (which you yourself will not deny) the will of God must be preferred to our own feelings and needs. How, were it not for Christ's sake, could I suffer you to be so far away from me, you who are my dearest and most necessary companion, because always obedient in all you do; most helpful in conference; most zealous in learning, most prompt in remembering. Blessed shall we be if we can thus persevere until the end, always and everywhere seeking the glory of Jesus Christ and not our own interests.

LETTER 76

TO THE SAME

To his very dear son Rainald, Abbot of Foigny, the spirit of fortitude.

WHEN you wring your hands, dearest Rainald, over your many troubles I too am moved to tears by your affectionate complaints.[1] When you are sorrowful, I cannot but be sorry; nor can I hear of your worries and troubles without being myself worried and troubled. But as I foresaw and warned you of the very ills which you declare have befallen you, you should have been forearmed against what was foreknown so as to have endured them with a lighter heart and, if possible, spared me the vexation of hearing all about them. As it is I suffer more than enough by not having you by me, by not being able to see anything of you and enjoy the comfort of your company, so that I am at times tempted to regret having sent you away. True it was at the behest of charity that I did so, yet whatever the need might have been, because I cannot see you, I mourn for you as lost to me. And so, when on the top of all this you who should be a staff to support me use your faintheartedness as a staff with which to

---

[1] *Piis querimoniis.* Eales translates, perhaps more literally, 'pious complaints'

belabour me, you are piling sadness upon sadness, one cross upon another.   Although it is a mark of your affection for me that you hide none of your troubles from me, it is nevertheless unfeeling of you not to spare me, who feel as I do towards you, any details of your sufferings.[1] Why should you make me, who am anxious enough about you, even more anxious?   Why should my heart, already torn by the absence of my son, be wounded still more by having to hear every detail of the trials he is enduring?   I have shared my burdens with you, as with a son and an indispensable and faithful helper.   But is this the way you help me to carry them?   You are not helping to carry them at all, but adding to their weight, and by so doing you are making things more difficult for me without helping yourself.

2. This is the burden of souls which are sick, for those which are well do not need to be carried and so are no burden. You must understand that you are especially abbot of the sad, faint-hearted, and discontented among your flock.   It is by consoling, encouraging, and admonishing that you do your duty and carry your burden and, by carrying your burden, heal those you carry.   If there is anyone so spiritually healthy that he rather helps you than is helped by you, you are not so much his father as his equal, not so much his abbot as his fellow.   Why then do you complain that you find the company of some of those who are with you more of a burden than a comfort? You were given to them as abbot not to be comforted but to comfort, because you were the strongest of them all and, by God's grace, able to comfort them all without needing to be comforted by any.   The greater your burden, the greater will be your gain; the easier your lot, the less your reward.   Choose whom you want, either those who by burdening you help you or those who by helping you burden you. The former win merit for you, the latter bilk you of merit.   Without any doubt those who share your labours will also share your reward. You should know that you have been sent not to be helped but to help, and realize that you hold the place of him who came not to be served but to serve.   I wanted to write you a longer letter for your consolation, but there is no need.   What need is there to fill dry pages with words, when the living voice is there?   I think that when you have seen the prior you will find that I have said enough, and that your spirit will revive in his presence, that you will be so refreshed by his words as to have no need to be consoled by a letter.   Do not have any doubt that I send to you in him and through him that spirit of mine which you begged me in your letter to send you if I could. As you know we are of one mind and one will.

[1] *Si mihi pium est nullas tuas angustias dissimulare, tibi tamen durum est sic affecto cunctas indicare.* I have translated this sentence in the same way as Eales who renders it: ' If it is a mark of your filial affection towards me that you do not hide any of your difficulties from me, yet it is hard to add trouble to one already burdened '. I cannot help feeling, however, that the contrast is meant to be between *mihi* and *tibi*, and so should perhaps be rendered: Although it belongs to my fatherly affection towards you to ignore none of your troubles, yet it is unfeeling of you. . . .

LETTER 77

TO THE SAME

I HAD hoped, dearest son, to find a remedy for my worrying over you in not being told of your difficulties. I remember I wrote to you in a former letter that although it was a mark of your affection towards me that you should hide none of your troubles from me, it was nevertheless unfeeling of you not to spare me, feeling towards you as I do, anything of the details. But now I confess I feel my anxiety for you increased by the very thing that I had hoped would relieve it. Hitherto I have only feared or grieved over what you told me about, but now there is hardly an evil that could happen which I do not fear for you. In fact, as your favourite Ovid says: *Quando ego non timui graviora pericula veris?*[1]

Uncertain about everything and therefore anxious about everything, I experience real sorrow for imaginary evils. He who is once fond of anyone, is hardly master over himself any longer. He fears, he does not know what; he is sorrowful when there is no cause for sorrow; he worries more than he wishes, and about what he does not wish, feeling compassion unwillingly and ruth in spite of himself. And so you see, my son, that neither my careful precautions nor your loving care has availed me at all in this matter, and I beg you no longer to hide from me all that is happening to you, lest your very efforts to spare me make me more uneasy. Please return as soon as you can those books of mine which you borrowed.

LETTER 78

TO ARTALD, ABBOT OF PRUILLY

Pruilly was founded in the year 1118. *It is situated in the diocese of Sens.*

To his dearest friend and brother, Abbot Artald, the greetings of Brother Bernard.

I THINK that we owe to each other as much kindliness and affection as it is possible for absent friends to bestow on one another, not only because we belong to the same Order and have taken the same vows, but also because of the mutual debt involved by our old friendship. And I do not think we could give better proof to each other and to ourselves of the warmth of our mutual affection than by not concealing what either of us may hear to the discredit of the other. I have heard that you are thinking of making a foundation in Spain from your monastery. I cannot possibly understand why you should

---

[1] *Quando*, etc. 'When have I not by fear made the dangers greater than they really were?' (*Ovid*, Ep. 1, verse 11).

want to do this, what point, what advantage there can be in exiling your sons to such a distant region, where the expense of finding a site and erecting a building will be very great, when you have quite near to you a place already built and ready for you.[1] Nor is it, in my opinion, any excuse to say that the place does not belong to you since I know very well that it could easily be yours, if you wanted it. Do you think that the Lord Abbot of Pontigny, who is the owner, would grudge it to you if you were to ask him? In fact he would be very glad if you were to take it off his hands, not because there is anything wrong with the place, but simply because he has no need of it. I think both you and I, because we are both young and for that reason apt to be suspected of levity, should be especially on our guard lest we forget the advice of the Apostle: ' Do not let anyone think the less of thee for thy youthfulness '. But I am confident that you will act cautiously and choose the place which is near to you and has a building on it already for you and which you know is necessary for yourself and a burden to our friend the owner.

LETTER 79

TO THE ABBOT OF THE CANONS OF ST. PIERREMONT

Mabillon was the first to restore the correct inscription of this letter from the Corbie MS. Until his time it had always been inscribed: To the Same. St. Pierremont was an abbey of Augustinian Canons in the diocese of Toul.

To the Most Reverend Father of the Canons of St. Pierremont in affectionate duty, from Brother Bernard.

SINCE it was the wish of your Reverence that this brother should consult a person of my mediocre attainments, I have counselled him to the best of my ability, but on the understanding that nothing I said should prejudice the opinion of wiser persons than myself. Not to bother you with an account of what you already know, this is the gist of the advice I gave. It is unsafe and perhaps unlawful for a man to return to the world after having worn for some time the habit in a religious house; it is also indecent and unbecoming for a man to involve himself in a second marriage after having lived for a long time a most staunchly continent life with the consent of his first wife while she was still alive. But because his marriage was celebrated in the usual manner with publicity and solemnity, no one disputing or opposing it, I do not think it safe for him to put her away without her consent unless he has first obtained the support of the bishop's sanction and authority or, at any rate, a canonical judgement of the

---

[1] The place here referred to is Vauluisant, where Artald, on the advice of St. Bernard, founded a monastery in the year 1127.

ecclesiastical courts. As I cannot help believing that the awkward
and dangerous position in which this wretched man finds himself is
largely your own fault, in as much as when he begged and implored
you to admit him to profession you deferred receiving him too long
and gave the evil one an opportunity for ensnaring him, I urge and
counsel you in the name of charity to spare no pains or expense in
trying by every means to set him right. You could do this, either by
persuading the woman to release him of her own free will and promise
to live in continence or the bishop to call them both together and, as I
believe could be quite properly done, separate them.

NOTE

A letter to Master Hugh of St. Victor (Benedictine Edition, 77) is, on account of its
importance, always included amongst the treatises of St. Bernard under the title:
Liber de præcepto et dispensatione.

LETTER 80

TO SUGER, ABBOT OF ST. DENIS

*Suger was born in the year 1081 and succeeded Adam as abbot of the royal
abbey of St. Denis in the year 1121–1122. Very soon after this he was
appointed chief minister by the King of France, Louis ' le Gros ', earning by
the services he rendered in this capacity the title ' Father of his Country '. It
is remarkable that Louis should have given him this appointment, for he had
already intervened against his king's interests in the battle over investitures.
His first direct contact with St. Bernard may have been when he secretly
sought his help in this affair. Suger was typical of the great ecclesiastical
statesmen of his time and is in many ways not unlike his redoubtable and rather
attractive English contemporary, Henry de Blois, Bishop of Winchester,
with whom Bernard came into conflict over the vexed affair of the York
election. No abbot lived in greater magnificence than Suger and no abbey
stood in greater need of reform than St. Denis. It had become little more
than a centre for the transaction of the great affairs of state. Probably
St. Bernard had the abbot and monastery of St. Denis in mind when he wrote
the* Apologia, *and without doubt his diatribes caused Suger much searching
of heart. It is a striking indication of the influence of the Cistercian reform
and of St. Bernard that the Abbot of St. Denis should have been moved to
reform, not only his own life, but also the lives of the monks under him,
so as to call forth the following letter.*

THE good news of what God has done in your soul has gone forth in
our land encouraging all the good people who hear it. To be
sure all those who fear God and have heard of it are amazed and full
of joy at this great and sudden change of the right arm of the Most
High. Everywhere ' your soul is praised in the Lord and the meek
hear and rejoice '. Even those who have not known you, but have

only heard how great has been the change from what you were
to what you are, marvel and praise God in you.   But what increases
both the wonder and the joy alike is that you should have fulfilled what
is written in the Scriptures, ' Let everyone who hears this say: Come ',
and, ' What I have said to you under cover of darkness you are to
utter in the light of day; what has been whispered in your ears you
are to proclaim on the house-tops ', by endeavouring to spread amongst
your monks the counsel of salvation which possesses your soul.   In
this you have acted like a resolute soldier, or rather like a devoted
and strong captain who, when he sees his men in flight and slaughtered
on all sides by the swords of the enemy, would be ashamed to survive
them and scorn to save his own life by flight, even if he could.   He
stands fast in battle, he fights stoutly, and he runs hither and thither
between the lines amongst the blood-stained swords trying with
sword and voice to dishearten the enemy and encourage his own men.
He is always on the spot where he discovers the enemy are breaking
through and his men being hewn down.   Where anyone is being
hard-pressed and overcome he is always there to assist him, being all
the more ready to die for each one in that he despairs of saving all.
And, while he is trying little by little to stem and stop the advance of
the enemy, it often happens that by his valour he snatches a victory for
his own men from the confusion of the enemy, all the more welcome
for being unexpected.   They in their turn now put to flight those
from whom they fled, and overcome those whom hitherto they have
barely been able to stave off from vanquishing them, so that those who
were lately all but victims now exult as victors.

2. But why should I compare such a religious and mighty achievement with secular things, as if religion itself did not provide many
examples?   Was not Moses fully confident in God's promise that if
the whole people of whom he was the leader were to perish he would
not only not perish with them but would on the contrary be put
at the head of a great nation?   And yet with what affection and zeal
and with what devotion did he not help them when they were
troublesome and try to meet them when they were rebellious !   In
the end he offered himself in satisfaction for their defection, praying
God to pardon them or else blot out his own name from his record.
He was a faithful advocate who easily obtained what he asked for,
because he was not seeking his own interests.   He was also a devoted
leader united by love to his people, as the head is united to the body,
so that he would rather perish with them than be saved without them.
Jeremias too, although he did not sympathize with the truculence of
his people, was inseparably bound to them by the bonds of compassion
for their infirmity and preferred to suffer exile and slavery with them
rather than to enjoy his native soil and liberty by himself.   When the
whole people were led off he was free to remain at home, but he chose

to share their captivity because he knew they would need him. And Paul was doubtless inspired by the same spirit when he wished to be doomed to separation from Christ for the sake of his kinsmen, knowing from personal experience the truth of those words: ' Not death itself is so strong as love, not the grave itself so cruel as love unrequited '. So you see whom you have proved yourself to be like! But I must add someone else whom I had almost forgotten. I mean the holy king David, who when he saw the slaughter of his people, was sad and made haste to stand before the angel who was smiting them and implore that the punishment might be transferred unto himself and his father's house.

3. Who suggested this perfection to you? I must confess that although I much desired to hear such things of you, yet I hardly dared hope that I ever would. Who would have believed that with one jump, so to speak, you would attain the summits of virtue, the pinnacle of merit? But God forbid that I should measure the immensity of God's love by the narrow limits of my own capacity for faith and hope. He can do whatsoever he wills. He can hasten the working of his grace and lighten the burden of his commands. It was your fault, not those of your monks, that good and zealous people censured. It was against you and not against the whole community that they murmured. In fact, it was you whom they held responsible. If you had corrected yourself, there would have been nothing left to criticize. If you, I say, had changed your ways, soon all the tumult would have died down, all the talk would have subsided. As for myself, the whole and only thing that upset me was the pomp and splendour with which you travelled. This seemed to me to savour of arrogance. If you had been content to put off your haughtiness and put away your splendid attire, the resentment of everyone would easily have died down. But you have done more than satisfy your critics, you have earned their praise, although this sudden change of so many great things should be deemed more the work of God than of yourself. In heaven the conversion of one sinner arouses great joy, but what about the conversion of a whole community, and a community such as yours?

4. From early times yours was a noble abbey of royal dignity. It served the palace and the armies of the king. Without any deception or delay it rendered to Caesar his dues, but not with equal enthusiasm what was due to God. I speak of what I have heard, not of what I have seen. They say the cloister of the monastery was often crowded with soldiers, that business was done there, that it echoed to the sound of men wrangling, and that sometimes women were to be found there. In all this hubbub how could anyone have attended to heavenly, divine, and spiritual things? But now everything is very different. God is invoked there, continence is cultivated, discipline maintained,

spiritual reading encouraged, for the silence is now unbroken, and the hush from all the din of secular affairs invites the mind to heavenly thoughts. Furthermore the labour of continence, the rigour of discipline, is relieved by the sweet tones of hymns and psalms. Shame for the past encourages the austerity of this new way of life. The men who pluck the fruit of a good conscience are inspired by a desire which shall not be frustrated, and a hope which shall not be confounded. Fear of future judgement gives place to a loving practice of brotherly charity, for 'Love has no room for fear'. The variety of holy observances keeps at bay tedium and *acidie*.[1] I have recalled all this for the honour and glory of God, who is the author of it all, but not without yourself as his collaborator in all things. He could have done it all without you, but he preferred that you should share in his work, so that you might also share the glory. Our Saviour rebuked certain persons for making his house a den of thieves. And so without any doubt he will commend one who applies himself to saving a holy thing from dogs, and pearls from swine; whose efforts and zeal have restored what was little better than a workshop of Vulcan to being a sanctuary of prayer and spiritual pursuits, what was a synagogue of Satan to its former use.

5. I have certainly not recalled all these past evils so as to taunt or shame anyone, but so as to make the new glories appear all the more important and comely by comparing them to the old infamy. Recent good things show up to all the better advantage when compared with former evils. We recognize like things by comparing them with like, but contrary things compared either please or displease the more. Join black things to white and the comparison will show up each colour the better. When ugly things are set against beautiful things, the beautiful seem more beautiful and the ugly seem more ugly. But so as to avoid any occasion for confusion or offence let me repeat to you also what the Apostle said: 'This is what you were once, but now you have been washed clean, now you have been sanctified'. The house of God is no longer open to seculars, the merely curious find no admittance to the holy places. There is no longer any idle gossiping, and the usual chatter of boys and girls is no longer heard there. According to the words, 'Here stand I and these children the Lord has given me', the place is free and open only to the children of Christ and is kept with becoming care and reverence only for the divine praises and sacred functions. How the martyrs, a great number of whom ennoble the place with their relics, must hear with joy the songs of these children, to whom they will reply with no less affectionate exuberance, 'Praise the Lord, ye children, praise ye the name of the Lord'; and again, 'A psalm, a psalm for our God, a psalm, a psalm for our king'.

[1] A traditional term for a state of spiritual aridity.

6. Now the vaults of the great abbey that once resounded to the hubbub of secular business echo only to spiritual canticles. Now breasts are bruised by the hands that beat upon them, and knees by the stones on which they kneel, and from the altars ascend vows and devout prayers. Now one can see cheeks furrowed with tears of repentance and hear the murmur of weeping and sighs. What can better please the citizens of heaven than this, what sight can be more welcome to the King of heaven than this sacrifice of praise with which he is now honoured here? Oh if only we could have our eyes opened to see what Eliseus by his prayers revealed to his servant! Without doubt we would see 'how before us go chieftains, and minstrels with them'. We would see with what attention and with what elation they assist in our singing, stand by us when we pray, join with us when we meditate, watch over us when we rest, and guide those of us who preside over and care for others. The powers of heaven know who are their fellow citizens, they earnestly delight over, comfort, instruct, protect, and care for in everything those who take the heritage of salvation. Although, being absent, I cannot see with my own eyes these things which you have done, yet I count myself happy even to have heard of them. But you, my brethren, I esteem still more happy, for to you it has been given to perform them. And more blessed than all is he whom the Author of all good has deigned to give the leadership in these things. On this great privilege I especially congratulate you, my dear friend, for it is due to you that all these wonderful things have happened.

7. Perhaps you are embarrassed by my praises? You should not be. What I have said has nothing in common with the flattery of those who 'call good evil and evil good', so that they betray whomsoever they praise. Theirs is a smooth but treacherous praise by which 'the sinner is praised in the desires of his soul'. Whatever kind of favour mine may be, it certainly proceeds from charity and, so far as I can see, it does not exceed the bounds of truth. He is safely applauded who is only applauded in the Lord, that is to say in truth. I have not called evil good, on the contrary I have called evil what was evil. I am all the more bound to lift up my voice and praise the good when I see it for having boldly denounced former evils or else, were I to cry out against what is evil and say nothing about what is good, I would prove myself a mere backbiter and not a reformer, one who would rather carp at evil than remedy it. The righteous man admonishes lovingly, the sinner praises wickedly. The former admonishes evil that he may remedy it, the latter praises that he may conceal what calls for remedy. You need have no anxiety that your head will be anointed with the oil of sinners as it used to be, by those who fear the Lord. I praise you because I consider you have done what is deserving of praise. I certainly do not flatter you; I am only

fulfilling what you sing in the psalm: ' They that fear thee shall see me, and shall be glad, because I have greatly hoped in thy works'; and again: ' This wisdom of his shall be praised on all sides '.   How many who used to abhor your folly now praise your wisdom!

8. I wish you to delight in the approbation of those who fear vice no less than they love virtue.   The praises of such men are true for they praise only what is good and do not know how to pander to evil. But there are others whose praise is not true, but false, who really disparage when they seem to praise, and of these we read in the Scriptures that they are ' Vain men, light weight sons of Adam as false coins in the scales, vain in all their conspiracies to deceive'. Clearly these are men to be avoided, according to the advice of the Wise Man: ' Turn a deaf ear, my son, to the blandishments of evil-doers that would make thee of their company'.   Therefore sinners do not lack either wine or oil, delicious certainly, but poisonous and deadly.   ' His words ', that is the words of the flatterer, ' are so gentle, they soothed like oil, but in truth they are weapons of destruction.'   And the righteous man also has his oil, but it is an oil of mercy, sanctifying and full of spiritual joy.   And he has his wine that he pours into the inflamed wounds of the soul.   With the oil of mercy he comforts the sadness of those who are sorrowful and whose heart he sees to be contrite.   When he admonishes he uses his wine; when he comforts, his oil.   But his wine is without rancour and his oil is without guile.   Not all praise is flattery, just as not all rebuke comes from spite.   Blessed is he who can say: ' In love some just man will chastise me, reprove me; never shall the sinner sleek this head with the oil of his flattery '.   By rejecting the oil of the sinners' flattery you have proved yourself worthy of the oil and milk of holy men.

9. Let these charming but savage mothers seek among the children of Babylon those whom they can feed with the milk of death, whom they may caress with their alluring favours, and nourish with ever-lasting fires.[1]   But when the nursling of the Church has fed from the breasts of wisdom and has tasted the sweetness of a better milk, already growing in grace, already satisfied with what he has received, he will say from the bottom of his heart: ' The milk from thy breasts is better than wine, the fragrance of rare perfumes cannot match it for delight '.   This is what he says to his mother the Church.   But when he has in a like manner tasted and seen how sweet is the Lord he addresses him as a very dear father and says: ' What treasures of loving kindness, Lord, dost thou store up for the men who fear thee '. Now my desires for you are satisfied.   When in the past I sadly watched you greedily suck from the lips of flatterers the food of death,

---

[1] *Quærant sibi jam in parvulis Babylonis dulces, sed truces matres, quibus lac mortis emulgeant, quos blandis mulceant favoribus, ac flammis nutriant sempiternis.*   Eales translates : ' Let the children of Babylon seek for themselves pleasant mothers, but pitiless, who will feed them with poisoned milk, and soothe them with caresses which will make them fit for everlasting flames '.

the fuel of sin, I used to say to myself, sighing: ' Would that you were my brother nursed at my own mother's breasts '. May they keep far away from you who would feed you with their alluring but treacherous milk of flattery, who expose you to the reproaches and mockery of everyone, while they are calling you blessed to your face ! Their applause was a byword the world over or rather made you a byword everywhere. If even now they still mutter in your ears, say to them in the words of the Apostle: ' If I were still courting your favour, I should not be the slave of Christ '. Those people whom we used to please with bad things we cannot please equally well with good, unless perhaps they too have changed and have begun to hate what we were and esteem what we are now.

10. Two unheard-of and detestable improprieties have arisen in the Church lately. If you will pardon my saying so, one of these was the arrogance of your way of life. But this, by the grace of God, is now mended to the glory of his name, to your everlasting reward, and to the edification of all of us. God can also bring it about that we will soon be consoled by the mending of this other matter. I fear to mention this hateful novelty in public, but I am loath to let it pass in silence. My grief urges me to speak, but fear binds my tongue. My fear is only lest I offend anyone by speaking openly of what is disturbing me, for the truth can sometimes breed hatred. But I hear the truth that breeds this sort of hatred comforting me with the words, ' It must needs be that scandals come ', and I do not consider that what follows applies to me at all: ' But woe to the man through whom it comes '. When scandal comes through vices being denounced, it comes through those who do what is blameworthy and not through those who blame it. And I do not set myself up as being more circum-spect or more discreet than he who said: ' It is better that there should be a scandal than that truth should be compromised '.[1] Although I do not know what good it would do if I did keep silent about what all the world is talking, if I alone were to try and cover up that foul thing the stench of which is in everyone's nostrils. I dare not hold my own nose against such a bad smell.

11. And who would not be indignant, who would not deplore, even if only in secret, that a man should against the Gospel both serve God as a deacon and Mammon as a minister of state, that he should be so loaded with ecclesiastical honours as to seem hardly inferior to the bishops, while being at the same time so involved in military affairs as to take precedence over the commanders of the army?[2] I ask you

[1] St. Gregory, *Hom. 7 in Ezech.*

[2] This is the notorious Stephen of Garlande. His family was very friendly with Louis ' le Gros '. Stephen came to court as a young man and succeeded his brother as seneschal of the royal palace. He was very active in affairs but became so swollen-headed that, after he had made himself objectionable to Queen Adela, he was deprived of his honours and banished from court. Besides seneschal, he was not only a deacon, but Archdeacon of Notre-Dame and Dean of Orleans.

what sort of monster is this[1] that being a cleric wishes to be thought a soldier as well, and succeeds in being neither? It is an abuse of both conditions that a deacon should serve the table of a king and that a servant of the king should minister at the holy mysteries of the altar. Who would not be astonished, or rather disgusted, that one and the same person should, arrayed in armour, lead soldiers into battle and, clothed in alb and stole, pronounce the Gospel in the church, should at one time give the signal for battle on the bugle and at another inform the people of the commands of the bishop. Unless perhaps something worse is true, namely that the man is ashamed of the Gospel in which the Vessel of Election gloried, is embarrassed at being seen as a cleric, and thinks it more honourable to be thought a soldier, preferring the court to the church, the table of the king to the altar of Christ, the cup of demons to the chalice of the Lord. This seems to be the more probable, in that although he holds many preferments from the Church, despite the unwilling toleration of the canons for such a number of offices being held by one man, yet they say he is more proud of the one name by which he is known in the palace than of all his other titles. Although he is archdeacon, deacon, and provost in many churches yet none of these titles gives him so much pleasure as Seneschal to his Majesty the King. What a novel and odious perversity it is that a man should think it more becoming to be known as a retainer of another man than a servant of God and consider it more dignified to be called an official of a king of this world than of the King of heaven. A man that puts the army before his clerical state, secular business before the Church, certainly proves that he prefers human things to divine and earthly to heavenly things. Is it more dignified to be called Seneschal than Deacon or Archdeacon? It is, but for a layman not for a deacon.

12. What a strange and blind sort of ambition this man has! He prefers the depths to the heights, a dung-hill to the pleasant places in which his lot has been cast, and he pours scorn on the desirable land. He completely confuses two different states of life, that of a minister of God and that of a minister of the king; and he abuses with great nicety both of them by choosing the honours, but not the labour of the army in the one, and the revenues, but not the service of religion in the other. Who cannot understand that the kingdom, just as much as religion, is disgraced by this, for it is just as unbecoming to the majesty of the king that hardy men should be commanded by a cleric, as it is to the state of a deacon that he should take the king's money to fight. What king would choose to have an unwarlike cleric at the head of his army rather than one of his most intrepid soldiers? And what cleric would consider it anything but unworthy of his state to be under obedience to a layman? His very tonsure

---

[1] It is very tempting to see here a reminiscence of the first verses of Horace's *De Arte Poetica*.

more becomes the kingly state than the condition of a retainer, and on the other hand it is not on psalms so much as arms that the throne depends. Certainly if perhaps, as sometimes happens, the one gains where the other loses so that, namely, the abasement of the king makes for the honour of the cleric or the derogation of the cleric adds something to the honour of the king, as for instance when some noble woman by marrying a man of humble birth lessens her dignity while raising his; if, I say, this is the case and from such a state of affairs either the king or the cleric gains something, the evil of it might somehow be tolerated. But as it is the loss of both has been to the advantage of neither, the dignity of both has suffered since it ill becomes a cleric to be called to be the seneschal of the king, just as much as it ill becomes the king to have in that position of government anyone but a strong and brave man. It is indeed very strange that either power should allow such a state of affairs, that the Church should not reject the military deacon and that the court should not expel its clerical chief.

13. I had intended and probably ought to have denounced this state of affairs more sharply than I have done, but the limits of a letter indicate an end. And I have spared a man whom report speaks of as your friend chiefly because I fear to offend you. I would not have a man your friend who is not true. If you persist in regarding him as your friend, prove yourself a true friend to him by doing what you can to make him a friend of the truth. True friendship is only possible between two who are united in the love of truth. And, if he will not yield to you in this, do you hold fast to what you have got and join the head to the tail of the offering.[1] By the grace of God you have received a robe of many colours, see that it covers you for it is no use beginning a work if you do not persevere to the end. Let my letter end with this warning to you to make a good end of what you have begun.

LETTER 81

TO ABBOT LUKE

Luke was Abbot of Cuissy, an abbey of the Premonstratensian Order, in the diocese of Laon.

You have shown, my dear friend, that you have a very good quality and one which is not common. It is that you not only listen to the advice of one junior to yourself, but are even grateful for it, very wisely regarding the truth of what is said and not the insignificance of the person who says it. I myself give thanks to God that my presumption has earned your thanks and not your wrath. And now,

[1] This means to join the end to the beginning of the work. It is an allusion to Exodus xxix, which commands the offering at the same time of the head and the tail of the victim.

counting on your outstanding humility, I shall venture with all the greater confidence to continue advising you. I implore you by the blood that Christ shed for souls to beware of the fearful danger incurred by souls bought at so great a price, when men and women live together under the same roof. It is a danger especially feared by those who have learned from long experience of the devil's wiles to say with the Apostle: 'We know well enough how resourceful is Satan'. The experience you have had of this brother's fall, about which you have consulted me, should have taught you to pay especial heed to the advice or rather the command of the Apostle to 'keep clear of fornication'. But I must say I am surprised that you should have considered it necessary to write to me on the matter when you have near at hand in William, Abbot of St. Thierry, a very experienced man of our Order who is especially fond of your house. And you must surely have at Prémontré men to advise you who are wise and faithful and well able to unravel difficult situations.

2. However, as for reasons best known to yourself you have asked me, I shall say what I think and not hold my tongue. If the brother had first confessed his fall however grave and disgraceful, then it would have been your duty to have kept him by you and cured him. But now that the evil odour of the crime has reached others, you must still try to cure him, but by different means. It is perhaps no longer expedient that he should be suffered to remain with you lest, as you say in your letter, you have cause to fear, your young and immature flock should become infected. On the other hand you must not entirely close your fatherly heart to this erring son however great his fall may have been. I think it is a sound and kindly counsel to find another house for him, one of Dom Norbert's remoter houses, where he can be taken in to do penance in a different place, but under the same vows, until you see fit to recall him. I do not believe it would be expedient for your own Order that he should pass over to ours. He has denied in my presence what you tell me in your letter about him saying that we have promised to receive him if he comes with your licence. Certainly if you do not wish to send him away to one of the houses I have suggested or if, in spite of your wishing to do so, he is not willing to go, or if you cannot find a place to receive him, then, owing to the urgency of the case, it will be necessary either to let him go to save his soul where he wants or, for the sake of pity, to keep him with you; but this only if you can see your way to removing completely all opportunity for him repeating or spreading defilement. Enough on this matter.

3. There is another matter concerning yourself which, with my usual presumption, I shall not hesitate to mention. I refer to that mill where the lay-brothers in charge have to submit to the company of women. If I am to be trusted there are only three courses open to you.

Either you forbid all access to women or you put the mill in charge of outsiders and not lay-brothers or else you give it up completely.

LETTER 82

TO GUY, ABBOT OF MOLESME

Guy was the second Abbot of Molesme after St. Robert.

G OD, from whom all good dispositions come and who is acquainted with all that we feel, knows how deeply I sympathize with you in the troubles from which I have heard you are suffering. But on the other hand, when I consider not through whom but from whom they have come, the sure confidence I have that before long I shall be able to rejoice with you over your prosperity equals the compassion I feel for you in your present difficulties. Only do not be carried away by your vexation but agree with me and, like holy Job, accept with equanimity whatever the Lord sends, whether it be good or bad, or rather, after the example of holy David, realize you should not be angry with the people from whom you have suffered these afflictions, so much as humbled under the mighty hand of God who undoubtedly sent them to try you. But as they are servants of the church committed to your care it is only right that you should mete out to them a suitable punishment for their abominable presumption, and that the damage suffered by your monastery should be in part made good from their own possessions, only you should aim rather at chastising their sins than avenging your injuries. I beg you, and in begging you I advise that you not only consider what they deserve, but also bear in mind what is becoming for you, or in other words that you should exalt mercy over judgement and glorify God by your moderation. My spirit advises through your mouth that son of yours who is so dear to me both on your own account and for his own sake that he does not allow himself to be so upset by his indignation, however just it may be, as to forget the command of our blessed Lord to turn the other cheek.

LETTER 83

TO GERARD, ABBOT OF POUTHIÈRES

Pouthières was an abbey of Benedictines in the diocese of Langres, founded by Gerard, Count of Nevers.

I DO not remember ever having written anything against you to the Count of Nevers. If I have written to this prince on behalf of your church, I did so to help you and not to accuse you. I had heard that he intended to pay you a visit to see whether there was any foundation in the evil reports that were going abroad about your house and who was to blame in the matter, so that if perhaps there should be anything wrong, with care and good-will he might put it right.   I do not see why you should complain that I have injured you if I have tried by encouragement to fortify him in his just and pious intention; in fact I consider that in my zeal for God's house I have done right to impress upon him his responsibility in this matter.[1]   You cite Scripture to prove that I have done wrong by not coming to you first, but I want you to realize that it is not with you that I have any quarrel, I am merely concerned out of charity for the peace of your monastery.   You will know the truth more fully if, as you say you intend to do, you bring the matter to me in person.   I am to be found here any day of the present[2] week you care to call.

LETTER 84

TO THE ABBOT OF ST. JOHN OF CHARTRES

This would probably be Stephen, who after being Abbot of the Augustinian house of St. John of Chartres became Patriarch of Jerusalem in succession to Germundus in the year 1128.

A T first I did not intend to answer your query about those matters on which you troubled to consult me, not so much because I was doubtful about what to answer as because it seemed impudent and superfluous to offer my counsel to a man of counsel like yourself. But when I considered that many or, I should say, almost all wise men, while they can easily solve the difficulties of others are apt to be doubtful and anxious about their own and place far greater confidence in the judgement of others, I decided (not unreasonably, I hope) to break my resolution and to tell you quite simply what I think, always providing that I do not thereby prejudice the judgement of those wiser than myself.   Unless I am deceived you have informed me by that religious man Ursus,[3] Abbot of St. Denis, that you are thinking of leaving your country, home, and those over whom it has pleased God that you should have charge, and of setting out for Jerusalem to live there to God alone and make your own soul.   I agree that it may be a good thing for a man who strives for perfection to leave his own country, according to those words: 'Go forth out of thy country and from thy kinsfolk'.   But I do not see how it follows that you are justified in deserting those who have been entrusted to your care. Why do you want to do so?   Are you attracted by the prospect of being free from the burden of responsibility?   But charity seeketh not its own.   Does the pleasant prospect of peace and leisure beckon you?   But you would be obtaining it at the cost of others.   For my

---

[1] A responsibility he had inherited from the founder, Count Gerard of Nevers.
[2] *instantis hebdomadæ.*   Eales translates.' of the coming week '.
[3] The fifth abbot of the Canons Regular of St. Denis at Rheims.

part I would gladly forgo the prospect of any spiritual advantage whatsoever if it could only be obtained at the price of giving scandal to others. Undoubtedly charity suffers when there is scandal, and I very much wonder what sort of spiritual advantage could be obtained at the cost of charity. How can anyone who prefers his own quiet to the common good possibly say with truth: 'For me life means Christ and death is a prize to win'; and where would those words of the Apostle come in: 'None of us lives as his own master, none of us dies as his own master'; and: 'This is my rule, to satisfy all alike, studying the general welfare before my own'; and: 'Christ died for us all, so that being alive should no longer mean living with our own life, but with his life who died for us and has risen again'.

2. Perhaps you will ask, 'If this is so, whence comes my great desire?' Pardon me if I say quite frankly what I think. No one who has any experience of the wiles of Satan can have any doubt that it is his angel under the guise of an angel of light that is trying to instil into your thirsty soul the false sweetness of 'stolen waters', a sweetness which in truth is far more bitter than wormwood. In fact who else would suggest scandal, stir up dissension, and trouble unity and peace, if not the ancient enemy of the human race, the enemy of the cross of Christ, the devil? He by whose envy death entered the world is even now envious of all the good he sees you are doing and, since he has been a liar from the beginning, he is lying now by promising you better things which he knows are not there. How could Truth suggest anything contrary to those most trustworthy words, 'Are you yoked to a wife? Then do not go about to free yourself.' And when has charity, which we know is on fire at every scandal, ever been known to instigate scandal? No, I tell you that it is the evil one, he whose envy makes him an enemy of charity, whose lies render him always hostile to truth, it is he who is now lying to you, mixing a false honey with a true gall, by promising what is doubtful as if it were certain, and by giving out what is true as if it were false, not so as to give you what you are vainly hoping for, but so as to rob you of what you are holding with such benefit. He is going about seeking how he may snatch from your flock the care of their shepherd, so that it may perish as, without anyone to save it, it undoubtedly will. And at the same time he is trying to make the shepherd subject to that terrifying curse: 'Woe to him through whom scandal comes'. But I trust that your God-given wisdom will prevent you from being led astray or deceived by any cunning ruse of the evil one to make you desert a certain good, and incur a certain evil for the sake of a good that is not certain.

LETTER 85

TO SIMON, ABBOT OF ST. NICOLAS

A letter of consolation and advice to Abbot Simon on account of the persecution he was enduring. Mabillon tells us that the persecutions came from his monks because Abbot Simon insisted on giving up certain parishes belonging to the monastery on account of a suspicion of simony attaching to them. Indeed we know that because he could not get his community to agree with him on this matter Abbot Simon resigned his office for a time. But the context of this letter gives the impression that his troubles arose from a well-meaning attempt to introduce into his monastery a stricter way of life. Abbot Simon became Abbot of St. Nicolas-aux-Bois in the diocese of Laon after being a monk of St. Nicasius at Rheims.

I COULD not but feel for you when I read in your letter of the persecutions you are obliged to endure for the sake of justice. Although Christ's promise of a kingdom should be enough for you, yet I will for my part faithfully offer you such consolation as I can and such advice as I deem wholesome. For who could watch without anxiety Peter amidst the waves holding out his hands for help; or hear without sorrow the dove of Christ no longer cooing but sighing, as if to say: 'How can we sing the songs of the Lord in a strange land'? Who, I ask, could see without tears the tears of Christ himself, as he even now lifts up his eyes to the hills whence comes his help? Although to be sure I, to whom in your humility you say you look for help, am on no hill, but am still labouring with great efforts in this vale of tears against the insidious stratagems of the relentless enemy and the violent malice of the world, so that with you I cry out: 'Our help is in the Lord who has made heaven and earth'.

2. 'All who will live devoutly in Christ Jesus, shall suffer persecution', so that even though they may never cease to have holy desires yet they are often unable to accomplish them. The multitude of wicked who make it their business to oppose the holy resolutions of good people is so great that there is nothing wrong in leaving them sometimes unaccomplished. So Aaron against his will gave in to the wretched demands of the turbulent people. So Samuel unwillingly anointed Saul to satisfy the same people, because they insisted on having a king. So David when he wanted to build the temple was prevented from accomplishing his pious design because he was a man of war obliged to wage constant war against the enemies who infested his frontiers. Just in the same way, venerable father, do I counsel you (yet not so as to prejudice the advice of those wiser than I) to moderate the full rigour of your purpose and of those who side with you, so as not to ignore the welfare of weaker souls. Those in the Order of Cluny over whom you have consented to rule should be

invited and not forced to a stricter way of life. And those of them who wish to live more strictly should be persuaded to accommodate themselves, so far as they can without sin, to the weaker brethren or, if it can be done without scandal to either party, they should be permitted to live their own life where they are, or else they might be allowed to go free from the congregation so as to find a community where they can live as they wish.

LETTER 86

TO THE SAME

YOU see it was for a very good reason and not for nothing that I have acted contrary to my usual practice by keeping your stray sheep here for a time. I did not do it for my own sake, but for yours and his, so that by this ruse or, I should say, by this timely assistance, I might be able to kill two birds with one stone and satisfy both his desire for a stricter life and yours that he should stay at home. I do not say this to show my good will towards you, that I could never do adequately, try as I might, but so as to demonstrate the truth of what I remember having told you before, namely that a monk who is unsettled and dissatisfied may be often quickly reconciled to the life in his own monastery by the experience of something a little stricter somewhere else. You say in your letter that you want my advice on how to treat this reconciled brother. But I do not think there is any need for it, because he is returning to you ready to do whatever you want, as it is only right he should, and not, as is too often the case, with the intention of persuading you to do what he wants. He is very much dreading the reception he will receive when he comes back, so I add my prayer to his and beg you to moderate the difficulties it is usual to make before re-admitting a fugitive monk, and to deal with him more kindly than is the custom in such cases. The deed is the same, but the motive for it demands a different verdict. There is all the difference between a religious who leaves his monastery from fear or hatred of the life, and one who from his love and desire for it leaves one monastery for another.

LETTER 87

TO WILLIAM OF ST. THIERRY

William of St. Thierry was born at Liège in the last quarter of the eleventh century. At some unknown date he became a monk at the Abbey of St. Nicasius, and afterwards, about the year 1120, Abbot of St. Thierry in the diocese of Rheims. He was early drawn into the orbit of St. Bernard and became one of his closest friends. It was at his instigation that the saint composed his Apology *and the two important treatises on* Grace *and* Free

Will and on the Errors of Abelard. He was also the biographer of St. Bernard.

William is an interesting character of whom we would like to know more, but his flame was eclipsed by the brighter light of his friend. He was certainly a man of God and also something of a scholar. He was the author of several treatises among them the very beautiful Golden Epistle to the Carthusians of Mont Dieu *which has been translated into English by Walter Shewring. Much against the wishes and advice of his friend he resigned his abbacy and became a simple Cistercian monk at the Abbey of Signy in the diocese of Rheims. We are told that the severity of the life nearly broke his resolution, which is not surprising considering that he must have been nearly fifty years old at the time and not strong physically. But he persevered and died a very saintly monk ' in great sweetness of spirit, in purity of body and soul, perfect in all the virtues '. The life of William of St. Thierry would be a fruitful matter for research.*

To the Lord Abbot William, the charity of a pure heart, a good conscience, and unfeigned faith, from Brother Bernard.

No one knows what is in man save the spirit of a man that is in him; man sees only on the surface and God alone can search the heart; yet you have been able to weigh and mutually to compare our affection for each other, so as to deliver a verdict not only on the state of your own heart, but even on that of another. I wonder how or on what grounds you have been able to do this, and I cannot wonder enough. It is an error to which the human mind is ever prone not only to consider good to be evil, what is true to be false, and what is false to be true, but also to be doubtful about what is certain, and certain about what is doubtful. You may be right when you say that my affection for you is less than yours is for me, but I am certainly certain that you cannot be certain. How can you know for certain what it is certain you cannot be certain about?[1] Paul himself mistrusted his own judgement and declared that he did not judge himself. Peter regretted that he was deceived by his own presumption when he said, ' Even though I should have to die with thee, yet I would not deny thee '. In the matter of our Lord's betrayal the disciples had no confidence in themselves, but each asked, ' Is it I, Lord?' David confessed his own ignorance and begged the Lord to overlook it. But wonderful to say, you have been able to assert, with I know not what grounds for your confidence: ' My affection for you is greater than yours is for me '.[2]

2. These are your very words, and I could wish they were not, for I do not know if they are true. If you know, how do you know?

[1] *. . . sed certe certum sum, certum non esse tibi. Quomodo ergo pro certo affirmas, de quo certum est, quia certus minime sis?*
[2] *ut plus amans, inquiens, minus diligar.*

What proof have you that my affection for you is less than yours is for me? Is it, as you aver in the postscript of your letter, that the messengers from here who pass to and fro by you never bring any token of my good will or affection? What sort of token, what sort of proof do you expect? Are you worried because I have not yet once answered your many letters to me? How could I possibly suppose your mature wisdom would be satisfied with my ignorant scribbling? I have not forgotten those words, ' Little children, let us love not in word, nor in tongue, but in deed and truth ', and when have you ever needed my help and not received it? O Lord, who searchest the hearts of men! O Sun of Justice, whose rays enlighten the hearts of men with divers graces! Thou knowest and I feel that by thy gift I love this man for the sake of his goodness. But how much I love him, that I cannot tell, thou knowest. It is thou, Lord, who givest the power to love, it is thou who knowest how much thou hast given him to love me and me to love him. Without thy telling him, how could any man say, ' I love more than I am loved ', unless he be one who has already seen his light in thy light, seen by the light of thy truth how much he burns with the fire of charity?

3. But, O Lord, I am for the time satisfied to see my own darkness in thy light, so long as thou dost visit those who sit in darkness and the shadow of death. In thy light the thoughts of men, the hidden places of the dark are made manifest. When the shadows are dispelled, then by thy light only the light is seen. By thy favour I feel that I love this man, but I have not yet the light to see whether I love him enough. I do not know whether I have yet achieved that love, greater than which no man can have, whereby I would be enabled to lay down my life for my friends. Who shall boast that he has a clean heart, much less a perfect heart? O Lord, who dost enlighten the lamp by which I see and hate my own darkness, enlighten, I pray thee, my very darkness that I may behold within myself and be glad, an ordered charity which knows and loves only what is worthy of love and in the measure that it is worthy of love and for the reasons that it is worthy of love, and be myself unwilling to be loved save in thee and in the measure that I deserve. Woe is me, if (as I greatly fear) I am either loved by this man more than I deserve or love him less than he deserves. If the better a man is the more he should be loved, but they are the better who love the more, what else can I say than that I must love him more than myself, because I have no doubt that he is better than myself, but less than I should, because I am capable of less?

4. But (it is you I now address, my father) that your charity is greater than mine is all the more reason why you should not despise my smaller capacity, because, although you love more than I do, you do not love more than you are able. And I too, although I love

you less than I should, yet I love you as much as I can according to the power that has been given me. Draw me after you that I may reach you and with you receive more fully whence comes the power to love. Why do you try to reach me and complain that you are not able? You could reach me if you but considered what I am; and you can reach me still whenever you wish, if you are content to find me as I am and not as you wish me to be. I cannot think what else you see in me besides what I am, what it is you are chasing which is not me. You do not overtake it, because it is not me, because I am not able to be what you would like me to be and, to use your own words, I do not fail you, it is God in me who fails you. And now if all this trifling pleases you, tell me and I will give you more, for, in obeying you, I shall not fear the reproach of presumption. That little preface[1] which you ask to be sent you, I have not got by me at the moment. I have not yet had it copied, because I did not think it worth while. May he who gives you the desire grant you the power to accomplish whatever you rightly wish for yourself or for your friends, most reverend father, worthy of all the affection I can bestow.

LETTER 88

TO THE SAME

To his friend all that a friend could wish, from Brother Bernard of Clairvaux.

IT was you who gave me this formula of greeting when you wrote ' To his friend all that a friend could wish '. Receive back what is your own, and in doing so realize that my soul is not far from one with whom I share a common language. Now, briefly and as I have the time, I must answer your letter. It came on the feast of Our Lady's Nativity and all my attention was absorbed in observing the festival, so that I could think of nothing else. But your messenger was so anxious to take to his feet again that he could scarcely wait until the next day, so that I should be more free to answer you something. As for that fugitive monk, after I had given him a harsh scolding suited to his hard heart I could do nothing else than send him back whence he came for our customs forbid me to keep any monk here without the consent of his abbot. You also should scold him sharply and incite him to make humble satisfaction, then comfort him with a letter to his abbot on his behalf.

2. With regard to the state of my health, I can only answer your kind enquiries by saying that I have been sick and still am sick, but not much more than usual nor much less. The reason why I have not sent that man as I intended is because I fear more the scandal of many

---

[1] This refers to the letter which precedes the *Apology*.

souls than the danger of one body.[1]   And now, so as not to pass over completely without mention the matter you wrote to me about, I come to yourself.   You say you wish to hear what I, as one who knows you well, think of your plan.[2]   If I am to say what I think, I must tell you that, unless I am mistaken, it is something I could not advise you to attempt and you could not carry out.   Indeed I wish for you what it has for long been no secret to me that you wish for yourself.   But putting aside what both of us wish, as it is right we should, it is safer for me and more advantageous for you if I advise you as I think God wishes.   Therefore I say hold on to what you have got, remain where you are, and try to benefit those over whom you rule.   Do not try to escape the responsibility of your office while you are still able to discharge it for the benefit of your subjects.   Woe to you if you rule them and do not benefit them, but far greater woe to you if you refuse to benefit them because you shirk the burden of ruling them.

LETTER 89

[TO THE SAME(?)]

It is not certain to whom this letter is addressed.   It might be William of St. Thierry, a friend of St. Bernard, who afterwards became a Cistercian against St. Bernard's advice, but Hüffer considers this doubtful.   The date is uncertain.

To his friend Wi, Brother Bernard.

As I drew myself in my letter to you, so I really am; except that I could not express on paper all that I felt in my heart.   You have not and never have had any reason at all to fear me.   And if I was ever afraid of you, now I am so no longer.   I do not ask for my friend back, because I am confident that I hold him; I do not receive him back, because I have never lost him.   I cling to him, and there is no one who can take him from me.   I embrace again as of old my friend because true friendship never wears thin, else it were no true friendship.   I shall hold on to him and ' I shall not suffer him to go until I bring him into my mother's house and into the chamber of her that bore me '.   When I speak of him as at leisure, I do not mean that he is idle, but that he is fortunate; for his is no leisurely leisure, but a leisure zealous for good and fruitful for eternity.   As for myself, unhappy man that I am, I am not worthy of holy leisure, I am not privy to the holy peace of contemplation.   But because you deem me worthy of yourself, I am yours and shall be yours as long as I live.

---

[1] *Quod vero non misi quem missurus eram, causa est, plus me animarum scandalum, quam unius corporis periculum timuisse.*

[2] William wanted to resign his abbacy and become a monk at Clairvaux under St. Bernard. See introductory note to Letter 87.

The sermons you ask for are not yet ready, but they shall be got ready and you shall have them.

LETTER 90

TO OGER, A CANON REGULAR

Oger was a Canon Regular of Mont-Saint-Éloi near Arras.   He had a great reputation for learning, and it is evident that he was on intimate terms with St. Bernard.   The saint submitted to him for approval his Apology *before even William of St. Thierry had seen it.*

In the year 1125 he was chosen by the Bishop of Noyon to introduce the Canons Regular into the parish of St. Médard in Tournai, and the foundation of Saint-Nicolas-des-Prés is largely his work.   He ruled this house as superior for fourteen years.   It was his resignation that elicited this vehement letter of reproach from St. Bernard.

Mabillon dates this letter about the year 1126, but it was clearly written after Oger had resigned from being the superior of Saint-Nicolas-des-Prés, and would therefore belong to about the year 1139, the year in which the Lateran Council met in Rome and St. Malachy on his way there stopped at Clairvaux.   According to Vacandard[1] this letter and the three which follow are set in an order diametrically reverse to the chronological, so that Letter 93 should come first, followed by 92 and 91, all written before the foundation of Saint-Nicolas-des-Prés, with the following letter last as written after Oger's resignation.   Oger is also referred to in Letter 96, written about the year 1133.

To Brother Oger, that he may walk worthily before God unto the end of his days, from Brother Bernard, monk but sinner, who loves him dearly.

IF I have seemed dilatory in answering your letter the reason is that I have lacked a messenger. I beg you to believe that this letter which you now read was written some time ago but, as I have said, for want of anyone to take it, time was lost before it was sent, although not before it was written. I gather from your letter that you found your pastoral charge irksome and have relinquished it after having not so much asked for your bishop's permission as exacted it by your insistence, and that even then you only obtained it on condition that, though dwelling elsewhere but in his diocese, you should not withdraw yourself from his authority, but that as this did not please you, you had recourse to a higher authority in the person of the archbishop, and then returned to your first home and to your abbot supported by his sanction. Now you implore me to instruct you how you should live after all this. Fine sort of doctor, incomparable teacher that I am, who when I begin to teach what I do not know may then be

[1] Vacandard, *Vie de Saint Bernard*, vol. I, p. 196, n. (1927 edn.).

expected to realize at last that I know nothing at all! A sheep might as well come to a goat for wool, a mill to a furnace for water, a wise man to a fool for knowledge, as you to me for guidance. Furthermore in all your letters you exalt me above myself, interlarding everything you say with praises of myself, praises which, as I am conscious I do not deserve them, I must ascribe to your good will and overlook your ignorance of the facts. You see only on the surface, God searches the heart. If I carefully examine myself under his awful gaze, it is certain that I will know myself better than you know me for the reason that I am closer to myself. And so I put greater faith in what I see when I examine myself than I do in your praises, who believe you see in me what I know is not there!

2. You apologize to me for not having taken my advice when I counselled and encouraged you not to give way to despondency but to be of good heart and carry patiently the burden imposed on you, which once undertaken cannot be put aside. I accept your apology, as you ask. I am fully aware of the aridity of my own wisdom and I always suspect my rash stupidity. As I always hope that people will act more judiciously than I have been able to instruct them, I have no right, I do not dare to be annoyed when the course I have advocated is not followed. Whenever my advice is followed, I confess that I always feel oppressed with a great burden of responsibility, and I can never be confident and always await the outcome with anxiety. But it is your responsibility, if advisedly you have not followed my counsel in the matter. It is also the responsibility of those whose more wholesome advice you have followed in preference to mine, if indeed you have taken any advice at all, whether you have acted reasonably or not. Let them see to it whether, when Christ was obedient to his Father unto death, it is permissible for a Christian to free himself before death of the yoke which obedience has laid upon him. You say you asked the bishop for his permission and obtained it. Well and good, but you asked for it in a way that you should not have done, so that you cannot be said to have received it so much as exacted it. A permission that has been extorted is no permission at all but an exaction.[1] What the bishop unwillingly did when he was overborne by your insistence was not to absolve you, but to cut you off.

3. I congratulate you on having disburdened yourself, but I very much fear that in doing so you have dishonoured God.[2] Without doubt you have, so far as you could, opposed his designs by casting yourself down from the post to which he had promoted you. If, by way of excuse, you allege the necessity of poverty, I reply that necessity wins a crown;[3] if you allege the difficulty or impossibility of your position, I reply that all things are possible to one who believes.

---

[1] *extorta seu coacta licentia, licentia non est, sed violentia.*
[2] *quod sis exoneratus . . . exhonoratus sit Deus.*
[3] *Rule of St. Benedict*, Chap. 7.

Better tell the truth and admit that your own quiet pleased you more than labouring for the benefit of others. I don't wonder at it, I admit that I feel the same way myself, but it should not please you too much. And it is too much, if a thing good in itself pleases no matter how it is obtained, even if it is obtained unlawfully, for nothing can be right to have, if it cannot be had rightly, as it is written: ' If you rightly offer and do not rightly divide, you have sinned'. Either you should not have undertaken at all the care of souls or, having undertaken it, you should on no account have relinquished it, according to those words: ' Are you married to a wife? Then do not go about to be free of her.'

4. What is the point of all these arguments of mine? Am I trying to persuade you to take up again the burden of your office, when it is clear that there is no place open to you? Or do I despair of you, as if you had saddled yourself with a sin you could not get rid of? Such is very far from my intention. But I do not want you to regard what you have done as if it were a trifling matter. I want you always to fear for it, always to be sorry for it, and never to regard yourself as safe, according to those words of Scripture: ' Blessed evermore is the timorous conscience'. You see what sort of fear it is with which I am trying to smite you? Not the sort that will lead you into the pit of despair, but the sort that will win you hope of eternal life. For there is a fruitless fear which is cruel and sad and which never obtains pardon because it never tries to; and there is a loving, humble, and fruitful fear which easily obtains mercy for anyone however great his sin. Such a fear begets, fosters, and preserves humility, and also gentleness, patience, and meekness. Who would not be delighted with such a fair progeny? But the other sort of fear begets a sorry brood: obstinacy, immoderate sadness, hatred, terror, scorn, and desperation. So I would not have you regard your fault with the sort of fear that begets desperation, but with the sort that engenders hope, fearful lest you do not fear or do not fear enough.

5. There is another thing which I fear even more for you, it is that, like those of whom it is written, ' Sin and shame is all their liking', you may be deceived not only into thinking that you have done no wrong, but even into congratulating yourself on having done something which very few are wont to do, in scorning high office and preferring to place yourself under another's rule when you were freed from ruling others yourself. This is a false humility which foments real pride in the heart that thinks such things; for what could be more proud than to attribute to a spontaneous and free act of the will what was really due to the force of necessity or the infirmity of faint-heartedness. And even if you had done it voluntarily and not because you had been overcome by work or compelled by necessity, there still could be nothing more proud than to plume yourself on it; for you

have preferred your own will to the designs of God, choosing quiet for yourself rather than the work for which he had selected you. If therefore having scorned God you make matters worse by congratulating yourself on it, your self-congratulation is hardly a good thing! Avoid all self-congratulation, put away all complacency, so that you may always be profitably anxious about yourself, always humbly fearful for yourself, but, as I have said already, with the fear that mitigates and does not provoke wrath.

6. If this horrible fear should ever besiege your heart, silently suggesting that your worship of God is not acceptable and that your repentance is fruitless because you cannot correct the matter in which you have offended him, do not for one moment give way to it, but answer it faithfully by saying to yourself: I have done evil, but it is done and cannot be undone. Who can tell whether God has not foreseen that it would profit me, that he who is good has not wished that good should accrue to me out of the evil I have done? May he punish me for what I have done amiss, but let the good which he has provided for me remain. The goodness of God knows how to use our disordered wishes and actions, often lovingly turning them to our advantage while always preserving the beauty of his order. What loving care the divine goodness has for the sons of Adam! Never does it cease to pour forth its blessings, not only where it can see nothing to deserve them, but often where it sees everything to the contrary! But to return to yourself: according to the two kinds of fear which I have distinguished above, I wish you to fear and not to fear; to presume and not to presume. To fear, in order that you may repent; not to fear, in order that you may presume; to presume so that you do not lose heart, not to presume so that you become slothful.

7. Behold how great is my confidence in you! I have scolded you sharply, and I have not hesitated to judge your conduct before knowing all the facts so that, for all I can tell, you have better reasons for it than I am aware of. You might not have wished to put in your letter all the reasons that would have excused you, either from humility, or for the sake of brevity. So I leave the verdict undecided, for it is clear I know nothing about the matter. There is however one thing you have done for which I have nothing but praise. I refer to the way that, when you had put off the yoke of office, without any thought of keeping your freedom you without hesitation immediately put yourself again under the discipline you loved, not ashamed to become once more a disciple after you had been a master. When you had been freed of your pastoral duties you could have remained your own master, since a religious is dispensed from obedience to his former superior when once he becomes an abbot. Yet you did not take advantage of this privilege, but as you had refused to rule others so you feared to rule yourself; believing yourself incapable of ruling

others, you had no confidence in yourself and scorned to become your own master, deservedly so because he becomes the disciple of a fool who sets up to be his own teacher. What the experience of others may be I do not know, but my own experience is that I can far more easily command and far more safely rule others than I can myself. You were prudently humble and humbly prudent when you did not at all believe that you were sufficient to your own salvation and decided henceforth to live under the authority of another.

8. I praise you also that you did not seek out a new master, but returned to the familiar cloister from which you had set out and to the father whom you had left. It would not have been fitting that a strange house should have profited by the loss of your mother house in which you were brought up, but which sent you out at the behest of fraternal charity. Yet I do not want you to think it a trivial matter that you have not received the permission of your bishop to return. Hasten therefore to make what satisfaction you can, either in person or through another. After you have done this, try to live simply amongst your brethren, seeking God, submissive to your superior, obedient to your seniors, friendly with your juniors, pleasing to the angels, profitable in speech, humble of heart, kind to all. Beware of thinking that because you were once in a place of honour, you should still be honoured above others, rather show yourself all the more humble, and more humble than any. It would be a shocking thing were you to exact honour when you have refused the labour.

9. There is another danger that can arise from this against which I would have you forewarned and forearmed. We are all of us so unstable that what we wanted yesterday we often do not want to-day, and what we reject to-day to-morrow we want. And so it can sometimes happen, at the suggestion of the devil, that the desire for honours that we remember will knock on the door of the soul, even so that what we were men enough to scorn we are childish enough to begin again to want. All that the soul once found bitter—high position, care of the house, arrangement of affairs, salutes of servants, freedom of action, power over others—all this it begins to find sweet after all, so that sorrow is felt for what it was once irksome to have. If you for one moment assent to this vile temptation (may it be very far from you to do any such thing!) your life will suffer no little harm.

10. Now you have all the wisdom of your wise and eloquent doctor whom you asked from so far away to teach you. This is the long desired and expected praise you so much wanted to hear. Or do you still expect something wonderful? You have it all. What more do you want? The spring is exhausted, and do you still expect water from a fountain that has run dry? Like the widow in the Gospels, of my poverty I have given you all I have got. Why so bashful? Why hang your head? You forced me. You asked for a discourse

and now you have got it.   A discourse long enough in all conscience, but saying nothing much; full of words and wind, but empty of sense. Not one calculated to order charity within you[1] as you asked for, but one which will exhibit my lack of knowledge.   How can such ignorance as mine be now excused?   Perhaps I might say that I have been suffering from fever or that I was preoccupied with the cares of office when I dictated it, since we are told that 'The wisdom of the learned man is the fruit of leisure'.   All this might have been some excuse, if I had composed something great and important, but for such a little thing as this these excuses cannot be adduced with any confidence at all.   No, my only excuse is, as I have already said so often, the meagreness of my knowledge.

11. But in my confusion I have one consolation.   Although I may have disappointed you by not sending what you expected, you can see by what I have sent you that I have tried.   When ability is lacking the will must supply for the deed.   Although what I have written may be of no use to you, it will certainly profit my humility.   'While he holds his peace, a fool may pass for a wise man', for his silence is attributed to humility and not to lack of understanding.   And so by holding my peace I could have passed for a wise man.   But as it is some will laugh at my stupidity, others will mock at me as a fool, and yet others will be indignant at my presumption.   All this will be of no small help to my sanctification,[2] because humiliations lead to humility and humility is the foundation of the spiritual life.   Humiliation is the only way to humility, just as patience is the only way to peace, and reading to knowledge.   If you want the virtue of humility you must not shun humiliations.   If you will not suffer yourself to be humbled, you can never achieve humility.   It is an advantage for me that my foolishness should be made public, that I whose lot it has often been to receive undeserved praise from those who do not know me, should now be discomforted by those who have found me out. The Apostle alarms me when, fearful for himself, he says: 'But I restrain myself, lest any man should think of me above that which he seeth in me, or anything he heareth from me'.   How aptly he has said: 'I restrain myself'!   The arrogant man does not restrain himself, the proud man does not restrain himself, the vain man does not restrain himself, nor does the boasting man, who either lies about himself or credits himself with what is not his own, restrain himself. Only the truly humble man can be said to restrain himself, sparing his own soul, because he prefers to conceal what he is, so that no one should believe him to be what he is not.[3]

12. It is very dangerous for anyone to hear himself spoken of above

---

[1] *Non quo, ut petieras, in corde tuo cavitas ordinetur.*   Eales translates: ' Such is the discourse which ought to be received by you with charity '.

[2] *religionis emolumentum.*

[3] The whole sentence is a play on St. Paul's use of the word *Parco.*

what he knows he deserves. I pray that I may be humbled before men for the truth, just as much as it has been my lot to be undeservedly praised for what is not true. I rightly apply to myself those words of the Prophet: 'I have been lifted up only to be cast down and discomforted'; and again: 'Play the mountebank I will and humble myself in my own esteem', for I shall play the mountebank that I may be mocked. A good sort of playing this, a playing calculated to enrage Michol and please God. A good sort of playing which is ridiculous to men, but a very beautiful sight to the angels. I say it is a good sort of playing by which we become an object of reproach to the rich and of ridicule to the proud. In fact what else do seculars think we are doing but playing when what they desire most on earth, we fly from; and what they fly from, we desire? Like acrobats and jugglers, who with heads down and feet up, stand or walk on their hands, and thus draw all eyes to themselves. But this is not a game for children or the theatre where lust is excited by the effeminate and indecent contortions of the actors, it is a joyous game, decent, grave, and admirable, delighting the gaze of the heavenly onlookers. This pure and holy game he plays who says: 'We are become a spectacle to angels and men'. And we too play this game that we may be ridiculed, discomforted, humbled, until he comes who puts down the mighty from their seat and exalts the humble. May he gladden us, exalt us, and glorify us for ever.

LETTER 91

TO THE SAME

I WILL pass over my lack of ability, I will not mention my humble profession or my profession of humility, and I will not plead my commonplace, not to say mediocre, position and name. Whenever I mention anything like this you do not regard it as a reasonable excuse, but as a mere pretext for not answering your letters promptly. According to your mood you call my quite legitimate modesty sometimes indiscretion and at other times false humility, and now you tell me it is pride. So I will not make any more of what you regard as dubious excuses, I will merely point out to you as a friend what you must believe to be a fact, namely that because of the short summer nights and the full days I have not had one moment of leisure in which I could attend to your business since your messenger left me . . . not the present one but the former. As it is, your letter has found me so occupied that even to recount all I have to do would take too long. I scarcely had time to read it when it came during my dinner. And now by getting up early I am just able to scribble, on the quiet, this brief reply. Whether or not you will be satisfied with its brevity is your affair.

2. To tell the truth, dear Oger, although my conscience bears witness that I am only trying to serve charity yet, for your sake, I cannot but be exasperated with all my cares. I bear them only for the sake of charity, because I am debtor to the wise and unwise; only for her sake am I prevented from complying with your requests. Does charity prevent me from doing what you ask in the name of charity? You have asked, you have implored, you have knocked, but charity has closed the door to you. Why be angry with me? If you wish, if you dare, you should be angry with charity. In the name of charity you have been bold to demand, and charity herself has refused you. Already she complains of this long screed and is vexed with you for imposing it. Not that she is displeased with your zeal, for she gave you that, but she would have you rule zeal with knowledge and not try to hinder greater matters with things of lesser consequence. See, even now I have become vexatious to lady charity, who urges me to make an end, but drawn on by my delight in conversing with you and by my desire to please you I am loath to be torn from a long letter and still have not finished. There is so much to answer in your letter. If only it were right for me to do as I please, I could probably satisfy both you and myself. But she who commands otherwise is mistress or, I should say, lord for 'God is charity'. Such is her authority that I must obey her rather than you or myself. So although I do not refuse what you ask, I must unwillingly and sadly defer it for the time, because I must obey charity, which is God, rather than men. Otherwise I, a mere worm of the earth, in my desire humbly to please you, would be setting myself, under the cloak of humility, but with a real pride, against that stronghold of authority which, as you well say, can command even the angels in heaven.

3. As for that booklet of mine, even before your messenger arrived I had asked for it back from the man to whom I had lent it. But I have not got it yet. I will do what I can to have it here when you come (if you ever do come), so that you may see it and read it, but not copy it.[1] That other one I lent you I had meant you only to read, but you tell me you have had it copied. What use that can serve or whom it can possibly benefit is your responsibility. I did not intend that you should send it to the Abbot of St. Thierry, but I do not mind. Why should I mind him seeing it when I would gladly lay bare my whole soul for him to see if I could. Alas that the mention of such a man should arise in so short a letter which even now clamours to be finished, when I would gladly dwell on his welcome memory! Do not hesitate, I beg you, to find an opportunity of going to see him, and do not on any account allow anyone to see or copy the aforesaid

---

[1] It is said that St. Columba was sued in the court of the king at Tara by St. Finnan in the 6th century for having secretly copied a manuscript which belonged to him, and that St. Finnan won his case, and St. Columba was ordered to give up the copy he had made.

booklet until you have been through it with him, discussed it with him, and have both made such corrections as may be necessary, so that every word of it may be supported by two witnesses.[1] I leave to the judgement of you both whether it shall be published, or shown to only a few, or to no one at all. I also leave to you both to decide whether the preface you have put together out of my other letters will stand or whether it would not be better to compose another.[2]

4. I had almost forgotten the complaint at the beginning of your letter that I had accused you of falsehood. I do not remember saying any such thing about you. But if I did (I would sooner believe I had forgotten than that your messenger had lied), it could only have been in fun that I said it and not seriously. How could I possibly believe that you were a trifler or one of those to whom Yes and No are the same. May such a suspicion of you be very far from me who know full well that you are happy to carry the yoke of truth from your youth and restrain the years of indiscretion[3] with the gravity of your conduct. I am not so simple as to believe that a simple statement from the lips without duplicity of heart can ever be a formal lie, nor am I so indifferent to you as to have forgotten what you have had at heart for so long and the obstacle that impedes its accomplishment.

LETTER 92

TO THE SAME

I FEEL you may be annoyed or at least surprised that I answered your long letter with only a short note. But I beg you to remember those words of the Wise Man, ' All things have their season: there is a time for speaking and a time for keeping silence '. And what time would there be for silence if conversation claimed even these holy days of Lent, and a sort of conversation all the more laborious for being so engrossing? When we are together it is possible quickly to say what we want, but being absent from each other we must laboriously compose what we want to ask or reply. And where, I ask you, is the leisure, where the quiet of silence when one is thinking, composing, and writing? You say that all this can be done in silence. I am surprised that you can seriously mean this. How can the mind be quiet when composing a letter and a turmoil of expressions are clamouring and every sort of phrase and diversity of senses are jostling one another? When words spring into the mind, but just the word one wants escapes one; when literary effect, sense, and how to convey a meaning clearly, and what should be said, and in what order it

---

[1] *ut in ore duorum testium stet omne verbum.* Literally: ' That in the mouth of two or three witnesses every word shall stand ' (*Deut.* 19.15 and *Matt.* 18.16).

[2] The booklet referred to here is plainly the *Apologia* of St. Bernard. It was inscribed to Abbot William of St. Thierry, which accounts for why Oger sent it to him without instructions. There is a reference to the preface here mentioned in Letter 87.4.

[3] *lascivos annos morum superas gravitate.*

should be said, has to be carefully considered; all the things which those who understand these matters scrutinize carefully? And do you tell me there is any quiet in all this? Can you call this silence, even if the lips are not moving?

2. It is not only that I have not the time, it is also that the sort of work you want me to do is not suited either to my profession or ability. Not teaching, but lamenting is the duty of the monk I am supposed to be and of the sinner that I am. There could not be anything more silly than for an untaught man such as I confess I am, to presume to teach what he knows nothing about. An untaught man is not competent to teach, a monk does not dare to do so, and a penitent does not want to do so. It is in order to avoid this that I have flown far away and dwelt in solitude, and like the Prophet have determined to ' take heed of my ways that I sin not with my tongue ', because, according to the same Prophet, ' a glib tongue shall not have its way upon earth '; and according to another, ' the tongue holds the keys of life and death '. Isaias calls silence ' the work of justice ' and Jeremias says that ' it is good to await the salvation of the Lord in silence '. Therefore so that I shall not seem entirely to ignore your request I invite and incite you, who by speaking press me to teach what I do not know, and, if not by my teaching, at any rate by the example of my silence, all those who like you wish to grow in virtue, to foster this ' work of justice ', the mother, the support, the guardian of all the virtues.

3. But what am I doing? I wonder you do not laugh. For, while appearing to condemn strongly much speaking, I still continue to pour out words, and in recommending silence to thwart silence by my verbosity. Our dear Guerric,[1] concerning whose life of penance you wish to be assured, to judge by his fruit is walking worthily, you may be sure, before God, and bringing forth worthy fruit of penance. But the little book you ask for I have not by me, for another friend, who was just as anxious to read it as you are, has had it for a long time and not yet returned it. However, so as not to ignore your request completely, I am sending you another booklet which I have lately published, in praise of the Virgin Mother. As I have not got the original I beg you to return it as soon as you can or, if you are coming here in the near future, to bring it with you.

LETTER 93

TO THE SAME

I HAVE answered your short letters with short letters, glad to have an excuse in your brevity for being brief myself. For true and, as you rightly say, eternal friendships are not helped by exchanging vain

[1] Guerric was made Abbot of Igny in 1138.

and empty words. However much you try to show your friendship by verses, phrases, and quotations, I feel sure you express less than you feel; and you would not be wrong if you believed the same thing of me. When your letter was delivered into my hands, you were already in my heart. While I write this letter you are present to me, as I am sure I shall be present to you when you read it. We wear ourselves out in scribbling to each other, and we exhaust our messengers in sending them backwards and forwards between us. But is the spirit ever weary with loving? Let us stop this tiring business of exchanging letters and turn ourselves to what the more we do the easier it becomes. Let us give our heads a respite from dictating, our tongues from chattering, our hands from writing, our messengers from running to and fro, and apply ourselves to meditating day and night on the law of the Lord, which is the law of charity. The more we rest from doing this, the less rested we become; the more we apply ourselves to it, the more repose we derive from it. Let us love and be loved: benefiting ourselves by loving, and others by being loved.[1] We find rest in those we love, and we provide a resting place in ourselves for those who love us. To love anyone in God is charity, to try and make ourselves loved for God's sake is the service of charity.

2. But what am I doing? I promise brevity but cling to prolixity. If you wish to know about Brother Guerric, or rather because you do, I can assure you that he so runs not as one uncertain of the course, and so fights not as one beating the air. But he knows that the effect comes from God's mercy, not from man's will, or man's alacrity, so he begs you to pray God for him that he who gives the power to fight and run may also give the power to conquer and achieve the goal. I greet your abbot through you, for he is dear to me not only on your account, but also because of what I have heard of him. It will give me great pleasure to meet him at the time and place you have arranged. I must tell you that for some time now the hand of the Lord has been heavy upon me. I reeled under it and had well nigh fallen, the axe was laid to the barren tree of my body, and I feared it was already being cut down, but on account of your prayers and those of my other friends the Lord has spared me this time, yet only in the hope that I shall show some fruit in future.

LETTER 94

TO THE ABBOTS ASSEMBLED AT SOISSONS

About the year 1130 the Benedictine abbots met at Soissons in the Abbey of St. Médard, a Cluniac house, under the aegis of Geoffrey, the Abbot of St. Médard, who afterwards became Bishop of Châlons-sur-Marne. The

---

[1] *Amemus, et amemur; in altero nobis, in altero nostris consulentes.* Eales translates: ' Let us love and be loved, striving to benefit ourselves in the other, and the other in ourselves '.

meeting was an attempt to establish among the monasteries of Black Monks in the province of Rheims the Cistercian custom of a yearly General Chapter. Its convocation was probably an outcome of St. Bernard's Apology, and it is to the credit of both parties that the saint was asked to attend. In the following letter he apologizes for his enforced absence and encourages the abbots with exhortation and advice.

To the Reverend Lord Abbots gathered together in the name of the Lord at Soissons, that they may see, establish, and observe the things which are right, from the servant of their holiness, Brother Bernard, styled Abbot of Clairvaux.

I AM vexed with my affairs because they prevent me from attending your meeting. But it is only my body they hinder, not my spirit, for neither the long distance nor my crowd of cares can impede my spirit and prevent me from praying for you, applauding you, and resting amongst you. I cannot, I say, fail this assembly of holy men, nor can distance of place and absence of body sequester me from this council and congregation of the righteous, especially as it will not be a council at which the traditions of men are obstinately defended and blindly observed,[1] but where the good, pleasing, and perfect will of God is carefully and humbly sought. Thither my whole heart carries me, there my devotion holds me, my love impels me, there do I cling with my approbation and remain by sharing in your zeal.[2]

2. So that those who now applaud you may have no occasion to mock and say that you have met for nothing, endeavour, I beseech you, to sanctify your lives and make your enactments good, for too good they cannot be. I grant that you might perhaps be too just, that you could be too wise, for it is written, ' Be not over just ', and ' Be not more wise than it behoveth to be wise ', but it is nowhere said, ' Be not over good ', or ' Be not more good than it behoveth '. No one can be more good than it behoves him. When Paul was already good, he was not content, but gladly stretched forth to those things that were before, forgetting those that were behind, striving ever to be better.

3. Let them depart from me and from you who say, ' We do not wish to be better than our fathers ', proclaiming themselves sons of lax and tepid fathers whose memory is accursed because they have eaten bitter grapes and the teeth of their children have been set on edge. If they glory in the memory of good and holy fathers, then let them at least imitate their sanctity while maintaining as a law their dispensations and indulgences. Although the holy Elias said: ' I

---

[1] A reference to the abuses prevalent in the houses of the Black Monks which the saint castigated in his *Apology*.

[2] *Illuc toto desiderio feror, devotione immoror, condelector amore, inhæro consensu, æmulatione persisto.*

am not better than my fathers', he did not say that he had no desire
to be better. Jacob saw angels ascending and descending the ladder,
but he did not see any standing still or sitting down. A fragile hanging
ladder is no place for standing still nor, in the uncertain condition of
this mortal life, can anyone remain fixed in one position. We have
not here an abiding city nor do we yet possess it, but we are still
seeking the one that is to come. Either you must go up or you must
come down, you inevitably fall if you try to stand still. It is certain
that the man who does not try to be better is not even good; when
you stop trying to be better, then you cease to be good.

3. Let them also depart from me and from you who call good evil
and evil good. What good thing do they call good who deem even
the pursuit of righteousness an evil? Once our Lord scandalized the
Pharisees by one thing which he said. Now it is not the saying even
of one thing, but silence which scandalizes these new Pharisees. You
can be quite sure of this: they are merely seeking for an opportunity
to attack you. Let them be; they are blind, leaders of the blind.
Consider the salvation of the little children and do not concern yourselves with the grumbles of the spiteful. It is not your concern to cure
the scandal of those who will not be cured unless you too become sick.
But neither must you wait to see if your enactments are pleasing in
every particular to everyone of your own monks, otherwise you will
decide nothing, or next to nothing. You must consider what is good
for them, not what they want. You will do better to draw the
reluctant to God, than to leave them to the desires of their hearts.
I commend myself to your holy prayers.

LETTER 95

TO HENRY I, KING OF ENGLAND

*This letter refers to the foundation of Rievaulx, which took place on March
5th, 1132. Rievaulx was the first daughter of Clairvaux in these islands
but not the first Cistercian house, for Waverley dates from the year 1129.
The first abbot was William, the scribe of St. Bernard's letter to Robert of
Châtillon and an Englishman, but the chief glory of Rievaulx is St. Ailred,
the third abbot. The founder was Walter Espec, who in 1138 rallied the
barons and yeomen of Yorkshire and drove back David, King of Scotland,
at the battle of the Standard.*

To Henry, the illustrious King of England, that in his earthly kingdom
he may faithfully serve and humbly obey the King of heaven, from
Bernard, styled Abbot of Clairvaux.

IN your land there is an outpost of my Lord and your Lord, an outpost
which he has preferred to die for than to lose. I have proposed to
occupy it and I am sending men from my army who will, if it is not

displeasing to you, claim it, recover it, and restore it with a strong hand. For this purpose I have sent ahead these men who now stand before you to reconnoitre. They will investigate the situation carefully and report back to me faithfully. Help them as messengers of your Lord and in their persons fulfil your duties as a vassal of their Lord. And may he for his honour, the salvation of your soul, and the health and peace of your kingdom, bring you safe and happy to a good and peaceful end.

LETTER 96

TO HENRY DE BLOIS, BISHOP OF WINCHESTER

Henry de Blois was a nephew of Henry I, King of England, and a brother of King Stephen. While a monk of Cluny and a young man he was appointed Abbot of Glastonbury in the year 1126. Three years after this he became Bishop of Winchester, while still retaining office as Abbot of Glastonbury. He remained Bishop of Winchester until his death in 1171, and during the whole of this time he was never in residence at his abbey. Nevertheless he took a great interest in Glastonbury and completely restored its material prosperity as well as effecting certain reforms in the observance of the monks. As Bishop of Winchester he concerned himself with high affairs of state and proved an upright and clearsighted statesman, as well as an administrator of genius. He was immensely rich, magnificent in every sense of the word, and highly ambitious; he even conceived the extraordinary idea of raising Winchester to a metropolitan see. In many ways Henry de Blois is one of the most attractive personalities of his time, but for all his colourful and strong character he stood at the opposite extreme to the school of reform which drew its inspiration from Clairvaux, and it was not long before he came into conflict with St. Bernard.[1]

To the illustrious Lord, Henry, by the grace of God Bishop of Winchester, greetings in the Lord from Bernard, styled Abbot of Clairvaux.

I AM overjoyed to hear from many persons that my unworthy self is privileged with more than a small share of your Lordship's favour. Although undeserving I am not ungrateful, and I return the compliment of your Lordship's favour, not indeed as you deserve, but nevertheless as I am able. I have no misgivings that you may scorn the little that I am able to offer in return, since you have so graciously forestalled it and so kindly deserved it. I forbear from writing more until I know from your reply, if you deem it fitting to send one, how you have received these few words. You can easily commit your answer either by word of mouth or in writing to Abbot Oger[2] who brings

---

[1] For an account of Henry de Blois see *The Monastic Order in England* by David Knowles, Vol. I, pp. 281–297.
[2] See Letters 90–93.

this letter, and whom 1 recommend to your Excellency as a man worthy of your esteem and confidence, commendable for his honesty, learning, and piety.

LETTER 97

TO DUKE CONRAD

This was Conrad, Duke of Zeringen. Mabillon dates this letter 1132 and quotes Samuel Guichen to the effect that Conrad was at this time contemplating hostilities against Amadeus I, Count of Geneva. This letter is just one example of St. Bernard's beneficent influence in curbing the sultry passions of the mediæval barons.

ALL power comes from him to whom the Prophet says: ' Thine, Lord, the power, of all princes art thou the overlord '. So it seems to me fitting, illustrious Prince, that I should write and admonish your Excellency to bow down before the terrible One who strikes with terror the hearts of princes. The Prince of Geneva, as I have heard from his own mouth, has offered himself to justice and is ready to make satisfaction to you in all that you have against him. So if, on the top of this, you set out to invade his territory, destroy churches, burn down homesteads, and shed human blood, there can be no doubt at all that you will seriously anger him, who is ' father to the orphan and gives the widow redress '. If he is angry it would advantage you nothing to fight no matter how great your military strength. It makes no difference to the omnipotent Lord whether armies are great or small, he gives victory where he pleases. When he wished he gave one man power to put thousands to flight, and two men ten thousand.

2. A poor man myself I am stirred by the cries of poor men to write to you knowing that it would be more honourable for you to yield to the humble than to submit to the enemy. Not that I believe your enemy to be stronger than you are, but I know the omnipotent God to be more powerful than either of you, and that he resists the proud and gives his grace to the humble. I would have had an audience with you on this matter, if it had been possible, but now I send in my place these brethren of mine in the hope that by their entreaties united with mine they may obtain from your Highness a complete treaty if possible, or at any rate an armistice until we can explore the ground for a firm peace to your honour, the good of your country and in accordance with the will of God. Otherwise, if you will neither receive the satisfaction offered you nor listen to my entreaties, or rather, if you will not heed the voice of God warning you through me for the good of your soul, then may he be your judge. I know full well that two armies can hardly close in combat without terrible slaughter on both sides, which is what I fear so much.

LETTER 98

FULK, Abbot of Epernay, had already written to me about the very question which you have asked me through Brother Hescelin. I did not answer him at once as I have been hoping to find something bearing on the subject in the Fathers, which I would rather have sent him than anything new of my own. But as it has not been easy to find anything I am sending you both, for the time being, what I think on the question, on the understanding that if any of you should think of some better solution, or should hear or read of one, you will not fail to pass it on to me. Your question is why the Machabees, alone of all the righteous of the Old Law, have been accorded by the Fathers the unique privilege of an annual feast and veneration equal to our own martyrs. To say that they were deemed worthy of the same veneration because they showed the same virtue in martyrdom is perhaps to give the reason why they should be so honoured, but not why they alone should be. There are others among the ancients of the Old Law who are known to have laid down their lives with just as much zeal for religion as the Machabees who yet are not commemorated with a like festival. And if it is said that there is no reason why the death of the other ancients should be commemorated because the time at which they died deprived them of the honour which their courage deserved, why is not the same reason valid for the Machabees if they too, because of the time at which they laid down their lives, did not immediately enter heaven but descended into the darkness of Limbo? For the first fruits of them that sleep had not then come, he who was to open the gates of heaven, the Lamb of the tribe of Juda, ' he that openeth and no man shutteth ', he at whose entry into his kingdom the heavenly powers sing: ' Swing back the doors, captains of the guard; swing back, immortal gates, to let the King enter in triumph '. So if it seems unfitting to commemorate with joy the passing of those whose passage was not joyful, why is it fitting to celebrate with joy the passing of the Machabees?

2. Or should one say that although both the Machabees and the other ancients had with our martyrs the same cause of righteousness for their death, they had not the same kind of martyrdom as ours? All the martyrs, both of the Old and the New Law, laid down their lives for righteousness, but the difference is that the martyrs of the New Law laid down their lives because they were righteous, while those of the Old Law did so because they denounced those who were not. The former died because they were righteous, the latter because they taught that those who were not would perish. To make the whole difference clear in a few words, I would say that righteousness itself earned for our martyrs their martyrdom and zeal for righteousness

earned it for the others. But the Machabees, alone of all the ancients, had in common with our martyrs not only the same cause for their martyrdom, but also the same kind of martyrdom, and so they have attained in the Church equal honour with our martyrs. Just as our martyrs, they too were forced to pour out libations to strange gods, to forsake the laws of their country or rather of their God, and they died because they refused to do so.

3. Not so did Isaias die, not so did Zacharias or even the great John the Baptist die, of whom the first, it is said, was cloven asunder, the second killed between the altar and the temple, and the third beheaded in prison. If you ask at whose hands these men met their death, I say at the hands of the wicked and irreligious. If you ask for what reason they were killed, I reply for the sake of righteousness and religion, but more because they upheld it than because they professed it. They upheld the truth against those who hated it and the truth earned them hatred, and hatred death. Although they were wicked and irreligious men who killed them, yet they were more protecting themselves from religion than attacking religion itself, they were not so much persecuting righteousness as defending their own wickedness. There is all the difference between attacking another's goods and defending one's own, between rejecting the truth and persecuting the truth, between envying believers and being enraged by their denunciations, between closing the mouth which professes the truth and being unable to endure the taunts of those who denounce. ' Herod sent and laid hold of John ', but why? Because he preached Christ, because he was a good and just man? No, on the contrary Herod respected him for this and ' having heard him, did many things ', but rather because John rebuked him ' on account of Herodias, the wife of his brother Philip '. That was the reason why John was bound and beheaded. Certainly he suffered for the sake of truth, but only because he was zealous for it; he was not forced to deny it. Hence the passion of this great martyr is celebrated with less festivity than the passion of lesser men.

4. If the Machabees had suffered in such a manner and for such a reason, there would not be any mention of them at all. But we rightly accord them a veneration equal to that of our own martyrs because a not dissimilar confession has rendered them similar. The fact that they did not suffer expressly for Christ need not worry us because it does not make any difference whether anyone suffers under the Law for the observances of the Law or under grace for the commands of the Gospel. Both equally suffer for truth and therefore for Christ who said: ' I am the truth '. It is the nature of their martyrdom rather than their valour which has earned for the Machabees their unique status; the other fathers who suffered under the Old Law with equal valour are not accorded the same veneration by the Church. I suppose that the reason for this is that it seems unfitting to

commemorate with a festival the death of those who, although they died gallantly, yet nevertheless did so before the death of Christ, especially as, before the saving Passion of Christ, no festal joy but the darkness of the grave received the dead. Without doubt the Church has judged that the Machabees should be excepted because what the time of their death deprived them of, the nature of their martyrdom has bestowed upon them.

5. Yet we commemorate with a solemn festival not only the Machabees but also those who chanced to die before the death of him who was Life manifested in the flesh, even if they died in his life time, like Simeon and John the Baptist; or for him like the Innocents whom, although they too went down to Limbo, we celebrate with a solemn rite, but for a different reason. In the case of the Innocents it would be unjust to deny all present fame to the innocence which died for justice. And John too, who knew that from his day the Kingdom of Heaven suffered violence and cried out: 'Do penance, for the Kingdom of Heaven is at hand', and joyfully embraced death because he knew that Life was following him close at hand. He took pains to make sure of this when he was near to death for he asked: 'Lord, art thou he who is to come or do we await another?' And he deserved to be reassured by the Lord who, after recounting his miracles, said to him: 'Blessed is he who is not scandalized by me'. By these words the Lord signified that he was to die and that his death would be such as might prove a scandal to the Jews and foolishness to the Gentiles. When he heard this, John, the friend of the Bridegroom, joyfully preceded his master to the grave where he could no longer doubt that he would soon come, and by dying so joyfully deserved that his death should be commemorated with joy by the Church. And the old man Simeon, as full of virtues as he was of years, carrying Life in his hands when death was close to him, said: 'Now thou dost dismiss thy servant, O Lord, according to thy word in peace, because my eyes have seen thy salvation'; as if to say, 'I can confidently go down into prison because I believe that my redemption is close at hand'. And so this man too who died with such joyful confidence and such confident joy is rightly commemorated with joy by the Church.

6. But what reason can there be for considering a death joyful which was not accompanied with any festal joy, or how could anyone derive joy from the knowledge that he was about to die if he knew that he would go down into darkness with no certainty that he would be consoled by a speedy release? One of the saints of the Old Law when he was told to put his house in order because he was going to die, turned his face to the wall and wept bitterly and implored some deferment of the hated death. When at last the dreaded time had come he said, miserably lamenting it: 'I must go down to the gates of the world beneath, in the noontide of my years'; and a little later:

'No more shall I lift my eyes to the Lord God in this land of the living, nor shall I see again the faces of men and quiet homes'. And another says: 'Ah, if the grave were only a place of shelter, where thou wouldst hide me away until thy anger was spent, with a time appointed when thou wouldst bethink thyself of me again'. And Israel said to his sons: 'Thou wouldst send down my grey hairs sorrowing to the grave'. What joy or occasion for festive celebration is there in deaths such as these?

7. On the other hand, our own martyrs desire to die and be with Christ, for they know that where the body is there too will be gathered together the eagles. Soon shall the righteous keep holiday there and rejoice at the sight of him, glad and content. There, most loving Jesu, there shall thy countenance fill the holy man with joy as soon as he is taken out of this wicked world. There one voice shall cry with everlasting jubilee, one voice of joy and salvation in the dwellings of the just: 'Safe, like a bird rescued from the fowler's snare; the snare is broken now, and we are safe'. How could those who sit in darkness and the shadow of death sing this song, while there is no one to redeem them and none to save them; when the day star from on high, Christ the firstfruits of them that slept, had not yet visited them? Rightly therefore does the Church, who knows how to rejoice with the joyful and weep with the sorrowful, distinguish because of the time they died between those whom she judges equal in valour, believing that the descent into Limbo should not be honoured with the same veneration as the passage into life.

8. And so while the cause makes the martyrdom, yet the time and nature of it determine a distinction. Time separates the Machabees from the new martyrs and unites them with the old, but the nature of their death has separated them from the old, and united them with the new. And, for the aforesaid reasons, these differences are observed by the Church. But the Prophet tells us what is common to all the martyrs in the sight of God when he says: 'Precious in the sight of the Lord is the death of his saints', and he explains why their death is said to be precious when he tells us: 'When he shall give sleep to his beloved: behold the inheritance of the Lord are children; the reward, the fruit of the womb'. But we must not think that only the martyrs are beloved of God, for we must remember what was said of Lazarus: 'Lazarus our friend sleeps'. And then it is said: 'Blessed are the dead who die in the Lord', meaning that not only are they blessed who die for the Lord like martyrs, but also they who die in the Lord like confessors. There are then two things which seem to me to render a death precious; the life which preceded it, and the cause of the death, and more the cause than the life. But most precious of all is that death which is recommended both by the cause of it and the life which preceded it.

LETTER 99

TO A CERTAIN MONK

THE messenger by whom you say you have been disturbed was sent by Brother William, not in his interests, but in yours. He is a man who by the grace of God habitually acts bravely, making quite sure that the saying ' A double minded man is inconstant in all his ways' does not apply to himself. Because he walks before God simply, and therefore confidently, he is not subject to that curse which says: ' Woe to the sinner that will go two ways about it to enter the land of his desire '. But I had heard that you had been involved in some quarrel and, to the grave scandal of your abbot and brethren, had left your monastery and gone to live in I don't know what sort of inaccessible place. I was much worried by this rumour and anxiously asked myself how I could help you and could think of nothing better than to ask you to visit me, so that I might first reassure myself by seeing you and speedily help you while we were together. But by my letter to you and yours to me we have both repelled any shadow of suspicion we might have had of each other and can now set our minds at rest on the matter. The sincerity of our affection has been proved by this false rumour, and I think it has been not unfruitfully renewed by our mutual anxiety for each other. I would now gladly enjoy this fruit if you are at liberty to visit me; but if you are not, it were better for me to be content with my own sterility than to enjoy the fruit of your company at inconvenience to yourself.

LETTER 100

TO A CERTAIN BISHOP

IF I had known you to be less in earnest than you are in what you have undertaken, then I should have had to exhort and conjure you. But now, as your devotion has run ahead of my intention, it remains only for me to render thanks unto God and to pray that he may give you the strength to accomplish what he has given you the grace to desire. Yet I will not hide my joy from you. You cannot guess how your intention has filled my heart with gladness. ' My soul will be delighted with good things' when I see you tireless in good and salutary works. I rejoice in your good intentions, not because I am seeking gifts, but because I look for the fruit in you; I gladly accept your favours because they benefit you, otherwise I would be devoid of that charity which ' seeketh not its own '. Indeed you are benefiting yourself even more than me for ' it is more blessed to give than to receive '. Your generosity highly becomes a bishop, it graces your priesthood, it is a precious jewel in your crown, and it is a credit to your high position. If a man is prevented from being poor because of the position he holds, then let him prove himself a lover of poverty by his actions. ' Blessed are the poor ', but ' poor in spirit ', not in goods.

LETTER 101

TO A CERTAIN CHANCELLOR

To the noble and honourable S., Chancellor, health in the Lord, from Bernard, Abbot of Clairvaux.

GOD has given you many good things in this life, but it is much to be feared that, unless you derive from your worldly and temporal goods some profit for your soul, you will lose the eternal joys of heaven for the sake of the passing and deceitful pleasures of time. In all simplicity, I would therefore suggest that some . . .[1] of our brothers wish to divide and build an abbey. If you wish to keep them by building for them a place on your property, as you can easily do, I beg you to notify me by the bearer of this letter. Surely your great sickness, of which I have heard, is a warning from God that you should succour your soul endangered among the false pleasures of the world, by this or some other good work.

LETTER 102

TO CERTAIN RELIGIOUS

I AM returning Brother Lambert to you. When he arrived here he was rather unsettled in certain respects, but your prayers have restored calm to him and he is no longer troubled by his former scruples. I have carefully enquired into the cause of his coming here and also the reason and nature of his leaving you. His intentions seem to have been above reproach, but there is certainly no excuse for his leaving you in the way he did, namely without permission. And so having scolded him for this as he deserved, I am returning him to you suitably chastened and now quite composed. When he comes back I beg you, dearest brothers, to be lenient in the matter of his presumption, for he is quite simple about it and without any malice whatsoever. He came straight here without turning to right or left, because he knew that all of us here are your loyal friends and faithful followers. As spiritual men, I beg you to receive him in the spirit of gentleness, confirming the charity which is in him and forgiving, on account of his good intentions, his mistaken departure. I am sure that, by the mercy of him who is all-powerful, any annoyance you may have felt at his irregular exit will soon vanish when you see the change in him for the better.

[1] MS. here defective.

LETTER 103

TO A CERTAIN ABBOT

This letter is an excellent commentary on the 28th chapter of St. Benedict's Holy Rule.

ABOUT that troubled and troublesome brother who has no respect for his superiors, my advice to you is brief but trustworthy. It is the devil's endeavour to go around the house of God seeking whom he may devour, and it is your duty to keep a sharp look-out so that he does not find a way in. The more he tries to separate a weak lamb from the rest of the flock, so that he can carry him off all the easier for there being no one to rescue him, the more it behoves you to withstand him with all your might, so that he can never snatch a lamb from your hands and boast: ' I have prevailed against him '. Do all that charity requires of you to save the brother, spare neither kindness, wholesome advice, rebukes in private, exhortations in public, and if necessary sharp words and sharp floggings, but above all, what is usually more efficacious than anything in these cases, do you and the brethren pray for him.

2. If you have tried all this and availed nothing, then you must have recourse to the advice of the Apostle and ' put away the evil one '. The evil one must be put away lest he lead others into evil. A bad tree can only give bad fruit. So I say ' put him away ', but not in the way he would want. That is to say do not let him go with your licence, for if you do he will deceive himself into thinking that he can legitimately live contrary to his vows outside his monastery, beyond all reach of discipline, as his own master and according to his own sweet will. But turn him out as a diseased sheep is turned out of the flock, as a gangrenous limb is cut off from the body. Let him under-stand clearly that from henceforth you will regard him as ' a heathen and a publican '. Do not have any fear that by thus preserving the peace of all at the cost of one,[1] you will be acting contrary to charity. The malice of one brother can easily disturb the unity of the whole. Let those words of Solomon comfort you: ' No man can set him straight at whom God looks askance ', and those of our Saviour: ' Every plant which my heavenly Father hath not planted, shall be rooted up ', and what the blessed John has said about schismatics: ' They went out from us because they were not of us ', and again the words of the Apostle: ' If the unbeliever depart, let him depart '. The godless ought not to be left in the domain of the just, else the just will stretch out their hands to wickedness. Better that one should perish than the unity of all.

---

[1] *Ne timeas esse contra caritatem si unius scandalum multorum recompensaveris pace.*

LETTER 104

TO THE BROTHER OF WILLIAM, A MONK OF CLAIRVAUX

The William mentioned in this letter is said to be the same as the William mentioned in Letter 99.

ALTHOUGH I have not met you and although, as regards the body, you live a long way from me, yet you are a friend, and my friendship for you renders you present and well known to me. This friendship has been given you without your knowledge: a gift not of flesh and blood, but of the spirit of God which has united your brother William to me in the bonds of spiritual love and everlasting friendship, and you through him to me, if you think it worth your while. Be wise and do not spurn the friendship of those whom very Truth calls blessed and proclaims the kings of heaven. We do not grudge you this blessedness, for we lose nothing by sharing it with you. Our kingdom would not be restricted if you were also king. Why should we grudge you a share in a kingdom which the multitude of those who share takes nothing from the share which each one enjoys? I wish you to be a friend of the poor, but I would rather you were poor yourself. The former is the stage of the proficient, the latter of the perfect. By friendship with the poor we consort with kings, but by love of poverty we become kings ourselves. The Kingdom of Heaven belongs to the poor, and kings have the power to make their friends happy when they wish. ' Make friends of the mammon of iniquity, that when you shall fail, they may receive you into everlasting dwellings.' You see how great is the dignity of holy poverty. It does not seek patronage for itself, but it is able to extend it to those who need it.[1] What sort of thing is this that, without the help of angels or men, simply by trusting in divine grace, is able to penetrate of itself to the vision of glory, to reach the summits of existence, to scale the very heights of all splendour?

2. Now I want you to consider without any self-deception how material things are keeping you from all this. Alas, it is but smoke, here now and then gone, which blocks your way to everlasting joy, which clouds the brightness of the light eternal, which cheats you of true knowledge, which robs you of great nobility! Why do you prefer to such glory the mere grass which is here to-day and on the fire to-morrow, the flesh and all its false glamour? For ' the flesh is but grass, and the glory of it but grass in flower '. If you are wise, if you have any heart, if your eyes are at all open to the light, cease

[1] An interpretation of this rather difficult passage, not uncommon among the Fathers. St. Bernard probably had in mind the twenty-first book and fourteenth chapter of St. Gregory's *Moralia* where we are told that we should consider our alms as gifts to patrons who will receive us into their eternal dwellings.

trying to chase what, when you do attain, is nothing but tribulation. Blessed is the man who does not go after such things, for they are only a burden; they soil the man who sets his heart upon them, and in their passing they cause untold suffering. Is it not better honourably to spurn them than sorrowfully to lose them? Is it not better to give them up for the love of Christ than to lose them in death? Death is a robber in ambush from whose clutches you cannot save either yourself or your goods. Nor can you protect yourself against him, for he comes as a thief in the night. You have brought nothing into the world and assuredly you will take nothing out. You sleep your sleep and lo! in the morning your hands are empty. But you know all this. I must not waste time in teaching you what you know already, I will do better to pray that you may be granted the grace to act according to the knowledge that has already been given you.

LETTER 105

TO MASTER WALTER OF CHAUMONT

I AM filled with sadness for you, my dear Walter, when I think of the flower of your youth, the brightness of your intelligence, the ornaments of your knowledge and scholarship and, what more becomes a Christian than all these, your noble bearing, all being wasted in futile studies and the pursuit of what is merely passing, when they would be so much better used in the service of Christ. God forbid that a sudden death should snatch them from you, that all should suddenly wither like grass in the fury of a burning wind, fall from you like leaves from autumn trees. What fruit will you have then of all your labours upon earth? What return will you be able to make to God for all that he has given you? What will you have to show for all the talents he has entrusted to you? What will happen to you, if with empty hands you stand before him who, although he willingly gave you all your gifts, will nevertheless exact a strict account of how you have used them? He will come, he will soon come, who will demand back with increase what was his own. He will take away all those gifts which have earned you such spectacular, but such treacherous, applause in your own country. Noble birth, a lithe body, a comely appearance, a distinguished bearing, are great acquisitions, but the credit of them belongs to him who gave them. You may use them for your own advantage, but there is one who will enquire into it and judge if you do.

2. Let us suppose that you may, for the time being, claim all the credit for yourself, that you may glory in your renown and the title you have of master, and win for yourself a great name on earth. What will happen to all this when you are dead? What will be left of it but the memory, and even this only upon earth, for it is written:

' There they sleep on, empty handed, the warriors in their pride '?
And if this is to be the end of all your labours, will you pardon me for
asking, what more have you than the beasts of the field? When your
charger is dead, what more can be said of it than that it was a good
beast? Ask yourself how you will answer at that terrible judgement
for having received your soul, and such a soul, in vain, if you have
paid no more attention to your immortal and rational spirit than any
brute beast whose soul ceases to exist the moment it ceases to animate
its body. Wherein, think you, lies your worth, you who are made
in the image of your creator, if you care not for this, your sole title
to the great dignity you enjoy as a man? Because you do not understand this, because you concern yourself with nothing spiritual or
eternal but, like the brute beasts whose soul dies with their body, are
content only with passing and material things, because you are blind
to the counsel of the Gospel: ' Labour not for the bread that perisheth
but that which endureth for life everlasting ', you are become ' like
the brute beasts and not better than they '. It is written that only
he shall go up the mountain of God who ' has not received his soul in
vain ', and not even he shall do so unless he be also ' guiltless in act
and clean of heart '. It is for you to decide whether you can dare
say this of yourself. If you cannot, then consider that reward will
be meted out to wickedness, if mere unfruitfulness incurs damnation.
Certainly thorns and briars will not be spared when the axe is laid
to the unfruitful tree, stinging plants will not escape when the unfruitful
tree is threatened. Woe therefore, and woe again to him of whom it
can be said: ' He should have borne grapes, but he bore wild grapes
instead '.

3. I know that you can think all this out clearly and fully without
my prompting you, but that the love you have for your mother
prevents you from following your convictions by completely
abandoning what in your heart you despise. What can I say about
this? You live with your mother and were I to tell you to leave
her it would seem inhuman. But on the other hand it is not for her
good that she should be the cause of your perdition. Perhaps you
can serve both the world and Christ? But no man can serve two
masters. Your mother wishes what will impede your salvation and
so impede hers as well. Choose which you prefer: you can either
serve her wishes or both her salvation and yours. If you truly love
her, it is for her good that you should leave her. If you leave Christ
in order to be with your mother, on your account she too will perish.
She who gave you birth would be ill paid if she were to perish on your
account. But how could she not perish who has destroyed the son
to whom she gave birth? I have spoken in this way in consideration
to the flesh and in deference to natural affection. But it is a true
saying, worthy of all acceptance, that although it is wicked to disregard

one's mother, yet to do so for Christ's sake is most righteous, for he who said, ' Honour thy father and mother ', also said, ' He who loves father or mother more than me, is not worthy of me '.[1]

LETTER 106

TO ROMANUS, A SUBDEACON OF THE CURIA AT ROME

To his dear friend Romanus, all that he could wish for a friend, from Bernard Abbot of Clairvaux.

You did well, my dear friend, to renew by your letter the pleasant memory I have of you and excuse the tiresome delay.   Forgetfulness of you can never steal you from the hearts of those that miss you but, I must confess, I had begun to think you had almost forgotten about yourself.   Have done with delay and do at once what you say in your letter you intend to do !   Prove by what you do the sincerity of what you write.   Why delay to give birth to the spirit of salvation which you have conceived already?   Nothing is more certain for mortals than death, nothing more uncertain than the hour of death: like a thief in the night it will come.   Woe to them that are with child in that hour !   If it should come upon and forestall that life-giving birth, alas, it will undermine the house and destroy the holy seed: ' For when they shall say peace and security; then shall sudden destruction come upon them, as the pains upon her that is with child '. I do not wish you to escape death, but I do wish that at any rate you should have no cause to fear it.   The righteous man, although he does not guard against death, yet he does not fear it.[2] ' Though he should die before his time, rest shall be his.'   He dies certainly, but his death is safe, for as he departs this life he enters a better one.   It is a good death which dies to sin that it may live to righteousness.   And this death to sin must come first if that final death is to be safe.   While you are still in this life, lay up treasure which will last for ever in the next.   Die to the world while you are in the body that after the death of the body you may live for ever in God.   What matter if death does rend your bodily raiment if it straightway clothes you in joy?   How ' blessed are the dead, who die in the Lord ', they shall hear the Spirit say ' from henceforth now you may rest from your labours ' !   And not only shall they rest from their labours, they shall also experience a great joy from the newness of life which will be theirs, and the safety that will last for ever.   The death of the righteous is good because of its rest, better because of its new life, and best of all because of its safety.   On the other hand, ' the death of the wicked is very evil '.   It is very evil because for them loss of the world is grievous, separation from the body worse, and the twofold suffering of worm and

---

[1] St. Jerome, *Ep.* 14.
[2] *Justus quippe mortem, etsi non cavet, tamen non pavet.*

fire worst of all. Come then, make haste, go forth and depart, die the death of the righteous that your end may be the same as theirs. How precious in the sight of the Lord is the death of his saints! Fly, I implore you, and linger no more where sinners walk. How can you live where you would be afraid to die? And, you can be sure, I shall be ready, according to the words of the Prophet, ' to bring out bread ' to you in flight.

LETTER 107

TO HENRY MURDAC

For Henry Murdac, see Letter 174, *the introductory note to Letter* 173, *and the note on ' The Dispute over the Election of the Archbishop of York', pp.* 259–61.

To his dear friend Henry Murdac, health, and not only in this life, from Bernard, styled Abbot of Clairvaux.

WHAT wonder if you are tossed about between prosperity and adversity since you have not yet gained a foothold on the rock. But if you have sworn and are determined to keep the just commandments of the Lord, neither prosperity nor adversity can sever you from the love of Christ. Oh if you only knew, if only I could explain to you! ' Such things as were never known from the beginning, as ear never heard, eye never saw, save at thy command, thou, O God, hast made ready for all that await thy aid.' I hear, brother, that you are reading the Prophets; think you that you understand what you read? If you do, you will perceive that it is to Christ which they refer. And if you would grasp him, you will do so sooner by following him than by reading of him. Why seek the Word amidst written words, when in the flesh he stands before your eyes? He has long since left his hiding place in the Prophets and appeared unto the Fishermen. Like a bridegroom from his bridal bed he has leapt from the shady coverts of the mountain sides and run into the open pastures of the Gospels. Let him who has ears to hear, hear him crying out in the Temple: ' Whosoever thirsts, let him come to me and drink ', and: ' Come unto me, all ye who labour and are burdened, and I will refresh you '. Are you afraid that you will break down where Truth himself has promised to refresh you? Certainly if the ' dark waters from the clouds of the air ' please you so much, you will be more than delighted with the clear water that springs from the fountains of the Saviour.

2. If you could but once taste for a moment the ' full ears of corn on which Jerusalem feasts ' how gladly would you leave the dry husks for Jewish hacks to gnaw! If I could but have you as my fellow in the school of piety of which Jesus is the master! If only I might submit the vessel of your heart when it has been purified to the unction which

teaches all things! How gladly would I share with you the warm loaves which, still piping hot, fresh, as it were, from the oven, Christ of his heavenly bounty so often breaks with his poor! Would that when God sweetly deigns to shed on his poor servant a drop of that heavenly dew which he keeps for his chosen, I might presently pour it forth upon you and in turn receive from you what you feel! Believe me who have experience, you will find much more labouring amongst the woods than you ever will amongst books. Woods and stones will teach you what you can never hear from any master. Do you imagine you cannot suck honey from the rocks and oil from the hardest stone; that the mountains do not drop sweetness and the hills flow with milk and honey; that the valleys are not filled with corn? So many things occur to me which I could say to you that I can hardly restrain myself. But as it is for prayers and not a sermon that you have asked me, I will pray God that with his laws and his commandments he may open your heart. Farewell.

P.S. Ivo and William join me in saying the same.[1] What more can I add to what I have said? You know very well that I wish to see you and the reason why; but how much I wish to see you, that you could never guess, nor I tell you. I pray God that he will give you the grace to follow me where you should have led the way. I believe you to be so great a master in humility that you would not object, although a master, to following your disciples.

LETTER 108

TO THOMAS, PROVOST OF BEVERLEY

To Thomas, Provost of Beverley, and a youth of great promise, that he may learn by the example of his namesake, the Apostle, from Bernard, the servant of the Poor of Christ at Clairvaux.

IVO who knows you has suggested to me, whom you do not know, that I should write to you; and charity prompts me to do so. He has told me all he wished of what he knew about you, and charity, which believes all things, could not hear and remain idle. Not idle, I say, as regards myself, because as soon as I had heard what Ivo had to say of you, I was compelled by charity to write to you, to exhort you, to pray for you. Whether with any effect or not rests with you. I confess that what I have heard of you from those who know you, pleases me. I do not mean your noble lineage, your courtly bearing, your handsome figure, your riches, or your exalted rank. All these and the like are mortal things and will fade like the flowers of the field. I refer to your strong character, your noble demeanour, and

---

[1] *Idipsum ipsi Willelmus et Ivo.* Eales translates: ' Let William and Ivo too have share in this my prayer '. Mabillon believes that Ivo is the brother of William to whom Letter 104 is addressed.

especially to that love of holy poverty which, I am told, you have lately conceived amidst your riches. And so while warmly congratulating you, I have conceived great hopes for you, which I trust will not be disappointed. May this my joy speedily reach even to the angels in heaven who are prepared to make great joy over you, as they are over the conversion and repentance of all sinners. If only it were to fall to my lot to husband the flower of your youth, to gather such an example of good dispositions; if only I were permitted to save it intact for God, to offer it unblemished, a sweet fragrance acceptable to the Lord.

2. Perhaps your conscience will answer to this that I have spoken too late, that your youth has already been soiled with too many sins for it to be possible to preserve it unblemished. This does not dismay me. A sinner myself, I feel no repugnance towards a sinner. I do not spurn the diseased, since I am aware that I too am diseased. Even if you believe me to be whole, I do not refuse ' to become weak to a weak man, that I may gain the weak '; I gladly listen to Paul in this matter, when he says: ' You who are spiritual, instruct such an one in the spirit of meekness, considering thyself lest thou also be tempted '. The gravity of the sickness is nothing to me when I consider the skill of the Physician, and also his pity which is so well known to me in my own grievous ills. No matter how great your sins may be, how foul may be your conscience, even though you may be conscious that your youth is polluted with dreadful atrocities, even though grown old in years ill spent ' you have become rotten like a beast on a dung heap ', yet you shall be cleansed and become whiter than snow, and your youth shall be restored as the eagle's plumage. I know who it is that says: ' Where sin abounded grace did more abound '. The good Physician heals all mortal ills, and contents all our desires for good.

3. A good conscience is a mine of wealth. And in truth what greater riches can there be, what thing more sweet than a good conscience? What is there on earth to give such peace and such serenity? A good conscience fears no material loss, no invective can touch it, and no physical pain can hurt it; death itself cannot bring it low, but only lift it up. What, I ask, amongst the goods of the earth is there to compare with such happiness as this? What thing like this can the world, for all its blandishments, offer to its lovers? What thing like this can the world, for all its lies, hold out to fools? Vast estates, a prelate's robes, the sceptre of a king; all this, yes. But not to mention all the hazards without which such things cannot be won or held, is it not true to say that at the first touch of death all is lost? It is written: ' There they sleep on, empty handed, the rich men in their pride '. But the wealth of a good conscience lives again, it does not wither away in travail, it does not pass away in death, it flowers again. It gives joy to the living, it consoles the dying, it

refreshes the dead. But why dwell in words upon the truth of what I am ready to prove by deeds. It is for you to prove me a liar or yourself a rich man. Only come and see. With what joyous steps will I not run out ' with bread to meet the fleeing man ', with what glad embraces shall I not receive my youngest son. ' Quickly shall the first robe be brought forth for you and a ring put on your finger, and I shall say:' This my son was dead but he lives again, was lost and is found.'

LETTER 109

TO THE SAME

This Thomas had promised himself to Clairvaux.[1] *But as he showed great reluctance to fulfil his promise, St. Bernard wrote the following letter to encourage him. But the warning and encouragement of the saint fell on deaf ears, for Thomas died suddenly, his promise still unfulfilled.*

To Thomas, his dear son, from Bernard as to a son.

WHAT need of words? A fervent spirit and eager heart cannot be expressed by the tongue alone. I need your presence also to tell me of your good will. If you were present you could both explain yourself and know me better. Even now we are tied to each other by a mutual debt, I by a debt of faithful care for you and you by the debt of humble obedience to me. I wish you to apply to yourself and to prove in me that saying of the Only-Begotten: ' The works which the Father has given me to perfect, they give testimony of me '. So in truth, even so the Spirit of the Son bears testimony to our spirit that we too are sons of God when he lifts us from the works of death and bestows upon us the works of life. It is not from the leaves or the blossom but from the fruit that we can tell a good tree from a bad, for it is ' by their fruits that ye shall know them '. It is therefore by their works that the sons of God are distinguished from the ' sons of unbelief', and it is by works that you too will prove the sincerity of your own desire and put mine to the test.

2. I long for and, indeed, require your promised and expected presence here. Do you ask why? It is not because I look for any natural satisfaction in your presence, but simply because I wish both to profit you and profit by you. The nobility of your birth, the strength of your body, the comeliness of your appearance, the grace of your youth, your estates, mansion, and gorgeous furniture, the marks of your high station, and on the top of all this your worldly wisdom; all these are of the world, and the world loves its own. But for how long? Certainly not for ever, since the world will not last

---

[1] *Thomas iste Ordini Cisterciensi in Claravalle sese devoverat . . .* , so Mabillon. But surely not as Eales translates: ' Thomas had taken the vows of the Cistercian Order at Clairvaux '.

for ever, but not even for a long time. The world will not acknowledge all these things in you for long because you will not have them
for long: the days of man are short. The world and its glory pass;
and it will part with you before it passes. Why does this love, which
you will so soon lose, please you so unboundedly? I love you for
your own sake and not for the sake of your possessions, let these go
to where they belong. Remember your promise and do not deny
me any longer the satisfaction of your presence, I who love you so
truly and will love you for ever. United by a pure love in life, we will
not be separated in death. Those things which I desire in you, or
rather for you, do not belong to the body, they are not subject to time,
so they do not fail with the body or pass with time, rather when the
body has been laid aside the joy of them increases and they last for ever.
They have nothing in common with the things I have enumerated
above, things with which the world, but not the Father, has endowed
you. These all vanish at the hour of death, if they have not vanished
before.

3. It is the best part which will never be taken away. And what
is this best part? ' Eye has not seen, ear has not heard, nor has it
entered into the heart of man to conceive it.' A man who lives as a
man or, to speak more clearly, a man who complies with flesh and
blood, knows nothing of it, because flesh and blood do not disclose it,
but only God by his Spirit. The merely animal man is never admitted
to this secret, he does not perceive the things that are of God. Blessed
are those who hear, ' I have called you friends, because all things,
whatsoever I have heard from the Father, I have made known to you '.
How wicked is the world, which only favours its friends so as to make
them the enemies of God and accordingly unworthy of the counsel
of the blessed. Clearly the world which wishes to be your friend is
the enemy of God.[1] And if the servant knows not what his lord does,
how much less does the enemy! Moreover the friend of the Bridegroom stands and is so overjoyed at the voice of the Bridegroom that
he says: ' How my heart melted at the sound of his voice!' And
so the friend of the world is excluded from the counsels of the friends
of God, who have not received the spirit of this world but the Spirit
of God that they may know what God has given them. I praise thee,
my Father, because thou hast hidden these things from the wise and
prudent and revealed them to children. Even so, Father, because it
seemed good in thy sight, not because they have deserved it of themselves. For all have sinned and are destitute of thy glory, so that thou
sendeth thy Spirit, without their deserving it, crying in the hearts of
these, thy adopted sons, ' Abba, Father '. Those who are led by thy
Spirit are thy sons, and will not be left out of the counsels of their
Father. Within them they have dwelling the Spirit which searches

---

[1] *Plane enim qui amicus vult esse tuus, inimicus Dei constituitur.*

even the hidden things of God. Of what could they be ignorant who are taught all things by the unction of God?

4. Woe to you, children of this world, foolish in your prudence, knowing nothing of the life-giving spirit, nor sharing in the counsels which well up only between the Father and the Son and him to whom the Son will reveal them. For ' who has known the mind of the Lord or who has been his counsellor?' Not indeed no one ever, but only someone sometimes, only those who can truthfully say: ' The only-begotten Son who is in the bosom of the Father, he hath declared to us'. Woe to the world for its clamour! The Only-Begotten cries among the people like an angel of great counsel: ' Who hath ears to hear let him hear '. And since he can find no ears worthy to hear the secret which the Father has imparted to him, he disguises it under parables for the crowd, that hearing they may not hear and seeing they may not understand. But to his friends he whispers apart: ' To you it has been given to know the mysteries of the Kingdom of God ', and he also says to them: ' Fear not, little flock, for it has pleased your Father to give you a kingdom '. And who are these friends of his? Without doubt those ' whom he foreknew and predestined to be made conformable to the image of his Son, so that he might be the firstborn among many brethren'. This is his great and secret counsel. The Lord knows who are his own, but what was hitherto only known to God has now been revealed to men. He does not deign to allow others to share in this great mystery, unless they are those whom he has known and foreordained to be his own. Those whom he has foreordained, he has also called. Who else indeed would be admitted to the counsels of God but those who are called? And ' those whom he has called, them he has also justified '. Over them the Sun rises, not the sun which is seen to shine every day on the good and bad alike, since only to those who are called is the prophetic promise made: ' Unto you that fear my name the Sun of Justice shall rise '. While the sons of unbelief stay out in the darkness, the sons of light go out from the power of darkness into this new light, providing they can truthfully say to God: ' We partake with all them that fear thee '. Do you see how fear must go first so that justification may follow? Perhaps it can be said that we are called by fear and justified by love. Finally: ' The just man lives by faith ', the faith surely ' that worketh by charity '.

5. And so let the sinner hear and be afraid and approach the Sun of Justice to be enlightened and see what he has to love. What is that? ' Those who fear the Lord know no beginning or end of his mercy.' They know no beginning on account of their being preordained, and they know no end because their blessedness shall never end. The first has no beginning and the latter has no end. Those whom he has foreordained from the beginning, he makes blessed without end, their

calling and justification, at least in the case of adults, coming between. Thus from the rising up of the Sun of Justice, the great mystery concerning predestination and beatification, hidden from before the beginning of time, begins at last to come forth from the depths of eternity, while each one who is called by fear and justified by love dares to believe that he also may be among the blessed, knowing that 'whom he has justified, them also he has glorified'. What then? The soul hears her call and is struck by fear. She then feels herself to be justified and is swamped with love. Does she doubt that she is also to be glorified? Initiated and then lifted up, can she despair of the consummation? If fear of the Lord, in which I have said the call consists, is the beginning of wisdom, what else is the love of God but progress in wisdom, the love, that is, which for the time being comes from faith and is the source of our justification? If this is so, what else but consummation in wisdom is that glorification from the divine and deifying vision which we hope for in the end? ' So one depth makes answer to another amid the roar of the floods ', when in terror of his judgements, that immense eternity and eternal immensity, of whose wisdom none can make a reckoning, leads in terror of his judgements but with wonderful goodness and power the corrupt and inscrutable heart of man into his eternal light.

6. For example, let us suppose a man in the world still held by love of the world and the flesh; a man carrying the image of an earthly man, still resting in earthly things. Who, but one himself sitting in the same shadow of death, could not see that such a man is wrapped about with horrible darkness? No sun of salvation has yet shone on him, no interior inspiration bears testimony to him of his eternal salvation. But if at some time the mercy of heaven should graciously regard him and send down on him the spirit of compunction, so that he comes to his senses with a groan, changes his life, calls upon God, and decides in future to live for God and not the world, would not such a one, in this undeserved visitation of heavenly light, in this sudden change of the right hand of the Most High, see himself to be no longer a son of wrath but of grace? Would not such a one, having experienced in himself the effect of divine goodness which had hitherto been so hidden from him that he could not know whether he was worthy of hatred or love, but seemed by the witness of his life to be worthy of hatred, for darkness was over the face of the abyss, would not such a one appear to have been rescued from a most deep and dark pit of horrible ignorance, and plunged into a pleasant region bright with eternal light?

7. Then at last the darkness is, as it were, divided from the light when the sinner is enlightened by the Sun of Justice, casts aside the works of darkness and puts on the arms of light; when he who by his former life and conscience was doomed as a true son of perdition

to the eternal flames, draws breath in such a great visitation of the day star from on high and begins, beyond all expectation, to glory in the hopes of the children of God.   As he is ravished by the near prospect of this vision, gazing upon it in the light which has newly come to him, he cries: ' The sun of thy favour shines out clear above us; thou hast made me glad at heart'. ' O Lord, what is man that thou shouldst notice him, or the son of man that thou shouldst give heed to him?' Already, O loving Father, that most vile worm, worthy of everlasting hatred, is confident that it is loved because it feels that it loves: or rather because it divines that it is loved, it is ashamed not to love in return.   Now in thy light, O Light Inaccessible, it becomes clear what good things thou hast had in store for that miserable thing man even when he was evil.   He loves indeed, but not without reason, for he knows that he is loved without desert; he loves without end because he knows that he was loved before the beginning of time.   A great secret which from all eternity has remained hidden in the bosom of eternity has now been revealed in the light of day for the consolation of the wretched: God does not want the death of a sinner but that he should be converted and live.   As a witness, O man, to this secret you have the Spirit which justifies testifying to your own spirit, that you, even you, are a son of God. See the design of God in the justification of yourself and declare and say: ' Thy decrees are my counsellors!'   Your present justification is both a revelation of the divine plan and a preparation for future glory.   Or rather predestination itself is the preparation for it and justification the approach to it.   It is said: ' Do penance, for the kingdom of heaven is at hand'.   Now hear how predestination is the preparation for it: ' Possess you the kingdom prepared for you from the foundation of the world '.

8. Let no one who loves God have any doubt that God loves him. The love of God for us precedes our love for him and it also follows it. How could he be reluctant to love us in return for our love when he loved us even when we did not love him?   I say he loved us.   As a pledge of his love you have the Spirit, and you have a faithful witness to it in Jesus, Jesus crucified.   A double and irrefutable argument of God's love for us.   Christ died and so deserved our love.   The holy Spirit works upon us and makes us love him.[1]   Christ has given us a reason for loving himself, the Spirit the power to love him.   The one commends his great love to us, the other gives it.   In the one we see the object of our love, by the other we have the power to love.   The former provides the occasion for our love, the latter provides the love itself.   How shameful it would be to look with ungrateful eyes upon the Son of God dying for us!   But this could easily be were the Spirit lacking. ' The charity of God is poured forth in our hearts by

---

[1] *Spiritus afficit et facit amari.*

the Holy Ghost who is given to us.' Loved we love in return, and loving we deserve to be still more loved. If while we were still his enemies we were reconciled to God by the death of his Son, how much more being reconciled shall we be saved through his life. Why so? ' He that spared not even his own son, but delivered him up for us all, how hath he not also, with him, given us all things? '

9. Since then we hold a twofold token of our salvation, the double pouring forth of Blood and Spirit; neither avails without the other. The Spirit is not given to any but those who believe in Christ crucified, and faith avails not unless it is actuated by love. But love is the gift of the Holy Spirit. And if the second Adam (I mean Christ) became not only a living soul, but also a quickening spirit, by one dying and by the other raising the dead, how can that which died in him avail me without that which gives life? ' The flesh profiteth nothing, it is the spirit that quickeneth.' And what else does quickeneth mean but justifieth? Since sin is the death of the soul (for the ' soul that sinneth, the same shall die ') the life of it is undoubtedly righteousness, for ' the just man lives by faith '. And who is just, but he who pays his debt of love to God who loves him? And this can never be except the Spirit reveal by faith the eternal designs of God for his future salvation. And this revelation is nothing else but an infusion of spiritual grace through which, while mortifying the works of the flesh, a man is made ready for the kingdom which flesh and blood cannot possess. He receives at the same time and in the same Spirit both the audacity to believe himself loved and the power to love in return, so that he should not be loved without return.

10. This is that holy and secret counsel which the Son receives in the Holy Spirit from the Father, and communicates to his own whom he knows, by the same Spirit, justifying them by communicating it, and communicating it by justifying them. Thus a man is justified so that he begins to know himself even as he is known; that is, he begins to experience something of his future blessedness, as it has lain hidden from all eternity in God who foreordained it, to appear all the more plainly in him when he confers it. And for this great blessing which he has received let him rejoice for the time being in hope, but not yet in security. How pitiful on the other hand are those who as yet hold no token of their call to such a joyful council of the just! ' What credence, O Lord, to such news as ours! ' Oh that they may be wise and understand. But except they believe they shall not understand.

11. O unhappy and foolhardy lovers of this world, you too have your counsels, but they are far apart from the counsels of the just! Scale adheres to scale, there is no vent between you.[1] You too, I say, even you, O impious ones, share a counsel together, but one against God and against Christ. For if, according to Scripture, ' piety is the

---

[1] *Squama squamæ conjungitur, et non est spiraculum in vobis.*

worship of God', it follows that whoever loves the world more than God is guilty of idolatry and impiety in that he worships and serves creatures rather than the Creator. But between the counsels of the impious and those of the righteous there is fixed a great gulf. For as the righteous keep far aloof from the counsel and council of evil-doers, so the wicked shall not rise to plead their cause, nor sinners have any part in the reunion of the just. For there is a counsel of the just, a grateful shower, which God has kept for his chosen, a truly secret counsel, coming down nevertheless like dew on to fleece. It is a sealed fountain of living waters of which no stranger may partake. It is the glory of the Sun of Justice which rises only on those who fear God.

12. When the Prophet adverts to the impious who remain in their aridity and blindness and are not privy to the rains and light of the just, he mocks at them and points them out as persons wrapt in gloom, confused and overcast, saying: 'Here is the people who will not listen to the voice of God'. O wretched people, you will not say with David: 'Let me listen to the voice of the Lord God within me'. You pour yourselves out on the vanities and follies, and will not listen to the intimate and most excellent words of truth. 'Great ones of the world, will your hearts be always hardened? Will you never cease setting your hearts on shadows, following a lie?' Will you always remain deaf to the voice of truth, ignoring the counsel of God who bears peace in his mind and speaks words of peace to his people, his holy ones, those whose hearts are turned unto him? 'Now you are clean', he said, 'by reason of what I have spoken to you.' And accordingly those who do not hear what he has said to them are not clean.

13. But do you, dearest son, if you would prepare the ear of your heart to hear the voice of God, sweeter than honey and the honey-comb, fly exterior cares, so that, with your spiritual sense free and unimpeded, you can say with Samuel: 'Speak, Lord, for thy servant heareth'. This voice is not heard in the market place nor does it sound in public. A secret counsel demands a secret hearing. Without doubt it will give you great joy and delight if you lend a prudent ear to it. Abraham was commanded to go forth from his country and from his kinsfolk that he might see and possess the land of the living. Jacob when he left his brother and home crossed the Jordan and was received by the embraces of Rachel. Joseph, after he had been sold in secret and taken from his father and home, ruled in Egypt. The Church is commanded to forget her nation and the house of her fathers, so that her beauty may delight the king. The child Jesus was sought by his parents among their friends and relations, but he was not found there. So do you also fly your brethren if you would find your salvation. Fly from the midst of Babylon, fly from the sword of the North wind. In the words of the Prophet, I am ready 'to meet

you with bread' when you are in flight. You call me your abbot: for the time being I will not refuse that title for the sake of complaisance. Complaisance, I say, not that I may demand it from you but that I may show it to you, just as ' the Son of man came not to be ministered unto, but to minister and to give his life a redemption for many '. If you deem me worthy, accept me as your fellow disciple whom you have chosen as your abbot. One master in Christ we will both have, and so let this letter end with his name, for ' the end of the law is Christ unto the justice of everyone that believeth '.

LETTER 110

TO THOMAS OF SAINT OMER, AFTER HE HAD BROKEN HIS PROMISE TO BECOME A MONK

To his dearest son, Thomas, that he may walk in the spirit of fear, from Brother Bernard, styled Abbot of Clairvaux.

You do well to admit the debt you have incurred by your promise and to admit your guilt in delaying the payment of it. You must consider not only what you have promised but also to whom you have promised it. I too remember well your making the promise, but although you made it in my presence you did not make it to me and I claim no share in it. So you need not fear that I, who was only the witness and not the Lord of it, shall upbraid you for your futile delay in the fulfilment of it. I saw and was glad; and now it only remains for me to pray that my joy may be complete, but this will only be when you have honoured it. You set yourself a limit which you ought not to have passed. You have passed it, but that is not my responsibility: ' To your own Lord you stand or fall '. But because the danger of your position is so menacing I have decided, not indeed to threaten or reprove you, but to advise you, and this only in so far as you can take it in good part. If you hear me, well and good; if you do not, it will not be for me to judge you; there is one who will see and judge, even the Lord who judges us all. What is especially a matter for fear and remorse is that you have lied, not to man, but to God. You have asked me to spare your blushes before men and I will do so, but is your shamelessness to be left unashamed before God? Why are you afraid of what men might think of your conduct and yet not afraid of God's frown? ' Perilous is his frown for wrong-doers.' Are you more afraid of the reproaches of men than the torments of hell? Do you fear the tongue of flesh and scorn the sword that smites all flesh? Are these the fine principles which you tell me you are acquiring in your pursuit of knowledge, the knowledge you follow with so much love and zeal that you do not care if the fulfilment of your promise is impeded?

2. I ask you, what sort of tribute to virtue is this, what sort of advance in knowledge, what sort of result is this of your erudition, to fear where there is no cause to fear and yet to have no fear of the Lord? How much better for you to learn Jesus, Jesus crucified. This, of course, is not an easy knowledge to acquire, save for one who is crucified to the world. You deceive yourself, my son, if you think you can learn from the masters of this world what is a gift of God and can be obtained only by those who follow Christ and scorn the world. This is a knowledge imparted, not by books, but by grace; not by the letter but by the Spirit; not by mere book learning but by the practice of the commandments of God. ' Sow for yourself in right doing and reap in mercy and be enlightened with the light of know-ledge.' You see the light of knowledge cannot properly be acquired unless there first enter the soul the seed of righteousness from which may come the grain of life and not the straw of vainglory. Do you who have not yet sown for yourself in right doing nor yet gathered your sheaves of mercy, fancy that you are following true knowledge? Perhaps you fancy that the knowledge which puffs up is true know-ledge? If so you err stupidly ' by always spending and having no bread to eat, always toiling and never a full belly '. Come to your senses, I implore you, and consider that this extra year which you have permitted yourself at the cost of offending God, is not at all a year acceptable to him, but a seed-bed of disunion, an incentive to wrath, a feeding ground for apostasy, a year which will extinguish the spirit, impede grace, and induce the tepidity which God vomits from his mouth.

3. Alas, it seems to me that you are led by the same spirit as your namesake Thomas, one time Provost of Beverley. He, like you, promised himself with all his heart to our Order and this house; then, like you, he began to make delays, and little by little to grow cold until a sudden and terrible death snatched him away while he was still a complete secular and in bad faith, a double child of hell. May the all-merciful God save him, if possible from the terrible conse-quences! The letter which I wrote to him in vain still exists. By doing what I could to warn him of what must soon befall him, I only succeeded in saving myself from any responsibility for him. If he had only listened to me, how happy he would have been! But he equivocated and I am innocent of his blood. Yet I am not satisfied by this. Although I am not to blame in the matter, yet I am impelled by the charity which seeketh not its own to lament for the parlous state in which he died by his own fault. How mysterious are the judgements of God! How fearful his counsels for the sons of men! Here is one to whom he gave his Spirit, but only to take it away again, so that thereby he sinned a sin beyond all measure. Grace was given to him and for this his transgression was all the greater.

Yet this was not the fault of the giver, but of him who rejected the gifts and so added sin to sin. Using ill the freedom which was his he saddened the free Spirit by his own free choice, he scorned the grace which was given him, and failed to put into effect the inspiration of God, so as to be able to say: ' The grace of God has not been rendered void in me '.

4. If you are wise you will wash your hands in the blood of the sinner by learning from his folly and taking pains quickly to escape from the pit of perdition and release me from the terrible fear I have for you. I confess that I feel your turning away just as if my heart were being torn from my body, for you are very dear to me and I regard you with all the affection of a father. For this reason every time I think of you I feel a sword of anxiety pierce my soul, and I feel it all the more bitterly when I consider that you yourself have no fear at all in the matter. Of such as you it was written: ' For when they shall say peace and security, then shall sudden destruction come upon them '. I see many fearful things threatening you while you delay to come to your senses, for I have had much experience and only wish that you could profit by it too. Believe me who have had experience, believe me who am fond of you, and understand that because of my experience I am not deceived, and because of my affection for you I would not deceive you.

LETTER III

TO THE DISTINGUISHED YOUTH, GEOFFREY OF PÉRONNE, AND HIS COMPANIONS

Geoffrey of Péronne was one of a band of noble youths whom St. Bernard converted when he was in Flanders. They are said to have numbered thirty in all.

To his dear son Geoffrey and all his companions, the spirit of counsel and strength, from Bernard, styled Abbot of Clairvaux.

THE news of your conversion has resounded abroad edifying many and rejoicing the whole Church. ' The heavens rejoice, the earth is glad ' and every tongue praises God. ' How the earth shook, how the sky broke at the coming of God ', pouring down more copiously than usual the gracious shower that God keeps for his chosen. Never more will the Passion of Christ appear of no effect in you, as in the many ' children of unbelief'. While they put off their conversion from day to day they are snatched away by an unexpected death and in the twinkling of an eye they are plunged into the pit. Like a tree in spring the cross has burst into flower, the cross on which the Lord of glory hung not only for the Gentiles, but also for the scattered sons of God that he might gather them together in one. It is he and no other who has gathered you together, he who loves you so well has gathered you as the precious fruit of his cross, as the worthy reward of the blood he shed. If the angels of heaven rejoice over the conversion of one sinner, what will they do over the conversion of so many who were sinners too, who for their very renown in the world, for their birth and youth, were such a bad example to so many? I read that God did not choose 'many noble, many wise, or many mighty' but now contrary to the usual rule he has converted by his wonderful power a whole band of such. They have deemed the glory of this world worthless; they have trampled on the flower of their youth; they have held their noble lineage of no account; they have considered worldly wisdom foolishness; they have defied flesh and blood; their natural affection for relations and friends they have renounced; all the privileges, honours, and dignities of their position they have treated as things no better than dung that they might gain Christ. If I thought you had done all this of yourselves, I would praise you; but it is the finger of God, the power of his right hand that has done it. It is that best of gifts, that most perfect of gifts, which has come without doubt from the Father of lights. Therefore it is right that we should sing our praises to him who alone does marvellous things, who has seen that the copious redemption which he has to offer has not been wasted in you.

2. What remains for you to do, my dear sons, but to endeavour to put your praiseworthy intention into effect. See that you persevere, for perseverance is the only virtue which is crowned. Do not be of those who say 'yes' one minute and 'no' the next, but true sons of your heavenly Father 'in whom there is no change nor shadow of alteration'. May you be 'transformed into the same image, going from glory to glory as by the spirit of the Lord', being ever watchful that you do not become fickle, unstable, wavering. It is written: 'A double-minded man is inconstant in all his ways', and again: 'Woe to the man who will go two ways about it to enter the land of his desires'. I congratulate you, my dear sons, and myself also, for I have heard that I am deemed worthy to help you in your good purpose. I will do what I can to advise you and I promise to help you as I am able. If I seem necessary to you or at least if you deem me worthy, I shall not grudge the trouble and I shall try not to fail you. If it should be the will of heaven, I will earnestly take this burden on my shoulders, although they are already bowed with care. Joyfully and, as the saying is, with open arms I will receive you as fellow citizens of the saints, servants of God's household. How gladly will I not, in the words of the Prophet, 'bring out bread' to those who fly from the sword; water to those who thirst. I leave the rest for my or rather your Geoffrey to say. Whatever he tells you in my name you can regard as coming from me.

LETTER 112

TO THE PARENTS OF THE AFORE-MENTIONED GEOFFREY, TO CONSOLE THEM

IF God is making your son his own, as well as yours, so that he may become even richer, even more noble, even more distinguished and, what is better than all this, so that from being a sinner he may become a saint, what do either you or he lose? But he must prepare himself for the kingdom which has been prepared for him from the beginning of the world. He must spend the short time which remains of his life on earth with us in order to scrape off the filth of secular life and shake off the dust of the world, so as to be fit to enter the heavenly mansion. If you love him you will surely rejoice because he is going to the Father, and such a Father! It is true that he is going to God, but you are not losing him, on the contrary, through him you are gaining many sons. All of us at Clairvaux or of Clairvaux will receive him as a brother and you as our parents.

2. Knowing that he is tender and delicate perhaps you are afraid for his health under the harshness of our life. But this is the sort of fear of which the Psalm speaks when it says: 'Fear unmans them where they have no cause to fear'. Have comfort, do not worry, I shall look after him like a father and he will be to me a son until the Father of mercies, the God of all consolation, shall receive him from my hands. Do not be sad about your Geoffrey or shed any tears on his account, for he is going quickly to joy and not to sorrow. I will be for him both a mother and a father, both a brother and a sister. I will make the crooked path straight for him and the rough places smooth. I will temper and arrange all things that his soul may advance and his body not suffer.[1] He will serve the Lord with joy and gladness, 'his song will be of the Lord's, for great is the glory of the Lord'.[2]

LETTER 113

IN THE PERSON OF ELIAS, THE MONK, TO HIS PARENTS

In the early printed editions it is claimed that the following letter was written by St. Bernard in the person of one of his monks. Why, it is hard to say, for the letter reads like a parody of the master's style. But the half-baked rhetoric and exaggerated sentiments might well come from a very raw though

---

[1] . . . *ut spiritus proficiat*—a reminiscence undoubtedly of the *Holy Rule* of St. Benedict, where he says of the monk who has been ordained priest that he should not make his priesthood an occasion for pride but *magis ac magis in Deum proficiat:* 'advance ever more and more in God'.

[2] Cf. *Holy Rule*, Prologue. 'We have, therefore, to establish a school of the Lord's service, in the institution of which we hope to order nothing that is hard or rigorous. But if anything be somewhat strictly laid down, according to the dictates of equity, for the amendment of vices and preservation of charity, do not therefore fly in dismay from the way of salvation, whose beginning cannot but be strait. But as we go forward in our life and faith, we shall with hearts enlarged and unspeakable sweetness of love run in the way of God's commandments.'

doubtless fervent junior monk of the period. It is hard to escape the impression that he was a prig.

To his dear parents, constant prayers from Elias, a monk but a sinner.

THE only lawful reason for disobeying parents is God, for he himself has said: 'He who loves father or mother more than me is not worthy of me'. If you really love me as good and religious parents, if you have a true and honest affection for your son, why do you keep worrying me when I am trying to please God, and why do you keep trying to take me from the service of him whose service is perfect freedom? Now I know for a fact that 'a man's household are his enemies'. In this matter it would be wrong for me to obey you, in this matter you are not my parents, but my enemies. If you loved me you would surely rejoice that I am going to my father and your father, the father of all. What have we in common, what else have I received from you but sin and misery? Only this corruptible body which I bear; this I acknowledge and admit I have received from you. Unhappy parents, are you not content with having unhappily brought me into this unhappy world! Sinners, are you not satisfied that by your sin you have given birth to a sinner! Or perhaps you envy me the mercy which I am hoping to obtain from him who does not wish for the death of a sinner, I whom you well know to be a child of hell!

2. Heartless father, savage mother, cruel parents, not so much parents as murderers, whose only grief is the salvation of their offspring, whose one consolation is the death of their son! Do you prefer that I should perish with you rather than reign in heaven without you, is this the reason why you call me back to the wrecked ship from which I eventually escaped naked, to the fire from which I barely got away with my life, to the robbers at whose mercy I lay, but from whom I have recovered a little by the mercy of the Samaritan? Why else do you strive to draw me back to the world like a pig to its filth, like a dog to its vomit, from the very gates of glory just when I, as a soldier of Christ, had almost captured heaven, though not by my strength, but by the strength of him who has conquered the world? What extraordinary behaviour! When the house is on fire and the flames close behind, you forbid me to leave and, having left, you persuade me to return! And you do this while you yourselves are in the midst of the conflagration and with an obstinate insanity and insane obstinacy refuse yourselves to fly the danger! What frenzy! If you care nothing for your own death, why should you desire mine too? Is it your only fear that you should perish without me? What sort of consolation can one who is himself burning offer to others in a like case? What consolation is it to the damned that they have fellow

sufferers in their damnation? What remedy for the dying to see others dying too? This is not what I am taught by that rich man who, despairing in his torments, asked that his brethren might be warned lest they should suffer a like fate, being fearful lest his own agony should be increased by the sufferings of his own kinsmen.

3. What! Shall I go and console my weeping mother by a short visit, so that both she and I should weep for ever without consolation? Shall I go and comfort my father furious at my short absence in time and be myself comforted for a time by his presence, so that each for himself and both for the other should be forever desolate with unconsolable sadness? Should I not rather, after the example of the Apostle, fly flesh and blood, that I may hear the command of the Saviour saying: 'Suffer the dead to bury their dead', and sing with David: 'My heart is steeled against all consolation', and with Jeremias: 'It was no wish of mine that calamity should befall mankind'. How could I fall for worldly prospects and be deceived by the consolations of the flesh, when 'portion is none more to my liking and I welcome the lot's choice'? There is no appetite for carnal pleasures when spiritual joys have once been tasted; earthly things are no satisfaction to one who expects the joys of heaven; passing things have a mawkish savour for one who thirsts for the delights of eternity. Cease, therefore, I beg you, my parents, cease to afflict yourselves by tears and to disturb me by your fruitless efforts to recall me. If you continue to worry me by your messengers I shall only have to betake myself farther off. 'Here is my resting place, here is my destined home', here I shall never cease to pray for you as well as for myself, here by my incessant prayers I shall obtain, if I can, that he for whose love we have parted for a while, may unite us together once more in a happy and eternal union, one in his love for ever and ever.

LETTER 114

TO GEOFFREY OF LUXEUIL OR LISIEUX

There is doubt as to whether the Geoffrey to whom this letter is addressed was of Luxeuil or Lisieux, because the Latin form of the two names is very similar and often confused.

I AM sorry for you, my son Geoffrey, and I have good reason to be. For who would not be sorry that the flower of your youth which, amid the rejoicings of the angels, you offered still fresh to God as 'an acceptable fragrance' should be now trampled on by demons and soiled by foul vice and worldly filth. How could you turn your back upon God to follow the devil, how could you suddenly withdraw from the threshold of glory when Christ had begun to draw you after him? In you I find verified the truth of those words: 'A man's enemies will be of his own household', for your 'friends and neigh-bours came to meet you and stood against you', they called you back into the jaws of the lion, set you once more in the gates of death, ' in dark places like the forgotten dead', and now it wants but little for you to be swallowed up in hell where the lions are ready to devour you.

2. Turn back, I implore you; turn back before you ' sink under the flood, swallowed up in its depths, and the well's mouth closes over you'. Turn back before you go down to whence there is no return, before you are ' bound hand and foot and cast into outer darkness where there shall be weeping and gnashing of teeth', before you are thrust down into a place of darkness and shadow of death. Perhaps you are ashamed to return, because for the moment you have given up the battle. You would do better to be ashamed not to return to the fight and give battle again after having run away. The fight is not over yet, the lines are still closed in combat, the victory is still to be won. If you will join us we do not wish to conquer without you nor do we grudge you your share in the glory. We will gladly run to meet you, ready to welcome you back, saying: ' There is good reason for this merry making and rejoicing because this son of ours was dead and has come to life again; was lost and is found'.

LETTER 115

TO BALDWIN, ARCHBISHOP OF PISA

The Baldwin to whom this letter is addressed was a monk of Clairvaux. He became Cardinal in 1130 and Archbishop of Pisa in 1137. The founda-tion mentioned at the end of the letter might be a reference to one in Sardinia, as there was no foundation in the diocese of Pisa. It is difficult to say the exact date of this letter, but it was written sometime between 1139–1146.

To his Lord and cordial friend Baldwin, by the grace of God Arch-bishop of Pisa, that he may flourish in the hope and power of the Holy Spirit, from Brother Bernard.

I HAVE received your letter expressing your desire to see me and your great devotion. Your affection is fully returned, for I too desire to see you and ' you love him who loves you'. I can tell you, if it should be any comfort to you, that I have read your letter with great pleasure and would have even greater pleasure in your presence. I wish that we could always be together or, as this is hopeless, that at least we could see each other from time to time, but that too rests with God. You and I serve under the same Lord and we are both bound to do his will, so that we can neither of us do whatever we like. He has put you in a high position to give light to the nations. If you give

light as you should, it will be known to everyone; it will also be known
to everyone if you do not give any light. 'A city set on a hill cannot
be hid' nor can 'a candle on a candlestick'. When a candle is thus
set on a candlestick everything is seen, both the light it gives and the
light it does not give. Either everyone rejoices in the light of it, or
else everyone reviles it for not giving light. How much better to be
'hid under a bushel' than to be set on a candlestick and give no light!
A light that has gone out not only plunges everything in darkness,
but it also smokes unpleasantly. A candle on a candlestick must either
shine or smoke. Paul was a candle that shone, and he was salt that
had kept its savour. How could he have been anything else when
everywhere he brought glory to his ministry? He was everywhere a
sweet odour of Christ. For how many to-day is he not still 'an
odour of life unto life'! Blessed is the man to whom it can be said:
'We will run after thee in the odour of thy ointments', it is as if to
say: 'We will run in the rays of your light', which is the same as
'We go forward by the example of your life and works'. The
sweet odour of the saints is their light. How many sinners ran to
repent through the example of St. John! He gave both light and a
sweet odour by the good report of his life and by his virtues. He was
'a burning and shining light' set up on high, as if on a sort of candlestick of virtues, scattering on all sides light and a most sweet odour.
I want you to be like St. John. Let your light shine before men, yet
so as to burn before God as well, so that men may say of you: He was
a burning and shining light. For your own good it is necessary that
you should burn, and for the good of those who look to you it is
necessary that you should shine. He shines well who is lit by his own
fire. Those who do not shine with their own light, shine as hypocrites
with a borrowed light, not being on fire themselves. Of the two it
were better to burn without shining than to shine without burning.
So the Lord says: 'I am come to cast fire upon earth and what will I,
but that it be kindled?' The moon shines, but it by no means burns,
and the light of it fades because it only shines, so they say, with the
light of the sun. Perhaps this is why Scripture says: 'The fool is
changed as the moon, but the wise man continueth as the sun'. The
wise man is compared to the sun because, like the sun, he shines with
his own light and does not fade, for 'charity', without which no man
can be wise, 'never falleth away'. When a man is content with the
testimony of his own conscience, he does not care to shine with the
light of another's praise. But what am I doing saying all this to you
as if it were necessary? 'Out of the fulness of the heart, my mouth
speaketh', I do not know, but for an anxious love nothing is safe
enough. And so I will say something else that occurs to me. They
tell me that you have those about you who like to take gifts so that,
it is said, one of your household secretly took a bribe for removing a

steward.   Such things do not wound the conscience which does not consent to them, but they stain the reputation.   It is necessary ' to bring forth good things not only before God but also before men ', although I know not how the consent of anyone to this can be excused if he does not correct it when he is able.

I humbly greet Brother Angelus[1] with your whole household. I will send the community for the foundation through him who, God willing, you send to the Chapter, if you command.

LETTER 116

TO THE VIRGIN SOPHIA

BERNARD, Abbot of Clairvaux, to the virgin Sophia that she may never sully her virginity, but attain its reward.

' VAIN are the winning ways, beauty is a snare; it is the woman who fears the Lord that will achieve renown.'   I rejoice with you, my daughter, in the glory of your virtue whereby, you tell me, you have cast away the false glory of the world.   It is well to be rid of it, and you deserve praise for not having been deceived in a matter concerning which many people, wise enough in other respects, are exceedingly foolish.   What is the glory of the world but the flower of grass, a mere vapour that passes away !   Whatever its degree, there is more anxiety in it than joy.   When you are advancing claims, protecting yourself, envying others, suspecting all, ever wanting what you have not got, never satisfied with what you have but always wanting more, what rest can there be in your glory?   If there should be any, the pleasure of it soon goes, never to return, and only anxiety is left.   Moreover you can see how many for all their efforts never attain it and how few ever learn to despise it, because what is a necessity for many is a virtue for few.   I say for few, and this is especially so of the nobility: ' Not many noble, but the base things of the world hath God chosen '.   Hence you are indeed blessed amongst others of your rank, because while they are contending for worldly glory you, by your very contempt for it, are exalted much more gloriously and by a far truer glory.   You are far more distinguished and honourable for being one of so few than for being one of a great family.   For what you have been able to do by the grace of God is yours, but what you have by your birth is the gift of your ancestors. And what is yours is all the more precious for being so rare.   Moral vigour amongst men is ' a rare bird on earth '[2] but it is even more so among refined and noble women.   ' Who will find a vigorous woman?' the Scriptures ask, but it is much harder to find one who is

[1] Nothing is known of this Brother Angelus.
[2] Horace, *Sat.*, 2, 26.

also of high birth. God is not at all a respecter of persons and yet, I don't know why it is, virtue is far more pleasing in the nobility. Perhaps because it is more evident. It is not easy to know whether the baser sort lack the glory of the world by their own choice or by force of circumstances. I certainly praise anyone who is virtuous through necessity, but I praise far more her who is virtuous by the free choice of her will.

2. Let other women who know no better contend amongst themselves for the tawdry and fleeting glory of short-lived and deceitful things, but do you strive to set your heart upon what can never fail. Do you, I say, strive for that 'eternal weight of glory which our present momentary and light tribulation worketh for us above measure exceedingly'. And if those daughters of Belial who 'put on airs, walk with heads high, and with mincing steps' got up and adorned like a temple, abuse you, answer them: 'My kingdom is not of this world'; answer them: 'My time has not yet come, but your time is always ready'; answer them: 'My life is hid with Christ in God. When Christ shall appear, who is my life, then I also shall appear with him in glory'. Although, if one must glory, you too can do so quite simply and quite safely, but only in the Lord. I will not mention the crown which the Lord has prepared for you in eternity. I will say nothing of the promises he has given you, that as a happy bride you will be admitted to contemplate face to face the glory of the Bridegroom, that 'he will bring you into his presence glorious, without spot or wrinkle or any such thing', that he will receive you into his eternal embraces, that his 'left hand will pillow your head, and his right hand embrace you'. I will pass over in silence the special place reserved for virgins amongst the sons and daughters of the kingdom. I will not mention the new song which you will sing as a virgin amongst virgins, but with special and most sweet tones all your own, rejoicing in it yourself and giving joy to the whole city of God, whilst you sing and dance and follow the Lamb whithersoever he goeth. 'The eye has not seen, nor the ear heard, neither has it entered into the heart of man to conceive' what the Lord has prepared for you and for what you must prepare yourself.

3. So I will pass over what is promised to you in the future and concern myself solely with the present, with what you have already, with the 'firstfruits of the spirit', the gifts of the Bridegroom, the pledges of betrothal, the 'abundant blessings with which he has met you on the way', he whom you await to follow you and complete what is lacking.[1] May he come out into the open to be seen by his bride in all his beauty and admired by the angels in all his glory. If the daughters of Babylon have anything like this, let them bring it forth, 'whose only glory is their shame'. They are clothed in

---

[1] . . . *quem et subsecuturum, atque quod deest completurum, exspectas.*

purple and fine linen, but their souls are in rags. Their bodies glitter
with jewels, but their lives are foul with vanity. You, on the contrary,
whilst your body is clothed in rags, shine gloriously within, but in
the sight of heaven, not of the world. What is within delights because
he is within you who is delighted, for you cannot have any doubt
that ' Christ dwells in your heart': ' All the splendour of the king's
daughter is within '. Rejoice and be exceeding glad, O daughter
of Sion, shout for joy, O daughter of Jerusalem, for the King has
greatly desired thy beauty ' if confession and beauty are thy clothing
and light is a garment thou dost wrap about thee ' since ' confession
and beauty wait on his presence '.[1] On whose presence? On his
who is ' beautiful above the sons of men ' and ' on whom the angels
desire to look '.

4. You hear to whom it is you are pleasing? Love what enables
you to please him, love confession if you would desire beauty. Beauty
is the handmaid of confession. ' Confession and beauty are thy
clothing ' and ' Confession and beauty wait on his presence '. In
truth where there is confession, there too is beauty. If there are
sins, they are washed away in confession; if there are good works,
they are commended by confession. The confession of what you have
done amiss is ' a sacrifice to God of a contrite heart '; the confession
of God's mercies to you is ' a sacrifice of praise '. What an excellent
ornament of the soul is confession! It cleans the sinner of his sin
and renders the righteous man more unsullied. Without confession
the righteous man is insensible, the sinner dead: ' Confession perisheth
from the dead '. Confession therefore is the life of a sinner and the
glory of a righteous man. It is necessary for the sinner and becoming
to the righteous: ' Praise becometh the upright '. Silk, purple, and
paint have their beauty, but they do not impart it. They show their
own beauty when applied to the body, but they do not make the
body beautiful. When the body is taken away, they take their beauty
with them. The comeliness which goes on with clothes, comes off
with clothes, it belongs to the clothes and not the clothed.

5. Therefore do not emulate evil-doers and those who borrow their
beauty elsewhere when they have lost their own. They prove themselves destitute of any proper or natural beauty who go to such pains
and such expense to make up after the fashion of the world that passes
away so as to be admired by the foolish people who see them. Consider it wholly beneath you to borrow your appearance from the furs
of animals and the work of worms, let what you have be sufficient

---

[1] *Confessio et decorem induis, Confessio et pulchritudo in conspectu ejus.* In the above contexts
Mgr. Knox translates quite legitimately ' *confessio* ' as ' glory ' and ' honour ' respectively.
The Douai has ' praise ' in both cases. But St. Bernard takes the word literally and then proceeds
in the following paragraphs to play upon the double meaning of it, to confess sins in our current
use of the word, and to confess the praises of God or to give thanks to God in the sense which
St. Augustine uses it in his *Confessions.*

for you.   The true and proper beauty of anything needs no help from
other sources.   The ornaments of a queen have no beauty like to the
blushes of natural modesty which colour the cheeks of a virgin.   Nor
is the mark of self-discipline a whit less becoming.   Self-discipline
composes the whole bearing of a maid's body and the temper of her
mind.   It bows her head, smoothes her brow, composes her face,
binds her eyes, controls her laughter, bridles her tongue, calms her
anger, and governs her steps.   Such are the pearls which adorn the
vesture of a virgin.   What glory can be preferred to virginity thus
adorned?   The glory of angels?   An angel has virginity, but he has
no body.   Without doubt he is more happy if less strong in this
respect.[1]   Excellent and most desirable is the adornment which even
angels might envy !

6. There remains another thing concerning the same subject.
Without any doubt the more your adornment is your own the safer
it is.   You see women burdened rather than adorned with ornaments
of gold, silver and precious stones, and all the raiment of a court.
You see them dragging long trains of most precious material behind
them, stirring up clouds of dust as they go.   Do not let this trouble
you.   They leave it all behind them when they die, but you will take
your holiness with you.   What they carry about does not belong to
them.   When they die they will not be able to take a thing with them,
none of all their worldly glory will go down with them to the grave.
These things of theirs belong to the world and the world will send the
wearers naked away and keep all their vanities to seduce others equally
vain.   But your adornments are not like this.   They remain securely
yours, secure because yours.   You cannot be deprived of them by
violence nor lose them to guile.   Against them the cunning of the
thief and the cruelty of the madman are of no avail.   They are not
corrupted by moth and they do not wear out with age, nor are they
spent with use.   They survive death, for they belong to the soul and
not the body.   They do not die with the body, but leave the body
in company with the soul.   Even those who kill the body are
powerless against the soul.

LETTER 117

TO A NUN

*A letter of exhortation and encouragement to a nun who, after living a
worldly life for many years, had been converted to a better way of life.*

IT was with great pleasure that I learned of your wish to strive for the
true and perfect joy which is not of this earth, but of heaven;
which is not of this vale of tears, but of that ' city of God which is

---

[1] *Angelus habet virginitatem sed non carnem; sane felicior quam fortior in hac parte.*   Eales
translates: '. . . in that respect his happiness exceeds his virtue '.

enriched with deeply flowing rivers'. The only true joy is derived not from creatures but from the Creator, no man can take it from you, and compared to it all earthly joy is no better than sorrow; all pleasantness, grief; every sweet thing, bitter; every seemly thing, mean; and finally everything else which might give pleasure, wearisome. You yourself are my witness for the truth of this; ask yourself, you know yourself best. Is this not the very thing which the Holy Spirit is crying out in your heart? Were you not persuaded of this by the Holy Spirit before ever you were persuaded by me? Unless you had been strengthened and charmed by interior graces in comparison to which every sensible consolation seemed dross, how could you, a mere girl, beautiful and well born, have had the power to overcome the weakness of both your sex and your age, and to repudiate the privileges of your position and beauty?

2. But you have acted wisely. The earthly things which you have rejected are fleeting and of little worth, whereas what you are seeking now are great and eternal. Let me tell the truth and say more: you are leaving the shadows and entering the light. From the depths of the sea, you are coming into harbour; after a wretched slavery, you are breathing the pure air of a happy liberty, in a word you are passing from death to life. So long as you were living according to your own will and not God's will, according to your own law and not God's law, although alive you were no better than dead. While living for the world you were dead to God or, to speak more truly, you were alive neither to the world nor to God. While you were trying to live as one of the world under the habit and name of Religion, you alone had rejected God by your own will. But you found that you were not able to do what you stupidly thought you could: the world rejected you, but not you the world. So while you turned away from God, the world turned away from you and you fell, as the saying goes, between two stools. You did not live for God because you did not wish to, nor for the world because you were not able to. You were dead both to God and to the world. To the former willingly and to the latter unwillingly. This is what is apt to happen to those who make vows and do not keep them; who according to their profession are one thing and in their heart another. But now by the mercy of God you are beginning to live again, not to sin, but to righteousness; not for the world, but for Christ, knowing full well that to live for the world is death, but in Christ even to die is to live. ' Blessed are the dead who die in the Lord.'

3. We will not discuss any more your broken vow and violated profession. From now the integrity of your life will not be undermined by the corruption of your heart, nor will you any longer sully the title of virginity by your evil life. From now on there will be no deception in the name you bear, and the veil you wear will not any

longer be meaningless.   Why have you hitherto been called ' nun '
and ' Reverend Sister '[1] when under the cover of your holy habit you
were living a life that was not holy?   Why did you feign by the veil
on your head a gravity that your impudent glances belied?   The veil
you wore covered a haughty brow, under the outward guise of modesty
you carried a saucy tongue in your head.   Your unrestrained giggles,
wanton bearing, good attire, were more becoming to a coiffure than
a veil![2]   But under the leadership of Christ the old habits have passed
away and all things are made new and you now attend more to the
care of your soul than your body and adorn your life rather than your
dress.   You are doing what you should and, indeed, what you ought
to have done long ago, for it is long since you made your vows.   But
the Holy Spirit who breathes, not only where he wills, but also when
he wills, had not then breathed upon you.   Here perhaps is some
excuse for your former way of life.   But if you suffer the fire of the
Holy Spirit which now burns in your heart, that divine fire which
enkindles your heart in meditation, to die out, you can be sure that
there will be nothing else for you but that other burning fire which
shall never be put out.   Rather let the fire of the Spirit extinguish in
you the concupiscence of the flesh lest (which God forbid) the holy
desires which you have newly conceived be extinguished by it and
you hurl yourself into the flames of hell.

LETTER 118

TO A NUN OF THE CONVENT OF ST. MARY OF TROYES

I HAVE been told you are thinking of leaving your convent under the
pretext of seeking a harder way of life, and that although you will
not listen to your Reverend Mother and sisters trying every argument
to dissuade you and every means to prevent you from doing this,
you are yet prepared to take my advice in the belief that whatever I
suggest would be for the best.   You had done better to have chosen
someone more experienced to counsel you on this matter, but as you
have preferred myself I will not hide from you what I think best.   I
have been turning this plan of yours over in my mind ever since I
heard of it and I am still puzzled as to your motives.   It might be that
you are inspired by zeal for God, in which case your plan would be
excusable.   But all the same I do not see how it can be wise for you to
follow it.   Do you ask why?   ' Is it not wise ', you say, ' to fly riches,
crowded towns, and delicate meats?   Would not my modesty be
safer in a desert where I could live in peace with a few others or even
quite alone, so as to please him alone to whom I have pledged myself? '

---

[1] *Ut enim hactenus Nonna et Sanctimonialis vocitata es.*   St. Benedict rules that junior monks
should call their seniors *Nonnus*.   There is no exact translation for this word.
[2] . . . *wimpalæ magis quam velatæ congruerent.*

By no means.   For anyone wishing to lead a bad life the desert supplies ample opportunity.   The woods afford cover, and solitude assures silence.   No one can censure the evil no one sees.   Where there is no fear of blame the tempter approaches more boldly, and evil is committed with greater freedom.   In a convent, if you would do good there is no one to stop you; if you would do evil, you are not able. Soon everyone would know about it, it would soon be blamed and corrected, just as on the other hand all would admire, respect, and imitate the good they saw.   Therefore you see, my daughter, that in a convent greater glory awards your deserts, and a more prompt correction your faults, for amongst others you set an example by a good life and give offence by a bad one.

2. But I will take away from you all excuse for error by the distinction made in the Gospel.   Either you are one of the foolish virgins (if indeed you are a virgin) or you are one of the wise.   If you are one of the foolish, the convent is necessary for you; if you are one of the wise, you are necessary for the convent.   If you are one of the wise and well tried virgins, the reform which has been lately introduced into your convent and praised on all sides would be much discredited and weakened were you to leave, which is what I fear.   It would be said that had the convent been good you would never have left.   But if you are known to be one of the foolish virgins and depart, we will say that you left because being evil you could not live up to the high standards of the convent and had gone off to seek somewhere where you could live as you pleased.   And there would be some reason for this inasmuch as before the reform of your house you never, so I am told, mentioned this plan of yours, but only when Religion began to flourish there did you suddenly become holy and, fired by an unexpected fervour, begin to think of the desert.   I recognize, my daughter, I recognize in this, and only wish you could do so too, the poison of the serpent, the guile of the deceiver, the imposture of the trickster.[1]   The wolf lurks in the wood.   If you, a little sheep, penetrate the shadows of the wood alone, you are offering yourself as a prey to the wolf.   But listen to me, daughter, listen to a faithful counsel.   Whether you are a saint or a sinner do not cut yourself off from the flock or you will fall a prey to the wolf and there will be none to rescue you.   If you are a saint, try to edify your sisters by your example.   If you are a sinner, do not pile one sin on the top of another but do penance where you are, for if you leave your convent you will incur great danger, as I have tried to show, give scandal to your sisters, and set the tongues of many wagging against you.

----

[1] *versipellis astutiam.*   When an adjective, as we assume it is here, *versipellis* means ' that changes its form or shape ', as the devil is apt to pose as an angel of light.   On the other hand, the word may be used as a substantive in which case it can mean ' were-wolf ' or one that can change himself into a wolf.

LETTER 119

TO ERMENGARDE, FORMERLY COUNTESS OF BRITTANY

Ermengarde was the wife of Count Alan, and a great benefactress of Clairvaux. She built the monastery of Buzay, near Nantes. Her son relates that after the building had begun he and his mother were persuaded by ill-disposed persons to discontinue the project. At length St. Bernard visited the neighbourhood and finding the building incomplete and the monks in difficulties, severely rebuked the founders and threatened to take his monks away. After this the property was restored to the monks and the building completed. Apparently it was not St. Bernard, but Godfrey, Abbot of Vendôme, who urged Ermengarde to resume her purpose of entering the religious life, which she seems to have abandoned for a time.

In the following letter the saint expresses his esteem and affection for the countess who had by then become a nun. It appears that he was what we should now call her spiritual director. To modern tastes the wording of the letter may seem rather extravagant, but it has ample sanction in the taste and custom of the times. The treatise of St. Ailred on Friendship shows that a spiritual friendship can be none the less real for being wholly spiritual, and may quite naturally find expression in terms of more human love, in the same way that the pure love of a soul for God has traditionally found its expression in the erotic language of the Song of Songs.

To his beloved daughter in Christ, once a distinguished countess, but now a humble handmaid of Christ, the respectful affection of a holy love, from Bernard, Abbot of Clairvaux.

I wish I could find words to express what I feel towards you! If you could but read in my heart how great an affection for you the finger of God has there inscribed, then you would surely see how no tongue could express and no pen describe what the spirit of God has been able to inscribe there. Absent from you in body, I am always present to you in spirit and, although neither of us can come to the other, yet you have it within your power, not yet indeed to know me, but at any rate to guess something of what I feel. Do not ever suppose that your affection for me is greater than mine for you, and so believe yourself superior to me inasmuch as you think your love surpasses mine. Search your heart and you will find mine there too and ascribe to me at least as great an affection for you as you find there for me. But your modesty is so great that you are more likely to believe that he who has moved you to esteem me and choose me as your spiritual counsellor has also moved me with a like feeling of affectionate concern for you. It is for you to see that you have me always by you; for my part, I confess, I am never without you and never leave you. I wanted to scribble these few brief lines to you from the road while travelling,[1] and I hope, if God wills, to write to you more fully when I have the leisure.

LETTER 120

TO THE SAME

I HAVE received what has given delight to my heart, the news of your peace. I am glad because you are glad. Your evident joyfulness is a great refreshment to my mind. It has nothing about it of flesh and blood, for now you are living humbly instead of in state, as one of no consequence instead of as a great lady, as poor instead of rich, and you are deprived of the consolation of your brother, son, and home. So without doubt your joyfulness can only be of the Holy Spirit. After having long since conceived of the fear of God you have at last given birth to the spirit of salvation, and love has cast out fear. How much sooner would I converse with you in your presence than write to you in your absence! Believe me, I become angry with the affairs by which I always seem to be hindered from seeing you, and I greet with joy the opportunities of seeing you which I seem to get so seldom. Such opportunities are rarely given, but I confess that their very rarity is dear to me, for it were better to see you even if only occasionally than never at all. I offer you a foretaste of joy which will soon be satisfied for I hope to come to you quite soon.

LETTER 121

TO BEATRICE, A NOBLE AND RELIGIOUS LADY

I MARVEL at the zeal of your devotion and the strength of your affection. My good lady, what can I mean to you? Why are you so anxious for me? If I were related to you by any tie of blood, if I were your son or nephew, I could regard your many kindnesses, your frequent messages, and the innumerable and daily marks of your esteem, as the fulfilment of a duty and no matter for surprise. But since I know you only as a great lady by birth[2] and not as my mother, it is no wonder that I wonder, it would only be wonderful if I were able to wonder enough. Who of my relations and friends show the same care for me? Who ever even enquires after my health? To my friends, relations, and neighbours, 'I am discarded like a broken pitcher'. Only you never forget me. You ask after the state of my health, about the journey from which I have just returned, and the monks whom I have moved to another place. To all of which I briefly reply that 'from a wilderness, from fearful desert spaces'

---

[1] *Hæc tibi interim de via breviter in transiter scribere volui.* Eales has: 'I was anxious to write this short note to you *about my journey* while on the way' (italics mine).

[2] *Nunc autem cum genere tantum dominam, non matrem te cognoscamus.* Eales has: 'But as, in common with the rest of mankind, we recognize in you only a great lady, and not a mother'.

the brethren have come unto an abundance of everything, of buildings and friends; into a fertile land and a dwelling place of greaty beauty. I left them very contented and peaceful and came home myself also contented and at peace, except that for a few days, but in no small way, my fever returned and I became so ill that I thought I should die. But God had mercy on me and I soon got over it so that now I feel stronger and better than I did before the journey.

LETTER 122

TO ADELAIDE OF MAURIENNE, WIFE OF LOUIS VI

To Adelaide, Queen of France, health and prayers from Bernard of Clairvaux.

I ADDRESS myself to your Majesty, not because of the notice you have taken of me or the friendship you have shown to me, but because I trust in your well-known liberality and kindness.

Wicard, your man, complains that, through no fault that he is conscious of, you have unjustly driven him into exile and deprived him of all his goods. Because I know this man and the good intention he has of leaving the world and turning to God, I do not think it would be inappropriate either for me to desire or for you to consent that he should be reinstated in your favour and in some, if not all, of his goods. I commend unto you, that we may both find favour in your eyes, this holy Religious, the Abbot of Beaulieu, who on this account is exposing himself to the fatigue of the long journey to you with this letter.

LETTER 123

TO THE DUKE AND DUCHESS OF LORRAINE

To the Duke and Duchess of Lorraine that they may so rejoice in a pure and mutual love that only the love of Christ is supreme in them, from Bernard, Abbot of Clairvaux.

EVER since necessity compelled us to send into your land for goods, we have always found you favourable and friendly. Whenever there was need you have bestowed liberally of your bounty on our people. You have liberally remitted all tolls and other dues for our merchants passing through your territory. Without doubt your reward for all this will be very great in heaven, if we believe those words of our Lord in the Gospel: ' As long as you did it to one of these the least of my brethren, you did it to me '. But why is it you allow your servants to take away again what you have given? It is worthy of you and honourable that none of your servants should dare to ask for again what you have been pleased to give for the good of your souls. If therefore you do not regret your favours (God forbid) it cannot be your will that we should be deprived of the gifts it has been your pleasure that we should receive from you. May you then be pleased to command as a firm and inviolable rule that our people shall not be troubled by any of your ministers. Otherwise, after the example of our Lord who did not refuse to pay custom for himself, we too are ready freely to render unto Caesar the things that are Caesar's, tribute to whom tribute is due, custom to whom custom is due, especially as according to the Apostle we ought not to seek your gifts so much as the fruit that may abound to you from them.

LETTER 124

TO THE DUCHESS OF LORRAINE

I GIVE thanks to God for the devotion which I know you have towards him and his servants. Whenever even the smallest spark of heavenly love seems to glow in a human heart exalted by earthly dignities, there can be no doubt that it is not a merely human virtue but a gift of God. I most gratefully receive the generous offer you have made in your letter to me. But as I know you to be engaged on an unforeseen and very serious matter just now I have thought it better to await your convenience, as it shall please you. I would not wish to burden anyone especially in the things of God, in which it is our duty to seek not so much the gift as the reward of the giver. So will you please name the day and place, answering by this messenger, on which, God helping and your present affair satisfactorily settled, you would be near these borders. Brother Wido[1] will meet you, so that if he finds anything in your territory suitable for our Order, you will be able to fulfil your promise all the more quickly and joyfully for ' the Lord loves a cheerful giver '. I am anxious to obey your wishes in this matter as far as is reasonable, so if this delay does not suit you, please let me know. Through you I salute the Duke and admonish you both that if you know this castle, for which you are making war, does not belong to your domain, for the love of God to leave it alone, ' for what does it profit a man, if he gain the whole world, and suffer the loss of his own soul? '

LETTER 125

TO THE DUCHESS OF BURGUNDY

THE special friendship which your Highness is supposed to have for me, a poor man, has now grown to such a pitch that whoever thinks he has offended you believes that the surest way back to your favour is through me. Hence when I was in Dijon a short while ago,

---

[1] Mabillon considers that his Wido may be Guy, the Abbot of Trois-Fontaines, who frequently went to Lorraine.

Hugh de Bese beseeched me with many prayers that I should placate your anger which he has called down on himself and that for the love of God and the friendship you have for me you should give your assent to the marriage of his son. Although this marriage did not meet with your approval he had irrevocably determined to make it because he believed it advantageous for himself. Now he is again besieging my ears concerning this affair not only with his own prayers but with those of his friends as well. I am not greatly concerned with his worldly advantage, but since the matter seems to have reached such a pass that he cannot prevent it without a breach of faith, I thought it well to mention it to you. It must needs be something of very special importance indeed if it is to be preferred to the good faith of a Christian and one of your own men. A man cannot break faith and yet still remain faithful to his Prince. I see no gain, but rather great danger to you, if you should happen to disturb the union of two people whom it may be God's pleasure to join together. May God pour out his grace upon you and upon your sons, lady most noble and dear to me in Christ. ' Behold, now is the acceptable time; behold, now is the day of salvation ': pour forth your corn on Christ's poor that you may receive your reward with increase in heaven.

FROM HILDEBERT, ARCHBISHOP OF TOURS, TO ST. BERNARD

Hildebert ruled the Church of Mans from 1098 until 1125, when he became Archbishop of Tours. In the following rather prosy letter he asks for the friendship of St. Bernard.

I BELIEVE that most people are aware that balsam is known by its smell and a tree by its fruit. In just the same way, dearest brother, by your reputation I know that your life is holy and your doctrine pure.[1] Although I live a long way from you yet the report has reached as far as me of how happy are the nights you spend in contemplation, how many are the sons that are born of your activity,[2] and how wholly you are given to cultivating the virtues and dominating the flesh. Whoever speaks of you to me has this same tale to tell. Like oil poured forth, such is the perfume of your name, such already the reward of your goodness; the ears of grain which you gather from your field before the final harvest. A notable and deathless tribute is some reward for virtue in this life. This is what it wins of itself and keeps for itself. The splendour of it is not diminished by jealousy nor augmented by any external efforts. Detractors cannot rob us of the esteem of good men nor can it be increased by the fawning of flatterers. It rests with each of us either to augment it by our virtues or to diminish it by our faults. Without doubt great hope is cherished in the Church that you will never fall away from your fair reputation because it is founded on a rock.

2. From all that I have heard of you I have come to love you and to desire with a great desire to be admitted to the sanctuary of your friendship and remembered by you when you steal from converse with men to speak to the King of Angels on behalf

---

[1] . . . *et quam sis ad sanctimoniam compositus, et integer ad doctrinam.* Eales: ' . . . how you are steadfast in holiness and sound in doctrine '.

[2] . . . *quam jucundas noctes cum tua Rachel ducas, quæ progenies ex Lia tibi exuberet.* Literally: ' What happy nights you spend with your Rachel, what abundant an offspring is born to you of Lia '. Rachel who was beautiful but sterile and Lia who was fruitful but blear eyed have traditionally been taken as types of the contemplative and active lives. The rendering given in the text seemed to us preferable and more intelligible than the involved metaphor.

of men. Now this desire of mine has been much increased by Gébuin, Archdeacon of Troyes, a man outstanding both in virtue and learning. I would have believed it my duty to commend him to you were I not sure that one whom you deem worthy of your favour needs no commendation of mine. If you do not know it, it was from him that I learned that you are qualified to be a spiritual guide in the Church both by example and by word. And now, so as not to burden you with my verbosity, I must bring this letter to an end, but my desire for your friendship will not end until I hear from you. I beg you to let me know how you are disposed by return of letter.

LETTER 126

TO HILDEBERT, IN ANSWER TO THE ABOVE LETTER

' A GOOD man out of the good treasure of his heart brings forth good things.' Your letter was so much to your own credit as well as to mine that I was most happy to receive it. It enables me to honour you while deriving from it great honour for myself. The condescension of a man in your high station and the regard which you express for such an insignificant person as myself, certainly afford me great satisfaction. There is nothing more rare or more dear to God than a man in a high position who is not high minded but stoops to those of low estate. No man can be accounted wise except he harken to the counsel of Wisdom saying: ' The greater thou art, the more in all things abase thyself'. And you have done this by abasing yourself to me, a great man to a small, an elder man to a younger. I could praise your well-proven wisdom and my praises would be justified, perhaps more justified than those you bestow upon myself. In estimating the grounds for our certainty we should realize that there is a world of difference between the evidence of mere hearsay and that provided by unmistakable facts, and then what we have learned for certain we can proclaim with confidence. You should look to the proofs for what it has pleased you to write in praise of myself. I have a proof of your goodness in the letter you have written so full of my praises. Another might be pleased with the learning it shows, with its sweet and pure language, with its limpid style, or with its welcome and praiseworthy brevity, but for my part I value most the wonderful humility with which a great man like you troubles to approach a person of my insignificance, and overwhelm me with your greeting, praises, and reverence. As for what you say of myself, I see in it not what I am, but what I should like to be, and what I am ashamed of not being. But such as I am, I am yours; and if, by God's gift, I should ever be any better than I am now, I shall still be yours, most reverend and loving father.

NOTE

THE following letters are concerned with the unfortunate schism in the Papacy, when, on February 14, 1130, the people of Rome surpassed themselves by proclaiming, on the same day and within a few hours of each other, two different Popes: Gregory, Cardinal Deacon of S. Angelo, and Peter Leonis, Cardinal Priest of St. Calixtus.

The rather obscure roots of this affair seem to lie in a decree of Pope Nicholas II in the year 1059, by which it was ruled that when a Pope died the Cardinal Bishops were to deal with the election of his successor and then associate themselves with the Cardinal Clerks, and finally demand the agreement of the rest of the clergy and people of Rome.　It seems clear from this that the election was vested in the Cardinal Bishops absolutely, but in course of time the text became corrupted and, in certain copies, the word ' Bishops ' was dropped out altogether.

Peter Leonis was the son of a converted Jew and a member of the powerful and rich family of Pierleoni.　As soon as he became Cardinal, his faction began to manœuvre for his eventual election to the Papacy, a prospect to which they were entitled by their fortune, if not by their virtue.　So when Pope Honorius fell ill, the Chancellor, Cardinal Haimeric, foreseeing possible trouble over the election, quietly moved him up to the Monastery of St. Andrew on the Cœlian hill, and under the protection of his own faction, the Frangipani.

In its simplest terms what happened after this was as follows.　When Honorius died the matter was kept quiet, and he was hurriedly buried in accordance with the letter, if not with the spirit, of the law, which forbade an election to take place before a Pope had been dead and buried for three days.　Then the fourteen electors whom Cardinal Haimeric had gathered together (four Cardinal Bishops, five Cardinal Priests and five Cardinal Deacons) proceeded to elect a new Pope.　Their unanimous choice fell on Gregory, the Cardinal Deacon of S. Angelo, and he, after a moment's understandable hesitation, accepted the redoubtable charge they had placed upon him. After this they lost no time in taking him to the Lateran Basilica where he received the devotion of a crowd of people, and then on to the Palladium, a monastery which stood on the Palatine hill, to be invested with the insignia of his office.　All this was performed under the protection of the Frangipani, and took place at nine in the morning of February 14, 1130.　By midday Peter Leonis, also under the protection of his faction, hastened as fast as he could go to the Church of St. Mark, where he too was proclaimed Pope by nine Cardinal Deacons, thirteen Cardinal Priests, all anxious to take this opportunity of asserting their pretended right to vote in the election of a Pope, and two Cardinal Bishops.　After this his faction proceeded in the accepted fashion of the Roman people to sack the Lateran and other strongholds of their opponents, while the principals exchanged fulminations and excommunications from a safe distance.

On February 23 the two Popes were duly consecrated, Gregory in the titular church of Cardinal Haimeric, S. Maria Novella, by the Cardinal Bishop of Ostia, under the title of Innocent II, and Peter in the Basilica of St. Peter by Peter, Bishop of Porto, under the title of Anacletus II.　Then having once more excommunicated each other, they both appealed to Christendom for support.　Innocent alleged in his favour the support of the greater number of the Cardinal Bishops and the saner part of the Sacred College.　Anacletus based his claim on the irregularity of his opponent's election in view of its secrecy and on the quantity, if not the quality, of his supporters.

There seems to be little doubt at all that Innocent had the better claim.　If the secrecy of his election was irregular it was amply justified by the circumstances and he had a clear majority of the Cardinal Bishops and all the more conscientious of the Sacred College behind him.　And when one compares the persons of the two claimants, there can be even less doubt that Innocent had the moral advantage.　Even Peter the Venerable, usually so careful and moderate, described Anacletus in a letter to the Bishop of Tusculum as guilty of ' ambition, cupidity, perjury, and yet worse '. A formidable indictment coming from such a man.

But the struggle was long and hard and the supporters of both sides were not always influenced by the highest motives.　But St. Bernard did not hesitate: he threw himself into the fight on the side of Innocent, and by his tireless energy succeeded in overthrowing the rival Pope.

LETTER 127

TO HILDEBERT, ARCHBISHOP OF TOURS

A letter written by St. Bernard to try and persuade Hildebert to support Pope Innocent. But Hildebert was quarrelling with the King and hesitated to support the Pope who claimed the allegiance of the King. He hesitated up to the last moment and beyond, for he died still opposed to Innocent. This letter was probably written about the year 1131.

To the great and renowned Priest of God, Hildebert, by the grace of God Archbishop of Tours, that he may walk in the spirit and search all things by the light of the spirit, from Bernard, styled Abbot of Clairvaux.

I WILL speak to you in the words of the Prophet and say: ' Comfort is hidden from mine eyes because death hath divided the brethren '. For it seems that, according to Isaias, they have made a covenant with death and a compact with hell. Innocent, the anointed of the Lord, has been set up for the fall and rise of many. Those who are of God have freely chosen him, but he who stands over against him is either Antichrist or his follower. The abomination of desolation is standing in the Holy Place, to gain possession of which he has set fire to the sanctuary of God. He persecutes Innocent and with him all who are innocent. Innocent has fled from his face, for ' When the lion roars, who shall not be afraid? '[1] He has obeyed the words of the Lord: ' When they persecute you in one city flee unto another '. He has fled and by the flight that he has endured after the example of the Apostles he has proved himself really an apostle. Paul was not ashamed to slip through the fingers of those who sought his life, by being let down the walls of a city in a basket. He fled away, not because he was afraid, but because he wanted to ' give place unto wrath ', not to run from death but to achieve life. With good reason therefore does the Church concede to Innocent the place of Paul, when she sees him following in the footsteps of Paul.

2. But his exile is not fruitless, he is labouring that he may be ' enriched with his toil '. His city has cast him out, but the world has received him. From all over the world they have ' brought out bread ' to the fugitive, although, like Shemei in his wrath, Gerard of Angoulême[2] has not yet entirely ceased to curse David. Whether

---

[1] This is a play upon the family name of Anacletus II, Peter Leonis. It occurs frequently in the letters of St. Bernard written during the schism.

[2] Gerard, Bishop of Angoulême, is an enigmatic character. Undoubtedly he was a very learned man and quite fearless . . . he had the courage to rebuke William, Count of Poitiers, for living in adultery, and William was formidable and not very gentle. But Gerard was ambitious and had come to look on his Legatine authority as a personal right. He immediately applied to Innocent to confirm him in his legateship in a very flattering letter on May 1, 1130, but Innocent refused to do so, and Gerard promptly threw in his lot with Anacletus, who made no difficulty in the matter.

that sinner who sees it and is enraged likes it or not, he cannot prevent Innocent from carrying a crown of glory, and being exalted before kings. Do not all the Princes know that he is truly the chosen of God? The Kings of France, England, Spain and, last of all, the King of Rome, have received Innocent as Pope and recognized him alone as the Bishop of their souls. Only Achitophel does not see that his schemes have been exposed and brought to nothing. In vain does that wretched man labour maliciously to devise schemes against the people of God and to hatch plans against the saints who adhere firmly to the saintly Innocent and refuse to bow the knee to Baal. No guile shall obtain for his parricide the kingdom of Israel, that holy city, which is ' the Church of the living God, the pillar and ground of the truth '. ' A triple cord shall not be lightly broken ' and the choice of the most worthy of the Sacred College, the approbation of the majority of the people, and (what is more than all this) the witness of a pure life, all combine to commend Innocent to everyone and establish him beyond doubt as the Supreme Pontiff.

3. And so, my father, we all expect your support, late though it may be, to come upon us like dew upon fleece. We do not blame your slowness, because it savours of gravity and banishes all suspicion of levity. Mary did not at once answer the greeting of the angel, she first considered what sort of greeting it might be; and Timothy was warned not to be too ready to lay hands on anyone. But I who am known to you say: ' Nothing in excess '. I who am your friend say to you: ' Do not try to be more wise than it behoves you to be wise '. I confess it is a shame that the old serpent should have left his silly women to coil himself round your heart, to attack such a strong column of the Church as you are. But I have every confidence that though he may attack you he will not overthrow you, for ' the friend of the bridegroom stands and rejoiceth at the bridegroom's voice ', the voice of gladness and healing, the voice of unity and peace.

LETTER 128

TO MASTER GEOFFREY OF LORETO

Geoffrey of Loreto was well known for his learning and afterwards became Archbishop of Bordeaux. He took his name from the Loreto close to Poitou in the diocese of Tours.

WE look for fragrance from flowers and flavour from fruit. Attracted by the fragrance of your good reputation which ' soothes the heart like flow of oil ', I am hoping, dearest brother, to know you by your fruit in deeds. And not I alone but God himself, although he has need of no one, needs your co-operation in this time of crisis, if you are not false. It is a wonderful thing for you to be able to co-operate with God; but not to do so, when you can, would be damnable. You have favour with God and men, you have learning, the spirit of liberty, and a gift for living, effective, and pointed eloquence; you cannot, being a friend of the Bridegroom, fail his bride in such a crisis. A friend is known in the hour of need. Can you sit by idle while your mother, the Church, is troubled? There has been a time of rest. Holy leisure has hitherto exercised its arts freely and lawfully. Now is the time for action, because the law has been broken. That beast, spoken of in the book of the Apocalypse, to whom power has been given to blaspheme and make war on the saints, occupies the See of Peter like a lion ready for its prey. There is another beast snarling at your side like ' the whelp of a lion that lies hidden in its lair '.[1] The former is more savage, the latter more cunning, and they are both united against the Lord and against his anointed. Let us set to work at once to ' break away from their bondage, and throw off their yoke '.

2. I for my part, together with other servants of God aflame with the divine fire, am labouring with the help of God ' to assemble the kings and people together ' to break this conspiracy of evil men and destroy ' every height that exalteth itself against the knowledge of God '. Nor have we laboured in vain. The Kings of Germany, France, England, Scotland, Spain, and Jerusalem, with all their clergy and people, support and follow the lord Innocent, as sons their father, as members their head, and they zealously preserve unity in the bond of peace. The Church supports him with good reason, for it has learned that his reputation is more fair and his election more sound, in that his supporters prevailed both in numbers and excellence. But you, my brother, why do you still stand aloof? How long will you doze in false security while the serpent lies at your side? I know very well that you are a son of peace and that no possible reason could bring you to leave unity. But it is not enough to remain passive when unity is threatened. You must defend it and try with all your strength to overthrow those who are disturbing it. Do not fear your loss of peace, it will be rewarded by no small gain in glory if you succeed by your efforts in taming or even silencing that wild beast near you, and if the goodness of God rescues by your hand so great a prize for the Church as William, Count of Poitiers.[2]

LETTER 129

TO THE BISHOPS OF AQUITAINE, AGAINST GERARD OF ANGOULÊME

To his Lords and Honoured Fathers, by the grace of God holy Bishops of Limoges, Poitiers, Perigueux, and Saintes, constancy in adversity, from Brother Bernard, styled Abbot of Clairvaux.

[1] Gerard of Angoulême.
[2] The same William whom Gerard fearlessly rebuked for adultery. Eventually he was brought over to the side of Innocent by the personal influence of St. Bernard.

COURAGE is gained in peace, proved in adversity, and confirmed in victory. The time has come, most reverend and holy fathers, for you to take courage, if you have any, and bestir yourselves to action. Once more the sword of the enemy seems to be threatening death to the whole body of Christ, but it is at you that it is being especially pointed, it is over you especially that it is being wheeled. You have the choice of either strongly resisting these daily attacks upon you or of shamefully yielding to them. That Diotrephes,[1] who covets pre-eminence amongst you, has not accepted you and does not recognize him whom the whole Church, together with you, has received as coming in the name of the Lord. And no wonder! for even at his time of life he craves for a great name. In remarking the vanity of this man, I am not being led away by any false or uncertain report; I am judging him by his own words. In an intimate letter he lately wrote to the chancellery he obsequiously and unworthily begged to be honoured with the burden and prestige of legate. Would that he had got it. Perhaps if his ambition had been satisfied, he would have hurt you less than he does now that it has been frustrated. He would then have only harmed himself or almost only himself. Now he rages against the whole world. You see what love of glory can do? The office of legate is a burden even to more youthful shoulders than his. All the world knows this. Yet here is a very old man who finds it an agony to spend even the few days that remain to him without this burden.

2. Perhaps he would argue that I am judging him on grounds of mere suspicion and that I have no right to blame him for the secrets of his heart which I cannot know and of which I cannot have any proof. I confess I am suspicious in this matter and I do not know whether even the greatest simpleton could judge otherwise than I have of a matter that is so obvious. To refer briefly to a perfectly unmistakable action of his: the first thing he did, or one of the first things, after the election of Pope Innocent, was to write and beg the legateship. When this was refused to him, in his rage he turned against Innocent and went over to the other man, pluming himself on being his legate. If he had not first asked for the legateship from Pope Innocent or if he had afterwards refused to accept it from the other man, I might have believed that he had some other motive for his double-dealing, although it could not have been a good one. But now he has no excuse for his ambition. Let him lay aside the legateship which he now enjoys, although it is only an empty name without any substance, and I, if I can, will cease to suspect him or, if I cannot prevent myself, I will, at any rate, do so unwillingly and accuse myself of rashness in doing so. He is a man who has for so long lorded it over others that he is ashamed to hold any place but the

[1] Gerard of Angoulême.

first. We see in him the truth of what the Scriptures say: ' Shame, that is the grace and glory of a man, may yet make a sinner of him '. And is it not a very great sin, the most grave offence, this proud shame which renders a man not only ashamed to be under others, but even so that he cannot endure not to rule over others?

3. It was because of this and nothing more that the man left him whom he once called ' Holy Father Innocent ' (for that is what he did call him when he wrote to plead for the legateship) and his holy mother the Church, to cleave unto his schismatic, so that they became two in one vanity. They have made a pact together and ' maliciously plot against the people ' and ' scale has pressed on scale so as to leave no vent between '. He calls him ' Pope ' in return for being himself called ' legate ', that ' by their vanity they may together deceive '. They comfort each other, support each other, and advocate each other, but each for their own sakes and not for the sake of the other. They are men in love with themselves. With equal zeal they ' make common cause against the Lord and against the King he has anointed ', but with very different intentions. They support each other in seeking their own interests and (what is shocking) they do so at the expense of Christ's heritage. What else are they trying to do before our very eyes, but banish Christ? Even now the legate wants new bishops for his Pope, so that he shall not be alone in his support of him. He does not wait until the sees become vacant by death, but, supported by tyrannical power, he intrudes men into sees while the bishops are still alive, taking opportunity for this of the spite of secular princes who are persecuting their bishops for motives of personal hatred: ' He agrees with the rich to lie in wait at dark corners and kill the man who never wronged him '. By such a door he enters the sheepfold.

4. We must not think that all this activity of the legate on behalf of his Pope is disinterested. He boasts that he has added the whole of France and Burgundy to his legatine jurisdiction. If he wants he can add Media, Persia, and the coasts of Decapolis ! In fact there is no reason why he should not extend his empty jurisdiction over Samaria or, indeed, anywhere his feet have trodden ! A man as stupid as he is conceited. A man void of both the fear of God and self-respect. He thinks that no one notices his absurd ambition when, in fact, he is the laughing stock of all those around him. And this is nothing to wonder at for he uses the sanctuary as a market place and, like some fussy businessman out for quick returns and searching every-where for the cheapest market, he anxiously seeks high and low for ecclesiastical dignities, finally choosing for himself a Pope who will consent to his being legate. Where does he get this privilege? Who gave him this prerogative? Does he possess the sanctuary of God by inheritance? Why does he accuse Pope Innocent of being in schism? He was his ' Holy Father ' so long as there was the slightest chance of

securing from him the favour he had the effrontery to ask for. His papal dignity and holiness vanished at the same time as his vain hope for the legateship. How wonderful that in so short a time sweet and bitter waters could flow from the same source! Yesterday Pope Innocent was holy and Catholic and the Supreme Pontiff, but to-day he is a wicked and schismatic disturber of the peace! Yesterday he was Holy Father Pope Innocent, but to-day he is simply Gregory, Cardinal Deacon of Sant' Angelo! So from a double heart out of one mouth come two contradictory statements: 'False hearts and treacherous lips'. How can there be any reserve or self-respect in a man whose conscience is thus ruled by his desires and whose tongue is forked, saying first 'Yes' and then 'No'? How can anyone, according to the words of the Apostle, 'study his behaviour not only in the Lord's sight, but in the sight of men', if, like the unjust judge, he neither fears God nor respects man?

5. It is quite certain that when ambition bursts out into blatancy it defeats its own purpose; that when it brazenly reveals itself, it loses its power to accomplish its purpose. Ambition is the mother of hypocrisy and prefers to skulk in corners and dark places. It cannot endure the light of day. It is an unclean vice wallowing in the depths, always hidden, but with ever an eye to advancement. And no wonder for, if it does not hide itself, it will always fail in its purpose. The more we are seen to want honours, the less likely are we to achieve them; what can be more dishonourable in a bishop than the desire for honours? The true Christian only glories in the cross of Christ. The ambitious man is only esteemed so long as he hides his purpose and walks by night. The hypocrite will seem holy and just to men only so long as his desire for filthy lucre is hidden in the shadows. But when, through impudence or imprudence, he happens to show what is skulking in his heart, his unrestrained desires will lead the more readily to his confusion for being so obviously set upon honours. And so the truth of those words are proved: 'Their own shameful doings are their pride, whose minds are set upon earthly things', and: 'If I seek my own honour, my honour is nothing'. And on such persons the curse which, unless I am mistaken, the Prophet calls down on hypocrites, is fulfilled: 'Let them be like the stalks on a housetop that wither there unharvested'. Men have not so lost all sense of propriety that they can esteem blatant and unashamed ambition, especially when it is evident in an elderly priest in whom childish vanity is all the more unbecoming since gravity and holiness are proper to his age and position. And, even if some flatterer should fawn before his face, nevertheless everyone will laugh behind his back. But there is a restrained sort of ambition which works cautiously though none the less equivocally. In order to succeed it keeps itself hidden and takes shelter under cover of propriety. Such a man,

although he does not fear God unto salvation, has a certain natural delicacy and retains for a time some modesty, because he fears the opinion of others and is ashamed to show himself in public.

6. What else is it but foolhardy and shameless, this desire to lord it over others so that a man spares neither his old age nor respects his priesthood in order to secure for himself a temporary legateship. The side of Christ, which redeemed the people in the unity of faith by pouring forth blood and water, he tears open again; and by dividing those whom Christ saved by uniting, he makes himself not a Christian but Antichrist, guilty of the cross and death of Christ. What impatient and unbridled desire for gain! What unrestrained greed! What blind and shameless greed! First quite openly and brazenly, as I have said, and he does not deny, he proceeds to assail the Holy See with a petition sufficiently unworthy of himself; and then smarting under his repulse, he immediately turns to the schismatic and, when he has sacrilegiously received from him the power he wrongly desired, he is not afraid once more to wound the side of the Lord of glory. He tears asunder the Church for which the side of Christ was torn. But the day will come when he shall see him whom he has thus pierced. The Lord when he comes to give judgement will recognize him from whom he now patiently suffers. When ' to every wronged soul he gives redress ', when he ' rights the wrongs of the defenceless ', is he likely to turn a deaf ear to his beloved bride, the Church, appearing ' boldly to meet her old persecutors, that thwarted all her striving '? No! he will not be able to be deaf to her complaint: ' Friends and neighbours that meet me keep their distance now, old companions shun me. I am assailed by enemies that grudge me life itself.' How should he not recognize the bone of his bone and the flesh of his flesh, yea rather already, by then, the spirit of his spirit? Is she not that beloved one whose beauty he has loved so well, whose form he adopted, whom with wonderful condescension he held in loving and chaste embraces, so that they were two in one flesh, to be united forever hereafter in one spirit? And she, although she had ' known Christ according to the flesh, now she will know him so no longer ', because before her face he shall be a spirit and it shall be Christ the Lord. When death is swallowed up in victory, when that which is weak in the flesh shall vanquish in the power of the spirit, when her Bridegroom shall show her to himself as his glorious, perfect, and beautiful dove, having no stain of sin or wrinkle of corruption, then shall she be united to him in oneness of spirit.

7. While I linger so willingly over these things I become forgetful of my subject: ' redeeming the time because the days are evil ' and carried away by my thoughts, but I am brought back by the urgency of my subject, and forced to abandon the pleasant prospects which my thoughts have conjured up to bewail the sad state of our present

condition. This enemy of the cross has had the audacity to drive from their seats the holy men who refuse to fall down and worship the beast who opens his mouth to utter blasphemies and blasphemes the name of God in his tabernacle. He tries to set up altar against altar, to banish what is right and establish what is wrong. He strives to impose abbots over abbots and bishops over bishops, to exile Catholics and impose schismatics in their place. Pitiable and to be pitied are those who consent to receive promotion from such a man. He encompasses sea and land to make one bishop and, when he has made him, he renders him a child of hell twice as bad as himself. What, think you, is the reason for all this frenzy? No other, surely, than that he does not like that distinction the angels made when they announced glory to God and peace to men. So by arrogating to himself the glory that belongs to God, he disturbs the peace that belongs to men. To him alone belongs glory ' who does wonderful deeds as none else ' and, as the Apostle says, ' to him alone be honour and glory '. As for us men, we ought to consider ourselves merci-fully treated and very fortunate, if we are permitted to enjoy the peace of God and peace with God. But how can the peace of men before God and with God possibly endure if God cannot be sure of his glory amongst men? How foolish are the sons of Adam to lose both peace and glory by despising peace and craving for glory! For this very reason has the ' God who takes vengeance ' ' shaken and torn the land asunder ', for this very reason has he ' made us witness cruel sights, such a draught as to make our senses reel '.

8. Whether we like it or not, the truth of the Holy Spirit must be fulfilled; the scandals foretold in the Scriptures must come to pass. But woe to the man through whom they come! It would have been better for him had he never been born. And who else can he be but that man of sin who, notwithstanding that a Catholic had been canonically elected by Catholics, invaded the holy place, which he wanted, not because it was a holy place, but because it was the highest place. He invaded it, I say, and he invaded it with arms, with fire and with bribes, not by the merits and virtues of his life. And he has arrived there, and he stands there, by the same means that brought him there. That election of his supporters of which he makes so much, was not an election but a faction, a mere shadow and excuse, a cover for his malice. It could be called an election of a sort, but to do so were an impudent lie. The authentic decree of the Church still holds: after the first election there cannot be a second. When the first election has taken place, a second one is no election at all, it is completely null. Even if the first election did take place with less solemnity and order than the second, as the enemies of unity contend, how can anyone presume on holding a second without first discussing the manner of the former and suppressing it by judgement.

For this reason whoever hastens to thrust himself forward and rashly to lay hands upon a usurper, in spite of the Apostolic injunction: 'Do not inconsiderately lay hands on anyone', they, I say, have the greater sin, they are the authors of the schism, they are the principals of this great mischief.

9. And now they demand judgement which they ought to have waited for before acting. Now they are prepared to offer a tardy justice which they had the opportunity of doing at the proper time, so that if you now refuse they will appear to have right on their side, and if you accept something may turn up favourable, during the delay caused by the disputes of the two parties. Or do they despair of their cause and believe that things could not be worse for them than they are, however their case is decided? They say that whatever may have happened in the past, all they want now is a hearing and that they are prepared to abide by the results. This is a mere subterfuge. What else is there left for them to do, what else can they do better calculated to confuse the simple, arm the evilly disposed, and palliate their own malice? What else but this could they say? But God has already judged the case which man is trying to re-open too late, and he has judged it by the evidence of the facts, not by the wording of some decree. Can any man be so rash as to dare to change the judgement of God? Will not God cry out in accusation: 'Men have taken away my right of judgement'.[1] 'Counsel is none that can be matched against God's will.' 'His word runs swift' in bringing the people and kings together in one that they may serve and obey Pope Innocent. Who can appeal against this? It is recognized as the judgement of God by Walter of Ravenna, Hildegard of Tarragona, Norbert of Magdeburg, Conrad of Salzburg, Archbishops. It is known and accepted as the judgement of God by the Bishops Equipert of Münster, Hildebrand of Pistoia, Bernard of Pavia, Landulf of Asti, Hugh of Grenoble, and Bernard of Parma. The singular prestige, the outstanding sanctity and authority of these prelates, respected even by their enemies, have easily persuaded me, who occupy a lower position both in office and virtue, to follow them whether right or wrong. I do not mention the great multitude of others, the archbishops and bishops of Tuscany, Campania, Lombardy, Germany, Aquitaine, of France too and all Spain, as well as the whole Eastern Church, whose names are in the book of life (but cannot find a place in a short letter).[2]

10. All these men, with one accord, with no inducement of money, undeceived by any fallacy, not led by considerations of human relationship, nor under duress from the civil power, but with eyes fully open to God's will, which they perceive most clearly, reject Peter Leonis,

[1] Doct. SS. Pat.
[2] The authenticity of the phrase in parenthesis is open to question.

and without any hesitation acclaim Gregory as Pope Innocent. Of our own prelates I do not mention one in this letter, because there is not space to mention all; and to mention some would be invidious and expose me to suspicions of flattery. But I ought not to pass over those holy men who, being dead to this world, lead a better life to God alone; whose life is hid with Christ in glory, where they zealously seek and, doubtless, find what is the pleasure of God, and whose only care is to please him. Of these the Camaldolese, Vallambrosians, Carthusians, Cluniacs, brethren of Marmoutiers, my own Cistercians, the brethren of Caen, Tiron, and Savigny, in a word all the brethren, both secular and regular, with unanimous consent, adhere to Innocent, sincerely approve of him, humbly obey him, and loyally recognize him as the true successor of the Apostles.

11. What about the kings and princes of the world, are they not united in the same spirit together with their subject peoples, acclaiming Innocent and confessing that he is the Pope and Bishop of their souls? What man is there of good repute and illustrious in any rank of life who does not believe the same? And yet those people, with I know not what contentious importunity and importunate contentiousness, still cry out in contradiction. They call the whole world to judgement and, few as they are, they are yet anxious that the whole universe should be judged. Having been over hasty in their election, they endeavour to re-open the case in order to have their position confirmed. First they acted recklessly, and now they want to undo what they have done. But who could bring together such a great army of princes, ecclesiastical and lay, not to speak of the people, so as to submit the matter to their judgement? Who would have the power to persuade so many thousands of holy men to pull down what they have built up and thus place themselves in a false position? Then what place could be found large enough and safe enough for so great a multitude? It is a matter that concerns the whole Church and not just the cause of a private person. You see they have made an impossible suggestion, so as to provide an occasion for calumniating their mother the Church. But, in fact, they have dug a pit for themselves into which they will be thrown, they have contrived a snare in which they themselves shall be caught, so as never to return to the bosom of their mother, the Church. A pretext is never lacking to him who would break with a friend.

12. But let it be so. Let us grant, for the sake of argument, that God may change his decision, call a council together from the ends of the earth, and suffer the matter to be judged twice over. Whom, in such a case, would they choose as judges? All have taken sides in the matter and would not easily agree upon a judgement. Such a council would be rent by faction and led to even more quarrelling rather than to peace. Then I should like to know to whom that schismatic would entrust Rome which, after having desired it for so

long, he has at last got into his clutches at great labour and expense, and which he possesses with such great pride and would be so ashamed to lose. If he should lose his suit but not his city, the whole world would have assembled for nothing. Why, otherwise, should Pope Innocent, who has been despoiled of everything, enter upon the cause? Neither the laws nor the canons oblige him to do so. I say this, not because I doubt the justice of our cause, but because I distrust the cunning of our adversaries. 'The Lord has made his justice as clear as light and his judgement as the noonday' although the light is not seen by the blind man nor does the midday sun shine upon him, because for him 'light and dark are as one'.

13. The question is this: which of these two men seems to be the Pope? There is a great difference between the two persons but, so as not to seem to flatter or abuse either, I will say what you will find being said everywhere and what I do not think anyone will deny, namely that the character and good name of Innocent need fear no comparison with that of his adversary, while his is not safe even amongst his friends. Then if you examine the elections you will at once see that ours is more honest, more creditable, and the first in time. The two first points are proved by the virtues and dignity of the electors, and the last is obvious. You will find, I cannot doubt, that this election was made by the more reputable of the electors. There are the Cardinal Bishops and Priests and Deacons and a sufficient number of those who are especially concerned in the election of a Pope to render it valid according to the decrees of the Fathers. But what about the consecration? Did we not have the Bishop of Ostia, to whom the consecration of a Pope especially appertains? Since then the person elected is the more worthy, the election more honest and regular, what reason or what pretext have these people to try and depose him and, against all right and justice and the wish of all good men, against the will of the Church of God, to set up another over and above him?

14. It must be clear, most reverend and illustrious fathers, that it is our solemn duty to resist with all our might this malicious, unworthy, and rash effort. This is a matter that concerns every child of God, but it especially concerns you and yours, if you are really devoured by zeal for the house of God. You, I say, and yours especially, must watch and pray lest you give way to temptation. And there is especial need of strength and caution in that quarter where the enemy are pressing hardest and bringing the major part of their forces to bear. You know from your own experience how savage and cunning is the enemy. Alas! how great is the spite with which he has acted in your neighbourhood, raging with the twin arms of malice, force and cunning. But can malice ever conquer wisdom finally? Now is his time and the time of the powers of darkness. But it is his last hour, and his power will soon pass away. Do not be afraid, but do

not let yourselves be deceived. Christ, the power and wisdom of God, is with you always, he is on your side. Be confident for he has overcome the world. He is faithful and will not allow you to be tried beyond your strength. You see the fool firmly rooted now, but the time will come when you will see his beauty wither under the curse of God. The Lord will not for long allow ' the rule of sinners in the domain of the just '. But now it is your duty to watch and to take care, as becomes your office, that your good people ' do not soil their hands with guilt '.

NOTE

In the Benedictine Edition (No. 127) there is a letter to William, Count of Poitiers and Duke of Aquitaine, said to have been written by St. Bernard in the name of Hugh, Duke of Burgundy.

It is addressed to the same Count of Poitiers mentioned in Letter 128. He took the side of the Anti-pope under the influence of Gerard of Angoulême. He was finally converted by a personal meeting with St. Bernard.

It is hard to understand why St. Bernard was thought to have written this letter. Nothing in it, but the sentiments, belongs to the saint. It is a brief exhortation to abandon Anacletus and embrace the cause of Innocent. The blameless life and character of the latter are enlarged upon.

LETTER 130

TO WILLIAM, COUNT OF POITIERS AND DUKE OF AQUITAINE

I HAVE not forgotten, most excellent Prince, how I lately left your presence full of good will towards you, and determined to do all in my power to help you and yours, by neglecting no opportunity for promoting your spiritual and temporal welfare. I left you thus disposed, because my visit had not been fruitless. Contrary to the expectations of many, and much to everyone's delight, I had been able to bring away from you an assurance of your peaceful intentions towards the Church. But now you have not scrupled to arouse again the wrath of God against you, even more than before, by expelling the clergy of St. Hilary from their city, greatly to the harm of the Church. I cannot but wonder by what advice, and under whose influence, that wonderful ' change of the right hand of the Most High' in you, should suddenly have been changed again for the worse. Who can have beguiled you to leave so soon the path of salvation and truth? Whoever it is shall surely bear his judgement. ' Would that they should be cut off, these authors of unrest.' Turn back, I pray you, turn back, or you too will be cut off. Turn back, I say, and restore peace to your friends and their church to your clergy, or you will irrevocably alienate him ' that is feared by awe-struck princes, feared amongst the kings of the earth '.

LETTER 131

TO THE PEOPLE OF GENOA

To the Consuls, Councillors, and all the people of Genoa, peace, health, and eternal life, from Bernard, styled Abbot of Clairvaux.

M Y visit to you last year was not fruitless, as the Church, in whose service I came, was soon to discover in the hour of her need. You received me with honour and you tried to persuade me to stay longer. This was more than one in my humble sphere deserved, but it did you great credit, and I have not forgotten it and am not ungrateful. Only God can reward you, and I pray that he may do so, for it was in his name that you received me. What have I to offer you for the honour you did me, but my good will and affection, my love and gratitude? I could not believe myself worthy of your applause, but I appreciated the devotion it showed. What joyous days those were, I only wish I could have stayed longer! Never shall I forget you, O faithful people, noble race, glorious state of Genoa! ' Evening, morn, and noon ', like the Prophet, ' I cried aloud and made my plea known to you ' and your readiness to listen was matched only by my love of the listeners. I brought to you words of peace and, finding you the sons of peace, I left my peace with you. I went forth to sow seed, God's seed, not mine, and the good seed I sowed fell on good ground yielding a hundredfold with wonderful speed, because the necessity was great. I experienced no difficulty or delay, but almost on one and the same day I both sowed and reaped, ' returning with joy as I carried with me the sheaves ' of peace. And this was the harvest I reaped: a joyous hope of release and home for men in captivity, chains, and prison; and fear for our enemies, disgrace for the schismatics, glory for the Church, and great joy for everyone.

2. Nothing now remains, dear friends, but for me to encourage you to continue as you have begun. Is it not only by perseverance that men earn their glory, and virtues their reward? Clearly without it there can be no victory for the soldier or honour for the victor. It is the backbone of character, and the crown of virtue; it is the mother of merits and mediator of rewards. It is the sister of patience, the daughter of endurance, the friend of peace, the link of friendship, the bond of concord, and the bulwark of holiness. Take away perseverance and service will be without reward, kindness without favour, and valour without renown. It is not the man who begins, but the man who perseveres unto the end that shall be saved. Saul, when he was but a child in his own eyes, was set up over Israel; but he lost both his kingdom and his life through not persevering in humility. If Samson had persevered cautious and Solomon devout, the former would not have lost his strength and the latter would have kept his

wisdom. I exhort and pray you to hold firmly on to this mark of the highest honour, this sole reliable protection of integrity. Keep carefully the words you heard eagerly. Remember that Herod was glad to hear John, but he would have been better off had he observed what he heard as gladly as he had listened. Happy are those who not only 'hear the word' but also 'keep it'.

3. Preserve peace with your brothers of Pisa, faith with the lord Pope, loyalty to the King, and honour amongst yourselves. This is desirable, becoming, and just. I have heard that you have received messengers from Count Roger of Sicily, but I do not know what they brought or with what they returned. To tell the truth, in the words of the poet 'I fear the Greeks when they come with gifts'.[1] If you should find that anyone amongst you has been so depraved as to have held out his hand for filthy lucre, take prompt cognizance of the matter and judge him as an enemy of your good name and a traitor, as one who has not scrupled to barter the honour and honesty of the commune. If you should discover anyone trying to sow discord amongst you by whispers, anyone assuming the rôle of the devil, who is ever a lover and author of strife, by disturbing your peace, meet the evil at once by the remedy of a severe judgement, for an evil is the more dangerous the more deeply it is in our midst. A hostile army can lay waste our lands and destroy our houses, but 'bad company corrupts good manners',[2] a little leaven is enough to leaven the whole. Sow, plant, and contrive, not only that you do not fall again into your old evil ways, but that you even make amends for them by good works, for it is written: 'A man's wealth may be his own life's ransom', and again: 'Give alms and at once all that is yours becomes clean'. If you must go to war, if you wish to prove your valour by a contest in arms, do not fight your neighbours and friends. It were better for you to work off your warlike spirit by subduing the enemies of the Church and defending your own honour against the Sicilians. From them your booty would be more honourably gained and more justly held. May the peace and love of God abide with you always.

LETTER 132

TO THE PEOPLE OF PISA

To my friends the Consuls, Councillors, and Citizens of Pisa, health, peace, and eternal life, from Bernard, styled Abbot of Clairvaux.

MAY God befriend you and remember the loyal service, the loving compassion, consolation, and reverence you showed and still show to the bride of his Son in her time of difficulty, in the days of her

[1] Virgil, Æneid, 2.49.
[2] Menander.

tribulation. And indeed this my prayer is already being fulfilled in part, is already bearing fruit, a fitting award is being quickly allotted to you.[1] By choosing you out to be his own people, by setting you apart quite for himself, as a people ambitious of noble deeds, God is already showing you the favour your conduct has deserved. Pisa has been raised to the status of Rome, it has been chosen out from all the cities of the world to be the stronghold[2] of the Apostolic See. This is not a matter of chance or human prudence, it is the providence of heaven, the gracious favour of God towards those who ' have earned his love by loving him '. He has said to Innocent his anointed: ' Here let thy dwelling be, and I shall bless it. Here will be my dwelling place, here my destined home. With my support the Pisans stand firm under the attacks of the Sicilian tyrant, not shaken by threats, enticed by bribes, or hoodwinked by cunning.' O citizens of Pisa, ' favour indeed the Lord has shown you, and our hearts are rejoiced '. Is there a city that does not envy you? Keep safe what has been entrusted to you, loyal city, recognize the favour that has been shown you, and try never to be found ungrateful. Reverence him who is your father and the father of the whole world, reverence the secular princes and the judges of the earth who are amongst you. They bring great glory, splendour, and fame to you. Otherwise, ' If thou knowest not thyself, O fairest amongst cities, thou shalt follow with the shepherds' flocks, and feed those goats of thine beside thy dwellings '. A word is enough to the wise. I commend to you the Marquis Engelbert, who has been sent to help the Pope and his friends. He is a strong and active young man and, unless I am mistaken, loyal. Let my recommendation win for him your favour, especially because I have spoken very well of you to him and have advised him to defer to your wishes.

LETTER 133

TO LOUIS ' LE GROS ', KING OF FRANCE

On November 8th, 1134, Pope Innocent promulgated a bull, convoking a Council at Pisa for May 26th of the following year. For some reason, Louis ' le Gros ' was not at all favourably disposed towards the project. It is not easy to understand why this was so. He may have been jealous of the Emperor Lothair, or his amour propre may have been injured in some way by the Pope. In any case he forbade the French bishops to attend the Council on grounds that the heat would be too great. This called forth the following letter from St. Bernard, and Louis was sufficiently mollified to withdraw his ban on the Council.

---

[1] *digna plane retributio celeri jam compensatur effectu.* Eales: ' Conduct that deserves a reward has already met with rapid recompense '.

[2] *ad Apostolicæ Sedis culmen eligitur.* Eales: ' . . . is chosen to be the *home* of the Apostolic See '.

To the most excellent Louis, King of France, and to his beloved wife and children, Bernard, styled Abbot of Clairvaux, sends health from the King of kings and Lord of lords.

THE kingdoms of this world and their prerogatives will certainly only remain sound and unimpaired for their lords so long as they do not contravene the divine ordinances and dispositions. Why, my lord, does your wrath rage against the elect of God, whom your Highness has also received and chosen as a father for yourself, as well as a Samuel for your son?[1] Your royal fury is arming itself, not against a stranger, but against yourself and your family. How well do the Scriptures say: 'The anger of man worketh not the righteousness of God', for it not only renders you insensible to the damage you are doing to your own interests and honour, but it also often blinds you to what everyone else can see is dangerous to yourself. A Council has been convoked. What is there in this to detract from your royal honour or menace your royal interests? There it will be commemorated and remembered how you, with a ready and special devotion to the universal Church, were the first of all the kings, or among the first, to set forth as a Christian in strong defence of your mother against the rabid fury of her persecutors. There the thanks which are due to you will be rendered by the assembled multitude. There prayers will be offered up for you and yours by a thousand holy men.

2. No one is ignorant that a council of all the bishops is most necessary at this time, unless it be some hard-hearted individual who pays no attention to the straightened circumstances of the Church. You say the heat will be too great. We are not made of ice! Or is it that our hearts are frozen within us, so that, in the words of the Prophet, 'there is none who care for the ruin of Joseph'. But of this another time. Now I, who of your subjects am the least in dignity, though not in fidelity, tell you that it is not desirable for you to try and hinder such a great and necessary good as this Council will be. I have very good reasons for saying this which would make the matter quite clear to you, and I would state them more fully were I not convinced that I have already said enough for a wise man such as you are. But if the Apostolic See has, in its severity, issued decrees which have deservedly troubled your royal serenity, then all your loyal subjects who are present at the Council will endeavour with all their power to have them changed or revoked in accordance with your honour. Amongst these I too will not hesitate to do anything I can.

---

[1] A reference to the consecration of Louis *le Jeune* at Rheims in 1131.

LETTER 134

TO THE CLERGY OF MILAN

MAY you be blessed by the Lord for, by your zeal and energy, your city has been cleansed of error, and has abandoned schism in order to return to Catholic unity. The glad tidings has gone abroad among Catholics, Sion has heard and rejoiced, and you have honour before God and men. How happy was the Church to have received to her bosom so large a multitude of worthy sons for whom she had been grieving as lost! With what a glad and serene countenance God, your Father, has received this sacrifice of your hands! Now, as the sons of peace, you must work for the peace of the world. I shall come to you as you have asked me, because I wish to share and partake in your joy, and I shall bring with me your messengers, my dear brothers. Then I shall try, according to the pleasure of God, to explain those matters of which you have written fully and reasonably. But, as the time in which I have to hasten to the Council is short, I hope it will not inconvenience you to wait until my return.

LETTER 135

TO SOME NOVICES LATELY CONVERTED AT MILAN

The following letter was written by the saint in reply to a message from certain persons in Milan who wished to become Cistercians. St. Bernard visited them on his return from the Council of Pisa, which ended on June 6th, 1135. This led to the foundation of the first Cistercian house in Italy, known as Chiaravalle Milanese, ' Clairvaux of the Milanese '.

To his most dear brothers at Milan, lately turned to God, a spirit prudent and strong that they may bring to a worthy conclusion what they have begun so well, from Bernard, styled Abbot of Clairvaux.

BLESSED be God who has enabled you to despise the glory of the world so that he might give you his own. ' How empty are those sons of Adam, light weight as false coin in the scales ', who, in the words of the Gospel, ' seek glory from one another, and do not want the glory which God alone can give.' They are deceived by their own vanity. But with you it is not so. From this reproach the divine mercy has freed you, so that in every place you might be ' a sweet fragrance of Christ unto God ', for his own glory, for the delight of angels, and for an example to men. If there is joy in heaven over one sinner who repents, how much greater joy will there be over the conversion of so many men like you of such a great city as yours. Stirred by my joy and invited by the most dear brothers, Otto and

Ambrose, whom you had sent for this purpose, I had determined to come to you with them. But believing it better not to come for just a short time in passing, I have decided to put off my visit until I am on my way back from Pisa. I am now on my way there and, by God's help, I shall return by you, so as to forward your holy intentions by such counsel and help as I can give.

LETTER 136

TO PETER, BISHOP OF PAVIA

There were two Bishops of Pavia of this name. The following letter was addressed to the first of the two, who was elected about the year 1130.

IF good seed sown on good soil seems to have brought forth fruit, the glory belongs to him who gave the seed to the sower, the fertility to the soil, and the life to the seed. What part have we in all this? Certainly I will not give to anyone else the glory which belongs to Christ, still less will I take it for myself. ' The perfect law of the Lord brings souls back to life, not I. The Lord's unchangeable decrees make the simple learned, not I.' The credit for good writing belongs to the writer, and not to the pen. It is much if I can claim for myself that ' my tongue is the ready pen of a swift writer '. What credit, you ask, have the feet of them who bring good tidings? Much in every way. First, they are the children of their heavenly Father and do not consider the glory they render him of no interest to themselves. For, being his children, they are also his heirs. Second, they regard the salvation of their neighbour as they regard their own, for they love their neighbour as themselves. Third, ' the labour of their lips ' cannot be completely lost to them, for ' everyone shall receive a reward according to his labour '. I did not close my lips but you opened your heart, therefore yours will be the greater reward because you laboured more. I am quite sure it will not be lost to you that you ' brought out water to meet the thirsty, and bread to meet fleeing men '. No kindly action, no exhortation whereby the poor, who are the children of Christ, are comforted, is ever without reward. We are both fellow workers and fellow helpers of God; let us both hope for a reward in the sight of the holy souls. May God grant that I may never forget you or you me.

LETTER 137

TO POPE INNOCENT

To his most loving father and lord, the Supreme Pontiff Innocent, the humble devotion of Brother Bernard.

THE opposition of Cremona has hardened, their prosperity is their undoing; the Milanese have become arrogant, their over-weening self-confidence deceives them. I am undone and my efforts are frustrated by those who put their trust in horses and chariots. I was sadly leaving when I received some consolation from you. Although the trials I endure for the sake of Christ are many, so also are the consolations I receive through him. When I received your welcome letter my heart was gladdened by the assurance it gave of your safety, of the misfortunes of the enemy, and of the successes of our allies. But when I came to the sad conclusion, my joy was a little damped. Who would not fear your anger? I admit that it is reasonable, and therefore all the more to be feared. My opinion is that what has not yet been accomplished, should be done; but in God's good time. Then you can just as readily do what you intend, and perhaps with less risk. By intemperate action, how soon could all you have accomplished with these people by the mercy of God, and at the cost of so much labour on the part of yourself and your servants, be reduced to nothing! And it would be surprising if such an action were to please him who exalts mercy over justice. Unhappy the lot of that bishop who has been transferred to Ur of the Chaldees from a sort of paradise, ' to have dragons for his brothers, and ostriches for his company '. What can he do? He would like to obey you, but the beasts of Ephesus bare tbeir teeth at him. Very prudently he is trying to disguise his sentiments for the time being, but oniy to incur thereby the very much more fearful wrath of yourself. On all sides he is beset by difficulties; unless he should find it more satisfactory to be without a people than without a lord, since he very properly prefers the favour of his Pope to his See of Milan. Can you doubt his loyalty? If any evil-minded person has tried to suggest to you the contrary, he only proves himself disloyal by spitefully persecuting with venomous tongue a man of excellent character. I implore you, most loving father, to have consideration for this most loyal servant of yours, for the work that has only just been started, for this newly planted tree; I beg you to spare the people who have only lately attached themselves to you and to remember the benefits which, as you rightly say, you have only recently conferred upon them. Remember, dear lord, those words of your Lord: ' I have been coming to look for fruit on this fig tree for three years, and cannot find any '. You have waited scarcely three months, and yet you are already preparing the axe! If you had waited already three years, we would still be entitled to expect a faithful servant of the Lord to wait yet a fourth. Therefore I say: Let it be for this year and permit him to whom you have entrusted the sterile ground of Milan, to dig it about with the spade of penance, to dung it with his tears, so that he can induce it to bring forth fruit.

LETTER 138

TO THE PEOPLE OF MILAN

I LEARN from your letters that I enjoy some favour with you. But, as I can find no reason for this in myself, I must attribute it to a gift of God. I do not refuse the favour of such a great people, on the contrary I willingly accept it, and devotedly embrace with open arms the devotion of so renowned a city, especially now that you have cast aside schism and, to the joy of everyone, returned to the bosom of the Church. It is a matter of great satisfaction to myself that I should have been invited to negotiate the peace; that, although a poor person of no consequence, I should yet have been asked to assume the rôle of ambassador in such an excellent cause. And I consider it not a little to your honour that you should be ready to be turned to peace with your neighbours by such a person as myself when, as everyone knows, the hostile invasions of many cities have been powerless to force this on you. I am now hastening to the Council, but I propose to visit you on the way back, so as to experience the good will of which you assure me. May God who has inspired you thus to trust me grant that you may not do so in vain!

LETTER 139

TO THE EMPRESS OF ROME

WHEN I reconciled the Milanese I did not forget your instructions. Even if you had not mentioned it, I would have borne in mind the interests of yourself and your kingdom, as I always and everywhere do, so far as I am able. They were not received back into the favour of the lord Pope and the unity of the Church until they had openly defied and denied Conrad, received our lord Lothair as their master and king, and with all the world acknowledged him as the august Emperor of Rome; until with their hands upon the Gospels they had promised, according to the wish and command of the lord Pope, that they would make full satisfaction for the injuries they have inflicted in the past. I give thanks to the divine goodness who has thus laid your enemies at your feet without any of the risks of war or human bloodshed; and I beg that when the time comes for them to seek through the lord Pope, as their mediator in this matter, to be received into your favour, they may experience that leniency which I myself know so well, so that they may not regret having followed good advice and may render you due service and honour. It is not fitting that the faithful servants who have worked so hard for your interests should be put to shame. But put to shame they would be if you were found to be inexorable and were to disappoint the hopes of forgiveness which they have held out to the Milanese.

LETTER 140

TO THE PEOPLE OF MILAN

The Milanese, after having been reconciled to Pope Innocent, began again to waver in their allegiance. In this letter the Abbot of Clairvaux exhorts them to loyalty and reminds them of the unfortunate results of their last rebellion.

GOD has favoured you and the Roman Church has favoured you; he as a father, and she as a mother. What more could have been done for you, that has not been done already? You asked that eminent persons might be sent to you from the Curia for the honour of God and yourself, and it was done.[1] You asked that the unanimous election of your venerable Father should be confirmed, and it was done. You asked that your See might be raised to metropolitan rank,[2] a thing which the canons deem unlawful, except in cases of great necessity, yet it was permitted. You asked that your citizens might be released from their bondage to the people of Piacenza, a thing which I am neither willing nor able to pass over, and it was done. In fact what petition which a daughter could reasonably have asked from a mother has there been even any delay in granting you? And to crown all, you will soon have the pallium. Now listen to me, renowned people, noble race, glorious city. Listen to me, I say, who love you and am anxious for your good. I speak the truth and do not lie to you. The Roman Church is very forbearing, but nevertheless she is powerful. I offer you good advice, worthy of attention: do not try too far her forbearance or you will feel her power.

2. But someone may say: I will show her due reverence, but nothing more. So be it, do as you say. If you show the reverence that is due to her, it will be a reverence without reserve, for the Apostolic See, by a unique privilege, is endowed with a full authority over all the Churches of the world. Anyone who withstands this authority sets his face against the decrees of God. She can, if she judge it expedient, set up new bishops where, hitherto, there have been none. Of those which already exist she can put down some and raise up others just as she thinks best; so that, if she deem it necessary, she can raise bishops to be archbishops or the reverse. She can summon churchmen, no matter how high and mighty they may be, from the ends of the earth and bring them to her presence, not just once or twice, but as often as she sees fit. Furthermore she is quick to punish disobedience if anyone should try to oppose her wishes. This you

---

[1] They had stirred up a schism after the deposition of their Archbishop Anselm. Guy of Pisa, Matthew of Alba, and Geoffrey, Bishop of Chartres, were the 'eminent persons' sent to reconcile her to the Holy See.

[2] Milan had always been a Metropolitan See. But in punishment for schism it was reduced to a suffragan status for a time.

have discovered at your cost. What advantage did you derive from your last rebellion and opposition to which you were unfortunately incited by your false prophets?[1] The only result was that, under your suffragans, you were deprived of all your power, honour, and glory. Who was able to stand up for you against the most just severity of the Apostolic See when, provoked by your excesses, it determined to deprive you of your ancient privileges and cut off your members? And even to-day you would be lying shamed and stripped had not the Apostolic See been merciful rather than firm with you. But now, were you to provoke her again, none could save you from far greater penalties. So be careful that you do not suffer a relapse, because, unless I am very mistaken, you would not find a remedy for the consequences so easily. If anyone should advise you, to obey in some things but not in others, you should know, since you have experienced once the severity of the Apostolic See, that he is either deceived or a deceiver. Do what I say, for I do not deceive you. Be humble and patient because God gives his grace to the humble and the patient inherit the land. Be careful to keep in the good graces of your mistress and mother now that you have returned to them, and try in future to please her, so that she may be pleased, not only to keep safe for you what she has given back, but even to add what she has not yet given.

LETTER 141

TO HENRY, KING OF ENGLAND

To Henry, the most illustrious King of England, honour, safety, and peace, from Bernard, styled Abbot of Clairvaux.

IT would be sheer stupidity or ignorance to want to teach you anything that concerns your honour. For this reason it will be enough for me to state my case quite simply, and in few words. Many words are superfluous to one who easily understands everything. We are on the threshold of the city, delivery is at the gates, justice is on our side; but the Roman soldiers cannot live on such fare. So we try to please God with the justice of our cause and cower the enemy with our arms, but we lack the bare necessities of life. What you could do to finish the good work you began with that magnificent and gallant reception you gave to the lord Pope Innocent, you would know better than I do.[2]

---

[1] A reference to the schism and the consequent penalty.

[2] Henry had nobly acknowledged Innocent at Chartres and loaded him with presents, some of which he obtained from the Jews. But it does not appear that he was able to send the help asked for in this letter.

LETTER 142

TO THE EMPEROR LOTHAIR

To Lothair, by the grace of God Emperor of Rome and Augustus, the prayers of a sinner for what they are worth, from Bernard, styled Abbot of Clairvaux.

B LESSED be God who has raised you up to be a sceptre of salvation amongst us for the honour and glory of his name, to restore the Imperial dignity, to support the Church in an evil hour, and finally to work salvation even now upon the earth. It is his doing that the power of your crown spreads and rises more each day, ever increasing and growing in dignity and splendour before God and men. And it was certainly by his strength and power that you were able to make such successful progress in the difficult and dangerous journey you undertook for the peace of your kingdom and the liberation of the Church.[1] You have magnificently achieved the full summit of Imperial dignity and, what is more, the greatness of your soul and faith shone out all the more clearly from your having achieved this with no great show of power. If the earth trembled and was silent before so tiny an army, how much more will terror seize upon the heart of the enemy when the king begins to show the full strength of his arm! The goodness of his cause will inspire him and a double necessity will urge him. It is not any of my business to incite to battle, but I do say, without any hesitation, that it is the concern of a friend of the Church to save her from the mad fury of the schismatics; that it is the duty of Caesar to uphold his own crown against the machinations of that Sicilian usurper. Just as it is to the injury of Christ that a man of Jewish race[2] has seized for himself the See of Peter, so it is against the interests of Caesar that anyone should make himself the King of Sicily.

2. If the double duty of rendering unto God what is God's and unto Caesar what is Caesar's is incumbent upon Caesar, why are the possessions of God at Toul diminished without any gain to Caesar? It is much to be feared that neglect of trifles will end in the loss of great things. What I refer to is this. The Church of St. Gengulphus in that city is, so I hear, being grievously and most unjustly oppressed. And I have heard that you, deceived by some cunning trap of the enemy, prevented the lord Pope from interfering when he was prepared to see that justice was done. I advise and implore you to

[1] This is the journey undertaken by Lothair, on the advice of St. Bernard, from Germany to Rome, in order to place Innocent on the throne and in turn to receive from him the Imperial Crown. As the Anti-pope held St. Peter's and all the strongholds in Rome, this took place in the Lateran.

[2] The father of Peter Leonis was a converted Jew.

be more prudent. Remove your opposition and permit justice to be done before that Church is quite destroyed. I am but an insignificant person, but I am your friend, so that, if I should seem importunate, it is perhaps because of that. I send my devoted greetings in Christ to her Imperial Royal Highness the Empress.

LETTER 143

TO THE SAME

I WONDER at whose instigation or advice you have allowed yourself to be so hoodwinked that a people who have, beyond any doubt, deserved of you a double honour, should have been treated quite to the contrary. I refer to the Pisans who were the first and, at one time, the only people to stand out in defence of the Empire. How much better it would have been if the royal wrath had flamed up against those who dared to take any occasion they could for attacking a bold and devoted people, at a moment too when they had set out in their thousands to encounter the tyrant, avenge the injury inflicted on their territory, and defend the interests of the imperial crown. I may very aptly apply to this people what was said of David, and ask you, 'What city of thine was ever so loyal as Pisa; one who ever does thy errands, obedient to thy commands?' These were the men who raised the siege of Naples and put to flight your only powerful enemy. These were the men who, wonderful to say, at one attack overcame Amalfi, Ravello, Scala, and Atrani, all rich and well protected cities, hitherto reputed impregnable by all who had tried to take them. How much more right and fitting, how much more reasonable and just it would have been had the territory of these loyal men been protected from hostile invasion, at any rate while they were engaged on these campaigns, both out of respect for the presence of the Supreme Pontiff whom they sheltered and served with great honour, and still do, when he was exiled from Rome, and in the interests of the Emperor in whose service they themselves were suffering banishment at that time? But the contrary has happened. Those who were hostile to you have met with favour from you, and those who were loyal have incurred your wrath. Perhaps you did not know. But now that you do know, it is vital and, what is more, only right and proper that you should change your attitude both in word and in deed towards these people. Let them receive from you in future the royal favour and liberality to which they are entitled. How well have the Pisans deserved of you, and how much they could still do for your interests! But a word is enough for a wise man.

LETTER 144

TO THE MONKS OF CLAIRVAUX

To his dear brethren at Clairvaux, monks, lay-brothers, and novices, a lasting joy in the Lord, from Brother Bernard.

Y OUR own experience can tell you how much I am suffering. If my absence is irksome to you, you can be sure it is much more so to me. You are suffering from the absence of one person, but I am suffering from the absence of each and all of you, and this is something quite different and much more hard to bear. I cannot but have as many anxieties as I have sons at Clairvaux; I cannot but fear for the safety, and grieve for the absence of each one of you. This twofold grief will never leave me until I am restored to you, for you are part of my life. I have no doubt of what you are feeling for me, but I am only one person. You have only one reason for your grief, but I have many because I grieve for each of you. It is not only that I am obliged, for the time being, to live away from you, when even to be king would be but a sorry servitude without you; but also because I am forced to move in affairs that trouble the peace of my soul, and are not perhaps very compatible with my vocation.

2. As you know all this you ought to sympathize with me and not be angry at my delay which the needs of the Church render necessary. Indeed I hope that my presence here may not be necessary for very much longer, but you must pray that it may bring forth fruit. We must reckon as gain the loss we suffer, for it is all in the cause of God. He can easily make good, and more than make good, what we lose, for he loves us and is all-powerful. So we must be of good cheer for God is with us and, no matter how great the distance which seems to separate us, we can always be united to each other in him. Any of you who are well disposed, humble, reverent, zealous in reading, attentive in prayer, fervent in fraternal charity, can be quite sure I am not far away from them. How could I not be present in spirit to those with whom I am thus united in heart and soul? But if there should be any one amongst you scheming, double-faced, grumbling, rebellious, insubordinate, restless and flighty, or unblushingly eating the bread of idleness, then even though I were present to such a one in body, yet my spirit would be far from him, in manner of life if not in material space, because he would be alienating himself from God.

3. In the meantime, dear brothers, serve God with fear until I return, so that the time may come at last when, delivered from the hand of the enemy, you may serve him without fear. Serve him with

hope, because he is faithful in his promises. Serve him thankfully, because he has claims on our gratitude. He has every right to claim that we should devote our lives to him, if for no other reason than that he gave his own life for us. Who is better entitled to my life than he who gave his that I might live, than he who has purchased for me eternal life at the cost of his own? And whom can it be more necessary for me to serve, than him who threatens me with everlasting fires? But I serve him willingly because charity sets me free. To this willing service I exhort you, dearest brethren. Serve him with the 'charity which has no room for fear', for which nothing is too much, which looks for no reward, and which yet impels as nothing else can. No fear has the same power to spur us on, no reward can so attract us, no sense of obligation can demand so much of us. Let this be the bond between us, by this let me be ever present to you, especially at the hours of prayer, dearest brothers.

LETTER 145

TO THE CISTERCIAN ABBOTS IN CHAPTER AT CÎTEAUX

WEAK in body and (God knows) anxious of heart I write to you— a wretched man, born to labour, but yet your brother. Would that I might merit to have the Holy Spirit, in whose name you are come together, as my advocate to impress upon your hearts the misfortunes from which I suffer, to portray to your loving eyes the picture of myself sad and on my knees before you. It is not my prayer that he should create in you a new spirit of pity, for I know how habitual to you is that virtue. But I do pray that you may understand from the bottom of your hearts how badly I need your pity. Then I am sure tears would well up from the fount of your love, and that with sighs and groans you would storm the gates of heaven so that God should hear you and have pity on me and say: 'Go back to your brothers, you shall die amidst your own and not amidst strangers'. I am afflicted by so many labours and worries that life itself often becomes a burden to me. To speak in a human way because of my great weakness, I desire to be spared until I can return, so that I shall not die until I am with you.[1] For the rest, dear brothers, 'amend your lives and your likings' and determine and observe what is good, what is honest, and what is wholesome; but above all endeavour to preserve unity in the bonds of peace, and so the God of peace will be with you.

---

[1] How ill the Abbot of Clairvaux was when he wrote these letters, we have no means of ascertaining precisely; but we do know he lived an active life for many years after writing them.

LETTER 146

TO THE MONKS OF CLAIRVAUX

M Y soul is sorrowful and will not be comforted until I return to you. What consolation can there be for me in this evil hour, in this land of my exile? There is only yourselves. Wherever I am, your dear memory never leaves me. But for this very reason your absence is all the more hard to endure. Unhappy am I to be doomed to an exile ever prolonged! In the words of the Prophet, ' Hard was my hurt to bear and these have added to it ', who separate me from you. The exile from God, which we all endure while we are in the body, is hard enough to bear; but added to this I have to endure an exile from you which almost renders me impatient with my lot. To be involved for so long in the vanity of everything here, to be shut in by the rotton feculence of the body, to remain still bound by the bonds of death and still subject to sin, to be for so long without Christ, this is a continual affliction, a wearisome suspense. I had but one remedy for all this, a truly heaven-sent gift, and it was the sight, instead of God's glorious countenance which is as yet hidden from us, of you who are his holy sanctuary. From this it seemed an easy passage to that glorious sanctuary for which the Prophet sighs when he says: ' One request I have ever had of the Lord, let me claim it still, to dwell in the Lord's house my whole life long, gazing at the beauty of the Lord, haunting his sanctuary '.

2. What more can I say? How many times has not that one comfort of mine been frustrated! Unless I am mistaken this is the third time that my sons have been torn from me, weaned before their time. I am prevented from rearing the sons I have ' begotten in the Gospel '. I am obliged to leave my own to undertake the cares of others. I do not know which is the more painful: to be taken away from the former or to be saddled with the latter. O good Jesu, ' for very misery my strength ebbs away, my frame is wasted, and my years are but sighs '. For me ' death is more welcome than life ', only let it be amongst my own brethren, my own family, my own dear sons! As everyone knows, it is sweeter, safer, and more natural to die thus. It were a loving act ' to give me some respite, some cooling breath of comfort, before I go away and am known no more '. If it please my Lord, let my sons be allowed to close the eyes of their father, albeit I am not worthy to be their father; let them be present at my last end and console my passing away; if it should seem good to thee, let my soul be lifted up on the wings of their prayers to the company of the blessed; let my poor body be buried by their hands amongst the bodies of the poor. If I have found favour in thy eyes, grant this my one great desire for the sake of the prayers and merits

of my brethren. Yet not my will, but thine be done. ' I do not wish to live as my own master or die as my own master.'

3. As I have told you of my sorrows, it is right that I should also mention my consolations. First, it is for God's sake that I am suffering all this grief and misfortune; it is in the cause of him for whom all things live. Whether I wish it or not, I cannot but live for him who has purchased my life by laying down his own; for the merciful judge who is able and willing to reward on that last day the sacrifices we have made for him. If I should fight his cause unwillingly, it will only be by his dispensation that I am doing so, and I shall be a wicked servant; but if willingly, then I shall have glory. It is this thought that gives me some respite amidst my troubles. And it is true to say that, for no merits of my own, he has given my labours a happy issue; I can tell from many things that ' the grace he has given me has not been without fruit ', something of which you will probably know. I should like to tell you, for your consolation, how necessary my presence here is or was at this juncture, were it not that it would savour of boasting. It is better that you should learn this from others.

4. Sorrowfully and reluctantly, weak and sickly, and (I must admit) ever haunted by the wan spectre of pale death, I have bowed before the urgent request of the Emperor, the command of the Apostolic See, the prayers of the Church and of secular princes, and suffered myself to be dragged to Apulia.[1] Pray for the peace of the Church, pray for my health, pray that I may see you again, live with you, and die with you. So live that your prayers may avail. Pressed for time and with ebbing strength, my words are broken by tears and sobs, as our dear brother Baldwin,[2] who has taken this letter down for me, can testify. He has been called to serve the Church in another sphere and in another post. Pray for him, because he is my only comfort now and my spirit finds great refreshment in his company. Pray for our lord the Pope who cherishes myself and all of you with fatherly affection. Pray for the lord Chancellor who is like a mother to me, and for all those who are with him . . . my lord Luke, my lord Chrysogonus, and Master Ivo, who are as brothers to me. Brothers Bruno and Gerard[3] are with me and they too beg you to pray for them.

---

[1] The Emperor Lothair, having come to Italy in order to help the Pope, was preparing to return home without having finally defeated the redoubtable Roger of Sicily. As soon as Lothair's back was turned he fell upon Campagna. It was left to St. Bernard to face him. He warned Roger that if he showed battle he would be defeated. Roger scorned his words and attacked the forces of Pope Innocent. But the saint's prophecy was fulfilled, and Roger was forced to leave the field in disorder.

[2] Baldwin, the first Cistercian Cardinal, was raised to the sacred purple by Innocent at Clermont in 1130.

[3] Gerard, Bernard's brother.

LETTER 147

TO PETER THE VENERABLE

To his most reverend lord and father, Peter, Abbot of Cluny, the entire devotion of his Bernard.

MAY the day star from on high visit you, O most excellent man, for you have visited me in a foreign land, and consoled me in the place of my exile! You have done well thus to 'take thought for the poor and needy'. You are a great man concerned with great affairs, and yet you do not forget me when I am absent, even when I have been absent for a long time. Blessed be your holy angel for putting the kind thought into your mind, and blessed be our God for prompting you to follow it! In your letter, that letter wherein you have poured forth your soul to me, I have something to be proud of amongst strangers. I am proud to think you keep me, not only in memory, but also in favour. I am proud to enjoy the privilege of your affection, and I am refreshed by the great goodness of your heart. I am also proud of my troubles, if I may be counted worthy to suffer them for the sake of the Church. But most of all it is the triumph of the Church of which I am proud and which keeps my head erect. If we have shared in her labours, so also shall we share in her consolation. But we must work and suffer with our Mother, or else she will complain of us, saying, 'Old companions shun me. I am assailed by enemies that grudge me life itself.'

2. I give thanks to God who has given her victory, who has 'cherished her and brought her safely through all her strivings'. Our sorrow has been turned to joy, and our tears to the praises of the harp. 'Winter is over now, the rain has passed by, the flowers have begun to blossom, the pruning time has come', the fruitless growth, the rotten branch has been lopped off. That impious one, who made Israel to sin, has been swallowed up in death and gone down into the pit. In the words of the Prophet he 'made terms with death and a compact with hell' and therefore, according to Ezechiel, 'only ruin was left of him, for ever vanished and gone'. That other one too, the greatest as he was the worst enemy of all, he also has been cut off.[1] He had been a friend of the Church, but one of those of whom she complained, saying: 'Friends and neighbours keep their distance now'. If any remain, we can only hope that they may soon meet with a like fate. The time is approaching for me to return to my brethren and, if I should live to do so, I hope to visit you on my way back. In the meantime I commend myself to your holy prayers, and beg you to

---

[1] This was probably Gerard of Angoulême.

remember me to brother Hugh the Cellarer[1] and to the others who are with you, as well as to all your holy brethren.

LETTER 148

TO GODFREY, THE PRIOR OF CLAIRVAUX

To Brother Godfrey the greetings of Brother Bernard.

ON the very octave day of Pentecost God fulfilled our desires by giving unity to the Church and peace to the city of Rome.[2] On that day all the supporters of Peter Leonis prostrated themselves at the feet of the lord Pope to take the oath of fealty and become his liege men.   And the clergy who had been in schism, together with the idol they had set up,[3] also prostrated themselves at the feet of our lord the Pope, and according to custom promised obedience.   There was great joy amongst the people.   At last the peace has come which I felt so sure would come, although I could not tell when.   Now nothing remains to keep me here any longer, and I can change ' I will come ' for ' I am coming ', as you have been imploring me to do. ' I am coming soon carrying with me my award ': the victory of Christ and the peace of the Church.   My departure from the city will be on the Friday after that day.[4]   And so ' I shall come back rejoicing, carrying with me my sheaves of peace '.   These are fine words, but the facts are even finer, so fine that whoever is not glad about them must be either wicked or a fool.

LETTER 149

TO POPE INNOCENT

IF things always went wrong, no one could endure it; if they always went well, anyone would become arrogant.   But Wisdom, who orders all things sweetly, varies the lives of the elect with most necessary vicissitudes, so that they are neither broken by adversity nor weakened by property.   Thus prosperity is rendered more welcome, and adversity more tolerable.   Blessed be God in all things: he has turned our sorrow into joy and anointed our wounds first with wine and now with oil.   The thieves and robbers have been smitten with compunction and brought low.   They have sent back with honour the priest

---

[1] *salutamus fratrem Hugonem Camerarium.*   Eales translates *Camerarium* as ' chamberlain '. This may be correct, but Du Cange quotes Peter the Venerable describing the office as that of a procurator or cellarer: . . . *hoc est fratrum procuratorio officio functus.*

[2] May 29th, 1138.

[3] The anti-Pope Victor who succeeded Anacletus.

[4] *Sexta feria post diem illum egressus est noster de civitate.*   Eales translates: ' The messenger whom I sent you left Rome on the Friday after that day '.

of God on whom they had dared to lay hands[1]; and the spoils which they had plundered, they have got together without delay and returned without cheating.   If any part of them are missing, Dalphin will make satisfaction to you according to your pleasure.   He has sworn with his hand in mine to do this.   If he should present himself to your Majesty in order to honour this pledge of his, as he has undertaken to do, I beg that the young man may be treated more kindly than he deserves.   I do not suggest that his crime should go unpunished but, on the other hand, I would not wish the satisfaction demanded of him to be such as to exasperate him beyond endurance and make him regret having followed my advice.

LETTER 150

TO HUMBERT, ABBOT OF IGNY

Humbert had been a Benedictine at La-Chaise-Dieu for twenty years before entering Clairvaux.   After nine years as a monk of Clairvaux he became Abbot of Igny in the diocese of Rheims.   In the year 1138 he called forth the following strong letter from St. Bernard by attempting to lay down his heavy burden for one that was lighter.   However it appears that fuller information as to the circumstances modified the saint's attitude, for Humbert retired to Clairvaux and when he died in 1148 the Abbot preached the funeral sermon and referred to him in it as a man after his own heart.

GOD forgive you, what have you done!   Who could believe that one so highly endowed as you, should break out into such evil! How is it that such a good tree has been able to bring forth fruit so very bad?   'How terrible is God in his dealings with men!'   I do not wonder that the devil has been able to do it, but I do wonder that God should have permitted it after all your years of what I believe to have been humble and sincere service.   What will he do with me who am but a slothful and careless servant if, even for a time, he can deliver up you, his faithful servant, to the will of his enemies? What sense is there, or rather what is not impious in your flight from duty, over which your sons lament and your adversaries make merry? I wonder that you were not scared by the example to Abbot Arnold.[2] His audacity was not unlike yours, and it met with a speedy but fearful retribution.   Yet he, as I know well, had some excuse, while you have none at all.   You have no disobedient monks, none of your lay-brothers are slothful in their work, you have no neighbours laying violent hands on your property, you do not suffer from scanty or insufficient means of support, so that you might feel obliged to leave those whom you can neither feed nor rule.

---

[1] Is this possibly a reference to the unfortunate capture and subsequent release, upon terms, of Pope Innocent by Roger of Sicily in 1139?
[2] Cf. Letters 4, 5 and 6.

2. Have a care lest those words of God 'They have hated me without cause' be applied to you. What ought he to have done for you that he has not done? He has planted for you a chosen and beautiful vineyard, and hedged it about with the vows of continence. He has dug therein a winepress of the strictest discipline and built a tower of poverty reaching almost to the heavens. He has put you in as husbandman and set you over it as the guardian. 'He has cherished you and will bring you safely out of all your striving' if you but permit him. 'But you are shamefully levelling his wall for every passer-by to rob his vineyard of its fruit. Ah! who will now prevent the wild boar from ravaging it, and the lone dweller in the woods from finding his pasture therein?' I am surprised that you think this is a proper way to prepare for death, as you say in your letter; that you have no fear at all of death finding you in a state of such great scandal and under the anathema of the Pope. If it were really necessary for you to do this, could you not have found some other time for it, but just now when I am kept by the needs of the whole Church so that I cannot come to the help of the poor community you have left exposed to danger. I implore you by him who was crucified for you, spare to torture those who are already sufficiently afflicted; and cease, I beg you, from adding to my already accumulated sorrows. To tell the truth I am so upset by this general and grave schism of the Church that life has become a burden to me, even if you and yours are able to live in peace.

LETTER 151

TO THE MONKS OF THE ABBEY IN THE ALPS

This letter is to the monks of St. Jean-d'Aulps, in the diocese of Geneva. The early history of this house is interesting as showing that the spirit which animated St. Robert and St. Stephen was alive before their day. About 1090 two monks left Molesme and settled at a place called Les-Harpes. In 1094 St. Robert appointed a certain Guy as their first Abbot. This Guy was succeeded by one Guerin. In 1120 Pope Calixtus II dispensed the house from the jurisdiction of Molesme and later, on June 28th, in the year 1136, it was affiliated to Clairvaux. The following letter was written by St. Bernard on the occasion of the election of their Abbot to be Bishop of Sitten in the upper valley of the Rhone.

YOUR good father and mine has been promoted, by the will of God, to a higher place. We must therefore do as the Prophet tells us when he says: 'The sun has been lifted up, the moon stays in her place'. The sun is he by whom your Alpine community was rendered glorious, even as the moon by the sun. But now that he has been lifted up, we who have ' willingly chosen to lie forgotten in the house of God, so that we might dwell no more in the abode of sinners' must keep our place. Our place is the bottom, is humility, is voluntary poverty, obedience, and joy in the Holy Spirit. Our place is under a master, under an Abbot, under a rule, under discipline. Our place is to cultivate silence, to exert ourselves in fasts, vigils, prayers, manual work and, above all, to keep that ' more excellent way' which is the way of charity; and furthermore to advance day by day in these things, and to persevere in them until the last day. I trust that this is what you are busily doing.

2. There is one thing you have done at which everyone marvels. It is that, although your lives were holy, you thought nothing of this but made it your business to share the holy lives of others that yours might become yet more holy. Thereby you have fulfilled what we read in the Gospel: ' When you have done all these things that are commanded of you, say: We are unprofitable servants'. You have proved yourselves truly humble by thus judging yourselves unprofitable servants. It is so rare that anyone leading a good life is ready to do this that when it happens everyone admires it. You were celebrated before, but this has made you more celebrated; your life was holy before, but this has made it even more holy. And wherever word of this your action has gone abroad, it has filled everything with the fragrance of its sweetness. In my opinion this virtue is to be preferred to long fasts and protracted vigils, in fact to every bodily exercise, as it is the ' true godliness profitable to all things'. The Cistercian multitude welcomed you with open arms, and the angels looked down upon you with smiling faces. Those holy spirits know very well that what pleases the omnipotent God more than anything is brotherly concord and unity, since the Prophet says: ' It is good to be joined together'; and another says: ' Gracious the sight and full of comfort, when brethren dwell together united'; and again: ' When brother helps brother, theirs is the strength of a fortress'.

3. I have said that this deed of yours is redolent of humility. We are taught how acceptable this virtue is to the divine majesty by him who has said: ' God resisteth the proud, and giveth grace to the humble'. And God shows how he is the master of this virtue when he says: ' Learn of me for I am meek and humble of heart'. What can I say of my little flock at Clairvaux to whom you have joined yourselves? I cannot describe how great and special is the love with which they welcome you. No words can express the mutual charity which the Holy Spirit has marvellously inspired between us. It now remains for you, my brothers, to invoke the Holy Spirit and set about electing your father. If you wait until I come, the delay would be dangerous, for I fear it would be a long time before I were able to do so. But summon to you Godfrey, the Prior of Clairvaux

and my dear brother, and with his advice or the advice of those he will send in his place, if he cannot come himself, as well as with the advice of your father Guerin, choose such a person as may be able to work for the honour of God and your salvation.

LETTER 152

TO BURCHARD, ABBOT OF BALERNE

The Abbey of Balerne was founded by a few monks from Molesme. The exact date of this is uncertain; some authorities give it as 1097, others as 1107. Later, in 1135, it became affiliated to the Cistercians. Abbot Burchard was sent from Clairvaux to rule it. He was a man utterly devoted to St. Bernard and, in a postscript to the Vita Prima, *he refers to the Abbot of Clairvaux as a second Benedict.*

YOUR words are exceedingly fiery. They blaze with the fire the Lord sent down upon earth. As I read them my heart was warmed within me. I blessed that fiery furnace of yours for sending out such glowing sparks. Was not your heart on fire while you were writing? A good man brings good things out of his good treasure. If I have laboured for you, as you humbly aver, I do not regret it. I ploughed the land in the hope of a great harvest, and I have not been disappointed. My heart is satisfied in a strange land with the fruit of my labours. I can see that the seed I sowed did not fall by the wayside, nor upon rocky ground, nor among weeds, but on good land. If I laboured in sorrow, now I remember my sorrow no more for joy that a child has been born into the world. A child not in understanding, but in malice. Such a child as the Saviour held up for the imitation of older men, when he said: 'Unless ye be converted and become as one of these little children, ye shall not enter the kingdom of heaven'; a child that could say: 'More learning have I than my elders, I that hold true to thy charge', and: 'Very young and despised, I do not forget thy charge'.

2. I thank you, Father, Lord of Heaven and earth, that thou hast hidden these things from the wise and prudent, and revealed them to children. So be it, my father, because it has seemed good to you. By thy good will they are what they are, not by any merit of their own. You do not seek merit in anyone, but you anticipate it. We are all sinners and need that you should first come to meet us. Do you, my brother, acknowledge that you have been met on the way and 'met on the way with abundant blessing', not by myself who am of no account, but by him who went before, inspiring me to admonish you for your good. It is very much if you attribute to me the planting and the watering, but where would I have been without him who gives the increase? Prostrate yourself before him in all

humility, cling to him with all the strength of your devotion.   Regard
me as his servant, your brother servant, a companion for your journey
to the homeland where we are fellow heirs, if I have loyally fulfilled
the service for which I was sent to you, if I have done all I could that
you might win the heritage of salvation.   This is my answer to your
enquiries.   I shall concern myself with your needs and my own
when I return.

LETTER 153

TO PETER THE VENERABLE

To the lord Peter, Abbot of Cluny, the humble affection of Bernard.

I RECEIVED your letter and was overjoyed that such a man as you are
should have ' met with abundant blessing' someone of no account
like myself.   When and where shall we have a suitable opportunity
for the meeting and talk which you suggest?   In the meantime I send
these few words in answer to yours, and will gladly send more if I
can be sure that I will not be troublesome to you.   How could a
person like myself dare to approach you, unless you should stoop to
give me access to your presence?

LETTER 154

TO THE SAME

BECAUSE I am sure that you realize how unwilling I am to oppose
your Reverence in any way, I do not hesitate to make any suggestions to you that I believe are necessary.   Concerning the monastery
of St. Bertin, I could wish that you would act with greater moderation
than you have done.   Even if you were able to bring it into subjection
to yourself quite peacefully and without any opposition, even so I
do not see what you would gain.   I do not believe you are a person
who would find any pleasure in an honour which is accompanied
by such a burden of responsibility.   As it is, since you cannot claim
this monastery without great trouble and disturbance, it seems to me
that reluctance to stir up strife affords you an excellent pretext for
retiring gracefully from the attempt.

LETTER 155

TO POPE INNOCENT II

*This letter concerns the misdemeanours of a young man called Philip.   When
the See of Tours fell vacant through the death of Hildebert in 1133, Geoffrey,
Count of Tours, expelled the Chapter from the city.   His reasons for this
rather high-handed behaviour are difficult to divine.   When the Chapter
met, elsewhere than in their own city, one party of them elected, quite*

uncanonically, a young monk of Fontaines-les-Blanches, by the name of Philip,
a nephew of Hildebert's predecessor, Gilbert.   Philip went off to Anacletus
to have his election confirmed.   He then returned to Tours and took
possession of his See.   The other party in the Chapter had in the meantime
elected a certain Hugh, who was consecrated at Le Mans.   Philip fled from
Tours and took with him the treasure of the Cathedral.   When the matter
was referred to Pope Innocent he entrusted St. Bernard with Apostolic
Authority to institute an enquiry into the matter.   The upshot of this was
that Philip's election was annulled by St. Bernard.   The supporters of
Philip appealed over St. Bernard's head to Innocent himself.   It is at this
juncture that the saint wrote the following letter.   Innocent supported the
decision of St. Bernard, and Philip sought refuge with Anacletus.   He later
repented his misdeeds, became a monk at Clairvaux, and was Prior there
when the saint died.

MAY the members share in the health of the head! May the balm
that was poured over Aaron's head until it flowed down his
beard, reach to the very skirts of his robe! If the sheep are scattered
when the shepherd is smitten, when he is well and strong may they
return to their pasture without fear. What I mean is this. The city
of God has been rejoiced by messages of your many glorious successes.
It is therefore only right that your triumphs should invigorate the
whole Church; that when God honours the chosen of his people,
they too should feel themselves honoured and all the stronger for the
increase of vigour in their head. The Church has suffered with you,
therefore she ought to reign with you. This is something worthy
of you and necessary for us. If the arm of justice was not shortened,
if zeal for it did not languish in times of fear and suffering, shall we
give up now when victory is within sight? Shall the courage that
shone in weakness fade away in the time of triumph?

2. With what a strong hand was that noble monastery of Vézelay
set in order![1] The Majesty of the Apostolic See did not even consider
giving away one inch to the insane rabble of armed people, to the
frenzied fury of undisciplined monks, or to what is more powerful
than all this, the forces of mammon. What shall I say of St.
Benedict's?[2] Was the anger of a king able to shackle the liberty of
spirit armed and stirred against flesh and blood? So also were the
churches of SS. Memmius and Satyrus wonderfully transformed from
synagogues of Satan to sanctuaries of God, whether wicked men
liked it or not.[3] And at Liège too, a choleric and furious king was

---

[1] The monks of Vézelay rebelled against the authority of the Abbot of Cluny when he tried
to impose an Abbot upon them.
[2] This was the Abbey of St. Benedict on the Po.   The trouble was similar to what happened
at Vézelay.
[3] St. Memmius was a famous church of Canons at Châlons.   Innocent II made them follow
the Rule of St. Augustine.   St. Satyrus was a church of secular Canons at Bourges.   Owing
to their worldly lives they were expelled by Innocent and replaced by Augustinian Canons.

unable to enforce, with his barbaric and menacing sword, acquiescence to his shocking and shameless demands.[1]   Who can praise enough the shafts that have been just lately hurled by the same hand, although from afar, against the disturbers of the Church of Orleans?   Truly the arrow of Jonathan did not turn back nor was his sword returned empty.   At the word of this the King was troubled, but not all Jerusalem with him.   Rather he mitigated his wrath at last, ashamed and fearful to be armed in vain against the Lord and against his anointed. Because of all this the majesty of your name fills all the earth and your greatness is above the heavens, but such a good beginning deserves the ornament of a worthy end.   This is what all who love you eagerly hope for, this is what they beg may soon occur.

3. With a like zeal and with an equally powerful arm it is necessary that the Church of Tours should be immediately succoured.   Unless you bring it speedy aid, she also will be on the point of perishing. They say that the spirit of Gilbert lives on in Philip, that he is heir to his ambition as well as his nephew by blood.   The prolonged agony of his mother Church indicates clearly enough how that young man is consumed with the lust to rule.   The wretch has disembowelled her in order that he may beget honour for himself.   By God's will an end has been put to his misdeeds at last, if the authority of the Apostolic See should be pleased to ratify what has been enacted against him at the demand of justice, under compulsion from his wickedness, for the preservation of peace.   God forbid that you should put to shame the loyal children to whom you graciously committed the settling of this business.   God forbid that raging ambition should find a protector in the defender of innocence.   How great is the audacity of this man to attempt such a thing, how great his madness to hope for it!   Twice over has the wretch despised the Apostolic mandate, and now even more brazenly he is venturing to present himself before justice itself in your person.   Who does not see clearly that despairing of his case he is impiously planning to undermine the tower of your strength with the power of his riches.   But there is no danger of this, for he is Innocent whom he is tempting, and the son of iniquity will have no power to injure him.

4. While we sigh for your presence, dearest father, we recall the memory of your kindness, and in this we find our consolation for your absence.   You are ever in our hearts, often on our tongues.   Your name is the salt of all talk, it is sweet to the ear, becoming to the lips, refreshing and warming to the heart.   It is extolled at meetings of holy men, it is the chief topic of their conversation, their prayers are full of it, it is an invitation to prayer.   We are all anxious for you just

---

[1] Lothair at the Council held at Liège made it a condition of his support for Innocent that the right of investiture should be restored to him.   The situation was saved by St. Bernard, who fearlessly rebuked Lothair and reduced him to submission.

now and pray for you and yours that the Eternal God, for whom and on behalf of whom you are labouring in time, may hold you worthy of everlasting memory.

LETTER 156

TO POPE INNOCENT II, CONCERNING THE ELECTION OF PHILIP TO THE SEE OF TOURS

The text of this letter gives the impression of having been hastily dictated to an incompetent scribe.

I HAVE called a meeting, venerable father, to settle the quarrel of Tours, and I have convened it at Blois since it is in the neighbourhood and both convenient and safe for those concerned.   When we met in that place the opponents of Philip's election advanced many reasons against it.   So as not to bother you with all the details, the two chief arguments against the election were that the candidate was under age and that there was a defect in both the number and the status of the electors, since all the archdeacons, the dean and cantor as well as all the priests of his church and most of the clergy, in fact all the persons of any consequence in the Church, had been expelled from their homes and the Church, and could not therefore be present.   On the other hand, they maintain that their election of Hugh was fair and canonical because he was the choice of those best qualified to elect. They deny that it is any valid argument against their election to say that it was held outside the city and church contrary to the usual practice, for the persecution rendered this necessary;   or that the representatives of the other party were not present, for they had been informed and summoned, but had refused to come.   They say that the place chosen had been agreed upon by both parties, but that their opponents stole a march on them by anticipating the day and hurriedly electing Philip on the quiet without them knowing anything about it: that they did not even wait for any of the suffragan bishops, who are more in favour of their election and have given their assent to it.[1]   To this the party of Philip reply: We have a full and adequate answer to all this if only a day convenient to us is chosen.   We do not deny that the present day is the one appointed, but we affirm that our candidate was not informed of it.   Since the case concerns him personally, he ought to be cited by name.   To this the others reply: Not at all, the dispute is between the electors concerning the election and not between the candidates concerning the See.   It is a matter for the litigants to decide, it is they who should be cited, and it would

---

[1] *nam nec de suffraganeis episcopis quempiam expectatum, suæ vero eos magis favere electioni et assensum præbuisse.*   Eales: ' Nor did they wait even for any of the suffragan bishops; but these are said to favour the election, and to have assented to it '.

be a most serious and improper thing to count the candidates amongst the litigants. No one was excluded by the letters of citation, and it is quite enough that Philip was summoned generally with the others. In fact you were clearly told to seek him out.[1] But he had gone away and was not found, so that it was exceedingly improbable that he should be present on the day. But there was nothing to be gained by absenting himself, for the case could be settled without him. And if you say that he should have been allowed to speak for himself as the matter chiefly concerned him, we can only reply that the fault is either his for disappearing or yours for not finding him. If a man chooses to be absent, not only from his city, but even from his kingdom and country, or what his intentions may be for so doing, is no concern of those whose duty it is to send out general letters of citation to the church and city. If he has any confidence in the justice of his case, what is there lacking for a fair trial? We see him surrounded by a crowd of supporters, men experienced and skilled in litigation. He even has armed men to guard him, as though he would have any need for these! He also has the support of bishops and an excellent promoter. Was he then so unprepared? If so, why this large crowd of supporters? And if he was unprepared, the judge offers him all he can need. These things we say, if it should appear that Philip really was ignorant of the day; but how can he now maintain that he has not been informed of the day and place of the hearing since the Abbot of Clairvaux himself told him when he met him hiding in the See of Cambrai, as he chanced to be passing by eighteen days ago?

2. When I had heard all this it seemed best both to me and to the religious and wise men, bishops, abbots and clergy, who were with me, to put an end to this prolonged ordeal of the Church and tolerate no longer the subterfuges and delays of those who cared only for their own interests and nothing for the fate of the Church. We therefore decided that, in the interests of justice, the case ought to be opened immediately and that the pretexts for further delay were not valid. Thereupon the partisans of Philip, having but small confidence in their case, adopted their usual evasive tactics, and appealed. Then we produced the Apostolic rescript which commanded us to settle the case definitely and obliged both parties to abide by our decision. But the partisans of Philip refused to pay any heed and walked out. They were twice recalled, but they refused to come back. So we turned to the other side, but with full judicial procedure, and proceeded with the case as you commanded. When we had received canonical proof of the two points mentioned above, examined all the witnesses, and offered Mass for guidance,[2] we quashed the election of Philip on the

---

[1] . . . *quin vobis manifeste denunciatum fuerit eum quærere.* Eales: ' . . . although you cannot deny that it was openly announced by you that Philip was being sought for '.

[2] . . . *post peracta sacrificia.* Eales: ' . . . and completing all formalities '.

authority of the Apostolic See. With regard to Hugh, since it is evident that he was elected while still below sacred orders, we leave the decision of his case, as is proper, to your mercy.

LETTER 157

TO PHILIP, THE INTRUDED ARCHBISHOP OF TOURS

In this very 'Bernardine' letter, the saint addresses himself to Philip. Almost certainly it was written before the previous letter, when Philip had gone to Rome to have his election ratified by Anacletus, but before he had returned to Tours, and been forced to retire again.

YOU are causing me great sorrow, my dear Philip. I beg you not to mock at my grief, because, if you do not see why I should grieve for you, then there is all the more reason why I should do so. Whatever you think of yourself, I think that your condition calls for a whole fount of tears. My grief is no matter for mockery, but for sympathy. My sorrow has no mere human cause, it is not occasioned by the loss of any fleeting chattels, but of you, Philip. I cannot better describe how great is the cause of my sorrow than by saying that Philip is the cause of it. When I have said this, I have declared what is a great source of distress for the Church, who once cherished you in her bosom when you were growing like a lily, and blossoming with every heavenly gift. Who would not have said then that you were a youth of fair hopes, a young man with great gifts. But alas! how your blossom has faded. From what great hopes has France fallen who gave you birth and nourished you![1] Oh, if you did but know, even you! If you set yourself to learn, you soon will know grounds for grief; and then in your grief, my grief will bear fruit. I would say more were I to follow my inclination, but I do not wish to say much while I am still uncertain, lest I be like one beating the air. I have written this, so that you should know how greatly I care for you, and that I am always at hand if God should inspire you with the wish to talk to me and afford me the pleasure of your company. I am at Viterbo and you, I hear, are in Rome. Be so good, I beg you, to answer this letter and tell me how it strikes you, so that I may know what to do, whether I should grieve more or less for you. And if you scorn everything I have said and refuse to hear me, I will not lose the fruit of this letter, for it proceeds from charity, but you will have to answer for your contempt before that fearful tribunal.

---

[1] *A quanta spe decidit Francia.* Watkin Williams (*op. cit.*) sees here a reminiscence of the *Quanta de spe decidi* from the *Heautontimor* of Terence (II.iii.9).

LETTER 158

Written on behalf of the Bishop of Troyes, who had got himself into trouble by trying to reform the clergy.

THE insolence of the clergy is being everywhere a nuisance and troubling the whole Church. The cause of it is the negligence of the bishops. The bishops throw what is holy to the dogs, and cast pearls before swine, who turn upon them and tread them down. But it is only right that they should have to suffer for those they foster. Because they do not correct those whom they endow with the riches of the Church, they have to put up with their misconduct. The clergy fatten on the sweat of others, they devour the fruits of the earth without charge, and so ' malice distils from their pampered lives '. The old saying of Scripture is true even to-day: ' The people sat down to eat and drink, and rose up to take their pleasure '. The mind accustomed to delicate meats, and uncultivated by the rake of discipline, contracts much filth. And if you attempt to clean it away, they will not permit you to so much as touch it with your finger tips, but act like those of whom the Scripture says: ' A people well loved and pampered, would throw off the yoke and revolt against their deliverer '. Now ' false witnesses have stood up to accuse ', men who delight to be for ever carping at the lives of others, while neglecting their own. Your son pleads with you for the Bishop of Troyes whose only fault in this quarrel is, so far as I can make out, to have rebuked the faults of the clergy. So much for the bishop. Now I must make my own excuses. The letter in which you were good enough to beg me to come to you when you could quite well have ordered me to do so, did not arrive before the Nativity of Our Blessed Lady. Therefore I do not say I have bought a yoke of oxen or a house or that I have married a wife, but I confess quite simply that, as you very well know, I have children and must nourish them, and so I do not see how I could come to you without grave scandal and danger to them.

LETTER 159

YOU earnestly entreat me and I firmly refuse you, but only because I want to spare myself, not because I scorn you. I wish I could compose something worthy of your zeal and intelligence. I would give you my very eyes, even my life, were I able to, my most dear friend, for I especially have every reason to love you spiritually in

Christ with all the power of which I am capable. But how can I find the ability, let alone the leisure, to do as you ask? It is not as though you were asking me to do some little thing that would be quite easy and ordinary. You would not be so insistent were it only a small matter. Your many letters, and the vehemence which animates them, are a clear enough indication of how serious you are in the matter and what great store you lay by it. And the more anxious I feel you to be, the more diffident do I become. Why so? Simply because I do not want to bring forth an absurd mouse in return for your great hopes.[1] This is what I so much fear, and this is the reason for my delay. It is not surprising that I should fear to give you what I should blush to see published. I am most unwilling to produce what I should regard as more fit for contempt than for publication. Who would wish to give anyone something that it would shame him to give and be no advantage to receive? I willingly give you what I have, but I am not so willing to lose it. Everyone knows how disappointing it is to receive something small when something great has been expected. And what is received with disappointment is not given but lost.

2. It is your endeavour, as a man of leisure and freedom, to seek on all sides fuel for the fire that burns within you, so that you may burn the more, and thus fulfil the words of the Lord to you: ' What would I but that it be kindled? ' I have nothing but praise for this, but I beg you to look where you may not be disappointed in receiving. You are mistaken if you think you can find anything in me to satisfy you. It is I who should beg from you. I know very well that it is more blessed to give than to receive, but only if the gift is creditable to the giver and useful to the receiver, such a gift as I doubt whether I have got to give. Were I to give you what I have, I am afraid that you would feel ashamed to have asked for it, and would regret having received it. But still, perhaps it would be better for you to make your own excuses for me, that your own eyes should provide you with evidence of the truth of what I say. And so I will accede to your importunity, so that you may have no doubts about my insufficiency. It is a matter between friends. I will not try any more to spare my modesty, I will forget my own foolishness in trying to satisfy your demands. I am having copied a few sermons I wrote recently on the first verses of the Song of Solomon, and as soon as they are ready I will send them to you. When I have the time, when Christ sees fit to calm the storm of cares that beset me, I shall continue with them, but you must encourage me. I send my devoted greetings to my lord and father, your Prior, and to your other brethren, and I humbly beg them to remember me before God.

[1] *parturient montes, nascetur ridiculus mus.* Horace, *De Arte Poetica.* ' The mountains will give birth and an absurd mouse be born.'

LETTER 160

TO THE SAME

M Y dearest Bernard, I cannot hide my sorrow nor can I disguise from you any longer the grief which I suffer. I have not forgotten my long-standing promise to you, I have for long had the firm intention and great desire to pass by you, so that I may see again those whom my soul loves and, in their company, find consolation for my journey, relief for my labours, and healing for my sins. But in punishment for my sins it has come about that regretfully I find that I am not able to do so. I acknowledge this not as a fault, but as a punishment for my faults. I beg you to understand, man of God, that it is not at all that I do not care for my friends, nor is it that I am lazy or negligent in the matter, but simply that I am prevented by the work of God which I cannot ignore. My vexation gnaws at me like a worm, and my grief is ever with me. I am troubled enough on other accounts but, I must confess, on none so much as on this. It vexes me more than all the labours of my journey, than the discomfort of the heat, than the anxiety of my responsibilities. Now that I have exposed my wound to my friend, it is your business to have pity on me and relieve me by sharing my burden. I implore your prayers, and the prayers of the holy men with whom you live. I am sending you the sermons on the beginning of the Song of Solomon, as you have asked me to do and as I have promised. When you have read them, I beg you to write as soon as you conveniently can and tell me whether you think I should continue with them or not.

LETTER 161

TO POPE INNOCENT

This letter was written on behalf of the Carthusian Bernard, to whom the two previous letters are addressed, when he was chosen to be Bishop of Pavia. In the event he became Bishop, not of Pavia, but of Belley.

I HAVE heard, venerable father, that Bernard of Portes, a man beloved of God and men, has been obliged by your invitation to shoulder the burden and work of a bishop. It seems very likely to be true, for it is a thing highly becoming to your apostolate to place a hidden light where all men may see it, so that he shall live not only for himself but bring others too into the light. How long is one who can give light to others to burn and shine in hiding? If it should please you, let him be set upon a candlestick that he may be a burning and shining light to others; but let it not be where the force of great winds prevail lest (which God forbid) the light should be put out. Who does not know of the effrontery and turbulence of the Lombards? And who knows it better than you? You know better than I do how weak is the power of the episcopacy in those parts, and what an ungovernable household it is. I cannot think what a young man, broken in bodily health, accustomed to the peace of a hermitage, would do amongst such a turbulent, uncivilized, and tempestuous crowd of people. How could such perversity and such sanctity, such craftiness and such simplicity, ever mix? If it should please you, let him be kept for a more suitable See and for a different sort of people who could benefit by his rule. Do not allow the fruit which he will be able to give in due season be lost through too great hurry.

LETTER 162

TO THE SAME, ON BEHALF OF THE CHURCH OF ORLEANS

For how long will the misery of the Church of Orleans appeal in vain to the heart of the father of orphans and the judge of widows? For how long shall the noble virgin of Israel lie prostrate in the dust, deprived not only of her husband, but even of her children? And for shame! there is none to lift her up. How long will it be before you attend to the children and their mother who are crying after you for mercy? I refer to those who have lost their homes and goods, and have only been able to save their lives by flight. Why do you stay that strong hand of yours, which has never before failed to avenge the down-trodden and smite the arrogant? Why are you hesitating to rescue the afflicted from the power of the bully and mete out vengeance to the haughty? If you must delay, let it not be for ever. Help when it comes late should come with all the greater strength and should afford succour all the more effectively. If it should so please you, may it be some compensation for your delays that those who have proudly abused the patience of the Apostolic See may gain nothing by it in the end; and that those who have suffered so patiently, trusting in you, may at last have no reason to regret their patience.

LETTER 163

TO CARDINAL HAIMERIC, ON BEHALF OF THE SAME

To his special friend, Haimeric, by the grace of God Cardinal Deacon and Chancellor of the Apostolic See, that he may shine with the light of wisdom and virtue, from Brother Bernard of Clairvaux.

If I did not already know your great compassion for the afflicted and your disgust for the shameless, I would implore you in season and out of season on behalf of Master William of Meun and his companions. I would compel you to take action against their oppressors and calumniators. But it is enough to have mentioned it to you; now it is up to you to prove that it really is enough!

LETTER 164

TO POPE INNOCENT, CONCERNING THE MURDER OF MASTER THOMAS, THE PRIOR OF ST. VICTOR'S AT PARIS

The following letters concern a double tragedy, arising from the confusion occasioned by the schism. Some four years before this letter was written, about the year 1129, St. Bernard had played an important part in reforming the Chapter of Notre Dame in Paris. Strongly supported by Stephen of Senlis, Bishop of Paris, who introduced the Canons Regular of St. Victor, the reforms were carried through in the teeth of opposition from the secular power. Thomas, the Prior of St. Victor, was the instrument of St. Bernard's policy of reform. A man of the greatest zeal and probity, his first concern was to restrain the venality of Theobald Notier, the Archdeacon of Paris. In order to obtain some sort of justice in the courts of this Archdeacon, the clergy had to pay him very large fees. To remedy this Thomas introduced far-reaching administrative reforms.

The result of this was that when Thomas was on a journey accompanied by the Bishop of Paris, Stephen of Senlis, and several other clergy, just as they were passing by the castle of Stephen de Garlande at Gournay-sur-Marne, Theobald, Notier's nephew, rushed upon Thomas and brutally murdered him in the arms of his bishop. Because it was a Sunday the company were unarmed and obliged to fly in order to save their lives. Stephen took refuge at Clairvaux.

The other murder was that of Archibald, Sub-Dean of Orleans. Apparently a certain John had usurped the Archdeaconry of Orleans during the vacancy of the See. The issue is a little difficult to unravel, but it appears that Archibald strongly opposed the pretensions of John and, for his pains, got murdered. This was the climax of a long period of unrest in the Church of Orleans.

To his most loving father and lord, Innocent, by the grace of God Supreme Pontiff, the entire devotion and service, for what it is worth, of Bernard, the unworthy Abbot of Clairvaux.

A WILD beast has devoured Joseph and, unable to meet the attacks of our dogs, it has fled to you, they say, for protection. The wretch must be mad to think that he, a wanderer and fugitive on earth, can find a refuge just where he should have most cause for fear. The scoundrel! Does he think that the seat of supreme justice is a den of thieves or a lair of lions? Does he seek refuge with the mother whose son he has butchered, does he dare to appear before his father, still licking his chops, his jaws still red with the blood of their son? Yet if he should ask to do penance, it should not be denied to him. But if he should only ask for a hearing, let him receive the answer that Moses gave to the people when they were worshipping the molten image, or that Phinees gave to the fornicating Israelite, or that Mattathias gave to the man who sacrificed to devils or, to take examples from nearer your home, let him hear from you what Ananias heard from the blessed Peter, or what the Saviour said to the money changers in the temple. Do we not know that the sins of some men go before them to judgement? Does not the voice of your brother's blood cry out against him to heaven? I believe that the spirit of our martyr, whom he has brutally killed during the last few days, with the souls of all the others who have been slain, is crying out with a strong voice from beneath the altar and demanding a vengeance all the more urgently for his blood having been poured forth so recently.

2. Do you ask, wretch, 'Was it I who killed him?' No, not you, it is true, but your people on your account. Whether by your designs, God shall see and judge. If you have any excuse, you whose teeth are spears and arrows, you whose tongue is a sharp sword, then the Jews are not to be blamed for the death of Christ, for they were careful to keep their hands off him. When the archdeacon found his cupidity restrained by blessed Thomas, a lover and protector of justice, so that he could no longer levy the illegal exactions which, on the score of his archidiaconate, he had been in the habit of doing for some time, he hated him so much that with bloodthirsty intent he was wont to threaten that he would murder him. There are now many witnesses of this, and they should not be ignored. Let the archdeacon say, if he can, what else than this his nephews had against him that they should have laid their murderous hands upon him, a holy man of God. If this man who is the cause, instigator, and also (as everyone suspects) the plotter of this crime; if, I say, this man should go unpunished by the Holy See (which, with unbelievable audacity, is just what he is hoping for) it will be an enormous incitement to other evils in the Church. One of two things would then have to follow: either no one noble or powerful according to the world could be admitted to ecclesiastical honours, or the clergy would have to be permitted everywhere to use their holy office for unworthy purposes, for fear that if anyone, fired by zeal for God's glory, should try to restrain them, they would be immediately butchered by the swords of soldiers as an upholder of justice. And then what would become of the spiritual sword, ecclesiastical penalties, Christian law and order, reverence for the priesthood, and finally the fear of God, if through terror of the secular power, no one should dare to so much as whisper against the effrontery of the clergy? Could there be any worse disorder, anything more unworthy of the Church, than that anyone should claim for himself ecclesiastical dignities by virtue of brute force and not of a holy life? Judge this man, my lord and father, as it shall seem good to you, but let your judgement be such as to benefit the Church and assure security, not only for the present time,

but for future generations. Let coming generations know not only of the crime that was done in our times, but also of the punishment that rapidly followed. Otherwise, if the poison should creep through the body without the antidote being administered, it is much to be feared that it will destroy many, and may God forbid this!

NOTE

IN a letter to Pope Innocent on the same subject (Benedictine Edition, 159), Stephen of Senlis, Bishop of Paris, tells how Thomas the Prior was brutally murdered in his arms. He recounts how Thomas, excellent in good works, had zeal and helped to bear the burden of his bishop. He describes Theobald Notier as the cause of the crime and his nephews as the perpetrators of it, and he begs that justice may be done, warning the Pope not to believe anything the criminals may say until he has heard from him more fully.

In another letter (Benedictine Edition, 160), the Bishop of Paris reminds Haimeric, the Chancellor, of his professions of friendship towards him and begs him to prove his sincerity by his zeal in bringing Notier to justice.

LETTER 165

TO POPE INNOCENT, CONCERNING THE MURDER OF ARCHIBALD, THE SUB-DEAN OF ORLEANS

THE voice of the blood of the Sub-Dean of Orleans increases in strength! Alas now, in the words of the Prophet, 'bloodshed never ends, but it begins again' and cries out to you with a strong voice from France. The blood cries out, I say, and lifts up its voice in a cry strong enough to shake the very palace of heaven, piteous enough to soften even a heart of stone. What are you about, O friend of the Bridegroom, guardian of the bride, and shepherd of Christ's sheep? Do you believe it is enough to think out a remedy for such a fearful, such an unheard-of disease as this? Certainly it is necessary to find something that will heal the wound that has been lately inflicted on the Church and act as a deterrent for the future, but it must also be applied. Gird your thighs with a sword, most powerful one! The destruction will not cease until Phinees rises up and makes amends. If the strength of the Church should spare these two, I mean John and Theobald Notier, by whom innocent blood has been shed, if not by their own hands, certainly by their consent, and perhaps by their design, who cannot see what must follow? How many amongst the clergy would the impunity of these men help to high preferment against all right and justice, not for their good lives, but for fear of their armed friends. A new disease must be met with a new remedy. Many think that it would be a good thing and most beneficial if you should cut these men off from all ecclesiastical dignities, so that they may be deprived of what they have and prevented from rising to others.

LETTER 166

TO HAIMERIC, THE CHANCELLOR, ON THE SAME MATTER

I HAVE often told the lord Bishop of Paris how you are always speaking kindly of him to me. And now the time has come for you to prove, not by word or tongue alone, but in deed and truth, that I am no deceiver and you no liar. This matter concerns you not only on account of the bishop, but also on account of your other friends, who would certainly be most anxious for you and very disturbed were this case to go otherwise than as they hope.

LETTER 167

TO JOHN OF CREMA, CARDINAL PRIEST, ON THE SAME SUBJECT

I SHALL never forget the love and condescension you have shown me, an individual of no importance whatsoever. It is ever my prayer and constant hope that the austerity and holy life whereby you please and delight the angels, may bring forth worthy fruit. This fruit the Church of France, as well as myself, is now expecting, and I believe not out of due season. It concerns both my good name and yours, that I shall not be disappointed in you. May it be as clear as daylight to all men that your zeal for justice and truth burns against these murderers of the clergy, and against those who are behind them, so that I may never have reason to regret of having boasted of you.

LETTER 168

TO GEOFFREY, THE ABBOT OF ST. MARY'S ABBEY, YORK

The fat slumbers of the great Benedictine abbeys were stirred with uncomfortable dreams when the Cistercians arrived in Yorkshire. St. Mary's Abbey, York, was the first to suffer a dramatic awakening. The abbey had become rich and had adopted all and, if one may believe the hints of early chronicles, rather more than all the traditional modifications of the Holy Rule. Yet there remained an élite who were not satisfied with the comfortable life of the abbey. At length, Richard, the prior, and Gervase, the sub-prior, presented on behalf of their followers a scheme of necessary reforms to Geoffrey, the abbot. The abbot, who appears to have been a weak character and was certainly old, instead of giving a clear answer tried to temporize. The reforming party were not satisfied and asked for permission to break away and live a life strictly in accordance with the Rule. The abbot refused and bitterly reproached them with levity, disobedience, and causing dissension in the community. Richard appealed to Thurstan, Archbishop of York. The archbishop summoned the abbot, the prior, and the sub-prior to conference before witnesses at his house. During the conference the abbot said he could do nothing without the consent of his chapter. Whereupon the archbishop offered to meet the chapter and hear the matter discussed. On the appointed day he arrived at the abbey and was forbidden entrance by the abbot. When he expostulated, the monks raised a clamour and attempted violence. He thereupon laid the abbey under an interdict, at which one of the monks cried out that a century of interdict would be preferable to episcopal interference. An attempt was made to seize Richard and his party and thrust them into prison. They took refuge in the entourage of the archbishop who returned to his home taking them with him. That was October 17th, 1132. There were thirteen monks altogether and they remained with the archbishop for three months. During this time two of them, Gervase and Ralph, returned to their mother house; but Gervase rejoined the reformers later on. It was at this moment that the Abbot of St. Mary's appealed to St. Bernard and received the following letters.[1]

On Christmas day of the same year Archbishop Thurstan installed Richard and his companions on land of his own in Skeldale, a solitary and uncultivated wilderness. And then, having presided at the election, he blessed Richard as the first abbot of the new community. Such were the turbulent beginnings of the great Cistercian abbey of Fountains.[2]

YOU write from across the sea to ask my advice, and I could wish you had gone to someone else. You have put me into a dilemma, for if I do not answer you my silence will appear rude; if on the other hand I do answer you it is difficult to know what I can say without offending anyone or without seeming to favour anyone unduly or to countenance anything unwisely. I can say that it was not with the knowledge, advice, or encouragement of myself or of any of the brethren here that your monks have left you. But I believe it to have been by the inspiration of God because, in spite of all your efforts, they remain firm in their purpose. And I believe that those very brothers feel the same who implore me for my advice about themselves, I suppose because their conscience gnaws at them for going back, otherwise, according to the words of the Apostle, if they are not troubled in their conscience for what they have done, ' they are fortunate '.[3]

---

[1] Vacandard dates this letter and the following two letters at the May or June of 1133.

[2] For the story of Fountains see *Monastic Order in England*, Knowles, Vol. I, pp. 231–239.

[3] *Credimus autem ex Deo fuisse, quod nec tantis potuit dissolvi conatibus. Credimus hoc idem et ipsos sentire fratres, qui nostrum tantopere de seipsis consilium flagitant, credo remordente eos conscientia quod retro abierint. Alioquin beati sunt secundum Apostolum, si se non judicant in eo quod probant.*

The whole tone of the letter, as well as the background of it, and the words and syntax, seems to make it clear that this passage refers to the two monks who left the reformers and returned to St. Mary's. They were Gervase and Ralph. Evidently they must have been uneasy about themselves and given Abbot Geoffrey no peace until he had written to St. Bernard. Gervase, we know, rejoined the reformers. Likewise at the end of the letter, it seems quite clear that the saint is referring to the two monks who returned to St. Mary's when he says, *Quidnam vero majus aut minus, superius aut inferius, arctius sive remissius sit, quod videlicet reliquerunt, an ad quod redierunt.*

However, Dr. Eales has thought differently and translated accordingly. The words *remordente eos conscientia quod retro abierint* he translates, ' their conscience troubling *them because they quitted you* ', i.e., the Abbot of St. Mary's. And the words . . . *quod videlicet reliquerunt, an ad quod redierunt* he translates, ' the state which they have left or that which *they have embraced* '.

And now what shall I do so as not to give offence either by not answering your letter or by what I answer? Perhaps it would be best for me to send you to one more learned than myself, one whose prestige and holiness entitle him to speak with greater authority than I. In his book on Pastoral Care[1] St. Gregory says: 'The second best is unlawful for one who has chosen the best'. And to confirm this he quotes the words of the Evangelist: 'No man who puts his hand to the plough and then looks back is fit for the kingdom of heaven'. From this he concludes that anyone is guilty of looking back who, having once undertaken great things, leaves them for something less perfect. And likewise in his third homily on Ezechiel he says: 'There are some who while leading as good a life as they know, decide, while leading it, on something more perfect, but afterwards change their minds and retract the good intentions they had. They continue in the good way they had begun, but fall away from the better one they had intended. Such persons appear to do well before the eyes of men, but before God they have fallen away.'

2. Behold a mirror! May they consider in it not only their bodily features, but the facts of their turning back. Herein let them examine and judge themselves, their thoughts answering for and against them, according to what that spiritual man has said who judges all things, but is himself judged by no man. It is not for me rashly to decide, but for them to make up their minds whether what they have left or what they have returned to is greater or less, higher or lower, harder or easier. St. Gregory has spoken to them. But to you, reverend father, I can say with the assurance of complete certainty and the naked truth that it would not be well for you to try to extinguish the spirit: 'Suffer him to do good who may, and thou thyself, when thou mayest, do good'. Rather should you take a pride in the progress of your sons, because it is written that a wise son is the pride of his father. For the rest let no one be offended with me because I have not hidden the righteousness of God in my heart,[2] unless it should seem to anyone that in order to avoid giving offence I have said less than I should.

LETTER 169

TO THE SAME

To the venerable Dom Geoffrey, Abbot of the Church of St. Mary at York, greetings in the Lord from Bernard, styled Abbot of Clairvaux.

IT has pleased your Reverence to consult me by letter on some doubtful matters. But I am fearful of delivering a decided opinion on these and like matters in proportion as, regarding as clearly as a man may

[1] Chap. 28.
[2] Cf. *Rule of St. Benedict*, Chap. 2.

9

the designs of Divine Providence, I hesitate to shock others by saying what they do not wish to hear.[1] And this is especially the case with those whose conscience is troubled by the worries of a too subtle mind and bemused in a fog of difficult and tortuous reasoning. But it is the avenger of its own voluntary blindness because, while it tries to justify to itself what it has done it suffers pricks and twinges from the truth which it remembers. The psalmist bewails the bitterness of such a frame of mind and prays: ' Bring my soul out of prison, O Lord, that I may praise thy name '. Do not therefore, I beg your Reverence, attribute it to any craftiness on my part if I am not able to answer your enquiries in the way you want, or if I do not venture to say what I want quite openly. Your letter takes its complexion from the complaints with which it begins. You bemoan the fact that in your old age some of your monks should have dared to desert you in order to pass to a more straight and safe way of life. Take care that your grief is not the grief of this world which ' worketh death '.

2. Surely if reason counts for anything in the opinions of men it should not be a matter for grief that someone should sometimes try to observe the laws of his Creator more strictly. And indeed we superiors are not watching over the souls of our sons with sufficient holiness and fatherly care if we resent their spiritual progress. If you want sound counsel, as I have no doubt you do, then I advise you not only to make it your business to see that those who remain with you in a mitigated observance of the Rule do not fall away, but also, according to the words of the Prophet, to ' bring out bread ' to meet those whose conscience did not suffer them to continue living in a manner out of keeping with the full purity of their vows and who have passed from the good way in which they began to a higher state of life. It should be your especial care to see that the former do not become reckless to their own ruin, and to encourage the latter that they may progress to their own glory. Surely those who have ' set their heart on the upward journey ', who go from virtue to virtue, will deserve all the more joyously to see the God of gods in Sion for having tried to follow more exactly a purer way of life.

3. And now about those two monks, Gervase and Ralph, who set out in the company of the others with the paternal and episcopal sanction of the Lord Archbishop Thurstan, having been released (as you admit) by yourself. I am sure that had they persevered in the pure state of life to which they had risen, they would have done, not wrongly,

---

[1] The text here is not quite obvious. *Verum de his et similibus tanto quid certum respondere pertimescimus, quanto minus divinæ voluntatis beneplacitum, sicut homines, ad purum intuentes, proximorum animos, si quicquam aliud quam volunt edicimus, offendere dubitamus.* Eales, who claims to have translated the text of the letters literally, has: ' But I am afraid to give any decisive answer; and hesitate the more to do so, inasmuch as if men with the purest intentions are unable to discern the minds of their nearest companions, they are still less able to discern the secret designs of the Divine Will. Again, I am afraid in so speaking to wound those who do not share my own opinion . . .'

but well. But I am also sure that if they wished to resume again that pure state from which they heedlessly fell away, they would be all the more praiseworthy on account of their courage, as soldiers are all the more glorious for their victory when they have returned willingly to the field of battle after having once shamefully deserted. It is my opinion that although the release you gave can be revoked, yet it cannot be rendered void before the judgement-seat of God. You admit their way of life is more holy yet you say that on account of the frailty of the flesh and the ties of personal relationship they cannot sustain for long the hardship of it. But you go on to say that their presence is necessary to you and to express grave doubts as to whether they can remain without fault in a position in which they did not place themselves without scandal.

4. One must distinguish between different sorts of scandal, and carnal affections must be completely cut off for the love of Christ. The Gospels thunder exceedingly, the whole of Scripture cries out on every page, that worldly advantage must be abandoned for the good of the soul, and to ignore this is not only wrong, it is almost heretical. I am not at all sure that such a return as you hope for ought not to be regarded as a grave sin. It is a most dangerous thing, not far short of a catastrophe, to presume on the mercy of God at the expense of his justice and, as it were, to play one off against the other, or in the words of Scripture ' to add sin to sin, and say: The mercy of God is great '. It is a mistaken sort of discretion to put small things before great, and to place the worse on the same footing as the better.

5. After this you go on to demand vigorously why those who return should be called apostates seeing that they are only trying to fulfil their vows according to the recognized customs of their house. It is not for me to condemn them. The Lord knows who are his own and everyone shall bear his own burden. He whom the darkness does not comprehend shall be known as the Lord on the day of judgement, and ' the wicked shall contrive their own undoing '. Let everyone judge of himself as leniently as he likes, but I shall say what I think of myself. I, Bernard, if I had in will and deed passed freely from something good to something better, from something dangerous to something safer, and then afterwards wilfully returned again to what I had changed for the better, I would very much fear that I had rendered myself not only an apostate, but also unfit for the Kingdom of God. And this is what blessed Gregory says: ' Whoever ', he says, ' attempts the best renders the second best unlawful for himself, since it is written: " No one who puts his hand to the plough and then looks back is fit for the Kingdom of God ". And whoever once he has undertaken great things falls back on something less excellent is guilty of looking back.' With regard to a certain excommunication you wish to discuss, to my mind it would not profit you to consider it, nor me to

give an opinion on it. The law judges no man without a hearing and it is rash to launch an excommunication against an absent person.

LETTER 170

TO THURSTAN, ARCHBISHOP OF YORK

To his most dear father and reverend lord Thurstan, by the grace of God Archbishop of York, greetings from Bernard, Abbot of Clairvaux.

THE splendour of your work and your reputation amongst men have combined greatly, as I know, to your credit. Your deeds prove that yours is no undeserved or empty reputation for facts themselves bear out what hitherto has everywhere been reported of you. How, especially of late, has your zeal for righteousness shone forth, your priestly activity stood out and been strong in the defence of poor monks who had no helper! All the Church has told of your deeds of mercy and alms-giving, but this you have in common with many others for it is the duty of all who possess the substance of this world. But this episcopal work, this eminent example of fatherly piety, this truly divine fervour and zeal wherewith he without doubt has inspired and girded you for the protection of his poor, who ' has made his angels like the winds, the servants that wait upon him like a flame of fire ', all this is wholly yours, the ornament of your dignity, the mark of your office, a glorious jewel in your crown. It is one thing to fill the belly of the hungry, and another to have a zeal for poverty. The one is the service of nature, the other the service of grace. ' Thou shalt visit thy kind and not sin ', the Scriptures say, therefore we care for others that we may not sin, but when we honour the holiness of another we benefit ourselves. Hence it is also said: Let your alms grow warm in your hand until you find a just man to whom you may give them. For whose advantage? ' He that receives a just man in the name of a just man, shall receive the reward of a just man.' It is because you do both these things, fulfilling both the service of nature and the service of grace, that I admire you and recognize that it is given to you from above to do this, so that the praise of all you have done to relieve our temporal necessities may mingle for ever with the divine praises, O most truly reverend and most deservedly lovable father !

LETTER 171

TO RICHARD, ABBOT OF FOUNTAINS, AND TO HIS BRETHREN

Vacandard dates this letter at 1133–34.[1] *The Geoffrey mentioned at the end of the letter is Geoffrey of Ainai, an experienced and elderly monk, whom St. Bernard sent to Fountains in order to instruct the religious in*

[1] Vacandard, *Vie de S. Bernard*, 1927 edn., Vol. I, p. 413 u.

Cistercian observance.   The formal affiliation to Clairvaux took place about 1134–35.

WHAT great things have I heard and known, and our brothers, the two Geoffreys, have told me of you! How you have been inflamed anew by the fire of God, how from weakness you have risen to strength, how you have blossomed afresh into a holy newness of life! This is the hidden work of the finger of God, sweetly renewing and wholesomely changing the spirit within you, not, indeed, from evil to good, but from good to better. Who will grant that I may come over and see this great sight? Your progress from good to better is no less wonderful, no less gratifying, than a conversion from evil to good. It is much more easy to find many men of the world who have been converted from evil to good than it is to find one religious who has progressed from good to better. Anyone who has risen even a little above the state he has once attained in religion is a very rare bird indeed.[1] But your most salutary and remarkable action has not only given great joy to myself who wish so much to serve your holiness, but also to the whole Church, since it is all the more celebrated for being so rare. The merest prudence demanded that you should rise above that mediocrity which is so near to apostasy and leave behind you that tepidity which God vomits from his mouth; but it was also a matter of conscience. You yourselves discovered whether or not it were safe for those who have vowed to observe the Holy Rule to remain in a stage below what is required by it. I regret deeply that the pressure of my daily cares and the impatience of the messenger oblige me to limit the expression of my full heart and to compress my affection for you within the compass of a short note. But Brother Geoffrey will supply for my brevity by word of mouth.

LETTER 172

TO DAVID, KING OF SCOTLAND

This letter was written about 1134 *in favour of the new foundation at Fountains.*

To the Lord David, the most excellent King of Scotland, worthy of all love in Christ, greetings and eternal life, from Bernard, styled Abbot of Clairvaux.

I HAVE long since learned to love you, most illustrious king, your fair renown has for long stirred in me the desire to meet you in person. This is my desire and relying on the words, ' The Lord has heard the desire of the poor ', I am confident in the Lord that one day I shall see you in the body whom even now I delight to gaze upon in spirit and imagination, and whom I constantly think of with such pleasure and

[1] Horace, *Satire*, 2.26.

joy.   Our brothers at Rievaulx were the first to experience the effects of your mercy.   You opened to them the treasury of your good will and anointed them with the oil of your compassion and kindness, so that the house of the King of heaven was filled with the odour of your ointments.   I am not ungrateful for this, I am as grateful as if you had shown your favours to me personally.   And now there are other brothers in the same neighbourhood who have lately joined us.   I do not think that your Highness can be ignorant of how these brothers, inspired from on high, came forth into a desert place from the Church of the blessed Mary at York where the observance was perfunctory. They have had to endure many persecutions and injuries inflicted on them sometimes with force and sometimes with guile.   They were rich and they abounded in the goods of this world, but they have chosen to become poor for the love of Christ, true followers of the apostolic life and sanctity.   If they had been of the world, the world would have loved them, according to the words of the Lord. But now that they are not of the world, the world persecutes them. With the help of God they bear patiently whatever the world does to them but we, who fear God, should help his servants in their troubles.   To you therefore, most merciful king, I commend these aforesaid servants of Christ that you may comfort them in their poverty, looking to Christ, the King of kings, for the meed which he will distribute to the just in his eternal kingdom.

LETTER 173

TO ALEXANDER, THE PRIOR OF FOUNTAINS, AND TO HIS BRETHREN

Richard, the first Abbot of Fountains, died on the last day of April, 1139. The community elected as abbot his namesake, Richard, who had been the sacristan at St. Mary's, York, before the breakaway.   This Richard died at Clairvaux in the year 1143–44, and Henry Murdac was elected as his successor.

Murdac was a Yorkshireman of fiery and combative temperament and both these qualities were to find ample scope when he was elected Archbishop of York in opposition to William Fitzherbert in the year 1147.   His arrival at Fountains was signalized by strong disciplinary measures.   He enforced the full observance of every Clairvaux use and tradition.[1]

In the Benedictine edition the death of Richard, the second Abbot of Fountains, is mistakenly given as 1138 and this letter is dated for the same year.[2]   More probably it was written in the year 1143–44, when Richard II died and Murdac was elected in his place.

To his very dear brothers in Christ, Alexander the Prior and all the convent of Fountains, greetings and his humble prayers, from Brother Bernard, styled Abbot of Clairvaux.

---

[1] Knowles, *op. cit.*, pp. 255, 139.
[2] *Richardus secundus mortuus in Clara-valle anno 1138, die 15 Maii.   Op. Snti Bernardi Abbatis* M.DCC.XIX.   See Knowles, *loc. cit.*, and Watkin Williams, *Life of St. Bernard*, p. 173.

Your venerable father has finished his course and fallen asleep in the Lord. I have always had a fatherly care for you as if you were my own sons, and now all the more so for the great predicament in which you find yourselves. I would have sent someone to you long ago, but I have been waiting until I could do so conveniently and helpfully, because the venerable Abbot Henry,[1] whom I had from the first destined for you, as he is capable and would, I believe, be very useful to you in the present business, has been prevented by affairs from coming immediately. Receive him, dearest brothers, with the love and honour he deserves, and listen to him in all things, as you would to myself, in fact more than you would to myself for his virtue and judgement far exceed mine. I have given him full authority to act in the matter of this election and in anything that may need regularizing or correcting in your monastery or the others. I have sent with him William, a very dear son of mine.

2. And now I entreat you, dearest sons, to be all of one mind in this election and not to suffer factions to arise amongst you, but that you, one and all, with one mouth, glorify God. He is not the God of discord but of peace, and so his dwelling place is in peace and he says: ' He that gathereth not with me, scattereth '. May the enemy never be able to gloat over those whose master is the Holy Spirit in the school of Christ and glory in their dissensions because their souls are thereby endangered and all the labour of their penances rendered void, because the fair name of our Order is sullied and those whose especial duty it is to glorify the name of Christ cause it to be blasphemed. Rather, as befits holy men and servants of Christ, choose for yourselves with one voice, as I have every confidence you will, a worthy shepherd of your souls, in company with the Abbots of Rievaulx and Vauclair,[2] whose advice I wish you to follow as if it were my own.

LETTER 174

TO HENRY MURDAC

Henry Murdac was first Abbot of Vauclair, then Abbot of Fountains, and finally Archbishop of York.

To his very dear brother Abbot Henry, greetings and prayers, from Brother Bernard, styled Abbot of Clairvaux.

I charge you, Brother Henry, that you submit out of charity to the choice of our brothers at Fountains if, with the advice of the venerable Abbot of Rievaulx, they elect you as their abbot. I do this very unwillingly, knowing that by your absence a great comfort will

---

[1] Henry Murdac, Abbot of Vauclair.
[2] William, the first abbot of Rievaulx, and Henry Murdac.

be lost to me. But I am afraid of resisting the choice of our brethren at Fountains, since I believe that when so many religious agree together, their decision is the will of God, according to the words I read in the Gospel: 'Where two or three are gathered together in my name, there am I in the midst of them'. So stir yourself, dearest brother, and receive their professions of obedience and care for them as the shepherd of their souls. Have no fear for the house which you have been ruling. It is quite near to me so, God willing, I shall be able to see that it has a capable administrator. And do not hesitate for the sake of the bishop, you can leave that to me.

LETTER 175

TO THURSTAN, ARCHBISHOP OF YORK

Thurstan remained at his post as archbishop until he felt the approach of death, and then he went to the Abbey of Pontefract, where he died a monk of Cluny in the year 1141.

To his reverend father and lord, Thurstan, by the grace of God Archbishop of York, health more of the soul than of the body,[1] from Bernard, styled Abbot of Clairvaux.

I PRAISE your desire for quiet and your wish to rest peacefully in the Lord. But the reasons you give do not seem to me in themselves sufficient for abandoning your pastoral care, unless perhaps (which I am sure is not the case) you have committed some grave sin or have obtained the permission of the Holy See,[2] for I am sure you are not ignorant of those words of the Apostle: 'Are you married to a wife? Then do not go about to free yourself'. No promise such as you say you have made[3] can be binding on a bishop so as to impede the ministry to which he is called.

2. It seems best to me, if I can say so without prejudice to the wiser opinions of wise men, that you should stay where you are and exhibit in a bishop the dress and holy life of a monk. But if there is some secret reason for your resignation or if the Lord Pope has gratified your wish for quiet, my advice, such as it is, is that you should not be put off from joining some house where you see great purity of observance by fear of any degree of poverty or rough clothes and victuals. Bear in mind that in such houses, although the soul is the first concern, yet due regard is always given to physical weakness and age. I am your servant so as always to pray God fervently for you that he may

---

[1] . . . *salutem non tam in via, quam in patria.* Eales translates: '. . . wishes health in the present life and in the future life eternal '.

[2] St. Bernard recognizes two reasons which would justify a bishop relinquishing his office, *viz.* some grave crime or the permission of the Holy See.

[3] Thurstan made a promise in his early youth to become a monk of Cluny.

inspire you to do what is best and grant that you may bear the burden and heat of the day, so as to receive in the evening of your life the meed of your labours in coin that bears his image.

LETTER 176

TO THE MONKS OF GRACE-DIEU

This letter is to a foundation known as ' Grace-Dieu'. There were two foundations of this name in St. Bernard's time. One of these was from a daughter house of Morimond in the year 1139, and the other was in Poitou from Clairvaux in 1135. It seems clear that this letter is addressed to the latter.

To his most dear brothers who are at Grace-Dieu, Bernard, styled Abbot of Clairvaux, strength in the Lord and in the power of the Most High.

'WHO will give me the wings of a dove that I may fly away' and see the good zeal of my sons, their progress, peace, order, and discipline? I want to see the new inhabitants in their new site, how they observe their Rule[1] among strangers, how they ' sing the song of the Lord in a strange land'. Already I have flown to you in imagination and am with you in spirit but, according to the words of the Lord, ' the spirit indeed is willing, but the flesh is weak' and cannot just now follow the spirit. But later on I will come, if ever I receive back from the Lord my old strength. But do you, in the meantime, stay where you are, yea, and progress in what you have undertaken, for, so soon as anyone begins to falter, immediately he ceases to progress.

LETTER 177

TO ST. AILRED, ABBOT OF RIEVAULX[2]

In this letter St. Bernard urges St. Ailred to write something on charity. This letter always appears as an introduction to St. Ailred's Speculum Charitatis *as from Gervase, Abbot of Louth Park, but Dom André Wilmart*

---

[1] *Quomodo apud extraneos militant;* Cf. *Sti Benedicti Regula Monach.,* p. 1 *et passim.*

[2] The ' Bernard of the North'. One of the most attractive figures in English monasticism. Not only a true Cistercian and a true disciple of St. Bernard, but also an able administrator. His works are printed in *P.L.,* t. cxcv, col. 209–796, with the exception of the *Sermon on the Saints of Hexham,* edited by J. Raine and published by the Surtees Society; the *Regula Inclusorum,* printed by the Maurists as an appendix to St. Augustine; and *De Jesu Puero Duodenni,* printed by the Maurists in St. Bernard's works. He was by birth completely English and connected with landed families between Hexham and Durham. He became associated with the Scottish Court and held the post there of steward or seneschal. *Vide The Monastic Order in England,* by David Knowles, Vol. I; also *Vita Ailredi,* by his disciple Walter Daniel, and an appreciation of his character by his friend Gilbert, Abbot of Swineshead, written on hearing of his death: *Gilberti Hoilandensis, Serm.* 41 *in Canticum,* printed in the appendix of St. Bernard's works by Mabillon.

has proved conclusively that the writer of it is St. Bernard of Clairvaux.[1]
And indeed, as Prof. David Knowles observes,[2] *the style* clamat dominum.

THE great virtue of the saints is humility, but a sincere and discreet humility. True humility does not consort with untruthfulness and it is in no way helped by the sacrilege of disobedience. I have besought you, I have commanded you, I have even charged you in the sacred name of the Most High, to write some little thing for me whereby the grievances might be answered of those who are trying to follow the narrow way after a life of self-indulgence. I do not condemn, I do not blame your excuses, but I do reproach your obstinacy. It was an act of humility to make excuses, but it is not humble to disobey. Where is the humility in refusing to consent to my wishes? Indeed to defend oneself in this way smacks of the sin of the soothsayers, such stubbornness is like the sin of idolatry. You complain that it would be too heavy a burden for weak shoulders and that it would be more prudent to refuse to undertake it than to break down under it. I grant that I am placing on you a heavy burden, that it is hard, even impossible. But even so you have no excuse. I persist in my opinion and I repeat my command. What will you do? Surely what he, to whose Rule you have vowed obedience, has said that a monk should do in such circumstances: ' If a superior still persist in his command, let the young monk know that it is expedient for him; and let him obey out of love, trusting in God '.[3] You have done what you ought to have done to excuse yourself, if not more than you ought to have done. You have gone as far as is allowed. You have pointed out all the reasons why you cannot obey. You have said that you are ignorant of grammar, that you are almost illiterate; that you have come to the desert, not from the schools, but from the kitchen; that you have since lived a rustic and rough life amidst rocks and mountains, earning in the sweat of your brow your daily bread with axe and maul; and that flights of oratory ill become your poor fishermen's clothes.[4] I most gratefully accept your excuses, they serve rather to inflame than extinguish the spark of my desire, because knowledge that comes from the school

[1] André Wilmart, *L'Instigateur du Speculum Charitatis d'Aelred Abbé de Rievaulx* in *Revue d'Ascétique et de Mystique*, Oct., 1933.
[2] David Knowles, *op. cit.*
[3] For the understanding of this passage it is necessary to read the whole reference in the Rule of St. Benedict, Chap. 68: ' If on any brother there be laid commands that are hard and impossible, let him receive the order of his superior with all meekness and obedience. But if he sees that the burden altogether exceeds his strength, let him lay before his superior the reasons of his incapacity patiently and in due season, without showing pride, or resistance, or contradictoriness.'
[4] The ' kitchen ' is a reference to the post St. Ailred held as steward in the Scottish Court. But in speaking of himself as ' ignorant of grammar ' and ' almost illiterate ' (*minus grammaticum et pene illiteratum*) he was using a very strong hyperbole. St. Ailred would have been better educated than most so-called educated people of to-day. Though he was not trained in the schools he had clearly been well taught by one who was familiar with the new humanism. *Vide* David Knowles, *op. cit.*

of the Holy Spirit rather than the schools of rhetoric will savour all the sweeter to me and because you ' have this treasure in an earthen vessel, that the excellency may be of the power of God '. What a joyous thing it is, what a presage of the future, that you should have come to the desert from the kitchen, so that as one who has been entrusted for a time with providing food for the body in a royal kitchen, you may now provide spiritual food for spiritual men and feed the hungry with the food of God's word in the house of the King of kings. What you say about your mountains and rugged rocks does not disconcert me at all, nor am I horrified at the thought of your great valleys, for now ' the mountains drop down sweetness, the hills flow with milk and honey, and the valleys are filled with corn ', now ' honey is sucked out of rocks and oil out of the hardest stone ', and rocks and mountains are the pasture of the Lord's sheep. And so I think that with that maul of yours you will be able to strike something out of those rocks that you have not got by your own wits from the bookshelves of the schoolmen, and that you will have experienced sometimes under the shade of a tree during the heats of midday what you would never have learned in the schools. Not unto yourself, not unto yourself give the glory, but render it unto him who has not only rescued you from ' the pit of misery and mire of dregs ', from the house of death and the unclean place, but ' hath made a remembrance of his wonderful works, being a merciful and gracious Lord ', and so as to raise more generously the hopes of sinners he has given sight to the blind, knowledge to the ignorant, instruction to the unskilled. And so why do you blush and hesitate to give what I ask, when everyone who knows you will know it is not yours that you give? Why do you dissemble? Why do you refuse to give even at the command of him who gave you all you have to give? Do you fear the envy of some or to be thought presumptuous? As if anyone has ever written anything useful without incurring envy! Or as if anyone could accuse you of presumption who are only obeying your abbot! I therefore order you in the name of Jesus Christ, and in the Spirit of our God, that you do not delay to write down those thoughts that have occurred to you, in your long meditations, concerning the excellence of charity, its fruit, and its proper order, so that we may see in what you write, as if in a mirror, what charity is, how great sweetness there is in the possession of it, how much heaviness and sorrow there is in cupidity which is the contrary of it, and that exterior troubles, so far from diminishing it, as many believe, only serve to increase it, and finally what discretion there should be in the exercise of it. But, for the sake of your modesty, let this letter be put at the beginning of the work, so that whatever in the *Mirror of Charity* (for that is the name I give it) should displease the reader shall be imputed to me who have commanded it and not to you who have obeyed by writing it.

LETTER 178

This letter was written to Albero of Montreuil, Archbishop of Trèves, 1131–1152, concerning the troubles of the Convent of St. Maur at Verdun.

To the venerable lord and most beloved father Albero, by the grace of God Archbishop of Trèves, Legate to the Apostolic See, from Bernard, Abbot of Clairvaux, that he may find grace before God.

IF you bear with me when I seek my own interests, how much more ought you to bear with me when I seek the interests of Christ and not my own? But the interests of Christ are my own, for he is our flesh and our brother. I take upon myself the mercy of Christ who took upon himself the chastisements I deserved, ' even unto death, the death of the cross '. ' The servant is not above his lord.' I do not consider any of the reproaches Christ suffered at the hands of men as no concern of mine, who, on my account, became ' the reproach of men and the outcast of the people '. I pity his lot who had pity on mine and gave himself up for me. O God, the women ' have come into thine inheritance, they have defiled thy holy temple '. I refer to the Convent of St. Maur at Verdun. Behold there the inheritance of the Lord, because it is his inheritance, it is his temple, but a defiled temple, a temple defiled by a double sacrilege, for by alienating themselves from Christ, they have taken from God what belongs to him. ' Holiness becomes thy house, O Lord ', but the house of prayer has become a house of ill-fame and a den of robbers. The dwelling-place of thy glory has become a lair of dragons, and no one heeds it. Does it satisfy your Lordship that God should lose his inheritance in your diocese while you are bishop? Will you return evil for good? God ' hast exalted thee above thy fellows ' and therefore you should take his part. If you say it is nothing to do with you, I ask you how you can extricate yourself from the implications of that saying: ' He shares another's guilt who does not prevent his sin when he can '? The ' Virgin of Jerusalem ' has fallen, and shall she rise no more? Clothe yourself with pity and hold out the hand of mercy. If you are a friend of the Bridegroom bring the bride out of ' where the mire has settled deep '. Write to them that they must abide by the decision of those to whom they entrusted the election, for otherwise there would be great embarrassment for her who was elected, for those who elected her, and for the church of Rheims of which she is the daughter. Or else, if you do not persuade them by fear and by your prayers, I tell you that your reputation will suffer much in the neighbourhood. I do not presume to judge your conscience, but I pray the Spirit of all truth that he may teach your heart ' to refuse evil and choose the good '.

THE LANGRES CONTROVERSY

THE following letters are concerned with a controversy over the election of the Bishop of Langres, which took place between St. Bernard on one side and the Archbishop of Lyons with Peter the Venerable on the other.

After the schism, but before he had left Rome, St. Bernard was approached by the Archbishop of Lyons; Robert, the Dean of Langres; and Ulric, a canon of the same church, to enlist his help in obtaining permission to fill the vacancy caused by the recent death of the Bishop of Langres. The Pope had insisted that they should be guided by the advice of ' religious persons ' in the matter of electing a successor. It is not easy to say what is the exact significance of the term ' religious persons ' in this context. Probably it meant men of sound faith and piety, and not necessarily only abbots of monasteries. Bernard was not quite easy about the matter and he only consented to help if they would give him some assurance that they would elect a worthy man. After much discussion, two names were eventually selected out of a great number of possible candidates. All agreed that they would choose either one or other of these two. The permission of the Pope to go forward with the election was granted on the express condition that the electors should abide by this arrangement, and they promised to do so.

But no sooner had the archbishop got back to Lyons than he threw over the agreement he had made with Bernard, and chose a totally different candidate. Whether or not he was the evil man that Bernard implies, it is not easy to say. Peter the Venerable hotly denies the slur cast on the character of the man by the Abbot of Clairvaux and attributes it to mere Cistercian prejudice. On the other hand although we cannot identify the man for certain, we do know that he was a Cluniac monk, and so cannot be surprised that he was supported by his abbot. As soon as he had been chosen, Peter presented him to Louis *le Jeune*, King of France, to be invested with the regalia of the see, and not long afterwards he was consecrated Bishop of Langres by the Archbishop of Lyons, the Bishop of Autun, and the Bishop of Mâcon. The electors were the very men who had met Bernard in Rome and made the aforesaid agreement with him. Bernard immediately appealed to Rome on the grounds that the election had been uncanonical. Whatever the moral character of the man might have been, there is no doubt at all that the matter had been carried through with a high hand and that the saint's attitude was impregnable from a canonical point of view. The outcome of all this was that the Pope quashed the election; but to the extreme embarrassment of Bernard his delegates immediately nominated himself. He refused to accept the nomination. In the end Bernard's *alter ego*, Godfrey de la Roche, Prior of Clairvaux, was chosen. There still remained the king to be placated. He had invested the former candidate in the temporalities of his see and felt it might be beneath his regal dignity to annul his action. However he at last yielded to the persuasions of Bernard and confirmed the appointment of Godfrey. The consecration followed soon afterwards, in October, 1138. Peter the Venerable took his defeat graciously and maintained unimpaired his love and admiration for the Abbot of Clairvaux.

LETTER 179

TO POPE INNOCENT II

WHILE I was still in Rome the lord Archbishop of Lyons happened to arrive there, bringing with him Robert the Dean of Langres and Ulric, a canon of the same church. They were hoping to obtain for themselves and for the Chapter of Langres leave to elect a new bishop. The Pope had forbidden them to attempt this except under the advice of religious men. When they asked me to help secure the Pope's permission to go forward with the election, I said that I would have nothing whatsoever to do with the matter until I was satisfied that they were going to elect a good and worthy man. They replied to this that it was their intention to leave the matter entirely in my hands and take no step without first consulting me. And this they promised me. But as I was still uneasy in my mind about the matter the archbishop himself came to persuade me, and he too firmly promised the same thing. He said that if the clergy acted otherwise than by my advice, he would refuse to confirm or ratify their action. The chancellor was brought forward as a witness. Still unsatisfied I sought out the lord Pope so that this arrangement might be confirmed by his authority, but I did not take this step before we had discussed the election at great length. As a result of these discussions, out of the great many names that were mentioned we finally chose two, and agreed that none of us would have any objection to the election of either one or the other of these. After this the lord Pope commanded that we should firmly abide by this arrangement we had come to, and this both the archbishop and the clergy promised to do. When they had gone I too set out for home, after remaining on in the city for a day or two in order to obtain leave for my departure from the lord Pope.

2. As I crossed the Alps news reached me that a man had been chosen for the see of Langres of whom I could have wished that I had heard better reports, and that a day in the near future had been settled for the consecration. I do not wish to repeat what I only heard about him with great reluctance. Certain religious persons, who had come to meet me and welcome me back, were for my turning aside and passing through Lyons so as to prevent, if I could, such a disaster. I had intended to return the shorter way for I was tired and ill and did not put much trust in the rumours that had reached me. For who would believe that such a man as the Archbishop of Lyons could be so fickle as to disregard not only his recent promise to me but also the mandate of his lord the Pope, and lay hands without misgiving on a man of such evil report? But in deference to the advice of these religious persons who had come to meet me I turned my steps towards Lyons. When I arrived there I found everything had transpired just as I had been told. Preparations were on foot for the great or, rather, the disastrous event. Yet the dean and, unless I am deceived, the greater part of the canons of Lyons were firmly and openly opposed. But the shameful and shocking news, spreading and growing on all sides, had filled the city.

3. What could I do? I approached the archbishop respectfully and

reminded him of the agreement we had made and of the mandate he had received from the lord Pope. He admitted everything, but laid the blame for his faithlessness at the door of the duke's son[1] who, he said, had recoiled from the arrangement he had made, so that he had been obliged to act in this capricious way in order not to upset him, or in other words to keep the peace. He added that whatever he might have done hitherto, he would act from now on as I wanted. ' Not as I want ', said I, ' but as God wants.' And I told him that he might best discover God's will in the matter by laying it all before a council of the bishops and other religious persons who had come, or were coming, to Lyons on his invitation: and that if, after invoking the Holy Spirit, they should feel moved to agree to the necessity for proceeding with the affair as it had been begun, then by all means let him do so; but if not, then in obedience to the apostolic injunction he should refrain from laying hands rashly on any man. He appeared to be satisfied with my advice. In the meantime news came that the man had arrived, but at a hostelry, not at the palace. He came on Friday night and left on Saturday morning. It is not for me to say why he did not present himself at the curia, when he had come a long journey expressly for this purpose. It might have been attributed to monastic modesty and contempt for honours if what happened afterwards did not indicate the contrary. For what else but the contrary to this could anyone believe when the archbishop, returning from seeing him, said in public that the man would not agree to what we had arranged for him, but had rejected it utterly?

4. Finally the archbishop commanded the election to be held forthwith. This is borne out by certain canons who were present at the time, as well as by a letter that can be produced. When this letter was read in the Chapter at Lyons, another in a contrary sense was immediately produced and read out, to the effect that the consecration was postponed and not cancelled, and that a day and place were appointed for deciding the matter which the first letter had said was already decided. You would have thought that these letters came not only from different people, but from people in flat opposition to each other, were it not that they bore the same seal and every page the same signature, declaring thereby that they were from a source which flowed with sweet and bitter waters. These letters are in our hands, and it would be impossible to obey the one without disobeying the other. If you follow the first, you stand condemned by the second; if you follow the second, you are blamed by the first. It were much to be desired that the second letter could as well defend itself against a third, as it had been able to nullify the first. They are letters against letters, one command against another, not in the sense of the Prophet,

---

[1] Son of Hugh II, Duke of Burgundy.

'A command here, a command there', but rather command and countermand.

5. In the meantime the man who had fled from consecration and rejected election hastened to the king, and secured his investiture in the temporalities of his see, but on what grounds he alone could say. Soon afterwards letters were sent out to change the place which had been arranged for the election and to anticipate the day, so that many of those who opposed it might be kept away by the inconvenience and an appeal against it forestalled. But no contriving of man can avail against the will of the Lord, and it so happened by his providence that, in fact, there was no lack of those to oppose and appeal against the election. Falk, the Dean of Lyons, appealed: Pontius, an archdeacon of Lyons, appealed; Bonami, a priest and canon of Lyons, appealed; an appeal was also lodged by our brothers Bruno and Geoffrey; and all these, knowing nothing of the schemes that seethed in the hearts of their opponents, arrived at the meeting quite by chance, but without any shadow of doubt under the providence of God. When I heard of the new arrangements there was but little time left for my messenger to arrive at the meeting and stop the sacrament or rather the sacrilege; in fact barely four days. But he did arrive nevertheless, and he was in time to oppose it and summon both the consecrators and their candidate to the Apostolic See. And he was a canon of Lyons. All that I have said is the very truth and no lie. The truth itself shall be my witness that I have said nothing out of personal hatred but, solely for the love of truth, have stated the facts as they stand.

LETTER 180

TO FALK, THE DEAN, AND GUY, THE TREASURER, OF THE CHURCH OF LYONS

As you see, my dear friends, the sickness of our church is very great. It will take much to cure it, and speed too. We must be unremitting in our prayers to the heavenly doctor, saying: 'Come, Lord, before it dies'. What greatly aggravates the trouble and renders it almost desperate is that it has its source just where one would be most entitled to expect help. For who is it that has brought all this evil upon our unhappy church? Certainly not any enemy or anyone who hates it, but an upright man, in fact its own leader and metropolitan. How comes all this evil from the south and not now from the north?[1] There is no grief like unto our grief, because it is just from those on whom we had put our hopes that we are suffering. The church of Lyons, our loving mother, has chosen a monster and

---

[1] *Quomodo ab austro et non jam ab aquilone panditur omne malum.* A reference to Jeremias 1.14: *Ab aquilone pandetur malum:* ' And it is from the north that calamity is brewing '.

no bridegroom for her daughter. In this we feel her to have acted more like a stepmother than a mother. How far has this her son-in-law fallen away from that ancient uprightness, gravity, and honesty for which she was so renowned! How can I call that an honourable marriage and unsullied bridal-bed which has been contrived in such a way by such a man? Regardless of all law, order, and right reason everything has been so upset or, rather, everything has been evidently ventured on so deceitfully, inconsiderately, and rashly, that anyone would be ashamed to have a steward or tax-collector, let alone a bishop, appointed in this way. But how can I praise you enough, my dear friends, who alone have had pity on our afflicted church and, not once but twice, have stood up for her when she was oppressed, rising up against her persecutors and protecting her like a wall around the house of Israel. In the whole congregation there has not been found anyone like you to keep the law of the Most High, obey his holy canons, and emulate the zeal of Phinees by smiting the fornicators with the sword of your tongue. These actions of yours make for both God's glory and your own honour, and it now only remains for you to bring the laudable work you have begun to a fitting end and thereby join the tail to the head of the victim.

LETTER 181

TO POPE INNOCENT

ONCE more I cry to you, once more I knock upon your door, with tearful sighs if not with loud cries. Repeated injuries by abandoned persons and by those who prolong their evil have forced me to repeat my cries. They are triumphant in their faithlessness. They add guilt to guilt and their insolence knows no bounds. Their rage grows strong while their shame and their fear of God grows less. Regardless of our appeal to you, Holy Father, and despite your just and prudent ruling, they have actually consecrated that same man whom they had dared to elect. And they who have done this are the Archbishop of Lyons, and the Bishops of Autun and Mâcon; all friends of Cluny. Their deceit and effrontery will cause great vexation to many holy men if they should be obliged to bear the burden imposed on them by such means. They would regard it as being obliged to bow the knee before Baal or, in the words of the Prophet, ' to make terms with death and a compact with the grave itself'. Where, I ask you, are justice, law, the authority of the sacred canons, the reverence due to your Majesty? The right to appeal to you is not denied to any oppressed person, only to myself is it of no avail. Where gold rules and silver sits in judgement, the laws and canons are silent, the scales of justice are loaded, and right reason has no sway. And, more outrageous even than this, these men are threatening to storm with the same weapons the very citadel of the Apostolic See. But that would be absurd for it is founded on a rock.

2. But what am I saying? I confess I have gone too far. It is not my business to accuse or censure anyone. It is enough for me to voice my grief. When at last it pleased your Serenity to permit me to return to my brethren after the many disappointments and toils I had endured in the service of the Roman Church, I came back safely to my monastery, broken indeed in physical health, as a useless servant, yet nevertheless rejoicing for the sheaves of peace I was able to bring with me. I believed that I had left all my troubles behind me and come at last to peace, I hoped that I might be permitted to repair the hurt I had suffered in spiritual things while outside my monastery, the loss I had incurred in recollection; but sorrow and distress have found me out. Now I lie prostrate on my bed, suffering more in my mind than in body. It is not any temporal inconvenience that I am mourning. 'My soul is continually in my hands' and its salvation is at stake. Would you wish that I should trust my soul to that man who has lost his own? I know you would not. For this reason I have said to myself that it were better to take flight than consume the rest of my days in grief, yet nevertheless in peril of my salvation. But it were better that God should inspire you with a better course of action. May he bring to your mind (if you should deem me worthy) how I have served you, and cause you to look with pity on your child and free your troubled son from his distress. Bear in mind what great things God has done for you and, as some little return for it all, annul and undo what has been done amiss.

LETTER 182

TO THE SAME, ON THE SAME SUBJECT

Most loving father, did you not strictly command that a religious and suitable person should be chosen to fill the vacancy in the church of Langres, and that the advice of myself, your child, should be followed in the matter? And did not my lord of Lyons receive from your Holiness in person these instructions, to be as loyally followed as they had been firmly enjoined and persistently repeated? And, in fact, did he not promise to do this? What then, I ask, does he mean by wanting to change what has been beneficially and advisedly decreed, and by trying on his own initiative to do something quite different and most unbecoming, so as to bring your Majesty into contempt and my own insignificant person into ridicule? How can that good man not blush to be found saying 'Yea and Nay' to the same things while, in the teeth of your decree and his own promise, he tries to impose on the necks of so many religious persons, your servants, such a shameful yoke? Enquire, my father, enquire very carefully into the references of that man on whom he is hastening to lay hands. Enquire both from those who are near at hand and from those who are far off. As for me, very shame forbids me to repeat what common report says of him or, rather, what his evil reputation openly declares of him. What can I say? My soul is sorrowful unto death. I might already have fled away had I not been held by hope of consolation from your merciful heart. I did intend to write the whole sorry story from the beginning, but my hand is paralyzed with sorrow, my mind is clouded with grief, and my tongue refuses to tell of the evil fraud, the deceit, the villainy, the trickery, and the audacity that have been perpetrated. But your son, Ponce the archdeacon, who has conducted himself with great firmness and loyalty in the affair, will explain to you what has happened and what we implore to be done. Trust him as you would myself. There remains one thing I must say, as though in travail: unless these men are made to desist from their evil and audacious machinations, I feel that, as I am now, ' my strength will ebb away for very misery; my years in mourning '.

LETTER 183

TO THE BISHOPS AND CARDINALS OF THE ROMAN CURIA, ON THE SAME SUBJECT

YOU will remember, if you consider it worth recalling, how I lived with you when the times were evil, going out and coming in and setting forth again at the king's bidding; staying with you and standing by you in your trials, until my strength became so worn out that, when heaven gave back peace to the Church, I was scarcely able to return home. I recall this, not for the sake of boasting or as a reproach to you, but so as to provoke, implore, advise, and beg of you the pity that is my due. Dire need now obliges me to appeal to all my debtors. As for myself, according to the words of the Lord I do not reckon myself as anything but a useless servant even when I have done all that I ought to have done. But do I deserve to be beaten for having done my duty? Yet since leaving you, I have met with nothing but trouble and sorrow. I called upon the name of the Lord, but did not prevail; and I called upon your name too, but it availed me nothing for ' the gods of the earth '—that is to say the Archbishop of Lyons and the Abbot of Cluny—' are exceedingly exalted '. These men, ' trusting in their own strength and boasting of their great possessions ' ' have drawn near and stood against me '. And not against only me, but also against a great number of the servants of God, against you also, against themselves, in opposition to God, and all justice and honour.

2. In fine, they have set up a man over our heads whom the good abhor and the evil scorn. By what right or, rather, by what wrong

they have done this thing, let God see and judge; and let the Roman Curia also see: let it see and grieve, let it have pity upon the unfortunate and gird itself in their defence, and for the honour of the good. What? Does it please thee, who art mistress of the world, set over all to execute vengeance on the proud and show mercy to the weak, does it please thee, I say, that ' the heart of the poor man should burn within him because the schemer that has entrapped him is so triumphant ', the heart of that poor man who has poured out his sweat and blood in your service because he had nothing else to give? Does it seem right that you should enjoy your peace and care nothing for ours, that you should not share your consolations with us who have supported you in your trials? If I have deserved well of you, then ' rescue the poor and deliver the needy out of the hand of the sinner '. Otherwise I will labour as I can amidst my grief, and tears will be my portion day and night. But to you I will read that verse: ' Who defies the Lord's vengeance more surely than the friend who refuses compassion to a friend?' and: ' Friends and neighbours that meet me keep their distance now, old companions shun me. I am assailed by enemies that grudge me life itself.'

LETTER 184

TO UMBALD,.A CARDINAL DEACON

There were two cardinal deacons called Umbald at that time and it is not certain to which of the two this letter is addressed.

To my dear lord, friend, and master, Umbald, by the grace of God and favour of the Apostolic See, Cardinal Deacon, from Brother Bernard, styled Abbot of Clairvaux, that he may hunger and thirst after justice.

IF you truly love me, then you must love me not only in word and tongue, but in deed and truth. And what is more if you truly love justice, as you have hitherto professed or pretended to do, then you must deplore the affliction which Christ is now suffering at the hands of impious men at Langres, and who cries to you with the voice of the church there: O Umbald, help me, for I am being persecuted by wicked men! For at Langres Christ is once more suffering and persecuted in his members because the clergy and faithful there have a man as bishop who has not been elected in a proper and orderly manner, but who has been imposed upon them by fraud and force. He is a man of unworthy life, bad reputation, and quite unsuited for the office, and he has been neither canonically elected nor licitly consecrated.

LETTER 185

TO POPE INNOCENT, ON THE SAME SUBJECT

YOUR affability has made me familiar, and my familiarity makes me bold. May you retain your accustomed kindness, or else my boldness will make you angry. Yet listen patiently, not only to what I have done, but also as to why I have done it, for perhaps my motives may be some excuse for my actions. I have been so bold as to retain the clergy of Langres whom you had summoned to your presence, but not before peace had been established between them. They have been persuaded to abide in future by the instructions they have received in their letters and hold an election according to your wishes and the advice of good men. It was most necessary that they should remain just now for the sake of the lands and possessions of the church, which are pillaged and plundered as soon as there is no one at hand to look after and protect them. If it should so please you, may the duty of electing someone pleasing to God be entrusted to men above suspicion, men who are seeking the glory of Jesus Christ and not their own interests, and so at last we shall be finished with this interminable and unhappy state of affairs in the church. All that remains to be said I have entrusted to Dom Herbert the Abbot of St. Stephen at Dijon, the Archdeacon of Langres, and their companions. I might also add that I hope you will receive under your protection the persons and goods of the Archdeacon of Langres and Bonami, a priest of the same church, for they have proved themselves loyal supporters of God's cause, and the labourer is worthy of his hire.

LETTER 186

TO LOUIS THE YOUNGER, KING OF FRANCE

The Pope had quashed the irregular election and consecration, and Bernard had been obliged to accept the choice of his prior, Godfrey de la Roche, for the see of Langres, after having refused it for himself. But the king was making difficulties about investing the new candidate with the temporalities or regalia of the see. He had already invested the former candidate with them and considered it beneath his royal dignity to countermand his action. But the following letter was successful in persuading him to do so.

THOUGH all the world were to combine in making me attempt something against your royal Majesty, yet I would fear God and not dare to oppose the king whom he had ordained. I know where it is written, ' He that resisteth the power, resisteth the ordinance of God '. But I shall speak the truth to you because I also know how wrong it is for any Christian to lie, especially for one of my profession. What happened at Langres concerning my prior happened contrary to all my expectations, and contrary to the intentions of the bishops and myself. But there is one who is able to secure the assent of unwilling men and compel them to serve the purpose he wishes, even against their wills. Never have I feared a danger for myself that I have not also feared just as much for him whom I love as myself. Never have I not shrunk from the company of those who would bind heavy burdens on the backs of men, and not lift a finger to move them. But what has been done, is done; against you nothing, against myself a lot. The support of my weakness has been taken from me, the light of my eyes has been snatched away, my right hand has been cut off. All these great storms and high waves have passed over me; wrath has come upon me and there is no way of escape open to me. By flying from burdens I have brought them upon myself, unwelcome and unwanted. I find it hard to kick against the pricks. Perhaps it would have been more tolerable had I willingly accepted the burden instead of kicking against it and refusing it.[1] For if there is any strength in me, would it not be easier for me to carry it on my own shoulders rather than in the person of another?

2. But I submit to one who has disposed otherwise. To rebel against him, either in judgement or in action, would not be safe or even possible for me, nor would it be for you, because he is feared amongst all the kings of the earth. It were an awful thing to fall into the hands of the living God, awful even for you, O king. How sorry I am to hear things of you so contrary to the fair promise of your beginnings. But how much more bitter would be the sorrow of the Church if, after having tasted such fair joys from you, she were to be deprived (which God forbid) of the glad hope of having a shield in your good dispositions, such as she has had hitherto. Alas the virgin, the church of Rheims, has fallen, and there is none to lift her up! And the church of Langres has also fallen, and there is no one to hold out a hand to her. May the goodness of God take from your heart any intention of adding to our grief, of piling up sorrow upon sorrow for us! I would rather die than see a king of such a fair reputation and of even better hopes, attempt to oppose the will of God and stir up against himself the wrath of the supreme Judge, bathe the feet of the Father of orphans in the tears of the afflicted, cause the portals of heaven to resound with the cries of the poor, the prayers of the saints, and the just complaints of the chaste bride of Christ who is the Church of the living God. May God forbid such a thing! We hope for better things, we expect more joyful things of you. God will not forget to be merciful, nor will his wrath set bounds to his pity. He will not permit his Church to be saddened through him and on

---

[1] *Tolerabilius fortasse spontaneo, quam nolenti et renuenti fuisset.* Surely a reference to Bernard's rejection of the see for himself which led to his being obliged to part with his prior instead. Eales translates: ' It would perhaps be more tolerable for a willing horse than for one who is restive and obstinate '.

account of him by whom he has already given her such joy on so many occasions. And if you think otherwise, this also he will reveal to you, schooling your heart in wisdom. This is our wish and our prayer day and night. Believe this of me, and believe it of my brethren. This truth will never be denied by us, and the honour of our king and the welfare of his realm will never be diminished by us.

3. We render thanks to your goodness for the kind answer you deigned to send us. But nevertheless this delay terrifies us who see the land given up to pillage and plunder. It is your land; and in this we clearly see and deplore a disgrace to your kingdom, that you should have commanded us to forgo our rights, because there is none to defend them.[1] What else has been done that can be rightly said to have diminished your royal dignity? The election was duly held and the elected is faithful. But he would not be faithful if he wished to hold your lands otherwise than by you. He has not stretched forth his hand to your lands, he has not entered your city, and he certainly has not put himself forward in any matter although strongly urged to do so by the clergy and people, by the sufferings of the downtrodden, and by the wishes of all good men. The state of affairs being what it is, you will see that you should take speedy counsel in the matter, as much for your own sake as for ours. Unless your Highness can answer this petition by the messengers who bring it according to the wishes of the expectant people, your people, the hearts of many religious men who are now devoted to you will be troubled, which would be most unfortunate; and I fear too that your very *regalia*, which appertains to the church, will suffer not a little damage.

THE DISPUTE OVER THE ELECTION OF THE ARCHBISHOP OF YORK

THE following letters concern the dispute over the election of the Archbishop of York. We do not intend to enter into all the details of this rather involved affair. Even after the careful researches of scholars there remains much that is not clear, and it is not easy to say on which side the rights lay. But in order to understand the letters some knowledge of the background is necessary.[2]

The See of York became vacant on the death of Archbishop Thurstan in the year 1140. It was clear from the first that the election of his successor would not be easy. One of the candidates, Waldef of Kirkham, a Cistercian, was vetoed on political grounds by King Stephen. After long negotiations William Fitzherbert, the treasurer and a son of Emma the king's sister, was elected. But his reputation at

---

[1] *Terra vestra est: et in hoc plane cognoscimus et dolemus dedecus regni vestri, quod vos jure abhorrere mandastis, si non fuerit qui defendat.* Eales translates: ' The land is yours; and we plainly see and mourn the disgrace brought on your kingdom by your orders that we should abstain from our rights, inasmuch as there is no one to defend them '.

[2] For all the facts of this vexed affair we are indebted to Prof. Knowles, *Monastic Order in England*, Vol. I, pp. 254 sqq; Watkin Williams, *St. Bernard of Clairvaux*, pp. 168 sqq, and the important monograph of Dr. C. H. Talbot, *New Documents in the Case of Saint William of York, Cambridge Historical Journal*, Vol. X, no. 1, 1950. Those wishing to study the matter further will find all they need in *The Case of St. William of York* by Prof. Knowles, *Cambridge Historical Journal*, Vol. II (1936), 162-77, 212-14.

this time was not all that could have been hoped for in an archbishop, and his election was open to the gravest suspicions of intrusion and simony.

The Cistercian abbots of Rievaulx and Fountains and the Augustinian priors of Kirkham and Gisburn made trouble. By virtue of the rights given them by the Lateran Council in 1139, they took an active interest in the election, and their responsibilities in the matter very seriously.

Henry de Blois, the Papal Legate and Bishop of Winchester, advised William to take his case to Rome. Henry supported William all through the dispute. He was a forcible character and an ambitious one. He had plans for raising his see to metropolitan rank, with York a mere appendage.

As soon as William Fitzherbert had left for Rome the Yorkshire abbots, probably at the instigation of St. Bernard, sent a deputation posthaste after him to put their side of the case. They paused on their way at Clairvaux to receive instructions from the abbot. Something that Fitzherbert omitted to do.

What brought St. Bernard into the dispute we do not know, but he had already thrown himself into the fray with all his characteristic fire and energy before the deputation from the Yorkshire abbots had arrived. He immediately set about strengthening their hand with letters of introduction to powerful friends in Rome.

The case was heard in Rome during March, 1142. The evidence was strong against the archbishop-elect, but the case broke down because the canons of the Church forbade the acceptance of secondhand evidence as grounds for proceeding against anyone. Pope Innocent II packed the litigants back to England, and ordered the principals to come in person to Rome the following year on the third Sunday in Lent.

It should be borne in mind that the Cistercian abbots were running the gravest risks in appealing to Rome against the election of the king's candidate. Their monasteries were in danger of confiscation and their Order of expulsion. Even their lives were not safe. The subsequent raid on Fountains and the mutilation of one of their party, Walter of London, prove that the danger was very real.

Both parties arrived in Rome for the final hearing of the case on March 7th, 1143. But no settlement ensued, as William Fitzherbert appealed to the testimony of William of St. Barbe, Dean of York, who was not present in Rome. The case was therefore referred back to England, and the Pope made his approval of the election contingent on William of St. Barbe undertaking to swear that pressure had not been brought to bear upon the Chapter by the king's men.

William of St. Barbe astutely avoided the issue by obtaining permission to substitute another approved witness in his stead. How he arranged this is not clear, perhaps on the grounds that his see of Durham, to which he had been lately elected, demanded all his attention just then.

The substituted witnesses found no difficulty in swearing as they were required to do, so that on September 26th, 1143, William Fitzherbert was consecrated Archbishop of York by Henry de Blois, Bishop of Winchester. But he had yet to receive the pallium.

With the decline of their cause and the increasing violence of their opponents the resistance of the Yorkshire abbots began to weaken. St. Bernard planned to come himself to give them heart and strengthen their spirit. But the journey was too much for his weak health, and he arranged to send Henry Murdac in his stead. He could hardly have chosen a better substitute. Although a Cistercian of Clairvaux and an *ex animo* disciple of the abbot, Murdac was a Yorkshireman with influential connections in the county and a resolute character. Unhappily circumstances postponed his departure until the following year. In the meantime the cause of the Yorkshire abbots suffered another blow in the death of Richard, Abbot of Fountains. When Murdac arrived at Fountains in 1144 he was elected abbot in his place.[1]

[1] *Vide* Letters 173 and 174.

Innocent II had died in September, 1143, and was succeeded by Celestine II. During the short reign of this Pope Henry de Blois fell from favour and lost his legatine authority.   Celestine died in 1144 to be succeeded by Lucius II, a friend of St. Bernard's.   As soon as the new Pope was elected, Henry de Blois tried to regain his position as Legate, but without success.   Hincmar, Cardinal Bishop of Frascati, was appointed in his stead and immediately dispatched to England with the pallium. He paused at Clairvaux on the way.   The following year he returned to Rome without having bestowed the pallium.   But he had met Henry Murdac.   Lucius II died in 1145 and Hincmar was in time to assist at the election of his successor, Eugenius III, the first Cistercian Pope, a disciple of the Abbot of Clairvaux, and a fellow religious of Henry Murdac.   Undoubtedly things were more hopeful for the Cistercian opponents of William Fitzherbert.

Eugenius III took resolute action.   He suspended William Fitzherbert until such a time as William of St. Barbe, now Bishop of Durham, should take the formal oath required by Innocent II.   Once more he tried to evade the issue, but he had already expressed his misgivings about the case of Fitzherbert in a letter to Hincmar, the Legate.   At this moment Fountains was raided and damaged by the king's supporters, but they failed to lay hands on the abbot as they intended.   Finally on St. Barbe still refusing to take the oath the Pope deposed William Fitzherbert and ordered another election.   This election took place at Richmond on July 24th, 1147, and the Pope confirmed it on December 7th of the same year.

William sought refuge with the Bishop of Winchester, and the majority of the clergy, supported by the king, refused to receive the newly elected Murdac.   He was not fully recognized by his clergy and the king until January, 1151.

In fairness to William Fitzherbert it must be said that his cause did not lack the support of devout and serious men.   One has the impression that he was being used by the Bishop of Winchester for his own purposes.   After all he became Archbishop of York in succession to Murdac and, whatever his former life may have been, he left behind him the reputation of a saint.   The crude violence of his supporters and the tergiversations of St. Barbe undoubtedly served to prejudice his case.

LETTER 187

TO POPE INNOCENT II

William Fitzherbert, the Archbishop-elect of York, has set out for Rome. St. Bernard tries to forestall him with this letter.

To his dear lord and loving father, Innocent, by the grace of God Supreme Pontiff, from Bernard, styled Abbot of Clairvaux, his humble duty.

SINCE many are called and few are chosen, it is no great argument in favour of something doubtful that many approve of it.   The Archbishop of York is coming to see you, the same of whom I have repeatedly written to your Holiness.[1]   He is a man who puts not his trust in God his helper, but hopes in the abundance of his riches.   His case is a weak and feeble one, and I have it on the authority of truthful men that he is rotten from the soles of his feet to the crown of his head.   What can this unrighteous man want with the arbiter of

---

[1] Unhappily all these letters are lost.

righteousness, the guardian of justice? Does he think he can swallow
up righteousness in the Curia, even as he has done in England? ' The
flooded river he drinks unconcerned; Jordan itself would have no
terrors for his gaping mouth.' He comes to you with many whom he
has won over by entreaties and treasure. Only this one has escaped
that he may bring you word, only this one has stood out at the risk of
his life like a wall around the house of Israel, only this one has refused
to bow down with the others and worship the idol at the command
of the king. He is alone except that righteousness bears him company.
' She has welcomed him as a mother welcomes the son who cherishes
her.' What can Peter's successor do in this business but what Peter
did with him who thought to purchase with money the gifts of God?
If the Church is founded on that rock the gates of hell will not prevail
against her. I do not speak on my own, but on the testimony of those
who are guided by the spirit of God.

LETTER 188

TO THE SAME

*By this time the deputation from the opponents of the York election, led by
Ailred of Rievaulx and Walter of London, the Archdeacon of York, have
arrived at Clairvaux, and the following are letters of introduction to friends
in Rome which St. Bernard gave them.*

To his most dear father and lord, Innocent, the Supreme Pontiff,
all the little that he has to offer, from Brother Bernard, styled Abbot
of Clairvaux.

THESE men whom you see before you are true, honest, and God-
fearing. They have been led by the spirit of God into your
august presence with the sole intention of seeing and obtaining justice.
Let your eyes rest upon these weary and poor men for not without
reason have they come to you from afar, undismayed by the great
distance, the dangers of the sea, the snows of the Alps and, being poor
men, the great expense of such a journey. They seek not their own
interests but those of Jesus Christ and so let my lord take them under
his protection lest, by the deceit or ambition of any person, all their
labours should be brought to nought. Their only motive is the love
of God and I do not think that even their worst enemy could suspect
them of being inspired in this business by either private interest or
personal rancour. If anyone is of God, let him stand by them.
Whose fault is it if the unfruitful tree cumbers the ground, but his
who holds the axe?

LETTER 189[1]

TO GERARD, CARDINAL PRIEST AND CHANCELLOR OF THE HOLY SEE

Gerard Caccianemici, Canon Regular, created Cardinal Priest 1124, was elected Pope in succession to Celestine II, March 12th, 1144, and took the name of Lucius II. He died October 15th, 1145.

To his most reverend father and lord, Gerard, by the grace of God Cardinal Priest and Chancellor of the Apostolic See, from Brother Bernard, styled Abbot of Clairvaux, his humble devotion.

THE bearers of this letter, being true, honest, and God-fearing men, have undertaken the fatigues of their long journey for God's cause and not their own. It is all the more certain that they are inspired by love of justice and zeal for the house of God since it is so very evident that they stand to gain nothing for themselves and do not hope to. This fact alone should powerfully recommend them to anyone who is a friend of religion and truly zealous for justice. But I know that the recommendation from me, your friend, will not come amiss, and so I faithfully and cordially recommend them and their cause to your fatherly care that they may learn that they are as much your friends as they are mine. Help, I pray you, as you conveniently can and with all your power, the cause of God which they serve.

2. A word for yourself. If the gains of the chancellery are growing, let your mercy grow in proportion. May your charity rather than the number of your chapels grow and a greater sum be set aside for the benefit of the poor. It would be a shocking thing if a priest of the Lord lined his pockets with the proceeds of his office. I say this not because I suspect you of any such thing, but because, as your faithful friend, I am anxious for you. I could wish that you were equally anxious for yourself.

LETTER 190

TO GUY OF CASTELLO

Guy Castello was created Cardinal in 1128; succeeded Innocent II September 25th, 1143, as Celestine II; died March 8th, 1144.

To his most reverend father, Guy, by the grace of God Cardinal Priest of the Apostolic See and a friend, greetings and prayers, from Brother Bernard, styled Abbot of Clairvaux.

THE bearers of this letter, being true, honest, and God-fearing men, have undertaken the fatigues of their long journey for God's cause and not their own. It is all the more certain that they are inspired

---

[1] Letters 189–198 and 201 were discovered by Dr. C. H. Talbot. See *New Documents in the Case of Saint William of York* by C. H. Talbot, the *Cambridge Historical Journal*, Vol. X, No. 1, 1950.

by love of justice and zeal for the house of God, since it is so very evident that they stand to gain nothing for themselves and do not hope to. Trusting in your affection, I presume faithfully and cordially to commend them and their cause to your care. Stand by them, I pray you, and help our cause for the sake of God and in the interests of the Church.

LETTER 191

TO CARDINAL ALBERIC

Alberic was Abbot of Vézelay, 1130; created Cardinal in 1136; and died in 1148.

To his most reverend father and friend, Alberic, by the grace of God Bishop of Ostia and Legate to the Apostolic See, greetings and such prayers as he is capable of in the Lord, from Brother Bernard, styled Abbot of Clairvaux.

I DO not believe that the bearers and their cause need much recommendation to one who is a friend of religion and truly zealous for justice. Their piety, which is well known to you, as well as the obvious justice of their cause, should be a sufficient recommendation even ' if their testimonies are not become exceedingly credible '. It is manifest that they are not seeking anything for themselves and put their trust, not in the foolish words of human wisdom, but in the truth alone, who solely for love of justice and zeal for the house of God have undertaken their long journey regardless of the expense and fatigue. But I know that the commendation of your friend cannot come amiss, so, with all my heart, I commend them and their cause to your fatherly care. May they discover that they are as much your friends as mine.

LETTER 192

TO CARDINAL STEPHEN

Stephen was a Cistercian, created Cardinal in 1140. He died in 1144.

To Stephen, by the grace of God Bishop of Palestrina, greetings and such prayers as he is capable of in the Lord, from Brother Bernard, styled Abbot of Clairvaux.

I DO not think that you who have on so many different occasions helped so many different people, can fail to help your own friends concerned in a cause which is entirely your own. I call it your own cause, because you always make the cause of God your own, and who does not know that all my friends are equally yours. So I pray you to receive the bearers as truly your own friends and to take in hand the cause which they serve as truly the cause of God and therefore of yourself.

NOTE

POPE Innocent II wrote on April 22nd, 1142, commanding the opponents of the election, Abbots William of Rievaulx, and Richard of Fountains, the Priors Cuthbert of Gisburn, and Waldef of Kirkham, and Robert, Master of St. Leonard's, York, to come to Rome in person on the third Sunday in Lent in the following year. He says that although William Fitzherbert may be guilty the canons of the Church forbid taking secondhand evidence as sufficient grounds for proceeding against anyone.

In another letter Cardinal Alberic, writing from the security of the Curia, appeals to the detachment and renunciation of the abbots and encourages them to accept the crown of martyrdom if necessary.

LETTER 193

TO AN UNKNOWN PERSON

The abbots have now arrived at Clairvaux on their way to Rome for the trial to take place on the third Sunday in Lent, 1143. *St. Bernard gives them the two following letters of introduction.*

To I., greetings and prayers, from Bernard, styled Abbot of Clairvaux.

THESE abbots have come from our house. I commend them to your sympathy that they may learn how much you care for me. What you do for them I shall regard as a personal favour to myself.

LETTER 194

TO A LADY OF RANK

Dr. Talbot tentatively suggests that this lady may be Sybil, daughter of Foulques of Anjou, second wife of Thierry of Alsace, Count of Flanders.

To the most noble and dear lady in Christ, S., greetings and prayers, from Bernard, styled Abbot of Clairvaux.

THESE abbots are from our house. They are devout and thoroughly praiseworthy men. I am anxious to send you my greetings in the Lord by them lest you should think I have forgotten your kindness to me. Very gladly do I secure you such friends as these and I faithfully commend them to you for I have no doubt that you will be pleased to welcome them. You may afford them any help or services they need with complete confidence, as they have come a great distance. Have no doubt that what you do for them, you do for the Lord.

LETTER 195

TO HENRY DE BLOIS, BISHOP OF WINCHESTER

Henry de Blois was Abbot of Glastonbury about 1126; consecrated bishop November 17th, 1129, and appointed Legate March 1st, 1139. He died in 1171. Clearly this letter was written by St. Bernard when the case had been referred back to England after the second hearing.

To his lord and truly reverend father, Henry, Bishop of Winchester and Legate of the Roman See, greetings and such prayers as he is capable of in the Lord, from Brother Bernard, styled Abbot of Clairvaux.

WE are told of how Joab when he had almost taken a city reserved the credit of the final victory to David. In just the same way I believe that now the final credit of finishing this dispute of the church of York, which has been discussed for so long and is now almost terminated, is reserved to you. For this reason I advise you in all friendliness, exhort you reverently, implore you earnestly, to conclude the affair in such a way that there shall be no breath of unpleasant suspicion to tarnish the credit that will be due to you. And, if that man should fall, act, I pray you, in a manner that becomes you and according to the powers you have received by arranging an election that shall be worthy of God and useful to the Church in which the canons are secured freedom to elect whom they will.

LETTER 196

TO ROBERT, BISHOP OF HEREFORD

Robert of Bethune, Prior of Llanthony, was consecrated bishop June 28th, 1131. He died at Rheims on April 16th, 1148, during the council convened to judge Gilbert de la Porrée.

To his most reverend father and lord, Robert, by the grace of God Bishop of Hereford and his cordial friend, greetings and his prayers for what they are worth, from Brother Bernard, styled Abbot of Clairvaux.

I AM glad and full of confidence now that your Lordship has been called upon to help in terminating the dispute of the church of York. Would that all disputes could be thus terminated! I have no doubt that the honour of God, the liberty of the Church, and the salvation of souls would then prosper. I pray you that you may see to it and take every care that this iniquity should not be any further drawn out or the condition laid down by our lord the Pope be at all changed by the guile of any person or the efforts of any deceiver. I do not say this because I have any doubt at all of your honesty or of your zeal for justice, but so that I can be all the more grateful to you when this affair reaches the desired end and make it an occasion for offering you my due acknowledgement. Begging you to remember me in your prayers, for I am gravely ill, I bid your Lordship farewell.

LETTER 197

TO KING STEPHEN

Another letter on the same subject.

To Stephen, by the grace of God King of the English, greetings and his prayers for what they are worth, from Brother Bernard, styled Abbot of Clairvaux.

THE King of kings has for long chastised your royal Majesty, for he is more powerful than you. Yet I believe that he has done it more in mercy than in fury because we know that he never forgets to be merciful in his anger. For this reason I humbly advise you and on bended knee implore you that on those matters for which above all God is especially chastising you and your realm, to wit the affairs of Church and State, you give not the spouse of the Church further cause for chastising you yet more harshly and even completely destroying you. Especially in the case of the church of York do I implore you with my whole heart to change your attitude and not attempt to hinder the termination of the affair according to the manner laid down by the Lord Pope. And if that man should fall, permit, I beg you, the canons to be left free lawfully to elect another, as not only the church of York but all the churches should be left free; then, if you do this, the Lord will be with you, he will render you glorious and exalt your throne.

LETTER 198

TO MATILDA, QUEEN OF ENGLAND

To his dear daughter in Christ, Matilda, by the grace of God Queen of the English, that she may reign for ever with the angels, from Brother Bernard, styled Abbot of Clairvaux.

I GLADLY take this opportunity of affectionately greeting in the Lord your Majesty and not only gladly but also faithfully suggesting certain things which I know to concern your own salvation and the glory of your kingdom. If you fear God and if you wish at all to harken to my counsel, do everything you possibly can to prevent that man from occupying the see of York any longer. I have heard all about his life and the manner of his election from religious men who are utterly trustworthy. This is the cause of God and I entrust it to you. It is for you to see that my trust is not betrayed. I commend to you all who are labouring in the cause that you may see they do not suffer from the wrath of the king nor any hurt whatsoever, for they are doing a good work. Further, if you could arrange that the king should abjure before his bishops and princes the sacrilegious intrusion on the liberty of the chapter, so that it alone should have the decision to which it alone is entitled, know that it would be greatly to the honour of God, the well-being and security of the king and his friends, and to the profit of the whole realm.

LETTER 199

TO WILLIAM, ABBOT OF RIEVAULX

This letter was written after the consecration of William Fitzherbert by the Bishop of Winchester on September 26th, 1143. Abbot William was evidently rather impetuous, and St. Bernard was afraid of what he might do.

To his dear brother and fellow-abbot, William, Abbot of Rievaulx, ' a spirit wise and discerning, a spirit prudent and strong ', from Brother Bernard of Clairvaux.

I HAVE heard what has been done about that archbishop. So I am writing to console you, for your zeal is well known to me and it would ill become our Order and not help your house if it were to flare up beyond the bounds of prudence and discretion. Since our own consciences are clear in the matter we should bear it calmly. I say with complete confidence that what has happened is not your fault and you are in no way to blame for it. You have done all you could to resist the evil and now, according to St. Augustine, you have no responsibility in it. We clear ourselves of all responsibility for another's evil deeds, he tells us, by disowning them in our hearts and rebuking them with our lips. You have done both these things, so be of good cheer and do not worry. As for ordination and the other sacraments, you must bear in mind that it is Christ the Lord and Pontiff of our souls who baptizes and consecrates. If anyone is reluctant to receive ordination, no one obliges him to do so. Yet I say with all confidence that if you receive it with the Church, there is no danger. We should have to leave this world altogether if we would fly from all the bad men tolerated by the Church. Finally, it will not be long now before the Pope hears of what has happened and whatever he orders and decrees do you hold to and follow with a good conscience. In the meantime wait calmly the issue.

LETTER 200

TO THE SAME

This letter was written after Hincmar, the Cardinal Bishop of Frascati, had set out for England with the pallium.

WE have done all we can against our common bane and, if we have been less successful than we hoped, we can still look to him who allows no good to go unrewarded for the fruit of our labours. ' There is awaiting us the prize we have earned, and the Lord, the judge whose award never goes amiss, will grant it to us when the day comes': this should be the great consolation for us, and for all who have struggled with us in the cause of truth. I would have you remember that if we suffer for the sake of justice we are blessed; and that we share no responsibility in the evil deeds of another, if we have refused to approve them and have even rebuked them. And this too should console us and enable us to possess our souls in patience, and look for the help that men have denied us, to the Lord who never betrays those who put their trust in him. I have every confidence in the mercy of our heavenly Father: ' He will root up every plant which he has not planted ' and the sterile fig-tree will wither at his curse, to encumber the land no longer. Therefore, my brother, I beg you to remain calm and not trouble the flock of God entrusted to your care. On the contrary you should be consoled ' playing the man and keeping your courage high ', so that ' we may live without fear in his service, delivered from the hand of our enemies '. For my part, I have done what I can to advise His Lordship, the Bishop of Frascati,[1] who, as Legate for those parts, has been entrusted with this business. He has faithfully promised me that, even if he can do nothing better, he will not bestow the pallium, but refer the matter back to the Pope, if the Bishop of Durham, the man who was formerly Dean of York, does not take the oath on which the whole matter was made to hang.

LETTER 201

TO THE ABBOTS OF RIEVAULX AND FOUNTAINS

With the consecration of William Fitzherbert and the growing violence of his supporters the purpose of the Yorkshire abbots was beginning to weaken, so the Abbot of Clairvaux writes this letter and tells them that he has arranged to send them his disciple the Abbot of Vauclair, Henry Murdac, to make the visitations prescribed and encourage them in their trials. As it happens, troubles of his own prevent Murdac from leaving that year.

[1] Hincmar.

10

To his very dear brothers in Christ and fellow-abbots, William of Rievaulx and Richard of Fountains, and all the others united with them in the same necessity, that they may preserve unity of spirit in the bonds of peace, from Bernard, styled Abbot of Clairvaux.

'WHO will give me the wings of a dove, that I may go up to this people of ours which is girded for battle', that I may behold the joy of your fraternal love, that I may take my share in the troubles that abound in your place of pilgrimage, that I may save those who 'perish from fears and the storms around them'. I am obliged to go out of my house on visitations by the Rule of our Order, by the duty of our fraternity, but charity spurs me more and more to attempt something greater than this.

2. Willingly would I go and see how my brethren and their flocks are faring and bring back word to my father Jacob; willingly would I come over to see the Lord of battles in the camps of Israel 'who makes your hands strong for battle and your fingers skilled in fight'. I am the least of my brethren, but I would not fear to smite the Philistine while he upbraids the hosts of Israel with a stone from my sling. Would that I might receive assurance from the Holy Spirit that I should not see death until I had eaten my fill with you and not of bread alone, but 'of every word that proceedeth from the mouth of God'. With a great desire do I desire to eat this feast of the Passover with you before I die. In this 'my heart would be filled as with some rich feast' and 'in such things is the life of my spirit'. For this I wait and wait hoping to be given the strength to follow my ready will, but up to now I have been prevented. The way is hard and difficult, and my body is weak. On the top of all this, apart from my own weakness, the journeyings I have to make on the business of my brethren and in the cause of the Church 'tower high above me and hang on me like a heavy burden'. Because of this, beloved, I am sending for your visitation my brother and dear friend, Henry, Abbot of Vauclair. Hear him, I beg you, as if he were myself. He is an upright and reasonable man who has taken on his shoulders some of my own cares and burdens and shares my powers for the correction of faults and the maintenance of the Order.

3. For the rest, as 'we all offend in many things' and being often among men pick up much dust from the world, I commend myself, dearest brothers, to your prayers and those of your friends. You must throw me a rope of prayer, for I am labouring far out to sea while you are safe in port. I believe that at the word of the Lord, the winds and the seas will be still. But he sleeps and you must waken him with your prayers.

LETTER 202

TO POPE CELESTINE II

*Innocent II had died, to be succeeded by Celestine II, and William Fitzherbert
had managed to get himself consecrated Archbishop of York in spite of St.
Barbe's evasion. It is, perhaps, not easy to escape the impression that the
Abbot of Clairvaux has rather overstated his case in this letter; certainly
he has displayed a gift for vituperation. Even some of the saint's most ardent
admirers are inclined to admit that he relied too much on the reports of secondhand evidence. The hot denunciations of this letter are in contrast with the
cool impartiality displayed by the Holy See. Yet it must be remembered
that the Abbot of Clairvaux was in a better position to judge the facts than
we are. He was in close contact with those who were on the spot at the time
and they were men of undoubted integrity. It is not easy to see how he
could have taken any other line or how he could have informed himself
better of the facts apart from undertaking a personal investigation. This we
know he wished to do, but was prevented by his ill-health. And certainly
the evasions of St. Barbe set the case of Fitzherbert in a sinister light.*

IT behoves your Holiness to raise up seed to your dead brother
according to the righteousness of the law. This you will best do
by maintaining the decrees of your predecessor Pope Innocent and
completing the work he had begun, but left unfinished. You have a
case on hand now in which you can do this. Everyone knows that
the dispute of the church of York has been decided by him. I would
that we did not all know how his decision has been implemented!
Who will grant that ' this secret will be kept in Gath and never a
word of it uttered in the streets of Ascalon'? To make a long story
short so as not to burden one so preoccupied, I will tell my lord
briefly what has been said and done in the matter. After the man
who had disgracefully tried to secure the see of York for himself had
been charged with many things of which intrusion was one, the
matter was made to rest on the word of William of St. Barbe, the
dean, so that the man would be foiled of his ambition unless the dean
should be ready to swear in person that there had been no untoward
intrusion on the liberty of the chapter. This was not a sentence so
much as an act of mercy, for the man had undertaken that the dean
would clear him. It was a very lenient decision, since he had been
confronted with many shocking charges of which he could not clear
himself. But would that it had all finished there! I am not complaining of the laxity of the sentence, that hurt nobody. If justice
had not been satisfied, at any rate the liberty of the Church had been
vindicated. But the indulgence he had received, although so great,
did not benefit the adversary one bit, for he was not able to carry out
what he had undertaken. The dean, on whose support he had counted,

preferred to fail him than fail himself by perjury. How could a man sponsor one who stood condemned by his own deeds as well as by public opinion? The dean very properly refused to do so, yet that man became a bishop!

2. This is something that would be better kept quiet and, if possible, completely hushed up. But too late! This victory of the devil is known all over the world. On all sides it is greeted by the derisions of the uncircumcised and the lamentations of the good. The shame of the Church is pointed out, Innocent has been stripped and left for dead by a wicked servant and his nakedness is mocked at! But Innocent is not dead, he lives on in you. If the affair was to end like this, why was the unclean business ventilated in Rome? It would have been better to have arranged it in some corner on the quiet. Why should so many have been obliged to endure all the fatigues and dangers of a long journey by sea and land? Why should religious men have been brought from the ends of the earth to give their evidence in accusation and why should the pockets of the poor of Christ have been emptied on the expenses of such a long journey? Could not this vile and infamous person have been made a bishop (I say it reluctantly) without all France loathing and all Rome learning what had already horrified England? How much better if it had not been dragged to Rome at all, if the stench of it had never invaded the sacred precincts! How much better for the Holy See to have been ignorant of such an intolerable state of affairs than publicly to have tolerated it! What incredible rashness! A man publicly infamous, accused before the Courts and not cleared, but rather condemned, has become a bishop! Let him who laid hands on him consider whether I would not do better to say he had been ' execrated ' rather than ' consecrated '. He will not deny that all these things are true, nor will he deny that they were stated in letters to him from the Apostolic See. Perhaps someone will say that sentence was never pronounced against the man, that he was never proved guilty. But I say that his action in trying to shelter behind William the dean so as to avoid judgement because he could not clear himself was tantamount to a confession of guilt and that he stands judged and convicted out of his own mouth by the refusal of the dean to sponsor him.

3. Things being in this state you must see to it, my lord and father, that your heart does not decline unto wickedness for, according to the Prophet, ' feet that stray into the snare, the Lord will punish as he punishes wrong doers '. What advice do you propose to give those wretched abbots who were dragged all the way to Rome as witnesses against the man and to all the other good men from the diocese? Are they to obey and receive the sacraments from one who has been twice intruded on his Church, by the king and the legate? It was the legate who, when he could not get him through the door, dug a way

for him into the sanctuary with a spade of silver, as the saying is, against all law and order, against the commands of the Supreme Pontiff, and much to the injury of the Apostolic See and the whole Roman Curia. Rather than bow down to this idol I fancy they would resign their positions unless forbidden by all your authority. How much more worthy of your apostolic zeal it would be to draw the sword of Phinees and shame those shameless fornicators than to allow such good and holy men to resign or to force them against their consciences to remain. (I have written with such confidence because I am fully aware of your love for righteousness. I pray that this love may never grow cold but wax ever warmer, most holy and loving father. Master Walter[1] was prepared to come to Rome even now, but having lost all the money he had set aside for the journey, he is forced to remain. But he will come nevertheless as soon as he conveniently can.[2])

LETTER 203

TO ALL THE ROMAN CURIA

To his reverend fathers and lords, the Bishops and Cardinals in Curia, greetings and such prayers as he can offer, from Brother Bernard, styled Abbot of Clairvaux.

I MUST write to all on a matter that concerns all. I am not afraid of being thought presumptuous because, although the least of all, I consider as my own any injury to the Roman Curia. I am on fire! I tell you that I am so consumed that I am weary of life. In the house of God I have seen a horrible thing. I am not able to correct it myself, all I can do is to appeal to those whose concern it is. If they set it right, well and good; if not, then I am free from all responsibility. But you will not have any excuse. You will remember the sentence given by the lord Pope Innocent of happy memory with your consent and with the general consent of all the Roman Curia, that the election, or, I should say, the intrusion, of William of York would be null and void unless that other William, then the dean, were prepared to clear him by his own oath of the charge against him. Nor will it have escaped your notice that this sentence was an act of mercy rather than of judgement, for it was what William, the archbishop-elect, had asked for. I would that the matter had rested there, that what has since been done contrary to it should not be suffered to stand. For what has happened but that the dean never took the oath, yet that man now sits 'in the chair of pestilence'. Would that Phinees might arm himself against this fornication, would that Peter still lived who

---

[1] Walter of London, Archdeacon of York, who came with Ailred of Rievaulx on the first deputation to Rome. He fell into the hands of the supporters of Fitzherbert, and was mutilated.
[2] The final passage in parenthesis was discovered by Dr. C. H. Talbot. It is missing from the Benedictine text. See C. H. Talbot, *op. cit.*

slew the impious with the breath of his lips. Many are crying out in their hearts to you to take appropriate steps for the punishment of this sacrilege. There will be a great scandal, I tell you, in the Church of God, and I very much fear that the authority of the Holy See will suffer great loss and injury unless steps are taken to punish this man who has subverted its general decree, in such a way that others may see and be afraid.

2. What can I say of that William's boast that he has received secret letters, verily letters of darkness ? I wish I could think that they were from the princes of darkness and not from the princes of the Church. The Roman Curia has become a mockery to the sons of uncircumcision who are saying that it has sent secret letters in a contrary sense to its open and public decree. What can I say to you? If you are not on fire at this grave scandal, not merely a scandal to babes, but to great and holy men; if you have no compassion for those poor abbots whom the Apostolic summons dragged all the way to Rome from the ends of the earth; if you have no pity for those great and goodly monasteries which are threatened by imminent destruction at the hands of this intruder, if (what I ought to have said first) you are not devoured by zeal for God's house; has not the cunning of the evil one so far prevailed that the princes of the Church bear with equanimity the contempt in which they are held and the shame of the Church? What even if that man has received a consecration that is sacrilegious? Were it not a more glorious thing to cast Simon down from his throne than to prevent him ascending it? What do you propose to do for those religious men who cannot bring themselves to receive with a sound conscience even the ordinary sacraments from this man's leprous hands? I fancy that they would rather flee their country than clasp hands with death, prefer exile to eating the meat of idols. And if the Roman Curia should oblige them to bend the knee to Baal against their consciences, then may God look to it and judge, then may that heavenly Curia whose judgements cannot be subverted by ambition see to it. Finally your son implores you by the mercy of God, if there is any zeal for God's house in you, to have pity on the Church, at least you who are its friends, and refuse your consent to this vile deed.

LETTER 204

TO POPE LUCIUS II

Hüffer is clearly quite mistaken in understanding this letter to refer to a dispute between Winchester and Chichester. It is concerned with the behaviour of Henry de Blois, Bishop of Winchester, in the vexed and complicated affair of the election of the Archbishop of York. There is an answer to this letter in Jaffre No. 8665.

To his most beloved father and lord, Lucius, by the grace of God Supreme Pontiff, his humble duty, from Bernard, styled Abbot of Clairvaux.

I RETURNED home to my own affairs from that excellent meeting of your Curia strengthened by the grace of God and delighting in your own most efficacious help as a rich man delights in his treasure. Since then I have been awaiting the hoped-for issue of the affair we settled. I have been waiting to see if the flower of the decision you made in Rome would bear the appropriate fruit in Winchester, so that the cup of my joy might be filled. Gladness is mingled with anxiety when the vine is still in flower, only when the flowers have given birth to fruit is joy complete. Hence we read in the Canticle: ' Let us see if the flowers be ready to bring forth fruit '. I have been watching the vine at Winchester, the second Rome as it is called in their song, to see if it brought forth grapes and lo ' it is turned into the bitterness of a strange vine and has brought forth wild grapes '. O happy Winchester, O second Rome, happy in your choice of so great a name! O city so powerful that you can withstand the authority of your mighty fathers in Curia, change their decrees, pervert their judgements, defame truth, and with a great voice confirm what Rome has most rightly judged shall not be confirmed without the prescribed condition of an oath.[1] For when the dean[2] was invited to take the prescribed oath, he not only refused in public to do so, but even declared himself willing to make an oath to the contrary. Yet that Philistine[3] in a spirit of turbulence does not blush to set up that idol Dagon[4] next to the very ark of the Lord. Surely he has the effrontery of the harlot spoken of by Jeremias the prophet. What will not the *auri sacra fames*[5] drive a man to do! Winchester has arrogated to herself the venerable name of Rome, and not only the name but the prerogatives as well. She suffers nothing to be done without her consent. Absolution and the dignities of the Church she regards as her own to be disposed as she will. Not happy but cursed is she, for she has cast precious pearls before swine and what is holy she has thrown to the dogs; she has not turned from the temple those who buy and sell doves, she has brought them in; and in a wonderful way is able to oppose the hitherto invincible Curia of the Roman Senate . . . for shame! O father, O glory of Rome, O upholder of justice, who carries alone the burden of so many great affairs, who protects the republic of the Church with the arms of justice, and adorns her life with virtues, we in our weakness call upon

[1] This refers to the oath that no undue influence had been exerted on the electors demanded by a Council in Rome during Lent, 1143, and presided over by Innocent II, from William of St. Barbe, Dean of York and Bishop-elect of Durham.
[2] William of St. Barbe, Dean of York, and thus the chief witness of the election. He was consecrated Bishop of Durham on July 1st, 1143, and thereby avoided taking the oath.
[3] Henry de Blois, Legate to the Holy See and Bishop of Winchester. A colourful and strong character. He had designs to make his diocese a Metropolitan see.
[4] William Fitzherbert, the Archbishop-elect. After his death he was honoured as a saint.
[5] Virgil, *Aeneid*, III, 57. ' The cursed lust for gold.'

you to avenge these outrages, to make for yourself a whip of cords and upset with the strong hand of Rome the tables of those who buy and sell and drive them forth from the temple. Were the primates of Rome to take lots their choice would rest on you for this ministry. How happy are we in the just defender of our cause! How happy in our avenger of such great insolence! The sword is with you, ' draw it forth and close the way ' against them that resist the authority of Rome. Behold here, here, I say, is the enemy, here is the man who walks before Satan, the son of perdition, the man who disrupts all rights and laws. This is the man who has ' set his face against heaven ', who has repudiated, reprobated, rejected, and renounced, the just judgement of the apostle, confirmed, consolidated, promulgated, and clearly defined in solemn conclave. This is the man that has set up that foolish figure-head, that idol, such a man as the sins of the people have deserved. Let Rome arise and gird herself with the zeal of Phinees at the sight of one man who puts his trust in mammon pulling up and destroying what her mighty sons have planted and built up. That unworthy man, they say, has set up that idol of resistance to the Roman tiara despite your judgement because he was jealous of your authority; he has set it up, they say, to break your authority. I leave it to your judgement to decide how far the prestige of Rome has suffered in this matter. Would that the song in which they sing that Winchester is greater than Rome could be silenced on their lips. They say that they have no need to send to Rome now that they have a legate. And what the Lord of Rome ordains and confirms, this steward, the legate, perverts and whittles down. The man whom the wisdom of the Roman Curia does not accept without the sanction of Blessed Peter, that deceiver of Winchester, that prevaricator of the judgements of Rome, him he sets up on high and exalts. Lest such contumacy should become a custom and an example, lest the dignity of Rome should be torn to shreds, lest the authority of Peter succumb to these new and great humiliations, lest religion should grow cold in the diocese of York, yea, lest it be wholly up-rooted and scattered to the winds, let Rome in the sole interests of justice, crush the contumacy of this stubborn man, and with the hammer of severity throw down that idol he has set up, and break his throne to pieces. If any of them should come to Rome for the pallium, it behoves your Holiness manfully to resist them, despising Ananias and Sapphira with their money bags. For we fear and dread lest that old whore of Winchester should be asked in some way by the new prophet[1] he has set up to share in the government, yea in the full power of the diocese.[2] Therefore be prudent and crush the head of the serpent that lies in wait for your heel in that realm lest the Church there should succumb and be totally suppressed. May your Holiness grow and flourish.

[1] William Fitzherbert again.
[2] A reference to the Metropolitan ambitions of Henry de Blois.

LETTER 205

TO POPE EUGENIUS III

A letter to the first Cistercian Pope in which the Abbot of Clairvaux expresses his pride and also his anxiety in the elevation of one who had once been his son in religion.   He also touches on the troubles of the Church of York.

To his most loving father and lord, Eugenius, by the grace of God Supreme Pontiff, his entire devotion for what it is, from Bernard, styled Abbot of Clairvaux.

THE glad tidings of what the Lord has done for you has been heard in our land and is on everybody's lips.   I have not written sooner because I have been thinking it over in silence.   I was waiting to hear from you, ' to be met on the way with abundant blessings '.   I was waiting for a trusty messenger from your person to tell me everything exactly as it all happened.   I was waiting to see if perhaps one of my sons would not come back to soothe the grief of his father and say: ' Thy son Jacob still lives, and it is he that rules the whole land of Egypt '.   So I am writing not of my own free will but of necessity, constrained thereto by friends to whom I cannot deny whatever little may remain to me of my life. (Few are the days left to me, now there only remains the grave.[1])   Now that I have begun, I will not keep silence but I will speak to my lord.   I do not dare to call you a son any longer.   You were my son, but now you have become my father.   I was your father, but now I have become your son.   You who came after me have been preferred before me.   But I am not jealous, for I am sure that you who not only came after me but also, in a manner, through me, will make up in your person for what is lacking to me.   For, if you will pardon my saying so, it was I who, as it were, begot you in the Gospel.   What is it that I hope will be my joy and a glorious crown for me?   It is you before God.   A wise son is the pride of his father.   From now on you will not be called son, but you will be called by a new name ' given you by the Lord's own lips '.   This is surely a change of the right hand of the Most High. Just as Abram became Abraham and Jacob became Israel or better still, to quote your predecessors, just as Simon became Cephas and Saul became Paul, so has my son Bernard been promoted to be my father Eugenius.   I hope it will be a joyful and beneficial change.   This is the finger of God ' raising up the poor man out of the dust, the beggar from his dung-hill to sit among princes and reach the honour of a throne '.

2. It only remains for the bride of the Lord who has been thus

---

[1] This passage is lacking in all but 2 MSS.

entrusted to you, to benefit by the change and be called no longer
'Sarai' but 'Sarah'.   Understand what I say, for the Lord has given
you understanding.   If you are a friend of the Bridegroom you should
say not 'his beloved is my princess' but 'his beloved is a princess',
claiming for yourself nothing of what is hers, save only the privilege
of dying for her if necessary.   If you are come from Christ, you are
come, don't forget, not to be served, but to serve.   Let the successor
of Paul be able to say with Paul: 'We are come, not because we
exercise dominion over your faith, but because we are helpers in your
joy'.   Let the heir of Peter be able to say with Peter: 'We are come,
not to lord it over the household of God, but to be an example to the
flock'.   So shall the bride, no longer a servant but beautiful and free,
be delivered by you into the arms of her fair Bridegroom.   From
whom else can she expect the liberty to which she is entitled if you
(which God forbid) seek your own profit from the inheritance of
Christ, you who long ago learned not to call anything your own, not
even your own body.[1]

3. The whole Church rejoices and glorifies God, because she has a
confidence in you such as she does not seem to have had for a long time
in your predecessors.   But especially does she rejoice who bore you
in her womb and who suckled you at her breasts.   And why should
not I too rejoice?   Why should not I be one of those who are glad?
I do indeed rejoice but I confess that I do so not without trembling.
I rejoice indeed, but in the very act of rejoicing fear and trembling come
upon me.   Although I have laid aside the name of father, neither the
fears nor the anxieties of a father have left me, least of all the affection
and heart of a father.   When I think of the heights to which you
have been lifted up, I fear a fall.   When I think of your great dignity,
I look down into the jaws of the gulf that yawns below you.   When
I ponder on the honour which is yours, I fear the danger which is at
hand.   I do not think that the words 'Man when he is honoured
does not remember what he is' refer so much to the time as to the
cause and mean that honours blind the judgement of a man, so that
he forgets that he is human.

4. You chose to be the last in the household of God, you took the
bottom seat at his feast, but now your Host has said, 'Friend, go up
higher'.   So you have gone up on high.   But do not let that make
you high-minded, lest when it is too late it should befall you to cry
out, 'I shrink before thy vengeful anger, so low thou hast brought me,
who didst once lift me up so high'.   You have been called to hold a
high position, but not a safe one; a sublime position, but not a secure
one.   How terrible, how very terrible is the place you hold!   The
place where you stand is holy ground.   It is the place of Peter, the
place of the Prince of the Apostles, the very place where his feet have

---

[1] Cf. *Rule of St. Benedict*, Chap. 58.

stood.   It is the place of him whom the Lord made master of his house-hold and chief over all his possessions.   He is buried there in that very place to watch over you and bear witness against you if your feet should ever stray from the path of righteousness.   Happy was the Church when still young, when still in her cradle, to be entrusted to the care of such a shepherd, of such a nurse, and to be taught to trample all earthly things under foot by the example of one who would sully his fingers with no gifts and who could say with a clear conscience and a pure heart: ' Silver and gold have I none '.

5. But my reason for writing to you before I meant to, is this. The Bishop of Winchester and the Archbishop of York are not of one mind with the Archbishop of Canterbury.   It is the old quarrel about the office of legate.   But who are they and who is he?   Is not the Archbishop of York that very person whom, in your presence when you were still in a manner one of us, your brethren resisted to the face because he was to blame?   But he put his trust in the abundance of his riches and, in the vanity of his heart, he has prevailed.   Yet he is a man who did not enter the fold by the door but climbed up another way.   If he had been a shepherd of souls, he would have been lovable; if he had been a mere hireling, he would have been tolerable; but as it is he is a man to be shunned and repelled for he is a thief and a robber.   What can I say of his Lordship of Winchester?   His deeds speak of themselves.   But the Archbishop of Canterbury to whom these two are opposed is a devout man with a fair reputation.   On his behalf I beg that his goodness may answer for him, and that their evil may be upon the others, as it is written: ' Good will befall the good, evil the evil '.   When you have time, deal with them according to their works, so that they may know a prophet has arisen in Israel.

6. Who will grant me before I die to see the Church as she was in the days of old when the Apostles let down their nets to catch not gold and silver but the souls of men?   How I hope that you will inherit the words as well as the office of him who said: ' Silver and gold have I none '.   What words of thunder !   What magnificent and virtuous words !   At the very sound of them all those who hate Sion are shamed and turned back in confusion.   This is what your mother looks for from you and longs for with all her heart.   This is what the sons of your mother, both young and old, hope and sigh for, so that every tree your father has not planted may be torn down with your own hands.   You have been set up over peoples and kingdoms for this purpose, to pull up and to destroy.   Many said when they heard of your election: ' Now the axe is laid to the tree '.   Many said in their hearts: ' At home the flowers have begun to blossom, the pruning time has come'; the dead branches will be cut away so that those which are left may bear more abundant fruit.

7. Have courage and be of good heart.   You hold your enemies

by the neck; claim for yourself with a strong hand and a firm purpose the land which your omnipotent father has allotted to you above that of your brothers, the land he took from the Amorite with his sword and bow. But in all your actions remember that you are human, and have the fear of him who 'strikes awe into the hearts of princes' ever before your eyes. How many are the deaths of Roman Pontiffs which your own eyes have seen in a short time! Let the sudden and sure deaths of your predecessors be a warning to you. Let the short span of their power remind you of how short is the time allotted to you. Remember, by constant meditations amidst the blandishments of your fleeting glory, that your last end will come. Without any doubt you too will follow to the grave those men you have followed to the throne.

LETTER 206

TO THE SAME

This letter urges the deposition of the Archbishop of York. The second half of it was discovered and published by Hüffer.

I AM importunate, but I have reason to be and my reason is the apostolate of Eugenius! For they are saying that it is not you but I who am the Pope and from all sides they flock to me with their suits. In such a crowd of suppliants there are some whom I cannot refuse to help without scandal, even without sin. And now I have another reason for importunity and one no less compelling for it is in a very good cause. My pen is again directed against that idol of York,[1] with all the more reason because my other attacks with this weapon have not gone home. They have not gone home for the reason that my weapon has not been wielded with the strength of Jonathan's sword which was never ineffective. The fault lies not with the weapon but with him who wields it. Clearly it has not been directed with the necessary strength. And what wonder, for who is able to shoot arrows with a powerful hand 'save the son of them who have been shaken'? He holds the place of Peter and can strike down with one blow Ananias and Simon Magus. Let me speak more clearly: it belongs to the Roman Pontiff to command the deposition of bishops for, although others may be called to share his cares, the fulness of power rests with him alone. If I may dare say it, he alone is at fault if he does not strike down a fault which needs to be struck down, and with the necessary strength. But I leave to your conscience to decide with what strength you should, I do not say strike down, but blast to pieces the fault of the aforesaid Archbishop of York. What remains to be done is reserved for you to do, so that the Church of God, over which you have been placed by the Founder, may see

---

[1] William Fitzherbert, Archbishop of York.

the fervour of your zeal, the might of your right arm, and the wisdom of your soul, and all the people may fear the priest of the Lord and harken to the wisdom of God commanding righteousness through his mouth.

[1] I speak with confidence to ' the heart of Jerusalem ' or rather to the heart of him whom ' the Lord has appointed watchman on the walls of Jerusalem ', for you know the sins which ' go before to judgement ' of that man, and you are quite aware of what such a man deserves by behaviour such as his. If anyone should suggest anything else to you, even should it be myself or an angel from heaven, ' let him be anathema ' by him whom he does not fear to contradict, even the Lord of lords who speaks in your heart. For ' He speaks peace unto his people and unto his saints ' whom I call your brothers, even brothers of the womb, who, as you know full well, have withered away at the zeal of this man, at what they regard with horror in the house of God and hear with dismay in his holy place. For how long a time have they ' laboured in their groanings ', ' withering away for expectation of what might come '. ' We have looked about and there was none to help; we have sought and there was none to give us aid.' Blessed be the Lord who has given us a Pontiff who has compassion on our sorrows, who cannot but grieve for the ' afflictions of Joseph '. To him the poor lift up their voices from the ends of the earth that he may deliver their brothers from the hands of them that seek their souls and not suffer them to be sold unto the merchants of Ishmael. May the Lord be in your heart that you may not turn a deaf ear to our sobs and cries; that the sighs of your brothers may pierce your heart, so that you will deliver their souls from such dangers and such sadness. It is not worldly harm or temporal hurt of which we complain, but our souls once bought for a great price, ' not with corruptible gold or silver, but with the precious blood of Christ, the unspotted lamb ', are ' ever in our hands ' and cannot with safety be entrusted to this new and insolent buyer. By him who redeemed our souls, we beseech you; yea, his very blood cries out to you: ' Do not leave the rod of sinners upon the lot of the just, that the just may not stretch forth their hands to iniquity '. And he who cries through us has given you the power, if only you have the will. For his Eminence of Frascati,[2] who, by the order of your predecessor, the Lord Lucius, is papal legate in that region, has (so we are told) heard such things of this man that his nostrils would not be able to endure the stench of them were the power not given him from on high. This then is my petition, this my plea, this the desire of my heart, that you give the legate full power to throw down that image[3] without listening to any subterfuge of appeals, should he find a just and

[1] Here begins the fragment discovered by H ffer.
[2] Cardinal Hincmar, Bishop of Frascati. He went to York with the pallium but returned to Rome without having given it.
[3] Again the Archbishop of York.

reasonable cause.   And now I appeal on behalf of his Lordship of Canterbury as I have done before, and truly he deserves your consideration both on account of his religious life and on account of my love for him, in which he places such confidence.   He is a friend of our brethren on whose behalf I also plead before you, and by his love for them he has deserved your compliance.   For the rest I have only to ask how much longer you will keep me in suspense; I listen for your messenger with anxious ears, but he does not come.   I beg you not to put the matter off from one day to another.   Tell me what you are doing about it and what you want me to do.   May God preserve you and multiply for you his graces!

LETTER 207

TO THE SAME

I HOPE I shall always hear of you what is to the glory of God, the credit of your office, and the joy of my heart!   That is why I am delighted beyond the power of words to describe to hear of the answer you gave to certain persons who were being too ambitious and anxious for the office of legate.   Not only myself, but all those who have your good name at heart are exceedingly gratified.   Moreover, when I read your letter written in the cause of the Church of Rodez, ' then was my mouth filled with laughter, and joy upon my tongue '. These and the like actions of yours are a credit to your office, they add lustre to your supreme position, and they become very well the Bishop of the world.   I kneel before the Author of your unique primacy and pray that he may give you the wisdom always to act like this in pulling up and planting, in destroying and in building. You have ascended your throne for the downfall and resurrection of many.   Let them fall, let them fall who have no right to be standing, and let them stand who are worthy to do so.   Lay the axe to the root of the unfruitful tree and prune the fruitful tree that it may bring forth fruit yet more abundantly.   Under the humble Eugenius let the mighty be put down from their seats, and the humble exalted; let the hungry be fed with good things and the rich sent empty away, as has happened recently, to the delight of everyone, in the case of a certain poor bishop.

2. Come now apply your zeal for piety to that unhappy Church across the sea.   It is time to have pity on it.   It is a vineyard of the Lord, a choice vineyard and a beautiful one.   But now alas! it is little better than a wilderness, because ' the wild beast ravishes it '.   Why are the people saying: ' Where is its God?   Where is he whom they put to watch over it?   Where is the hand of the pruner, the fork of the gardener?   For how much longer will useless growths be allowed to cumber the soil and suffocate the fruit?'   Surely the time has come for pruning.   The man of peace[1] whom he hoped would

---

[1] William of St. Barbe, Dean of York, and afterwards Bishop of Durham.

sponsor him and clear him of his guilt has said that the need is rather for cutting down than sponsoring. There is in existence a letter from him to the Apostolic legate[1] in which he frankly denies that there was any election at all and asserts that it was a clear case of intrusion. So he now finds that the very man he was counting on to sponsor him has become his accuser. The things that are said of him on all sides would be, quite rightly, enough to lose a knight his belt.

3. How can you allow this man to stand when you have so many good reasons for throwing him down? And I know you do not lack the will to do so. I have read in your letters of your zeal for that Church and I now ask you to show it. It is not for me to tell you, a wise man, how you should go about it, but it does seem to me there is more than one way in which you could do it. I am not much concerned where the unfruitful tree falls, so long as it does fall. A man who stakes his title to possession of a see on a clandestine traffic in letters is a knave and a robber. It is either true that he has these secret letters authorizing his ' execration ' or it is false. If it is true, then he is guilty of knavery and is a calumniator of the Supreme Pontiff. If it is false, then he ought to hear the words: ' Thou hast killed and taken possession '. Lying lips were ever soul destroying. But God forbid that we should believe such duplicity, as this man would want us to, of a man like Pope Innocent. If he were here to answer for himself, I have no doubt that he would say: ' I gave sentence against you openly and in secret I said nothing '.

LETTER 208

TO THE SAME

This letter was evidently written after the suspension of William Fitz-herbert, but before his deposition. Word had reached the Abbot of Clairvaux of the raid on Fountains, and like most news of this sort it was probably exaggerated. It does not seem certain that any blood was shed in the raid, but great damage was done and probably the abbot would have suffered if the raiders had been able to lay hands on him. It is difficult to say how far William was behind this outrage, but the impression is that it was carried out by his violent supporters, the king's men, and that he knew nothing about it or was powerless to stop it.

THWARTED ambition is raging, it is indeed mad with despair. That man of perdition is careering towards his fall and has been hastening for some time the final sentence of condemnation. Even now his sins have become evident and are leading him off to judgement. That tree accursed and full not of fruit but of thorns is anticipating the hand of the feller and provoking him to execution. How much better

---

[1] Hincmar, not Henry de Blois.

if he had fallen long ago rather than those good men whom by standing he has overthrown, against all law and justice. If he had never stood he would have been powerless against them. Now they who were standing to such better purpose than he, have fallen in their innocence and for their innocence. But their harmless blood shall be required of those who by their secret support lent that poisonous tree strength to stand lest it should fall immediately. The blood of the saints calls out against them from the earth, the blood of those who are in the hand of God and beyond the reach of torment. Yet they were my children and they have been scattered. Words are no consolation, and if they were some comfort and remedy, they fail me for grief, sorrow shuts them off, my sighs interrupt them. But I have one thing to say and it is my last, something that it is easier to write than to speak. Listen, or rather read! If this man should still survive, I very much fear that his survival will be your fall, and whatever more he should do, like an evil tree that cannot give good fruit, will be held to your account and not any longer to his.

LETTER 209

TO POPE INNOCENT

Raynald, the Archbishop of Rheims, died on January 13th, 1138, and the people of Rheims seized the opportunity of the interregnum to obtain from Louis le Jeune, in return for a substantial payment, the authority to establish in the city a commune with a mayor at its head. Probably the king regarded this arrangement as a means of curbing the power of Theobald of Champagne, and there was a precedent for it at Laon, a city not far distant from Rheims. But there was this difference between the arrangement at Laon and Rheims. At Laon, the commune was established in agreement with the bishop, at Rheims it was set up sede vacante so that the new archbishop would have to take office on terms unknown to his predecessors and in the framing of which he had had no voice. This led to endless trouble and the chapter appealed to the king who wrote to the mayor and commune commanding them to respect the ancient rights of the cathedral and churches of the city. This order was ignored and communal rule replaced the ecclesiastical. After an outburst of anger the king accepted the fait accompli, the more readily, perhaps, for the advantages that he hoped would accrue to him from it. A state of open feud ensued between the chapter and the city. There is no doubt that the populace had been guilty of the gravest excesses and violence. St. Bernard intervened with the following letter and then visited Rheims and harangued the mob in the market place. As a result of this, peace was patched up and St. Bernard was elected archbishop. But in spite of a cordial letter from the king urging him to accept the office, he refused, and Samson de Mauvoisin was elected, a man of whom the saint was to speak in terms of the highest praise.[1]

[1] See *St. Bernard of Clairvaux*, by Watkin Williams, pp. 165–167.

To his most loving father and lord, Innocent, Supreme Pontiff, the humble devotion of Bernard, styled Abbot of Clairvaux.

THE church of Rheims has fallen into ruin, the glorious city has been brought into contempt. She cries out to those who pass by that there is no sorrow like unto her sorrow. Without there is fighting, and within there is fear. But there is also fighting within, for her own sons are fighting against her and she has no father[1] to set her free. You are her only hope, only Innocent can dry her eyes. But how long must she wait to be protected by your shield? How long will she be trodden under foot before anyone raises her up? The king has humbled himself, and his anger has subsided. What remains but for the apostolic hand to be held out to that afflicted church and to apply to her wounds remedies and fomentations? In my opinion the first thing to be done is to hasten on with an election of an archbishop, for the insolence of the people of Rheims will scatter what little remains if their madness is not checked by a strong hand. If this election should be rightly held, I am sure that the grace of God will give a happy issue to the other matters.

LETTER 210

TO THE KING OF FRANCE

It is very probable that the following letter was written by the saint on his election to the see of Rheims.

I AM very glad you are so sincere in all that appertains to the glory of God. For, not to mention other things, you would surely not be so very anxious to promote such a wretched person as myself except for the glory of God; what other reason could you have since I am poor and destitute? You were not satisfied with simply consenting to my election, you also added your request that I should accept it. You show me favour, you open wide to me your kind heart and, so that I should not be scared of the burden, you promise to help me with your royal protection. Whence such condescension in a king, such maturity in one so young? But, O king, I am a timorous character, broken in body, and there only remains for me the grave, I cannot on any account ' stretch forth my hands to great works '; unfitted and unequal to such a holy office, I cannot possibly venture to accept it. Those responsible for my election should have considered this. If they are able to overlook my insufficiency, I cannot because I have read ' thy own self befriend, doing God's will '. Or if they believe me suitable because of the religious habit I wear, they must understand that in the habit there is the appearance of

---

[1] *non habet generatorem qui liberet eam.* ' . . . nor has she a spouse to set her free ' (Eales).

holiness, but not the virtue. No one is better known to me than myself, no one knows me so well as I know myself. I cannot believe against my conscience those who only see me from without and judge me only by appearances. I and the sons God has given me are here and, although sinners, we pray for your kingdom and your person. To part us would be difficult and cruel, and would induce sorrow rather than prayers. So much for myself. Now, I beg you, deign to listen to what is in my mind about the church.[1] The queen amongst the churches sits in sorrow, ' her cheeks are wet with tears ', all dim now and discoloured the beauty that once shone so fair, faded her ancient glory, her splendid apparel is trodden under foot, her nobility has been brought into contempt, her liberty turned to servitude. I am tortured in this flame, and can find no thought to comfort me, until he shall come who will console her. May reverence for her spouse touch your heart, the spouse by whose blood she was redeemed, in the likeness of whom she was adorned, and with whose heritage she was endowed. And may you remain firm in your purpose lest this well loved bride of our Lord be overwhelmed even now with such a mass of evil, that she is no longer pleasing to his eyes. I tell you, I tell you as your true friend, that such a thing would certainly not advantage you. So may you administer your kingdom of France, great and mighty king, as to obtain the Kingdom of heaven.

LETTER 211

TO POPE INNOCENT, ON BEHALF OF FALK, ARCHBISHOP–ELECT OF LYONS

Concerning this Falk, see Letter 180. He had been Dean of Lyons in the recent trouble.

I HAVE been heard so often in the affairs of other people that I do not think I shall be rebuffed in something that concerns myself. My dear lord, I consider the cause of the Archbishop of Lyons as my own, for a member cannot but be concerned in what touches the head. I would not be saying this had the man taken the honour on himself without being called thereto by God, even as Aaron was. And I cannot but think it was the work of God, the way that all the votes of so many men were so easily united in him without any delay, much less any disputes. And rightly so too, for he is a man distinguished not less for the breadth of his mind than for the nobility of his birth, for his knowledge, and for his praiseworthy life. His blameless reputation has nothing to fear even from the snarls of an enemy. It is surely fitting that the favour of the Apostolic See should follow such an election of so good a man, and that it should fulfil the joy of the people by according to him with its accustomed benevolence, or rather

---

[1] The church of Rheims?

with its well deserved liberality, the fulness of honour which is all that is lacking.[1] This is what the whole Church with urgent supplication begs of you, and it is what I, your child, implore of you with my usual boldness.

NOTE

In the Benedictine Edition (No. 172) there follows after the above letter a very short note from Godfrey de la Roche, now Bishop of Langres, but said to have been written in his person by St. Bernard, begging Pope Innocent to confirm the election of Falk as Archbishop of Lyons.

LETTER 212

TO THE SAME FALK

THE lord Bishop of Langres and myself have both written on your behalf, as we thought we ought to do, to the lord Pope, and you have a copy of both the letters. We are resolved always to stand by you so far as we can, because we hope for much good from you. It is in your interest to see that our hopes are not disappointed. If I have found any favour in your sight, I beg you to bear in mind those poor and needy monks at Bénissons-Dieu.[2] What you do for one of these you do for me, or rather for Christ. They are poor and they are living amongst poor people. I especially beg you to prevent the monks of Savigny from molesting them; for they are calumniating them unjustly, as I believe. If they think they have reason for what they say, then do you judge between them. I beg that our son, Abbot Alberic, although his own virtues are commendation enough, may be in even greater esteem by reason of my recommendation. I love him tenderly, even as a mother her only son. He who loves me will love him too. Let me experience your affection for myself in his person. He has all the more need of your paternal consolation for being so far away from me.

LETTER 213

TO POPE INNOCENT

This letter concerns Falk who was elected Archbishop of Lyons in 1139. He was a great friend of the Carthusians, and he was archbishop at the time that St. Bernard wrote his famous letter to the canons of Lyons on the Immaculate Conception.

To his most beloved father and lord, Innocent, by the grace of God Supreme Pontiff, his humble duty, from Bernard, styled Abbot of Clairvaux.

[1] The pallium.
[2] Bénissons-Dieu was founded from Clairvaux in 1138. Alberic was its first abbot. In the neighbourhood was a daughter house, Savigny, a congregation of Black Monks who became affiliated with the Cistercians on Sept. 17th, 1147.

IF I have lied to my lord in the testimony I gave of the Archbishop of Lyons, may it be far from me to have done so knowingly. If I have been deceived in my judgement, how many are they who have been deceived with me, or who have deceived me! And what should render my mistake, if I have made one, the more excusable is that neighbouring religious, to whom the man is so much better known, have also either deceived me or been deceived with me. And this is proved by the unanimity of his election by the clergy and people, and by the solemn consecration he received at the hands of the local bishops, without there being the slightest breath of suspicion, without even an enemy opening his mouth to protest. Where have these tardy opponents to the archbishop come from? If they have come from far off, can they know the man better than his neighbours? If they are neighbours, why did they not object at the time? For, as I have said, everything was done openly, and nothing behind closed doors. Is it more credible that all those who elected the man, yea, and the very Holy Spirit himself who made them of one mind on the matter, were deceived, than that there are a few men who are lying about him because they hate him? Let the man who would persuade you of the contrary prove his words. As for me, as I can think of no reason for believing otherwise, there only remains for me to consider it a case of a bad man bringing forth from a bad treasure, bad things. Let him see to it that those words, ' He who does not gather with me scatters ', do not apply to him. And I am quite sure that the successor of the first shepherd reverences and loves the man who gathers with Christ, and will no longer countenance the man who scatters the flock.

2. I remember that I wrote to your Holiness in commendation of the archbishop, and I do not regret having done so, for almost as many as know the man approve of my testimony in his favour. And if I have also commended his election, I have only commended what the unanimity of all the electors confirms. But if popular judgement seems open to suspicion, then let the opinion of the religious be sought, and if these too do not dissent, there are two courses of action open to your Holiness: you can either abide by the general verdict of all those concerned, or you can deliver up the man into the hands of his enemies. For my part, I have no doubt which of these two courses would most become your judgement.

LETTER 214

TO LUKE, CARDINAL

This letter concerns the same subject.

To Master[1] Luke, by the grace of God and favour of the Apostolic See, Cardinal, from a man who loves him much, that he may ever abide in the love of God.

---

[1] The MS. is worn and illegible just here.

Those who persecute the Archbishop of Lyons wound themselves, not justice. But it behoves us to fight for the man vigorously and not half-heartedly, because his enemies attack him in force. Let my love, which you understand is offended by the injury done to my archbishop, spur on your zeal.

LETTER 215

TO THE CANONS OF THE CHURCH OF LYONS

The Canons of Lyons had instituted a feast of the Conception of the Blessed Virgin and by doing so called forth the following well-known remonstrance from the Abbot of Clairvaux. St. Bernard maintains that it is impossible on purely rational grounds for her conception to have been holy; that there is no evidence at all for it in Scripture, the Fathers, or the tradition of the Church, and that if her conception were not holy there could be no justification for a feast in its honour. It remains to say that he uses the term ' conception ' in a different sense to the Church in her dogma of the Immaculate Conception. In this doctrine the Church teaches that the Blessed Virgin was, by a unique privilege and solely by virtue and in anticipation of the redeeming death of our Blessed Lord, preserved from all taint of original sin from the first moment of her existence, that is to say from the moment she was quickened in her mother's womb. There is no real evidence that the use of the term ' conception ' in this sense ever occurred to St. Bernard. He believes that the Blessed Virgin was cleansed from original sin, or sanctified in the womb, after her conception but before her birth, in the same way as St. John the Baptist, but more abundantly, so as to preserve her from all actual sin throughout her life.

The authenticity of this letter has occasionally been questioned in the past, ostensibly on the grounds that in it St. Bernard speaks of himself as ' the especial son of the church of Lyons '. But he was born and lived his whole life in the province of the metropolitan church of Lyons, and was therefore perfectly justified in regarding himself as a son of that church. Furthermore, the style of the letter is unmistakably the saint's: . . . clamat dominum.

Among all the churches of France the church of Lyons is well known to be pre-eminent for its dignity, sound learning, and praiseworthy customs. Where was there ever so flourishing strict discipline, grave conduct, ripe counsels, and such an imposing weight of authority and tradition? Especially in the offices of the Church, has this church, so full of judgement, appeared cautious in adopting novelties, and careful never to permit its reputation to be sullied by any childish levity. Because of this I marvel exceedingly that some of you should wish to tarnish the lustre of your good name by introducing at this time a new festival, a rite of which the Church knows nothing, of which reason cannot approve, and for which there is no authority in tradition. Are we more learned or more devout than the Fathers? To introduce something which they, with all their prudence in such matters, passed over in silence, is a most dangerous presumption. It is not as if they would have passed it over without good reasons, for it is a thing that could not have escaped their attention.

2. You say that the Mother of the Lord should be highly honoured. You are right, but ' the honour of the queen loves justice '. The Virgin has many true titles to honour, many real marks of dignity, and does not need any that are false. Let us honour her for the purity of her body, the holiness of her life. Let us marvel at her fruitful virginity, and venerate her divine Son. Let us extol her freedom from concupiscence in conceiving, and from all pain in bearing. Let us proclaim her to be reverenced by the angels, desired by the nations, foretold by the patriarchs and prophets, chosen out of all and preferred before all. Let us magnify her as the channel of grace, the mediatrix of salvation, the restorer of the ages, and as exalted above the choirs of angels to the very heights of heaven. All this the Church sings in her praise and teaches me too to sing. What I have received from the Church I firmly cling to and confidently pass on to others; but, I confess, I am chary of admitting anything that I have not received from her.

3. Certainly the Church has taught me to keep that day with the greatest veneration on which, when she was taken up from this evil world, she brought a festival of great joy to heaven.[1] But I have also learned in the Church to celebrate the birth of the Virgin, and from the Church to hold it as a festival and holy, believing most firmly with the Church that she entered the world already holy because she had been sanctified in the womb.[2] And I read of Jeremias that he too was sanctified before he left the womb, and I believe the same of John the Baptist who from the womb felt the presence of the Lord in the womb. It is a matter for consideration by you whether it would be permitted to think the same of David, in that he said to God, ' By thee I have been confirmed from the womb, from my mother's womb thou art my protector '; and likewise, ' From my mother's womb thou art my guardian, depart not from me '.[3] And to Jeremias it was said: ' I claimed thee for my own before ever I fashioned thee in thy mother's womb; before ever thou camest to birth, I set thee apart for myself '. How beautifully the divine Word distinguishes between formation in the womb and birth from the womb. It shows that the former was only foreknown, but that the latter was blessed

---

[1] *Accepi sane ab Ecclesia illum diem cum summa veneratione recolendum, quo assumpta de sæculo nequam, cælis quoque intulit celeberrimorum festa gaudiorum.* Eales translates this sentence: '. . . when I have received from the Church that day to be reverenced with the highest veneration, when being taken up from this sinful earth, she made entry into heaven; a festival of most honoured joy.'

[2] . . . *firmissime cum Ecclesia sentiens, in utero eam accepisse ut sancta prodiret.*

[3] See par. 8 *ad fin.*

beforehand with the gift of sanctity, so that no one should consider the privilege of the prophet to have been only a matter of fore-knowledge or predestination.

4. Let us grant this in the case of Jeremias. What shall we say of John the Baptist whom the angel pronounced would be filled with the Holy Spirit while yet in his mother's womb?[1] Certainly I do not think that this can refer only to predestination or foreknowledge. Without any doubt the words of the angel were fulfilled in their own time, as he said they would be; and it is not permissible to doubt that he was filled with the Holy Spirit as the angel had foretold, and in the time and place that he had foretold. And certainly the Holy Spirit sanctified him when he filled him. But I would not venture to say how far this sanctification availed over original sin either for John the Baptist, or for the prophet, or for anyone else who was thus prevented by grace. Yet I have no hesitation in saying that they were sanctified whom God sanctified, and that they came forth from the womb with the sanctity they received in the womb, and that the original sin they contracted in conception had no power at all to hinder or rob them in their birth of the blessing they had already received before their birth. And who would venture to say that a child filled with the Holy Spirit still remained a child of wrath, and that he would suffer the penalty of damnation if he should happen to die in the womb, having received the fulness of the Spirit? This is very severe. But I would not at all venture to define anything about it on the strength of my own opinion. However this may be, the Church, which judges and declares the death but not the birth of the saints precious, makes a unique exception in favour of him concerning whom the angel said, ' Many shall rejoice in his birth ', and honours his nativity with festal joy. And why should not the birth of him be holy and so a festival and joyous, who was able to rejoice even whilst in the womb?

5. We cannot for a moment suppose that a privilege which has been accorded to some, though very few, mortals, was denied to that Virgin through whom all mortals have entered life. Beyond all doubt the Mother of the Lord was holy before she was born. Holy Church is certainly not mistaken in keeping the day of her birth holy and celebrating it every year throughout the world with a glad and joyous festival. I, for my part, believe that she received a more ample blessing which not only sanctified her in the womb, but also preserved her thereafter free from sin throughout her life. This is something which we do not believe to have been accorded to any other born of woman. This unique privilege of sanctity whereby she was enabled to live her whole life without sin surely well becomes the Queen of

---

[1] The Vulgate: *Adhuc ex utero matris suæ.* St. Bernard quotes *adhuc in utero matris suæ.* Eales translates according to the Vulgate.

Virgins who, in giving birth to him who destroyed sin and death, obtained for all of us the reward of life and righteousness. Therefore her birth was holy because great sanctity from the womb made it so.

6. Is it possible to think of any other honours that we can add to these? That her conception which preceded her honoured birth should also be honoured because there would have been no birth to honour if there had been no conception? What if another should maintain for the same reason that festal honours should be accorded to both her parents? And the same thing could also be claimed with the same reason for her grandparents and her great-grandparents, and so on without end, so that there would be festivals beyond count. Such a repetition of joys would be more fitting for heaven than for here below, for citizens than for exiles.[1] But they show records of, so they say, heavenly revelations; as if anyone could not equally well show records of how the Virgin had been seen commanding the same honours for her parents, according to the commandment, 'Honour thy father and mother'. I find it hard to be moved by records of visions which are unsupported by sound reason or good authority. How does it follow that her conception would be holy because her birth was holy? Was it because it preceded a holy birth? It preceded so that there should be a birth, but not so that the birth should be holy. Whence that holiness which could be passed on to what was to follow? Would it not be more true to say that, because her conception was not holy, she was sanctified after she had been conceived so that her birth was holy? Or shall we say that perhaps the conception shared in the holiness of the birth which followed it? It would certainly be true to say that the sanctification of what had already been conceived could be transmitted to the birth that followed, but it is quite impossible that the holiness of the birth could be retrospective and sanctify the conception which preceded it.

7. Whence therefore the sanctity of the conception? Can it be said that she was conceived holy because she was already holy before her conception, so that, on account of this, her conception would be rendered holy, just as her birth was rendered holy because of the sanctification she received while in the womb before her birth? But she could not have been holy before she existed, and before her conception she did not exist. Or was sanctity present in the act of her conception, so that she would be holy at the same time as she was conceived? But reason cannot accept this, for how can anything be holy without the presence of the Sanctifying Spirit, and how can the Holy Spirit have any part in sin, and how can there not be sin where there is carnal lust? Perhaps someone might say that she was

---

[1] In fact an ordinary Calendar of the Church now has a good 280 feasts, not counting Sundays, out of the 365 days of the year. But whether everyone regards this as a foretaste of heaven is a matter open to enquiry.

conceived of the Holy Spirit and not of man, but this is a thing hitherto quite unheard of. I read that the Holy Spirit came upon her, but not that it came with her, when the angel said: 'The Holy Spirit shall come upon thee'. If it is permitted to say what the Church thinks, and the Church thinks what is true, I say that she conceived of the Holy Spirit, not that she herself was conceived of the Holy Spirit; that she gave birth as a virgin, but not that she was born of a virgin. Otherwise where would the unique privilege of the Mother of the Lord be, whereby she alone is believed to be able to glory in both the birth of a child and in the virginity of her body, if we concede as much to her mother? This is not to honour the Virgin, but to detract from her honour. If therefore it was quite impossible for her to have been sanctified before her conception, because she did not then exist; or in the act of her conception, because of the presence of sin; it remains that she was sanctified after her conception, when she was already in the womb, and that this sanctification excluded sin and rendered her birth, but not her conception, holy.

8. And so, although it has been given to very few of the sons of men to be born holy, it has not been given to any to be conceived holy, so that the prerogative of a holy conception might be reserved for him alone who sanctified all of us; the only person who, being conceived without sin, cleansed all sinners. It is true for all the sons of men what one of them humbly and truly admitted of himself: 'I was born in sin; guilt was with me already when my mother conceived me'.[1]

9. This being so, what reason can there be for a feast of the Conception? How, I ask, can a conception be holy which was not of the Holy Spirit, not to say that it was of sin; and how can a feast be kept in honour of what was not holy? Gladly will the mother of God forgo an honour by which either sin is honoured or by which a false holiness seems to be implied. A novelty, the mother of rashness, the sister of superstition, the daughter of levity, presumed against the practice of the Church, can in no wise at all be pleasing to her. If you thought such a feast advisable, you should have first consulted the Holy See, and not have followed so hastily and so unadvisedly the simplicity of the uneducated. In fact I have before now observed this very error amongst some persons, but in order to spare the devotion of simple hearts for the Virgin, I have overlooked it. But when I find this superstition amongst learned men in the noble church of which I am specially the son, I doubt whether I could overlook it without grave offence to you all. I have said all this in submission to the judgement of anyone wiser than myself, and especially in submission to the authority of the Roman Church, to whose decision I refer all that I have said on this or any other such subject, prepared to modify anything I may have said, if it should be contrary to what she thinks.

[1] See par. 3 *ad fin.*

LETTER 216

TO THE PATRIARCH OF JERUSALEM

William, a monk of Tours, was Patriarch of Jerusalem from 1130–1145, and almost certainly it is to him that this letter is addressed.

IT would appear churlish of me not to answer the many patriarchal letters I have received from you. But what more can I do than greet you in return for your greetings to me? ' With abundant blessings, you have met me on the way ', you have taken the initiative by being the first to greet me with letters from across the sea, and by so doing you have robbed me of the opportunity of being the first to make the advances of humility and charity. What worthy return can I make? You have left me no return that I can make equal to what you have given me. You have also shared with me the treasure of all the ages, by bestowing on me a part of the Cross of Christ[1]; and what return can I possibly make for this? But that I cannot give you what I ought is no reason for not giving you what I can, even though it be only to show a ready heart and will by writing back and saluting you. For the present this is all I have to offer you across such a great distance of land and sea. But if the opportunity ever comes, I will prove that it is not only in word that I love you, but in very deed. Regard, I beg you, the Knights of the Temple, and open your loving heart to these brave champions of the Church. It would be most acceptable to God and welcome to men, if you would care for these men who are ready to lay down their lives for their brethren. Brother Andrew will tell you what I have in mind for the place to which you have invited us.[2]

LETTER 217

TO WILLIAM, PATRIARCH OF JERUSALEM

To his venerable lord and most dear father William, by the grace of God the Patriarch of Jerusalem, the Spirit of Truth which proceedeth from the Father, from Bernard, Abbot of Clairvaux.

A BUSY man myself I am taking this opportunity of writing a few words to you, a busy man too, by the present bearer, a good and loyal friend of mine. And if anyone should think this presumption on my part, it is a pardonable presumption for it arises from affection. But, so as not to be drawn into a long letter when I have promised to

---

[1] . . *de thesauro sæculorum mihi impertire curasti, id est de ligno Domini.* Eales translates: ' Even of your worldly treasures you have been careful to make me a sharer in giving me a part of the Cross of the Lord '.

[2] ' Brother Andrew ': this may have been an uncle of St. Bernard, who was a Knight of the Temple.

write only a short one, let me come at once to the point. When God the creator was pleased to reveal the depths of his design for the salvation of the human race, he so loved the world that he gave his only-begotten Son. And he, for the sake of men, became man, and out of the sons of men he called some to himself, men especially chosen, especially loved. And of this chosen band, there was one especially chosen by him; out of this body of well-loved friends, there was one especially loved whom he set apart for a special mark of his favour. When he was lifted up on the cross and with raised hands was offering his eventide sacrifice, but before he commended his spirit to his Father, he chose this man to take his place with his mother; a virgin he entrusted his virgin mother to this virgin disciple, as brother to brother. But why am I saying this? Attend carefully.

2. The Lord has chosen many people, and of them he has made some leaders, so that they might have the dignity of the priesthood. But you, as a certain intimate favour, he has placed in the house of his child David. To you alone of all the bishops of the world he has committed that land which ' yielded grasses that grow, and a fruit tree giving fruit of its own kind ' from the root of which sprang that flower of the field, that lily of the valleys. You alone, I say, have been chosen out by the Lord to be his own bishop, to enter his tabernacle each day, and to adore him in the very place whereon his feet have stood. We read that holy Moses was once told, when he was to deliver a command from the Lord to the Children of Israel: ' Take the shoes from thy feet, thou art standing on holy ground '. That too was a holy place, but only as a figure of this other holy place where Truth was manifested by the sign of holiness. The first was holy, but this place is more so. What is there like to truth? What has that which is only seen in a glass darkly to compare with the glory which, when the veil has been rent, is seen with face revealed? And yet, since all these things were happening in figure and in illustration or what was to come, it was said to Moses: ' Take the shoes from thy feet, thou art standing on holy ground '. And I say to you: ' Take the shoes from thy feet, thou art standing on holy land '. If your heart is still somewhat wrapped in the works of darkness, quickly set it free: thou art standing on holy land. What a fearsome place is this! For here, by the merciful kindness of God, the Day Star from on high first dawned upon us. What a fearsome place is this! For here the father first met the son returning from his place of exile[1] and, falling on his neck, clothed him in the robe of immortality! How fearsome is this place! For here the dear Lord poured wine and oil into our wounds, and the merciful Father, the God of all consolation,

---

[1] . . . *filio revertenti de regione dissimilitudinis. Regio dissimilitudinis* is a technical phrase of St. Bernard. Man, created in the image of God, has exiled himself from God so as to become disfigured by sin. *Vide* Gilson, *La Théologie Mystique de Saint Bernard*, p. 62—quite the best study on the subject.

made a pact with us. I give thanks to thee, O Lord, because thou hast brought deliverance to the earth and revealed to it thy grace. When thou wast angry thou didst not forget thy mercy. This is a place far more holy, far more renowned than where Moses stood, because it is the place of the Lord, the place of him who came by blood and water, not by water only like Moses, but by blood and water. Behold the place where they laid him! 'Who dares climb the mountain of the Lord or who will stand in his holy place?' Only he should do so who has learned from the Lord Jesus Christ how to be meek and humble of heart.

3. Only the humble man can safely climb the mountain, because only the humble man has nothing to trip him up. The proud man may climb it indeed, yet he cannot stand for long; for the proud man is like one who would stand not on his own feet but on the foot of another, that foot of which the Prophet spoke in abhorrence saying: 'Let not the foot of pride come unto me'. The proud man has only one foot to stand on: love of his own excellence. And so he cannot stand for long, because he is like a man standing only on one foot. Who can stand long on that foot, the foot on which they stood who did wickedness and fell: the angel in heaven, the man in paradise? If God did not spare the man whom he crowned with glory and honour, whom he had set over the work of his hands, nor yet the angel who was the first of his works, full of wisdom and comeliness, how much more should I fear that he will not spare me when I am proud, I who live not in a paradise of delights, nor in a heavenly palace, but here in this vale of tears? Therefore to stand firmly, we must stand humbly. So that our feet may never stumble we must stand, not on the single foot of pride, but on the two feet of humility. Humility has two feet: appreciation of divine power and consciousness of personal weakness. How fair are these feet and how strong, neither involved in dark ignorance nor defiled by deceitful excess! Take care that being set up on high you do not become high-minded; but be fearful and humble yourself under the powerful hand of him who treads the pride of the haughty in the dust. You must know that your church has been entrusted to you not as a handmaid to a lord but, so as to return to what I said at the beginning, as a mother to a son, as Mary to John, so that it might be said to you of her, 'Son, this is your mother', and to her of you, 'Mother, this is your son'. Thus you can safely undertake to rule in the name of him who, although he is 'high above us, stoops to regard the lowly things in heaven and earth'.

THE ARCHBISHOP OF TRÈVES AND POPE INNOCENT II

IN a letter to Pope Innocent (Benedictine Edition, 176), Albero, Archbishop of Trèves, regrets the impossibility of getting to Rome to see the Pope himself, learn how he was prospering, and inform him of his own affairs. He tells him that he is sending in his stead a reliable messenger in the person of Hugh, Archdeacon of

Toul. And he informs the Pope of the unity and complete loyalty to his cause of the Church in France, and that the loss of Benevento, Capua, even if need be of Rome itself, could not shake his confidence in the ultimate victory of Pope Innocent over the schismatics. The king, Lothair, he tells him, is preparing a large army for the liberation of the Church.

In another letter to Pope Innocent (Benedictine Edition, 177), Albero says that he never wanted a bishopric and that if he ever had done so it would not have been that of Trèves, for the people are an exasperating and stiff-necked lot. He has done a lot for them, he says, but his labours have not been appreciated. Among his many difficulties the chief is his young and nobly born suffragans who, so far from supporting him as they should, oppose him in every possible way. He begs the Pope to help him, saying that he has borne with all his difficulties patiently, if not willingly, so as not to seem disobedient towards him. He concludes by telling the Pope that he has many things to complain of in his behaviour towards him; that, although he was prepared to die for him, yet he had not received from him the support he felt entitled to expect.

LETTER 218

TO POPE INNOCENT, ON BEHALF OF THE ARCHBISHOP OF TRÈVES

To his most loving father and lord, Innocent, Supreme Pontiff, the entire devotion of his Bernard.

I SPEAK confidentially because I love sincerely. The love which retains any dregs of doubt or suspicion is no true love. The Archbishop of Trèves is not alone in his complaints, many are murmuring about the same thing, especially those who are most sincerely devoted to you. What all who conscientiously fulfil their pastoral charge are saying, is, that righteousness is perishing in the Church; that the keys of the Church are abolished; and that the authority of bishops is being brought into contempt because they are not able to avenge the offences given to God and are not allowed to punish any unlawfulness at all, even in their own dioceses. They refer the matter to you and the Roman Curia and you, so they say, demolish what they have done well, and set up again what they have rightly demolished. Any mischievous or troublesome person, be he from the people, or from the clergy, or even expelled from the monasteries, runs to you. When they come back they boast and swagger that they have found protectors amongst those very persons by whom they ought to have been corrected. Was not the sword of Phinees promptly and rightly drawn to punish the incestuous alliance between Drogo and Milis? But now the blade is being turned off and blunted by the protecting shield of the Apostolic See. For shame! What glee this has caused amongst the enemies of the Church, especially amongst those people by the fear or favour of whom we have perhaps been led from the right course. Our friends are put to the blush, the faithful are insulted, and the bishops are everywhere shamed and despised. When this happens, when no one pays attention to their just decisions, then your authority also suffers.

2. Yet these are the people who are zealous for your honour; these are the people who labour loyally for your peace and victory, but I fear that their labours may be in vain. Why are you weakening their strength like this? Why are you undermining their influence in this way? For how much longer will you continue to blunt the arms of your loyal warriors and cast down the horn of your strength and salvation? The church of St. Gengulph at Toul mourns her desolation with bitter tears, and there is none to comfort her. For who can withstand the strength of a strong arm, or the force of a torrent in spate, or the authority of the Supreme Pontiff? The Blessed Paul complains that he has to sustain the same violence on his church at Verdun.[1] The archbishop is unable to defend it any longer from the mad excesses of the monks since, as though they were not insane enough, they have been further strengthened by the force of the Apostolic See. What new reason, I pray, have you discovered for re-opening the question of what has been granted by a wise and necessary dispensation to canons of blameless life, and bringing it to judgement again, after it had been once granted, and then confirmed, and then, so they say, ratified? And indeed both the matters above mentioned are said to have been settled by you and then abolished. By such sacrifices God is not pleased. Alas, his anger is not mollified by this, nor his grace won, nor his pity moved. Over these and the like the anger of the Lord is not turned away, his arm is still stretched out, and the rod spoken of by Jeremias is over our sins still.

3. The Lord is wrath indeed with the schismatics, but he is by no means pleased with the Catholics. Also the church of Metz is in grave danger, as you know very well, from the quarrel between the bishop and clergy. You know your own mind in this affair; but there is no peace yet, nor any prospect of it in the near future. To tell the truth, it seems to my insignificance that this and the troubles of the churches of Verdun and Toul could be more safely and conveniently settled by their metropolitan who knows all the facts, has experience, and of whose fidelity the Church is witness. Have a care what you do in those two dioceses of Metz and Toul for, as things are, they might just as well be without bishops.[2] I wish I could say they were without tyrants. When men like these are defended, upheld, honoured, and

---

[1] The Bishop of Verdun had transferred the monastery of St. Paul of Verdun to the Premonstratensians because the Benedictines to whom it had belonged had become very relaxed. The monks resisted the change and Peter the Venerable supported them. Innocent was prepared to reconsider the case, but was persuaded by St. Bernard to let the matter stand.

[2] Stephen was Bishop of Metz and Henry, Bishop of Toul. Stephen is well spoken of in the records of those times. St. Bernard himself warmly greets him in Letter 30. It is possible that Stephen had displeased St. Bernard by having stirred up trouble in his diocese. He also caused great ill feeling by attempting to impose upon the canons of Liège his own nominee as bishop, and Innocent tried to settle the matter by passing over the jurisdiction of the metropolitan, the Archbishop of Trèves. It is this that St. Bernard complains of here. With regard to Henry, Bishop of Toul, it seems that St. Bernard may have been wrongly informed of certain negotiations he was carrying on with Frederick, Count of Toul.

encouraged, many people are surprised and shocked, because they are very well aware that there are things in their lives which, even in the lives of the laity, not to say bishops, would deserve to be utterly condemned and reprobated; things of which I should be ashamed to write and of which it would not be seemly for you to hear. Granted that without anyone to charge them they cannot be deposed, but is it necessary that the Apostolic See should honour and exalt by its special favour these men whom common report accuses?

4. On what grounds of personal merit, of either priestly holiness or of episcopal worthiness, has the Bishop of Metz been permitted to deprive the church of its liberty by annulling at his pleasure the election made by the canons, and causing his nominee, the provost,[1] to be elected against the privileges of the church? How much more right and proper it would be, should it seem good to your judgement, that a man worthy of greater honour should not be deprived of the honour to which he is entitled. I refer to the Archbishop of Trèves who, not without the dissatisfaction of God-fearing persons, has been prevented by you from settling both this and other affairs in his diocese as though he were a man under suspicion or of no experience. Believe me, your loyal son, this is not, to my mind, a good thing for the diocese.

5. I might have feared the stigma of presumption by writing to.you like this were it not that I know to whom I am writing and myself who am writing. I know your great goodness, and I know that you are fully aware of the great affection for you with which I have ventured to write this. Again with regard to the Archbishop of Trèves, I should inform you that his messenger holds a great position in that kingdom; that he is a man loyal and constant in the support of you and the Church of God; that he is not at all an evil minded man, prone to listen to the seditious persons by whom he is often sorely troubled. I tell you this so that you may know how to receive and listen to him, for you would be exposing him to ridicule were you to rebuff him. I wished to conclude by these words in favour of the messenger, but in fact his own virtues are a sufficient commendation, especially his great devotion to you. If I did not believe this of him I would not on any account entrust such a personal letter as this to him.

LETTER 219

TO THE BISHOPS OF OSTIA, TUSCULUM, AND PALESTRINA ON BEHALF OF THE SAME

GOD has set you up on high in order that the greater your authority the better you may serve the Church. But the Father of the household will put down from their seats the mighty whose great

[1] *Primicerius.*

position is not justified by their service. How great is the loss sustained by the bride of Christ in the bishopric of Metz! I do not think you can be ignorant of it, although we feel it more for being so near. It is a great wolf that is daily trying to break into the sheepfold of Christ both by guile and open attack, and to scatter the sheep that have been gathered together by the blood of Christ. It is not merely from yesterday or the day before that he has assailed the flock of the Lord with all his might, he has harassed it with robbery, fire, and murder ever since he was a cub. I do what I can to indicate the wolf and set the dogs on him. You will see where your duty lies. It is not for me to teach my teachers.

LETTER 220

TO POPE INNOCENT, ON BEHALF OF THE SAME

How is it that evil triumphs over wisdom? Do you know, dear lord, the Archbishop of Trèves? I am sure you do. And do you also know that unholy Abbot of St. Maximin? I think not. Who could be more deserving of honour than the archbishop, or who more deserving of disgrace than that abbot? What wrong has the archbishop done? He has recovered the stolen property of his church, and he has freed a captive church from the clutches of laymen. Is he not being repaid with injury for the good he has done, with hatred for his love? Let your loving glance rest upon him, I pray. Put by for a while your occupations and consider how ill he has been treated, that such a good man as you know him to be should be made a laughing stock to his neighbours and enemies by such a man as I would be ashamed to describe. My dear father, it is my filial affection that speaks. Hitherto I have sympathized with the unfortunate and unhappy archbishop. But henceforth, if this injustice from which he suffers is not set right, I will take all my deep compassion and sorrow to him by whom it could be. There are other wrongs from which he is suffering and I have no doubt that in alleviating them you will be benefiting yourself. Whatever tarnishes the good name of my dear lord wounds my heart.

LETTER 221

TO THE SAME, ON BEHALF OF THE SAME

Still my prayers, still my entreaties, though they be repeated ten times, shall continue. I shall not cease to plead with you because I shall never cease to have faith in you. I have a good cause and I have a just judge, who will not delay to cancel the fraud when the truth appears. Then he who had hoped to jeer will laugh no more. As it is written, ' malice is self-betrayed '. The principle of the Holy See has never been ashamed to revoke what it discovers to have been obtained from it by fraud, and not honestly deserved. It is a most excellent and praiseworthy principle that no one shall gain by a lie, especially from the Holy and Supreme See.   Knowing this, your child confidently pleads for the Archbishop of Trèves, and so entreats not as one uncertain of the result.   For indeed I know very well the merits of that man, his cause, and his purpose.   For which of these do those monks want to stone him?   Because he has deserved ill of them?   But he has stood by them loyally and helped them in many things.   On account of the injustice of his cause?   But no one would question his justice save one who is himself unjust.   Is it because he has liberated the monastery, or rather, I should say, won it back for the episcopal see from the clutches of laymen, as Hercules' club might be wrested from his hands by one stronger than he?   Or is it for his evil intentions?   But it is a holy thing to do as he intended and reform the life of a monastery.   May the Lord enlighten the heart of my lord, that a march may not be again stolen on him by those monks who are not, as they pretend, so anxious for liberty as they are for licence.

LETTER 222

TO THE SAME, ON BEHALF OF THE SAME

How often, my lord, have I not experienced your kindness and affection!   It now remains for me to experience it in the hour of need.   May God forbid that I should ever ask you for anything that I believed to be contrary to the honour of God or your interests.   My heart is quite at ease on that score, therefore I have every confidence that you will hear me, especially as I am petitioning a father for his son, Innocent for an innocent man.   There is no need for me to tell you, for you must surely know, how from his youth up the Archbishop of Trèves has had at heart the honour of the Apostolic See and the peace of the Roman Church; how anxiously and firmly he has stood by it in times of tribulation and, while others rested in the shade, has borne the heat and burden of the day; and how steadfastly and bravely he has upheld the truth before kings in defence of his brethren.   Moreover ' to speak of what I know and testify what I have seen ' so that you may receive my testimony, what great prudence and foresight he showed in rescuing the goods and possessions of the Church from the power of alien foes; how generously and kindly he has always used his own possessions for the common good, and especially for those of the household of the faith; and how carefully and watchfully he has preserved his good name from ' treacherous lips and perjured tongues '.

2. What, then, has he done to displease you?   Is it that he has rescued the church of blessed Maximus from the power of the king and subjected it to ecclesiastical authority?   Is it that he did not receive that man who, they say, wished to be a general before he was a

11

soldier, an abbot before he was a monk? If he has displeased you by this or something else, he certainly does not deserve to lose so easily the old affection of his loving father, but rather that his fault should be covered up by his father's affection, and that the memory of his many good works should excuse him, a man blameworthy in so little and praiseworthy in so much. But now, my lord, you have exalted the men who were persecuting him and given joy to all his enemies. Many people are wondering for what reason of personal merit, or on what reputation for virtue, a man who could not rule his own soul has been set up to rule over the souls of others. How can such a man rule others, when he could not be ruled by others? How can he dare to be over others, when he has never learned to submit to others? How can he command obedience from others, when he has never known how to obey others? ' If a man knows not how to rule his own house, how shall he take care of the Church of God?' Finally, as the father so shall the sons be; and of his sons, of their manners and way of life, who have cruelly torn their mother so as to foment schisms and quarrels, it were better to be silent than to speak. But I have not said this so as to pass judgement on the servants of another: for their own lord they stand or fall. All I know is that, if the wretched schemes of these men prevail, dissolute youths will follow their example by throwing off the yoke of discipline and roaming to and fro about the earth. And even if they do not completely succeed in this, they will at any rate be able to boast that they were able to resist their superiors. Alas! How many men, and some of considerable consequence, who are confident of their claims on your mercy, will find their hope and confidence shaken, if a son who was once so loved by you, should be cast from your grace and favour by the first breath of trouble.

3. If my prayers are of any avail with you, Holy Father, I beg you earnestly, I who love you for your own sake, that you should not cast off now that your affairs prosper the man who has stood by you in your troubles, or suffer his influence with you to be at all diminished, when he has every right to expect that it should be increased. Otherwise, if contrary to the hope of all, and contrary to the deserts of the man himself, it should happen that strangers rob him of the fruit of his labours, that his good deeds are repaid by evil, and his love by hatred, then he alone would suffer a wound from a quarter he did not expect, but many would grieve at his persecution. May the Spirit of Truth which proceedeth from the Father, teach you to distinguish in all things between light and darkness, so that you may know how to reject the evil and choose the good.

LETTER 223

TO CARDINAL HAIMERIC, CHANCELLOR

I MIGHT as well try to meet arrows with straws as to repay with words the kindnesses you have showered upon me; except that the former would seem a mere joke, whereas the latter might appear deceitful. Deeds ought to be repaid by deeds. But that would be too much for me, poor as I am in all but good will. Therefore I will match your good deeds with my good will, because that is all I have to give. I am rich in desires, I abound in good wishes, and certainly a real benefactor does not look for any more than this. For how can anyone be a benefactor without being also benevolent? And nothing is more precious to a benevolent man than the benevolence by which he is known as benevolent, and is beneficent. Benevolence is a fruit of beneficence, unless perhaps there is someone who regards as a benefit what has been bestowed in the hope of a return, or forgone through fear of the consequences. But who does not see that the latter is abandoned, the former sold, and neither given? A real benefit should be without self-interest. He who has received cannot repay to him who has given anything more welcome than gratitude for what he has received gratis. And this benevolence is created in the mind of him who receives by the benevolence of him who gives through the medium of beneficence. I confess myself rich in this benevolence, and from a full heart I offer it as a fitting return to my benefactor. I devoutly offer it up, a sacrifice of praise, to the maker of all things, for the salvation of my benefactor.

LETTER 224

TO HENRY, ARCHBISHOP OF SENS

This is the same Archbishop of Sens to whom St. Bernard addressed the long and important letter, included among his regular treatises, on the life and duties of a bishop. He seems to have been a strong-willed prelate, not to say imperious. He was surnamed ' The Wild Boar '. In the year 1136 he seems to have got himself into serious trouble and been suspended for a time.

I CONFESS that I have often intended to write to you for your own sake on behalf of other people, and then have decided not to do so on account of your hateful hardness: but charity shall prevail. I want to keep your friends for you, but you will not condescend to it. I wish to reconcile your enemies to you, but you will not suffer it. You will not have peace, you are set on rushing to your own shame, confusion, and deposition. You are multiplying your accusers and driving away your supporters. In everything your own sweet will is law, you think only of power and not at all of the fear of God. All your enemies are laughing about you, all your friends complaining. How could you have unfrocked that man when he had not been, I do not say convicted in court, but even summonsed. Everyone will be shocked by this, everyone will be whispering about it, everyone will jeer at it, everyone will be indignant. Do you really think that the whole world is as void of all sense of justice as you seem to be, so that you can deprive a man of his archdeaconry in this way without causing remark? Or perhaps it pleases you more to give it and then take it away, than to retain his gratitude for the gift of it?[1] Do not, I pray, do not do this thing, which will shock everyone and please no one. Perhaps I have written more boldly and more bitingly than you could wish, but if you will correct your ways you will see it has been for your good.

LETTER 225

TO CONRAD, KING OF THE ROMANS

To Conrad, by the grace of God the illustrious and glorious king of the Romans, from Bernard, styled Abbot of Clairvaux, the loving prayers of himself and his brethren.

ALTHOUGH we are situated a long way from you, yet we love you and desire your honour with all our hearts. The knowledge of this renders us bold and confident, especially in matters that we know concern your honour and salvation. And now we petition you concerning a certain business, which is not so much ours as his from whom all power comes and whom you have to thank for your glory and world-wide fame. To be as brief as possible to one so busy as you are, we have entrusted the affair to our brother the Abbot of Eberbach,[2] and we implore your royal Majesty to lend a favourable ear to his petition, or rather to our petition through him.

LETTER 226

TO THE SAME

I HAVE received your letters and greetings with a devotion equal to my unworthiness; the unworthiness of my position, not of my devotion for you. The complaints of the king are mine as well, especially those which you fittingly express concerning the invasion of the empire. I have never wanted the king to be dishonoured or the empire to be diminished, and my soul hates those who do, for I have read, ' let every soul be subject to the higher powers ', and, ' he that resisteth the power resisteth the ordinance of God '. And I would

---

[1] *Sed vos forsitan plus amatis reddere, et perdere, quam gratiam de beneficio retinere.* Eales: ' But you perhaps are better pleased to give it back after seizing it, rather than to deserve his gratitude by suffering him to retain it '.

[2] A Cistercian house founded from Clairvaux in 1131.

advise you too to remember this sentence in showing reverence to the Supreme and Apostolic See, and to the representative of St. Peter, just as you would wish it to be shown to you by the whole empire. I have certain other things to say to you that were better not written; it would be more suitable to tell you them in person.

LETTER 227

TO POPE INNOCENT

WE have received Brother Andrew safe and happy, bringing with him glad tidings of your safety and glory, of the peace and prosperity of the Church, of the flourishing and strong condition of the Curia, and finally of the favour and benevolence with which you still regard us. 'God in his mercy has shown us favour, and our hearts are rejoiced.' But your wish that we should send you brothers cannot easily be fulfilled, principally because we have not the usual large numbers with us. Besides those who have been sent in twos and threes to other places, three new monasteries have been wholly founded from here since I left you,[1] and there remain others to be founded in the near future. Yet I shall take measures to summon some from other houses whom I can send you, since I wish in all things to be obedient to you.

BERNARD, ABBOT OF ST. SAVIOUR

IN a letter to Pope Innocent (Benedictine Edition, 343), Bernard, the Abbot of St. Saviour, near Farfa in Italy (the monk sent by the Abbot of Clairvaux, at the behest of the Pope referred to in the preceding letter, to make a foundation in Italy), complains that he has encountered nothing but difficulties since leaving Clairvaux and his abbot, and that he has not received the support promised him by the Pope.

In another letter (Benedictine Edition, 344), Bernard writes to St. Bernard bitterly lamenting that he ever left Clairvaux, and complaining that, although he was sent at the behest of the Pope, the Pope has not kept his side of the engagement by confirming his donation of the place. He concludes by saying that he has received nothing but kindness and support from the Abbot of Farfa. It is to be noted that both these letters are from the same Bernard who afterwards became Abbot of Tre Fontane near Rome, and finally Pope as Eugenius III.

LETTER 228

TO EUSTACE, THE OCCUPIER OF THE SEE OF VALENCE

To the illustrious man Eustace, from Brother Bernard.

THOUGH I do not say so in letters, I do want your salvation, my illustrious friend. And who is to stop me wanting? Laws cannot command the will, nor can princes rule it. The will is free, especially when it is led by the spirit, because ' where the spirit of the

---

[1] These were: La-Bénissons-Dieu, Les Dunes, and Clairmarais. This letter would therefore have been written soon after the foundation of the last-named monastery in 1140.

Lord is, there is liberty'. And so my spirit has become bold and, although unbidden, unasked, and uninvited, I am writing to you as though I were myself a person of consequence. But what if charity should bid me? Another, perhaps, might act differently but I have undertaken, in the spirit of charity, to address in this letter a nobleman and advise him as far as I am able as to his salvation, arouse him from his slumbers, incite him to search his heart, and stir him to follow grace. Who knows, I tell myself, whether God may not relent and forgive and leave a blessing behind? Indeed who does not know how abundant are the riches of his goodness and forgiveness which the merciful and compassionate God has already laid up for him? He has been merciful, patient, forgiving, and long-suffering even up to now; 'he has become like a man that heareth not, that hath no reproofs in his mouth', slow to anger, ever prone to forgive. To you, most excellent man, I say: how long will you hesitate, how long will you scorn to turn to him? It is hard for you to kick against the pricks. 'Knowest thou not that the goodness of God leadest thee to repentance? But according to thy hardness and impenitent heart, thou treasurest up for thyself, wrath against the day of wrath, and the revelation of the just judgement of God.'

2. Or is it more from shame than hardness of heart? But what matters it from what you are perishing? O shame void of all sense, hostile to salvation, empty of all honesty and honour! This is the sort of shame that the Wise Man says 'makes a sinner of a man'. Is it such a shameful thing for a man to yield to God or such a disgrace to be humbled under the powerful hand of the Almighty? Did not that glorious king David say: 'Thee only my sins have offended; thou wast witness of my wrong doing; thy warnings were deserved, and if thou art called in question, thou hast right on thy side'? To yield to the Divine Majesty is the highest sort of victory, to submit to the authority of mother Church is the highest glory. What extraordinary perversity not to mind befouling oneself, and yet to mind being cleansed! According to the Wise Man there is also a shame that is 'the grace and glory of a man'; if, that is, he is ashamed to sin, but not ashamed to repent for having sinned: thus you will not lack glory even though it come late in the day, shame bringing back the glory that sin put to flight. They hold the second place of blessedness whose sins are forgiven, whose 'transgressions are buried deep'. Honourable indeed is that burial cloth of which we read: 'Honour and beauty are before him'. Who will grant that I may see you in this golden vesture, that I may say to you: 'Glory and beauty are thy clothing'? 'Come back, maid of Sulam, come back; let us feast our eyes on you.' Arise, arise, clothe yourself in strength, and put on the vesture of salvation. Arise, you who sleep, arise from death and Christ will enlighten your darkness. 'Linger not in the false

path of wickedness, give thanks while breath is in thee; the dead breathe no more, give thanks no more.'

3. For how long will you forget yourself? For how long will you sleep in death, the ornament of the nobility, but the grief of the faithful? How long will you stubbornly resist your better nature, estranged from honour, opposed to salvation? Why do you persist in pursuing an end so inconsistent with your eminent life and actions?[1] How can your old age, which ought to be spent in quiet and fruitful acts of mercy, support the punishment due to the sins of your past life, and wipe out their guilt? Why should your venerable grey head alone be robbed of its honour, why should it pass away unhonoured, when honour especially becomes it? ' Thy soul befriend, doing God's will '; ' God has put to confusion those that please men, for he hath despised them.' Brief are the days of men, death is at the door of an old man. You have only a short time, a very short time, with those who say to you, ' Well done ! ' Consider it a small thing to be judged by them, or by the standards of men, you who are already about to appear before the scrutiny of heaven, a pitiful old man being even now dragged before the terrific tribunal of Christ by the failure of nature. You should be preparing yourself for judgement, you should be conforming yourself to that other world and, fearful of rebuff, you should be cultivating friends in that court. Why heed the opinions of those whose praise will not help you, whose abuse cannot condemn you? ' Man is but emptiness, light weight sons of Adam as false coin in the scales; vain are all their conspiracies to deceive.'

4. For these reasons those who call you blessed, deceive you. They give you words only in exchange for your gifts. Both are vain, especially words. You deceive from vanity; but you are the more deceived, they the less. What you give is, at any rate, worth something; and you give to ungrateful people, to undeserving people. They are not seeking either you or your interests, they are out only for themselves. They hunt, as they can, your gifts with false and empty praises. ' Their words soothe like oil, but they are weapons of death.' Therefore David said: ' Never shall the sinner sleek this head with the oil of flattery '. By these ' the sinner is praised in the desires of his soul and the unjust man is blessed '. Not I, but the Wise Man warns you to be careful of these, saying, ' Turn a deaf ear, my son, to the blandishments of evildoers who would make thee of their company '. Attend rather to him who judges with equity the meek of the earth who look up to you and are not fed, but who are oppressed by your worldly power. You would not have any power at all over them were it not given you from above. This is your hour, and the

---

[1] *quid illos egregios mores, actusque tuos tam dissimili pergis exitu consummare?* Eales translates: ' Why do you proceed to consummate your previous excellent character and actions with so different an ending? '

power of darkness. But listen: ' Strictly his doom falls on those whose heads are lifted high; for greatness greater torment is reserved '. If you fear this, you will take care; if you are heedless of it, you will fall into it, and ' it is a fearful thing to fall into the hand of the living God '. May the one true God save you from such a thing, ' he who does not wish for the death of a sinner, but rather that he should turn from his evil ways and live '. Sharp words are not popular, although they are right; wholesome counsels are not well liked because they are sour. And so I will put my finger to my lips and say no more until I know how you have taken this. Believe me, I wish to do what I can to please you, but in deed and truth, not with pen and tongue.

LETTER 229

TO SIMON, THE SON OF THE CASTELLAN OF CAMBRAI

The Abbey of Vaucelles mentioned in the following letter, was founded by St. Bernard in person in the year 1132. Ralph, the first abbot, was an Englishman, and Nivard, St. Bernard's youngest brother, was the first novice master.

WHEN I learned, my dear friend, from Ralph, the Abbot of Vaucelles, of your desire to see and talk to me, I was greatly moved by your devotion; and surely I am not ungrateful for your good will. You must know that I want to satisfy your desire, but that I am prevented by bodily weakness from doing what I wish not only in this matter but in many other matters as well, and in much necessary business. But although absent in body, I am present to you in spirit, until it pleases God that I should be present to you in both body and spirit; if however we love not in word only, but in truth and very deed. And so this is what I ask of you: will you, as an outstanding mark of your generosity and a clear proof of the charity you promise, love for my sake what you have of mine amongst you, I mean the brethren of Vaucelles and their church, caring for them and helping them if necessary? And I should like now to make a first proof of your charity by asking you to ratify and not render void your father's gift to me of the forest of Ligecourt for the support of that monastery. We also, for our part, while rendering thanks to you for your kindness in the past and hoping for the same in the future, pour forth our prayers for you and yours to him ' who does the will of them that fear him and hears their prayers '. We pray for the welfare of your wife and of all who belong to you.

LETTER 230

TO COUNT WILLIAM OF NEVERS

This letter is addressed to the Count of Nevers who became a Carthusian at the Grande Chartreuse in 1147, *and appears to refer to his intention of doing this.*

To the pious Count William of Nevers, the greetings and prayers of Bernard, Abbot of Clairvaux.

I WANT to meet you at the time and place we arranged, but there is a reason why I cannot do so; a reason which you, unless I am mistaken, will consider just and reasonable when you know it. I am glad that you value and remember wholesome advice, even when it is given you by insignificant and common persons. Therefore I advise and implore you by the salvation you hope for, that you nevertheless go to the Abbot of Pontigny as you had intended, for he is a wise and religious man and your firm friend, and decide the matter with his advice as well as with the advice of those other men of counsel, whom you have judged it expedient to call together for the purpose. In the meantime we will pray for you; and I trust in the Lord Jesus that, though I shall not be there, he will be present, and make known to you his will through his servants. Farewell.

LETTER 231

TO THE SAME

To his dear friend in Christ, William, greetings from Bernard, styled Abbot of Clairvaux.

B ECAUSE you show yourself so ready to obey, I must be all the more cautious in what I advise or command you. It is indeed fitting that you should complete as soon as possible the good beginnings of your conversion. Having acted manfully in disdaining your worldly goods, it remains for you to leave yourself as well by living no longer under your own will, like a true follower of Christ who became obedient to his Father even unto death and who, when he could do all things, declared that he could do nothing of himself but as the Father had taught him. But as you assure me that the needs of the time, the necessities of the poor, and the care of your household seem to forbid that for the time, I too, in so far as it rests with me, do not prohibit you from what charity dictates in the matter, providing you do not overstay the time you have settled with yourself. I would only warn you not to waste wantonly this liberty which has been conceded to you for a time in following your whims, or even (may such a thing be far from you!) in occupying yourself with secular affairs, rather than in concerning yourself with the things of God.

LETTER 232

TO J., COUNT OF NEVERS, THE SON OF THE ABOVE

To J., Count of Nevers, greeting and prayers from his friends and brothers at Clairvaux.

WE believe that you have an abundance of this world's goods, but the servants of God at Molesme are suffering from such great poverty that, so we have heard, they have not any bread, nor can they easily find an income for the support of their great numbers that would be sufficient to correct the situation. We have taken care to suggest this to you privately, they being quite ignorant of our action and expecting nothing at all of the sort from us, so that if it should be in your heart to give an alms to God, you may know that there is at present great want in that monastery. But if not, if you have nothing to give them, or if you do not want to give them anything, you can refuse without any offence to them as they do not know we have approached you in the matter.

LETTER 233

TO COUNT EBAL OF FLORE

This letter was written on behalf of the monastery of Benedictine monks at Liesses.

BERNARD, Abbot of Clairvaux, to his dear son Ebal of Flore, that he may decline evil and do good.

BY humbly commending yourself to my prayers, by devotedly associating yourself with our community, by not hesitating to put me to the fatigue of a long, albeit a fruitless journey, you have given me confidence to rebuke you when necessary. What do you think my prayers can avail you when every day you thwart them by your evil deeds? I have heard that besides the innumerable other evils which you unceasingly inflict on the monastery which your devout mother built for the monks of Liesses, you deny the liberty (not that is . . . that they may leave it free and letting go what is their own withdraw from it completely[1]). Who advised you to do this? This

---

[1] As it stands it is not easy to see what this sentence means. The condition of the MS. is very bad just here. This is the Latin as published by H..ffer: *Tu enim sicut audivi preter alia mala innumera que committere non cessas monasterio, quod monachis Lesciensibus tua religiosa mater exstruxit, libertatem contradicis, non videlicet . . . et ipsi a se liberum relinquant et de manu sua, quod suum abicientes absolutum dimittant. Quis tibi hoc consulit? Hec libertas quam illi monasterio queris peior est omni servitute.*

liberty which you seek for that monastery is worse than any slavery. If you will believe me and acquiesce in my advice, if you wish my prayers, I do not say to benefit you, but not grievously to injure you, from now on you must put aside this obstinacy of yours and, without excuses or delay, confirm the gift as it was made by your mother to these holy brothers, yet so that they promise to keep there as many monks as may conveniently and wholly maintain the life, while you and your mother undertake to provide food and clothing so that the monks may be supported in the service of God.

LETTER 234

TO BERALD, ABBOT OF ST. BENIGNUS, DIJON

To the venerable Berald, Abbot of St. Benignus at Dijon, his lord and friend, the spirit of pity, from Brother Bernard, unworthy Abbot of Clairvaux.

I APPEAL to your loving heart for this little sheep of yours who has strayed from the fold. I beg you to have mercy and compassion on him, after the example of the Good Shepherd. I know full well how capricious he is, I know that he has left his monastery twice before this and been received back. Nevertheless your paternity knows very well that mercy must be preferred to justice and Blessed Benedict, who says that a monk is to be received back up to three times, is especially to be obeyed. It is for this that Brother Henry implores your kindness. But if you are not minded to attend to me on this, as a last resource Brother Henry begs that you should give him dimissorial letters so that with your licence he may make his soul in some other monastery. As for myself, I can tell you that ' the Lord has chastised me, chastised me indeed, but would not doom me to die '.

BUGGO, BISHOP OF WORMS, AND ST. BERNARD

IN a letter addressed to the Abbot of Clairvaux, Buggo, Bishop of Worms, complains that his many letters to the abbot had been ignored. He rather peremptorily tells Bernard to respect at least his importunity and satisfy his request by sending him a monk to guide the young Cistercian foundation in his diocese for which he is supplying the material needs.

In another letter in much the same vein as the first, but less peremptory, the same bishop says that he is surprised that his repeated letters to the Abbot of Clairvaux have received no response, and attributes it to his sins. A letter written ' more in grief than in anger '. Both these letters appeared in the *Bulletin de l'Académie royale,* Brussels, 1861.

LETTER 235

TO BUGGO, BISHOP OF WORMS

St. Bernard's answer to the letters mentioned above. This letter is notable for the saint's avowal that it was his habit always to answer his letters, even when they were from people of humble station. Unhappily a large part of the MS. is defective.

To his venerable lord and very dear father Buggo, by the grace of God Bishop of Worms, that he may see the Lord's mercies in the land of the living, from Bernard, styled Abbot of Clairvaux.

I HAVE received your letters, reverend father, with due veneration, and ' my heart was in awe of your words '. You say that you are surprised, and take it ill, and attribute it to your sins that, after having written to me very often, you have not only failed to obtain what you asked for, but that you have not even received a word in answer. If this is so, I attribute to myself your words and say that I am surprised and take it ill and ascribe it to my sins. If I have done this thing willingly and knowingly, it is pride and a slight on the Lord Christ. But it has hitherto always been my habit to answer all my letters, even when they are from people of humble station; how much more so therefore when they are from those who are seen to be the columns of the Church of God. I believe on account of this . . . of answering you on account of my affairs which grow daily . . . I am, or without letters to have answered you by word of mouth through a messenger, whose tongue I hold in as great esteem as ' the pen of a scrivener that writeth swiftly '. For besides these two . . . I find a third reason. Concerning brother E., I say briefly . . . because he is a brother of great hopes; but since he is, as it were, still an unfledged bird in the nest . . . it does not seem safe to send him back amongst his neigh-bours and friends . . . lest he be involved in some crisis.[1] But when ' his hands are skilled in battle, and his right arm a match for any bow of bronze ', then according to the will of heaven, so be it. If it should seem hard to you that you have not been sent Brother A., consider how necessary he is to us.

THE CONTROVERSY WITH PETER ABELARD

THE following letters concern the controversy between St. Bernard and Peter Abelard. Everyone is familiar with the story of Abelard's romantic although illicit love affair with Héloïse, but with this we are not concerned: Peter Abelard has a surer title to fame than a romantic love affair.

Abelard was born at Le Pallet near Nantes in the year 1079. Destined for the army, he soon abandoned a military career for the schools: ' Mars for Minerva ', as he expresses it in the fashion of the times. He sat under Roscelinus, a well-known

---

[1] MS. very defective in all these places.

nominalist philosopher of those days whose doctrine was condemned at Soissons in 1092. He then went to Anselm of Laon, a teacher of the opposite school, and finally left him for William of Champeaux, who afterwards became Bishop of Châlons-sur-Marne and a friend of St. Bernard. Otto of Freising, a contemporary who had himself sat under Abelard, wrote that Abelard was so arrogant and self-opinionated that he would scarcely demean himself to listen to his masters. And Abelard himself boasts of how vexatious he made himself to William of Champeaux by refuting his arguments and reasoning against him.

Eventually he left William of Champeaux to set up a school of his own at Melun, and then, nearer Paris, at Corbeil. Here his health broke down through over study and he was obliged to give up his school and retire to Brittany in order to recuperate. Soon afterwards we find him back again in Paris. But the schools had had enough of him and closed their doors to him. In the year 1113 he founded his own school on Mont St. Geneviève. Here he wrote his book on 'The Divine Unity and Trinity' which was condemned at Soissons in 1121. After this he retired to the Abbey of St. Denis in Paris, to leave it a year later in order to live on his own in a remote spot in the territory of Theobald II, Count of Champagne. Very soon he was joined by disciples, and an oratory was built dedicated first to the Holy Trinity and afterwards to the Paraclete. It is said that the life he led here with his disciples was so severe as to rival that of the Cistercians. After three years of this life he was elected Abbot of St. Giles de Rhuys in Brittany but, finding himself totally incapable of ruling others, he retired again to the Paraclete. Here, under the combined direction of himself and Héloïse, a small community of nuns was formed. But in 1136 he is back again in Paris, teaching at St. Geneviève.

It was William of St. Thierry who first gave the alarm to St. Bernard in a letter describing the novel and dangerous doctrines of Abelard. A meeting was arranged between him and the saint. It is not clear exactly what transpired at this meeting, but we know that soon afterwards Abelard was clamouring to be faced with St. Bernard before a council of bishops.

The Council of Sens met on the octave of Pentecost in the year 1140. The king and most of the bishops of France were present, including the legate. Abelard came full of confidence and surrounded by his disciples and friends. There can be no doubt that he hoped to make a show in which the Abbot of Clairvaux would retire discomfited. But to the amazement of everyone, when St. Bernard arose at the Council and before the whole assembly called upon him to defend himself on the points in question, Abelard refused to answer a word and appealed direct to Rome. The bishops thereupon sent to Rome a list of the chosen passages from his works which they considered erroneous.

Abelard immediately set out to defend himself in person before the papal court, but he was met at Cluny, where he had paused on the way, with the news that his books had been publicly burned in Rome and that he had been condemned by a rescript dated July 16th, 1140.

After this he remained at Cluny under the kindly protection of Peter the Venerable, and on April 21st, 1142, he ended his life with a pious and edifying death at St. Marcel near Châlons-sur-Saône. It is pleasant to record that before he died he was reconciled with St. Bernard.

The character of Peter Abelard still remains a matter of controversy. On one side his admirers hail him as a sort of Hesperus of the free thought that dawned with the Reformation, as a brilliant and original thinker brutally suppressed and persecuted by an obscurantist monk and an ignorant body of bishops. On the other, there are those who denounce him as an unprincipled and unscrupulous heretic, filled with his own conceit. The truth appears to lie between the two extremes. There can be no doubt at all of Abelard's brilliance and charm. He certainly was a brilliant and original thinker. But his character seems to have been marred by many of the attributes of a precocious undergraduate, by a certain intellectual bumptiousness, and by a hot-headed intolerance for men older than himself, which alienated many who might have helped him.   Nor can there be any doubt that many of his tenets, if not all blatantly heretical, were at least extremely hazardous, conceivably safe in the hands of the master, but very apt to be misunderstood and wrongly explained by enthusiastic disciples.   On the other hand it is certain that he had no intention whatever of teaching heresy, and that his faults were largely on the surface, concealing a truly devout and religious spirit.   Even Otto of Freising, a Cistercian and Abbot of Morimond, remarks in this context that St. Bernard was apt to show a certain credulity in listening to reports unfavourable to those who seemed to rely too much on secular learning, and who founded themselves too exclusively on human reasoning.[1]   Yet there can be no doubt that the saint was justified in his attitude of suspicion to the novelties taught by Abelard.   The only question is whether in his abhorrence of intellectual pride and his anxiety for the faith of simple people, he chose the best possible way of dealing with the situation, and did not perhaps over-state his case against Abelard.

'I do not want to be a philosopher', wrote Abelard towards the close of his life, 'at the price of being rejected by Paul; nor yet an Aristotle at the price of being rejected by Christ, for there is no other name under heaven whereby I can be saved. I adore Christ reigning at the Father's right hand.   With the arms of faith I embrace him working divinely in that glorious virginal flesh which he received of the Holy Ghost.'   It would be a good thing indeed if all his modern apologists could say as much.

A testimony to Abelard and Héloïse, quite remarkable considering its source, together with an appreciation of the protection afforded him by Peter the Venerable, is to be found in a rare book published at Paris in the year 1720 by Dom François-Armand Gervaise, Abbot of La Trappe: *La Vie de Pierre Abélard, abbé de saint Gildas de Ruis, ordre de saint Benoit, et celle d'Héloïse, son epouse, première abbesse du Paraclet.*

WILLIAM OF ST. THIERRY ON ABELARD

WILLIAM of St. Thierry warned the Abbot of Clairvaux and the Bishop of Chartres of the new and strange doctrines being taught by Peter Abelard (Benedictine Edition, 326).   'It is not a question of trivialities', he says, 'but of belief in the Trinity, of the person of the Mediator, and of the mystery of our Redemption.'   And these new opinions of his are being broadcast far and wide, they have crossed the seas and have passed the Alps, reaching even Rome itself.   They are so often preached, and maintained with such impunity, that people suppose them to have the authority of the Roman Curia behind them.   He concludes by saying, 'God knows I love this man; but in a case like this no one is my relative, no one my friend'.

LETTER 236

TO WILLIAM OF ST. THIERRY

To his dear friend William, from Brother Bernard.

IN my opinion your misgivings are well called-for and reasonable. This is evident from your booklet in which you bruise and close 'the lips that mutter wickedness'.   Not that I have yet had the opportunity to read it with the attention you require, but, from what I have been able to see by glancing through it, I like it very much and consider it well able to overthrow the iniquitous teaching.   As you

[1] It is fair to say that Otto recanted this on his death bed.

well know, I am not in the habit of trusting much my judgement, especially in such grave matters as these, so I suggest that it would be worth our while to meet somewhere, as soon as we have an opportunity, and discuss the whole thing.   But I do not think this can be arranged before Easter, lest we are distracted from the prayer that is proper to this season of Lent.   I beg you, in the meantime, to suffer patiently my own patience and silence, for at present I know little or nothing at all of these matters.   Yet in answer to your prayers God can give me the power for what you are urging me to do.   Farewell.

LETTER 237

TO SUMMON TOGETHER THE BISHOPS OF THE ARCHDIOCESE OF SENS

WORD has gone out amongst many and I believe it to have reached your ears that I have been summoned to Sens on the octave of Pentecost and challenged to a fight in defence of the faith, although ' the servant of God must not wrangle but be mild towards all men '. Even if it were only in defence of himself, your child might, perhaps not unreasonably, pride himself on your protection.   But now because it is your affair, nay, more yours than mine, I advise and earnestly beg you to prove yourselves friends in adversity.   I call you friends, not my friends, but Christ's friends; Christ whose bride calls out to you that she is being strangled in the forest of heresy and amongst the undergrowth of errors which are cropping up under your care and shelter.   The friends of the Bridegroom will not desert the bride in time of peril, in the hour of tribulation.   Do not wonder that I have called upon you so suddenly and at such short notice, for it is a part of the cunning and shrewd design of our opponents to attack us while we are unprepared and to engage us in battle while we are unprotected.

LETTER 238

TO THE BISHOPS AND CARDINALS IN CURIA

To the lords and reverend fathers, the Bishops and Cardinals in Curia, from the child of their holiness.

NO one has any doubt that it belongs especially to you to remove scandals from the Kingdom of God, to cut back the growing thorns, to calm quarrels.   For this is what Moses commanded when he went up the mountain, saying: ' Wait here till we come back to you.   You have Aaron and Hur with you; to them refer all matters of dispute.'   I speak of that Moses who came through water, and ' not by water only, but by water and blood '.[1]   And therefore he is

---

[1] ' This is he that came by water and blood, Jesus Christ; not by water only but by water and blood ' (1 John 5.6).

greater than Moses because he came through blood. And because by Aaron and Hur the zeal and authority of the Roman Church are signified, I do well to refer to her, not questions about the faith, but wounds to the faith, injuries to Christ, insults and dishonours to the Fathers, the scandals of the present generation and the dangers of those to come. The faith of the simple is being held up to scorn, the secrets of God are being reft open, the most sacred matters are being recklessly discussed, and the Fathers are being derided because they held that such matters are better allowed to rest[1] than solved. Hence it comes about that, contrary to the law of God, the Paschal Lamb is either boiled or eaten raw, with bestial mouth and manners.[2] And what is left over is not burned with fire, but trodden under foot.[3] So mere human ingenuity is taking on itself to solve everything, and leave nothing to faith. It is trying for things above itself, prying into things too strong for it, rushing into divine things, and profaning rather than revealing what is holy. Things closed and sealed, it is not opening but tearing asunder, and what it is not able to force open, that it considers to be of no account and not worthy of belief.

2. Read, if you please, that book of Peter Abelard which he calls a book of Theology. You have it to hand since, as he boasts, it is read eagerly by many in the Curia. See what sort of things he says there about the Holy Trinity, about the generation of the Son, about the procession of the Holy Spirit, and much else that is very strange indeed to Catholic ears and minds. Read that other book which they call the *Book of Sentences*,[4] and also the one entitled *Know Thyself*, and see how they too run riot with a whole crop of sacrileges and errors. See what he thinks about the soul of Christ, about the person of Christ, about his descent into hell, about the Sacrament of the Altar, about the power of binding and loosing, about original sin, about the sins of human weakness, about the sins of ignorance, about sinful action, and about sinful intention. And if you then consider that I am rightly disturbed, do you also bestir yourselves and, so as not to bestir yourselves in vain, act according to the position you hold, according to the dignity in which you are supreme, according to the power you have received, and let him who has scanned the heavens go down even into hell, and let the works of darkness that have braved the light be shown up by the light, so that while he who sins in public is publicly

---

[1] . . . *quod eas magis sopiendas, quam solvendas censuerint.* Eales, apparently understanding *sopiendas* as *sapiendas* translates: '. . . because they held that such things are rather to be tasted than solved'.

[2] . . . *more et ore bestiali.*

[3] 'No part must be eaten raw, or boiled, it must be roasted over the fire . . . whatever is left over, you must put in the fire and burn it' (*Exodus* 12.9).

[4] Abelard denied that he had ever written a book with this name and implied that St. Bernard could not distinguish between Peter Lombard and himself. But Bernard was familiar with the works of Peter Lombard, and also his *Book of Sentences* was not published when this letter was written. Undoubtedly he is referring here to Abelard's book *Sic et Non* which starts: 'Here begin sentences taken from the Holy Scriptures which seem opposed to each other . . .'

rebuked, others, who speak evil in their hearts and write it in their books, may restrain themselves from putting darkness for light, and disputing on divine matters at the crossroads. Thus shall the mouth that mutters wickedness be closed.

LETTER 239

TO POPE INNOCENT

To his most loving father and lord, Innocent, by the grace of God Supreme Pontiff, the entire devotion, for what it is worth, of Brother Bernard, styled Abbot of Clairvaux.

THERE must be scandals; they are an unpleasant necessity. Therefore the Prophet says, ' Had I but wings as the dove has wings, to fly away and be at rest ', and the Apostle desires to be dissolved and be with Christ, and Elias declares, ' I can bear no more, Lord; put an end to my life; I have no better right to live than my fathers '. This I have in common with the saints, although it is a matter only of the will and not of merit, that I too wish to be taken out of it all, overcome, I admit, by ' the fears that daunt me and the storm around me '. But I fear that I should not be found so well prepared as I am well disposed. I am weary of life; and I know not whether it would be well for me to die. Perhaps for this reason I am removed even in my wish from the saints who were spurred on by their desire for better things, whereas I am constrained to go forth only to escape scandals and troubles. In fine he says, ' It were better to be dissolved and be with Christ '. Therefore in the saint the desire was uppermost, in me feeling. But in this most miserable life he was not able to have the good he desired, nor I to be free of the anxieties which I suffer. And so while we are both alike in our wish to go forth, we differ in our motives for wishing it.

2. Fool that I am, I was but now promising myself rest, when the madness of the lion had been quelled and peace restored to the Church.[1] And now the Church is at peace, but not I. I did not realize I was in the vale of tears, I was forgetting that I was still in ' a land where all is forgotten ', I did not stop to consider that the earth on which I dwell brings forth thorns and troubles for me, and that, when they have been cut back, new ones will grow again, and other new ones after these, and so on without end. I had heard this to be sure, but experience, I have now discovered, gives a better comprehension to the hearing. Grief transcends and never ends for me,[2] my sorrows have increased because evils have gained strength; first the frost, then came the snow. Who can endure this cold? In it charity grows

[1] A reference to Peter Leonis, the anti-Pope.
[2] *Innovatus est dolor, non exterminatus.*

cold so that iniquity abounds. We have escaped the lion only to fall victims to the dragon who is, perhaps, more dangerous lurking in his lair than the lion raging in the open. Although he is no longer lurking in his lair: would that his poisonous writings were still lurking in their shelves, and not being discussed at the crossroads! His books have wings: and they who hate the light because their lives are evil, have dashed into the light thinking it was darkness. Darkness is being brought into towns and castles in the place of light; and for honey poison or, I should say, poison in honey is being offered on all sides to everyone. His writings 'have passed from country to country, and from one kingdom to another'. A new gospel is being forged for peoples and for nations, a new faith is being propounded, and a new foundation is being laid besides that which has been laid. Virtues and vices are being discussed immorally, the sacraments of the Church falsely, the mystery of the Holy Trinity neither simply nor soberly. Everything is put perversely, everything quite differently, and beyond what we have been accustomed to hear.

3. Goliath advances tall of body, girt in the noble accoutrements of war, and preceded by his armour-bearer, Arnold of Brescia.[1] Scale is joined to scale, and there is no breathing space between.[2] The bee that is in France[3] has murmured to the bee in Italy, and they have joined forces against the Lord and against his anointed, 'they have strung their bows, have arrows ready in the quiver, to shoot from their hiding places at unoffending hearts'. In food and clothing they have all the appearances of piety, but they reject its virtue, and they deceive all the more people by transforming themselves into angels of light, whereas they are Satan. Therefore Goliath, standing between the two armies with his armour-bearer, cries out with a loud voice to the ranks of Israel, and taunts the forces of the saints, all the more audaciously for there being no David to defy him. He insults the Doctors of the Church by holding up the philosophers for exaggerated praises. He prefers their ideas and his own novelties to the doctrines and faith of the Catholic Fathers; and, when all have fled before him, he calls me out, the least of all, to single combat.

4. At his request the Archbishop of Sens wrote to me fixing the day of the meeting, on which Abelard, in his presence and in the presence of his brother bishops, should establish, if he could, his perverse doctrines, against which I have dared to croak. I refused because I am but a child in this sort of warfare and he is a man habituated to it from his youth, and because I deemed it an unworthy action to bring the faith into the arena of controversy, resting as it does on sure and immutable truth. I said that his writings were evidence enough against

---

[1] A pupil of Abelard, heretic, and demagogue.
[2] *Squama squamæ conjungitur, nec spiraculum incedit per eas.* Eales translates: 'Scale overlaps scale, and there is no point left unguarded'.
[3] The French bee is Abelard; the Italian, Arnold of Brescia. Perhaps an allusion to *Isaias* 7.18.

him, and that it was the business of the bishops to adjudicate on the doctrines of which they were the ministers, not mine. But he lifted up his voice all the more for this, called upon many, and assembled all his accomplices. I would rather not say what he wrote about me to his disciples. He spread it about on all sides that he was going to answer me at Sens on the day appointed. The word of it went forth to everyone, and I was not able to hide myself. At first I did nothing, not greatly caring for what people were saying. Yet, unwillingly and sorrowfully, I bowed to the advice of my friends, who saw how everyone was preparing as if for a show, and feared that my absence would serve only to increase the influence of the man and the scandal of the people, also it seemed that his errors might appear to be confirmed if there were no one to answer and refute them. And so I went to Sens at the time appointed, unprepared, unprotected, except by those words which I had in my mind at the time: ' Take no thought how or what to speak: for it will be given you in that hour what to speak ', and ' With the Lord to aid me, I have no fear of the worst that man can do '. Besides the bishops and abbots, there were many religious men present, and also masters of the schools from the cities, and many educated clerics, the king too was there. And so, in the presence of all, face to face with my adversary, I took certain headings from his books. And when I began to read these, he refused to listen and walked out, and appealed from the judges he had chosen, which I do not think was permissible. When these aforesaid headings from his books had been examined, they were found by the judgements of all to be contrary to the faith, to the truth. I have written all this on my own behalf in case I should be thought to have shown levity or at least rashness in so grave a matter.

5. But you, successor of St. Peter, will judge whether this man who has attacked the faith of Peter should find a refuge in the see of Peter. You, I say, the friend of the Bridegroom, will find a way of freeing the bride ' from treacherous lips, the perjured tongue '. But, to speak a trifle more boldly to my lord, look also to yourself, most loving father, and the grace of God that is within you. Did not God set you up over nations and kingdoms when you were yet small in your own eyes? And for what other purpose than that you should pull up and destroy, build and plant? Consider, I beg you, how much he has done for you who took you from your father's house, and anointed you with the oil of his mercy; how much for his Church, by means of you; how many things in the field of the Lord, heaven and earth being witnesses, have been powerfully and wholesomely pulled up and destroyed; how many things have been well and truly built, planted, and propagated. God has raised up crazy heretics in your time that by your hand they may be crushed. I have seen a fool well rooted, and straightway his beauty was cursed. I have seen, I say, an impious

man lifted up and exalted like the cedars of Lebanon; and I passed by, and lo! he was not. There must be heresies and schisms, that they also, who are approved, may be made manifest among you.[1] God has proved you and found you true. But so that nothing should be lacking to your crown, heresies have now arisen. For the perfection of your virtue, it now only remains for you not to be found to have done less than the great bishops, your predecessors. Catch for us, most loving father, the foxes that are destroying the vine of the Lord, while they are yet young; lest, if they should grow and multiply, what was not done for their extermination by yourself, may be the despair of those that come after you. Although now they are no longer so small or so few, but well grown and numerous, and only to be exterminated by your strong hand. Jacinctus has borne us much ill-will, but he has not hurt us because he could not. I thought I ought to bear patiently in my own person, what he has not spared either yourself or the Curia. All this my Nicholas, who is yours too, can tell you better by word of mouth.

THE ERRORS OF ABELARD

St. Bernard wrote a long letter (Benedictine Edition, 190) on the errors of Abelard but, on account of its doctrinal importance and great length, it is included among the treatises of St. Bernard.

The Archbishop of Rheims, in a letter to Pope Innocent (Benedictine Edition, 191), begged the Holy Father to suppress the evil teaching of Abelard. In much the same phraseology as St. Bernard he describes how many are being led astray by Abelard's false doctrines and hints at the fear that there may be some in the Curia itself who favour his errors. He describes what happened at Sens, and ends by saying that the remedy now rests with the Pope.

LETTER 240

TO GUY OF CASTELLO

Guy was said to have been a disciple of Abelard. In 1143 *he became Pope as Celestine II.*

To his venerable lord and most dear father, Master Guy, by the grace of God Cardinal Priest of the Holy Roman Church, that he may not swerve either to the right or to the left, from Bernard, styled Abbot of Clairvaux.

IT would be to wrong you were I to believe that you would so love anyone as to love also his errors. Whoever loves anyone thus, does not yet know how he ought to love him. Such love is earthy, animal, diabolical, and harmful both to the lover and the loved. Let other people think as they wish of others, I am still not able to think of you otherwise than as a man reasonable and just. Some people judge first and learn afterwards, but I do not judge a drink to be either

---

[1] See Vincent of Lérins, *Commonitorium,* x.15.

sweet or bitter until I have tasted it.   Master Peter has used in his books phrases that are novel and profane both in their wording and in their sense.   He argues about faith against the Faith; he assails the law in the words of the law.   He sees nothing ' through a glass, in a dark manner ', but views everything face to face ' dwelling on high matters, on marvels beyond his reach '.   It were better for him to know himself according to the title of his book, and not to exceed his limitations but to be wise according to sobriety.   I do not accuse him before the Father, there is that book of his, in which he takes such mistaken pleasure, to accuse him.   When he speaks of the Trinity, he savours of Arius; when of grace, he savours of Pelagius; when of the person of Christ, he savours of Nestorius.   I do not question at all your judgement, in having for so long begged you not to prefer anyone to Christ, in the cause of Christ.   But know this, that it is expedient for you to whom power has been given by the Lord, expedient for the Church of Christ, and expedient for the man himself, that silence should be imposed upon him because ' his mouth overflows with curses, and calumny, and deceit; his tongue is a store house of misery and shame '.

LETTER 241

TO CARDINAL IVO, ON THE SAME SUBJECT

To his dearest Ivo, by the grace of God Cardinal Priest of the Holy Roman Church, that he may love justice and hate iniquity, from Bernard, styled Abbot of Clairvaux.

MASTER Peter Abelard is a monk without a rule, a prelate without responsibility.   He is neither in order nor of an Order.[1]   A man at variance with himself: a Herod within, a John without; a most doubtful character, having nothing of the monk about him except the name and the habit.   But this is not my concern.   Let each one bear his own burdens.   There is another thing which I cannot overlook, a thing which concerns everyone who loves the name of Christ.   He speaks iniquity openly.   He corrupts the integrity of the faith and the chastity of the Church.   He oversteps the landmarks placed by our Fathers in discussing and writing about faith, the sacraments, and the Holy Trinity; he changes each thing according to his pleasure, adding to it or taking from it.   In his books and in his works he shows himself to be a fabricator of falsehood, a coiner of perverse dogmas, proving himself a heretic not so much by his error as by his obstinate defence of error. He is a man who does not know his limitations, making void the virtue of the cross by the cleverness of his words. Nothing in heaven or on earth is hidden from him, except himself. He was condemned at Soissons with his work before the legate of the Roman Church.   But as if this were not enough, he is again acting

[1] . . . nec ordinem tenet, nec temetur ab ordine.

in such a way as to get himself again condemned, and how his last error is worse than his first. Yet he feels himself to be quite safe, because he boasts that he has disciples amongst the cardinals and clerics in Curia and supposes that they, whose judgement and condemnation he ought to fear, will defend him in his past and present error. If anyone has the Spirit of God, let him remember that verse: 'Lord, do I not hate the men who hate thee, am I not sick at heart over their rebellion?' May God free his Church by means of you and your sons of 'the treacherous lips and perjured tongue'.

LETTER 242

TO POPE INNOCENT, ON THE SAME SUBJECT

To his most loving lord and father, Innocent, the humble duty of Bernard, styled Abbot of Clairvaux.

'BE sure the bride of Christ weeps; there in the darkness her cheeks are wet with tears, and of all that courted her there is not one left to console her.' While the Bridegroom delays the Sunamite has been entrusted to you in the land of her exile. There is no one to whom she acknowledges more readily her wrongs, no one to whom she discloses more intimately her anxieties and her complaints than the friend of the Bridegroom. You love the Bridegroom and so you will not spurn his bride when she cries to you in her sorrow and trouble. Amongst all the kinds of enemies by which the Church is hedged about, like a lily amongst thorns, there is none more dangerous, none more troublesome, than the sort who tears at her while he is being held to her bosom and fed at her breasts. It is while she is suffering and sorrowing from such enemies that she utters these words: 'Friends and neighbours that meet me keep their distance now; old companions shun me. I am assailed by enemies that grudge me life itself.' There is no pest so noxious as an enemy in the guise of a friend. Examples for us of this are the friendliness of Absolom and the kiss of Judas. A new foundation is being laid besides that which has been laid. A new faith is being forged in France. Virtues and vices are being discussed immorally, the sacraments falsely, and the mystery of the Holy Trinity neither soberly nor simply, but over and above what we have been taught. Masters Peter and Arnold, the pest of which you rid Italy, have made common cause against the Lord and against his anointed. Scale is joined to scale and there is no breathing space between. Their lives are corrupt and hateful and by the leaven of their corruption they are corrupting the faith of simple people, upsetting moral values, defiling the purity of the Church. After the manner and likeness of him who transforms himself into an angel of light, with the appearances of piety but without the virtue of it, they are girt about like the temple that they may shoot from their hiding places at unoffending hearts. We have escaped the roaring of Peter the Lion who occupied the see of Simon Peter only to encounter Peter the Dragon who assails the faith of Simon Peter. The former openly persecuted the Church of God, like a lion going about and seeking whom it may devour; but the latter lurks like a dragon in hidden places that he may kill the innocent. But thou, Lord God, will humble the proud with their haughty looks and tread under foot the lion and the dragon. The former was harmful only so long as he was alive, death put an end to both his life and the harm he could do; but the latter by writing new dogmas has made provision for passing on his virus to future generations, for poisoning every generation that is to come. In fine, to say a lot in a few words, our theologian lays down with Arius that there are degrees and grades in the Trinity; with Pelagius he prefers free will to grace; and like Nestorius he divides Christ by excluding the human nature he assumed from association with the Trinity. But in all this he boasts that he is held by all the cardinals and clerics in Curia to be a fountain-head of knowledge, that his books and sayings have found their way into the hands and hearts of the Romans, and he summons to protect his errors those very men by whom he ought to be judged and condemned. What can this persecutor of the faith be thinking of, how can he have the effrontery to turn for protection to the Defender of the faith? How can he face, how can he dare to set eyes on the friend of the Bridegroom? If only I were not kept by my care for the brethren, if only I were not hampered by the weakness of my body, how glad I would be to see with my own eyes the friend of the Bridegroom defending, heart in hand, the bride in the absence of her spouse! I can no more bear to see the Church suffering than I can ignore the injuries done to my lord the Pope. Do not, most beloved father, withhold your help from her. Already the charity of many is growing cold through the abundance of iniquity and, unless you hold out to her your hand, now, even now, the bride of Christ ' will wander abroad and follow with the shepherd's flocks, and feed her flocks beside the Shepherd's encampment '.[1]

LETTER 243

TO CARDINAL STEPHEN, BISHOP OF PALESTRINA

To his venerable lord and very dear father, Stephen, by the grace of God Bishop of Palestrina, that he may play the man and keep his courage high, from Brother Bernard, Abbot of Clairvaux.

[1] . . . *egreditur et abiit post vestigia gregum, et pascit greges juxta tabernacula pastorum.* Evidently a quotation from the Canticle of Canticles 1.7: . . . *egredere, et abi post vestigia gregum, et pasce hædos tuos juxta tabernacula pastorum.* Eales translates: ' . . . I foresee the day when the Spouse of Christ will go forth and follow strange paths, and be led astray by false pastors '.

I TELL you of the difficulties and sorrows of the bride of Christ all the more readily for knowing you to be the friend of the Bridegroom and very glad to hear his voice. If I have rightly judged your dispositions, I am certain that you do not seek your own interests but those of Jesus Christ. Peter Abelard proves by his life, by his behaviour, and by his books, which are now issuing from darkness into the light of day,[1] that he is a persecutor of the Catholic Church, and an enemy of the cross of Christ. Outwardly he appears a monk, but within he he is a heretic having nothing of the monk about him save the habit and name. He opens up the old wells and the trodden-in pools of heretics, so that the ox and ass may fall in. He had long been silent, but while he kept silence in Brittany he conceived sorrow, and now in France he has brought forth iniquity. He has come out of his hole like a twisting snake, and like the hydra when one head is cut off he grows seven more in its place. A single head was cut off, a single heresy of that man, at Soissons; but already seven greater ones have grown up in its place, an example of which I have sent to you. Raw and inexperienced listeners hardly finished with their dialectics, and those who can hardly, so to speak, stand the first elements of the faith, are introduced by him to the mystery of the Holy Trinity, to the Holy of Holies, to the chamber of the King, and to him who is ' shrouded with darkness '. In fine, our theologian has laid down degrees and grades in the Trinity like Arius, with Pelagius he puts free will before grace, and with Nestorius he divides Christ by excluding from association with the Trinity the human nature he assumed. Thus he runs through almost all the sacraments, and ' boldly sweeps from world's end to world's end ', ordering all things mischievously. Besides this he boasts that he has infected the Roman Curia with the virus of his new ideas, that his books and sayings have found their way into the hands and hearts of the Romans, and he summons to protect his errors those very men by whom he ought to be judged and condemned. May God care for his Church for which he died, so that he may behold it without spot or wrinkle, and so that perpetual silence should be imposed on that man, ' whose mouth overflows with curses, calumny, and deceit '.

LETTER 244

TO CARDINAL G.

To his venerable lord and beloved father G., Cardinal of the Holy Roman Church, a spirit prudent and strong, from Bernard, Abbot of Clairvaux.

---

[1] . . . *libri jam de tenebris in lucem procedentes.* Eales translates: ' . . . the books already published '.

I cannot keep silent about the injuries done to Christ, the difficulties and sorrows of the Church, the misery of the needy, and the grievances of the poor. We have fallen on dangerous times. We have teachers with itching ears and scholars who ' turn away their hearing from the truth, and are turned to fables '. We have in France one Peter Abelard, a monk without a rule, a prelate without responsibility, an abbot without discipline, who argues with boys and consorts with women. He puts ' stolen waters and hidden bread ' before his household in his books, and in his discourses he introduces profane novelties of phrase and meaning. He approaches the dark cloud which surrounds God, not alone as Moses did, but with a whole crowd of his disciples. Catholic Faith, the childbearing of the Virgin, the Sacrament of the Altar, the incomprehensible mystery of the Holy Trinity, are being discussed in the streets and market places. We have escaped the roaring of Peter the Lion, only to encounter the hissing of Peter the Dragon. But thou, Lord Jesu, will humble the proud with their haughty looks, and tread under foot the Lion and the Dragon. The former was only harmful so long as he lived, death put an end to both his life and the harm he could do. But this one has already made provision for passing on his virus to posterity, for harming every generation that is to come. He has put on record his leprous novelties with pen and ink. I have secured his books and sent them on to you. Judge the author from his work. See how our theologian like Arius makes grades and degrees in the Trinity, how with Pelagius he gives free will greater importance than grace, how with Nestorius he divides Christ by denying to the human nature he assumed the fellowship of the Trinity: but this is by no means all. Is there no one amongst you who grieves for Christ, no one who loves righteousness and hates iniquity? If this mouth that utters evil should not be stopped, let him look to it and judge who alone considers our troubles and sorrows.

LETTER 245

TO GREGORY, CARDINAL DEACON OF SS. SERGIUS AND BACCHUS

To his venerable friend Gregory, Cardinal Deacon of the title of SS. Sergius and Bacchus, greetings and love, from Bernard, Abbot of Clairvaux.

According to your custom you ought always to rise for me whenever I enter the Curia. I may seem to be joking, but it is a serious matter. I am entering the Curia now, not in person but in the cause that is before it. Do you rise for me as you used to do, rise up now for my cause, or rather for the cause of Christ, because Christ is concerned in this cause and the truth is in danger. Rise up then, rise to confront him who disputes about faith[1] against the faith, who

---

[1] Surely here and *passim* in this context, it is ' faith ' and not ' the faith ' as Eales translates. Abelard tried to define faith as an ' opinion '.

assails law in the words of the law, whose hand is against all, and against whom is every hand. This is Peter Abelard who writes, teaches, argues and distinguishes as he likes concerning morals, sacraments, and even the Father, Son, and Holy Ghost. He now enters the Curia after having disturbed and troubled the Church, not that he may heal the sorrow that he has caused her but so as ' to cover sin with smooth names '. If you are her son, defend the womb that bore you and the paps that gave you suck.

LETTER 246

TO GUY OF PISA

This is Guy Moricot de Vico, a native of Pisa, created cardinal by Innocent II.

To Guy of Pisa, a sound mind in a sound body, from Bernard, Abbot of Clairvaux.

BECAUSE of our mutual affection I would feel quite safe in trusting a cause of mine to you. And I now entrust to you this present cause all the more readily for the great love that we owe to him whose cause it is. It is the cause of Christ, rather Christ himself is concerned in the cause, and the truth is in danger. The garments of Christ are being divided, the sacraments of the Church torn to shreds. But the tunic of Christ remains whole for it has no seam, having been woven all in one piece from the top. The tunic of Christ is the unity of the Church which does not admit of being torn or divided. What has thus been woven, what the Holy Spirit has thus unified, cannot be torn up by men. Though they sharpen their tongues like serpents and draw their stings of ingenuity to disturb the peace of the Church, yet, because they are the gates of hell, they shall never prevail against her. If you are indeed her son, if you recognize her as your mother, do not desert her in danger, do not withdraw your support from her in trouble. Master Peter has entered the Curia so that he may have the authority of the Holy See as ' a wall and breast-work ' to protect the errors he has written and taught, and with which he has assailed the Church.

LETTER 247

TO A CERTAIN CARDINAL PRIEST

To the Cardinal Priest . . . , affectionate greetings from Bernard, Abbot of Clairvaux.

LET no one despise your youth. It is not a grey head that the Lord expects from you, but a mature mind; not weight of years, but a blameless life. Although both Jeremias and Daniel were children yet they did not stand in awe of or fear the disgraceful old men, grown old with years ill spent. I would have good reason for calling anyone disgraceful who soils the beauty of the Church, the purity of the Faith. Such a one is Peter Abelard who argues and distinguishes just as he pleases and beyond what we have received about faith, sacraments, and the mystery of the Holy Trinity. After disturbing the Church he now enters the Curia, not that he may heal her wounds, but because he has ' turned his heart towards thoughts of evil, to cover sin with smooth names '. They will stand by the Church with confidence who know themselves to be the sons of the Church.

LETTER 248

TO A CERTAIN ABBOT

To his most dear brother and co-abbot, the zeal of God according to knowledge, from Bernard, Abbot of Clairvaux.

' THERE must be heresies, that they who are approved may be made manifest amongst you.' If anyone is of the Lord, let him now take his side. For God is in this cause. Truth is endangered. The garments of Christ are being divided, the sacraments of the Church torn. The good estate of the Church is being corrupted from the sole of the foot to the crown of the head, the simplicity of the faithful is being ridiculed. The lion is on the point of arising from his lair to confront the Church and prey upon the nations. Peter Abelard has gone before the face of Antichrist to prepare his way, holding forth on faith; the sacraments of the Church; on the Father, Son, and Holy Ghost, over and above what we have received. Like Arius he puts degrees and grades in the Trinity; like Pelagius he emphasizes free will at the cost of grace; he excludes from the fellowship of the Trinity the human nature assumed by Christ, thereby dividing Christ like Nestorius. But in all this he boasts that he has reconciled to himself the Roman Church, and that his books and sayings have found their way into the hands and hearts of the Romans. In defence of his errors he summons those very men by whom he ought to be judged and condemned. Let God see to it and judge if the mouth that is muttering treachery be not speedily closed. The bearer will explain the rest more fully.

ST. BERNARD AND ABELARD

IN a letter to Pope Innocent from Henry, Archbishop of Sens; Geoffrey, Bishop of Chartres and Papal Legate; Elias, Bishop of Orleans; Hugo, Bishop of Auxerre; Atto, Bishop of Troyes; and Manasses, Bishop of Meaux (Benedictine Edition, 337), their lordships, after saying that what has been settled by the Holy See is settled once and for all, and cannot be changed, describe how the teaching of Abelard has stirred all France, so that the highest and most sacred matters are openly discussed by all classes of people, and often quite wrongly. They then give an account of how the

Abbot of Clairvaux had met Abelard privately and before witnesses to remonstrate with him, and of what happened at the Council of Sens. They say that Abelard had got together all his disciples to support him at the Council, but that when the abbot confronted him he seemed at a loss, refused to say a word, and appealed to Rome. They conclude by saying that his books seem to be full of errors and that if his Holiness should see fit to condemn them and impose silence on their author, the harmful results of his doctrine and teaching would be thereby eradicated.

Eventually Pope Innocent condemned the errors of Abelard (Benedictine Edition, 194).

LETTER 249

TO CARDINAL HAIMERIC

To his most intimate friend, the illustrious Haimeric, Cardinal and Chancellor of the Holy Roman Church, that he may show good things before God and man, from Bernard, Abbot of Clairvaux.

' As we have heard so have we found ' the books and maxims of Peter Abelard. I have noted his words and marked his enigmas, and I have found them to be ' mysteries of iniquity '. Our theologian assails law in the words of the law. He casts what is holy before dogs, and pearls before swine. He corrupts the faith of simple people and sullies the purity of the Church. As the poet says: *Quo semel est imbuta recens servabit odorem testa diu.*[1] His book has passed through fire, and he has now been brought into a place of repose.[2] Now the enemy of the Church rests in the Church; the persecutor of the faith, in the bosom of the faith. He has been wasted as water poured forth. ' Never may he thrive who has defiled his father's bed.' He has defiled the Church; he has infected with his own blight the minds of simple people. He tries to explore with his reason what the devout mind grasps at once with a vigorous faith. Faith believes, it does not dispute. But this man, apparently holding God suspect, will not believe anything until he has first examined it with his reason. When the Prophet says, ' Unless you believe, you shall not understand ', this man decries willing faith as levity, misusing that testimony of Solomon: ' He that is hasty to believe is light of head '. Let him therefore blame the Blessed Virgin Mary for quickly believing the angel when he announced to her that she should conceive and bring forth a son. Let him also blame him who, while on the verge of death, believed those words of One who was also dying: ' This day

---

[1] ' The jar will long preserve the odour of what it was once steeped in when new ' (Hor., *Ep.* I.ii.68). The cheaper unglazed jars sometimes used in those times absorbed what was first put into them when they were new.

[2] *Transierat per ignem liber ejus, et inductus est in refrigerium.* An allusion to *Transivimus per ignem et aquam, et eduxisti nos in refrigerium:* ' Our way led through fire and water, but now thou hast brought us into a place of repose ' (Ps. 65.12). It seems that the first part of the sentence refers to Abelard's book which was publicly burned, and the second part to Abelard himself who had retired to Cluny. Eales however makes both parts refer to the book and translates: ' His book has passed through the fire, and was brought into a place of refreshment '. It is easy to understand how a book can be burned, but not how it can be brought into a place of refreshment.

thou shalt be with me in Paradise'. And let him praise the hard hearts of those to whom it was said, ' O foolish and slow of heart to believe in all things which the prophets have spoken ', and commend the slowness of him to whom it was said, ' And behold, thou shalt be dumb and shall not speak because thou hast not believed my words '.

2. So that this letter shall not be too long, I will only say a little about very much. This most excellent doctor put degrees and grades in the Trinity like Arius; with Pelagius he prefers free will at the expense of grace, and with Nestorius he divides Christ by denying to the human nature he assumed association with the Trinity. But in all this he boasts that he is a perfect fount of knowledge for the cardinals and clerics of the Curia; that his books and sayings have found their way into the hands and hearts of the Romans; and he summons to the protection of his errors the very men by whom he ought to be judged and condemned. Jacinctus has shown me much ill will, but he has not done anything to hurt me because he could not. This does not upset me, because he does not spare either the person of the Pope or the Curia. My Nicholas, and yours too, can tell you better by word of mouth, all the rest which he has seen and heard.

LETTER 250

TO THE BISHOP OF CONSTANCE, CONCERNING ARNOLD OF BRESCIA

Arnold was born at Brescia in Italy and, after studying in France under Abelard, he received minor orders and returned to his native country. As soon as he had got back to Italy he began to stir up trouble by denying the right of bishops, priests, and monks to hold any property and affirming that all property owned by the clergy belonged to the prince. He also seems to have held heretical views on the Sacrament of the Altar and Infant Baptism. Quick witted and eloquent he stirred up trouble and inflamed the passions of the baser sort of the populace wherever he went. In 1138 he was condemned to silence and banished from Italy. But as soon as Innocent II died (1143) he returned to his country and troubled the reigns of all the popes of his time by inciting the turbulent Roman populace to rebuild the capitol and restore the republic, until he was finally caught by the English Pope Hadrian IV in 1155 and condemned to death by the Emperor Barbarossa.

' IF the good man of the house knew at what hour the thief would come, he would surely watch and not suffer his house to be broken into.' Do you know that a thief has broken into your house during the night, not indeed your house but the Lord's house, yet entrusted to you? Surely you do know what is happening amongst you, for the news of it has reached even me who lives such a great distance from you. It is not to be wondered at that you were not able to foresee the hour or observe the nocturnal entry of the thief; but it will be surprising if you do not recognize him when he has been caught, if you do not hold him fast, if you do not stop him from carrying off your vessels, even Christ's most precious possessions: the souls which he has marked with his image and redeemed with his blood. Perhaps you are still perplexed and wondering to whom I can be referring. I speak of Arnold of Brescia, a man whom I could wish was as praiseworthy for his doctrine as for his way of life. If you want to know, he is a man who comes neither eating nor drinking, that he may sup alone with the devil on the blood of souls. He is one of those whom the vigilant Apostle noted as having the appearances of virtue but denying the power thereof. And the Lord himself also noted the same thing when he said: 'They come in sheep's clothing, but inwardly they are ravening wolves'. Up to the present wherever he has lived for any time he has left behind him such foul and fell tracks, that he dare not on any account return to where he has once set foot. He has quite atrociously stirred up and troubled the land in which he was born. When accused before the lord Pope of a most wicked schism, he was expelled from his birthplace and forced to swear he would not return except by the Pope's permission. For a like reason this notable schismatic was turned out of the kingdom of France. Cast off by the Apostle Peter he promptly joined up with Peter Abelard, and with him and before him tried hard and stubbornly to defend his errors which had already been exposed and condemned by the Church.

2. His madness has not yet abated, his hand is yet stretched out. For, although a fugitive and wanderer, he does not cease to do amongst strangers what he is no longer able to do amongst his own countrymen; like a raging lion he goes about seeking whom he may devour. And now, I am told, he is working iniquity amongst you, and devouring your people like bread. His mouth is full of cursing and bitterness, and his feet are swift to shed blood; destruction and sorrow are in his ways, and the way of peace he does not know. He is an enemy of Christ's cross, a sower of discord, a fabricator of schism, a disturber of the peace, and a divider of unity. His words are smooth as oil, but they are very weapons of destruction. It is his habit to attract the rich and powerful by soft words and the pretence of virtue, according to those words: 'He will agree with the rich to lie in wait at dark corners, and kill the man who never wronged him'. When he has obtained their good will and feels sure of their friendship, then you will see the man openly confront the clergy and, with the support of military power, rise up against the bishops themselves, and rage on all sides against the ecclesiastical order. Knowing this, I do not see what better or more wholesome thing you can do than to follow the advice of the Apostle and 'put away the evil one from amongst you', though the friend of the Bridegroom will see that he is imprisoned rather than put to flight, so that he should not be able to run around

doing any more harm. This is the command which our lord the Pope put into writing when he was with us, because of all the evil he had heard of him; but there was no one to do the good work. If we are warned by the Scriptures to catch the little foxes which spoil the vine, how much more is a great and fierce wolf to be bound fast so that he shall not break into the fold and slay and destroy the sheep.

LETTER 251

TO CARDINAL GUY, LEGATE IN BOHEMIA

News had reached Bernard that this cardinal was befriending Arnold. It may have been under the influence of this same Guy that Arnold was able to return to Italy immediately after the death of Innocent in 1143, and there to create endless trouble.

IT is reported that Arnold of Brescia is with you, the man whose life is as sweet as honey and whose doctrine is as bitter as poison, the man with the head of a dove and the tail of a scorpion, the man whom Brescia has ejected, Rome rejected, and France repulsed; whom Germany abhors, and Italy will not receive. Have a care, I implore you, that he does not extend his mischievous influence under the cover of your authority. He has both the skill and the will to do it, and if your favour is added we shall have a triple cord such as is not easily broken; and the harm done will be, I fear, beyond measure. There are only two alternatives for me, if it is true that you have this man with you: either I must believe that he is not at all known to you, or (what is more likely) that you have hopes of converting him. It is much to be desired that you may succeed in this. But who can fashion a son of Abraham from this stone? What a welcome boon it would be for the Church to receive from your hands as a vessel of honour, one whom she has endured for so long as a vessel of dishonour. You can try; but a prudent man will be careful not to exceed the limit laid down by the Apostle when he says: ' A man that is a heretic, after the first and second admonition, avoid; knowing that he, that is such an one, is subverted, and sinneth, being condemned by his own judgement'. Otherwise to be friendly with him, to hold him often in conversation, not to say to entertain him, looks like favouring him, and is a powerful protection for any enemy. A friend of the Apostolic legate and member of his household will put forward with impunity what he likes, and will be readily believed whatever he says. Who would expect any wrong to come from the legate of the lord Pope? And who would dare to oppose one who comes from you, even were he openly to say what is perverse?

2. Consider too what foul traces this man has left behind him wherever he has been. It was not without reason that the strong

hand of the Apostolic See obliged him, a man born in Italy, to cross the Alps, and not to return home.   Who is there amongst those with whom he is driven to take refuge who does not heartily wish him back again in his own country?   That he should make himself so odious to everyone is a clear justification of the penalty under which he lies, so that no one can say that this was inveigled from the Pope. What possible excuse can there be for flouting the judgement of the Supreme Pontiff?   The actions, if not the tongue, of him against whom it was proclaimed testifies to its rightness.   And so, to favour this man is to contradict the Pope and even the Lord God.   A just sentence justly delivered by anyone soever, certainly proceeds from him who says in the words of the Prophet: ' I am one who speaks justice'.   I have every confidence in your prudence and uprightness and do not doubt that, when you have learned the truth of the matter from this letter, you will be firm and act in a way that is becoming to yourself and beneficial to the Church of God, on whose behalf you are discharging the office of legate.   You command my affection and may count upon my service.

LETTER 252

TO POPE INNOCENT, ON BEHALF OF ARNULF, BISHOP-ELECT OF LISIEUX

Arnulf was Archdeacon of Séez when he was elected Bishop of Lisieux in the year 1141.   He appears to have been a learned man.   Peter the Venerable also wrote to the Pope on his behalf.

To his most loving father and lord, Innocent, by the grace of God Supreme Pontiff, the humble devotion of Bernard, styled Abbot of Clairvaux.

BLESSED be God and the Father of our Lord Jesus Christ who has preserved free his Church, the bride of his beloved Son, and delivered her from the troubles and sorrows of evil things.   The schismatics are laid low, the heretics hold their peace, the necks of the proud and haughty are trodden under foot.   ' Until yesterday, I saw the sinner in schism enthroned high as the cedars of Lebanon; then I passed by and he was there no more.'   In the heresy I saw many old errors springing up revived, ' but silence fell on the lips that muttered treason'.   The tyrant of Sicily lifted up his heart on high, but now he has been humbled under the powerful hand of God.   There is no one of any rank whatsoever over whom the Church of God has not received victory through you, by the mighty hand and uplifted arm of God.

2. There remains however one adversary, the Count of Anjou, that hammer of good men, and destroyer of the peace and liberty of

the Church. He is persecuting the church of Lisieux so that her shepherd cannot find an entrance into the sheepfold, except by some other way. But what has been done cannot be undone. And if someone should look into the affair and examine it closely, he will see that everything, the person involved, the affair itself, and the agent of it, co-operates for good to the advantage of the cause, and the establishment of what has been done. If you look at the person involved, he is your beloved son in whom you are well pleased. If at the affair, it has been carried through in proper order and in accordance with the canons. If at the agent of it, he is a religious man who fears God. If at him who opposes it, you see a man who has not made God his helper, but an adversary of the Church and an enemy of the cross of Christ. It is a strong argument for imparting certainty in any doubtful matter that what pleases good people and disgusts bad people is the best. The Count of Anjou has appealed to the Apostolic See. I wonder why! What injury or loss has he sustained? He is not oppressed, he is on the contrary the oppressor. He is not appealing for relief of injuries, but simply to hold up the consecration of the bishop by interposing an appeal.

3. Since the religion of him who has carried this thing through, as well as your affection for the person chosen, and the justice of his cause, all coalesce, it would seem superfluous and unnecessary for me to petition for him where his humility has already had recourse. I speak to my lord, even I who am but dust and ashes. I, the servant of the bride, speak to the friend of the Bridegroom: let my words be welcome. To you, my lord, is entrusted the care of the Church from the rising up of the sun to the going down thereof. You ought to be for it a wall and a breastwork in the face of the enemy and those who persecute her. You ought to cherish her sons under the shadow of your wings. Receive the Bishop of Lisieux as a true son of the Roman Church, and send him back with your blessing, so that 'his enemies may never claim the mastery over him'. Gird on your sword, Holy Father, for the exaltation of your son, the overthrow of the enemy and the protection of the liberty of the Church,' for we are not the sons of the bondwoman, but of the free woman, free with the liberty wherewith Christ has made us free'.

LETTER 253

TO PETER, DEAN OF BESANÇON

Apparently Guy, Abbot of Cherlieu, was being persecuted by Peter, Dean of Besançon, and had gone to Rome in order to put his case before the Pope. News of this fracas called forth the following letter from the Abbot of Clairvaux. Cherlieu was a daughter house of Clairvaux, founded 1131.

12

I HEAR such an account of the journey of the Abbot of Cherlieu that I regard him as if he were already dead. I am sorry to say that you especially are to blame for any danger that threatens him,[1] any trouble that he has to undergo. I did not expect this of you because I have not deserved it. I thought you were a different sort of person from what I find you to be. Those who were present at the affair testify that you did not conduct yourself either sincerely or honourably. I partly believe them, for neither is the Abbot of Beauvais very pleased with you. Do not, I beg of you, persecute the servants of God, of whom you read what he himself says: 'He that touches you, touches the apple of my eye'. Do not utterly uproot from my heart whatever good opinion I may have had of you. I have written in this way to you, not because I am not fond of you, but because I wish to remove any obstacle there may be to my affection for you. Speaking as a friend, I tell you that it would not do either you or your church any good if the Pope were to hear of how you have acted.

LETTER 254

TO POPE INNOCENT, CONCERNING THE MATTER OF THE ABOVE LETTER

I THINK that the injury done by the aggressor, the innocence of the sufferer, and callousness of the judge are sufficiently evident in the case which my dear friend Guy, Abbot of Cherlieu, is bringing before you. The poor man has been compelled by the violence of his opponents as well as by the impossibility of obtaining justice, to have recourse to you, despite the trouble and expense of the journey, and the danger of the times. This lover of quiet has been obliged to shake hands with death in order to preserve his peace. Look kindly, I beg you, upon this poor and needy man, and lend a fatherly ear to his complaints, lest such a great expenditure of slender resources be all in vain. I have twice written to you in the past of that man who is assailing the abbot, to testify that he was violating his profession and squandering the goods of his monastery. And now I grieve to tell you that he is an enemy of the cross of Christ, an oppressor of the holy men in his neighbourhood, and a deceiver of the poor. As he now has almost nothing of his own to waste, he descends upon his neighbours with force and makes free of their possessions. His monastic habit is a lie for, in fact, he is a robber, completely unmindful of regular observance, and utterly regardless of the canons. He is brazen faced, quite unscrupulous, impervious to piety, prone to anger, bold in crime, ready to inflict injury. I am most surprised that the abbot of Chaise-Dieu, a religious man, can overlook or be ignorant of so many great vices in one of his monks.

---

[1] The journey to Rome in those days could never have been easy and not always safe. A chronicle records how once an envoy to Rome fell into the hands of an anti-Pope and had his nose cut off.

2. But what has all this to do with me? Let him look to it: he stands or falls to his own Lord. For me it is enough to be liberated from his hands, and this is what I earnestly implore of you. I have attempted to achieve it in other ways, but without success. ' I have looked around, and there was none to help me.' It has come to the common refuge to which we all fly, there we are sure to be set free. Only let there be pity in the heart, for power is not lacking to the hand. It is clearly one of the privileges of the Apostolic See that, in the last resource, men should have recourse to your supreme authority and power. Indeed it is the rescue of the poor man from the clutches of the strong which, among all the other notable marks of your primacy, has rendered yours a glorious apostolate. To my mind there is no more precious jewel in your crown than that zeal with which you are wont to strive for the down-trodden and prevent ' the rule of the godless in the domain of the just ', doubtless because of what follows, ' else the just too might soil their hands with guilt ', or because of what is written elsewhere, ' The heart of the oppressed burns within them, when the schemer that has entrapped them is triumphant ', and the bodily torture of the one, is the spiritual loss of the other.

3. There is a monastery not far from here,[1] which is similarly harassed by the grievous assaults of evil men, and ' there is none to rescue it, none to bring it aid '. And for this also your child does not hesitate to besiege your heart with his sorrowful prayers. The abbot who bears this letter will explain truthfully by word of mouth who these men are and what is the occasion of their machinations. May the Omnipotent God preserve you for many years to be the protector of all of us who live a poor life in the garb of poverty and under the vows of repentance, that ' delivered from the hand of our enemies, we may serve him without fear '.

LETTER 255

TO THE SAME, ON THE SAME SUBJECT

FOR how long will the schemer triumph, and the heart of the oppressed burn within them? For how long will such great innocence be harassed by such arrant impudence? It must be due to our sins that my lord is so late to discover those who lie to him, so slow to hear those who call upon him in this matter. In other cases I know it is the custom of my lord quickly to apprize the situation and readily to render help. For the sake of him who has chosen you, and made you a refuge for the down-trodden, now at last put an end to the wickedness of the oppressor, and the troubles of the afflicted: both have been sufficiently shown up and exposed. At the command of my lord the affair has been discussed and settled; it only remains

[1] Clairfontaine?

that the results should receive the confirmation of your authority. Shall that man of lies be heard if he comes to you against the witness of such great men as the bishops of Valence and Grenoble? Again I supplicate you and cast myself down before you with the greatest anxiety possible lest you should suffer that religious monastery to be wrecked by a treacherous and cruel foe. For he who has nearly destroyed his own is not likely to spare ours. Therefore with my usual presumption I add: if you believe me, your child, send this man who abuses your kindness back into his cloister, and command the Lord Abbot of Chaise-Dieu that he promote a religious man to the position which he uselessly holds, and that he set the monastery in order according to the Rule. Clearly this would be a thing worthy of your apostolate, a thing pleasing to God; this would be for the honour of the Lord Abbot of Chaise-Dieu and his monastery. So also you would free the soul of that aforesaid man and the monastery which he burdens.

LETTER 256

TO MASTER ULGER, BISHOP OF ANGERS, CONCERNING A QUARREL BETWEEN HIMSELF AND THE ABBESS OF FONTEVRAULT

Bishop Ulger was a prelate of standing with a great reputation for learning and piety. In spite of the scandal caused by his quarrel with Petronella, the Abbess of Fontevrault, St. Bernard seems to have held him in high esteem. The date of this letter would be approximately 1140–1142.

TEARS are more in place than letters. But because charity need not be lacking to either the one or the other, I must supply the latter while not forgetting the former. The letter is for you, the tears for myself and other weaklings who, like myself, are scandalized. Perhaps you will say that the scandal has not come through you? But can you deny that it is on account of you? I could bear the rest if only you were not in the affair. I dare not say you are in the wrong. It is not my business to enquire into that; there is one above who will look into it and judge. Woe to that man through whom scandal comes, certainly he will be punished whoever he may be. But now I am addressing you. Bear with my foolishness for a little while. I have taken upon myself to speak unto my lord, and speak I will. I will sufficiently, even though only partially, satisfy the zeal and affection that inspire me. I will not fear the age of Master Ulger, I will not be overawed by his high position, I will not be deterred by his great name. The greater the name, the greater the scandal. Because of this I will overstep my limits, and act the fool. I shall scold a man older than myself; I shall call a bishop to book; I shall try to teach a Master, to give advice to a wise man. The love and emulation which I once conceived for the sanctity and glory of your reputation must not make me fear any sort of presumption. It is no small matter either for myself or for the Church, which used everywhere to rejoice with a great joy in your noon-day light, that the spiritual fragrance of your reputation should be lessened through the envy of the devil.

2. It is clear enough how little you value your own high standing. This is to your credit, but not if you carry it so far as to offend God. I also praise your firmness in not yielding even to the highest powers when you consider that your rights are at stake, but only if in being firm you do not act obstinately. How glorious, and certainly much more holy, it would be were you to endure with fortitude the infliction of an injury, and so 'keep your good name for the glory of God'. I cannot think how you can be sure that your conscience is safe in this scandal. Nor would it be any excuse to lay the blame of it at the door of another, even if you could rightly do so. Granted that another has stirred up the scandal, you could certainly suppress it if you wished. How could it be anything but honourable to do this, or anything but culpable not to do it? If the evil you suppress is your own doing, it shall be counted to you for righteousness to suppress it; if another's, for your honour. It is incumbent on you to demand the suppression of the scandal whoever the author of it may be; and you would only be free from blame for not doing so, if you could not. It is the work of angels to 'gather up all the scandals out of the kingdom of God'. If you should say that that is nothing to do with you, then you would stand rebuked by that sentence: 'No utterances like a priest's for learning; from no other lips will men expect true guidance; is he not an angel[1] to them from the Lord of Hosts?' Therefore you are clearly not fulfilling your ministry if you do not gather up this scandal when you can. And it is for you to judge whether this is no fault. But I would not say that even this alone would be enough, if you did not also honour it by your life.

3. There is another thing I would add were I not more timid than I set out to be. But it were safer to quote the Master who, being a bishop himself, does not fear to speak the naked truth to a bishop. 'There is a fault amongst you', he says, 'that you have lawsuits one with another. Why do you not rather suffer yourselves to be defrauded?' He has held a mirror up to you. The sun of justice has shone forth. The truth has appeared. The flaw has been shown up. Of what importance is that trivial and accursed little property that it should be able any longer to obscure such an obvious truth or to hinder such a needful correction? May God give you the light to follow the advice which comes not so much from me as from all those who are 'jealous with the jealousy of God' for your good name, reverend father, worthy of all honour.

---

[1] Literally 'messenger'.

LETTER 257[1]

TO ULGER, BISHOP OF ANGERS

To the reverend father Ulger, by the grace of God Bishop of Angers, and to his beloved in Christ the dean and chapter of the church of blessed Maur, the greetings and prayers of Brother Bernard, styled Abbot of Clairvaux.

I HAVE heard with sorrow that a serious and horrible deed has lately been done in your city. I sympathize both with him who suffered from it and with him who inflicted it, knowing that both are pitiable and both to be pitied. Presuming much on your forbearance I have deemed it necessary to admonish you on behalf of both parties. What could be more necessary for both than that by our zeal in the matter the one should be found ready to make humble satisfaction and the other ready and willing to forgive? And so I earnestly beg and implore you in the Lord to do all you can to make peace between them, so that both may be induced in some way or other to do their duty in the matter. And if this seems a long task, it is the business of you especially, my lord bishop, to see that the way of salvation remains open to the repentant man, and that, if he can only be absolved by the Pope, he has no difficulty in obtaining from you the necessary letters. That soul is entrusted to your care. I beg you to do all in your power to rescue him from his great danger and to signify to our lord the Pope the whole story of his misfortune so that he can receive his penance and bring back mercy.

LETTER 258

TO POPE INNOCENT, ON BEHALF OF ULGER, BISHOP OF ANGERS

To his most loving lord and father, Innocent, by the grace of God Supreme Pontiff, the humble devotion of Bernard of Clairvaux.

WHO but a man destitute of all sensibility and human feelings could look on the Bishop of Angers broken by age, troubles, and dangers, and not be moved? As for myself, I cannot see without emotion this aged man whose life and learning renders him so venerable, and to whom but one reproach attaches. Concerning this I can only say that I am ignorant of what has transpired between himself and the abbey, and do not presume to write anything on a matter about which I am not informed. But if it turns out that he has done what he promised, I do not think there is any other course open but to restore him to favour and his office.

---

[1] The Berlin State Library, Latin MSS., fol. 118.

LETTER 259

TO BALDWIN, ABBOT OF THE MONASTERY OF RIETI

I WAS much touched by the affection with which your letter was redolent, and I only regret that I cannot reply as I feel. But I will not delay over excuses for I know you understand. You know how great is the burden under which I groan; and ' my groans are not hidden from you '. You must not judge my affection for you by the brevity of my letter to you, for my affection could never be expressed by mere prolixity. The misfortune of my many occupations can curtail my letters to you, but they can never diminish my affection for you. My work can never exclude or impede my affection, though it may well hamper the expression of it. As the affection of a mother for her only son, so was mine for you when you were with me, delighting my heart by your presence. But I will also love you while absent from me, lest it should seem that my love for you was merely for the comfort I received from your company. You were most necessary to me; and from this it can be seen how sincere is my affection for you because, had I been seeking my own interests, I would not be lacking you to-day. Now you can see how, regardless of my own convenience, I did not begrudge you your gain when I placed you in a position whence you might sometime be set over all the goods of your Lord.

2. But do you take care to be found a faithful and prudent servant, supplying your fellow servants with heavenly bread without stint, and disbursing without sloth.[1] Do not make futile excuses about your being new to the office and inexperienced, which might be sincere or might not. Barren modesty is not acceptable nor is humility praiseworthy when it is not in accordance with the facts. Attend to your duty. Put aside all false modesty by considering your position. Act as a master. You may be a greenhorn, but you are also a debtor; you must have realized that when you bound yourself. Will your inexperience be any excuse to your creditor for his loss of gain? Does a money-lender allow the first years of his loan to pass without any profit? You say you have no capacity for these things. As though you would have to answer for what you cannot do as well as for what you can! No, prepare yourself to answer for the one talent entrusted to you, and set your mind easy about the rest. If you have received much, then give much; if little, then give little. He who is not faithful in small things, will not be so in great things. Give all, because all will be required of you down to the last farthing; but certainly only what you have, not what you have not.

---

[1] . . . *absque desidia erogare.* Eales: ' pray without ceasing '. *Erogare* in the sense of to pray is exceedingly rare. There is no example of it in the Vulgate. The apostolic injunction ' pray without ceasing ' is *sine intermissione orate.*

3. Remember to ' give to your voice the voice of power '. That is to say, see that your deeds accord with your words, or rather your words with your deeds, by being careful to practise before you preach. It is a beautiful and sound order of things that you should bear first yourself the burden you are to place upon others, and so learn from your own experience how to temper all things for other people. Otherwise you will be mocked by the Wise Man, as one ' too idle to put hand to mouth '; scolded by the Apostle when he says, ' Thou that teachest another, teachest not thyself', and branded with the fault of the Pharisees who ' bind heavy and insupportable burdens, and lay them on men's shoulders, but with a finger of their own they will not move them '. The example given is indeed ' a living and effectual word ', easily making what is said persuasive, by showing that what is ordered can be done. Therefore on these two commands of word and example, understand that the whole of your duty and the security of your conscience depends. But if you are wise you will add a third, and that is devotion to prayer, so as to fulfil that threefold repetition of the command in the Gospel of St. John to feed the sheep. You will find that you can only fulfil the demands of the threefold sacrament if you feed your sheep by word, by example, and with the fruit of holy prayer. And so there are these three: Word, Example, and Prayer, but the greatest of these is prayer. For although, as I have said, the ' power of the voice ' is example, yet to both example and word, prayer gives grace and efficacy. Alas! I am called, torn away. I may not write more. Let me however briefly admonish you to set me free as soon as you can of one heavy care, by remembering to explain more clearly what you meant when you complained, amongst other things, that someone whom you would never have expected has wounded you. This gives me much anxiety.

LETTER 260

TO THE CLERGY OF SENS

This letter appears to have been written soon after the death of Henry, Archbishop of Sens. He was succeeded by the precentor Hugh, surnamed Toucy, and not, as Eales says, by Hugh, the Abbot of Pontigny, who became Bishop of Auxerre. The date of this letter would be approximately 1144.

DEAREST friends, you must now set about finding a new pastor in the place of the one you have lost. This is not something to be undertaken hurriedly, confusedly, or inconsiderately. Unless you approach this matter in due order and with careful reflection, you may find that your action is rendered void, and that you are involved in the same wearisome round as so many of your neighbours. Let their experiences be a warning to you; from their troubles learn how to act in your present circumstances. It is no trivial matter you have on hand, it is nothing less than the replacement of the pastor of the noble church of Sens. Certainly this is not something to be undertaken lightly. Await the advice of the suffragan bishops; await the consent of the religious in the diocese; arrange this matter which concerns all with the help of all. Otherwise, believe me, we shall have the mortification of seeing your church in tribulation, the mortification of witnessing your confusion. All this could easily happen if you should chance to take any action which you would have to retract afterwards. Let a fast be proclaimed, let the bishops be summoned, let the religious be invited; and God forbid that you should deprive the election of such an exalted priest of its due solemnity. I am sure that the Holy Spirit will be present to your prayers and that you will be honoured for honouring your ministry, if with mutual consent and counsel you zealously seek the glory of God and the good of the people.

LETTER 261

TO ATTO, BISHOP OF TROYES

See also Letter 24, addressed to the same Atto.

To his lord the venerable Atto, by the grace of God Bishop of Troyes, whatever the prayers of a sinner can avail, from Bernard, the useless servant of the brethren at Clairvaux.

WE have often been visited by your charity and now through dear Brother G. we have received a repetition. The bishops marvel at your consideration for the poor and your devotion towards strangers. You must know that if those for whom you do this are unworthy, they are not ungrateful, although you do not seek thanks from us but from God. He places himself in your debt by making you a debtor to the wise and the foolish, since he regards whatever you do for his people as done for himself. For the rest, we desire that the above mentioned Brother G. may deserve well of your paternity for, according to the Scriptures, ' a wise son is the pride of his father '. If he is as good as he appears to be, we believe that you will be benefiting yourself by whatever you do for him.

LETTER 262

TO ATTO THE BISHOP AND TO THE CLERGY OF TROYES

' MY brethren, if any of you err from the truth, and one convert him, he must know that he who causeth a sinner to be converted from the error of his way, shall save his soul from death, and shall cover a multitude of sins.' Our friend Anselm is erring, certainly he is and there can be no doubt about it. If we let him go as he is, it will not be long before others follow him in his error. How many will not follow the example of such a distinguished youth! And, in my opinion, those who could recall him but don't are just as much to blame as he is. I am innocent of this man's blood. I have told him by letter what I now tell you: he is taking on himself to do what is not lawful. It is not lawful for the clergy to fight with the arms of soldiers, nor for a subdeacon to marry. Tell the sinner his duty lest he die in his sin; but he who redeemed him by his own precious blood shall require his blood of your hands. He cries from heaven: ' The virgin of Israel is cast down and there is none to raise her up '. How long will the gold lie in mud? Remove this pearl, remove, lift up from the dung-heap this most splendid and precious gem; lift it up before it is trodden under foot by swine, that is by unclean spirits, and is no more a vessel of honour but of dishonour.

LETTER 263

TO ATTO, BISHOP OF TROYES

A letter of remonstrance to his friend Atto, Bishop of Troyes, for having conferred the archidiaconate on a mere child. The conferring of benefices on children was a custom of the times which incurred the strong disapproval of the saint.

To the venerable lord and father, Atto, by the grace of God Bishop of Troyes, all the devotion possible of Brother Bernard.

YOUR kindly condescension is responsible for my confident plain-speaking to you when necessary. I intercede with you for your venerable son G., or rather I am taking it on myself to advise you for your own good with regard to him. I cherish your good name and wonder very much for what reason or by whose advice you have so unfortunately, as I think, ignored your duty with regard to the archidiaconate by conferring it on a mere child who cannot rule himself, in preference to your aforesaid son G., who can administer it very well. God forbid that you should undo again all that you have accomplished! But I have said enough to an understanding man. If you fear men, the Gospel will teach you whom you ought to fear even more. You wish to please men, yet you would do better to obey God; and if you ought to render to Caesar what is Caesar's, you ought also to render to God what is God's.

LETTER 264

TO POPE INNOCENT, ON BEHALF OF ATTO, BISHOP OF TROYES

With regard to the six following letters see the reference to Atto in Letter 158 to Pope Innocent.

I BEG that my lord of Troyes may be heard for the justice of his cause, I wish that such concord should be re-established between him and his clergy by your kindly zeal, that they shall no longer apply themselves to harassing unjustly the old man against whom they have no reasonable grounds for complaint. There is one insignificant youth amongst them who is most insolent and haughty, and I consider that the bishop had better trounce him than be trodden under foot by him. The bearer of this letter will tell you who he is. May you therefore, in your discretion, deal with this man and the others so that the bishop who has your honour at heart may himself be held in honour and never suffer for his justice. His innocence is his protection, but it should be seen to that he is not injured by the hatred of anyone.

LETTER 265

TO THE SAME, ON THE SAME SUBJECT

MAY every precaution be taken in the cause of my lord of Troyes that he may be honoured as he deserves and that his clergy may not be deprived of the justice that is their due. Let peace be restored between them and a bridle put on spiteful persons, so that they may never again be able to rise against their aged bishop.

LETTER 266

TO THE SAME, ON THE SAME SUBJECT

IT behoves you to be a friend of my friends and help Brother N. in the cause which he brings to you; but with discretion, so that the clergy may, if possible, be subjected to their bishop and yet not crushed by his justice, and that there may be peace between them.

LETTER 267

TO THE SAME, ON THE SAME SUBJECT

THE necessity of the lord Bishop of Troyes, a reverend old man and my friend, obliges me to have recourse to your unfailing mercy, which both my friends and myself have experienced so often. This is the demand I make upon it: that you may have pity on an old man, entitled by his age to be left in peace, and not permit him to be harassed; and that you may deign to grant the request which he is sending you by his messenger.

LETTER 268

TO THE SAME, ON THE SAME SUBJECT

WHEN, for my sake, my friends find favour in your sight, you increase your favours to me and multiply my honours. Yet I am not seeking favours or honours from any man, but only the Kingdom of God and his justice, and I believe the same is true of the Bishop of Troyes. I commend him to you with confidence on two accounts: both as a just man and as my friend. I equally commend to your charity the youth of excellent parts, and very dear to me, by whom he is sending this letter.

LETTER 269

TO THE SAME, ON THE SAME SUBJECT

I COMMEND to you the cause of my lord of Troyes and the messenger, a dear friend, who is bringing it. Take it in hand because, unless I am mistaken, it is just. He is a friend of myself, your friend. See that you do not listen to any tales against him, but rather help his cause and his messenger as much as you can.

LETTER 270

TO THE ABBOT OF ST. AUBIN

ALTHOUGH I have never met you, I have heard of you; and even from this I derive no small or insignificant pleasure. By means of it you have stolen my heart so that, amidst my many occupations, I am easily carried away by the peace-giving thought of you, and very willingly dwell upon it and refresh myself with it. And the more welcome the thought of you, the more eager is my desire to see you. But when will that be, if ever? At any rate in the city for God, if ' we have not here a lasting city, but seek one that is to come '. There we shall meet and our hearts rejoice. In the meantime I rejoice and am glad at all that I hear of you while waiting for my joy to be filled by the sight of you on the day of the Lord. I beg you, most dear and longed-for father, to add the prayers of yourself and your monks to the many things I am always receiving from you and hearing of you.

LETTER 271

TO THE BISHOP OF ROCHESTER

This letter was apparently written about the year 1142 after Ascelin had been consecrated Bishop of Rochester. It concerns one Robert Pullen, an Englishman of great learning and the first English cardinal. He reconstituted the schools of Oxford.

I HAVE not deserved your severe letter.   What have I done wrong? I advised Robert Pullen to spend some time in Paris for the sake of the sound doctrine which is known to be taught there, because I thought it necessary and I still do so.   I asked your Highness to permit this and would ask the same thing again, were I not sensible of your anger at my first petition.   I said that he was supported by many friends whose influence in the Curia was not small, because I feared for you and I still do so.   I did not think your action in seizing the goods of a man after he had appealed was a matter for praise, and I am still of the same opinion.   But I never advised him to go against your will, and I do not do so now.   I am your servant and am always ready to uphold and honour your authority with due and fitting reverence. On the strength of my good conscience in this affair I venture once more to advise and pray you to allow Master Robert to depart for a short time to Paris with your full favour.   May God reward you for your kindness to my children, I mean my sons whom I have sent to Ireland.

LETTER 272

TO THE QUEEN OF JERUSALEM

This letter is addressed to Melisande, daughter of Baldwin II, King of Jerusalem, and wife of Fulk V of Anjou.   In the year 1143 Fulk of Anjou died, leaving the kingdom to his widow Melisande during the minority of her son Baldwin III, a boy of twelve years of age.

MEN say that I have some influence with you, and many who are to set out for Jerusalem beg me to commend them to your Excellency.   Amongst whom there is this young man, a kinsman of mine; a youth strong, they say, in arms and polished in manners. And I am delighted that for the time being[1] he has chosen to fight for God rather than for the world.   Act according to your custom and, for my sake, see that all is well with him, as it has been for all my other kinsmen who were able to introduce themselves to you by means of myself.   For the rest, take care that the pleasures of the flesh and the glory of the world do not hinder your journey to the heavenly kingdom.   What profit is it to reign for a few days on earth, if the eternal kingdom is lost?   But I am confident in the Lord that you will do better than this.   And if it is true what my dear uncle Andrew says of you, and he is a man in whom I have every confidence, you will reign by the mercy of God both here and in eternity.   Take care of the pilgrims, the needy, and especially the prisoners,[2] for God is gained by such sacrifices.   Write to me often because it will not hurt you and it will benefit me to know fully and for certain of your state and dispositions.

[1] . . . *ad tempus.*   Eales: '. . . at his age '.
[2] *inclusis.*

LETTER 273

TO THE SAME

A letter written to Melisande on the death of Fulk, her husband.

To the most illustrious Queen of Jerusalem, Melisande, that she may find favour with the Lord, from Bernard, styled Abbot of Clairvaux.

WERE I only to regard the glory of your kingdom, your power, and your noble lineage, my writing to you amidst all the many cares and occupations of your royal court might seem rather inappropriate. All these things are seen by the eyes of men, and those who have not got them envy those who have and call them happy. But what happiness is there in possessing what will ' soon fade like the grass and wither away like the green leaf'? These things are good, but they are transient and changeable, passing and perishable, because they are the goods only of the body. And of the body and its goods it has been said: ' Mortal things are but grass, the glory of them is but grass in flower '. So, when writing to you, I must not hold in too much awe those things of which we know ' the comeliness to be vain, and the beauty a snare'. Receive, therefore, what I have to say in a few words, for although I have many things to say to you, I will do so briefly because of your many affairs and mine. Receive a brief but useful word of advice from a distant land, as a small seed which will bear a great harvest in time. Receive advice from a friend who is seeking your honour and not his own ends. No one can give you more loyal advice than one who loves you and not your possessions. The king, your husband, being dead, and the young king still unfit to discharge the affairs of a kingdom and fulfil the duty of a king, the eyes of all will be upon you, and on you alone the whole burden of the kingdom will rest. You must set your hand to great things and, although a woman, you must act as a man by doing all you have to do ' in a spirit prudent and strong '. You must arrange all things prudently and discreetly, so that all may judge you from your actions to be a king rather than a queen and so that the Gentiles may have no occasion for saying: Where is the king of Jerusalem? But you will say: Such things are beyond my power; they are great matters which far exceed my strength and my knowledge; they are the duties of a man and I am only a woman, weak in body, changeable of heart, not far-seeing in counsel nor accustomed to business. I know, my daughter, I know that these are great matters, but I also know that although the raging of the sea is great, the Lord is great in heaven. These are great affairs, but great too is our Lord, and great his power.

LETTER 274

To his beloved daughter Melisande, Queen of Jerusalem, the mercy of God our saviour, from Bernard, styled Abbot of Clairvaux.

I AM surprised that I have not had any letter from you or received any of your accustomed greetings for such a long time. I cannot forget your old affection for me which I have put to the proof in so many ways. I have heard certain evil reports of you, and although I do not completely believe them I am nevertheless sorry that your good name should be tarnished either by truth or falsehood. But my dear uncle Andrew has intervened with a letter signifying better things of you, and I cannot disbelieve anything he says. He tells me that you are behaving peacefully and kindly; that you are ruling yourself and your kingdom wisely with the advice of wise men; that you love the Brothers of the Temple and are on friendly terms with them; and that, according to the wisdom given you by God, you are providently and wisely meeting the dangers which threaten the Holy Land with sound counsels and help.[1] These are actions which become a strong woman, a humble widow, a great queen. It is not beneath your dignity as a queen to be a widow, and you need not be one if you do not wish it. I believe that it is much to your honour, especially among Christians, to live as a widow no less than as a queen. You are a queen by succession, but a widow by virtue. You are the former by reason of your lineage, the latter by the grace of God. You have the former by the good fortune of your birth, the latter you have obtained by courage. A double honour is yours, the one according to world, the other according to God: but both are from God. Do not think the honour of widowhood is a small thing, for the Apostle says: ' Honour widows that are widows indeed '.

2. You are familiar with the wholesome and sound advice of the Apostle by which you are taught to ' watch your behaviour not only before God, but also before men ': Before God as a widow, before men as a queen. Remember that you are a queen whose worthy and unworthy actions cannot be hidden under a bushel, but are set up on high for all men to see. Bear in mind that you are a widow whose concern it is to please not a man but God. Blessed are you if you make the Saviour a wall for the protection of your conscience, a breastwork to ward off disgrace. Blessed are you if, alone and a widow, you give yourself wholly to God to be ruled by him. Unless you are well ruled, you will not rule well. The Queen of the South

---

[1] The fact is that Melisande exposed the whole Latin Kingdom to the attacks of Zengi, the Emir of Mosul, by breaking the alliance made by Fulk with the Emir of Damascus. In 1144 Edessa, the bulwark of Jerusalem, was captured by Zengi.

came to hear the wisdom of Solomon, that she might learn how to be ruled and so how to rule. Now there is one greater than Solomon here: I speak of Jesus and him crucified. Give yourself unto him to be ruled, and to be taught how you ought to rule. Learn of him as a widow, for he is meek and humble of heart; learn of him as a queen, because he gives the poor redress and rights the wrongs of the defenceless. When you think of your dignity, bear in mind that you are a widow because, to speak plainly, you cannot be a good queen unless you are also a good widow. You ask how you can tell a good widow? From what the Apostle says: ' If she have brought up children, if she have given shelter, if she have washed the saints' feet, if she have ministered to them that suffer tribulation, if she have diligently followed every good work '. If you do these things ' blessed thou art and all good shall be thine '. May the Lord that dwells in Sion bless thee, renowned daughter in the Lord, worthy of all respect. I send my admonition first, now I shall expect an answer. I have given you an opportunity and shall take no excuse if our friendship is not renewed in future by frequent and friendly letters and messages from you.

LETTER 275

TO THE SAME

YOU see how greatly I presume on your goodness by daring to commend others to you, although my commendation of these Premonstratensian brothers is more likely to be superfluous than presumptuous. They are commendable enough on their own account without anything that I can say. Unless I am mistaken you will find them prudent men and of a fervent spirit, patient in troubles, and powerful in word and deed. They have put on the arms of God, and girded themselves with the sword of the spirit, which is the word of God, not against flesh and blood, but against the ' spirits of wickedness in the high places '. Receive them as peaceful warriors, gentle with men, relentless with devils. Or rather receive Christ in them, for he is the cause of their pilgrimage.

LETTER 276

TO ROGER, KING OF SICILY

By the time this letter was written (1139?) Roger had repented of his evil ways.[1]

YOUR renown has spread far and wide over the earth. Is there a corner of the world to which the glory of your name has not penetrated? But harken to the advice of one who loves you. If you do not wish to ruin your glory or to be ruined by it, endeavour, so far

---

[1] See note 2, p. 349.

as you can, to refer it all to him from whom it comes. You will do this by discerning between[1] those whom the fame of your royal magnificence calls from afar and by stretching out your hand not so much to the greedy as to the needy. Truly 'blessed is that man who takes thought' not for the greedy but 'for the poor and destitute': the poor man who only begs with reluctance, only accepts with diffidence, and glorifies his Father who is in heaven for what he has received. Since therefore the destitute will faithfully glorify God for your gifts to them, the fountain of glory must necessarily flow to you with a fuller stream, because he loves those who love him and glorifies those who glorify him and 'he who soweth in blessings, shall reap also in blessings'. For this reason I beg you to receive the bearer of this letter; certainly it is necessity and not greed that brings him into your presence. And not his own necessity but the necessity of his brethren, the many faithful servants of God by whom he has been sent. Listen patiently to what he has to say of their trials, and listen with fellow suffering, for 'if you suffer with them you shall also reign with them'. To reign with such men is no trivial matter even for a king, for theirs is the kingdom of heaven because they have rejected the life of the world. 'Make friends for yourself of the mammon of iniquity, that when you fail they may receive you into their everlasting dwellings.'

LETTER 277

TO THE SAME

This letter refers to the monks sent from Clairvaux in 1140 to make a foundation in Sicily.[2]

I F you are seeking me, here I am with the children God has given me. It is said that my humble person has found such favour with your royal Majesty that you desire to see me. And who am I to disregard the good-pleasure of a king? I hasten to you, and here am I whom you seek, not in weak bodily presence, the presence in which Herod mocked the Lord, but in my children; for who can separate me from them? Wherever they go, I will follow them: 'if they should come to rest at the furthest ends of the sea', there shall I be with them. You have, O king, the light of my eyes, you have my heart, and my soul. What does it matter if the least part of me is absent? I refer to my poor bit of a body, to that wretched slave which my soul would gladly

---

[1] *si inter eos, quos regiæ magnificentiæ celebris opinio evocat de longinquo, discretionis oculos apertis.* . . . Literally: 'if you open the eyes of discretion amongst those whom the celebrated renown of your royal magnificence summons from afar'.

[2] Although this foundation started well and under good auspices it does not appear to have prospered, and it seems at any rate possible that the former letter to Roger was written after the new foundation had begun to encounter difficulties and should therefore come after this letter and the one immediately following.

relinquish did not necessity retain it.   It cannot follow the willing soul because it is weak, and the tomb is almost all there is left for it. But why care? 'My soul shall dwell in joy, while my seed shall inherit the land.'   My seed is good seed.   It will bear fruit if it falls on good land.   My soul shall be filled with joy because, I trust, she shall receive the fruit of her labour.   This is the hope laid up in my heart, so that I can patiently bear to be parted even from these my sons. Do not wonder, O king.   I would sooner have been parted from my body than separated from these, if God alone had not been the reason. Receive them as strangers and pilgrims, yet nevertheless as fellow citizens of the saints and of God's household; rather I should say not merely citizens but kings, for by the right and title of poverty theirs is the kingdom of heaven.   It is not right that they should be summoned from afar to no purpose; that, exiles from their homes, they should wander on a useless pilgrimage.   Do not think that they can sing the songs of the Lord in a strange land.   But perhaps I should not call it a strange land which has opened its heart to the good seed and has already taken the precious trust to its loving bosom.   I see well that the good seed has fallen on good ground, nay the best ground, and I hope in the Lord that it will take root and germinate, and multiply, and bring forth fruit in patience.   Then I shall share this with the king, and every man shall receive according to his labour.

LETTER 278

TO THE SAME

You have got what you asked for and you have done what you promised.   You have received with royal liberality those whom I sent forth at your word to journey abroad.   You have 'brought out bread to meet them ', ' you have brought them out into a place of repose ', ' you have settled them in a country of high hills, where they can eat the food their own lands yield '.   These are material things, but they can be traded with in return for heavenly things. This is the way to heaven, by such sacrifices God is won.   For to these men belongs the kingdom of heaven and, in return for your material gifts, they will be able to render you everlasting life and glory. I have sent you Master Bruno, at one time my inseparable companion for many days,[1] now the father of many souls who rejoice in Christ but are destitute on earth.   May he too experience the open hand of the king, so that the number of his friends, who will receive him into their everlasting dwellings, may be increased.   What you do for him you do for me, because what he lacks is also my need.   But my purse is not at all adequate, so I have with reason made it my business to direct him towards yours which is obviously better filled than mine !

[1] *individuum comitem.*   Eales: ' . . the companion of my solitude '.

LETTER 279

TO AMEDEUS, ABBOT OF HAUTECOMBE

To his dear brother in the Lord Amedeus, the Abbot of Hautecombe, greetings and affection from Brother Bernard, styled Abbot of Clairvaux.

I BEG you to send for us to Montpellier either your father or some other intelligent messenger, so that he should arrive there on the octave of the Assumption of the Blessed Mary. For on that day, and in that place, there ought to be messengers from the King of Sicily, who ' go down to the sea in ships ' in order to bring the daughter of Count Theobald to the son of their lord. But if perchance they should have brought ships for our brothers and ask for the community we were to send them, then your messenger will excuse us in these words: ' The brothers were ready and the community prepared; but the lord Alfan, the messenger of the King of Sicily, said that the king only required two brothers, who were to go ahead of the others and see the place. But when it should please the king, he will make known to us his will concerning the sending of the whole community; since it is dangerous for the Order and for religion that brothers should live in a strange land without discipline and without the protection of either their abbot or their brethren.

LETTER 280

TO POPE INNOCENT

A letter in commendation of Samson de Mauvoisson, Archbishop of Rheims.

I COMMEND my lord of Rheims to your Highness, not as one in many, but as one unique amongst many. And I do this with all the greater confidence for being so sure of his loyal devotion, sincere affection, and his obedient and yielding disposition towards you. Let him be honoured for he is a vessel of honour. May you do what you can to make him feel that he does not honour his ministry in vain, that it is not in vain that he excels in those virtues by which God is honoured, the Church adorned, and which become a priest of the Lord.

LETTER 281

TO THE SAME, ON BEHALF OF THE ARCHBISHOP OF CANTERBURY AND THE BISHOP OF LONDON

M Y lord of Canterbury,[1] who is a good man and highly thought of by good people, has been unjustly involved in a dispute and is prevented by violence from defending himself in it. He was ready to start out for Rome (because the affair was to be terminated in your

[1] Theobald.

presence) when he was turned back by the storm and tempest of wars.[1] I beg you to excuse him, for he is much vexed by the necessity of excusing himself because he is confident in the justice of his case, and also because he wishes to see you. Your son ventures to add this also: if this venerable priest has any other petition to make, let it be granted the more speedily for his being so worthy. 'I have taken it upon me to speak to my lord, and speak I will': your old friend, loyal servant, and devoted son, Robert, Bishop of London, cries out to you for help because the intruder,[2] who occupied before him the see for which he has been chosen by the providence of God, has taken away the securities[3] and lands of the church, and will not return them. It is not for a person of my humble station to teach such wisdom as yours how damaging this is or how it should be corrected.

LETTER 282

TO THE SAME, ON BEHALF OF THE BISHOP OF SALAMANCA

The bishop referred to is Peter who, when his diocese was rent by a threefold schism, was summoned to Rome, and, together with the other leaders, degraded from his office.

THAT distinguished man, the former Bishop of Salamanca, did not consider it was too much trouble for him to turn aside on his way back from Rome to visit me, your child; nor did he consider it beneath his dignity to implore the help of myself, good-for-nothing though I be. When I heard what he had to say, I thought of those words of the Prophet: 'Every mountain and every hill shall be levelled'. This is your amusement, to level down the high-minded, to repress those who are swollen with pride, and to reduce the overbearing to their measure. When the man told me the whole story of his tragedy as it had happened, I had nothing but praise for the judge and approval for the judgement; but, I must tell you, I was moved by pity for the judged. The whole theme of his story was those words of the Prophet: 'I have been lifted up only to be cast down and left bewildered', and 'so low hast thou brought me who didst once lift me up on high'. When I thought of your justice and your strong character, which I used to know so well, I thought at the same time of your great mercy which I have experienced on so many occasions, and I said: 'Who can tell whether he will not relent and forgive, and leave behind him a blessing?' Certainly, I say, he is ready everywhere and always to be jealous and yet to forgive; 'to subdue the proud, and yet to spare the vanquished',[4] except that, after the example

---

[1] Between Stephen and Matilda.

[2] This was probably Anselm who was elected in 1134 and afterwards set aside. Robert succeeded in 1141, which would date this letter some time not long after that year.

[3] *vadia.* According to Du Cange *vadium* equals *vadimonium.* Eales: 'goods'.

[4] *Aen.* 6.853.

of his master, he is also wont to prefer mercy to justice. I consented with my usual presumption to speak to my lord, even I who am but dust and ashes. And I found grounds for hope, confidence for my petition, a reason for my pity, in that I saw the man did not, as is usual in such cases, turn away in fury, and return to his native land, there to stir up scandals and foment schisms; but that he gave place to wrath, adopted an attitude of meekness, and turned his steps towards your monks of Cluny there to throw himself at the knees of the humble monks and fortify himself with their intercession, as with powerful arms from God. With these weapons he is determined to strive with you, and with these engines of devotion he will try, as he declares, to undermine that wall of your severity by which he is confronted. He is sure that you will hear the prayers of the humble, and not spurn their intercession, and that you, before whom the princes of the world tremble, will be overcome by piety. I too with confidence stretch out my hands in company with such men, bow my knees before you, and supplicate for the supplicant. I boldly pronounce that this poor man who has already been hindered enough by his haughtiness, ought now to be helped by his humility; that it is not right for only vice and not virtue to receive its due.[1]

LETTER 283

TO THE SAME, ON BEHALF OF PETER OF PISA

The reconciliation of the Cardinal Priest Peter of Pisa to Innocent II at the height of the schism was one of the great personal triumphs of St. Bernard. He met him at Salerno and after addressing him a moving appeal in the presence of Roger of Sicily, he took him by the hand and led him off to Pope Innocent. There can be no doubt at all that Innocent pardoned him and confirmed him in his office. But Innocent in difficulties was a very different person from Innocent victorious as, much to his disappointment, St. Bernard was to discover. Hardly was the schism ended than Innocent, who before had been so reasonable and long-suffering, began reprisals, much to the very openly expressed indignation of the saint. At a council held at the Lateran during the April of 1139, all the supporters of the anti-Pope were ignominiously deprived of office without any distinction being made between those who had remained in schism right to the very end, so that it was not so much they who left the schism as the schism which left them, and those who, like Peter of Pisa, were reconciled with Innocent while the schism was still at its height. This letter must have been written soon after 1139, but unfortunately it appears that its only effect was to lose St. Bernard the friendship of the Pope. It was not until four years later, during the pontificate of Celestine II, that Peter was reinstated in his honours.

---

[1] Peter might have been reinstated in his office had not envoys from King Alfonso arrived in Rome in haste to obtain the see for a friend of the king.

WHO shall judge between us? If I had a judge before whom I could bring you, I would soon show you (I speak as one in travail) what you deserve. There is the tribunal of Christ, but God forbid that I should summon you before that, far sooner would I stand up and defend you there, should such a thing be necessary for you or possible for me. And so I hasten to him whose duty it is in the present time to judge all things, and that is yourself. I arraign you against yourself, to judge between yourself and myself. What, I ask you, have I, your son, done to deserve so ill of you that you must brand and blazon me with the name and stigma of a traitor? Were you not pleased to appoint me as your representative for the reconciliation of Peter of Pisa, should God deign through me to call him from the foul condition of schism? If you deny this, I can prove it by as many witnesses as there were men in the Curia at the time. And after this was not the man received back to his position and honours according to your plighted word? Who is it then who has advised you, or rather beguiled you to revoke what you had once granted, and to go back on the word your lips had uttered? I say this not to blame your severity, or the zeal with which you were fired by God against the schismatics, the zeal and severity with which you ' wrecked the ships of Tharsis ' and, after the example of Phinees, slew the fornicators, according to those words of the Prophet: ' Lord, do I not hate the men who hate thee, am I not sick at heart over their rebellion? ' But it is clear that the punishment ought to fit the crime, it ought not to be the same for a small sin as a great one, nor is it right that he who forsook the schism should fall under the same sentence as those whom the schism forsook. For the sake of him who, that he might spare sinners, did not spare himself, remove this reproach against me and, by re-installing him whom you have once installed, honour your first wise and unbiased decision. I have written to you on this matter before, but because I never received an answer, I suppose my letter did not reach you.

LETTER 284

TO THE SAME, IN COMMENDATION OF NICHOLAS, BISHOP OF CAMBRAI, AND ABBOT GOTTSCHALK

IF any care for me, if any memory of me at all survives in the heart of my lord, and if there remains the smallest way open for me to your old friendship, let that noble and humble man, Nicholas, Bishop of Cambrai, experience it. I confess that I am beholden to him and that I owe him all that I can do for him, not only because he honours me and mine whenever he can, but also because of his sincerity, meekness, and righteousness, which should also commend him even to you. And, unless I am very much mistaken, the men who trouble him are knaves and quite untruthful. But you will discover this for yourself without my labouring the matter in words. There is, moreover, with him, a religious and holy man, the Abbot Gottschalk, and on behalf of him likewise I implore you to hear his petition, if anything that I say can add to his deserts. I do not believe he would make any petition that would not be worthy of a hearing.

LETTER 285

TO THE SAME, ON BEHALF OF THE BISHOP OF AUXERRE

ALTHOUGH a person of no consequence, I am always writing to you; and on this occasion my boldness is provoked by the appeal of friends. I may be audacious, but I am not mendacious.[1] Let not my lord suspect me of lying in anything that I write to him. I wish to please my friends, but not at the cost of my soul. I know very well that it is written: 'Lying lips were ever the soul's destroying'. I certainly deny any falsehood, but not my importunity: let that find pardon, for the rest I do not fear. My lord of Auxerre is a friend of mine,[2] a special friend of mine. Everyone knows this. He can communicate his anxiety to me, but not any falsehood. We offer you a genuine excuse for his dean, and demand[3] that he be absolved. We are the sons of one father (to speak with my accustomed boldness), who is yourself. I am confident that the father will not turn his sons away but 'will do the will of them that fear him, will hear their prayer and save them'.

LETTER 286

TO THE SAME, ON BEHALF OF ALVISUS, BISHOP OF ARRAS

Alvisus had been a monk of St. Bertin, then Prior of St. Vedast at Arras, and finally Abbot of Anchin before becoming Bishop of Arras in 1131. He was a devoted admirer of St. Bernard and the Cistercians. It is possible that some of his troubles as bishop had come from his imbibing the reforming ideas of St. Bernard.

To his most loving father and lord, Innocent, by the grace of God Supreme Pontiff, the humble devotion of Bernard, styled Abbot of Clairvaux.

IT is nothing new or wonderful for the human mind to deceive or be deceived. Both must be guarded against because from both there is danger. Against both the Angel of great wisdom sets before you a safeguard when he said: 'Be ye wise as serpents and simple as doves'. Wisdom will prevent you from being deceived, and simplicity from

[1] *Fatior audax sum, sed non mendax.*
[2] Hugh, formerly Abbot of Pontigny.
[3] Rather a strong word for even St. Bernard to use towards the Pope, but the Latin seems no less strong: *absolutionem exigimus.* Eales: 'We ask for absolution for him'.

deceiving.   The monks of Marchiennes have come to you in a spirit of deception and error, against the Lord and against his anointed.[1] They have spoken evil against the Bishop of Arras whose good character and life is for all a sweet fragrance.   Who are these men who snarl like dogs, who call good bad, and who put darkness for light?   Who are these men, I ask, who, in despite of the law,' miscall the deaf, and put a stumbling-block in the blind man's way'?   Why, my lord, are you angry with your son?   Why have you filled his enemies with glee?   Do you not remember those words of the Apostle: ' Believe not every spirit, but try the spirits if they be of God '?   I have every confidence in the Lord that their schemes will be thwarted, and that ' when that which is true is come, that which is false shall be done away', so that ' malice will be self-betrayed'.   I have heard how steadfastly he has spoken before the king and princes in defence of the Roman Church.   He will come to you in his innocence on the day that you summon him, in the meantime he has sent before him his archdeacon, the bearer of this letter, whose person and character I commend to you.   There also comes to you the Abbot of St. Vedast, a man who is clearly an enemy to himself, to his own people, and to his church, a man unworthy to be an abbot, for he seeks his own ends and not those of Jesus Christ.   The son who comes with him is not different from his father.   He is a man who cares for neither his soul nor his good name, so that he has become an object of ' scorn and derision to his neighbours ': I speak of G., his monk.   May the Spirit of truth grant you the power to distinguish between light and darkness, to know evil from good.

LETTER 287

TO THE SAME, ON BEHALF OF A FRIEND

To his most loving lord and father, Innocent, by the grace of God Supreme Pontiff, the humble devotion of Bernard, styled Abbot of Clairvaux.

I WOULD not keep for myself the favour I enjoy in your sight.   I wish to share it with friends.   I have no fear that there will not be enough both for them and for myself.   I can share it with many, and yet suffer no loss myself.   What I have freely received, I freely give.   Your liberality makes me liberal, but liberal with what is yours.   I commend to you the bearer.   He is a most commendable person.   He is a friend of the poor of Christ, a servant of your servants.   If he has any petition to make of you, I beg that you may hear him with your accustomed kindness for my sake, or rather for his sake, for he is such a good man that he deserves to be heard on his own merits.

---

[1] Marchiennes was a Benedictine abbey, situated at Scarpe, in the diocese of Tournai.

LETTER 288

TO THE SAME, ON BEHALF OF A RELATION

The young man referred to in this letter is probably the same young man referred to by the saint in a letter to the Queen of Jerusalem.

THIS young man is, they say, a courageous and active soldier. He is setting out for Jerusalem to engage in a better sort of warfare. He asks me, your child, to obtain your encouragement, prayers, and blessing for the good work he has begun. He is a relation of mine and, according to the Prophet, I must not turn away from my own flesh and blood.

LETTER 289

TO THE SAME, ON BEHALF OF CERTAIN POOR MEN

I AM always writing to you. Every day brings you my letters and petitions. I am torn in two ways. I do not want to fail my friends on the one hand, and on the other, I am loath to trouble you. Affection spurs me on, diffidence holds me back, and shame almost prevents me from fulfilling the demands of charity. The bride of Christ has nowhere to lay her head, no refuge in time of trouble, save with the friend of the Bridegroom. These poor men you see before you have come on behalf of poor men through many perils by land and sea,[1] and seek a refuge under the shadow of your wings, and in the bosom of your apostolic pity, for they are troubled in many things and afflicted by wicked men in almost everything. If you are faithful to the duty and traditions of the Apostolic See, you will not disregard the complaints of the poor for the sake of humouring the powerful. I intercede with you for them because they are my brothers and of my Order, and I beg you to hear their prayer for the sake of their cause and for the love of him who does not spurn the prayers of the poor.

LETTER 290

TO THE SAME, ON BEHALF OF A MESSENGER

Now that charity has grown cold, it is rare to find anyone faithful; and because charity is so precious, the fidelity and love of N., who has most faithfully transacted your business with us, should be encouraged with favours and kindness. May all be well with him, for he is very dear to me both as a faithful man and a reliable messenger!

[1] From England perhaps?

LETTER 291

TO THE SAME, ON BEHALF OF A CERTAIN FRIEND

I HAVE been almost consumed by all the business which constantly rages at Rome like a fire, and long to be refreshed by the welcome and gratifying sight of your writing. But alas! as your child has already told you so often, there are not secretaries in all Clairvaux for the needs of your servant. May you show every kindness and affection to N., both for his own sake as well as for ours, for he is our friend and an illustrious lover of our person and our Order, who also faithfully transacts the business of his friends.

LETTER 292

TO THE SAME, ON BEHALF OF HIMSELF

To his most reverend lord and father Innocent, the humble devotion of Bernard.

I USED to think I was a person of some importance, even if it were not very much, but now 'I am brought to nothing, I am all ignorance, standing like a dumb beast before you'. Yet I would not say that I was then a complete nobody, since in those days the eyes of my lord were upon me and his ears were open to my prayers, he welcomed all I wrote to him and took it all in good part, and answered all my requests kindly and fully. But now I have good reason to describe myself as a person not merely of small account, but of no account whatsoever, because since yesterday and the day before my lord has averted his face from me. But why? What have I done wrong? Much, I admit, if the money of Cardinal Ivo was distributed according to my will and not according to his instructions, which is what I hear my lord has been told. But I am sure that you have learned the truth of the matter by now, and that the truth shall set me free. I am not so stupid as not to know that what Cardinal Ivo left no instructions about, becomes the property of the Church.

2. But now hear the plain truth. If I utter falsehood I shall be condemning myself out of my own mouth. When the man put off his mortal body, I was absent, in fact I was very far away. But I heard from those who were present at the time that he made a will; and what he did he caused to be written down. He divided what he wished of his goods amongst those whom he wished, and what was left over he entrusted to the two abbots who were then assisting him and to myself who was absent, to be distributed, because the poorer religious houses were known to us.[1] When the abbots returned home

---

[1] *eo quod nobis nota essent loca pauperiora sanctorum.* Literally: 'because the poorer places of the saints were known to us'.

and did not find me (I was detained at that time, according to your instructions, by the negotiations for peace), they nevertheless distributed the money as they thought best, not only without my consent but even without my knowledge.   Now, I beg you, let your anger give way before the truth; cease to regard me any longer with frowns and indignation, but let your countenance assume once more its accustomed serenity and bright joy.

3. As for the report I have heard about your displeasure at my many letters, there is no need for me to worry further about that for I can easily remedy it.   I know very well that I have presumed more than I should have done without paying sufficient heed to myself and to whom I was presuming to scribble; but you will not deny that it was your own kindness that fortified me with this boldness.   I was urged on by love for my friends for, if I remember aright, I wrote very little on my own behalf.   But there can be too much of a good thing.   In future I shall temper my zeal with prudence and place a seal upon my lips.   I would sooner offend some of my friends than the anointed of the Lord.   Also I have not dared at this time to write to you about the dangers that threaten the Church, about the great schism I fear, or about the many ills which we are enduring.   But I have written to the holy bishops who are in attendance on your person, and if you wish you can hear from them what I have written.

LETTER 293

TO THE THREE BISHOPS IN CURIA: ALBERIC OF OSTIA, STEPHEN OF PALESTRINA, HINCMAR OF TUSCULUM, AND TO GERARD THE CHANCELLOR

This is the letter referred to at the end of the one to Pope Innocent immediately preceding.   When, in the year 1142, the see of Bourges fell vacant, the king announced that the election of the chapter should be quite free, but at the same time he vetoed the election of Peter de la Châtre, who was the most likely and the most suitable candidate.   He took a public oath that so long as he lived Peter should not be Archbishop of Bourges.   In spite of this Peter was elected by the chapter and consecrated by the Pope himself.   When he returned to France the king, faithful to his oath, excluded him from his city. Peter took refuge with Count Theobald, and the Pope laid an interdict upon every place where the king set foot.   Thereupon the king considered yielding and St. Bernard wrote the following letter on his behalf.   Before the matter could be settled a further complication arose which will be explained by the subsequent letters.

THE notorious and horrible death of those men whom, in the past, the earth swallowed up and sent down alive into hell because of the scourge of schism, plainly shows how great an evil in the Church is schism and how it should be avoided by every possible means.   The same thing is shown by the persecution of Guibert and the foolhardiness of Burdin,[1] whom we have experienced inflicting in our own times an almost incurable wound and a cruel chastisement on us by setting the State against the Church. It is shown also by that Leonine madness[2] from which we have just been delivered by the mercy of God, after untold damage and loss to the Church. Well does our Saviour say in the Gospel, ' Woe to that man through whom the scandal cometh ', and woe also to us who live lamenting what we suffer, deploring what we feel, and dreading what we fear. And, what is worse, human affairs have come to such a pass that the guilty will not be humbled and the judges will not show mercy. We say to the wicked, ' Rebel no more; and to the transgressor, Abate your pride' and they will not listen ' for they are all rebels '. We implore those whose business it is to reprove sin and save the sinner, not to break the bruised reed, not to extinguish the smoking flax, and all the more they ' break up the ships of Tharsis with a violent wind '.

2. When, with the Apostle, we cry out to sons that they should obey their fathers in all things, we might as well be beating the air. When we tell fathers not to be provoked to anger by their sons, we turn their anger upon ourselves. Sinners will not make satisfaction, rulers and magistrates will not show forbearance. All follow their own sweet will and break the rope of unity by pulling it with all their might in different ways. The recent wound of the Church has hardly healed before they make ready to tear it open again, to nail the body of Christ again upon the cross, to pierce again his innocent side, to divide again his raiment, and, as far as they can, but in vain, they try again to rend his coat without seam. If you have hearts that can be moved by pity, do all in your power to combat these evils, lest a schism break out in the land where, as you well know, schism is wont to be healed. If the man by whom scandal comes is specially stricken by a great curse from the mouth of the judge, what blessings will not they deserve who combat and put to flight this evil?

3. For two things I cannot excuse the king. He took an oath unlawfully and he kept it unjustly. But the last he has done not willingly, but because he was ashamed to break it. As you well know, it is considered a disgrace by the French to break an oath however ill-advisedly it may have been taken, although no wise man can doubt that unlawful oaths ought not to be kept. Yet even so I cannot admit that he is to be excused in the matter. But I have undertaken to obtain pardon for him, not to excuse him. It is for you to consider whether, on the grounds of his youth, anger, or station, he can be excused. He could be without doubt if you would let mercy triumph

---

[1] Guibert, Bishop of Ravenna, set up by Henry IV as an anti-pope in opposition to Gregory VII. Burdin, Archbishop of Braga, was intruded into the Roman See by Henry V, and compelled by Calixtus II to retire to the monastery of Cava.
[2] The schism of Peter Leonis.

over justice, taking into account that he is a mere youth, albeit a king, and thus deserving of leniency on the understanding that he will not presume on it in future. I would say: let him be spared if it can be done without prejudice to the liberties of the Church, or to the reverence due to the archbishop who was consecrated by the Apostolic hands. This is what the king himself humbly begs for, and what our afflicted Church on this side of the Alps implores. Otherwise we join hands with death, pining and withering away for dread of what we fear will come upon the world. This has been my prayer for the last year; and, because my sins have called for it, my petition has met, nct with attention, but with anger, and the desolation of almost the whole world has followed on the anger. If in my zeal I have allowed some expressions to burst from my lips which ought not to have been said or which ought to have been said differently, ignore them, I beg you, but do not ignore what I have said when it has been well and rightly said.

LETTER 294

TO POPE INNOCENT, CONCERNING THE MARRIAGE OF RALPH, COUNT OF VERMANDOIS

Ralph, Count of Vermandois and seneschal to the King of France, had married Leonora, a niece of Theobald, Count of Champagne. Tiring of his wife, Ralph began to turn his attentions to Petronilla, the sister of Queen Eleanor of France, as a more attractive and more advantageous match for himself. In this he had the full support of the king. The difficulty was how to dispose of his first marriage. For this purpose he made use of an old ruse by pleading that his marriage with Leonora was invalid owing to the bar of consanguinity. The matter was submitted to the Bishops of Tournai, Senlis, and Laon; and they, in deference to the king, upheld the plea of Ralph. St. Bernard took the matter up and wrote the following letter to the Pope. The Pope ordered the matter to be submitted to a council. The council to decide the matter was convoked at Lagny, near Paris, in the year 1142, and was presided over by Cardinal Ivo, the legate of the Pope. This council upheld the first marriage of Ralph, declared his second marriage to Petronilla void, and laid his territory under an interdict. The king was furious and invaded the territory of Theobald, laying waste the countryside and burning the townships. The outcry against this brutal behaviour was such that the king began to feel qualms and declared that he would evacuate the territory of Theobald if the Pope would lift his interdict on Ralph. St. Bernard then wrote to the Pope another letter advising a policy which has been considered by some to savour more of the serpent's astuteness than the dove's simplicity.

IT is written: 'What God has joined together let no man put asunder'. But shameless men have arisen who, despite the law of God, have not scrupled to separate what God has joined together.

Nor is this all. They have gone further and added one sin to another by uniting what should not be united. The sacred rites of the Church have been violated and the robes of Christ have been torn, and to make matters worse this has been done by those very persons whose business it ought to be to mend them. ' Thy friends, O God, stand against thee now ', for they who are breaking thy commandment are not outsiders, they are the men who to-day hold the place of those to whom it was said, ' If you love me, keep my commandments '. God joined together the Count Ralph and his wife through the ministers of the Church, and the Church through God who gave such powers to men. How then can a court separate those whom the Church has thus joined together? The sole and very convenient provision made in this matter was that the dark deed should be done in darkness. Those who do evil hate the light and avoid it, so that the evil which they do should not be shown up by the light. Why has Count Theobald deserved this? What has he done amiss? If it be a sin to love righteousness and hate iniquity, then he would be without excuse. If it be wrong to render to the king what is the king's and to God what is God's, then he would have no excuse. If at your command he gave asylum to the Archbishop of Bourges, this is his first and greatest sin.[1] This is the crime for which he is answering! Those who render evil for good, abuse him because his actions are good. Many are imploring you from their hearts that you should suitably avenge this injury done to your son and that you, who are able to act in the matter as you please, should restrain with your apostolic authority the perpetrators of this crime and their leader so that their wickedness may fall upon their own heads.

LETTER 295

TO THE SAME, ON THE SAME SUBJECT

DISTRESS and troubles are upon us! The earth shivers and shakes at the death of men, the banishment of the poor, and also the imprisonment of the rich. Religion itself is being brought into contempt and shame. Even to mention peace amongst us is counted a disgrace. Nowhere is faith, nowhere is innocence safe. That great lover of innocence and piety, the Count Theobald, is almost at the mercy of his enemies. ' He has reeled under the blow and well nigh fallen, but still the Lord is there to aid him ', and he is glad to be suffering for the sake of justice and his obedience to you, because of those words of the Apostle, ' If you suffer anything for justice' sake, blessed are you ', and, ' Blessed are they that suffer persecution for justice' sake '.

[1] This was Peter de la Châtre whom the Pope consecrated Archbishop of Bourges, disregarding the king's veto and remarking that he was too young to judge of these matters and had need of instruction. The king refused to acknowledge Peter as archbishop and forbade him entry into his city. At this, the Pope asked Theobald to shelter him and excommunicated the king.

All this I was able to see, but alas! not able to prevent.   What more is there to say?   So that the whole land should not be laid waste, and the whole kingdom, being divided against itself, fall, that most devoted son of yours and lover and defender of the liberties of the Church has been obliged under oath to have lifted that sentence of excommunication and interdict which was promulgated by your legate Ivo of happy memory against the person and territory of the tyrant who is the head and author of all these ills and sorrows, and also against the adulteress.   The aforesaid prince did this at the entreaty and on the advice of some loyal and wise men.   For they said it would be easy to obtain from you, without harm to the Church, a renewal and irrevocable confirmation of the same sentence which had been justly passed in the first place.[1]   Thus artifice would be outwitted by artifice, and peace obtained without the tyrant who ' takes pride in his own malice, in his own ill-doing ' gaining anything.   I have much to say to you, but there is no need to write everything, since there is present to you one who knows everything I want to say, and can explain it all to you more fully and more clearly by word of mouth than I can in a letter.

LETTER 296

TO LOUIS, KING OF FRANCE

You yourself deign to admit, and your own conscience bears witness, that I gladly do and will do all that is within my small power for your honour and for the good of your realm.   But as for the complaint you make to your humble servant about the anathema which is to be renewed against Count Ralph, and the wish you express that I should do all I can to prevent it on account of the many evils which you think will come from it, I cannot at all see how I can do this and go against the Apostolic mandate; and, even if I could, I do not see how it would be reasonable for me to do it.   I am sorry about the evils which you fear, but all the same I cannot do evil that good may come of it.   It is more satisfactory and safer to leave all this to the judgement and providence of Almighty God who can bring to pass and preserve the good he wishes, and either prevent the evil which wicked men are trying to bring about or at any rate see that it falls upon the heads of those who wish it and seek it.

2. But there is one thing in the letter of your Highness that greatly grieves me, namely that this anathema will conflict with the peace which has been arranged between yourself and Count Theobald. Do you not realize how great was your offence in obliging Count Theobald, by the violence of the war you waged against him, to take an oath contrary to God and all justice that he would not only seek

---

[1] Whatever may be thought of this advice, it should be noted that the saint only quotes it, and does not give it.

but also obtain an undeserved and unlawful absolution of the interdict on Count Ralph and his lands? Why do you want to add one sin upon another and heap up the wrath of God against yourself? What has Count Theobald done to deserve this recurrence of your anger? He obtained with great difficulty and trouble the absolution of Count Ralph although, as you very well know, it was quite undeserved and, so far from seeking or ever having sought its most just renewal, for fear of you he has even protested against it. Do not, my lord king, do not, I beg you, dare to resist so flagrantly your King, or rather the Creator of all, in his kingdom and territory, and with such rash and repeated audacity to raise your hand against the terrible one, even him who is ' feared by awestruck princes, feared among all the kings of the earth '. I have spoken to you sharply because I fear sharper things for you, and I would not fear them so much were I not so fond of you.

LETTER 297

TO THE SAME

G OD knows how fond of you I have been ever since I first knew you, and how I have always wanted your honour. You too know with what anxiety and trouble I, with other faithful servants of yours, have striven during the last year to obtain peace for you. But I begin to fear that we have laboured in vain, for it is evident that you are too ready to kick aside frivolously and hastily the good and sound advice you receive; and, under I know not what devilish advice, to hasten back while their scars are still fresh to your former evil ways, which with good reason you were only lately deploring. From whom but the devil could this advice come under which you are acting, advice which causes burnings upon burnings,[1] and slaughter upon slaughter, and the voice of the poor and the groans of captives and the blood of the slain to echo once more in the ears of the Father of orphans and the Judge of widows ? Clearly the ancient enemy of our race is delighted with this hecatomb of slaughtered men, because ' he was a murderer from the beginning '. Do not try to ' cover sin with smooth names ' by citing Count Theobald as a futile pretext for your wrongdoing, for he says that he is ready and indeed very willing to abide by the terms which were arranged between you both when peace was made, and that he is prepared to make immediate satisfaction in everything if those who love your name, that is to say the mediators between you both, should find him to have offended your honour in any way, which he does not think he has.

2. But you will not receive any peaceful overtures or keep your own truce or accept sound advice. On the contrary, by some

---

[1] When the king invaded the territory of Count Theobald he committed untold atrocities. One village he burned to the ground with its inhabitants, and even to this day it is known as Vitré-le-Brûlé.

mysterious judgement of God, you insist on turning everything round so perversely that you deem disgrace to be honour and honour to be disgrace and fear what is safe and scorn what you should fear. According to the rebuke that Joab gave the holy and glorious king David, you have 'nothing but love for your enemies and nothing but hatred for your friends'. Those who are urging you to repeat your former wrongdoing against an innocent person are seeking in this not your honour but their own convenience, or rather not so much their convenience as the will of the devil; they are trying to use the power of the king to secure the mad purposes which they are not sure of being able to achieve by themselves, and are clearly the enemies of your crown and the disturbers of your realm.

3. But whatever you may be pleased to do with your own kingdom, crown, and soul, we, the sons of the Church, cannot overlook the injuries, contempt, and ignominy to which you have subjected our mother, and we perceive that all this, besides what we grieve that she has already had to suffer from you, is partly being inflicted on her again and partly threatened. Certainly we shall make a stand and, if necessary, fight even to the death for our mother with the weapons that are permitted to us, that is with prayers and lamentations to God, not with shields and swords. And, for my part, besides the daily prayers which, God is my witness, I offer in supplication for peace, for your kingdom, and for your salvation, I have also endeavoured to further your cause with the Holy See by letters and messengers almost, I must admit, against my conscience and, I cannot deny, even to the extent of arousing against myself the just anger of the Supreme Pontiff. But now I tell you that, provoked by the constant excesses you commit almost daily, I am beginning to regret having stupidly favoured your youth more than I should have done, and I am determined that in future to the best of my limited capacity I shall expose the whole truth about you.

4. I shall not withhold the fact that you are again trying to make common cause with excommunicated persons, that I hear you are associating with robbers and thieves in the slaughter of men, the burning of homesteads, the destruction of churches, and the scattering of the poor, according to those words of the Prophet, 'Swift art thou to welcome the thief who crosses thy path, to throw in thy lot with adulterers'; as if you are not able to do evil enough by yourself! I shall not conceal the fact that you have not even now corrected that unlawful and accursed oath you took against the church of Bourges, on account of which so many evils have arisen; that you do not allow a pastor to care for the sheep of Christ at Châlons; and moreover that you billet your brother and his soldiers, archers, and cross-bowmen in the houses of the bishops against all right and justice, thereby rashly exposing the property of the Church to be squandered in

13

disgraceful uses of this kind. I tell you, you will not remain long unpunished if you continue in this way. Therefore, my lord king, I admonish you in a friendly way and strongly advise you to give up your evil practices immediately, so that, like the King of Nineveh, you may be able to placate by humility and penance the wrath of God, if perhaps he is even now preparing to strike you. I have spoken harshly because I fear an even harsher fate for you. But bear in mind those words of the Wise Man: ' Better the love that scourges, than hate's false kiss '.

LETTER 298

TO JOCELIN, BISHOP OF SOISSONS, AND SUGER, ABBOT OF ST. DENIS

The subterfuge referred to in Letter 295 had the unfortunate result that such devices usually have. The king, finding that he had been tricked, renewed his attack against Count Theobald with greater fury. In the following letter St. Bernard remonstrates with the councillors of the king.

I WROTE to the king to rebuke him for the wrongs which are being committed in his realm with, I understand, his consent; and I deem it proper to submit his reply to you who are in his council. It is strange if he believes what he says; and, if he does not, how can he expect me to believe it when, as you very well know, I am aware of all that has been done for the re-establishment of peace? For, in an effort to try and show that the count has not kept his agreement, he says, as you can read in his letter: ' Our bishops still remain suspended, our land is still under an interdict '. As if it were within the power of the count to absolve from any ecclesiastical interdict whatsoever or as if he had ever undertaken to do so! ' Count Ralph ', he says, ' has been hoodwinked, and again cast off.'[1] But what has this to do with Count Theobald? Did he not faithfully exert himself in the matter of his promise, and successfully fulfil it? But the king has been caught by his own cunning and fallen into the pit he had himself dug. This is the whole reason why he would denounce the agreement which you vouched for with your own lips. Is it fitting that on this account the wrath of the king should flare up against God and his Church, against himself and his kingdom? Must he on account of this so far forget his honour as to send his brother to vanquish one of his own vassals with whom he had not broken off relations,[2] or even warned or reasoned with, and that too through Châlons, concerning which city in particular the king, as you know, had made an arrangement with Count Theobald ?

2. But the king adds that the count is trying to ally himself by marriage[3] to the Counts of Flanders and Soissons, against his fealty.

[1] In fact this is precisely what was done.

[2] . . . *quem non dico* diffidavit, *sed nec submonuit vel posuit ad rationem.*

[3] The Count of Flanders had betrothed his daughter to Henry, the son of Count Theobald. And Count Theobald was contemplating a betrothal between his daughter and the Count of Soissons.

That the count is doing this against his fealty is not a certainty, but a mere suspicion. You can form your own opinion on the morality of allowing a sure agreement to be prejudiced by a mere empty suspicion. Such a thing is not at all to be believed of a man like Count Theobald. They are not enemies of the king with whom the count is trying to ally himself, but rather his vassals and friends. Is not the Count of Flanders the king's kinsman by blood and an acknowledged supporter of his realm? How then does his vassal and faithful friend act against the allegiance he owes to his king if he allies himself to other friends of his king by matrimony? If the matter is regarded objectively, would not such an alliance seem rather to make for the peace, strength, and greater security of the realm?

3. But I am very surprised that the king should dare to say that he is aware of the fact that I know of Count Theobald's plan to attract Count Ralph to his side against himself. For, saying more to my messenger than he wrote in his letter, he declared that I have often confided to Count Ralph that I would take the larger part of his sins upon myself if he would support Count Theobald. If the man exists to whom I have given any such message, let him come out into the open and accuse me. If I have said it in writing, let the letter be produced. The king should take heed whom he is believing in this matter. I have no knowledge at all of what he alleges and the same is true of Count Theobald, he denies that he knows anything of it. Let God see and judge how Count Theobald is accused on mere suspicion by a man who, in defiance of the commandments of God and the decrees of the Supreme Pontiff, has consorted with an excommunicated person and adulterer, by openly flouting his solemn engagements and allying himself with Count Ralph.

4. The king says: 'I almost had on my hands two strong opponents'. To this the Prophet mockingly retorts: 'Fear unmans him where he has no cause for fear'. 'See', says the king, 'how I who have attacked no one am being attacked myself; how I who have persecuted no one am myself persecuted.' Who, I ask, is attacking him? Who is persecuting him? Is not Count Theobald entreating him and humbling himself before him? Is he not prepared to render him homage as his king, and to serve and obey him as his liege lord, while begging for peace and doing all he can to conciliate him? But supposing this were not the case, but that on the contrary it was the count committing all this evil against the king, should not the king have had recourse to what you are well aware has been arranged? For they made a covenant together that if any quarrel or controversy should arise out of the matters they had agreed upon, they would neither of them do or try to do any wrong to each other until the matter had been discussed and ventilated before us three and his lordship of Auxerre, for we were then the mediators and if any quarrel arose we

ought to have been the arbitrators. But this is just what Count Theobald is begging for and the king refusing.

5. Finally, supposing Count Theobald has deserved these evils at the hand of the king, what has the Church of God done to deserve them? What has not only the church of Bourges done, but also the churches of Châlons, Rheims, and even Paris? Suppose the king has some claim against Count Theobald, has he therefore any right to lay waste the territory and possessions of the Church, and to forbid the shepherds of Christ's sheep to care for their flocks? Has he any right to deny to some the promotion to which they are entitled by their election, and in other cases to postpone the elections until he has swallowed up everything, gorged himself with the patrimony of the poor, and laid waste the territory, which is a thing hitherto unheard of? Is it you who have advised this? It would be passing strange if the king has done this against your advice, but still more strange and mischievous if he has done it by your advice. Certainly to advise such outrages is to contrive schism, to resist God, and to make a tool of the Church and reduce her once more slavery. Any servant of God, any son of the Church, should certainly do what he can to oppose this and stand out like a wall in defence of the house of God. And you, how can you, if indeed you do desire the peace of the Church, if indeed you are the sons of peace, I do not say commit such evil things, but have any part in them by your advice. For whatever wrongs are committed, they are quite rightly attributed, not to the young king, but to his elderly advisers.

LETTER 299

TO JOCELIN, BISHOP OF SOISSONS

The saint denies in the following letter that he ever called either the Abbot of St. Denis or Jocelin of Soissons a schismatic or fomenter of scandal. It is certainly true that he did not do so, not in so many words.

I DO not think I have in me anything at all of the spirit of blasphemy, and I know that I have never cursed or wished to curse anyone, least of all a prince of my people. Notwithstanding this I do beg your pardon for whatever it is that I have done by which you consider yourself to have been hurt. I know who it is that says: 'We are blasphemed and we entreat'. Therefore I say with blessed Job: 'I have spoken the word I would fain unsay; more I dare not'. I thought that I had answered you both and done enough when I wrote to the Abbot of St. Denis concerning your common complaint. But because I see that your anger has not yet cooled, anger which would perhaps be more suitably turned against those who are treading the Church under foot, I say to you also: I neither said nor wrote nor

believed that you were a schismatic or a fomenter of scandal, and I say
this with complete ease of mind without any fear whatsoever that
my letter will accuse me of lying.   Examine it if you wish, and if
you find therein anything to bear you out I will confess myself guilty
of grave sacrilege and admit that I did, even as you remark, write it
while disturbed by the spirit of blasphemy.

2. But a humble apology must not exclude the spirit of liberty.
I confess I have grieved and still do grieve that I have yet to hear of
you avenging the injuries of Christ with that liberty which would so
well become you.   This grief compelled me to write to you severely,
but not to write what you say I did.   I thought (and I would still
think so were I not fearful of being troublesome to you) that it is not
at all enough for you simply not to have been the author of the
schism, unless you also hold in abhorrence those who are (whatever
their dignity) and shun their company and counsels.   I would consider
it very much to your credit if you could say: ' I have shunned the
company of the wicked, never sat at my ease with sinners '.   Does
that zeal only become the prophet, or is not the priest of the Lord
required also to say to-day: ' Lord, do I not hate the men who hate
thee, am I not sick at heart over their rebellion? '   Certainly I could
have wished (if I may say this without disrespect to you) that you had
shown some of this zeal towards that boy the king who has flouted
both your advice and his agreement for no reason at all.   He is
disturbing without cause his whole realm, he is stirring up war everywhere, he is devastating churches, desecrating holy things, setting up
on high impious persons, persecuting the good, and slaughtering the
innocent.   These are the things I would have you grieve over, these
are the things I would have you condemn and oppose for all you are
worth.   It is not for me to teach my master Jocelin, still less to call to
book a bishop, it is rather for him to rebuke me and other sinners and
to correct the erring.   See how much I fear you!   You looked askance
at my last letter because it was sent open, so you will have this one
closed.   But I had no other intention in not sealing with wax according
to custom my last letter than what is usual for those who address one
letter to different persons.   Now I ask your pardon for this also.

LETTER 300

TO STEPHEN OF PALESTRINA

Stephen was a Cistercian.   In the year 1140 *he was created Cardinal
Bishop of Palestrina, and he died in* 1144.   *From a phrase in the following
letter it would appear that he was born at Châlons.*

JEREMIAS said, when speaking of his ene mies to God, ' Bethink thee
how I ever stood up before thee to p lead for them, to avert thy

anger from them. Henceforth leave their children to famish or give them up to butchery', and more in the same vein. I remind your Reverence of this because I seem to be in rather the same plight as the Prophet. You know how I have stood up for the king to my lord the Pope; how absent in body yet present in spirit I spoke out on his behalf. Indeed the king made fair promises. But now he is returning evil for good, and so I am obliged to write in a contrary vein. I am ashamed of the mistake I made about him and of the false hopes I cherished of him, and I am very glad that I was not listened to when, in my simplicity, I spoke for him. I thought to serve a peace-loving king, and I find that I have helped a bitter antagonist of the Church. The Church amongst us is being crushed under foot and made to serve vile ends. Episcopal elections are forbidden; and whenever the clergy dare to hold one, their chosen candidate is prevented from fulfilling the duties of his office. The church of Paris is sorrowful because she is deprived of her pastor, and no one dares to utter so much as a whisper about finding another.

2. But the king is not satisfied with despoiling the episcopal residence of the goods they may have at the time, he must needs lift his sacrilegious hand even against the lands and men around by claiming from each the revenues of the whole year for himself. Your church of Châlons has indeed held an election, but the chosen candidate has been defrauded for a long time of his due honours and, as you know, this cannot be done without serious harm to the flock of the Lord. The king has charged his brother Robert with the administration of the diocese; and he, exercising episcopal powers over all the territory and goods of the church, is energetically offering sacrifices every day, but they are not the sacrifices of peace, they are the cries of the poor, the tears of widows, the lamentations of orphans, the sighs of captives, and the blood of the slaughtered. But he finds the bishopric a sphere far too small for his wickedness, and so he has fallen upon the church of Rheims and carried his evil into the land of the saints without sparing either clergy, monks, or nuns. The words 'They think to make God's sanctuary their spoil' are always being heard on all sides. So does the king improve on the evil he did at Bourges with his Herod-like oath.

3. The king, when we had taken some little trouble in the matter, made peace with Count Theobald and what we believed to be a firm pact of friendship. But he is now seeking excuses to be rid of his friend. He makes it an heinous charge against the count that he is arranging matrimonial alliances for his children with the barons of the king. This extension of charity[1] is held suspect by the king, he thinks that he is no king if the chiefs of his realm love each other. You can

---

[1] *Suspecta est illi dilatatio charitatis.* Eales: 'A loosening of friendship is suspected by the king in this'.

estimate the sort of dispositions he has towards his subjects when he considers himself to be all the stronger if there should be hatred and discord amongst them.   You can see for yourself and judge if this king is a man of God, who has put his trust in hostility rather than in charity, when God is charity.   He would not at all do this if he had the wisdom of him who said: ' Not death itself is so strong as love, not the grave itself so cruel as jealousy '.   He breaks his covenants of peace and openly oversteps the terms he has made, neither does he keep the promises his lips have uttered.   Lastly, he has recalled to his household and council an adulterous and excommunicated man whom he had undertaken to banish.   According to those words of the Prophet, ' Swift art thou to welcome the thief who crosses thy path, to throw in thy lot with the adulterer ', the king and defender of the Church has allied himself with many other wicked and excommunicated persons, perjurers, incendiaries, murderers, so as to commit even greater mischief against one who, without any doubt, truly loves and protects the Church.

4. In addition to all this, the king has obliged, after his own manner, bishops to curse those who should be blessed and to bless those who should be cursed.   And because not all will do as he wishes in this matter, he encompasses land and sea to find men ready to perjure themselves so that man may put asunder those whom God has joined together.   I ask you, how has he got the effrontery to try so hard to lay down laws for others about consanguinity when it is clear that he himself is living with his cousin within the third degree?[1]   I have never knowingly praised illicit marriage and do not do so now, indeed I do not know whether there exists any consanguinity between the son of Count Theobald and the daughter of the Count of Flanders or between the Count of Soissons and the daughter of Count Theobald; but understand this and see that my lord understands it too: the Church would be deprived of much protection and strength if these nuptials were to be forbidden when they could be in any way lawfully held.   I do not suppose that those who oppose these nuptials have any other intention than that of preventing those who are withstanding the threatened schism from finding a refuge in the territories of the aforenamed princes.   Thus far does my zeal carry me.   I am not able to correct the faults which I have been able to point out, but I am able to warn him who can.   The zeal of my lord can do this.   So I thought it necessary for him to be informed of this great trouble and danger of the Church, and I know of no one better able to do this than you who are united to him, not only in bodily presence, but also in spirit.   I pray you make my excuses to him for my change of tone

[1] The consanguinity between the king and Eleanor his wife is thus explained by John Besly in his *History of France*: Eleanor was the daughter of William Count of Aquitaine.   Aldeardis, great grandmother of Eleanor, was sister to the wife of Humbert II, Count of St. Jean de Maurienne, and so aunt to Adela, mother of King Louis.

in writing about the king who has changed, for you know what the Prophet of God said to God: ' With the innocent man thou shalt be innocent, and with the perverse man thou shalt be perverse '.

LETTER 301

TO JOCELIN, BISHOP OF SOISSONS

WE have worked hard, but it is questionable whether we have made any progress. We have sowed much, but gathered little. We confess that your presence and co-operation are needed. Our common friend, the Abbot of St. Denis, will tell you why we have not sought your help in our difficulties before now. We admonish you to cease dissembling, and to begin working for peace with the wisdom which God has given you. There ought to be no need to ask you to do this, since it is not only evident that your ministry would be greatly honoured by it, but also that it would be disgraced by your failure to do so. We hope to see you at the celebration to be held at St. Denis.

LETTER 302

TO LOUIS, KING OF FRANCE

To Louis, by the grace of God illustrious King of France and Duke of Aquitaine, that he may love righteousness and judge his land with wisdom, from Hugh, Bishop of Auxerre,[1] his humble servant, and Bernard, styled Abbot of Clairvaux.

IT is a long time since we set aside our own affairs and left our homes in order loyally, as God is our witness, to work for your peace and the peace of your realm. But we are sad that there should be no fruit to show for all our labour, or at the most only very little. The poor are still crying after us, and the desolation of the land increases every day. Do you ask what land? Your land and none other. It is in your realm and against your realm that all this mischief is being done; for, whether they be your friends or your foes who are reduced to poverty, led captive, and trodden under foot in this war, they are still your people in your realm. We see in this those words of the Saviour being even now fulfilled: ' Every kingdom divided against itself shall be brought to desolation '. On the top of all this, those who are dividing the land and rendering it desolate acclaim you as their head and leader in this wickedness, you whom they ought to fear as the protector and experience as the avenger of your people. But we were hoping that you had been touched and enlightened by the grace of God so as to see this wickedness, recognize your mistake, and wish to withdraw your foot from the snare with the help of saner counsels.

[1] Hugh of Mâcon, one of the first disciples of St. Bernard, Abbot of Pontigny, and then Bishop of Auxerre from 1136 to 1151.

2. However we lost almost all hope at the conference we lately had together at Corbeil. You know how unreasonably (if you will pardon our saying so) you withdrew from us on that occasion. Your annoyance allowed us no opportunity for clearly explaining what had displeased you in our discourse. If you had but deigned to wait calmly for this, even you might have perhaps recognized that nothing was said unbecoming or unsupportable to you, in the present state of your affairs. But as it is, being yourself annoyed without cause, you are keeping us too, who only desire and seek your good, on tenterhooks, anxious and doubtful about what we should do. What has upset you is nothing else than the fraud of wicked men and the idle chatter of silly people who do not know good from evil or evil from good. But although we are anxious, we do not entirely despair of the help of the Spirit whom we feel has wholesomely smitten your heart with remorse for past evils. We are still hoping that you may search your heart and successfully finish what you have prudently begun. For this reason we have sent you our most dear brother Andrew[1] of Baudimont, who will explain all this to you by word of mouth and truthfully report back to us what you may be pleased to answer. But if you persist in refusing good advice, then we are innocent of your blood. God will not allow his Church to be trodden under foot much longer, either by you or by your minions.

LETTER 303

TO JOCELIN, BISHOP OF SOISSONS

It is not clear what the saint is asking for in this letter, but from the last sentence it appears that it is some help for persons in trouble. Doubtless it is something arising out of the difficulties with which the former letters are concerned.

I HAVE never been able to dispense with the help of friends, for I am a pitiful object both in mind and body. But now especially do I need help and pity, for, goaded by my conscience and weighed down under the hand of God, I have given myself up to a hard prison and am sitting in harsh judgement on myself.[2] If you are still my father, as I admit you used to be, let your son experience it, that son who still cherishes for you a warm affection. I know, I know full well, how hard it is to wrest the club from the hand of Hercules, and I am the more insistent because I am asking for something difficult. The more difficult it is, the more earnestly do I try and deserve it. If I obtain it, I shall confess myself in your debt for a great, for a very great kindness. I know it is more blessed to give than to receive, but I yield to necessity,

---

[1] The procurator (what we would now call ' agent ') of Count Theobald.
[2] The seclusion of his monastery.

I go to meet danger, in my straits I take counsel, and I now openly ignore or forget my self-respect. I yield the more honourable rôle to you, as is only right, and I take for myself the more modest part by being not only shameless in receiving, but even more importunate in asking. I ask you humbly, I ask you urgently, I ask you in season and out of season. I am not asking you for anything it would not be right for you to give, or that I would afterwards regret having received; although it is not very becoming in me to ask for it now in this way. If you set the poor man free from the hand of the powerful, you will be rendering me a great service and yourself a greater. I have now made known to you how I feel, you know what it is I want, and the afflicted now await the results.

LETTER 304

TO POPE CELESTINE

Innocent II died in the year 1143, and was succeeded by Celestine II.

COUNT Theobald is a son of peace and what he asks for, I ask for too. He has a great zeal for peace, but asks you to carry it into effect. Yours is an apostolate of peace, your position obliges you to seek peace. All men desire peace, few deserve it. Your son admits that he is amongst those who desire peace, but whether or not he is amongst those who deserve it is for you to judge. Even if neither the count nor myself deserve it, the plight of the Church, the bride of Christ, demands it. The friend of the Bridegroom will not sadden the bride. The care of all the churches belongs solely to the Apostolic See that they may be all united under her and in her; its charge is to preserve the unity of all in the bonds of peace. Give us peace, send us peace. Although we may not deserve it, you owe it to the Church.[1] This for you is as good as a command.

LETTER 305

TO PETER THE VENERABLE, ABBOT OF CLUNY

It would certainly not be surprising if relations between the Abbot of Clairvaux and the Abbot of Cluny had become rather strained as a result of the rivalry between the two Orders, the dispute over the election at Langres, and the exemption of the Cistercians from paying tithe; and the following letter seems to indicate that this had indeed been the case. But the Benedictine editor of the letters refuses to admit that there had been any estrangement between the two men, and maintains that St. Bernard was writing only facetiously and rhetorically.

[1] . . . *etsi non quia debetis, certe quia obedire debetis.* Eales, literally: ' . . . if not to acquit yourself of an obligation towards us, at least because you ought to obey (the duty imposed upon you) '.

To the reverend father and lord Peter, by the grace of God Abbot of Cluny, the humble devotion of Bernard, styled Abbot of Clairvaux.

So you are pleased to jest? Courteously and kindly I would admit, if I could be sure you were not ridiculing me. Do not be surprised at my saying this, for your sudden and unexpected urbanity makes me a little uneasy. It is not so long ago that I greeted you in a letter with all the respect that is your due, yet you never answered one word. And it is not long since I wrote to you again from Rome, but even then I did not get a reply. Are you therefore surprised that I did not presume to trouble you with my trifles when you got back from Spain? If it is blameworthy not to have written for some reason or other, how can you be free of blame for having neglected, not to say disdained, to write in answer to my letters? So you see what I might urge in justice on my behalf (for that is what you implored me to do), if I did not prefer to welcome your renewal of favour towards me rather than to delay it by futile excuses or accusations. I have only said this so as to be quite open with you and not to keep anything back from you, for this true friendship demands. Because charity believeth all things, I have put away all my misgivings and am glad that you have warmed to the memory of an old friendship, and recalled a wounded friend. Being recalled I am happy to return, happy to be recalled. I have now put out of mind all grievances. Here I am, now as ever, your devoted servant, and full of gratitude for being once more your intimate friend, as you were kind enough to write. If I had perhaps grown cold towards you, as you reproach me for having done, there is no doubt that cherished by your love I shall soon grow warm again.

2. I welcomed your letter with open hands. I have read it and re-read it greedily and gladly, and the more often I read it the better pleased I am. I must say I enjoy your fun. It is both pleasantly gay and seriously grave. I do not know how it is you are able to be both gay and grave, so that your fun has nothing about it of frivolity, and your dignity loses nothing by your gaiety. You are able to keep your dignity so well in the midst of your fun that those words of the holy man might be applied to you: 'I smiled on them though they were never so ill at ease, and the encouragement of my glance never failed them'. So you see I have answered you, and now I think I am entitled to demand more than you promised! It is only right that you should know how things are going with me. I have decided to stay in my monastery and not go out, except once a year for the general chapter of Abbots at Cîteaux. Here, supported by your prayers and consoled by your good will, I shall remain for the few days that are left to me in which to fight, 'until the time comes for me to be relieved at my post'. May God be merciful and never alienate his mercy or your prayers from me. I am broken in body and have a

legitimate excuse for not going about as I used to do. I shall sit still and hold my peace, so that perhaps I may experience something of that inner sweetness of which the Prophet sings: 'If deliverance thou wouldst have from the Lord, in silence await it'. And, so as not to appear the only one to make fun of me, I suppose you will not now dare to reproach me with my silence and, in the way you have, to call it sloth! As a matter of fact I think Isaias has more suitably and properly called it ' the service of righteousness '; and, inspired by God, he also says, 'In quietness and in confidence lies your strength'. Commend me to the prayers of your holy brethren at Cluny having first, if you think fit, greeted them from me as the servant of them all.[1]

PETER THE VENERABLE TO ST. BERNARD

IN a very long reply to the Abbot of Clairvaux (Benedictine Edition, 229), Peter, in a most affectionate greeting expresses his delight with Bernard's last letter and describes how he could not refrain from kissing it before he read it out to his brethren. He excuses himself from the charge of not answering Bernard's letters on the grounds that the letter from Rome was in reply to one of his, and that he has no recollection of the previous letter. He then goes on to express his regrets for the mutual distrust and rancour which was dividing the monks of their two Orders. He attributes this first to the difference between their customs, and declares that it is childish and stupid, because quite unreasonable, to allow such things to cause any ill-feeling. If such differences in customs and observances were a valid reason for quarrelling there would be no charity left anywhere. The Church herself has a hundred different customs and usages in various parts of the world. ' What ', he asks, ' does it matter if monks, united by one profession, should observe different customs, so long as all alike attain to eternal life?' As for their different interpretations of the Rule, the Rule itself allows the greatest liberty to the abbot in the ordering and arranging of all things for the salvation of souls. In fact this is all that matters, the salvation of souls; and for this we should cultivate that single eye which renders the whole body full of light. He then urges his own monks who have adopted certain mitigations in the letter of the Rule, but not against the mind of the legislator, to cultivate this single eye which regards solely, not the mote in another's eye, but the glory of God and the salvation of souls. He prays that his Cistercian brethren may do the same and not scorn their Cluniac brothers, who, like them, are seeking only God's glory and the salvation of souls. As for the different colour of their habits, it were sheer folly to quarrel about such a trivial thing. Yet he had seen black monks looking askance at their white-robed brethren of Cîteaux, and vice versa! As if both white and black were not sheep of the same heavenly shepherd! What human shepherd, not to say God, would ever quarrel about the different colour of his sheep's wool? It is not the colour of the habit that matters, but the colour of the soul. The Rule itself allows the greatest latitude in the matter and enjoins the brethren not to grumble about the colour of their habits, but to be content with whatever can be got most cheaply. In fact there are excellent reasons and ample authorities for both the black habit and the white habit. In any case no one could be so stupid as to think that diversity of colours or customs could make any difference to the salvation of souls. In conclusion, Peter remarks that the real root of all the trouble between the two Orders is the dismay felt by his own black monks at seeing the tide of fashion turn

---

[1] *Commendate me orationibus sancti conventus Cluniacensis, salutato prius ex me servo omnium, si dignum judicatis.* Eales more literally: ' Commend me to the prayers of your sacred convent of Cluny; salute it first from me, the servant of all, if you think fit '.

against their venerable institution and the white monks, who are only a new Order, preferred to them everywhere. To this he replies by pleading for mutual tolerance and respect. He implores his black monks to abase themselves before their white-robed brethren for the love of Christ, and he prays that the white monks may put aside any censoriousness and humble themselves before their Cluniac brethren, and in accordance with the Rule they both claim to follow, ' not only to say in word that they are lower and more vile than all, but to believe it in the depths of their hearts '.

This letter from Peter the Venerable impresses one as the letter of a great and magnanimous man to whom all pettiness would be quite foreign and incomprehensible.

In another letter (Benedictine Edition, 264), Peter, after greeting the Abbot of Clairvaux as the great and glorious pillar of the monastic Order, and indeed of the whole Church, goes on to say that, if he were free to order his life according to his pleasure, he would choose to live with Bernard rather than to be a king amongst men. He calls Bernard a fellow citizen of the saints in heaven and once more repeats his great desire to be always with him, or at least to see him often. But as neither of these things is possible Peter asks whether he might be allowed, as the next best thing, to enjoy Bernard's presence in the person of his beloved secretary Nicholas. This Nicholas is none other than that notorious secretary of Bernard who, having insinuated himself into the confidence of his abbot and of Peter, finally fled from Clairvaux after grave misconduct, taking with him Bernard's personal seal.

LETTER 306

TO PETER THE VENERABLE, ABBOT OF CLUNY

O YOU good man, what have you done? You have praised a sinner, you have numbered a good-for-nothing amongst the blessed! You must now pray that I shall not be led into error. I should be led into error if, in my delight at such great praises, I were to forget the sort of person I am. This almost did happen when I read the letter in which you made me out to be blessed. If words could do that, how happy I would be. Even now I would call myself happy, but by your favour not by my own deserts. Happy to be loved by you and happy in loving you. Although I do not think that even that tit-bit, sweet as it is, can be swallowed whole or even, as they say, admitted to the teeth. Do you wonder why? It is because I can find nothing in myself to deserve such affection, especially from such a man as you. I know that a just man will never wish to be loved more than he deserves. Would that I could imitate as well as I can admire such humility. Would that I could enjoy your company, I do not say always, nor even often, but just once or twice in a year! It could not but be profitable for me to see such an example of all the virtues, such a model of regular observance, such a mirror of sanctity, nor would it be in vain that I should see with the eye of faith how meek and humble you are, which I admit is a thing I have not even yet learned from Christ. But if I go on to do to you what I complain of your doing to me, although I should

speak the truth, yet I would violate that rule of truth which says:
'Never do to another what you would not have done to yourself'.
And so I will now answer the trifling request with which you concluded
your letter. He for whom you have asked is not with me now, but
with the Bishop of Auxerre. I am told he is so ill that he cannot come
to us without grave inconvenience.

LETTER 307

TO THE SAME

YOUR son Galcher has now become ours, according to those words:
'All my things are thine and thine are mine'. Let him not be
loved any the less for his belonging to us both; but if possible let him
be loved all the more, and be all the more esteemed by me because he
belongs to you, and by you because he belongs to me.

LETTER 308

TO THE SAME

To his most reverend father and dear friend Peter, by the grace of God
Abbot of Cluny, health and greetings in the source of all true health,
from Brother Bernard, styled Abbot of Clairvaux.

WOULD that I were able to express in this letter all that I feel towards
you! Then you would certainly see clearly the love for you
which God has inscribed upon my heart and engraved upon my very
bones. But what need is there for me to commend myself to you in
this way? For a long time now we have been united in the closest
friendship, and an equal affection has rendered us equals. What could
a person of my lowly attainments have in common with a man like
you, if you were not so tolerant of my limitations? Thus it has
come about that both my lowliness and your magnanimity have been
so blended that I could not be lowly without you nor you
magnanimous without me. I say this because my son Nicholas,
who is your son too, is himself greatly disturbed and has greatly
disturbed me by telling me that he noticed that one of my letters to
you concluded with bitter words. Believe me who love you that
nothing could have come from my heart or left my lips which would
have offended your ears. My many occupations are to blame, because
when my secretaries have not fully grasped my meaning they are apt to
write too sharply, and I do not have time to read through what they
have written. Forgive me this time, for whatever I may do with
other letters, I shall in future look through my letters to you and trust
no one's ears or eyes but my own. The rest will be more fully and
more clearly recounted to you by our common son. Harken to him

as you would to myself who love you so dearly, not in mere words, but in deed and truth. Greet for me all your holy brethren, and pray them to pray for me.

PETER THE VENERABLE'S REPLY

PETER answers the preceding letter from St. Bernard with the utmost cordiality and affection (Benedictine Edition, 388). He disclaims all the high titles that the saint gives him and retains only that of 'dear friend'. As for the bitter words for which the saint apologized (they were in a letter concerning the business of an English abbot), Peter declares that he was not in the least offended by them, and if he had been the apology of Bernard would have been a more than ample amend. After this Peter refers to the will of one Baro, a Roman subdeacon. He says that although all that he had deposited at Cluny belonged by right to the abbey, yet he is quite willing for Bernard and his brethren to have it. In conclusion he refers to an election at Grenoble to which the Carthusians were objecting. He says that he has entrusted his opinion on the affair to Nicholas and asks Bernard to accept what Nicholas tells him as coming from himself.

LETTER 309

TO PETER THE VENERABLE

To his most dear father and lord Peter, by the grace of God Abbot of Cluny, health and greetings from Brother Bernard, styled Abbot of Clairvaux.

WHEN your letter first arrived I was only able to take a short but very affectionate glance at it. I was busy at the time with so many things as you alone know or can know, most loving father. Yet I tore myself away and escaped from the ceaseless questions and petitions of everyone, and shut myself up alone with Nicholas, of whom you are so fond. There I refreshed myself again and again with the charm which emanated from your letter. So fragrant was it with affection that my heart was moved. I was sorry, that, as I was situated, I could not sit down there and then to answer you. My many daily duties were calling me. A great crowd of people from almost every nation under the sun had arrived to see me. I had to attend to them all because for my sins I am born to be embarrassed and consumed with many and manifold cares. In the meantime I am scribbling this short note, but when I have more leisure I will write a careful letter expressing my sentiments more clearly. What you sent us from that will, we assure you in all sincerity, we have received not as a debt but as a gift. I am very glad to hear the truth about the Grenoble affair. I must tell you that my heart glowed at the words of our common son which you in part related to me.[1] I am ready and prepared to do your will wherever I can. At the chapter of abbots at Cîteaux a commemoration was made of you as our special lord,

[1] Guy, Prior of the Grande Chartreuse.

father, and very dear friend, and of all yours, living and dead. The elect of Beauvais greets you as your friend, which he is.

And I Nicholas add my undying affection for you and for all your household.

LETTER 310

TO THE BISHOPS OF OSTIA, TUSCULUM, AND PALESTRINA, ON BEHALF OF THE ABBOT OF LAGNY

Lagny was a renowned and rich abbey on the Marne, in the diocese of Paris. The abbot on behalf of whom the saint wrote the following letter was one Ralph, who was formerly Abbot of St. Nicholas in the Vosges. He was appointed as Abbot of Lagny by Count Theobald on the advice of St. Norbert.

To you I can venture to say whatever comes into my mouth. You must endure my foolishness for a while, and I am sure that your benevolence, which makes you debtors both to the wise and foolish, will enable you to bear with me. I am not saying this because I am thinking of breaking out into speech which would be beside the point, or because I intend to be frivolous, or because I want to be facetious, especially in writing to you who are columns of the Church; but because grief is stirring up the truth that lies within me impatient of restraint and my over-full heart is welling up into speech. For, I tell you, when I see evil by a cursed reversal of things everywhere overcoming wisdom, 'I come near to losing my foothold, feel the ground sink under my steps'. Everywhere the impious gain strength, and zeal for righteousness is disarmed. There is no one, I do not say who wishes to do any good, but who can do any good. The proud are working as much wickedness as they like and no one dares to whisper against it. Would that even innocence were safe, and righteousness were able to defend itself. What wrong has the Abbot of Lagny done? Is it his trouble that he is a good monk and a better abbot or that his reputation is good and his life even better? Or is it that he has adorned his monastery with a good observance, has increased its revenues, and filled it with a number of good brethren? Behold the crime which is laid at his door! If it is a crime to be loved by both God and man, then let him be taken away and crucified! No one can deny that he is this, heaven and earth bear witness to it. If it is a crime to be hospitable, kind, sober, chaste, and humble, then 'let him go away from his adversary's presence empty handed', for this cannot be denied of him, the holiness of his life and the lustre of his reputation are irrefutable witnesses.

2. It is alleged against him that he was unwilling to receive the messenger of my lord the Pope. Certainly a great offence, if it is true. The abbot does not deny that a man who was being sent over to England, after he had been honourably received asked to speak with

him, but as he was preparing to go out at the time, his prior, Humbert, offered to go and see the man in his abbot's place. I leave it to your judgement who was to blame, if there was any want of respect in the treatment this man received. He is also accused of violently seizing a letter of the lord Pope from the said Humbert and tearing it up. But the letter still exists whole and with its seal intact. The prior did not part with it under duress, as is falsely alleged, but under the advice of Count Theobald and myself he gave it up spontaneously. It is also said that he has imprisoned some monks. This too is false. All he did was to separate certain troublesome and scheming monks into different cloisters, believing that they would do less harm like that than if they were together; and who in his senses can blame him for this? As to the charge that he has squandered and alienated the property and goods of his monastery and given it to his relations, this has already been sufficiently answered in the presence of the Bishops of Soissons and Auxerre, with Count Theobald acting as the advocate of the monastery, but I will answer it again by saying that he gave to his relations just as he gave to others, that is according to the same measure and custom.

4. It is a thing never heard of before that a rebellious, proud, and ambitious monk should deserve to have his liberty by a privilege of the Apostolic See. From the time of Judas none have been found to rise against his master and betray innocent blood like this monk. Happy the master who can share with the Master the implication of those prophetic words: 'The very man I trusted most, my own intimate friend, who shared my bread, has lifted his heel to trip me up'. At one time this man used to lord it over the clergy against the teaching of the apostle Peter, and he also exercised dominion over the faith of the whole world against the teaching of Peter's co-apostle Paul. And now he has added something more to this by usurping to himself the same prerogative against religion itself. What remains for him to do but to lord it over the very angels? This last Judas seems to have surpassed the first in cunning and deceit, inasmuch as the first horrified all his co-apostles by his crime, whereas this one has been crafty enough to persuade not just anyone but the very chiefs of the apostles to wink at or rather to favour his wickedness. I do not blame my lord Pope, like any other man he can be deceived; and I pray that God may not blame him. But may it be far from him to permit the execrable and sacrilegious endeavours of this evil person to prevail, after he has learned the truth. With my usual audacity I would have written to him also about this matter, were I not aware that he receives what I write to him with less than his wonted favour. Do you, who are yourselves monks, weep for your master Benedict for, as you see, he is being thwarted in almost every direction, even to the destruction of almost all the force of monastic observance by monks who are able to oppose their abbots with a strong hand.

LETTER 311

TO THE SAME

IF the things which you hear about the Abbot of St. Theofred are true[1] you cannot ignore them without danger, both on account of your office and on account of your conscience. The conscience, I say, not only of yourself, but also of others. They are certainly likely to be true and I, for my part, believe they are true, because the bearer of this letter testifies to them, and he is a truthful man. You ask how I know all this? I have a pile of letters all from holy men, men whom I know to be holy and truthful, and all of them are as eloquent in praise of the bearer as they are vehement in denouncing the horrid blasphemies of the abbot whom he is accusing.

LETTER 312

TO JOHN, ABBOT OF BUZAY, WHO HAD LEFT HIS ABBEY AND BETAKEN HIMSELF TO SOLITUDE

The abbey of Buzay was founded in 1135 by Conan III, Duke of Brittany, at the request of his mother, Ermengarde. It was situated on the left bank of the Loire, in the diocese of Nantes.

To his very dear son John, that he may live by the Spirit and depart not from the fear of God, from Brother Bernard.

I CANNOT say with how great a bitterness of soul and sadness of heart I write to you, dearest John, now that I see that, for all my letters, I have made no progress with you, because my words have no effect on you. Unless I am mistaken, I have already written to you twice, and for my sins my labour has brought me no response from you. Now a third time I cast my seed, praying Almighty God that it may not return empty but flourish and accomplish its purpose by making my heart glad at last with the fruit of your obedience and salvation. If you hear me, or rather if God hears me, I shall have won my son; if not I shall betake myself once more to my accustomed arms, that is to prayers and lamentations, not against you but for you. I have shed bitter tears and shall continue to do so, and to heave heavy sighs from the bottom of my heart for him whom my heart loves. Who will grant me that you, my brother, may return once more to the bosom of our mother? Who will bring you back for me into that peace of soul, that community of life, brotherhood of spirit, and serenity of conscience in which I once held and possessed you?

2. Lest anything on my side should be causing you loss and holding you back, let me tell you that it is not true what I hear you have been

---

[1] St. Theofred was a monastery in the diocese of Le Puy—not Pau, as Eales says.

induced to believe, namely that I am thinking of removing you without reason or trial from the rule of souls which I have entrusted to you. This is not true, but hear in a few words what is true. If I had wished to do this, it would not have been lawful; and even if it had been lawful, I would never have wished to do it. If this is all that turns your heart from me, now that you have learned the truth, nothing remains for you but to recover your senses, search your heart, come back to us, and moreover rebuke yourself for your levity and heedless cruelty. If it only needs one accursed suspicion to alienate you and throw you over, how much more should an absolute certainty be able to pick you up and bring you back! It would be a shocking thing if you could be led astray by falsity, but not be brought back by truth! To have assented for a time to a disguised falsehood may be pardonable, but what a shameful thing it would be to continue to assent to it, and not rather to be angry with it, after it had been found out and exposed! Therefore, unless you want me, or rather God, to be angry with you, be angry with yourself and sin not. As to what you have lost, that is a matter for pity rather than anger. You are a man, sailing like the rest of us on this vast ocean of life stretching far and wide on every hand, and peopled with living things past number. Who can boast that he has never been driven about by strong winds and tossed by great waves? And you, you must understand, have been shipwrecked by them; you have fallen on the rocks of danger from false brethren. Once more I say: this is the truth. You have been deceived; a lying spirit in the mouths of false prophets has tripped you up.

3. But now that all deception has vanished before the rays of rising truth, if you still (which God forbid) persist in your obstinacy, I shall not in the meantime be your judge, but there is one who will see and judge you. Yet I shall spare you. I shall turn a blind eye and put off coming to you with a rod. Furthermore I shall try to attract you, if I can, by mercy and the spirit of meekness, for that is the rôle which comes most easily to me; and, I do not doubt, it would be more effective with you. But I shall not hesitate to unsheath against you the sword that lies hidden in my loving heart, the sword of constant sorrow and unceasing prayers to God for you. And if, in the hardness of your impenitent heart, you continue to steel yourself against the blows of this sword so lovingly wielded, unable ever to say in your heart, ' I have been wounded by love ', then look out for yourself, because not only will truth then set me free from responsibility for you, but also charity. But what am I saying? How can I, unhappy man that I am, how can I be ever free, while my son lies bleeding to death? My affection for him shall never die although it remain for ever without effect, nor shall my grief subside or my lamentations cease. As long as I live I shall act towards you as another Samuel,

O do not be for me another Saul. I will pray for you, and pray for your return. Come back, my son, come back before I die, that I who have loved you in life may not be separated from you in death!

LETTER 313

TO HERBERT, ABBOT OF ST. STEPHEN OF DIJON

The Brother John with whom this letter is concerned was a Canon Regular of the church of St. Stephen at Dijon.

IF Brother John has said anything against me, or written anything unbecoming, he has hurt himself more than he has hurt me. By writing in such a way he has proved his own levity rather than my error. Even if he had hurt me in anything, it is not my business to repay him in the same coin. Therefore, having regard to what becomes me rather than to what he deserves, I beg and implore you to forgive the young man this fault which seems to savour more of boastfulness than malice. But I think he should be restrained in future from writing or treating of matters which are above him. It is quite evident, even in this small thing he has taken on himself, that he is lacking in a mature style and mind. Regard him as a young man who, even in this short tract he has written, either cannot express what he means or does not mean what he should.

LETTER 314

TO POPE EUGENIUS III

This letter is to one of St. Bernard's own monks when he was elected Pope as Eugenius III in the year 1145.

' As cold water to a thirsty soul, so is good tidings from a far country'! I received with joy, as coming from your presence, our brothers Gg. and G. and I was much consoled by all they told me. I had heard from others a little time before of this great event which has happened, of what the Lord has done to his child. But they did not bring your blessing with them. So when your letter bearing upon it your own seal was unrolled, from the fulness thereof we all received good tidings, words of consolation, the greeting and apostolic benediction. When I heard this my spirit came to life within me and I cast myself prostrate on the ground in thanks to God, and your brethren and I all prostrated ourselves in your honour. I say this not so as to anoint your head with the oil of a sinner nor like ' the deceiver and him that is deceived' to call the poor and needy man blessed to deceive him, but . . .[1] who bless him whom the Lord has blessed.

---

[1] MS. here defective and for the rest of the letter.

For in other words or in another tongue ought I to speak to you. The words I speak are not the kisses of a flatterer. ' As he that taketh a dog by the ears, so is he that passeth by in anger and meddleth with another man's quarrel'; ' Like an earthen vessel adorned with silver, so are swelling words with a corrupt heart'; ' Be not anxious for the morrow, for thou knowest not what the day to come bringeth forth'; ' It is better to be rebuked by a wise man, than to be deceived by the flattery of fools'.

LETTER 315

TO THE ROMAN CURIA, WHEN THEY ELECTED THE CISTERCIAN ABBOT OF ST. ANASTASIUS TO BE POPE

On the death of Lucius II in 1145, Bernard Paganelli, formerly a monk of Clairvaux and latterly Abbot of St. Anastasius near Rome (now known as the abbey of Tre Fontane), was elected Pope.

To his lords and reverend fathers, all the cardinals and bishops in Curia, the greetings of their son.

GOD have mercy on you; what have you done? You have recalled a dead man from the grave and restored him to his fellow men. You have plunged once more into crowds and cares a man who had fled from both. You have made the last first and lo! his final stage is more fraught with danger than his first. A man crucified to the world has been brought back into the world by you, and a man who ' had chosen to lie forgotten in the house of the Lord' you have set up to be the lord of all men. Why have you thwarted the hopes of a needy man, why have you confused the decisions of a poor man, a beggar, a penitent? He was running his course well, what made you block up his path, turn his road, entangle his steps? He has fallen among robbers as though he had been going down from Jerusalem instead of coming up from Jericho. He who had resolutely shaken himself free of the powerful clutches of the devil, the snares of the flesh, the glory of the world, has not been able to escape your hands. Did he leave Pisa so as to receive Rome? Did he, who could not endure the responsibility of being second in charge of one church, covet the lordship of the whole Church?

2. What reason, what counsel, made you, as soon as the late Pope had died, suddenly rush upon this rustic, lay hands upon him when in hiding from the world, and, knocking away his axe, mattock, or hoe, drag him to the palatine, place him upon a throne, clothe him in purple and fine linen, and gird him with a sword ' ready to take vengeance upon the heathen, to curb nations, to chain kings, and bind princes in fetters'? Had you no other wise and experienced man amongst you who would have been better suited for these things?

It certainly seems ridiculous to take a man in rags and make him preside over princes, command bishops, and dispose of kingdoms and empires. Ridiculous or miraculous? Either one or the other. I have no doubts that this could be the work of God 'who does wonderful things as none else', especially when I hear everyone saying that it has been done by the Lord. I have not forgotten the judgements of God in times gone by or what the Scriptures tell us of many men taken from a private and even rustic life by the will of God, to rule over his people. To mention only one, did he not choose David somewhat after the same manner to be his servant, and 'take him away from herding sheep, and bid him leave off following the ewes that were in milk'?

3. And yet I am not happy in my own mind, for his nature is delicate, and his tender diffidence is more accustomed to leisure than to dealing in great affairs. I fear that he may not exercise his apostolate with sufficient firmness. What do you think will be the feelings of a man who from the secrets of contemplation and the sweet solitude of his heart, suddenly finds himself plunged into a vortex of great affairs, like a child suddenly snatched from his mother's arms, like a sheep being led to sacrifice and finding itself in unfamiliar and unwelcome surroundings? Unless the Lord support him with his hand, he must necessarily be overcome and crushed under such an excessive and unaccustomed load, formidable even for a giant, even for the very angels themselves. Nevertheless because it has been done, and many are saying it has been done by the Lord, it must be your concern, dearest friends, to help and comfort with your fervent support what is clearly the work of your hands. If you have in you any power to console, if there is in you any charity from the Lord, if you have any pity, any compassion, support him in the work to which he has been lifted up by the Lord through you. Whatever things are true, whatever things are seemly, whatever things are of good fame, suggest them to him, persuade him of them, encourage him to do them, and the God of peace will be with you.

LETTER 316

TO ROBERT PULLEN[1]

To his very dear friend, the lord Robert Pullen, by the grace of God Cardinal Priest of the Holy Roman Church, greetings and prayers from Brother Bernard, styled Abbot of Clairvaux.

I RECEIVED your letter with all the greater pleasure for having always retained such happy memories of you. I assure you that you have no need of commendations and letters of introduction to me. Unless

[1] See Letter 271.

I am mistaken the Spirit of truth, that Spirit by whom charity is poured into our hearts, bears irrefutable witness to both of us of our affection for each other. Blessed be God who, in his mercy, has met my, or, rather his, Eugenius with abundant blessings, to prepare a lamp for his Anointed; and has sent a faithful friend to be his helper and a great consolation to us. For even when he was called away and taken from me his friend to my great concern because I delighted in his presence, even then, as I see now clearly, God had ' thoughts of peace and not affliction ' and was saying, ' It is not for thee to know, now, what I am doing, but thou wilt understand it afterwards '. God has given you to him to comfort and advise him. Watch over him carefully, according to the wisdom God has given you, so that in the press of business he is not circumvented by the craft of evil-minded persons, and led into decisions unworthy of his apostolate.

2. Act in a manner that becomes your position and the high dignity you have obtained. Labour prudently and manfully with the zeal God has given you, for his honour and glory, for your own salvation, and for the benefit of the Church; then you will be able to say with truth: ' The grace he has shown me has not been without fruit '. Heaven and earth are witness that hitherto you have faithfully and usefully devoted yourself to the instruction of many; but the time has come to work for God and do all you can to prevent godless men from defying his law. Take particular care, dear friend, to be found a faithful and prudent servant of the Lord, displaying dove-like simplicity in your own affairs, and in the affairs of the Church, the bride of Christ, which has been entrusted to your care and loyalty; and the wisdom of the serpent against the cunning of that old serpent, so that in both God may be glorified. There are many things I want to say, but there is no need for a long letter when the living voice is at hand. In view of both your many occupations and mine, I have put my words into the mouth of the brothers who bring this letter. Hear them as you would myself.

LETTER 317

TO ALPHONSUS, COUNT OF ST. GILLES, CONCERNING THE HERETIC HENRY

The heretic Henry with whom this letter is concerned was a disciple of a fanatic called Peter of Bruys, who was a man reprobated as a dangerous heretic even by Abelard. The main heresies of Henry were that infants are not saved by baptism; that all churches should be destroyed as unnecessary; that the representation of Christ crucified was no fit object of veneration; that the body and blood of the Lord are not really offered on the altar; that prayers and alms offered for the dead are ridiculous.

WE have heard and known of the great evils which the heretic Henry inflicts every day on the Church. He is now busy in your territory, a ravening wolf in the guise of a sheep. But, according to the indication given by our Lord, we can tell what sort of man he is by his fruits. Churches without people, people without priests, priests without the reverence due to them, and Christians without Christ. The churches are regarded as synagogues, the holiness of God's sanctuary is denied, the sacraments are not considered sacred, and holy days are deprived of their solemnities. Men are dying in their sins, and souls are everywhere being hurled before the awesome tribunal unreconciled by repentance, unfortified by Communion. The grace of Baptism is denied, and Christian children are kept away from the life given by Christ. Although Christ cries out: ' Suffer little children to come unto me ', children are nevertheless kept away from salvation. Does God, who has ' multiplied his salvation so as to save man and beast ', withhold his mercy only from the innocent? The Saviour became a child for the sake of children, why grudge him to them? This is devilish jealousy, this is the jealousy which brought death into the world; or does this man think that the Saviour does not want children because they are children? If this is the case, then it was for nothing that the mighty Lord was born a child, not to say scourged, spat upon, crucified, and done to death.

2. How can this man be a man of God who thus acts and teaches against God? It is shocking that he should be heard by so many, and have such a large following who believe in him. Unhappy people! At the voice of one heretic you close your ears to all the Prophets and Apostles who with one Spirit of truth have brought together the Church out of all nations to one faith in Christ. Therefore the divine oracles are deceived and the eyes and hearts of those who believe what they said to have been fulfilled are also deceived. With what stupendous and more than Jewish blindness does this man alone either close his eyes to the clear truth or, because he resents its fulfilment, by some diabolical art persuade stupid and foolish people to ignore the obvious facts in front of them, and believe that the Prophets were deceived, the Apostles were in error; that the whole world, even after the shedding of Christ's blood, is going to perdition; and that the riches of God's mercy and his graces to the world are only for those who follow him? Because of this, although weak in body I have taken the road to those parts which this boar is more especially ravaging without anyone to resist it or save them. When he was chased from France for his wickedness, the only territory open to him was yours. Only under your protection could he ferociously ravage Christ's flock. But whether or not this is in keeping with your honour, you alone must judge. Yet it is no wonder that the cunning serpent has deceived you, since he has ' the appearance of godliness, but denies the power thereof '.

3. Now hear what sort of man he is. He is an apostate who, having abandoned the monastic habit (for he was once a monk), has returned to the world and the filth of the flesh, like a dog to its vomit. Ashamed to live amongst kinsmen and those who know him, or rather not permitted to do so on account of his monstrous crimes, he has girded himself and taken the road to where he is not known, becoming a gyrovague and fugitive on the face of the earth. When he began to seek a living he sold the Gospel (he is an educated man), scattering the word of God for money and preaching so that he might live. If he is able to secure something over and above his keep from simple people or some elderly women, he squanders it in gambling or more shameful ways. Frequently after a day of popular adulation this notable preacher is to be found with prostitutes, sometimes even with married women. Enquire if you like why he left Lausanne, Le Mans, Poitiers, and Bordeaux. There is no way at all of return open to him in any of these places, because of the foul traces he has left behind him. Do you really hope to collect good fruit from such a bad tree as this? He fouls the land in which he is and makes it stink in the nostrils of the whole world, because, according to the words of the Lord, ' a bad tree cannot bring forth good fruit '.

4. This, as I have said, is the cause of my coming. But I do not come now on my own, I am drawn both by the summons and the plight of the Church, to see if the thorns and evil things of that man can be uprooted from the field of the Lord while they are still young, not by my hand, for I am nothing, but by the hands of the holy bishops who are with me, and also with the help of your right hand. The chief amongst the bishops is the venerable Bishop of Ostia, sent by the Holy See for this very purpose. He is a man who has done great things in Israel and by him the Lord has given victory to the Church on many occasions. It must be your concern, most excellent sir, to receive him honourably and those who are with him; and, so that the good work which such a great man has undertaken on your behalf and on behalf of your people, shall not be in vain, give him all the help you can according to that power which you have received from above.

LETTER 318

TO THE PEOPLE OF TOULOUSE, ON HIS RETURN

I WAS delighted to hear what our dear brother and fellow-abbot, Bertrand of Grandselve,[1] had to tell me, on his arrival here, of your solid and sincere faith in God, of your persevering and devoted affection for us, and of your eager dislike of heretics, so that any one of you could make their own those words: ' Lord, do I not hate the

[1] The monastery of Grandselve was a Benedictine foundation in the diocese of Toulouse, and affiliated to Clairvaux about 1145.

men who hate thee, am I not sick at heart over their rebellion? Surpassing hatred I bear them, count them my sworn enemies.' I give thanks to God that our coming to you was not in vain. Our stay was short, but the fruit of it was not small. When I made the truth clear to you, not only by word but also by power,[1] the wolves who came amongst you in the guise of sheep and were devouring you like bread were found out; so too were the foxes who were spoiling that most precious vineyard of the Lord, your city, but they were not caught. And so, very dear friends, pursue them and seize them, until they have all gone, fled from your midst, for it is not safe to sleep near serpents: ' they agree with the rich to lie in wait at dark corners, and kill the man who never wronged them'. They are the ' thieves and robbers' pointed out by our Lord in the Gospel. Perverted men and ready to pervert others, they are clearly out to sully your good name and corrupt your faith. ' Evil communications corrupt good manners'; and, as the Apostle says, it is especially their ' word' which ' spreadeth like a canker'.

2. Would that I could find an opportunity for coming to you again. I am ready to do so, and if by God's will I can come to see you a second time for your instruction and salvation, weak and ailing though I be, I shall not count the cost. Obey the bishop and the other superiors and teachers of the Church. Be active in hospitality because this is very pleasing to God. Because of the care he was wont to show in entertaining strangers and travellers, your father Abraham deserved to receive angels as his guests. In the same way Lot because of a like devotion and pious custom was rejoiced by the presence of them. And so do you, in a like manner, receive not angels but the Lord of angels in the person of travellers, and feed him in the person of the needy, clothe him in the person of the naked, and redeem him in the person of captives. Such offerings deserve well of God and he will say to you at the judgement: ' Inasmuch as ye did it to one of these, the least of my brethren, ye did it unto me'.

3. And I also remind you, my dear friends, of what I said when I was with you, namely do not receive any outside or unknown preacher, unless he should be sent by the Supreme Pontiff or have permission to preach from your bishop, for ' how shall they preach unless they are sent?' These are they who take to themselves the appearances of godliness but deny the power thereof, and mix profane novelties of speech and meaning with heavenly words, like poison with honey. Avoid them like poison, and know that under the guise of sheep they are ravening wolves. I commend to you the bearer of this letter, the venerable Abbot of Grandselve, and his house which is also ours, having been lately handed over by him to us, and especially affiliated with Clairvaux. Show us in his person, and in the person of the holy

---

[1] One of the references of St. Bernard to his miracles.

men who are with him, what great progress you have made in works of mercy under our encouragement, and prove your love and devotion for us by showing it to them. What you do for them, count as done for us. May the grace and peace of God be with you.

LETTER 319

TO THE ROMAN PEOPLE, WHEN THEY REBELLED AGAINST POPE EUGENIUS

To the nobles, chief citizens, and all the people of Rome, that they may offend no more, but rather do good, from Brother Bernard, styled Abbot of Clairvaux.

ALTHOUGH I am a contemptible and insignificant person, a mere nobody, I am addressing my words to you, the great and famous Roman People. When I consider who I am, to whom I am writing, and at the same time how very different my action could appear to another, I am bowed down by the very burden of it, held back for very shame. But I consider that it is a lesser evil to be in danger of contempt from men than of condemnation by God for keeping silent, for not speaking out the truth, for hiding his justice, when he himself has said: 'Raise thy voice like a trumpet call and tell my people of their transgressions'. It will be something in my favour before God if I can say: 'Thy just dealings are no secret hidden away in my heart; I boast of thy faithful protection, proclaim that mercy, that faithfulness of thine for all to hear it'. Therefore I am not afraid, obscure and timid person though I be, to write from afar to the glorious people of Rome and by a letter from over the mountains to admonish them of their sin and of their danger, in case they should hear me and relent. Who knows if this people who yield not to threat of arms and quail not before the forces of powerful men may not be converted by the prayers of an obscure and poor man. Did it not happen once that the people of Babylon, who had been deceived by wicked judges, at the voice of a mere boy, reconsidered their judgement, so that the life of an innocent person was saved on that day? And so now too 'although I am very young and despised' (young in virtue not in years), God can still give power to my utterance, so that by it the people who have been led astray may reconsider their judgement. This is my answer to those who think that they ought to be indignant at my presumption in writing to you.

2. But if this is not enough, let me add that this matter is one that concerns everyone, it is the common cause of all, great or small. The trouble is in the head, and for this reason there is no member of the body so small or so insignificant as not to be affected by it, not even myself. This very great trouble affects even me although I am the least of all, because what affects the head cannot but affect the body

of which I am a member. When the head is suffering does not the tongue cry out for all the members of the body that the head is in pain, and do not all the members of the body confess by means of the tongue that the head is theirs and the pain too? ' For a little, leave me to myself that I may find some comfort in my misery' and not my misery but the misery of the whole Church. ' My head is suffering', are these not the words she is crying out everywhere? What Christian, even though he be the least in the world, does not glory in this head because of those two princes of the world, Peter and Paul, who exalted her by their victory and adorned her with their blood, the one bowing his head on the cross, the other under the sword? The suffering of the Apostles concerns every Christian, and as ' their utterance fills every land ' so their wounds are felt by all.

3. Why, O Romans, why do you offend the princes of the world who are your special patrons? Why do you arouse against you the king of earth and the Lord of heaven, by your intolerable ravings, and by attacking rashly and sacrilegiously the Holy and Apostolic See, which is uniquely exalted by divine and royal privileges; and why do you try to diminish its honour, you who ought to be ready to defend it single handed against the whole world? Thus, foolish Romans, without seeing or understanding what is right, thus do you endeavour to throw over your head and the head of all, in defence of whom you ought rather, if necessary, to sacrifice your own necks. Your fathers subjugated the whole world to the City, but you are coming near to making it ridiculous in the eyes of the whole world. The heir of Peter has been expelled by you from the throne and city of Peter. The cardinals and bishops, ministers of the Lord, have been despoiled by you of their goods and houses. O foolish and senseless people! O people void of brains and heart! Was he not your own head, and were not his eyes your own? What is Rome now but a body without a head,[1] a face with the eyes gouged out, a countenance darkened? Unhappy people, open your eyes and see the desolation which is even now upon you: ' All dim, now and discoloured, the gold that once shone so fair. Alone she dwells in the city, a widow now, once a queen among nations.'

4. But this is only the beginning of evils, I fear there may be worse to come. If you persist in your evil ways, I fear the end may be at hand. ' Come back, maid of Sulem, come back ' to your senses. Acknowledge now, late though it be, what great evils you have suffered, and from whom you have suffered it, and still are suffering it. Consider for what reason, for what purpose, by whom and for whose benefit, you have only lately squandered all the revenues and ornaments of your churches. Whatever gold or silver could be found in the vessels of the altar, on the sacred images themselves, has been torn off

[1] Cf. *Aen.*, 2.255-7.

and carried away by impious hands. How much of all this have you still got in your purses now? But the beauty of the Lord's house has been irretrievably lost. And now why are you trying to repeat all this mischief, and bring yourself once more on evil days? What hope of gain is luring you on? All that can be said at present is that your latest actions are more reckless than your former, because then not only many of the people, but also some of the clergy and princes of the world, took your part in that schism. But now your hand is against all, and the hand of all is against you. All the world is innocent of your blood, except you yourselves and your children with you. Woe to you, pitiful people, and woe doubly worse than before, not from outside nations, not from the frenzy of the barbarians, not from thousands of armed men, but only from yourselves. Woe to you from your own household and friends, from domestic strife, from cruel wounds self-inflicted, from the torture inflicted on you by your own children.

5. Do you understand now how all are not peaceably disposed towards you in your own household, not all are friends who seem to be so? Even if we had known it before, we are now being taught more plainly by your fate the truth of those words of our Lord: 'A man's own household are his enemies'. Woe to brother from brother in your midst and to children from their parents! Woe to them not from the sword but from treacherous lips and the tongue that utters guile! For how long will you evilly encourage each other to do evil and slay each other with your own tongues, so that you are consuming each other up? Gather together the scattered sheep, return to the meadows, return to your bishop, the shepherd of your souls. Lunatics, return to your senses. I say this not to revile you as an enemy, but to rebuke you as a friend. True friends sometimes rebuke, but flatterers never.

6. I now add entreaties. I entreat you for the love of Christ to be reconciled to God, to be reconciled to your rulers, I mean to Peter and Paul whom you have driven from your midst in the person of Eugenius, their vicar and successor. Be reconciled to the princes of this earth lest perchance the whole world should take up arms on their behalf against your folly. Do you not realize that with them against you, you are powerless; with them on your side, you have nothing to fear? Under their protection you will have no cause to fear the thousand peoples around you. Be reconciled at the same time to the thousands of martyrs who are in your midst, but who are against you on account of the great sin you have committed and still persist in committing. Be reconciled also to all the Church of the saints who everywhere are scandalized by what they hear of you. Otherwise this letter will bear witness against you and the very Apostles will 'stand forth boldly to meet their persecutors who thwart all their

strivings '. Let us now have an end to talking. I have proclaimed justice to you, I have foretold your danger, I have not hidden the truth, but I have exhorted you to better things. It only remains for me either to be delighted by your speedy correction or to be inconsolably saddened by the certainty of your imminent condemnation, withering away for fear and expectation of what will come upon your whole city.

LETTER 320

TO CONRAD, KING OF THE ROMANS

The saint urges Conrad to quell the rebellious Romans.

THE Crown and the Church could not be more sweetly, more cordially, or more closely united and grafted together than in the person of the Lord, since he came to us according to the flesh from the royal and priestly tribes, as both our King and our High Priest. And not only this, but he has also so mingled and combined both these characters in his body, which is the Christian people with himself their head, that the Apostle calls this race of men ' a chosen generation, a kingly priesthood '. And, in another part of the Scriptures, are not all those predestined to life called kings and priests? Therefore what God has joined together let no man put asunder. Let us rather try to concur with the divine plan by uniting ourselves in spirit with those to whom we are united by constitution. Let us cherish each other, defend each other, and carry each other's burdens, for Solomon says: ' When brother helps brother, theirs is the strength of a fortress '. But if they both snarl and snap at each other, they will both be destroyed. May I have no part in the counsels of those who say either that the peace and liberty of the Church will suffer from the empire, or that the prosperity and glory of the empire will suffer from the Church. For God, who founded both, did not unite them for their mutual destruction but for their mutual support.

2. If you are aware of this, how long will you persist in ignoring their common disgrace and common hurt? Is not Rome at once both the Apostolic See and the capital of the empire? To say nothing of the Church, is it to the king's honour to rule a dismembered empire? I do not know how your wise men and princes advise you on this matter, but I, speaking in my folly, shall not keep silence but speak out. From the beginning of our times the Church of God has suffered many things and has been many times delivered. Now hear what she says in the psalm, for it is her voice: ' Often have they assailed me even from my youth, but never once outmatched me. I bent my back, and sinners mishandled me; long their tyranny lasted, but the Lord proved faithful, and broke the sinners' necks in pieces.' You can be sure, O king, that the Lord will not even now permit ' the godless to

bear rule in the domain of the just'. The arm of the Lord is not shortened, nor has he become powerless to deliver his people. Even now he will surely save his bride whom he has redeemed with his blood, endowed with his spirit, adorned with heavenly gifts, and none-theless enriched with earthly goods. He will deliver her, I say, and if necessary by another's hand. It is a matter for the consideration of the princes of the realm whether this would be to the king's honour or the benefit of the kingdom. Of course it would not.

3. Wherefore I say unto you, gird your sword upon your thigh, most powerful one, and let Caesar restore to himself what is Caesar's and to God what is God's. It is clearly the concern of Caesar both to succour his own crown and to defend the Church. The one befits the king; the other the defender of the Church. Victory, we trust in God, lies in your hands. The pride and arrogance of the Roman people exceeds their strength. And, I ask you, would any great and powerful person, be he a king or an emperor, presume to conduct himself so abominably against both the empire and the Church? But this accursed and lawless people, who know not their own limita-tions, and do not stop to think or ponder on the purpose or result of their actions, in their folly and frenzy have dared to attempt this enormous sacrilege. God forbid that this mob rule, this audacity of the common people, should prevail for one moment against the king. I am only an obscure and mean person, and it is foolish of me to thrust myself forward on a great matter into counsels of such weight and wisdom, as if I were myself a person of some consequence. But I am all the more free to utter what charity suggests, for being so obscure and lowly. And so, in my folly, I will add this: if anyone else should try to persuade you to anything different from what I have said (which I do not think they will do), he is certainly not one who loves the king, or he has but small understanding of what becomes the king's Majesty, or else he is seeking his own interests and not those of God or the king.

LETTER 321

TO POPE EUGENIUS

I HOPE you will always act like this; that you will always consider the petition and not the petitioner. You refused to accept the king's petition on behalf of the Bishop of Orleans,[1] yet the king was not offended because his heart was in the hands of God. Even if he had been offended, you would have had to put up with it so as not to offend God. If righteousness is maintained and not abandoned, God will be all the more propitiated, and relieve us all the sooner from tribulation and sorrow. I cannot adequately express how it fills me with gladness to hear similar reports of your actions being spread abroad

---

[1] This was Elias who, on being accused of great crimes, resigned his see in 1146.

daily to the great joy of everyone. So much for that. For the rest, if anyone suggests to you that more might be put on me, know that as it is I am not equal to supporting what I carry. Inasmuch as you spare me, you will spare yourself. With regard to Brother Baldric, although he is most dear and useful to me, I have obeyed you without delay. As to sending an abbot to St. Anastasius, if it has not been done it will be immediately I know that it has not. Moreover, with regard to sending someone else, I have not presumed to do anything further in the matter because I have heard nothing further from you. But this will be done as quickly as you wish. My lord of Auxerre and Brother Baldric will tell you about all these things more clearly and more fully. I beg that what Baldwin, the Archbishop of Pisa, of happy memory, did in Sardinia concerning the excommunication of the judge of Avora, may remain firm and ratified by your authority, because I believe this good man acted justly. Finally let the judge of La Torre be commended to you and welcomed by you, for it is said that he is a good prince.[1]

LETTER 322

TO THE SAME, ON BEHALF OF THE SAME BISHOP OF ORLEANS

THE time has come for me to write to you on behalf of the humble and poor monk[2] who is now no longer a bishop; and what makes it all the more sad is that he has come to this after being rich and important. There is no occasion now for flattery, it is pity that is needed. Many wrote on his behalf to ask that he might remain a bishop; but this was asking a lot, I could not be persuaded to venture on that. However now I am obliged, out of common humanity, to do what before I avoided doing. The man had some grounds for hope, but now they are gone. He said to himself: The state of affairs has much changed since the sentence was imposed upon me. It is true that I submitted to this rather severe sentence, a sentence difficult even for an innocent person. But what can be done now, when things have happened to make it all but impossible? There is no bishop at Nevers, nor even at Troyes. The Bishop of Auxerre has crossed the Alps. This is a large part of the provincial bishops before whom I was obliged to clear myself of the charges against me. Certainly there are plenty of persons ready to clear me, but the bishops are lacking or absent. So what is to be done now? Can I be expected to find bishops who are not there to be found? If the judge should understand the situation, would it be surprising if he relieved me of an impossible sentence? Or if it is not utterly impossible, might he not overlook lightly or not examine too severely what is perhaps only a small matter, since it is mercy and not sacrifice that he wants? What

---

[1] This may be Gunnar who eventually became a monk.
[2] Before becoming Bishop of Orleans, Elias was a monk.

advantage is there for him in my blood, that he should search out my iniquity and examine my sin? Rather, because he is kind and merciful, will he not forget something of it, overlook part of it, and add something of his own? He is the lord, is it not lawful for him to do as he wills? Even if he does not care to supply me with a sufficient excuse, why should he not use his liberty, as a man of apostolic gentleness and authority, to prefer mercy to justice?

2. When, greatly afraid, he yet still had these grounds for hope, grounds not unreasonable in the opinion of himself and his friends, he yielded and entrusted himself entirely to my judgement. And, so as to save the Church any further trouble on his account, on my advice he anticipated the outcome, the blow of the axe, and resigned his bishopric. But there still remains to this eminent and humble man, one by no means small consolation in his unhappy plight. Would you know what that is? Certainly he is not concerned with great things or wonders above himself. He, who was once a bishop, only asks that by your mercy he may remain a priest; only that he may be shielded by your good will from infamy and perpetual disgrace. Surely this is a prayer that deserves to be heard! He who was once honoured is not now asking for honours, but only to be saved from dishonour. He will be content with a middle position. I beg that he may be permitted to stay his fall on whatever honourable step he can, and not be forced down to the lowest extremity of shame. He is a young man, he is of noble birth, he has held a high position; but he does not shun a modest place, only a shameful place. The impious Achab benefited from his humilation, and shall not humility profit a noble and loyal man? Far be it from the Holy See, far be it from your Holiness, to despise a humble and contrite heart!

3. If I were to say that because he has humbled himself he ought to be exalted, I should not be presuming too rashly. I might be excused on the strength of that rule in the Gospel which you know so well. But I do not say that he should be exalted, only that he should not be scorned, and that I should not be confounded in my hope. If we have received evil from the hands of the Lord, shall we not also receive good? Have you not the power to put down the mighty from their seats and to exalt the humble? To prefer to use power against evil rather than for good is to abuse it. Besides, he is worried by many debts, for he is now poor and needy. Command, I beg you, that these debts be paid out of the episcopal revenues. It is hard to be both deprived of honour and crushed by debt.

LETTER 323

TO THE SAME, ON BEHALF OF SAMSON, ARCHBISHOP OF RHEIMS

Eugenius had taken away the pallium from Samson, the Archbishop of Rheims, on the grounds that he had exceeded his rights by crowning King

14

*Louis at Bourges on Christmas day. Apparently the Archbishop of Bourges
had objected. This letter would have been written about the year 1146.*

To his most loving lord and father Eugenius, by the grace of God
Supreme Pontiff, the humble devotion of Bernard, styled Abbot of
Clairvaux.

G OD forgive you, what have you done? You have shamed a most
modest man; you have humiliated before the whole Church a
man whom all the Church praises. You have pleased all his enemies;
but how many do you think you have saddened? There is no means
of estimating the number, for his sympathizers are beyond count.
This man, who is beloved by God and men, has to expiate a great sin
when he has been found guilty of nothing and has confessed nothing.
We feel that this is the zeal of Phinees. But the Israelite is slain and
not the Midianite woman. It is laid to his charge that he has crowned
the king; but he did not believe that he had exceeded the limits of his
privileges in doing this. It is thrown up against him that he has
presumed to celebrate the divine mysteries in a church under interdict.
He denies this. In time this will be submitted to proof and he will be
cleared. But supposing all that his adversaries have been allowed to
say, or have been pleased to say, against him in his absence were true,
is it therefore right that a man whose whole life is so praiseworthy
should be so harshly smitten, so severely censured for one single
excess? If you and not his enemies were to judge him, to have
exceeded only once might be considered even a virtue. What could
he have done in such a difficult position? It was a day of celebration,
the court was assembled with all solemnity, the young king was there,
and what is of greater moment than all this, it was for the business of
God that they had assembled, namely for the expedition to Jerusalem.
Certainly these circumstances did not admit of any disappointment in
the matter of Masses and the solemn crowning of the king with all due
honour. Nor was it expedient for the Archbishop of Bourges to
hinder due honour being shown to the king.

2. This being the situation, I consider that there are not lacking
grounds for mercy since great necessity could excuse any appearance
of contumacy. Have you only the power to smite and not to heal?
You know who it was that said: ' It is mine to smite and to heal '.
Far be it from you who hold his place not to use his words too,
especially his words of mercy. For this once let the arrow of Jonathan
be turned back, if necessary on to myself. I confess I should rather
be forbidden to say Mass myself, than that the archbishop should be
deprived of the pallium. There is another consideration which might
well restrain your loving severity, it is that it may give occasion of
offence and anger to your son, King Louis. This would not be
expedient, especially just now; since the good work which he has so

whole-heartedly begun under your encouragement might not be brought to a favourable issue if he should undertake it in a spirit of irritation and annoyance. As for the rest, you have ordered and I have obeyed, and your authority has made my obedience fruitful. ' I have declared and I have spoken, and they are multiplied above number ': towns and castles are emptied, one may scarcely find one man among seven women, so many women are there widowed while their husbands are still alive.[1]

LETTER 324

TO THE SAME, WARNING HIM OF THE BISHOP OF SÉEZ

IT is not my habit, as it is of many, to preface anything I want to say to you, or to approach it in a roundabout way. So I will come to the point immediately. A deceitful man is coming to you, in order to deceive you, so I believe. May he not succeed! For this could not happen without danger, very grave danger, to many. As it is always evil to deceive, so it is commonly an evil to be deceived. But it makes a difference who is deceived, and in what. To cheat you, especially in ecclesiastical matters, is all the more dangerous and disgusting because your power and dignity are so great. If, for example, the fox of Séez, by his crafty machinations, is able, as he hopes, cunningly to deceive you so as to be able to return with your authority to the vineyard of the Lord where he did so much harm in so short a time, with what great ferocity will he not rage in the future! Alas, he will devour all that is left of it! He comes to you, a fox, but he will return a lion! And he will no longer use cunning but cruelty against many of the clergy and laity. Therefore we must be on our guard against his guile, so that his violence shall have no opportunity to break out again.

2. Do not let yourself be hoodwinked by the man's sad demeanour, mean clothes, pleading expression, lowly glance, humble words, nor even by his crocodile tears which, I am told, he has taught himself to shed as the occasion demands. All this is just appearances, and you know who it was that said: ' Judge not according to appearances '. The appearances of piety consist in these sort of things, but not always the virtue! These are merely the sheep's clothing, too often, as the Lord tells us, used by wolves so as to be able to slaughter more sheep, who do not hide themselves because they come amongst them disguised. For this reason even some of my own people have written to you on behalf of this man. They have been deceived by his tricks, not paying enough attention to what the Wise Man has so wisely said: ' Here is one that wears the garb of penance for wicked ends, his heart

[1] This last paragraph is a reference to the preaching of the crusade which the Pope had imposed on St. Bernard.

full of guile '. Pay no regard to what he says or to how he bears himself, consider what he has done. From his fruits you shall know him. Many deplorable things are said about him, and if there is one who sees and judges he will have to answer for them. I do not want to tell you all I have heard of him. One cannot believe everything, on the other hand one cannot discount everything. I will briefly tell you what occurs to me; it will be for you to judge whether I am right or not. I ask myself, why did he avoid his appointed judges? If the reason is that he has some personal complaint about them, they are men above suspicion. If it was because of the inconvenience of the place, it was in his neighbourhood, amongst his own kindred and he could easily have gone to them and explained his business at little expense and small trouble. It only remains to believe that the cunning man fled from a crowd of accusers who could not follow him outside their country for lack of money. I thank his Lordship of Lisieux who, moved by zeal for the house of God, has spared neither himself nor his purse. He is a good brother who desires to raise up seed to his dead brother.[1] Do you also thank him, for he has by his diligence added not a little lustre to your name, since by it the wicked man has been found out and overthrown, and this is to your glory.

LETTER 325

TO THE SAME, ON BEHALF OF THE PRIOR OF CHAISE-DIEU, WHO HAD BEEN ELECTED BISHOP OF VALENCE

IF rarity lends value then there can be nothing more valuable in the Church than a good and useful pastor. Such a pastor is indeed a rare bird. Whenever such a one can be found, hands should be laid on him at the first opportunity and every effort made to prevent his fruitful promotion from being thwarted by the force or cunning of evil-minded persons. I have heard that in the church of Valence the prior of Chaise-Dieu has been elected by the choice of both the clergy and the people. I should be very surprised if he were not a suitable man. Do you want to know why I believe this? It is because good men want him, and a man who pleases good men cannot but be good himself. It is also true to say the same of a man who displeases the bad men of his neighbourhood. It therefore behoves your Holiness to assent to the wishes of the good people who have chosen the prior of Chaise-Dieu lest, if you reject their choice, the efforts of wicked men might succeed in choosing someone whom you would not wish to have as bishop.

---

[1] This was Arnulf, Bishop of Lisieux. Bernard says that he is raising up seed to his dead brother, because he caused some secular canons to observe the rule of St. Augustine which had been given to them by his brother John.

LETTER 326

TO THE CARTHUSIAN PRIOR OF PORTES

I GATHER from your reply to my letter that you are perturbed because something I wrote to you has given the impression that I am upset. My dear reverend fathers, you have nothing to fear from me who love you sincerely as my friends, and who look up to you as holy men. Perhaps with fatherly affection it was not me whom you feared but for me, because I seemed to be disturbed without good reason, or at any rate more than I should have been. It is true that I was distressed, but for you, not with you, and that only very slightly. If even in this I have been rash, without any rashness I will accuse myself of rash judgement and you will forgive me. Pardon me, I pray you, for my nature is such that I am consumed with zeal for your house. I cannot bear to see such holiness as yours tarnished, if there is anything I can do to prevent it. I say tarnished, for God forbid that I should ever believe it could be corrupted. The slightest blemish, not to say disease, in the fair body of your brotherhood saddens me. Clearly it would be a dimming of your lustre for any one of you to take ill a humiliation since a perfect man would take pleasure in it and glory in it. For one who has determined to be perfect any imperfection is a blemish. Therefore this dimming of lustre, this blemish in Brother Noel saddens me. Even if he should be pure before God, what then? He should also watch his behaviour before men.

2. But you say: It was not he that bore it ill, but we who were grieved on his account. It comes to the same thing. Again I will say what I think. I cannot think why you should be grieved on his account unless it is because you feel that what has happened is grievous to him. It is for you to judge whether it is becoming for him to be grieved over such a matter, especially when he is so new to the life. For, if he will pardon my saying so, he was rather like this even before his entry, though whether by his fault only his own conscience can tell. Perhaps this is what was in the mind of the Pope when, as you say, he refused to confirm his election. I expect he forbade the hasty promotion of the new hermit because he was fearful of the tongues of detractors; because he did not want spiteful people to be able to say that this was the fruit that Brother Noel hoped to gather from the desert. But whatever may have been the Pope's intention, whether it was this or something else, you must know that he said nothing to me about it, so no one can say that he acted under my influence. For my part I am resolved that, so far as I can, I shall at my first opportunity, not only not stand in his way, but with all my strength, with both hands, as they say, draw him where the grace which is in him may best bear fruit for the glory of God. Who will grant me to see learned

and holy men as pastors presiding in the Church of God, if not every-where or even in many places, at least in some? What matter if it is remembered that once when still a youth Brother Noel acted after the fashion of a youth? The old things are passed away and all is made new. He is buried again with Christ by the baptism of the desert, and I shall not rake up again his buried vices.

3. I was very much upset when I heard of the Abbot of Chézy or of Troyes having written harshly to you. When I have the opportunity I shall not fail to tell them what I think as far as is in keeping with the love and friendship I have for them on account of their piety. I thank God that he has not permitted you to be overcome by evil, but has given you the strength to overcome evil by good, instead of returning evil for evil and cursing for cursing. As regards the letters you had written to me in the past against those aforesaid abbots, you may be quite sure that they did not learn about them through any wish or efforts of mine. And now enough of this.

4. It is time for me to remember myself. May my monstrous life, my bitter conscience, move you to pity. I am a sort of modern chimæra,[1] neither cleric nor layman. I have kept the habit of a monk, but I have long ago abandoned the life. I do not wish to tell you what I dare say you have heard from others: what I am doing, what are my purposes, through what dangers I pass in the world, or rather down what precipices I am hurled. If you have not heard, enquire and then, according to what you hear, give your advice and the support of your prayers.

LETTER 327

TO POPE EUGENIUS

To his most loving father and lord, Eugenius, by the grace of God Supreme Pontiff, the humble devotion of Bernard, styled Abbot of Clairvaux.

THE monks of Baume[2] have fallen seriously, but they have not escaped punishment. Because you have not kept silent about their fall, because you have not turned a blind eye to it or hushed it up, the whole Church owes you praise and thanks. You have bestirred yourself as you should have done and you have smitten them, yet only so that you might heal them. But if my lord should forget to have mercy and 'shut them for ever from his pity', from whence will come the healing? I wait with confidence for mercy to follow judgement so that I may sing to the Lord both of mercy and judge-ment. I know well that the vicar of Christ will not depart from the

---

[1] Chimæra: a triple-bodied monster, lion before, she-goat in the middle and a serpent behind.
[2] Baume in the diocese of Besançon. The monks had shown contempt for the Church to one Osbert.

footsteps of his Master, especially since he says: 'If any man minister to me let him follow me'. And the Prophet says of him: 'Who knows but he will relent, and be appeased, and leave behind him a blessing'! This is just what I am bold to demand from you who have come after him. It would not do for you to destroy the innocent with the guilty. Those who have done evil have been removed. Therefore what remains to be done but to save the rest? And why should they not be saved who have obeyed both yourself and your predecessor? I quote Paul who said: 'Put away the evil one from amongst yourselves'. Have pity on them and do not allow the evil of the wicked to prejudice the righteousness of the innocent. I say this because their cause with the monks of Autun comes before your Majesty, and they fear that the evil of others may damage them. Most of all I beg of you to work for their peace and harmony: I wish well to both of them and think it is expedient for both.

LETTER 328

TO THE ABBOT OF PRÉMONTRÉ

A letter to Abbot Hugh, the successor of St. Norbert who founded the Order of Premonstratensian Canons and was a friend of St. Bernard. All his contemporaries speak well of Abbot Hugh, but a rift had occurred between the Cistercians and Premonstratensians for the reasons explained in the following letter. Abbot Hugh had evidently written very strongly to St. Bernard, and the following letter is the saint's reply and explanation.

WHEN I had read what you had to say to me,[1] I was afraid. You have written very bitterly, but God forbid that the terrible things you say against me should be true. What have I done wrong? Are you angry with me because I have always loved you personally and have done what I could to cherish and foster your Order? If you do not trust my words, my deeds will speak for themselves. My conscience tells me that I ought to be thanked rather than abused by you. But as you have preferred to abuse me, I will support my words with the evidence of my deeds. It is distasteful for me to do this for I might seem to be casting up my good deeds as a reproach to you, and this would be most improper. But you compel me to act in this unwise manner. When have you or yours ever wanted my help and been refused it? First your own Prémontré itself, the place where you now live, was my gift to you, for brother Wido

---

[1] *Audivi auditionem vestram, et timui.* A quotation of *Hab.* 3.2, of which the literal translation is: 'I have heard thy hearing and was afraid' (Douay) or 'I have heard the tale of thy renown, awe stricken at the divine power thou hast' (Knox).

(this was the name of the first inhabitant of the place) had first given it to me by the hand of the bishop.[1]   Then it was due to my efforts that Beaulieu associated itself with you.[2]   At Jerusalem, King Baldwin, when he was still alive, gave me the site of St. Samuel and money to build there, but you have both the site and the money by my gift. Everyone knows how I worked that you should have the church of St. Paul at Verdun, and you have reaped the fruit of my success in the matter.   If you do not recognize this, my letters to Pope Innocent on the matter are still extant, true judges and all but living witnesses on my behalf.   The brethren at Sept-Fontaines had by my gift the place where they first lived which they call France-Vale.

2. For which of these things do you wish to leave your friends? Are you not returning evil for good by threatening to sever relations with us, banish the peace between us, leave our fellowship, and rend the bonds of unity?[3]   But I suppose it is not for the good I have done you that you stone me but for the injury I have inflicted on you by receiving Brother Robert and giving him the monastic habit when he was of your Order.   I do not deny that I have done this, he is with us now.   But I thought that I had satisfied you when I truthfully explained to you by word of mouth my reason for doing this and the obligation I was under in the matter, and this not once but several times.   But you are still upset, and as you do not mind repeating the charges against me which I had excused, I have no objection to writing again what I have already explained to you once.

3. I never once tried to induce the aforesaid Robert to leave you, on the contrary I restrained for many years his desire to do so, not once but several times.   How can you suspect me of having enticed him away when you have Master Otho as the adviser and instigator of his departure?   If you do not know this, ask him; unless I am mistaken in the man, he will not deny it.   I could perhaps name others, and not a few, both amongst those who have come to you and those who have come back to you, whom you would not have now had they not been persuaded and compelled by myself.   But I spare you, not because I am short of material but because I am not short of proper delicacy.   I found in your cloisters not a few who, touched and converted by the words of my sermon, decided to come to us; but they were persuaded by your brethren to change their minds and were received and retained in your Order and habit.   Afterwards their

[1] What St. Bernard says here seems at variance with the letters of the foundation of Prémontré, but the site occupied by Prémontré when this letter was written was not the site of its first foundation.   There is no reason why the saint should not have given the site which it occupied when he wrote the letter, and indeed it is apparent from the letter that he did.   Wido was a hermit who lived there.

[2] A house in the diocese of Troyes affiliated to the Premonstratensians in 1140.

[3] Under St. Norbert, a great friend of St. Bernard, a compact of unity was made between the Cistercians and Premonstratensians.   One of the terms of this compact was that neither should take men from the other without the consent of the superiors concerned.

conscience smote them and once more they decided to leave and, unless I am mistaken, they would have done so had they not been held firm where they were not only by my approval but also by my encouragement.

4. But now listen, as you wish to hear it all again, to how I came eventually to receive Brother Robert. The lord Pope, after he had been asked by him and his friends, commanded me to receive him. Brother Robert said that the consent of yourself and of his abbot had been granted in answer to his requests and had not been wrung from you by a papal command. If you deny this, it is none of my responsibility but his. If you wish to charge the Supreme and Holy Pontiff with duplicity, you cannot expect me to see anything wrong in trusting his Holiness and in obeying his great authority. Nevertheless the venerable Abbot Gottschalk, who is one of you and had been appointed by the Pope to look into this matter, clearly did not deny that he had brought from you the free liberation of this brother and your willing concession of it.

5. You have no ground for attacking me on the matter of Brother Fremund, since I certainly would not have received him without the free consent of his abbot. And that you are aware of this is quite evident from that bitter letter of yours in which you abuse me solely on the grounds of the unexpected connivance of the chapter. As if, indeed, that had been forbidden in our agreement, or as though the liberation of a religious was the business of the chapter and not rather of his abbot alone.

6. You add that I took away from you the house of your brethren at Basse-Font, although it was outside the assigned boundaries. I wish that before accusing me you had taken the trouble to enquire of the persons concerned not only who took the house but also why it was taken away from you. I am sure they would not have concealed the truth. But hear it now from me and then you can ask about it afterwards if you wish. The brothers began to build the house for some of their sisters and certainly it was a long way from their abbey, but it was adjoining two of our granges and quite near our sheep-walks. I asked them as their friend who might perhaps be useful to them, not to establish for posterity a fruitful ground for scandal and discord between us. But nevertheless they continued building. This is the whole story of my violence, this is how I took away your house. If to make a request is to use violence, then I am inexcusable.

7. What happened was that the bishop was annoyed that they had ventured, without consulting him, to build not only an oratory in his diocese but also a house on the property of the church and in the territory of his tenant. He tried to prevent the completion of the building, but in vain for they would not leave off work on it even when they were forbidden to continue. Afterwards, as I was passing

through that land, I met the Abbot of Basse-Font, and he pointed out to me that work on the building had ceased. But I gathered that it was not so much for love of me that this had happened as on account of the knight who appeared to have given them the land but who gave them cause for complaint by interfering with them in many things. Yet even if they had voluntarily given up the project solely out of charity towards myself, it would not have been an action unworthy of their profession, nor would it have seemed an undeserved kindness. I can only wonder where this complaint originated, since their late abbot died well disposed towards me and apparently very devoted, and his successor, who often consults me in the most friendly way on his difficulties, has never even mentioned it. Besides, I have since been received most hospitably and courteously in that house, and have heard nothing of the matter either from the abbot or from anyone else. And I do not remember hearing the slightest mention of the matter from either you or the abbot of that house, either at Clairvaux after the abbot had been here, or very lately at Bar when that chapter of yours was already beginning whence I received from you those letters of complaint or rather of abuse.

8. Then you complain of me because a lay-brother of Igny burnt down a hut of your brethren at Braine. What a hut it was too! A mere shelter of boughs where the brother, who looked after the crops in the field, might find shade. It was not burnt from malice but for the very good reason that it was on a field which belonged to the brethren at Igny and occupied land which it was necessary to cultivate. The place was hardly worth two pence and, unless I am mistaken, the Abbot of Braine has already received satisfaction for it, so that he makes no complaints whatsoever and has no reason to do so. But if he has not received satisfaction, I am ready to see that he does as soon as I know. And likewise with regard to the Abbot of Longpont, as soon as I heard your complaint that he was intending to build on your territory I forbade him to do so, and I believe that he has given up the project, but if he has not I will see that he does as soon as I know for certain.

9. But above all you are moaning because our Abbot of Villars has caused your church of St. Follian to be put under an interdict. But it would be more just for you to complain of your brother the Abbot of St. Follian than to find fault with the well-deserved punishment of the Pope. I know well that the truculence of this abbot has displeased many of your own men, and it would be very surprising if you too were not displeased by it. So I say to you: Turn your anger against this man, since it is due to his greed and stubbornness that the divine offices have been forbidden to your brethren. The whole business is tedious and involved, and it would be difficult to explain all the subterfuges of that abbot within the compass of a letter, but I will try

to give you the reasons for the interdict as shortly as possible.   After two or more compacts of peace, after a final sentence of the judge, promulgated by your abbots and ours according to the mandate of your chapter, the Bishop of Cambrai, in whose diocese St. Follian's is situated, was called in, and when he saw that the abbot was obstinately set upon breaking all his engagements, he wanted, so he said, to have him restrained by an ecclesiastical sentence.   But the abbot, in order to gain time, appealed to the Pope.   The matter duly came before him. But when he learned on the testimony of both your abbots and the abbots of other religious that the Abbot of St. Follian not only refused to keep any agreements, but was also withstanding the sentence passed on him by the judge, he laid his church under an interdict until he had made satisfaction.   Finally, in the presence of the bishop who had received the order to promulgate the interdict, the Abbot of Cîteaux was asked by you, by the man himself, and by me, to arrange some sort of peace and, in deference to the requests of many of your own men, he agreed to do this.   While the Abbot of Villars was absent, an agreement was drawn up and the bishop said that if the Abbot of St. Follian would keep it, he would not promulgate the interdict.   But the abbot broke the agreement as soon as the bishop's back was turned, and the house which by the sentence of the judge and by the agreement was to have been pulled down, and had already been destroyed, was again rebuilt in defiance of both the agreement and the sentence.   This house the abbot held and still holds, in fact he has built another.   So why should the bishop not execute the Apostolic mandate which he has received concerning the promulgation of the interdict, especially as there has been further prevarication?   Yet I, wishing to overcome evil by good, arranged for the sentence of interdict to be postponed until the octave of Epiphany, in the hope that the man might in the meantime think better of his actions, and resolve to abide by the judge's sentence or some agreement.   I still hope that this may happen, that the God of peace may grant that our peace may rest upon him.

10. Since this is the true state of affairs, I don't see what cause you have to complain of me, on the contrary it is I who have cause to complain of you.   It only remains for you to love those who love you and to take great care that unity is preserved in the bonds of peace, those bonds that have been forged between us in the interests of peace and charity, and are hardly less useful to you than to us.   You can sever them if you wish, but you would gain nothing by such an action nor do I think it would be right.   We have a common cause and, even if what you say of me were true, the guilt of one person ought not to be allowed to prejudice it.   For my part, I am determined to love you whatever you do, even if you do not return my love.   He who wants to part with a friend searches for pretexts.   It is my concern and wish

never to give any friend of mine a pretext for parting with me nor to search for it in another, for the first is the mark of a neglected friendship and the second of a false one. And because, according to the Prophet, ' gracious is the sight and full of comfort when brethren dwell in unity ',[1] you may be able to loose or rather break yourselves away from me, but not I from you. I shall cling to you, even against your will; I shall cling to you, even against my own will. Once I bound myself to you with a strong bond, with charity unfeigned, that charity which never fails, and so when you are angry, I shall be peaceful, and I will give place to the wrath of those who would quarrel with me lest I should give place to the devil. Overcome with abuse, I shall win with kindness. I will help those who do not wish for my help, I will give to those who do not thank me, and I will honour those who despise me. And now my soul is sorrowful because in some way I have offended you, and it will remain sorrowful until relieved by your forgiveness. If you delay I shall go and throw myself at your door, I shall continue knocking, I shall implore you in season and out of season until I deserve or extort your blessing. The winter is more than half over and, still thwarted, I await my tunic.[2]

LETTER 329

TO WARREN, ABBOT OF THE ALPS

To his reverend father, worthy of all veneration, Warren, Abbot of the Alps, and to all his brethren, that they may always go from good to better, from Brother Bernard, the servant of their holiness.

TRULY in you, my father, I find fulfilled those words: ' When a man hath done, then shall he begin '. You are an old man who has already earned his rest and well-deserved reward, yet like one of Christ's young soldiers you have thrown yourself once more into the fray; you have ventured once more to set your hand to high endeavour and provoke an almost unwilling old adversary to start the fight again. For when that first and greatest of all sinners sees you inspired to go against all your habits and all the traditions of your predecessors by giving up your churches and ecclesiastical benefices; by destroying those synagogues of Satan, the cells where three or four monks live without order or discipline; by closing your monastery to women; and by devoting yourself with greater energy to the maintenance of piety and discipline; I say when he sees all this, what can the old enemy do but look on and be wrath, gnash his teeth and wither away for fury? Let the devil rage, what does it matter? His confusion

---

[1] Actually the saint quotes *Isaias* 41.7, *Glutino bonum est*, but in the context this means nothing else but ' it is ready for the soldering ' (Douay) or ' all goes well with the soldering ' (Knox), so a text from the Psalms giving the obvious meaning of the saint has been substituted.
[2] *Viz.*, Charity.

will be your consolation, so that you can sing to God: ' Joy shall be theirs, thy true worshippers, to see the confidence I have in thy word '. There is no fear that a man who is able, like you, to overcome the infirmity of old age will succumb to the enemy. Your spirit has conquered your years; your holy heart glows with warmth in a body growing cold with age; and your ready spirit does not feel the weakness of your withered flesh. And no wonder, for why should you fear the decay of your old bodily dwelling when you see your spiritual tabernacle growing stronger every day, to continue to do so for all eternity: ' For we know, if our earthly house of this habitation be dissolved, that we have a building of God, a house not made with hands, eternal in heaven '.

2. Perhaps someone might ask: ' What if a man be cut off by death before his spiritual building is finished? ' I reply that the perfect can grow no further, and that anyone still growing is, by that very fact, proved to be not yet perfect. But there is an answer we can give with all confidence to this question; we can say: ' With him early achievement counted for a long apprenticeship '. Truly a man has achieved much who has achieved eternity. Has not he who passes into eternity fulfilled a long time? If a man be measured not by the length of time he has lived, but by the greatness of his mind; that is to say, if he be measured not by the number of his years or days, but by the devotion of his mind and the unquenchable desire of his heart for always progressing with which he has been able to run in the way of the Lord, then can he not claim for himself a reward equal to his merits as having made up in virtue for what he has lost in time? True virtue never comes to an end, it does not finish with life. For this reason it is said: ' Charity never fails ', and ' The patience of the afflicted shall not perish for ever ', and again, ' The fear of the Lord is holy and endures for ever and ever '. The righteous man never considers himself to have arrived, he never says, ' It is enough ', but he always hungers and thirsts for righteousness, so that even if he should never die he would always try as hard as he could to be even more righteous, always try with all his strength to go from good to better. He does not give himself to the service of God for a time, like a mercenary, but for ever. Hear what a righteous man says: ' Life-giving are thy commands, never by me to be forgotten '; and, ' Now and for ever to do thy will, to earn thy favour, is my heart's aim '— not therefore for a time. Therefore his righteousness endures not for a time but for ever. His everlasting hunger for righteousness merits everlasting consolation and, although his life may be completed within a short time, yet he can be reckoned to have fulfilled a long time by the perpetuity of his virtue.

3. How then can the unfailing devotion of good men be prejudiced by the mere shortness of its span, when the same brief span does not

suffice to excuse the stubborn malice of the reprobate? There is no doubt that the mind stubborn and inflexibly evil is punished for all eternity because the short span of its activity is clearly long with regard to the obstinacy of its purpose, so that even if such a man should never die he would never wish to leave off sinning, rather he would wish to live for ever so that he could always sin. The same thing could be said of him in another way as has been said of the good man: ' With him early achievement counted for a long apprenticeship ', because he who wishes never to change his will deserves to receive the reward of many or rather of all ages. But unwearied effort to progress, unflagging effort to be perfect, is accounted perfection.

4. If therefore to apply oneself to perfection is to be perfect, then it follows that not to wish to be perfect is to fall away. Where then do they stand who say: ' It is enough for us to be like our fathers, we do not wish to be any better '? Do you, a monk, wish to be better? No. Do you wish to become worse? Certainly not. You say then that you wish to live and to remain at the stage in which you have now arrived, without becoming any better or any worse. But this is to wish for an impossibility. What stands still in life? Certainly it is especially true of man to say: ' His life is brief as a flower that blooms and withers, fugitive as a shadow, changing all the while '. The Creator of both man and the world, as long as he was in the world and lived amongst men, never stood still. According to the Scripture: ' He went about doing good and healing all men '. He went about not fruitlessly, not lazily, he did not potter, but ' he exulted like some great runner who sees the track before him '. No one overtakes a runner without running himself. What good is it to follow Christ if one never reaches him? St. Paul says: ' So run that you may obtain '. Do you, Christian, fix the limit of your course where Christ fixed his. ' He became obedient even unto death '; therefore however far you run, if you do not keep on running even unto death, you will not obtain the reward. The reward is Christ. If you cease to run while he continues to run, you do not approach him but fall behind, and in that case it is much to be feared that you would be like those of whom David said: ' They that go far from thee shall perish '. If to progress is to run, when you cease progressing you cease running, and when you cease running you fall behind. From this it is evident that to cease wishing to progress is nothing else than to fall away.

5. Jacob saw a ladder and on that ladder he saw angels, but none was sitting down or standing still, all were either going up or coming down. From this we can learn that in this mortal life there is no half way between going up and coming down. The soul must either increase or decrease just as the body must. But the soul does not grow or decrease with the body. The vigorous souls do not always reside in strong and energetic bodies, sometimes they are in weak and sickly

bodies. And the Apostle tells us this was his experience when he says: 'When I am weak then I am powerful', and he freely gloried in his weakness 'that the power of Christ may dwell in me'.

6. What I have explained by examples I can show to be true in you, my father, in whom I see illustrated those words: 'Though our outward man is corrupted, yet the inward man is renewed day by day'. What else is your fervour in restoring the observance of your community, if it is not a renewal of your inward man? Thus a good man brings forth good things from his good treasure; thus a good tree brings forth good fruit. Your fruit is the first and best, but from what tree does it come but your pure heart? When has an impure heart ever been known to search for and choose with such zest the pure observance of the Rule? Pure thoughts do not come from an unclean mind any more than clean water comes from a foul well. Without any doubt what pleases us so much about you comes from within; it wells up and spreads abroad from the fulness of your heart. And what so pleases us in your actions shines first in your soul.

7. Sons, follow your father, imitate him as he imitates Christ. Say: 'We hasten after you, drawn by the fragrance of your perfumes', for he is 'the good odour of Christ in every place'. To say nothing of you who live near him and can perceive his fragrance from close at hand, the sweet fragrance of his good achievements has even reached to us who live afar off, so as to be a life-giving odour. I believe that even in heaven they have perceived this sweet fragrance, and that they sing with more festive joy than usual: 'Who is this that makes her way up by the desert road, erect as a column of smoke, all myrrh and incense, and those sweet scents the perfumer knows', and also, 'Thy plants are a paradise of pomegranates with the fruits of the orchard'. If anyone of you does not hear this joyous strain in heaven, he envies it; and whoever does not perceive this sweet fragrance on earth, if you will pardon me saying so, is himself rotten.

LETTER 330

TO POPE EUGENIUS, ON BEHALF OF BROTHER PHILIP

From the first words of this letter it appears to have been enclosed with another letter concerning other affairs. The Brother Philip on behalf of whom it was written had been Bishop of Taranto and was degraded for supporting Anacletus in the schism. He came to Clairvaux where he was allowed to act as deacon. He was prior when St. Bernard died.

THERE is a matter which I do not wish to mix with other things, because it touches and vexes me more than other things, and requires particularly urgent prayers from me. Our Philip has exalted himself and been humbled; he has humbled himself, but he has not been exalted, as though our Lord had not said both things. There has been strictness but no compensation; there has been judgement, but no mercy. It cannot be denied that many have meted this treatment out to others, but no one has ever wished to have it meted out to himself. If it is true that 'with what measure we mete, it shall be measured to us again', then there will be judgement without mercy for those who do not have mercy. Your apostolate is capable of both, of zeal for justice and of mercy. 'Dearly the kingly heart loves justice', but God forbid that the king should love it at the expense of mercy. The steward whose praises we read of in the Gospel, preferred to defraud his lord rather than to deny his neighbour mercy. For a hundred he accepted eighty on one occasion, and fifty on another. He is rightly praised for preferring the loss of his lord's goods to the loss of his neighbour. Because a man who does this is worthy of reward, by one such action that steward kept as friends those whom he had retained as servants.

2. But what am I doing? I seem to be arguing rather than pleading. This is not desirable. If I continue to write like this, I shall arouse judgement rather than mercy. I have no more confidence in these arguments than I have in spiders' webs: 'The snare is laid to no purpose if the bird is watching'. I know that much stronger arguments can be used against me, especially by someone of your acumen. Therefore my arms are the prayers of the poor, and I have any amount of such arms. To these weapons the strong and otherwise impregnable fortress must fall. The father of the poor and the lover of poverty will not turn away from the prayers of the poor. Who are these poor? I do not stand alone, though even if I did I might still venture to plead with you. All your sons, both those who are with me and those who are not, join with me in this petition. Only, of course, Brother Philip is not with them, because he does not plead for himself, nor does he ask others to plead for him, and I do not even know whether he wishes it. I think he would prefer to do all he can to remain forgotten in the house of his God. We are not pleading for the man, but for the Order, because we believe that a dispensation in this case would be of no small benefit to it.

LETTER 331

TO THE SAME, ON BEHALF OF BROTHER RUALENE

Brother Rualene had been sent from Clairvaux to the monastery of St. Anastasius to take the place of the abbot who had become Pope. But he did not take kindly to his new position and wished to return to Clairvaux.

I HAVE learned as a fact that Brother Rualene is still unsettled, and I have no hope now that he will ever be anything else. Therefore both he and I need a speedy remedy for the situation. I tell you that I shall be consumed with anxiety so long as he is upset and unsettled. You must not be surprised at this for we are both of one mind, except that I am the mother and he the son. The name and authority of father I have yielded to you. There only remains to me my affection which is the cause of my anxiety for him. A mother cannot forget the child she bore, and the grief I feel for him proclaims him to be my son. You ask whom I am complaining about? About myself. I do not complain about you, only to you. I am the cruel but loving mother who has not spared her own son, that she might bring her heart into subjection by loving obedience. I have offered a pledge of my love by the sacrifice of my son. I have obeyed him who can command whom he will to do what he will, but I admit that I did so willingly and not under constraint. Brother Rualene was not of this mind. He resisted, although in vain. He was forced both by you and by me. I had no grounds for believing that he would always oppose it so obstinately. But a merciful heart should yield to the appeals of one who cannot be reconciled to doing what he should. Otherwise, if he continues to perform unwillingly what he has been forced to undertake, it would be hard for him and profit nobody. If he continues to hold his office without doing any good in it, the office will suffer and you and I will be to blame. ' No one ', says the blessed Ambrose, ' does anything well if he does it unwillingly, even if what he does is good in itself; because the spirit of fear achieves nothing if it is not united to the spirit of love '.[1] I therefore beg you for the mercy of God, to show the heart of a father and return this child to his mother while he still lives. His whole trouble may only be that he was weaned too soon. It were better to suffer him to live than to divide him between us. What advantage would there be in his death? Of one thing I am quite certain and it is that those words ' Neither mine nor thine; let it be divided between us ' are not the words of either a mother or a father. Perhaps you are not afraid of this because you do not think it likely to happen. But I tell you his constant letters to me make me fearful. They are full of complaints and murmurings, and threaten his flight and division, or rather desertion, not only from you but also from me.

LETTER 332

TO THE SAME, ON THE SAME SUBJECT

ALTHOUGH at one time I wished for what you did not want me to wish, your kindly dispositions towards me inspired me to wish, and even strongly to wish for what you wanted. Does it please you

[1] St. Ambrose, *In Psal.* I.

that Brother Rualene should be Abbot of St. Anastasius? This had formerly been my wish, but because he was most unwilling I ceased to wish for it. Then again because your will was not in accordance with mine, I once more changed my mind, as it was right that I should. We can but try. Your command has been obeyed, not just because it was your command but because it was your wish. Therefore it was done willingly, not reluctantly or under duress. This ready execution of your command proves my obedience: let what I have written bear witness to my willing obedience. If I had been content simply to obey your command, would I not have been, according to the words of the Lord, ' an unprofitable servant in doing that which I ought to have done '? But now because I have not only done it, but done it willingly, I am no longer a servant but a son.

LETTER 333

TO THE ABBOT RUALENE

ALTHOUGH I am suffering more than enough from your absence, dearest Rualene, I am much more troubled to learn of your sadness. It would seem more fitting that I should mourn for you than for my own desolation and deprivation of you, although the deprivation is no small loss and not a little troublesome, since it is of a son so dear, a brother so useful, and a helper so necessary. But the more vividly I remember your dear self, the more deeply do I sympathize with your grief, feeling your trouble more than mine, and finding it far harder to endure than my own loss. I have not been unmindful, nor idle or silent in the matter, I have tempted God on account of it almost to the extent of angering the supreme and holy pontiff, that by some means or other, even at my own danger, I might recall you. But I have been thwarted in all my efforts and exertions to obtain this, and so I yield exhausted to the judgement of heaven and to an authority greater than mine; unable to achieve my own wish, I am forced to be content with what I can achieve. Do you therefore, most dear and greatly missed brother, be strong in the Lord, and cease to kick against the pricks any longer, for you will only hurt yourself and many others who love you in the Lord. Spare yourself and me, who for love of you have not spared myself. Be brave and confident, knowing that your strength is in the joy of the Lord. Be joyful with the joy of salvation that I too may rejoice in your gladness and give thanks and praise, both for your peace and my own consolation, to God who loves a cheerful giver.

LETTER 334

TO POPE EUGENIUS, ON BEHALF OF THE ABBOT OF ST. URBAN'S

A KNIGHT of the Temple wished to become a monk of our Order, and there were not lacking some of us who wished to have him. But since they did not dare to receive him because it was not lawful, they took him secretly to a certain abbey called Vaux and suggested to the abbot that he should have him given the black habit of another Order of monks, so that afterwards they could receive him and give him the habit of our Order. And so it was done.[1] When I learned of the matter I took it to the chapter, and by a decree of the chapter he was put out of the Order. But the Brothers of the Temple were not at all satisfied with this, so they must needs obtain from your Majesty letters to the Bishop of Châlons, ordering him to suspend the Abbot of St. Urban's (for it was he who gave the man the black habit) from entering his church until he had presented himself before you. And so the Abbot of Vaux is in a great state of anxiety and is sending you the brother who bears this letter to implore your mercy on behalf of the Abbot of St. Urban's, who gave the habit to this man at his request, not suspecting that there was anything wrong. The Abbot of Vaux feels that as it is by his fault that the Abbot of St. Urban's is in trouble he ought to do what he can to set him free, if he as well as myself, your sons, may obtain this favour from you.

LETTER 335

TO THE SAME, ON BEHALF OF THE MONKS OF ST. MARIE-SUR-MEUSE

I CANNOT fail my lord of Rheims in his petition, especially as it is so worthy of a hearing. I therefore beg and urgently implore you speedily to liberate the poor monks of St. Marie-sur-Meuse from the ill-treatment which they are suffering, and to protect them with your strong hand from the injuries and calumnies of evil-minded persons, about all of which the bearer of this letter can inform you. It is on account of this that these poor men have sent to you from afar, calling on you for help. May you learn from the righteousness and poverty of those who love you as well as from the reverence due to my lord of Rheims, who has intervened on their behalf, what sort of answer you should give to this appeal.

---

[1] The Cistercians had undertaken not to receive any of the Knights of the Temple, but there was nothing to prevent them receiving a black monk.

LETTER 336

TO THE BISHOP OF SOISSONS, ON BEHALF OF THE ABBOT OF CHÉZY

I BESOUGHT you when perhaps I might have bidden you, and I thought my plea had been heard. But, because I have learned that this is not so, it seems that I must not ask you in a simple and ordinary way, but must cry out with a loud voice. I cannot lightly or with equanimity endure a rebuff in this matter, and hitherto I have never met with one from you. Act as becomes you, act in your accustomed manner, for it is your custom to listen to me. Return to judgement: and if you will not do so because I ask you, then do so because I tell you. It does not seem just that a religious man, my friend and your son, the Abbot of Chézy, should lose the rights of his monastery all because of something he said without thinking and without the consent of his community. His opponent has no confidence in the justice of his suit and just repeats his accusation; but this ought not, in my opinion, to prevent the abbot from receiving a fair decision, especially as those men, by whose connivance the matter was brought up, know quite well that he did not mean what he said but rather the contrary. I hope that you will not in future sadden and trouble me.[1] May God give joy to your soul and preserve you from all anxiety, father most worthy of honour and love from all servants of Christ, but especially from myself.

LETTER 337

TO POPE EUGENIUS

To his well-beloved father and lord Eugenius, by the grace of God Supreme Pontiff, the humble devotion of Brother Bernard, styled Abbot of Clairvaux.

I F in our French church there is anyone capable of filling a place of honour in the household of the King of kings; if there is any trusty David to do the bidding of the Lord, then, in my opinion, that person is the Abbot of St. Denis. I know that he is a man loyal and prudent in temporal affairs as well as fervent and humble in spiritual matters and, what is most difficult, he concerns himself in both without cause for reproach in either. Before the king he behaves as one of the Roman court, and before God he behaves as one of the court of heaven. I beg and implore you to receive kindly the messengers of this great man and that you should write him such a letter as he deserves and as becomes yourself, showing affection and intimacy, love and esteem. By doing this, by thus showing him affection and honour, you will be honouring your own ministry.

---

[1] *Ex hoc credimus quia non contristrabitis nos, neque conturbabitis.* Eales: ' I hope you will not be put out with me because of this, nor be vexed '.

LETTER 338

TO THE SAME

LET others fear your Majesty, so that with trembling lips and fingers and by devious circumlocutions they can hardly come to the point of what they want to say. I have regard only for your honour and advantage and say what I have to say openly and at once; I am not afraid to say what is necessary without any delay or beating about the bush, just as if you were one of ourselves. Therefore I do not hesitate to tell you that you have been deceived and very gravely. Who advised you to thrust ecclesiastical preferment on a man who stands convicted and condemned for ambition? As if he were not anxious enough on his own account to push himself forward! Is this not the man whom Bishop Lambert of holy memory[1] caught red-handed in the most hateful misdeeds perpetrated under the spur of ambition, and degraded with all due solemnity not only from the position he held at the time, but from all prospect of promotion? There is nothing else for you to do but to revoke your decision, and this for the sake of those holy brothers of Corona who are so anxiously calling on you to do so, and on account of the holy and learned bishop who was the prime mover in this matter, as well as for the sake of conscience and no one else's conscience but yours. It only remains for me to satisfy my own conscience by quoting to you those words: ' Be angry and sin not '. You will sin if you are not angry with the man who gave you this deceitful advice, and inveigled from you such an unworthy decision.

LETTER 339

TO THE SAME

A SERPENT has deceived me! A double-faced cunning wretch, void of all righteousness, afraid of an interview, an enemy of his own conscience, battening on the injury of his brethren, has without my knowledge obtained letters of recommendation from me through the Bishop of Beauvais. For what would I not do for this man? If you do not wish my conscience to be even further burdened, see that this cunning villain gains nothing and is not able to use any letter of mine for persecuting innocent people. Although even this would not satisfy me if this evil swindler and greedy extortioner were not made to pay the penalty of his misdeeds.

---

[1] Bishop of Angoulême in succession to Gerard. The Benedictine monastery of Corona was in his diocese.

LETTER 340

TO THE SAME, ON BEHALF OF THE PRIOR OF THE GRANDE CHARTREUSE

The prior of the Grande Chartreuse, Anthelm, had caused trouble amongst his brethren by endeavouring to abolish certain relaxations that had crept in. Those who would not obey were sent away. Some of them, apparently, found their way to Rome and obtained absolution and reinstatement from Eugenius. The saint wrote the following letter to remonstrate with the Pope.

OUR tempters slumber not nor do they sleep. Once again ' on the mountains they give chase to them, and in the desert they waylay them '. The Carthusians have been troubled; ' they were troubled and reeled like a drunken man, and almost all their wisdom was swallowed up '. You know, my lord, an enemy has done this thing. But why do I say ' has done ', when he is still doing it? He is still quite sure that the fruit of their sanctity is his for the taking. It is his chosen food, as you know. He has already established traitors in their midst, and through them he is stirring up civil strife and domestic fury in the monastery. From the very beginning of the place and the Order it has been something quite unheard-of that anyone who had left should be received back without making satisfaction. The departure of these men was bad, their return is worse; they are adding treachery upon treachery. What think you, most holy father, will these men do, who have left their monastery in sin and returned in pride? They glory in the evil they have done, they insult their long suffering brethren, they boast of their victory: the prior is no longer prior, and ' the heart of the oppressed burns within them, so triumphant is the schemer that has entrapped them '. He wants to go away, for he cannot bear to look on at the destruction of his Order. He would have gone away already if he could have done so alone. This prior must be a good man, for I have heard that he depends on the advice of good men.

2. Do you see, most kind father, how gravely you have been deceived? Shall not the man responsible for this receive his deserts? If I know you at all, he will undergo judgement whoever he is. They came to you in the clothing of sheep, in the holy habit of their Order, and you were deceived by appearances. What wonder? You are a man. But now that their fraud has been exposed, let your zeal show itself and boldly fulfil its function against these evil men. Have no part in their counsels, let the plans of Achitophel be thwarted. But keep a watch on yourself. It is not so dangerous to be deceived without knowing as to allow zeal to sleep. Ignorance excuses the former, indolence renders the latter inexcusable. Perhaps he will come up to you with another tale. I pray that his malice may betray itself and not my lord. This is the truth, this is how the matter stands. Your

judgements are never more pleasing or more just than when, on occasions like this, the man who has tried to injure others falls into the snare of his own setting; than when his spite recoils on himself, and all his violence on his own head. I am confident that in his zeal my lord will accomplish this, and that he who was the prior will be prior again, so that evil may not completely triumph. Otherwise, if the prior is not reinstated, there is every reason to fear that the Order will not long remain in its present condition. May God inspire you to take all this in a fatherly way and to answer it favourably for the consolation of all of us who are sad and troubled about it almost beyond endurance.

3. My lord of Cîteaux has passed away to the great loss of the Order. But I have a double cause for sorrow, because in him I have lost both a father and a son. And now we have in his place Goswin, the Abbot of Bonneval. May it please you to support him with your apostolic rescript, and confirm by your sanction his election. You know him and he has no need to be commended to you, his life and God-given wisdom are commendation enough. My lord of Valence is better; when he is able he does great good. For this reason those who love a good man love him, and he loves them. It is for you to love and encourage such men. As for myself, your child, I am more feeble than usual. My life ebbs slowly away, drop by drop; probably because I do not deserve a quick death and prompt entry into life.

LETTER 341

TO COUNT THEOBALD

You know that I care for you, but how much I do so God knows better than you. I am quite sure that you too are fond of me, but for the sake of God. Therefore if I should offend God, you would have no reason for your affection since then God would not be with me. Why should a great prince like you care for an insignificant creature like me, unless you believed that God were with me? So perhaps it would not be to your advantage for me to offend God. But I would certainly offend God were I to do what you want me to do. For I know quite well that ecclesiastical honours and preferments are due to those who are able and willing to administer them worthily for the honour of God. So to obtain them by my influence for your young son would not be just to you or yours and would be dangerous for myself. It is not lawful for anyone, even for an adult, to hold benefices in many churches, except by dispensation on account of some great need of the Church or because of some outstanding advantage. Therefore if you feel this too hard a saying and are still determined to carry out your plan, I beg you to excuse me from having any part in it. I am sure that you would be able to obtain what you want by your own influence and that of your friends. And so you would achieve your purpose without my sinning. Certainly I wish your William well, but before all I would that he should stand well with God. Hence I am unwilling that he should do anything against the will of God lest he should lose God. But if anyone should wish differently, I would not be a party to it lest I too should lose God. When he wants something that he can have without offending God, then I shall prove myself a friend and, if necessary, do all I can to help him. To one who, like you, loves righteousness, there is no need for me to labour to excuse righteousness. Please make my excuses to the countess in accordance with what I have written.

LETTER 342

TO THE BISHOP OF LAON

I AM your devoted friend. If you are aware of this, or, I should say, because you are aware of it, allow me, I pray, to reconcile to you the bearer of this letter, and do you, in your turn, reconcile him to all those whom he appears to have offended. Otherwise you will offend me, whom you acknowledge as your friend; and this surely you would not wish to do. Ever since you have been a bishop I have never received any blessing from you, neither purse, nor wallet, nor shoes for my feet.

LETTER 343

TO POPE EUGENIUS

To his most loving father and lord, Eugenius, by the grace of God Supreme Pontiff, the humble devotion of Brother Bernard, styled Abbot of Clairvaux.

THE voice of the turtle dove has been heard in our chapter, and it has filled us with joy. Certainly a clear voice, and a voice burning with zeal, weighty with knowledge. The spirit of life breathed through your words, a mighty spirit, a spirit crying aloud, chiding, and arousing us to ' a jealousy that is the jealousy of God himself '. I must admit I am at a loss to say what pleased me most in your letter: the kindness you showed in it or the profit we were able to derive from it, your majesty bowing down or our humility being lifted up, your severity smiting us or your kindliness soothing us. Those of us who were hungering at all after righteousness were filled, those less zealous were smitten with compunction, those who cared nothing for it were put to shame. Act always like this, I beg of you. The loving care that you owe to all ought not to be withheld from those who are especially entitled to it, but ought to be given to them all the more generously. Charity is kind, she embraces all and excludes none. Let her gather others, but let her gather them in with us. To care especially for those who can say with the Apostle, ' Behold we have left all things and followed thee ' is a work that becomes your apostolate.   You must not abandon those who have abandoned themselves.   They are the little ones of the Lord who trust in him; and the faithful servant will not abandon them, especially when he is the one to whom all the world has been entrusted.   They are a part of that trust, a little flock indeed but, unless I am mistaken, they deserve to have God for their father, and he will bestow upon them the crown of glory, the diadem of his kingdom.   They do not reckon it usurpation to be the heirs of God, co-heirs with Christ, for they hear the words: ' Do not be afraid, my little flock.   Your father has determined to give you the kingdom.'   And now enough of this for the moment.

2. The Abbot of Trois-Fontaines was well planted because he was planted by running waters.[1]   But I am afraid that a good tree bearing good fruit may bear none at all if uprooted.   I have sometimes seen a vine fruitful at the first planting and barren at the second.   I have seen a well planted and flourishing tree wither when transplanted.   You will grievously wound my heart if you do not send him back, because he and I are of one mind and heart.   As long as it is divided both parts must bleed.   How can I, deprived of the staff of my old age, bear alone the burden which we were hardly able to bear together?   If it does not matter about me, I pray that you may be deterred from inflicting a certain harm for the sake of an uncertain good by the deep wound which the whole Order would incur from your action.   But if you are quite determined to keep him, I beg you to hold him in great esteem and to lift up your hands in prayer to God that he may deign to find a suitable man to take his place in that house.   For the rest, I earnestly beg your Holiness to give me a speedy answer not only in word but also in deed concerning those things which on behalf of the whole Order and other affairs too I have judged it fitting and even necessary to entrust to the same abbot to deliver to you.

LETTER 344

TO HUGH, ABBOT OF TROIS-FONTAINES, WHEN HE WAS IN ROME

I REGRET having written to you on behalf of that young man, and I could wish, if it were possible, to withdraw the approval I seemed to give, but certainly did not, to the judgement of a friend in his misguided bestowal of the office of provost.[2]   I must confess that I was prevailed upon to write as I did by my affection for the youth's uncle, a very great affection but, in this case, not so very supernatural.   I was greatly influenced by the sorrow I felt at his recent death.   I may seem fickle, but I would sooner jeopardize myself with my lord by writing

---

[1] This was Hugh.   He was made Cardinal Bishop of Ostia in 1150.
[2] This friend was Hugh of Mâcon, Bishop of Auxerre.

with haste, than with God by the appearance of a lie. I did not write very carefully and circumspectly to him about the provost-ship because I knew quite well that (as you remember) his two predecessors had ordered it otherwise and confirmed it with their authority. But, if you have any influence with him, you will do a good work if you can persuade him to restore to the church her privileges and render them effective with his authority. I hope that we can clear the bishop of this blot on his character, and provide for the youth in some other way.

THE AUXERRE ELECTION

THE following four letters concern an involved dispute over an election to the vacant see of Auxerre. The trouble started in the year 1151 with the death of the bishop, Hugh of Mâcon. Hugh had been one of the saint's earliest disciples and friends. He had entered Cîteaux with him, from Cîteaux he had become Abbot of Pontigny, and in the year 1136 he had been raised to the see of Auxerre. After his death he was found to have left all his property to a good-for-nothing nephew. St. Bernard wrote at once to Pope Eugenius begging him not to confirm the legacy. He contended that it was unthinkable that such a man as Hugh of Mâcon could have been in full possession of his faculties when he made such a will; that the whole matter had been arranged by a certain Stephen, a deacon and member of the house-hold; that, in fact, Stephen had probably made and sealed the will himself. In the meantime an election had taken place and a candidate chosen by eleven priests, nine deacons, and a number of clergy. The result of this election had not pleased William, Count of Nevers. Working behind the scenes the count had tried to get a candidate of his own chosen at a second election held by the treasurer, the cantor, the archdeacon, a priest named Hugh, and the above-mentioned Stephen. St. Bernard wrote again to the Pope warning him about the Count of Nevers and begging him to settle the affair by appointing a man of his own choice. Eugenius hesitated to take the extreme step suggested by the saint and appointed instead a commission of three with St. Bernard to look into the matter and see that a suitable candidate was chosen. The saint submitted the name of Alan of Regny, Abbot of l'Arrivour, a Cistercian house, but the commission would not agree to his choice. Once more the saint wrote to Eugenius, and the Pope in answer to this letter decided in favour of Alan. This called forth the accusation that the Pope was a tool in the hands of St. Bernard, a charge which the saint hotly rebutted. Then the king made difficulties on the ground that his *congé d'élire* had been granted only to the first election. The saint wrote to him pointing out that his attitude was unreasonable and unusual, quoting the precedent of Soissons where the clergy had met many times before they could agree on a candidate. Finally the king acquiesced, and Alan was consecrated Bishop of Auxerre to the satisfaction, at any rate, of the Cistercian faction.

LETTER 345

TO POPE EUGENIUS, AFTER THE DEATH OF THE BISHOP OF AUXERRE

I HAVE something to tell you which I would have mentioned before if I had known as much about it as I do now. Someone has made Israel, that is the Bishop of Auxerre, to sin.[1] When he was dying and

---

[1] This was Hugh, first Abbot of Pontigny. He died in 1151.

nearly unconscious, this man arranged that he should die almost intestate. He left little or nothing to the poor or to churches; but, at the suggestion and request of Stephen, he left to his nephew, a sensual and frivolous young man, almost all that he had saved from the episcopal revenue.[1] They say that he left him seven churches, and tithes and meadows in the episcopal demesne; and moreover, what is a disgrace to religion, of his movables all his gold vessels and equipages. And, as if all this were not enough, the young man has also commandeered the equipages of the monastery for his journey to you in order to get his legacy confirmed. Some people believe that the bishop was quite ignorant of all this and that Stephen made out the will as he wanted it and sealed it. I could well believe this for, when on a former occasion the bishop was thought to be on the verge of dying, they made him give a certain church to the same nephew. But, so I have been most credibly informed, when he recovered he did not at all recognize what he had done. Who could believe that such a holy man, and so spiritual, would have made such a will if he had known what he was doing and had been in full possession of his faculties at the time? Even a worldly man would hardly believe that this is a fitting will for an ecclesiastic. Can we believe that this is the will of a temperate and spiritual man, of one who judged all things but was himself judged by none? Who, either in heaven or on earth, would not blame him if this will were allowed to remain?

2. Do you therefore, servant of God, who hold the sword of Peter, cut away from religion this shameful disgrace; from the Church this scandal; from the bishop this sin; from all those spiritual men who loved him spiritually, but not according to the flesh, this sorrow; and from your own heart this bitterness and grief: ' Arise, Phinees, make a stand, and the destruction shall cease '. Make a stand, I say, unbowed in the face of flesh and blood, for this is the battering ram by which the children of the world will try to break down your firmness. To be ill-disposed towards his nephew in this matter would be the truest kindness to the uncle.

3. You must know that those devout men, the Dean of St. Peter's at Auxerre, the Prior of St. Eusebius, both on behalf of themselves as well as on behalf of the Abbot of St. Laurence, were prepared to come to see you about the first election in the church of Auxerre, but they were hindered and kept back by the opposing party in the person of the Count of Nevers. The count himself summoned them to him and with serious and quite blatant threats forbade them to interfere in the matter, as the prior himself, who was sent by the aforesaid abbot, by his brother according to the flesh, and by the dean to speak to me on the matter, revealed to me, complaining about it and begging me to

---

[1] It is not quite clear from the text whether Stephen was the name of the nephew or of a third party.

nform you of it. I have said once before, and I say again: Remember what was done at Nevers. Sometimes regularity can best be maintained by acting in an irregular manner. Those who are learned in these matters teach concerning your two keys that one represents discretion and the other power.

LETTER 346

TO THE SAME, CONCERNING THE ELECTION OF A BISHOP AT AUXERRE

WHEN I first wrote to you on behalf of the church of Auxerre, I had heard of the first election, but not of the second. I seem to have been something of a prophet, for shame has come upon that church as I suspected it might and things have turned out as I feared they would. Remember what happened at Nevers, and see whether by a similar ruse, or rather fraud, on the part of the same agent, a second election has not been planned, so that after one candidate has been chosen both may be rejected and a third manœuvred in. They sent to me that I might write on behalf of their side, but before doing this I thought it best to send one of the brethren from here to learn the facts of both sides and inform me of them. When he had arrived and enquired into everything, he found on the testimony of all who had come together that there was only one priest, namely Hugh, the brother of Geoffrey, on that side, and no deacons save only Stephen. I except of course those who had been the chief agents in the affair, the cantor, the archdeacon and, apparently, the treasurer, but he was not present. On the other side there were nine deacons and eleven priests besides those of lower degree. The twelfth, who is also the archpriest, does not wish to support either party, and declares that he is for neither one side nor the other although, of the two, he prefers the first. The aforesaid Hugh has the seal of the church, but he is not a man of peace, quite the contrary, and in the matter of handing over the seal he does not consider what he ought to do but what he wants to do. That is how the matter stands. And I, with my usual boldness, suggest one thing. I say malice should not triumph, wisdom ought not to be deceived, and it is not right that the church should be held in suspense any longer.

LETTER 347

TO THE SAME, ON THE SAME SUBJECT

I AM weary and faint-hearted and you do well to comfort and encourage me with your frequent and kindly attentions during the short time that is left to me. Such behaviour is certainly becoming in you, but I do not deserve it. I do not like to take advantage of such great kindness, and my conscience bears testimony that I am ready to accept with composure your denial as well as your indulgence of my wishes. Like all men, I wish to have my own way, but not to the detriment of justice, to the prejudice of truth, or at the price of your good pleasure. So much for myself, that you may not think I do not appreciate your kindness or am not grateful. Now let your Holiness hear what I have to tell you. As regards myself, to put up with insults and abuse is a small price to pay, and one that can be made good easily enough. Indeed I cannot think of any better medicine for the pricks of my conscience. There is no reason at all why neglect or scorn should upset a person of no consequence like myself. But if the abuse should reflect on the Lord's Anointed, then, I confess, my patience would begin to crumble and my long-suffering almost completely to vanish away. Have I ever asked for myself the ordering of churches, the disposal or creation of bishops? A fine instrument I should be for such things, no better than an ant harnessed to a cart! You wished to promote a man, a worthy man I have no doubt, against whom no one could find anything to say, not even those who did not wish for his promotion.

2. The secret of your good pleasure has been revealed to all whom it concerned. The secret has been published but, so far, we have been denied any fruit or benefit from it. Do you ask who is responsible for this? It is your man of peace, the man by whom you laid such great store. He is a man without any love for religion, a man who finds wisdom irksome and who is scared of justice. Yet a man who was not afraid to betray the secret of his lord and to render void his decree. No wonder that, since he does not mind showing himself in his true colours, he does not concern himself with the reverence that is your due in satisfying his rancour and malice. I have been put to shame, but what does that matter? I do not mind being put to shame for the sake of zealous obedience. This cup has not passed from me, but it has clearly passed through me to you, and it is evident that it is the author of the decree rather than his spokesman that is touched. When a decision of yours is scorned, not to say perverted, clearly it is you and not your spokesman that is affronted. Ought the promotion to be undermined of a man against whom no one can find anything to say? One of two things must happen. Either your decree which you have uttered through me will stand, or else I shall be considered a liar, as I am already. But it were better and more worthy of your apostolate if he who is mighty in iniquity did not take pride in his malice.

3. Your mandate has been obeyed in part, and in the greater part. It was entrusted to three persons, of whom two agreed to it and one would not. Nothing now remains but for you by your voice to supply what is lacking. You may do this safely. You have nothing to fear from the scandal of those persons concerning whom the Lord says: 'Let them say what they will, they are blind leading the blind'.

Of the rest, the people are pleased, and so is the better part of the clergy, the king himself, and all the Church of the saints. You have done much good in our time by the grace that has been given you, but in my opinion nothing will contribute more to your good name than this. I bear witness against the opposing party that their many nominations to the offices of the Church have not been inspired by a love of religion, but by a wish to see it weak and unable to control their wickedness by meeting strength with strength, so that they need not fear the power of those for whose holiness they have little regard. The Count of Nevers does not take after his father. He is opposed to him as he is opposed to all good men. He lies in wait to pounce upon the property and goods of the churches, like a lion preparing for its prey. He would sooner receive a Saracen or a Jew than this man whom he believes is the only one willing and able to resist his malice and cunning. For this reason, by means of covert threats and open persecution, he has imposed silence on certain clergy, so that his opponents may not glory in their numbers.

4. To say briefly what I think: unless you want the monasteries in that diocese to be reduced to poverty, the churches to be trodden under foot, religion to be held up to scorn, and every episcopal see to be reduced to servitude for the sake of its possessions, you must see that the man of Regny is consecrated bishop. Where is that spirit which you showed in the York affair? Shall not this man who is trying to do a similar thing be made to feel it? I hear that he is coming to Rome in the same spirit as the man who stirred up the Curia against you, to attempt the same thing himself. I remind you of the Bishop of Lund. All cause for delay is now removed, and there remains no reason for not doing what should be done.[1] And I would add this: to have a good and upright chancellor of good repute contributes not a little to the dignity of the Holy See, is no mean support for the apostolic administration, and no inconsiderable protection for the apostolic conscience. A mistaken appointment is always a subject of remark, but after long deliberation it is disgraceful.

LETTER 348

TO LOUIS, THE KING OF FRANCE, CONCERNING THE AUXERRE ELECTION

HAVE I ever, at any time, tried to diminish the honour of the king or the prestige of the kingdom? God knows I have not, and I think that in your heart you know it too. The men who are really acting against you are those who are stirring up trouble in the elections, so that they can have men to serve themselves rather than the king, out of the revenues of the churches. I was present at the Auxerre

---

[1] *Causa dilationis sublata de medio.* Eales: ' The charge of bribery has now been removed.

election. There was harmony amongst the clergy because having up till then taken opposing sides they were all, by the mercy of God, come together again. I know the man elected and I can assure you that he is a blameless character. I do not think that any of those present had any doubts about your consent because they already had your letter giving it. It would not have entered anyone's head that, once your consent had been given, it ought to have been sought a second time, especially when there had not been another election after that one. Must the favour of the king be obtained every time the clergy differ amongst themselves? There is no reason or custom for such a procedure. You remember how at Soissons the clergy met many times for an election and then went away without achieving anything? Yet I don't think they obtained your consent for each meeting after you had once given it.

2. As things stand, my lord king, you have no reasonable grounds for disallowing the elections that have been held, inasmuch as it is evident that your consent was already given. But some people are trying to confuse you and stir up trouble in the churches for their own ends; and, what is worse, they are attempting with devilish zeal to break the bond of mutual good-will and affection that exists between the king and the Supreme Pontiff. God forbid that they should succeed. They will undergo judgement whoever they may be, and the king will act in a manner worthy of a good king as he has always done hitherto. And so please give more happy instructions as soon as possible, so that the church which has been for so long vexed and troubled shall not continue any longer than necessary in her sad condition. You need have no misgivings about the elect. He will prove a loyal subject and merit the good-will of his king, or else I am very much mistaken. I trust you will not grieve the great number of holy men who are in that diocese or your servant myself for, to tell the truth, I have never had to endure from you anything quite so troublesome as this will be if you persist in your present frame of mind.

LETTER 349

TO POPE EUGENIUS, ON BEHALF OF PETER THE VENERABLE

IT would be silly for me to write to you on behalf of the Lord Abbot of Cluny; to act as if I wanted to befriend a man whom all the world befriends. But although he does not need me to write on his behalf, I am nevertheless doing so in order to satisfy my affection for him, for this purpose alone and no other. Although I cannot accompany him in body I shall be with him in spirit on his pilgrimage to Rome. Nothing can separate us, not the height of the Alps, nor the cold of the snows, nor the long distance of the journey. And I am present to him now, stretching out my hand to him in this letter.

He cannot go anywhere without me because I am so much in his debt
for the favour of his friendship.   But his favour itself acquits me of the
debt, for what was a duty has become a pleasure.   Honour this man
as an honourable member of Christ's body.   He is a vessel fit for all
honourable employment, a vessel full of grace and truth, full of all
manner of good things.   Send him back with joy to rejoice the hearts
of many by his return.   Show him great favour, so that when he
returns we may all receive of his fulness.   He should, of course, find
no difficulty in obtaining from you anything he asks for in the name
of the Lord Jesus.   For, if you do not know it, he it is that holds out
his hands to the poor of our Order; he it is that freely and frequently,
as far as he may without offending his own people, supports our
brethren from the possessions of his monastery.   But let me explain
why I say ' in the name of the Lord Jesus '.   It is because I fear and
suspect he may ask to be released from the rule of his monastery;
and no one who knows him would consider this a petition made in
the name of Jesus.   I am very much mistaken if he is not more self-
effacing than usual, if he has not become more perfect since he last
saw you, although it is well known that almost from the first instant
of assuming office he reformed his Order in many ways, in the matter,
for instance, of fasting, silence, and costly and curious clothing.

LETTER 350

TO THE SAME, ON BEHALF OF THE BISHOP OF BEAUVAIS[1]

I AM not writing to tell you that the requests of your son the Bishop
of Beauvais deserve your attention, for he is himself capable of
persuading your fatherly heart of what it is right and proper to do.
Nevertheless I do plead for him.   This devoted young man deserves
your encouragement, and his zeal for the good of his church should
be supported as well as praised.   He will become every day more
devout, more fervent, and stronger as he feels that you are behind him
to rescue him with the never failing help of your strong arm from the
wicked men who are always troubling and harassing his church.   I beg
that the request of Arnulph of Maïole may be granted.   Master G.
(for this is the name of the messenger) will tell you what the request is.
As for the petition of the Abbess of the Paraclete,[2] if you so wish you
can find out about it from the same man, and grant it if you see fit.

---

[1] This was Henry, brother of Louis the Younger.
[2] Heloïse, the friend of Abelard.

LETTER 351

TO COUNT HENRY, THE SON OF THEOBALD, COUNT OF CHAMPAGNE

THE Abbot of Châtillon, a good man, when he set out for Rome left all his property under my protection. And now the servants of Simon, men of Belfort, have taken off his pigs. I assure you I would rather have had my own pigs stolen. The King of kings has set you up as a prince upon earth so that by his power and for his sake you may encourage the good, restrain the evil, defend the poor, and give justice to those who suffer injuries. If you do this you will be fulfilling the functions of your state and can have every reason to hope that God will increase and strengthen your principality. But if you fail to do this it is much to be feared that the very honour and power which you seem to have may be taken away from you, and may God forbid such a thing!

LETTER 352

TO BRUNO, ABBOT OF CHIARAVALLE

Is your anger justified? I don't think so. Your own words accuse you, ' they were not ordered with judgement ', but poured forth without any consideration. A cool judgement knows that the scourges of love are better than the false kiss of hate. But you say I scourge you without cause. Maybe; but my words were spoken in a friendly spirit, indeed they were inspired by a father's anxious care. And so if you are not guilty I have not harmed you, for you are acquitted by your own conscience. But if you are guilty it is with yourself rather than with me that you ought to be angry. You complain that I did not believe you, as if you had ever mentioned the matter to me. Even if I had believed the complaints against you, how could I either have believed you or disbelieved you when you had said nothing? Keep your word and pay your debts as soon as you can, lest any scandal should arise amongst us or concerning us. Think well of me who thinks well of you and who does not disbelieve you, as you say unthinkingly without knowing what you are saying.

LETTER 353

TO POPE EUGENIUS, ON BEHALF OF THE MONKS OF MIROIR

The rancour between the Cluniac monks and the Cistercians took a more concrete shape after Innocent II had recognized the services of the Abbot of Clairvaux during the schism by exempting all Cistercian houses from paying tithe, thereby depriving the Cluniacs of one-tenth of their revenue. It came

15

to a head in the case of Gigny, a Cluniac priory in Burgundy. The monks
of Gigny organized an attack on the Cistercian abbey of Miroir and inflicted
damage amounting to some thousands of pounds in our money. The Pope
ordered that the monks of Gigny should make full compensation for all the
damage that had been done. A conference was held under the auspices of the
Abbot of Cluny to assess the damage and arrange for the payment, but no
satisfactory conclusion was arrived at and the matter remained unsettled at the
death of St. Bernard.

IN the hope of reaching a peaceful settlement I met the monks of
Gigny at Cluny. We worked hard for peace, but nothing came
of our endeavours except the ruin of our hopes. We repeated the
instructions you gave in your letter about the payment of compensation and the restitution of what had been taken away, but all to no
purpose. The damage was very great for, not to go into details, one
whole abbey was destroyed and the cost of rebuilding it is estimated
at not less than thirty thousand *solidi*. They thought that this was too
much for them to pay. Since we had lost so much I was prepared to
forgo full compensation, but the sum they offered was so trivial that
the venerable Abbot of Cluny, whose efforts on behalf of peace have
been more kind than successful, did not think it worth our while to
accept it. And so no agreement was reached because the compensation
they offered was so absurdly small. They said that certain evil-
minded persons amongst them had done this thing and that they should
see to it, that it was no concern of theirs. This is an absurd excuse.
It is notorious in the whole neighbourhood that the outrage was
committed by the men of the monastery, that some of the monks were
present at the time, and that all consented to it. Up to the present I
have not heard of any one of them being opposed to it. The abbot
himself has openly refuted and condemned this sort of shuffling by
declaring that a monastery is entitled to require full compensation for
any damages that it may suffer from another. We await the last word
in this matter from you, for it has been more than clearly proved that
it can only be settled with a strong hand.

LETTER 354

TO THE SAME, ON BEHALF OF THE ARCHBISHOP OF RHEIMS AND OTHERS

MY lord Samson, Archbishop of Rheims, is a vessel worthy of
honour in the household of the Father. If you are aware of
this, I trust you will maintain the honour due to him and to his church.
If I know anything of the man, the more you honour him the more
God will be honoured by him and in him. My lord Godeschale,
Bishop of Arras, a simple and upright man, is still as humble as ever

TO THE BISHOP OF OSTIA 431

and does not need to be any further humiliated by anyone or he will lose his authority and his usefulness. If you see fit, lend him, I beg you, further authority by your support, for he will never have it by his own efforts, being quite content, as far as he is concerned, with his own lowly condition. There is one who opposes him and flourishes. It would be well if this man were humbled before the bishop and in his own eyes. To resist the proud and favour the humble is ever the habit of your Lord, and you will have heard his words: ' If any man minister to me, let him follow me '. I beg that the Abbot of Ancourt, who is a good man, may be treated in a manner worthy of his goodness; that his needs may receive consideration; and that the apostate may not be heard against him. It would be well to confirm the Dean of Bethune with your authority in the good work for his church which he has taken in hand with the approval of his bishop and the consent of the advocate. In the same way I plead for the deans of Soissons and Cambrai, that their petitions may receive the hearing they deserve. I am in danger from false brethren. Many forged letters have gone out under a forgery of my seal. And, what I fear may have happened, these forgeries are said to have reached even you. This is why I have rejected my old seal and am, as you see, using a new one for the future, containing both my image and name. Do not any longer accept the other seal as coming from me, except in the case of the Bishop of Clermont to whom I gave a letter sealed with that seal before I had had this one made.

LETTER 355

TO THE BISHOP OF OSTIA, CONCERNING CARDINAL JORDAN ORSINO

YOUR legate has passed ' from country to country, the guest of king or people ', leaving everywhere amongst us the foul and horrid traces of his progress. This apostolic man has gone about everywhere from the foot of the Alps and the kingdom of the Teutons through almost all the churches of France and Normandy as far as Rouen, and he has filled every place he has been, not with the Gospel, but with sacrilege. It is said that he has committed foul deeds everywhere, that he has carried off loot from the churches, that he has promoted good-looking youths to ecclesiastical benefices wherever he could, and that where he has not done this it was not for lack of wanting to do so. Many bought themselves off so that they might be spared a visit from him. From those whom he could not visit he extracted payment by means of his messengers. In schools, in bishop's courts, in market places, he has become a byword. Seculars and religious all speak ill of him. Monks, clergy, and poor people, all complain of him. But it is the men of his own profession who are loudest in their condemnation of his life and reputation. Both within ecclesiastical circles and without his evil reputation is the same.

A very different person is John Paperon,[1] of whose praises the Church is full, because everywhere he is a credit to his ministry. Read this letter to my lord the Pope. It is for him to consider what should be done with a man like this. I have satisfied my own conscience. Yet with my usual impetuosity I say that it would be well for him to purge his court of such men, and so free himself of responsibility for them. I had determined to say nothing about this, but the venerable Prior of Mont Dieu[2] persuaded and encouraged me to do so. What I have said is very much less than what everyone is saying about him in public.

LETTER 356

TO POPE EUGENIUS, ON BEHALF OF THE CHURCH OF ST. EUGENDUS IN THE JURA

This monastery was formerly named after Eugendus, a certain holy abbot of the famous monastery of Condé, built by St. Romanus.

IF one can believe what is being said, the noble monastery of St. Eugendus, at one time famous for its riches and fervour, is now on the brink of ruin. I do not think this report is wholly to be discounted. I am grieved to see that the houses near here belonging to this monastery are all partly destroyed already and are being destroyed more every day. And I have learned that the mother house is in the same or even a more sorry condition than her daughter houses. But ought I to relate now the whole of this sad story of misfortunes beyond count? The bearer, a monk of the aforesaid monastery, and Archegaud, the prior, a man who has been for long dear to me for his uprightness and piety, can tell you what they know better than I, but not the whole story.

Who could do this? The ills are certainly so many and so great that it would be a wonder if they did not compel you, although you may be overlooking them and closing your eyes to them, to arise and strike with the apostolic axe. I have cleared my own conscience, but this will not be enough unless the monastery also is cleared. Whether it shall live or die rests with you.

---

[1] Legate to Ireland in 1152, where he distributed four pallia and instructed the people in the laws of marriage to which they were strangers.
[2] Gervase, a Carthusian.

LETTER 357

TO A CERTAIN LAYMAN

I HAVE never met you, but I have heard of you. You have the reputation of being a wise man and you enjoy a respected position in the world. But my dear son Peter, to whom you seem to be well known and related by blood, has asked me to write to you or, I should say, to write back to you. For you have written to him, and I could wish that your letter had been creditable to yourself and profitable for him. This is not the case, for you have had the audacity to try and dissuade a soldier of Christ from the service of his Lord. I tell you, there is one who will see and judge this. Are not your own sins enough for you that you must saddle yourself with the sins of another by doing your best to entice a repentant young man back to his follies and thus, in your hard and unrepentant heart, to lay up wrath for yourself on that day of wrath? As though the devil were not tempting Peter enough without the help of you who are supposed to be a Christian and his friend and leader. You have behaved towards him like another serpent, but he has not yielded to you like another Eve. He was shaken but not overthrown by what you wrote, for he is founded upon a firm rock.

2. I shall not return evil for evil, on the contrary I shall try to overcome evil with good by praying for you, by desiring better dispositions for you, and by trying to impart them with my letter. First of all, so that you may be in very truth as wise as people say you are, I send you to the Wise Man saying: 'Suffer him to do good who may, and thou thyself, when thou mayest, do good'. You have the time to do good, but for how long will you have it? How much of life is there left to you, especially now that you are an old man? 'For what is life but a vapour which appeareth for a little while, and afterwards shall vanish away?' If you are truly wise then that curse will not come upon you: 'Never yet did I see a fool secure in his possessions but I prophesied disaster, there and then, for his fair prospects'. The truly wise man did well to call the falsely wise fools, for the wisdom of this world is foolishness with God. 'Ah, if you would but take thought, learn your lesson, and pay heed to your final end.' If only you were wise in the things of God, if only you had a true estimation of the things of this world and paid more heed to the depths beneath you, surely then you would dread what is beneath you, crave for the heights above you, and scorn what lies to your hand! My mind, or rather my soul, suggests much that I might say to you. But until I know from your answer how you have taken what I have already said, I will refrain from adding anything more. I do not wish to become burdensome to one with whom I hope to be on friendly terms in

future, and whom I would gladly help to salvation if he would permit me. Although she has done nothing to deserve it, I greet your dear wife in Christ.

LETTER 358

TO PETER, ABBOT OF CELLES, ON BEHALF OF A MONK OF CHÉZY WHO HAD ENTERED CLAIRVAUX

M Y answer to what you have written is this. I am just as upset as anyone else at the annoyance of my lord of Chézy. But I suppose you know that, by his own wish and command, the monk has been mine for some time now, and that he has promised obedience to me and I have made myself responsible for him? I cannot easily remember how many times I staved him off when he wanted to come and sent him back when he did come. Finally he came and remained on in spite of my not wishing it, and I could not persuade him to return. He said that if I cast him out he would only go further off and never come back at all. But even so he did not have my consent, on the contrary he entered against my advice. I could not in conscience forbid him to enter or turn him out when he had, because, as I have said, once under my care I am responsible for him. - I admit that even so I ignored my conscience in the matter for fear of offending that good man his abbot; and I would still do so, if the monk would pay any attention to my advice. This being the true state of the affair, it is up to you to comfort the abbot, dry his tears, and make my excuses to him on the above reasonable grounds. Finally he too, as you know, is very undecided, and has often thought of leaving his house. If he should now put this plan of his into effect I would not stand in his way, for he is not contented where he is.

LETTER 359

TO POPE EUGENIUS, ON BEHALF OF THE BISHOP OF LE MANS[1]

T HE Bishop of Le Mans is here. If you are not already aware of it, I tell you that he is a man of whose integrity and uprightness no one has any doubts, except those who do not know him. I have known and loved him from his early youth both for his notable virtues as well as for his other sterling qualities. If your paternity has heard anything discreditable to him, then either I am very much deceived or his detractor has lied to his own undoing. Give him an audience and send him away with your full favour. I should be much mistaken if it were not well bestowed. I beg that the Abbot of Vendôme may

[1] William of Passavant, formerly archdeacon of Rheims.

find special favour with you and a ready hearing for his reasonable request. My lord of Angers is sending his messenger to request a favour both by himself and through me. Grant him a favourable hearing for the sake of his righteousness, and do not listen to the man who is muttering lies against him. It is only right that you who live for all should do good to all according to their deserts.

LETTER 360

TO CARDINAL HENRY, ON BEHALF OF THE SAME BISHOP

I WRITE to you as I would to myself, for I hope that I stand where you do, because I love you as myself. As your love for me is the same as mine for you, or rather because you love me, do what you can to see that my lord of Le Mans does not leave your presence disappointed in anything. Otherwise I too shall be disappointed because I love him for the sake of his goodness and would wish that you should love him too.

LETTER 361

TO THE BISHOP OF OSTIA, ON BEHALF OF THE SAME

A CERTAIN cleric is said to have gained the ear of my lord and attempted to discredit his bishop, who is a friend of mine, for the sake of his own greed. If you care for me, or rather if you care for the justice of God, see that this evil tale-bearer gains nothing from his lies and is prevented from injuring in any way an innocent bishop and a loyal friend.

LETTER 362

TO THE ABBOT OF MONTIER-RAMEY

THE bearer was lately admitted to your house at my request; but, moved by foolishness and instability, he threw off the habit and left you. Because he appears to be sorry and wishes to return to you and humbly begs to be received again, I too beg you for the love of God and myself to give this penitent man a second chance and to admit him once more to your house and the habit.

LETTER 363

TO POPE EUGENIUS

NICHOLAS has left because he was not one of us. But he has gone leaving behind him foul traces. I knew for some time what sort of man he was, but I was waiting either for God to convert him or for him to betray himself like Judas, and this is what has happened. When he left there was found on his person, besides books, money, and much gold, three seals, one his own, the other the prior's, and the third mine, not the old one, but the new one which I was obliged to have made on account of his cunning and frauds. I remember having written to you about this without mentioning any names, saying merely that I was in danger from false brethren. Who can tell to how many people he has written saying anything he wanted under my seal but without my knowledge? I sincerely hope that your Curia may be cleansed of his filthy lies, and that the very innocence of those who are with me may serve to excuse them to those who have been deceived and baffled by his lying. It has been partly proved and he has partly admitted that he has written to you falsely not once but several times. His foul deeds have poisoned the very ground and are a byword with everyone, but I will not pollute my lips or your ears by mentioning them. He boasts that he has friends in the Curia, so if he comes to you remember Arnold of Brescia because a worse than he is here. No one has better deserved life imprisonment, no one deserves more a sentence of perpetual silence.

LETTER 364

TO THE COUNT OF ANGOULÊME

D O not be surprised at my thinking that the rent you are charging my brethren for the domain of Boisse is too high, for we have not been accustomed to pay anything like that. We have founded many abbeys, but none of them has been liable to such exactions. But because you wish it and because the Lord loves a ready rather than a grudging giver, I will keep the agreement which my brethren have made with you, until God shall inspire you with better dispositions, which I have no doubt he will do. For the rest love, cherish, protect, and support them, because you will be able to appear with greater confidence before the tribunal of Christ if you have the poor to love you and intercede for you.

LETTER 365

TO THE COUNTESS DE BLOIS

The Countess de Blois was the wife of Theobald the Great, Count of Champagne.

I AM sorry your son[1] has behaved badly towards you. I deplore as much the conduct of the son as the wrongs of his mother. Yet, after all, such conduct is excusable in a young son. Youth is ever prone to such faults and is itself an excuse for them. Do you not realize that ' all the thoughts and imaginations of a man's heart are

---

[1] This was probably Henry, who succeeded his father in 1151.

bent towards evil from youth'? You may be sure that the merits and alms of his father will bring about a change for the better in him. You must offer more and more vows and prayers to God for him, because, even though at the moment his conduct towards you is not what it should be, yet nevertheless a mother ought not and cannot lose her maternal affection for her children. 'Can a mother ever forget the son she bore in her womb?' asks the Prophet, and he adds: ' even if she were to forget, I will not be forgetful of thee'. The young man has so many excellent qualities that we must offer prayers and tears to the Lord, that God may enable him (as I am sure he will) to emulate the goodness of his father. He must be treated with gentleness and kindly forbearance, because by such treatment he will be more encouraged to do good than if he were exasperated by nagging and scolding. I am sure that by these means we will soon be able to rejoice over a happy change in him. There is nothing I desire more than that he should change for the better. I wish I could find his conduct towards others as irreproachable as I have always found it towards myself, for I have never known him anything but most ready and willing to do all I wished. May God reward him for this! But, as you have asked me to do, I am always remonstrating with him about his conduct towards you, and I shall continue to do so.

LETTER 366

TO SANCIA, SISTER OF THE EMPEROR OF SPAIN

Ferdinand, the Abbot of Toldanos, a monastery of Black monks, resented, unreasonably it was said, the subjection of his monastery to the abbey of Carrezeda. As a means of escaping from this subjection he tried to affiliate his house to Clairvaux and was supported in this plan by the foundress of Toldanos, the Infanta Elvira. Thereupon Carrezeda appealed to Sancia who took the matter up with the Abbot of Clairvaux. In the end Carrezeda won its point. But in the year 1203 Carrezeda itself became affiliated to Clairvaux.

I BEG you to understand that I am not responsible for what was done in the matter of receiving the monastery of Toldanos: I was absent at the time and ignorant of what was on foot. I do not, however, deny that it was done by our own people, but quite openly and above board. They acted with the complete knowledge and consent of the bishops and at the request and with the consent of the foundress of Toldanos. They could see no reason why they should not quite freely accept a place which the foundress herself declared to have been founded with the freedom of God and to be exempt from subjection to any other religious house. They say that she had in her possession the documents to prove this. But as you write that the monks of

Carrezeda are complaining that they have been wronged and that, heedless of Solomon's words, ' suffer him to do good who may ', they are opposing this holy work, and also because the servants of God may not go to law, I mean to leave this matter in your hands.   I hope that you may take appropriate action and quell, by your authority, this silly and unjust calumny, so that an Order recognized by the Church may be left in peace for the glory of God and good of your soul.

2. Brother Nivard, who is very grateful to you, has advised me to put entire confidence in you, both because of your devotion towards our Order, and because of a good promise you have made to him. I cannot believe that those who are opposing us will not respect your salutary warning and advice, but if they do not, I suggest that the whole controversy should be submitted to the two bishops in whose dioceses the places in question are situated.   Whatever they should agree to decide on the matter will need to be ratified and executed by yourself. If you fear God, do not allow this very good work to be hindered or that good woman, the foundress of Toldanos, to be disappointed, or God to be robbed of the reformed Order's acceptable sacrifice.   I entreat you to show your affection towards the foundation of Espina, so that sustained by your kindness they may persevere unhindered in the service of God and their Order.[1]

LETTER 367

TO THE AUNT OF THE EMPEROR OF SPAIN

To the illustrious lady G., queen and aunt of the Emperor of Spain, the greeting and prayers of Bernard, styled Abbot of Clairvaux.

WHEN I heard of your devotion from my brother Nivard I gave thanks to God and prayed that, of his goodness, he would reward you for your faith and confidence in us.   With great pleasure I grant you the fellowship of our house and partnership in our prayers so that you shall enjoy the same privileges in life and after death as one of our own brothers.   For the rest, I am obliged to inform your Highness that the brothers of Carrezeda are both directly, of themselves, and by means of your granddaughter spreading calumnies about us.   Concerning the monastery . . . (*MS. here defective*).   Therefore we should ' watch our behaviour not only before God but also before men ', and take every precaution to proceed in this business so as not to bring into ill-repute the good we do or to give men any occasion for disparaging it.   Accordingly we entrust the matter to your hands

---

[1] Founded from Clairvaux in the diocese of Palencia in the year 1147.   St. Bernard's brother, Nivard, was there, but not as abbot.   Vacandard, however, is doubtful whether the Nivard mentioned in connection with this foundation was the brother of St. Bernard.

so that you may take the necessary measures to suppress it. And if they cannot be persuaded to desist by any other means, then may you be willing and ready to have it terminated by the judgement of the bishops of Zamora and Astorga. We are ready, by the help of God, so to order the matter that your devotion may be satisfied and God glorified by our work, as soon as it is made known, either by their own admission or by the judgement of the bishops, that they have no just cause for complaint against us.

LETTER 368

TO THE LEGATES OF THE APOSTOLIC SEE, ON BEHALF OF THE ARCHBISHOP OF MAINZ

In spite of this letter, the archbishop was found guilty and deposed. But he is said to have died a pious death in a Cistercian house.

To his lords and reverend fathers, the Legates of the Apostolic See, that they may please God in all things and return from their mission ' rejoicing as they carry their sheaves with them ', from their son Bernard, styled Abbot of Clairvaux.

ALTHOUGH absent in body I am close to you in affection and good-will. It is my earnest hope and prayer that your intentions and acts may be directed to what is fitting and expedient. I therefore venture to intercede for your good-will on behalf of the Archbishop of Mainz, since I have heard that he has been summoned to answer his accusers in your presence. I believe that you will honour your calling if, as far as justice permits, you support this weak and crumbling wall with the shoulders of your authority; if you prevent, as far as you are able, this bruised reed from being broken. May he find himself assisted by my petition and his own simplicity. They say that because of his very simplicity he was more outwitted by false brethren than found guilty of anything deserving deposition.

LETTER 369

TO LOUIS THE YOUNGER, KING OF FRANCE

IF that man from Brittany should wish to put away the adulteress so that he can be absolved from the bond of excommunication by which he is bound, and she should ask from you her paternal inherit-ance, which she has in accordance with the division she has arranged with her brother, perhaps it would be wiser not to refuse it to her although she does not deserve it, so that you may be able by this means to obtain the support and help of her powerful husband. Otherwise it is not the advice of your humble and faithful servant either that land should be granted to a stranger or your favour to an excommunicated and incestuous man, lest you too should hear those words: ' Swift art thou to welcome the thief who crosses thy path, to throw in thy lot with the adulterers '.   On the other hand, I would not advise a too hasty or sudden breach with the man.   I should treat with him through a loyal and prudent messenger, so that, if possible, terms may be arranged and time gained.   But if he should refuse to do this and prefer to plot against you, you must trust in God that he will not prevail, since justice is with you and will be on your side.   I do not know whether the bishop of that district would be a suitable person for your purpose; not that I have any doubts as to his fidelity towards you, for I know him to be most faithful, but because that man hates him and would not, I fear, have any confidence in his advice.   Yet he is ready and willing to do what he can with God's help in your service.   If he should make any suggestion to you in secret as coming from me, you may take what he says as if it came from my own lips. He is a man whom I love much and in whom I have great confidence; and, unless I am much mistaken, you can trust him implicitly with perfect safety.

LETTER 370

TO THE SAME

THE letter your Majesty deigned to send me has rejoiced my heart. May God, for whose sake you wrote it, rejoice you too.   Who am I, or what is my father's house, that my royal master should trouble whether I am alive or dead?   But now, as you have done me the honour to enquire after my health, I must tell you that I feel myself to be somewhat better, and I believe I am for the time being out of danger, but still very, very weak.   I must also tell you that Lord Robert, your brother, most graciously and kindly visited me when I was sick and spoke to me in a manner that filled me with joy and left me much more hopeful of him.   Show that you love him for, if his actions are as good as his words, you will be very satisfied with him. And if you judge fit let him see how pleased you are that he has promised to be guided in future by the advice of myself and of good men.   I have not my seal handy, but he who reads this will recognize my hand, for I have written it.

LETTER 371

TO POPE EUGENIUS, ON BEHALF OF THE BISHOP OF BEAUVAIS

The Bishop of Beauvais with whom this letter is concerned was Henry, brother of Louis the Younger, King of France.

YOUR son, the Bishop of Beauvais (I would call him my son, if it did not seem impertinent), was quite ready to come when you summoned him to your presence, for he has a clear conscience and is quite sure of your paternal good-will towards him. But I have hindered him, although he was so anxious to come that it was all I could do to keep him back. Chief among the many good reasons I had for doing this was the fact that I could not be sure why you wanted him. Then, besides the several other inconveniences that appeared to impede his going, he and his brother the king are not of one spirit, and it was not sufficiently safe for him to be absent for long from his people. Don't ask me whose fault this is; it is not my business to blame anyone, my only concern is to excuse the bishop. I have seen him showing the king every mark of respect and submission possible, but with no effect. Yet you may be sure that no matter what fears he may have or what may happen, he will come to you without delay as soon as he knows your pleasure. His person and his cause are in your hands. He has not conducted himself in the matter entrusted to him in any way that would give him reason to doubt your good-will. And so he has sent in his place this person in full confidence that he was sending him to his father. Would it please you to know what instructions he has given him? They are that he should not do anything without your directions, that he should follow in all things your advice on which he himself wholly depends. He is sure that you will not only act as his judge, but that you will also help, encourage, and befriend him. If it should please you to commit the matter to the Lord Archbishop of Rheims, I am sure that with the help of God it could soon be terminated, especially if the right of appeal were taken away from both parties.

LETTER 372

TO HUGH, CARDINAL BISHOP OF OSTIA, ON BEHALF OF
THE BISHOP OF BEAUVAIS

I WRITE this in haste, and consequently not very cheerfully,[1] because the traveller is anxious to be off at once. By a wonderful and most fortunate coincidence, Brother G— Fulcher arrived with both your letter and the letter of my lord at the same time as the man who is to take this letter. Certainly this is providential, since I now have someone by whom I can write back to you at once, and I could not do so quick enough to satisfy myself. I am writing this myself, ill though I be, as I have no one else to hand. You put the matter of the Bishop of Beauvais first, and so I will answer it first. He is a free agent. He is no longer under my authority. His behaviour is the concern of his own see. If he sometimes behaves himself as he should not or in an unbecoming manner, I can be sorry but, however much I may want to, I cannot correct him. Yet I ought to tell you that as

---

[1] *Festine ista dicto, et ob hoc minus festive. . . .* Eales: ' I write to you with haste and consequently with less care '. Certainly this letter is carelessly written.

regards what you have heard about his travelling abroad too much, I have not noticed it up to now nor have I ever heard it said; neither has it come to my ears that his brother Robert who is with him has committed any serious or unbecoming action or persuaded the bishop to do so since he came to him.   It would be surprising if you have heard anything that is concealed from me.   But I will do what you wish concerning his recall when I have an opportunity to do so without causing offence.   I would have done so already had I been able to without annoying the bishop, and if I did not fear that he would be replaced by someone even more useless.   The bishop came to us in Lent on his way to answer his summons to the Curia.   And he would have gone on had I not dissuaded him.   My reason for dissuading him was that I did not feel that he was prepared as a young bishop should be either in his counsellors or in his retinue.   But his intention is to set out at the first opportunity.   He is your brother, treat him kindly, so that his adversaries do not prevail against him.   I would have preferred you to have written to him rather than to myself and admonished him in a brotherly way concerning what you have heard about him.

2. I know that you are anxious about the state of my health.   What you have heard is true.   I am sick unto death, but for the time I have recovered although I do not think it will be for long.   I have been very weak now for longer than I could have believed possible.   But I say this without meaning to set any limits to the power of Divine Providence which can raise even the dead.   This is my answer both to you and to my lord.   Be so good, I pray you, to associate yourself with the Bishop of Tusculum in rendering to him with my fullest devotion my grateful thanks for his great condescension and loving care.

3. These are the true facts about the Archbishop of Lyons, and you can regard them as certain.   He had set out on a journey with all the money and retinue that becomes so great an archbishop, when, scarcely beyond his own territory, he fell suddenly into an ambush of his enemies.   What could such a man do?   He could not go forward, and to have abandoned his intention would have been worse than any captivity for him.   So part of his retinue he sent back and the rest he scattered.   He got rid of the greater part of his money, retaining just enough to enable him to continue his journey with a few men.   What more?   He went forward with three or four servants, disguised as a servant himself.   And so by the public road amidst a great and mixed crowd of pilgrims, just as one of them, he arrived at St. Gilles.   But being ill he went on to Montpellier, where he remained for some time and spent all he had and more.

LETTER 373

TO THE SAME, ON BEHALF OF THOROLD, ABBOT OF TROIS-FONTAINES

Hugh had been raised to the purple as Cardinal Bishop of Ostia from being Abbot of Trois-Fontaines, the first daughter house of Clairvaux. He took an interest in his successor and wished to impose a monk named Nicholas. But the brethren of Trois-Fontaines refused to accept Nicholas and chose a monk named Thorold who had been Abbot of Fountains in Yorkshire in succession to Murdac. The Abbot of Clairvaux acceded to their choice. But Hugh, whose new dignity had perhaps turned his head, resented this choice and complained of St. Bernard. It is interesting to note that the family of Thorold still flourishes.

'WOE to the world because of scandals'! Have I scandalized you? How could anyone believe such a thing possible unless he were ignorant of the mutual understanding between us, of our friendship, and of ' how lovingly we walked together in the house of God'? What a sudden and sorry reversal! He who used to support me is now preparing to overthrow me, he who used to defend me is now frightening me with threats, assailing me with curses, and accusing me of deception! Our first parents were not accused of their grave and unparalleled fault until they had admitted it; Nineveh was given an opportunity to repent; Sodom was punished at the sight of its sin, not on hearsay. But you treat me differently because you treat me scornfully. I am not considered the sort of person who should be allowed an opportunity of excusing himself, of making satisfaction, of defending himself, of justifying himself. I am judged without being heard, condemned without proof.

2. Now deign to hear my excuse. It may possibly fail to satisfy you, but it is nonetheless sincere. You wished to have Brother Nicholas as abbot. I do not deny that I remember this. We both agreed upon it. I gave my word for it because I believed it could be arranged. That it was not arranged was due, not to my duplicity, but to necessity. It became a matter of discord. But why do I say discord? It was rather a matter of concord, for all the brethren were found to agree completely in disagreeing with our plan for Nicholas. Not one monk or lay-brother, except two or three who were your own countrymen, would consent to having him. I tried to bring them round by arguments, by soft words, and by warnings, but they held their ground unanimously and stubbornly. I could bring force to bear, but may God save me from doing this, even as I saved that modest, timid, and retiring monk from all the turmoil. For, not to mention those external matters of which you too have experience of him, everything seems beyond his power. And so I took him together with his friends, and put him in a position which he will be able to bear easily because it will be shared with my own monks. A new

place has been started by the brethren quite near here, so I can easily visit it. I did not venture to do anything about a suitable abbot for your post because I had not your consent, but I wished to give you Brother Robert because, in lieu of anyone else at hand, he seemed most suitable. Then I got your answer to say that in your opinion he was not a fit person. What more is there to say? They have chosen the man who, so I have learned, displeases you.

3. The reason why you disapprove of this man is not far to seek, for, so they say, you publicly declare that he was turned out of the first monastery over which he ruled because of the stigma of uncleanness. It could have been so but I call God and his angels to witness that, so far as I can remember, up to now I have heard nothing against him on this score. Not even his archbishop, when he was trying in every way he could to remove him, told me anything like this about him either by letter or by messenger. Can you believe that I would lend my support to anything unclean or dishonourable? If you do believe this of me, have a care that the slur does not fasten itself on you too, for it is well known that you have been my intimate friend and that up till now you have valued our friendship. And what do you think and say of the archbishop? In spite of knowing the man well, as he could not help doing for he was widely known, he was the first to promote him to rule over his monastery in the place of himself. Not even for a moment could I entertain any suspicion of a man of such integrity as the Archbishop of York. I grant you that after he had promoted him he removed him. I would not deny this. Why he did so is his own concern. It is well known that many were very displeased at this action of the archbishop and considered it ill-advised, out of order, and high-handed. The archbishop acted as he pleased, and, so as not to cause unpleasantness, the man, on my advice, gave way to him peacefully and submitted to his displeasure.

4. One thing I do say: from the time he came here no one (and this is the testimony of all) has discovered in him any reason against this promotion. He has given no trouble. He is cultured, learned, and cheerful in looks and word. You may say that this is just because he has only been with us for a short time. I admit this. Perhaps he will do well, perhaps not so well. I have no confidence in any of my actions and cannot foresee their consequences. Not being sure myself, I cannot expect you to be so. But what has been done cannot well be undone. If I were a prophet I would certainly not have done anything which I would have known might offend my friend, upset a holy man, scandalize a bishop. What do you want me to do? I have acted under necessity and in a perfectly regular manner.

5. This is my excuse. If you are satisfied with it, let there be no more trouble between us; if you are not satisfied, I will accept your judgement whatever it may be. To undo what I have so recently

done would be painful to me unless I had some good reason, and this perhaps I shall have in time. If you wish to remove the man, you have the power. I will not stand in your way. I will not try to stem the tide. Unjustly I have not acted; but if I have acted stupidly, it is easy for you to correct my stupidity and, if you see fit, even to punish it. Yet I say that, being a just man, you will deal with me in a merciful and Christian manner; that you will correct me with mercy and not in your anger speak ill of me to others. I have put my position to you in this letter, and I only hope that by doing so I have not added fuel to the flames. I learned of your anger, not through you, but through others, and I have been careful not to answer you in a similar way through others but to complain to you of yourself in this letter. For the rest I bless God for having taken from me before I die this consolation in which perhaps I took too much pleasure, the favour, that is, of yourself and my lord, so that I might learn from experience not to put my trust in any man.

LETTER 374

TO HAIMERIC, THE CHANCELLOR

It is clear from the context that this must have been one of St. Bernard's first letters to Cardinal Haimeric.

To the illustrious lord Haimeric, Chancellor to the Holy Roman See, that he may live as becomes him in the house of God,[1] from Hugh, Abbot of Pontigny, and Bernard of Clairvaux.

THE goal of bishops is not, so we believe, different from the purpose of Christ. Therefore we who seek God should make common cause with them. If anyone refuses to do this, he shall hear from the Lord those words: 'He who is not with me, is against me'. Either we must obey the Apostle saying 'Extinguish not the Spirit', or we must hear with the Jews, 'You always resist the Holy Ghost', and from the Prophet, 'Woe unto you, the men who call evil good and good evil'. We cannot at the same time take pleasure in both good and evil, nor by one mouth can the righteous man be praised for his righteousness and the sinner in his evil desires. What is there to be surprised at if good should be for the good man the breath of life and for the ungodly the savour of death? He who is the fount and source of all good was born for the fall and rise of many, a sign which even to-day is contradicted. Even to-day the Saviour is found to be for many a stone to trip their feet, a boulder that catches them unawares. Yet there are not lacking those who say with a willing

---

[1] . . . *in domo Dei quemadmodum oportet conversari.* Eales: ' In the hope that their conduct in the house of God may ever be such as it ought to be '.

heart: 'He is our peace'. But how shall they find peace for whom peace itself is a scandal? How shall they be saved for whom salvation itself is a loss? The psalmist says, 'Glory and riches are in his house', meaning the house of the righteous man, but he immediately shows what he means by glory and riches when he adds, 'His righteousness shall endure for ever'. And truly there are no riches and glory to be compared with the conscience of a righteous man. What does the unrighteous lose? If Paul glories in the riches of his heart, saying, 'For our glory is this, the witness of our conscience', who is injured thereby? Yet the Prophet adds, 'Ungodly men are ill content to see it'. What malice! Are these riches like worldly possessions, so that the more one man has the less there is for another? Why then is the ungodly man angry? He loses nothing at all. Why does he envy the good man his good things? He does not want to have them. He is like the dog in the fable which kept others away from the hay it could not eat itself. Nevertheless, even if he gnashes his teeth in fury, what is of God cannot be altogether frustrated. Whether he likes it or not, 'the honest man will rejoice to witness it, and malice will stand dumb with confusion'.

2. All this only concerns those who can be suspected. To you we say: 'Use your talent and you will have your reward'. What good is it wrapped up in a napkin since the time must come when it will be demanded back with interest? Why do we fail to use it while we still have time to do so? Although for you, by virtue of the office you hold, it is always time to seek the rewards of piety, yet for this holy avarice there is no time like the present time. All you have to do is to bring forth the treasure you have received for this purpose from the Lord: 'Wisdom hidden is wasted, is treasure that never sees the light of day'. If it is not only your duty but, as we hear, your desire to do good to all, you ought especially to do so to the household of the faithful. Although this command of the Apostle is general to everyone, yet we make bold to point out that it is the special privilege and duty of your office; unless (which we do not for one moment believe) you are more concerned with your position than with the responsibilities of your position. There is hardly any good work done in the whole world which does not have to pass through the hands of the Chancellor of Rome, so that scarcely anything is considered good which has not been first scrutinized by him with judgement, moderated with his advice, furthered with his zeal, and confirmed with his help. And so what could be more right than that he should be held responsible for any good work found to be imperfect or defective, as well as for any that has been adequately and efficiently accomplished? I would say that the man who holds your office must be either blessed or pitiable, for he must prove himself always either a partner in all good or an enemy of it. Rightly therefore all praise or blame attaches

to him according to results and the part he has taken in them.   Happy he who can say to the Lord: ' I am a partaker with all them that fear thee and keep thy commandments '.

3. But we have become so engrossed in our theme that we have forgotten that we are pouring our remarks into ears already fully engaged.   Although if you are well disposed, if you remember not our deserts but the gifts by which you were the first kindly to solicit our friendship, we trust that we shall not seem to have been needlessly insistent.   We consider it an unmistakable sign of your friendship that an important man like your Excellency, always engaged in great affairs, should have seen fit even to greet such insignificant persons as we are, not to mention your gifts.   May God reward your gift of material gold with the spiritual gold of wisdom, that we may rejoice as much in your gain as we do in your gift.

LETTER 375

TO RAYNALD, ARCHBISHOP OF RHEIMS

To his most reverend father and lord Raynald, by the grace of God Archbishop of Rheims, greetings and whatever the prayers of a sinner can avail, from Brother Bernard of Clairvaux.

BLESSED be God who inspired you to comfort me with your letter. I can indeed return letter for letter, but can I ever make any return for the favour you have shown me?   I have good reason to feel proud that you should have deigned to meet me with your abundant blessing, to stir me with your exhortation, and to honour me with your greeting.   But I can never deserve the high names that you have given me in your ignorance of my true character, although I am not less grateful for being so undeserving.   Yet in so doing you have acted in a manner that becomes you, for you are a debtor by your office to both the wise and the foolish.   That report of me, by the fragrance of which you say that you have been moved to this condescension towards me, is certainly not a little gratifying, but it is dangerous. The result of it is very welcome and pleasing to me inasmuch as, although lacking all substance and having little resemblance to the truth, a priest of the Most High has been moved by it to greet me before ever I deserved his notice.   The monk who brings this letter will fully inform you concerning my arrival.   He will explain why I have not come and when I intend to do so, and any other question it may please your Excellency to ask about me.   It is for this reason that I have sent him ahead while I wait until I am free to come.

LETTER 376

TO MATILDA, QUEEN OF ENGLAND

To the most illustrious lady, and beloved daughter in Christ (which I say with affection and not presumption) Matilda, by the grace of God Queen of England, the greetings of Bernard.

IF I should seem to presume somewhat in thus addressing you, it is no matter for surprise, since almost everyone knows how you favour me and how great is your affection for me. Because of this I have been asked by a certain friend of yours,[1] the venerable Abbot of La Chapelle, to remind you of his plea for a certain tithe which, if you remember, I mentioned to you at Boulogne, and which, with your usual kindness, you favourably considered. But because my request has not yet been granted, the time has now come for it to be discharged. For the rest, keep well for me that son to whom you have lately given birth, for (if it will not displease the king) I claim some share in him.[2]

LETTER 377

TO HENRY, ARCHBISHOP OF SENS, AND TO HAIMERIC, THE CHANCELLOR

IT is surely a good thing when laymen wish to give up ecclesiastical benefices which they have no right to hold. And when they wish to hand them over to the servants of God, it is a twofold good. But when they cannot do this except by the hand of a bishop, it follows that the bishop will either be guilty of a twofold evil or the promoter of a twofold good according to whether he grants or withholds his assent. What a certain knight asks you in this matter, you ought to have asked him. For surely you cannot prefer that a sanctuary of God should be held as a family possession by a knight rather than by the servants of God? If you do, it would be very surprising. Do not act like this, I pray you, lest the sons of the uncircumcised hear of it and mock. Supposing that you were able to rescue a captive church from the hands of a powerful man and restore to it its rights, which I do not for one moment suppose you could, what heir and successor would you most willingly chose: a knight to do service for it in the armies of the king or monks to intercede for your sins before the King of kings? Do therefore what is right, what becomes you, what is pleasing to God, and what, even if there were no other reasons, I should ask you to do for love of myself.

---

[1] . . . *quodam amico vestro*. Eales: ' A certain friend of mine '.
[2] . . . *in eo mihi vindico portionem*. Eales: ' I claim some portion in him '.

LETTER 378

TO HUGH, A NOVICE, WHO AFTERWARDS BECAME ABBOT OF BONNEVAL

This Hugh was, apparently, the nephew of St. Hugh, Bishop of Grenoble.

To his very dear son in Christ, Hugh, 'a new creature in Christ', that he may take courage in the Lord, from Brother Bernard, styled Abbot of Clairvaux.

WHEN I heard the good news of your conversion, my heart was filled with joy. It is a cause of joy for men and angels. Already it is a festal day in heaven, a day resounding with songs of praise and thanksgiving. A noble youth, gently nurtured, has conquered the evil one, scorned the world, sacrificed his body, renounced the affection of his parents, and, taking to himself wings, leaped over the snares of riches. Whence such wisdom, my son? Not even among the ancients of Babylon was such wisdom to be found. They were those who, according to or rather against the teaching of the Apostle, ' wished to become rich and fall into temptation, the devil's snare for them '. But the wisdom of my Hugh is of heaven and not of this world: ' I give thee praise, Father, that thou hast hidden all this from the wise and revealed it to a child '. Do you also, my son, thank our Redeemer for his gift to you, and ' keep the innocence of a child, with the thoughts of grown men '. Do not let the roughness of our life frighten your tender years. Remember that the rougher the thistle, the softer the cloth.[1] The sweetness of Christ will take the bitterness from the prophet's broth. If you feel the stings of temptation, lift your eyes to the serpent on the staff, and draw life from the wounds of Christ. He will be your mother, and you will be his son. The nails which cleave his hands and feet, must also pass through yours.

2. But ' a man's household are his own enemies '. These are they who love not you but the satisfaction they derive from you. But let them hear from you those words: ' If you really love me, you would be glad that I am on my way to my Father '. And now hear what blessed Jerome says: ' If your mother should lie prostrate at the door, if she should bare her breasts, the breasts that gave you suck, if your nephew should be hanging by his neck, yet with dry eyes fixed upon the Cross go ahead and tread over your prostrate mother and father. It is the height of piety to be cruel for Christ's sake.'[2] Do not be moved by the tears of demented parents who weep because from being a child of wrath you have become a child of God. Why have these unhappy people sentiments so harsh? What cruel love, what mistaken

---

[1] A reference to the practice of beating new cloth with thistles to make it soft.
[2] *Ep. Heliod.*, 1.

affection is theirs! Bad company, it is said, corrupts noble minds. And so I advise you, my son, to avoid as far as you can idle talking with guests, it only fills the ears without filling the mind. Learn to pray, to lift up your heart to God, your eyes in supplication to heaven. It were an impious thing to believe that God could ever close his heart to you or be deaf to your cry and sighs. For the rest, remember always and in everything to obey the counsels of your spiritual fathers as well as the commandments of the Divine Majesty. Do this and you shall live; do this and a rich blessing shall come upon you so that for every single thing you have left you will receive a hundredfold in return, even during this life. Do not believe anyone who tries to persuade you that you have been overhasty and would have done better to have waited until you were older. Believe rather him who said: 'It is well thou shouldst learn to bear the yoke, now in thy youth'. Farewell and persevere, for only perseverance is crowned.

LETTER 379

TO ROBERT, ABBOT OF DUNES

It was this Robert who succeeded St. Bernard as Abbot of Clairvaux, having been expressly chosen by him as his successor when he was dying.

To his brother and most dear friend, Abbot Robert, all that is due to a most dear friend, from Brother Bernard of Clairvaux.

HARDLY had I got to know you, dearest Robert, when you were promptly taken from me. But I console myself with the thought that it is only your bodily presence I lack, for in spirit we are united. I could never have borne even this had it not been a matter of God's will. The time will surely come when we shall be restored to each other again, when each of us will be pleased for our own sakes, and both of us for the sake of each other, present to each other not only in spirit but also in body, and never again to be separated. God, who is the cause of our present only temporary separation, will then be the bond of our union. He will always be present to us and will render us constantly present to each other. I send my greeting to all your sons, whom I regard also as my own, and I beg them to pray for me.

LETTER 380

TO THE SAME

To his most loving brother abbot, Robert of Dunes, the greetings of Bernard, styled Abbot of Clairvaux.

WITH regard to this brother whom you say is not only useless but also a burden, quite apart from his hidden defects of character, I will tell you how I should act in your place. It seems to me that, on the grounds of what you have told me about him, namely that during his probation he did not show himself either a likely or an acceptable recruit, you could with a clear conscience ' banish the offender from your company '. But if you wish to prefer mercy to justice, you could keep him on for as long as you wish without professing him. I strongly advise you not to admit him to profession while he is in this state. Give him another trial, if you like, and see how he gets on. If there is no improvement, you must use your power of expulsion, lest by one sick sheep the whole flock should become contaminated.

LETTER 381

TO THE ROMAN PONTIFF, AGAINST THE BISHOP OF RODEZ

UP to the present I have been writing to you in season and out of season at the request of friends, but now even if I wished to keep silence the interests of the Christian religion would forbid it. ' Cursed be the man ', says the Prophet, ' who goes about the Lord's work grudgingly, nor stains his sword with blood.' Evil is making head-way every day and godless men are prospering more and more, for there is no one to stand up to them and make himself a rampart for the protection of Israel. Even during your pontificate corrupt men have tried might and main to enter the holy of holies, men who have made a pact with death and truce with hell. Why are you so patient with them? The clergy of Rodez have elected a man who conspires in their vices. They are not ashamed to conceal the truth from you with lies concerning the person of the elected and the manner of his election. This man, the choice of men but not of God, has many witnesses to his infamy but none to his repentance. In fact it were more decent to keep silent than to speak of him. God forbid that such a monster should receive preferment during your pontificate; that a man having no regard for the price of his own redemption, for the blood shed by Christ, should be given the cure of other men's souls! What scruple would such a man have at a cunning insinuation that he had been injured, that an appeal had been suppressed, if he could thus ingratiate himself with the Curia and promote his cause? Pay no heed to his lies! According to truthful men no appeal could have been suppressed because no appeal was made. It is vital that you should support with all your authority the action that has been taken in this matter on the advice of religious men by the archbishop. I wish ever more strongly to recommend the archbishop. I would not speak or wish to be heard on his behalf were he not a credit to his office.

LETTER 382

TO THE BISHOP OF LIMOGES

I AM not writing to you in my own interests or to seek any advantage for myself. I am writing to you for your own sake. The days of men are short. As long as you are Bishop of Limoges try to be a credit to your position by letting us see your good works. I am glad to hear that the Pope has entrusted the cause of the bishop-elect of Cahors[1] to you, with the power to conclude it canonically without appeal. You have it in your power to prove to the Church of God that the Pontiff has been justified in this action of his. But you will only succeed in doing this if you fear God, observe the canons, and love justice. In the church of Rodez there is a question of a shepherd and a bishop of souls, a successor of Christ, a man to raise up seed to his dead brother. Shall it be the man of foul life, burdened conscience, and scandalous reputation? Shall it be the man who has descended from abbey to abbey, or rather from abyss to abyss, so as to be at once a consecrator and violator of virgins?[2] What of that saying of the Apostle: 'A bishop must needs be beyond reproach'? Do not be inconsistent with yourself, let your actions correspond with your words, so that those words of the psalm cannot be applied to you: 'Their tongues shall be turned against them'. It rests with you. Keep a watch on your soul and have no share in the sins of others. Through you this man will either stand or fall, if the latter you will be blessed by the Lord.[3]

LETTER 383

TO MALACHY, ARCHBISHOP OF IRELAND

To the venerable lord and most blessed father, Malachy, by the grace of God Archbishop of Ireland, and Apostolic Legate, that he may find favour before God, from Bernard, Abbot of Clairvaux.

A MONGST all the many worries and troubles by which I am distracted, your brethren from a distant land, your letter, and your gift of a staff are my comfort. Your letter shows me your good-will, your staff supports my weak body, and your brothers serve God humbly. I have accepted all, all have given me pleasure, and all work together for my good. With regard to your wish that I should send you two of the brothers to prepare a place, I have discussed it with the

---

[1] *Catiniensis.* Perhaps it should read *Catorcensis.*

[2] *Numquid ille, qui de abbatia in abbatiam, vel potius de abysso in abyssum descendit, ut idem sit violator virginum, et consecrator.* Eales: 'A man who has sunk from abbey to abbey, or rather from one depth to another, and who has not scrupled to violate the virgins to whom he himself has given the veil'.

[3] *. . . sed si corruerit, manus tuas consecrabis Domino.*

brethren and we are agreed that it would not be well for them to be separated from us until Christ is more fully formed in them, until they are better equipped to fight for the Lord. When they have been instructed in the school of the Holy Ghost, when they are clothed with strength from on high, then they will return to their father to sing the songs of the Lord no longer in a strange land but in their own.

2. Do you, in the meantime, with the wisdom given you by the Lord look for and prepare a site similar to what you have seen here, far removed from the turmoil of the world. The time is not far distant when I shall be able with God's grace to send you men fashioned anew in Christ. Blessed for ever be the name of the Lord by whose gift it has come about that we have sons in common whom your teaching has planted, my exhortations have watered, and to whom God has given increase. I beg you to preach the word of the Lord so as to ' make known to his people the salvation that is to release them from their sins '. As you are both archbishop and apostolic legate you have a twofold duty in this matter. For the rest because ' we are betrayed, all of us, into many faults ', and moving much amongst men of the world we collect much of the world's dust, I commend myself to the prayers of yourself and your friends, so that Christ, the source of all pity, may deign to wash me clean in the waters of his mercy, since he said to Peter: 'If I do not wash thee, it means that thou hast no companionship with me '. Indeed I not only beg this of you as a favour, but ask for it in return for my prayers to God on your behalf, if the prayers of a sinner like myself can avail anything. Farewell in the Lord.

LETTER 384

TO THE SAME

To Malachy, by the grace of God bishop and legate of the Apostolic See, whatever the devotion and prayers of a poor sinner can avail, from Bernard, styled Abbot of Clairvaux.

I HAVE done what you commanded, if not as it should have been done, at any rate as it could have been done at the time. The calls on me have grown so many that I have been scarcely able to accomplish the little that I have done. I have sent you these few seeds that you see before you. They may suffice for the sowing of a small part of that field where Isaac had gone to meditate when Rebecca was brought to him by the servant of Abraham, to be happily united to him for ever after. Scorn not this seed that I have sent you, for in it I find fulfilled in our day those words of the Prophet: ' Except the Lord of hosts had left us seed, we had been as Sodom, and we should have been as Gomorrah '. I have sowed and now it is for you to water, then God will give the increase. I greet the saints who are with you and humbly commend myself to your prayers and theirs.

LETTER 385

TO THE SAME

To his most loving father and most reverend lord, Malachy, by the grace of God bishop and legate of the Holy and Apostolic See, the greetings and, for what they are worth, the prayers of Brother Bernard, Abbot of Clairvaux.

How agreeable are your words, how pleasant the thought of you, lord and father! You command all the affection, and all the devotion of which I am capable. There is no need for many words where such affection flourishes. I am sure that the Spirit of God bears testimony to your spirit that I am all yours, little though that be. Do not, most loving and longed-for father, do not forget the poor man who clings to you with such affection, never forget your needy friend. I do not commend myself to you as though our friendship were something new, for it is my boast in the Lord that for a long time now my insignificant person has found favour in your eyes. Yet I pray that this affection which is no new growth may yet grow anew every day. I commend to you my sons, who are yours too, and I do so all the more earnestly for their being so far away from me. You know how, after God, I put all my trust in you by entrusting them to you, because it seemed wrong to refuse your prayers. Do all you can to open your heart to them and cherish them. Never on any pretext let your care and ardour for them flag or fade, never allow to perish what your hand has planted.

2. I have learned from your letters and from those of my brethren that the house flourishes exceedingly both in temporal and in spiritual things. With my whole heart I render thanks to God for this, and my congratulations to you. But because there is still need for vigilance in a new country amongst a people little accustomed to the monastic life and unfamiliar with it,[1] I beg you in the Lord not to remove your care from them until the work you have so well begun has been perfectly finished. Concerning the brethren who have returned, I would have been well contented for them to have remained with you. But perhaps those natives of your country who are little disciplined and who found it hard to obey observances that were strange to them, may have been in some measure the occasion of their return.

3. I have sent back to you my very dear son Christian, having instructed him as well as I could in the observances of our Order, and I hope that in future he will be more careful about them. Do not be surprised that I have not been able to send many with him, for I could not find many suitable men who were willing to go, and I was loath

---

[1] In spite of partisan historians, it cannot be denied that the religious position in Ireland at this time was not healthy. See St. Bernard's *Life of S. Malachy.*

to oblige them to do so against their will. My dear brother Robert
acceded to my request this time like an obedient son. It will be your
business to help him in the buildings and other things necessary for
the well-being of your house. I would also suggest that you persuade
those religious who you are hoping will be useful to the new monastery
that they should unite with their Order, for this would be very advantageous to the house, and you would be better obeyed. Farewell, and
always remember me in Christ.

LETTER 386

TO THE BRETHREN IN IRELAND, ON THE PASSING OF BLESSED MALACHY

*St. Malachy died on November 2nd, 1148. He had been an intimate friend
of St. Bernard since first meeting him when he stopped at Clairvaux on his
way to Rome in the year 1139.*

To his brother religious in Ireland, and especially to those houses
founded by Bishop Malachy of blessed memory, the consolation of the
Holy Spirit, from Brother Bernard, styled Abbot of Clairvaux.

IF we had here an abiding city we might rightly shed many tears at
the loss of such a fellow citizen as Malachy;[1] and if we look, as
we should, for the one that is to come, the loss of such a valuable
leader will still be an occasion for sorrow, yet nevertheless in this case
knowledge should moderate our feelings and sure hope set a limit to
our grief. It ought to be no matter for wonder if our affection wrings
a groan from our hearts, if our sense of bereavement expresses itself
in tears, yet there should be measure in our grief, we should, in fact,
find some consolation for it in the contemplation, not of what we can
see, but of what we cannot see, for we see only what passes, what
endures we cannot see. We must be glad for the sake of this holy
soul, otherwise he would accuse us in the words of our Lord to the
Apostles: ' If you really loved me you would be glad to hear that I
am on my way to my Father '. The spirit of our father has gone ahead
of us to the ' Father of a world of spirits '. We would prove ourselves
not only wanting in charity but also ungrateful for all that we have
received through him, were we not glad for his sake that he has passed
from his many labours to everlasting repose, from the dangers of the
world to the safety of heaven, from the world to the Father. It is an
act of filial piety to grieve for the death of Malachy, but it were an
act of even greater filial piety to rejoice with him in the life that he has
found. Has he not found life? Surely he has, and a blessed life:
' In the eyes of fools he seemed to die, but all is well with him '.

---

[1] *Si habemus hic manentem civitatem, copiosissimis jure lacrymis plangeremus. . . .* Eales: ' If
we had here a continuing city, we should *not* have to shed abundant tears . . .'.

2. Even considerations of our own advantage suggest that we should rejoice and be glad that we have such a powerful patron in the court of heaven, a faithful advocate whose deep love will not permit him to forget us, and whose well tried holiness will obtain for him the favour of God. Who would dare to believe that the holy Malachy loves his sons less now or is less able to help them than he was? There is no doubt that since God loved him before he died he now enjoys a deeper and more sure experience of God's love; and that since he loved his own, he loved them to the end. May it be far from us, O holy soul, to consider your prayers less helpful to us now that you are offering them to the Divine Majesty with even greater eagerness, now that you are no longer living by faith but reigning by vision! Far may it be from us to believe that your charity is in any way less active that it was, now that you sit at the very fount of charity and are able to draw deep draughts of it instead of the drops for which you used to thirst. Charity is strong and cannot yield to death, it is even stronger than death. When he lay dying he remembered you and lovingly commended you to God, and he begged even me, a person of no consequence, always to remember you. For this reason I thought it well to write and tell you that I am ready with all my heart to give you such help as I can both in spiritual matters, if my incompetence in such things can achieve anything through the prayers of our blessed father, and in material matters if any opportunity should arise.

3. And also, dear sons, I feel the deepest compassion for the Irish Church in her great bereavement, and my sympathy for you is all the greater for my realization of the debt I owe you. The Lord has highly honoured us by favouring our place with the blessed death of Malachy and enriching it with the treasure of his precious body. Do not take it ill that he should have his tomb with us, since God out of his abundant mercy has so ordained it that you should have him while he lived and we when he was dead. For both you and us he was a common father, and still is, for this was the wish he expressed to us on his death-bed. Wherefore we embrace you all with deep affection as our true brothers for the sake of this great father of ours, just as we are inspired to regard you as such by the very spiritual relationship by which we are united.

4. I exhort you, my brethren, to follow carefully in the footsteps of our father, and all the more zealously for knowing from daily experience his holy way of life. You will prove yourselves his true sons by manfully keeping his teaching; and as you saw in him and received from him a pattern of how you ought to live, live by that pattern, and make more of it than ever: ' Wise sons are the pride of their father '. Even I have been stirred from my sloth and imbued with reverence by the pattern of perfection he set before me. May he so draw me after him that I may run willingly and eagerly in the

fragrance of his virtues, while the memory of them is still fresh.   May Christ have you all in his safe keeping praying as you are for us!

LETTER 387

TO JOCELIN, BISHOP OF SOISSONS

To the venerable lord and most dear father, Jocelin, by the grace of God Bishop of Soissons, that he may find favour with the Lord, from Bernard, Abbot of Clairvaux.

IT would only injure the kingdom and the princes if the king should make public his affairs and impetuously reveal his counsel without mature consideration.   I am very pleased indeed that the king trusts and confides in you.   I know you to be very zealous for the good and honour of the king and the kingdom.   This is as it should be.   Order and reason demand that a counsellor should be both prudent and devoted.   On these two things prudence and devotion, all good counsel depends.   If a counsellor unites in his person these two, then he will be able to bring forth good advice and direct the enterprises of the king.   But if, in the performance of his duty as administrator, his devotion should lack prudence, or his prudence lack devotion, then woe to the country whose king is a child!   May my soul not fall into the hands of counsellors whose devotion to me lacks prudence or whose prudence lacks devotion!   Thus fell the wretched Adam from immortality, when he followed the advice of Eve, who had devotion for him but not prudence, and of the serpent who had prudence but completely lacked all devotion.

2. Why is it that my lord the king is trying to draw the Archbishop of Bordeaux into a quarrel?   Is it by your advice?   I hope that you would never dream of giving him any such advice, and that I may never have reason to suspect you of doing so.   What harm has the man done?   Is it because with the consent, desire, and acclamations of the people of Poitiers, he consecrated the bishop, as he was quite at liberty to do by the canons?   Or is it because he gave to the poor churches, and the hungry of Poitiers, the money distributed by a dying man, and did not rob the Church of it?   Is this why he is blamed?   If it be a fault to give a pastor to straying sheep, to refrain from despoiling the widow and the orphan, to preserve intact the privileges of the Apostolic See, then there is no excuse for the Archbishop of Bordeaux.   What misguided guidance to reckon righteousness as wickedness, and innocence as a crime!   Look to yourselves, you bishops, for ' your own goods are in danger when your neighbour's house is aflame '![1]

3. But since you, my lord, are nearest to the king's side, and since

[1] Horace, *Ep.* I, s, 84.

his affairs depend upon your consent for their execution, it is incumbent on you to use your influence on behalf of your brethren, and to see that the anger of the king does not become inflamed against them. I tell you that in the Archbishop of Bordeaux you are dealing with a fearless man, powerful in word and deed. He will not budge from his rights. He holds a great position in his district. If things should get difficult for him, he will have no lack of supporters in his trouble. See therefore that no one pours oil upon the flames of the king's wrath, but that it is extinguished before it has time to grow: 'Too late is the doctor called, when sickness has grown bad through long delays'.[1]

LETTER 388

TO THE BRETHREN OF ST. ANASTASIUS

To his very dear sons in Christ, the brethren of St. Anastasius, greetings and prayers from Brother Bernard, styled Abbot of Clairvaux.

HEAVEN is my witness how greatly I love you all in Jesus Christ, and how great would be my desire to see you were such a thing possible, not only on your own account but also on my own. It would be an enormous joy and comfort for me to embrace you, my sons, my joy, and my crown. This is not yet possible for me, but I firmly trust in God's mercy that the day will come when I shall be able to see you, and then my heart will be glad and my gladness no man shall take from me. In the meantime it is certainly a great joy and consolation for me to hear of you from my dear brother-abbot, Bernard. I congratulate you on the satisfaction you have given him by your discipline and zeal in the matter of obedience and poverty; without doubt your reward for this will be great in heaven. I beg and implore you, dearest brothers, so to act, so to stand firm in the Lord, as to be always careful for the observance of the Order that the Order may always be careful for you. Be eager always to preserve unity in the bonds of peace, having towards each other, but especially towards your superiors, the humble charity 'that is the bond that makes us perfect'. Seek humility before all things and peace above all things for the sake of the indwelling Spirit of God which rests only on the peaceful and humble.

2. But there is one thing your venerable abbot has asked me about which does not seem to me at all good. And I believe that I have the Spirit of God and know the will of God in this matter. I fully realize that you live in an unhealthy region[2] and that many of you are sick, but remember him who said: 'I delight to boast of the weaknesses

---

[1] Ovid, *De Remed. Amor.*, 91, 92.

[2] The monastery of St. Anastasius was situated in the Campagna outside Rome. To within living memory this district has been riddled with malaria. St. Bernard's attitude towards medicine was probably wise in the state of medical knowledge at that time. Less wise was the selection of such an unhealthy region for a monastery.

that humiliate me, so that the strength of Christ may enshrine itself in me ', and ' When I am weakest then I am strongest of all '.   I have the very greatest sympathy for bodily sickness, but I consider that sickness of the soul is much more to be feared and avoided.   It is not at all in keeping with your profession to seek for bodily medicines, and they are not really conducive to health.   The use of common herbs, such as are used by the poor, can sometimes be tolerated, and such is our custom.   But to buy special kinds of medicines, to seek out doctors and swallow their nostrums, this does not become religious, is contrary to simplicity, and is especially inconsistent with the decency and simplicity of our Order.   We know that ' those who live the life of nature cannot be acceptable to God ' and for us who ' have received no spirit of worldly wisdom, but the spirit that comes from God ' the proper medicine is humility and the most suitable prayer is ' purge me of my sin, the guilt which I freely acknowledge '.   This is the health you must try to obtain, seek out, and preserve, dearest brothers, because ' vain is the help of man '.

LETTER 389

TO ARCHBISHOP THEOBALD, ON BEHALF OF JOHN OF SALISBURY

YOU do me a signal favour and honour me very much when you favour my friends for my sake.   Yet I seek not honour from any man, but the kingdom of God and the justice thereof.   I am sending your Highness John, the bearer of this letter.   He is a friend of mine and of my friends, and I beg that he may benefit from the friendship for which I count on you.   He has a good reputation amongst good men, not less for his life than for his learning.   I have not learned this from those who exaggerate and use words lightly, but from my own sons whose words I believe as my own eyes.   I had already commended him to you in person, but now that I am absent I do so much more and with all the more confidence for having learned from reliable witnesses about his life and habits.   If I have any influence with you, and I know that I have much, provide for him that he may have the means to live decently and honourably, and I beg you to do this without delay for he has nowhere to turn.   In the meantime provide for his needs, I beg you, and let me thus experience, most loving father, those depths of affection which you retain in your heart for me.

LETTER 390

TO HILDEGARDE, ABBESS OF MONT ST. RUPERT

Hildegarde was a well-known visionary, favoured with several rather surprising revelations.   Her prophecies were more widely known than generally understood.   But she enjoyed the favour of Pope Eugenius and several distinguished churchmen. In a letter to St. Bernard she congratulated him on his preaching of the Crusade and declared that she saw him ' as a man in the sun '. But in the following reply to one of her letters, the Abbot of Clairvaux seems to word himself with a certain circumspection.

To his beloved daughter in Christ, Hildegarde, whatever the prayers of a sinner can avail, from Brother Bernard, styled Abbot of Clairvaux.

THAT others should believe me a better person than I know myself to be, is due more to human stupidity than any special merits of my own. I hasten to reply to your sweet and kindly letter, although the multitude of my affairs obliges me to do so more briefly than I could wish. I congratulate you on the grace of God that is in you and admonish you to regard it as a gift and respond to it with all humility and devotion in the sure knowledge that ' God flouts the scornful, and gives the humble man his grace '. This is what I beg and implore you to do. How could I presume to teach or advise you who are favoured with hidden knowledge and in whom ' the influence of Christ's anointing still lives so that you have no need of teaching ', for you are said to be able to search the secrets of heaven and to discern by the light of the Holy Spirit things that are beyond the knowledge of man. It is rather for me to beg that you may not forget me before God, or those who are united to me in spiritual fellowship. I am sure that when your spirit is united to God you could help and benefit us much, for ' when a just man prays fervently, there is great virtue in his prayer '. We pray without ceasing for you that you may be strengthened in all good, instructed in interior things, and guided to what endures, so that those who put their trust in God may not fall by losing faith in you, but may rather derive strength, so as to make ever greater progress in good, from the sight of your own progress in the graces which you are known to have received from God.

LETTER 391

TO THE ENGLISH PEOPLE

The manuscript of this letter in the Biblioth èque Nationale, Paris (fonds latin, MS. 14845, fol. 257), has been known for some years but, to the best of our belief, it has never before been published or translated.

I ADDRESS myself to you, the people of England, in the cause of Christ, in whom lies your salvation. I say this so that the warrant of the Lord and my zeal in his interests may excuse my hardihood in addressing you. I am a person of small account, but my desire for you in Christ is not small. This is my reason and motive for writing, this is why I make bold to address you all by letter. I would have preferred to do so by word of mouth had I but the strength to come to you as I desire.

2. Now is the acceptable time, now is the day of abundant salvation. The earth is shaken because the Lord of heaven is losing his land, the land in which he appeared to men, in which he lived amongst men for more than thirty years; the land made glorious by his miracles, holy by his blood; the land in which the flowers of his resurrection first blossomed. And now, for our sins, the enemy of the Cross has begun to lift his sacrilegious head there, and to devastate with the sword that blessed land, that land of promise. Alas, if there should be none to withstand him, he will soon invade the very city of the living God, overturn the arsenal of our redemption, and defile the holy places which have been adorned by the blood of the immaculate lamb. They have cast their greedy eyes especially on the holy sanctuaries of our Christian Religion, and they long particularly to violate that couch on which, for our sakes, the Lord of our life fell asleep in death.

3. What are you doing, you mighty men of valour? What are you doing, you servants of the Cross? Will you thus cast holy things to dogs, pearls before swine? How great a number of sinners have here confessed with tears and obtained pardon for their sins since the time when these holy precincts were cleansed of pagan filth by the swords of our fathers! The evil one sees this and is enraged, he gnashes his teeth and withers away in fury. He stirs up his vessels of wrath so that if they do but once lay hands upon these holy places there shall be no sign or trace of piety left. Such a catastrophe would be a source of appalling grief for all time, but it would also be a source of confusion and endless shame for our generation. What think you, my brethren? Is the hand of the Lord shortened and is he now power-less to work salvation, so that he must call upon us, petty worms of the earth, to save and restore to him his heritage? Could he not send more than twelve legions of angels, or even just say the word and save his land? Most certainly he has the power to do this whenever he wishes, but I tell you that God is trying you. 'He looks down from heaven at the race of men, to find one soul that reflects, and makes God its aim', one soul that sorrows for him. For God has pity on his people and on those who have grievously fallen away and has prepared for them a means of salvation. Consider with what care he plans our salvation, and be amazed. Look, sinners, at the depths of his pity, and take courage. He does not want your death but rather that you should turn to him and live. So he seeks not to overthrow you but to help you. When Almighty God so treats murderers, thieves, adulterers, perjurers, and such like, as persons able to find righteousness in his service, what is it but an act of exquisite courtesy all God's own? Do not hesitate. God is good, and were he intent on your punishment he would not have asked of you this present service or indeed have accepted it even had you offered it. Again I say consider the Almighty's goodness and pay heed to his plans of mercy. He puts

16

himself under obligation to you, or rather feigns to do so, so that he can help you to satisfy your obligations towards himself. He puts himself in your debt so that, in return for your taking up arms in his cause, he can reward you with pardon for your sins and everlasting glory. I call blessed the generation that can seize an opportunity of such rich indulgence as this, blessed to be alive in this year of jubilee, this year of God's choice. The blessing is spread throughout the whole world, and all the world is flocking to receive this badge of immortality.

4. Your land is well known to be rich in young and vigorous men. The world is full of their praises, and the renown of their courage is on the lips of all. Gird yourselves therefore like men and take up arms with joy and with zeal for your Christian name, in order to ' take vengeance on the heathen, and curb the nations '. For how long will your men continue to shed Christian blood; for how long will they continue to fight amongst themselves? You attack each other, you slay each other and by each other you are slain. What is this savage craving of yours? Put a stop to it now, for it is not fighting but foolery. Thus to risk both soul and body is not brave but shocking, is not strength but folly. But now, O mighty soldiers, O men of war, you have a cause for which you can fight without danger to your souls; a cause in which to conquer is glorious and for which to die is gain.

5. But to those of you who are merchants, men quick to seek a bargain, let me point out the advantages of this great opportunity. Do not miss them. Take up the sign of the Cross and you will find indulgence for all the sins which you humbly confess. The cost is small, the reward is great. Venture with devotion and the gain will be God's kingdom. They do well therefore who have taken up this heavenly sign, and they also will do well, and profit themselves, who hasten to take up what will prove to be for them a sign of salvation.

6. For the rest, not I but the Apostle warns you, brethren, not to believe every spirit. I have heard with great joy of the zeal for God's glory which burns in your midst, but your zeal needs the timely restraint of knowledge. The Jews are not to be persecuted, killed or even put to flight. Ask anyone who knows the Sacred Scriptures what he finds foretold of the Jews in the psalm. ' Not for their destruction do I pray ', it says. The Jews are for us the living words of Scripture, for they remind us always of what our Lord suffered. They are dispersed all over the world so that by expiating their crime they may be everywhere the living witnesses of our redemption. Hence the same psalm adds, ' only let thy power disperse them '. And so it is: dispersed they are. Under Christian princes they endure a hard captivity, but ' they only wait for the time of their deliverance '. Finally we are told by the Apostle that when the time is ripe all Israel

shall be saved.   But those who die before will remain in death.   I will not mention those Christian money lenders, if they can be called Christian, who, where there are no Jews, act, I grieve to say, in a manner worse than any Jew.   If the Jews are utterly wiped out, what will become of our hope for their promised salvation, their eventual conversion?   If the pagans were similarly subjugated to us then, in my opinion, we should wait for them rather than seek them out with swords.   But as they have now begun to attack us, it is necessary for those of us who do not carry a sword in vain to repel them with force. It is an act of Christian piety both ' to vanquish the proud ' and also ' to spare the subjected ',[1] especially those for whom we have a law and a promise, and whose flesh was shared by Christ whose name be for ever blessed.

The above letter was also sent ' To the lords and very dear fathers, the archbishops, bishops, and all the clergy and people of Eastern France and Bavaria, that they may abound in the spirit of strength, from Bernard, styled Abbot of Clairvaux ' (Benedictine Edition, 363).

LETTER 392

TO THE DUKE WLADISLAUS, AND THE NOBLES AND PEOPLE OF BOHEMIA

To the Duke Wladislaus, all the other nobles, and to all the people of Bohemia, greetings in Christ, from Bernard, styled Abbot of Clairvaux.

I ADDRESS myself to you in the cause of Christ, in whom lies our true deliverance.   I say this so that the warrant of the Lord and my zeal for his interests may excuse my hardihood in thus addressing you. I am a person of small account, but my love for you in Christ is not small.   This zeal of mine impels me to write in a letter what I would far sooner inscribe upon your hearts with my voice, if I had the power to follow my will in the matter.   But the body is weak although the spirit is willing.   My corruptible body cannot comply with the inclinations of my spirit, nor can the burden of my flesh keep pace with its speed.   But although the great distance between us prevents me from reaching you in body, my heart stretches out to you, and this is what really matters.   Hear then the good news I have to tell you, news of deliverance, and open your arms wide with devotion to receive the rich indulgence that is offered you.   This time is not like any time that has gone before, new riches of divine mercy are descending on you from heaven, and happy are we to be alive in this year of God's choice, this year of jubilee, this year of pardon.   I tell

[1] *Aeneid*, 6, 853.

you, the Lord has never done the like for any former generation, never did our fathers receive so rich an outpouring of grace.   See, you who have sinned, to what artifice God has had recourse in order to save you, consider the depths of his pity for you and be amazed !   He places himself in need of you, or pretends to do so, in order to help you with the riches of heaven.   The earth is troubled and shaken because the Lord is losing his land, the land in which he was seen amongst men for more than thirty years.   His land, the land which he honoured with his birth, made glorious with his miracles, sanctified with his blood, and endowed with his tomb.   His land, the land in which the voice of the turtle dove was heard, the voice of the Virgin's Son calling men to a pure life.   His land, the land in which the flowers of his resurrection first blossomed.   This land evil men have begun to invade and, unless someone be found to withstand them, they will swallow up the holy sanctuaries of our religion, violate the couch on which our life fell asleep in death for our sakes, and profane the holy places adorned with the blood of the Immaculate Lamb.   Hear something more, something well calculated to smite the hardest heart of any Christian.   They accuse our King of betraying us, they charge him with pretending to be God when he was not.   Let those of you who are loyal to him arise and defend their Lord against the shame of such an imputation. Safe is the battle in which it is glorious to conquer and a gain to die. Why do you hesitate, you servants of the Cross?   Why do you, who want for neither strength nor goods, make excuses?   Receive the sign of the Cross, and to all of you who have confessed their sins with truly contrite hearts, the Supreme Pontiff, to whom it was said, ' What thou shalt loose on earth shall be loosed in heaven ', offers a full pardon.   Receive this proffered gift and hasten each to outstrip the other in taking advantage of this opportunity which will not come again.   I ask and advise you to put this business of Christ before everything else and not to neglect it for what can be done at other times. And so that you may know when, where, and how it is to be done, listen further: The army of the Lord is to set out next Easter, and it has been determined that a large part of it shall pass through Hungary. It has been laid down that no one shall wear any coloured, grey, or silk apparel, and the use of gold or silver harness has been forbidden. But those who wish may wear gold or silver when they enter battle, so that the sun may shine upon them and scatter the forces of the enemy with terror.   We have written in Latin because you have with you a learned and holy man in the lord Bishop of Moravia; and I pray him that, according to the wisdom he has received from the Lord, he may with all diligence exhort and instruct in this matter.   We have sent a copy of this letter to the Lord Pope, to whose admonitions you must listen with attentive ears and whose commands you must implicitly obey.

LETTER 393

TO HENRY, ARCHBISHOP OF MAINZ

In the year 1146, during the excitement of the Crusade, a certain monk, Raoul by name, a zealous but rather ill-educated religious, wandered round the Rhineland inciting thousands to take the Cross and begin the Crusade by setting about the Jews. In the following letter the Abbot of Clairvaux indignantly condemns the action of Raoul. Even to this day the Jews of that district have not forgotten the protection extended to their race by the saint, and in recognition of their gratitude they will sometimes call their sons Bernard.

To the venerable lord and most dear father Henry, Archbishop of Mainz, that he may find favour before God, from Bernard, Abbot of Clairvaux.

I RECEIVED your kind letter with due respect, but my answer must be brief because of the press of business. By revealing to me your troubles you have given me a sure sign and pledge of your affection and, what is more, a mark of your humility. Who am I, or what is my father's house, that I should have referred to me a case of contempt for an archbishop and of damage to his metropolitan see? ' I am no better than a child that has no skill to find its way back and forth.' Yet ignorant though I be, I am not unmindful of those words of the Most High: ' It must needs be that scandals come, but nevertheless woe to that man through whom the scandal cometh'. The fellow you mention in your letter has received no authority from men or through men, nor has he been sent by God. If he makes himself out to be a monk or a hermit, and on that score claims liberty to preach and the duty of doing so, he can and should know that the duty of a monk is not to preach but to pray. He ought to be a man for whom towns are a prison and the wilderness a paradise, but instead of that he finds towns a paradise and the wilderness a prison. A fellow without sense and void of all modesty! A fellow whose foolishness has been set up on a candlestick for all the world to see!

2. I find three things most reprehensible in him: unauthorized preaching, contempt for episcopal authority, and incitation to murder. A new power forsooth! Does he consider himself greater than our father Abraham who laid down his sword at the bidding of him by whose command he took it up? Does he consider himself greater than the Prince of the Apostles who asked the Lord: ' Shall we strike with our swords?' He is a fellow full of the wisdom of Egypt which is, as we know, foolishness in the sight of God. He is a fellow who answers Peter's question differently to the Lord who said: ' Put back thy sword into its place; all those who take up the sword will

perish by the sword'. Is it not a far better triumph for the Church to convince and convert the Jews than to put them all to the sword? Has that prayer which the Church offers for the Jews, from the rising up of the sun to the going down thereof, that the veil may be taken from their hearts so that they may be led from the darkness of error into the light of truth, been instituted in vain? If she did not hope that they would believe and be converted, it would seem useless and vain for her to pray for them. But with the eye of mercy she considers how the Lord regards with favour him who renders good for evil and love for hatred. Otherwise where does that saying come in, ' Not for their destruction I pray', and ' When the fulness of the Gentiles shall have come in, then all Israel will be saved', and ' The Lord is rebuilding Jerusalem, calling the banished sons of Israel home '? Who is this man that he should make out the Prophet to be a liar and render void the treasures of Christ's love and pity? This doctrine is not his own but his father's. But I believe it is good enough for him, since he is like his father who was, we know, ' from the first a murderer, a liar, and the father of lies'. What horrid learning, what hellish wisdom is his! A learning and wisdom contrary to the prophets, hostile to the apostles, and subversive of piety and grace. It is a foul heresy, a sacrilegious prostitution ' pregnant with malice, that has conceived only spite, and given birth only to shame '! I should like to say more, but I must forbear. To sum up briefly what I feel about this fellow: He is a man with a great opinion of himself and full of arrogance. He shows by his works and teaching that he would like to make a great name for himself amongst the great of the earth, but that he has not the wherewithal to achieve this.

LETTER 394

TO ALL THE FAITHFUL

This letter is chiefly concerned with the plan for an expedition against the idolatrous tribes to the east of the Saxons and Moravians. It was greatly feared that these peoples would make the vulnerable state of Europe an occasion for attacking in the rear of the crusading armies. This expedition was to enjoy all the spiritual privileges of the crusade to Jerusalem.

To his lords and reverend fathers, the archbishops, bishops, and princes, and to all the faithful of God, the spirit of strength and deliverance, from Bernard, styled Abbot of Clairvaux.

WITHOUT doubt it has been heard in your land, without doubt the news has gone forth in oft repeated words that God has stirred up the spirit of kings and princes to take vengeance on the pagans and to wipe out from Christian lands . . . [*MS. defective*]. How good and great is the bounty of God's mercy! But the evil one sees this and resents it, he gnashes his teeth and withers away in fury, for he is losing many of those whom he held bound by various crimes and enormities. Abandoned men are now being converted, turning aside from evil, and making ready to do good. But the evil one feared far more the damage he would incur from the conversion of the pagans, when he heard that their tale was to be completed, and that the whole of Israel was to find salvation. This is what he believes to be threatening him now at this very time, and with all his evil cunning he is endeavouring to see how he can best oppose such a great good. He has raised up evil seed, wicked pagan sons, whom, if I may say so, the might of Christendom has endured too long, shutting its eyes to those who with evil intent lie in wait, without crushing their poisoned heads under its heel. But the Scriptures say: ' Presumption comes first, and ruin close behind it '. And so God grant that the pride of these peoples may be speedily humbled and the road to Jerusalem not closed on their account. Because the Lord has committed to our insignificance the preaching of this crusade, we make known to you that at the council of the king, bishops, and princes who had come together at Frankfort, the might of Christians was armed against them, and that for the complete wiping out or, at any rate, the conversion of these peoples, they have put on the Cross, the sign of our salvation; and we, by virtue of our authority, promised them the same spiritual privileges as those enjoy who set out towards Jerusalem. Many took the Cross on the spot, the rest we encouraged to do so, so that all Christians who have not yet taken the Cross for Jerusalem may know that they will obtain the same spiritual privileges by undertaking this expedition, if they do so according to the advice of the bishops and princes. We utterly forbid that for any reason whatsoever a truce should be made with these peoples, either for the sake of money or for the sake of tribute, until such a time as, by God's help, they shall be either converted or wiped out. We speak to you, archbishops and bishops, and urge you to oppose any such plan for a truce with all your strength, and to watch with the greatest care this matter, and to apply all the zeal of which you are capable to seeing that it is carried through manfully. You are the ministers of Christ, and therefore it is demanded of you with all the more confidence that you should watch faithfully over God's work, which, because it is his work, should be especially your concern. And this is what we too pray for from God with our whole heart. The uniform of this army, in clothes, in arms, and in all else, will be the same as the uniform of the other, for it is fortified with the same privileges. It has pleased all those who were gathered together at Frankfort to decree that a copy of this letter should be carried everywhere and that the bishops and priests should proclaim it to the people of God, and arm them with the holy Cross against the enemies of the Cross of Christ, and that they should all meet at Magdeburg on the feast of the apostles Peter and Paul.

LETTER 395

TO G— DE STOPH

To his well-loved daughter in Christ G— de Stoph, the greetings and prayers of Bernard, styled Abbot of Clairvaux.

MY dear daughter, your brother Henry has been to see me. On my advice he has not laid aside the intention for which he took the Cross, he has done something far better. He has become poor for the sake of Christ, and he has decided to live in the habit of religion with the poor of Christ. Do not take it hard that he should thus have chosen with Mary that best part of all which shall never be taken from him, and have turned his face towards that true Jerusalem which does not stone the prophets, but which is ' united in fellowship '. Take comfort from these words and bear in mind our last conversation together. May you so act as always to deserve the mercy of God, and the thanks of your brother and myself. May you always prosper, my dear daughter.

LETTER 396

TO HIS BROTHER ABBOTS[1]

A hitherto unpublished letter for which the translator is indebted to the Reverend Father Joseph Canivez, O.C.S.O.

Apparently certain Cistercian monks had been attempting to join in the expedition of the Crusade, and in this letter to the abbots of the Order the saint declares that all monks and lay-brothers who leave their monastery to take part in the expedition are excommunicated.

To all his reverend lords and dear brother abbots, that they may abound in the grace of God, from Brother Bernard, styled Abbot of Clairvaux.

ALTHOUGH we are bound by our religion to exclude none from the warmth of our charity, yet our zeal is nevertheless greater towards those to whom we are united by the profession of a common life. Therefore while rejoicing in your well-being, I am just as much saddened by your adversities as I would be by my own. I have learned from the report of many that certain brethren are grumbling against you, and that they have scorned our holy way of life and are trying to mix themselves in the turmoil of the world. How is their case different from Abiron and Dathan who, while grumbling against Moses, were swallowed up by the earth, except that they are buried

---

[1] Codex 388, Nationalbibliothek, Wien, fol. 81 v.

by their earthly desires? What concern have they with crowds, when they are to be blamed for singularity? Why do they seek the glory of the world, when they have chosen ' to lie forgotten in the house of God '? What have they to do with wandering about the countryside when they are professed to lead a life in solitude? Why do they sew the sign of the Cross on their clothes, when they always carry it on their hearts so long as they cherish their religious way of life? To be brief, I say to all by the authority not of myself but of the Apostolic See that if any monk or lay-brother should leave his monastery to go on the expedition, he will place himself under sentence of excommunication.

LETTER 397

TO ALPHONSUS, KING OF PORTUGAL

To Alphonsus, the illustrious King of Portugal, whatever the prayers of a sinner can avail, from Bernard, styled Abbot of Clairvaux.

I HAVE received the letter of your Highness with great pleasure in him who sent ' deliverance to Israel '. What I have done in the matter will be evident from the outcome of it, as you will see for yourself. You will see with what promptitude I have complied with your request and with the exigencies of the affair. Peter, the brother of your Highness and a prince worthy of all honour, has acquainted me with your wishes. After having passed through France with his army, he is now soldiering in Lorraine. Soon he will be fighting the battles of the Lord. My son, Roland, is bringing you the documents which set forth the liberality of the Apostolic See. I commend to you both him and my brethren who are in your kingdom.

LETTER 398

TO PETER, ABBOT OF CLUNY

To his most loving father Peter, by the grace of God the venerable Abbot of Cluny, greetings and such prayers as he is capable of from Brother Bernard of Clairvaux.

I EXPECT the heavy sighs of the Eastern Church have reached your ears and penetrated to your heart. It is only fitting that a man of your high rank in the Church should show compassion for your mother and the mother of all the faithful, especially when she is so grievously afflicted, so seriously endangered. The higher the position a man holds in the House of God, the more he ought to be consumed with zeal for her welfare. If we harden our hearts, if we steel our affections and pay little heed to this great suffering and have small compassion for this sorrow, where does our love for God and our neighbour come in? If we do not try with all the attention of which we are capable to render advice and help in such great evils, such great perils, we surely prove ourselves ungrateful to him who ' hid us in his royal tabernacle safe from danger ' and deserving of severe punishment as men who care nothing for the divine glory and the salvation of our brother. I have ventured to speak my mind quite openly and as a friend because your Excellency has always deigned to treat me with honour.

2. Our fathers, the bishops of France, together with the lord king and the princes, are to meet at Chartres on the third Sunday after Easter to consider this matter. I hope that we may be favoured with your presence. It is clear that this is a matter which needs the counsel of all the eminent men of the kingdom. You will render a service acceptable to God if you consider this as a matter which concerns yourself and prove the zeal of your charity in time of peril. You know, most loving father, that a friend is known in the hour of adversity. I am sure that your presence would be a great benefit to the assembly both because of the prestige of the holy abbey of Cluny over which you preside, and because of the wisdom and grace with which God has endowed you for the benefit of your neighbour and the honour of his name. May you now be inspired by his grace not to hesitate but to come and confer your most desirable presence on his servants gathered together in his name in order zealously to serve him.

LETTER 399

TO POPE EUGENIUS

This letter is dated by Eales, following the authority of Mabillon, for the year 1146, and is taken to refer to the preparations for the ill-fated Second Crusade. To us it seems from the whole tone of the letter that it far more probably belongs to the year 1150 after the first expedition had met with disaster, and refers to an attempt to launch another expedition to retrieve the fortunes of the first. The phrase . . . nec terrebitur damnis prioris exercitus, quibus magis resarciendis operam dabit, '. . . he will not be deterred by the loss of our former army, but rather he will do his best to repair it', would seem to establish this beyond any doubt. If the phrase does not refer to the disaster of the first expedition, it could only refer to the loss of Edessa in 1144, and this would not meet all the facts, because an army had not been sent to defend Edessa. As is well known, the plan to launch another attack came to nothing.

St. Bernard urges the Pope to retrieve the fortunes of the Crusade with another expedition.

THE news is sad and grave.[1] Sad for whom? Or rather, I should say, for whom is it not sad? Only for the sons of wrath who do

[1] This can only refer to the news of the defeat of the Crusade.

not feel the wrath and are not saddened by the sad things which are happening, ' for sin and shame is all their liking '. But for these, it is sad for everyone, because it is a cause that affects everyone. You have done well to praise the most righteous zeal of the Church in France, and to encourage it with the authority of your letters. I tell you, such a grave and universal crisis is no time for half-hearted or timid measures. I have read in the book of a certain wise man: ' He is no brave man whose courage does not rise in the face of difficulty '.[1] I would say that a faithful man is even more to be trusted in disaster. The waters have reached the soul of Christ, the very apple of his eye has been touched. In this second passion of Christ we must draw those two swords that were drawn during the first passion. And who is there to draw them but you? Both of Peter's swords must be drawn whenever necessary; the one by his command, the other by his hand. It seems that Peter was not to use one of these swords, for he was told ' put up thy sword into the scabbard '. Although they both belonged to him, they were not both to be drawn by his hand.

2. I believe that the time has come for both swords to be drawn in defence of the Eastern Church. You hold the position of Peter, and you ought also to have his zeal. What could we think of one who held the primacy but neglected the responsibility? We hear the voice crying: ' I go to Jerusalem to be crucified a second time '.[2] Although some may be indifferent to this voice and others may be deaf to it, the successor of St. Peter cannot ignore it. He will say: ' Although all may be scandalized in thee, I will never be scandalized '. He will not be deterred by the loss of our former army, but rather he will do his best to repair it. Because God does what he wishes, it is no reason why we should not do our duty. But I as a faithful Christian hope for better things and think it great joy that we have fallen on divers trails. Truly we have eaten the bread of grief and drunk the wine of sorrow. Why are you, the friend of the Bridegroom, fearful, as though the kind and wise Bridegroom had not, according to his custom, saved the good wine until now? 'Who knows but he will relent and be appeased, and leave behind a blessing.' Certainly the Divine Goodness is wont to act in this way, as you know better than I do. When has not great good been preceded by great evils? To mention nothing else, was not that unique and unparalleled gift of our salvation preceded by the death of our Saviour?

3. Do you then, the friend of the Bridegroom, prove yourself a friend in need. If you love Christ as you should, with all your heart, with all your soul, and with all your strength; if you love him with that threefold love about which your predecessor was questioned, then

---

[1] Seneca, *Epistle to Lucilius*, 22.
[2] Hegesippus, *De Excid.*, lib. 3, cap. 2.

you will make no reservations, you will leave nothing undone while his bride is in such great danger, but rather you will devote to her all your strength, all your zeal, all your care, and all your power. An extraordinary danger demands an extraordinary effort. It is as if the very foundations of the Church have been shaken and we must put forth all our strength to prevent the building from falling. I have written boldly but also sincerely for your sake.

4. I expect you must have heard by now how the assembly at Chartres,[1] by a most surprising decision, chose me as the leader and chief of the expedition. You may be quite sure that this never was and is not now by my advice or wish, and that it is altogether beyond my powers, as I gauge them, to do such a thing. Who am I to arrange armies in battle order, to lead forth armed men? I could think of nothing more remote from my calling, even supposing I had the necessary strength and skill. But you know all this, it is not for me to teach you. All I beg is that with the love you owe me especially, you will not allow me to be the victim of men's caprice. Seek, as is especially incumbent on you, counsel from on high, and do all in your power to see that his will is done on earth as it is in heaven.

LETTER 400[2]

TO PETER THE VENERABLE

This letter was written after the assembly at Chartres on May 7th, 1150. St. Bernard exhorts the Abbot of Cluny to come to another assembly to be held at Compiègne, in an attempt to organize a second effort to save the Holy Places.

To his venerable lord and most dear friend Peter, by the grace of God Abbot of Cluny, health and deep affection, from Brother Bernard, styled Abbot of Clairvaux.

A GREAT and important enterprise for the Lord is on foot all over the world. It is already a great enterprise, for the Lord of heaven is losing his land, the land where his feet have stood. His enemies ' threaten the mountain where queen Sion stands, the very hill of Jerusalem '. The green and flower-girt bower where the virgin flower of Mary was laid amid linen and spices is being all but removed from the face of the earth, so that the sepulchre is no longer honoured but shamed, to the lasting shame of Christendom. The holy places are threatened, the places made illustrious by the prayers of the prophets and miracles of the Saviour and consecrated by his life and blood.

---

[1] Meeting held in May, 1150.
[2] Edited by Father Satabin in *Studies* for June 15th, 1894, from a manuscript in the Abbey of Anchin.

What does this mean but that the very grounds of our salvation, the riches of the Christian people are being taken away? 'The Lord looks down from heaven at the race of men, to find one soul that reflects, and makes God its aim', one soul that sorrows for him. But there is not one to help him. The hearts of the princes are untouched. In vain they carry the sword. It is sheathed in the skins of dead animals and consecrated to rust. They will not draw it when Christ suffers, where he is suffering again, unless his grievous suffering in one corner is seen to affect the whole world.

2. The Son of God turns to you as to one of the great rulers of his household. The nobleman who has gone off into a far country and entrusted to you much of his spiritual and material goods, now in the hour of need is forced to have recourse to you for help and counsel. Little or nothing was achieved by us concerning this enterprise of God at the meeting in Chartres. Your presence there was much needed and eagerly awaited. Another meeting has been arranged at Compiègne for July 15th, and we beg and implore you to be present. You must be there, necessity, great necessity, demands your presence.

3. For the rest I commend your Gaucher, the nephew of my Gaucher, who is yours too, to your favour. He is a young man who holds you in great affection as his father. Be even more friendly to him so that he may know that my intercession on his behalf is never in vain. My Nicholas greets you as though he were yours as much as mine, as indeed he is.

LETTER 401

TO SUGER, ABBOT OF ST. DENIS

This letter appears to have been written when the king, Louis the Younger, was setting out for the Crusade.

To the lord Abbot of Blessed Denis, the greetings and prayers of Brother Bernard of Clairvaux.

THIS is what I have written to the king: 'You have undertaken a great and weighty enterprise, one which no man, unless he were supported by God, could hope to carry out. It is something beyond the powers of man, yet " what is impossible to man's powers is possible to God ". If you know this, you should take great care not on any pretext to cast away such necessary help, not for any reason to offend God and so deprive yourself of his grace. You must beware now especially of ever offending God so that he should turn away his face from you in anger and withdraw his help. This is a danger that affects not only the king, but the whole Church of God, because now your cause is one with that of all the world. Listen to why I am saying this. I am hastening to your presence, even as this letter, on my way to keep the vigil of St. Mary Magdalen at Laon; but I have taken care to forewarn and fortify you by another letter.   For I have heard that the Count of Anjou is pressing to bind you under oath respecting the proposed marriage between his son and your daughter.   This is something not merely inadvisable but also unlawful, because, apart from other reasons, it is barred by the impediment of consanguinity.   I have learned on trustworthy evidence that the mother of the queen and this boy, the son of the Count of Anjou, are related in the third degree. For this reason I strongly advise you to have nothing whatever to do with the matter, but to fear God and turn from evil.   You have promised that you would not on any account do this thing without consulting me, and it would be very wrong for me to conceal from you what I think about it.   If you should do it, know that you do so against my advice, against the advice of many who love you, and also against God.   Do not think that after this your sacrifice would be acceptable to God, since it would not be complete.   While trying to save another kingdom you would be sacrificing your own by aligning it against God, against all right and justice, and against what is expedient and honourable.   I have delivered my soul from responsibility in the matter, and I only hope that God will deliver yours from " the treacherous lips, the perjured tongue ".'[1]

LETTER 402

TO THE SAME

To his most loving father and lord Suger, by the grace of God the venerable Abbot of Blessed Denis, greetings and prayers from Brother Bernard of Clairvaux.

Blessed be God who by your hand has brought salvation to the church of St. Geneviève so that this house of God is restored to order and discipline.   The Apostolic See itself thanks you for having undertaken faithfully and effectively a great work, and I too, with all those who truly love God, are as grateful to you as we can be.   I beg and implore that, in accordance with the instructions of the apostolic letter, you should do all in your power to see that the work you have begun so magnificently goes ahead from day to day until it is brought to a happy conclusion.   I do not think it is now necessary to trouble you on behalf of the church of St. Victor, because I am aware that the care of all the religious houses has been committed to you.[2]   But more care is needed for those houses in which the observances of religion are known to leave more to be desired.

---

[1] The proposed marriage with which this letter is concerned came to nothing.

[2] Suger had been left in charge of the religious houses of France as the regent of the king while he was away on the Crusade.

LETTER 403

TO THE SAME

To his very dear father and lord Suger, Abbot of St. Denis, greetings and affection from Brother Bernard, styled Abbot of Clairvaux.

YOU must discharge the duties of the king who has left you as his regent, or rather of God himself who has chosen you for this task. The restoration of the beauty and observances of St. Geneviève was plainly such a duty. This new plantation looks to you as its adviser and great protector. I write to beg you to bring to a satisfactory conclusion the work you have begun so well, and to stand out like a rampart in defence of the house of Israel, so that the godless man shall not prevail. May you deign to encourage the abbot of that place, for he is a timid man. Such an action would minister to the honour of your person and the salvation of your soul, especially in times such as these.

LETTER 404

TO THE SAME

To his very dear father and lord Suger, by the grace of God Abbot of Blessed Denis, the spirit of counsel and consolation, from Brother Bernard, styled Abbot of Clairvaux.

WHEN I saw a certain letter you had written to my lord of Tours, I rejoiced and was glad. And it was no ordinary joy that I felt but one exceeding great. May you be attended by the Day-Spring from on high for your attention to the realm of our glorious King, so as to relieve it from the stress of need and ill-fortune, which are already at the doors and would be on us but for your vigorous action. Surely it was an inspiration of God to summon a council of the princes both of the court and the Church, so that all the world may know that the king and his realm do not lack for a good friend, a prudent counsellor, and a strong helper. That king, I say, who is now on the service of the King of all ages; who is moving nations and peoples so that the King of heaven shall not lose his land, the land whereon his feet have stood. That king, I say, who, when he was full of glory and riches, when he was secure and at peace, victorious in battle, and still young in years, chose to exile himself from his own lands that, under foreign skies, he might serve him whose service is perfect freedom. Who would dare to trouble his realm? Who would dare to commit such treachery against the Lord and his anointed? O my lord king, would that they might be cut down who thus trouble you, who thus devise evil against you and yours whilst you are away, alone amongst strange peoples, saving from desolation the land which the Lord chose out of all others to make glorious with his name.

2. Play the man, then, and keep your courage high, for the Lord your God is with you in protecting the king in exile for his sake. He who can command the winds and the seas will easily calm these swelling waves. You have with you the Church of God to see that no one shall arise to make Israel to sin. All the burden, if it be burdensome to you, will be carried on the shoulders of all. Now is the time, now is there the need for you to act in accordance with the position, dignity, and power you have received, so that your name may be not only blessed, but admired and praised by this and all succeeding generations. You will have to see to it that such a large part of the Church is not put to this trouble for no purpose, and measures must be taken that render harmless or crush altogether the machinations of rebels. It is my desire to address myself to you all, gathered together in the name of the Lord, in a letter which, though it serve no useful purpose, will at least serve to show how I feel. May he who has given you this good purpose give you also the power to carry it through, and bring Satan down under your feet, so that God may be glorified, the Church honoured, the realm stabilized, and those who mutter and devise treason put to silence.

LETTER 405

TO THE SAME

To his venerable father and lord Suger, by the grace of God Abbot of St. Denis, the greetings and prayers of Brother Bernard, styled Abbot of Clairvaux.

Now is the time and the need to take up the sword of the spirit, which is the word of God, against a diabolical ruse which is sprouting up again. The men who have returned from the Crusade have arranged to hold again those accursed tournaments after Easter, and the lord Henry, son of the count, and the lord Robert, brother of the king, have agreed regardless of all law to attack and slay each other. Notice with what sort of dispositions they must have taken the road to Jerusalem when they return in this frame of mind! How rightly can it be said of these men: ' We sought a cure for Babylon, but curing her there was none '; ' and these, when thou smitest them, are unrepentant still; when thou crushest them to earth, will not heed reproof '. After so many hardships, after so many dangers, after being ' worn down by stress of need and ill fortune ', while the kingdom is at peace and the king away, those two come back to trouble and disturb the land. As you are the chief person in the kingdom, I beg and advise your Highness to oppose this thing with all your might, either by persuasion or by force. If you do this it will reflect great credit on yourself and on the kingdom, and it will benefit the Church. I appeal to force for the restoration of the discipline of the Church. I have written in the same vein to my lords of Rheims, Sens, Soissons, Auxerre, and to the Counts Theobald and Rudolph. You must oppose this evil thing for the sake of the lord king, and of the Pope, who is much concerned for the safety of the realm.

LETTER 406

TO THE SAME

To his dear lord Suger, by God's grace the venerable Abbot of St. Denis, the greetings and prayers of Brother Bernard, Abbot of Clairvaux.

M Y brethren of Maison-Dieu, in the diocese of Bourges, are in need of food. I have heard that the king has ample crops there and that they are going cheap. I beg you to command that they should be given as much of them as you, in your prudence, think fit. The king used to help them when he was in the district.

LETTER 407

TO THE SAME

To his lord and dear father Suger, by the grace of God the reverend Abbot of St. Denis, greetings and devoted prayers from Brother Bernard, styled Abbot of Clairvaux.

I AM sending a poor abbot to a rich abbot, that the needs of the one may be alleviated out of the abundance of the other. I am yielding to you the better part, according to that saying of the Truth that it is more blessed to give than to receive. I am sure that you would freely and liberally hold out your hand to this poor man of Christ if you knew as well as I do his piety and probity, and also the need in which he is placed. He is bowed down under debts and suffers from shortage of food because his fields give him baneful weeds instead of corn. But as no such sterility has affected your coffers, I beg and implore you in the name of your mercy to help him. You may be quite sure that whatever you should be pleased to give him would be well bestowed.

LETTER 408

TO THE SAME

Mabillon dates this letter for the year 1150 (St. Bernard died 1153), and in this case it would have been written after the failure of the Crusade and refer to the plan for making a second attempt. But it could just as well have been written before the Crusade had been conceived.

To his most loving lord Suger, by the grace of God Abbot of St. Denis, greetings and whatever the prayers of a sinner can avail, from Bernard, styled Abbot of Clairvaux.

THE news which the Master of the Temple and Brother John have brought I received with as much joy as if it had come from God. For the Eastern Church is now crying out in such misery that anyone who does not sympathize from the bottom of his heart with her is no true son of the Church.   But although glad at the news, I am distressed at the short notice you have given me, which makes it impossible for me to come to you at the time stated.   I have promised the Bishop of Langres that I would go to him on that day for a talk on grave and serious matters, and he is relying on me.   But I have mentioned a time when, if it suits you, I would gladly come and bring the bishop with me for he would be very useful at our conference.

LETTER 409

TO THE SAME

To his reverend father and dearest friend Suger, by the grace of God Abbot of St. Denis, greetings and the prayers, such as they are, of Brother Bernard, styled Abbot of Clairvaux.

I HAVE time only to answer your letter very briefly.   It came to-day and it is now already evening, and to-morrow I have to be at Cîteaux for the chapter.   And so I answer briefly and hope that you will never for one moment think that I have ever believed that you are in any way responsible, either by counsel or by consent, for the evils which we are deploring.   It was only that, impelled by my zeal, I was trying to express how I felt and to impress my own feelings on you so that you might be fired by like sentiments.   Also, although I was sure that your conscience was clear, I was much grieved to hear what was being said, and at the scandal in the Church.   And if they will not submit, especially in matters of this kind, what are you doing in their company?   Why do they flatter themselves on your support?   Should you not completely dissociate yourself from these transgressors of the law and have nothing at all to do with them?   Then you could say of yourself with perfect confidence: ' I have shunned the company of the wicked, never sat at my ease with sinners ', and all good men in the Church would know that you are unsullied by their company. Remember how the Prophet begins to speak to the Lord and you will find that the blessed man does not guide his steps by ill counsel.   But I beg you to believe that I have never thought ill of you, for I know your integrity too well.   Farewell, and pray for me.

LETTER 410

TO HIS UNCLE, ANDREW, A KNIGHT OF THE TEMPLE

YOUR last letter found me prostrate in bed. I received it with open hands, and read and re-read it with the greatest pleasure. But it would be an even greater pleasure if I could see you. I read in it of your desire to see me, and I read of your fears because of the danger threatening the land which our Lord graced with his presence and the city which he sanctified with his blood. Woe to our princes! They accomplished no good in the land of the Lord and in their own lands, to which they hastened back, they are doing unbelievable evil. They use their power for evil and know not how to do good. But I do not believe that the Lord will throw off his people and abandon his heritage. The hand of the Lord will triumph and his arm shall give his people courage, so that all men shall know that they would do better to hope in the Lord than to put their trust in princes. You do well to compare yourself to an ant, for what else are we, children of men, but ants of the earth, toiling for futile and useless things? What profit has man for all his labour under the sun? Let us rise above the sun and let our conversation be in heaven, going ahead with the mind to where we shall soon follow with the body. There, my dear Andrew, there you will receive the fruit of your labours, there you will have your reward. Under the sun you fight as a soldier, but for the sake of him who is above the sun. Let us who fight upon earth look to him for largesse. Our reward for fighting comes not from the earth, not from below, but is ' a rare treasure from distant shores'. Under the sun we have no profit, our reward is on high above the sun: ' good measure and pressed down and running over shall they give into our bosom'.

2. You wish to see me, but you say that the gratification of this wish depends on me, for you hint that you hope I shall send for you. What shall I say? I both wish for you to come and yet fear your coming. Poised between wishing and not wishing, I am torn between the two, and know not what to choose. On the one hand is the wish to satisfy both your desire and mine, on the other hand the doubt whether I should not believe your widespread fame which reports that you are so necessary where you are that no small disaster would follow your departure. And so I dare not send for you, yet I long to see you before I die. You are in a better position than I to know whether or not there is any way you could come without scandal or loss to the people there. And it is possible that your presence here would not be without use. Perhaps, by the mercy of God, there might be some who would return with you to help the Church of God, for you are known and loved by all. He could grant that you should be able to say with the patriarch Jacob: ' I had nothing but this staff with me, when I crossed the Jordan, and now I come back with two companies

behind me'. One thing I do say: if you are coming at all, come quickly lest when you arrive you should not find me. I am growing weaker, and I do not think I have long upon this earth. God grant that I may be refreshed for a little while with your lovable and dear presence ere I depart. I have written to the queen as you have asked me to do, and I rejoice at the good report you give of her. Through you I greet in the Lord the Master and all your brothers of the Temple, and also those of the Hospital. I also greet in the Lord through you those who are enclosed[1] and all the saints to whom you may have an opportunity of speaking, and I commend myself to their prayers. Take my place with them. I also salute with great affection our Gerard who was once with us here, and is now, I hear, become a bishop.[2]

LETTER 411

TO SUGER, ABBOT OF ST. DENIS

A letter to comfort Abbot Suger on his death-bed.

To his dear and intimate friend Suger, by the grace of God Abbot of St. Denis, Brother Bernard sends glory from within and grace from on high.

FEAR not, man of God, to put off the earthy man which is holding you down to the earth, and which would bring you down even to the regions under the earth. It is this which troubles, burdens, and aggrieves you. But why trouble about your clothing of flesh, when you are about to put on the garb of immortality in heaven? It is ready for you, but it will not be given to you already clothed; it will clothe you, but not while you are still clothed in the flesh. Wait patiently, and be glad to be found naked and unclothed. God himself wishes man to be clothed, but not while he is still clothed in the flesh. The man of God will not return to God, until what he has of the earth has gone back to the earth. These two, the man of God and the earthy man, are at variance one with the other, and there will be no peace for you until they are separated; and if there should be peace, it would not be the peace of God, nor would it be peace with God. You are not one of those who say: 'Peace, when there is no peace'. The peace which passes all understanding is awaiting you, and the righteous are waiting for this peace to be given you, and the joy of the Lord awaits you.

2. And I, dear friend, am torn by the desire to see you, that I may receive a dying man's blessing. But no man can arrange his life just as he wishes, and so I cannot dare to promise what I am not sure of being able to perform; yet I will try my best to do what I am not yet

---

[1] *Inclusos omnes.* Perhaps better Eales: ' all who are shut up '.
[2] Perhaps Gerard, Bishop of Bethlehem.

able to see my way to doing.   Perhaps I shall come, perhaps I shall not. But whatever happens I, who have loved you from the first, shall love you without end.   I say with all confidence that I can never lose one whom I have loved unto the end: one to whom my soul cleaves so firmly that it can never be separated, does not go away but only goes before.   Be mindful of me when you come to where I shall follow you, so that I may be permitted soon to come after you and come to you.   In the meantime be sure that I shall never lose the dear memory of you, although to my sorrow I lose your dear presence.   Yet God can keep you with us in answer to our prayers, he can still preserve you for those who need you, of this there can be no doubt.

LETTER 412

TO POPE EUGENIUS, ON BEHALF OF ODO, ABBOT OF ST. DENIS

Odo succeeded Suger as Abbot of St. Denis in the year 1151.   He is well spoken of in contemporary records.

EVEN if no one else were to write to you on behalf of the monastery of St. Denis and of Odo the abbot, yet I should not hesitate to do so.   It is a good cause and not open to any doubt on either count: the monastery is a noble one and the abbot a man of good reputation. The former is known all over the world and the latter is my neighbour and well known to me.   Furthermore both he and his monastery have a special claim on you.   For all these reasons I would not be ashamed to write to you even if I were the only one to do so.   As it is, others are writing as well as myself, and they are men who could not be discredited even if I were not writing.   They are familiar with the situation, they know exactly what the abbot has done, and they are not afraid to say what they know.   Backed by men of such irreproachable character, I have no misgivings in presenting my petition.   I have no misgivings in begging and entreating you to give some thought to that property of yours which Odo holds and which has been wickedly and cruelly harassed.   I beseech, I implore you to lift up your hand, to stretch out your arm, and cover him with your shield.   Let Peter's sword defend the patrimony of Peter.

2. It is in vain that they rise against this man whom public opinion exonerates, whom universal esteem commends.   Good sons, forsooth, are they to pry into the hidden secrets of their father and imagine I don't know what crimes unknown to everyone else.   They who hear of it are dumbfounded at this sudden and unexpected accusation. They are ashamed because never before has anything of this sort been said of Odo.   The Abbot of St. Denis is not a man hidden under a bushel.   He is a man set upon a candlestick; so even if he wanted to do so, he could not hide what he does.   Both his light and his smoke

must be seen by all. Have these men the eyes of a lynx to see what has never before been seen by anyone else? I confess I am very suspicious of their report. What makes me even more sceptical about it is that the ringleader of this wicked attempt on the abbot is said to be a man called Raymond. I have learned that he is a man garrulous in public and in secret a sneak; a man torn by ambition, fawning with flattery; a man wholly given to deceit and not less to stirring up trouble. I have pointed out the wolf under the clothing of a sheep, I have described him by sure signs, so that from now he will be afraid to bite and powerless to harm.

LETTER 413

TO THE SAME, ON THE SAME MATTER

IF whispers and craft should prevail against the Abbot of St. Denis, then I am innocent of his blood for I have already written to you against his detractors. But what an accusation they bring against that man! Or is it that they cannot find anything better with which to accuse him? How is it that, if their accusation is justified, he has the sympathy of all his honest neighbours? He is accused of accumulating debts, of mortgaging lands, and of neglecting property, but there can be good and even necessary reasons for all this. I have been given a full account of the situation by a meeting of the convent, and a reliable witness bears testimony that things are not as you have been told. But let there be an enquiry, for in matters of this sort the eye is a more convincing witness than an oath. Then if things are found to be as these men maliciously make out that they are, the abbot will be without excuse. But if not, then see that his delators gain nothing from their lies. They blame him for the death of a man. If he cannot clear himself of this charge, then let him die. Yet who cannot see it is most unlikely that he should deliver up to death a man whom he had recently saved from death? How can these men have the face to insinuate such a thing when they must have seen and experienced the zeal of their abbot in freeing men who have committed homicide, and in punishing those who have avenged the blood of a relation? If you knew these men well, you would not accept anything they said without corroboration. May God preserve you from permitting false lips to prevail against the innocence of the abbot!

LETTER 414

TO HUGH, BISHOP OF OSTIA, ON BEHALF OF THE ABBOT OF ST. DENIS

THE Lord Abbot of St. Denis is being accused by evil men, but by all good men, both in his monastery and round about, he is held to be without blame. I lovingly plead for your charity on his behalf because I have had and still have a very high opinion of him. May you, in your kindness, make a stand for him, not so much because he is my friend as because the charges against him are not true or even likely. If he is burdened with debt, then the needs of the time are evidently the reason, although they are nothing like so great as they are made out to be. As for his having alienated property, this is clearly proved to be false. I suppose not even his enemies have been able to suspect him of the death of G—, since he sheltered the said G— and all his friends from enemies and with much trouble rescued them from the very jaws of death. For all this, but especially because the cunning of Raymond is not unknown to me, I earnestly beg you to be attentive in upholding the innocence of the abbot.

LETTER 415

TO G—, CHANCELLOR

This was Guy Moricot, commonly known as Guy of Pisa. He succeeded Robert Pullen as Chancellor in the year 1146.

YOUR predecessor of happy memory, the Chancellor Haimeric, held the Lord Bishop of Metz in special affection. Whenever the bishop's messengers arrived in Rome he would commonly receive them in person and do all he could to help them. May you follow in his footsteps and help with the arms of the Church the noble bishop in his great necessity.

LETTER 416

TO GUY MORICOT, CARDINAL DEACON

To his dear friend and lord Guy, by the grace of God Cardinal Deacon of the Roman Church, greetings and prayers from Brother Bernard, styled Abbot of Clairvaux.

MAY you be blessed by the Lord for meeting me on the way with such abundant blessing. If there is to be found in my heart any mercy, any affection, any charity, your devout humility and humble devotion entitles you to claim it all for yourself. For some time I have been rejoicing and giving thanks for that good zeal of yours about which I have learned from my brethren. But now I feel myself to be even more indebted to you, if such a thing be possible, for the humble affection with which you have commended yourself to an insignificant person like myself. I was most careful to read to the brethren the devout and affectionate letter in which you lay bare your heart, to show them the blessing you sent them,[1] and to direct, as you asked, that the Mass should be celebrated in those very vessels. May God make you in his great house a vessel fit for noble use, so that of you too we, your devoted friends, may one day have the happiness

A gift of sacred vessels.

of hearing: ' This man is to me a vessel of election '. The Holy Spirit, ' by which the love of God has been poured out in our hearts ', is witness to my great love for you in Jesus Christ.

2. Because my jealousy on your behalf is the jealousy of God himself, not only do I pray to him for you but I also pray you to take heed how you should live in the house of God and in your appointed ministry. I tell you, not, God knows, from presumption, but from charity, that ' strictly falls his doom where heads rise high ' if they do not labour to be true to their commission, but that on the other hand ' those who have served well will secure for themselves a sure footing '. Do you, therefore, most dear and longed-for lord, turn from evil and do good. Take care not to be found seeking your own profit from the patrimony of Christ, but to be always mindful of that apostolic warning: ' Empty handed we came into the world, and empty handed, beyond question, we must leave it '. Therefore, beloved, watch over your soul for it is immortal, and see that you keep always rooted in your heart those words of the Lord: ' How is a man better for it, if he gains the whole world at the cost of losing his own soul? ' Pitiful, pitiful beyond measure, are those who spend their lives enjoying the good things of the world, so that ' full of ease, their life passes and they go down at last without a struggle to the grave '. For ' they cannot take all with them when they die, magnificence will not follow them to the grave ', because it is ' but a wisp of smoke, which shows for a moment and then must vanish into nothing '. Think of this, dearest friend, let it be your daily meditation, emblazon it on your heart, and never let it slip from your memory. Farewell.

LETTER 417

TO PETER, BISHOP OF PALENCIA IN SPAIN

The diocese of Palencia contained the Abbey of Espina, founded from Clairvaux in the year 1147. This letter seems to have been written to the bishop in reply to one in which he had expressed his appreciation of the writings of the saint.

To his venerable lord and most dear father Peter, by the grace of God Bishop of Palencia, that the Lord may meet him on the way with abundant blessings, from Bernard, Abbot of Clairvaux.

' HAD I but wings, as a dove has wings, to fly away and find rest ' in the fragrance of your ointments! My nostrils are filled with the sweet fragrance of your worthy life and blameless conduct, and it is ' the fragrance of the earth when the Lord's blessing is on it '. Truly my heart is filled with this fragrance ' as with some rich feast ', and ' the life of my spirit is in such things as these '. How can I not be filled with joy when I hear of a man who is both exalted in station and lowly in heart, who is busy and yet tranquil, and who holds the words of the Lord in reverence? ' A rare bird in our land ' is this blend of humility with great position, and this tranquillity preserved in the midst of business. O Lord, thou hast given joy to the heart of thy servant! May the Lord give joy to you also, so that you may ' share the joy of his people '. I have rejoiced with an exceeding great joy because I have heard things of you that I could have hardly expected to hear. My brethren, who are bringing this letter,[1] have told me how you ' buffet your body, and make it your slave ', of your lofty spirit, of your love for reading, of your kindly behaviour, and of the good you do to everyone but especially to the household of the faithful. Do not think, most dear friend, that I am intent on praising you. I have not forgotten that rebuke of the Prophet: ' False guides, that promised all was well; fools that gave them credence to their undoing!' Sinner though I be, I have no wish ' to sleek your head with the oil of a sinner's flattery ', but rather to anoint you with the oil of the joy that issues from a pure heart, a good conscience, and a sincere faith. I am no peddler of oil, it is all I can do to find enough with which to anoint myself in the wrestling ground of this world, yet I cannot keep silence from praising Christ. Praise is due not to the creature but to the Creator, not to him that receives but to him that gives, not to him that plants or to him that waters, for they are nothing, but to God who gives the increase. Therefore I shall praise not the man who holds out his hand but God who fills it. My mouth shall sing the praises not of the servant but of the Lord. Do you therefore, dearest friend, if you would be wise, or rather because you are wise, recognize that the grace which is in you does not come from yourself, for ' whatever gifts are worth having, whatever endowments are perfect of their kind, these come to us from above; they are sent down by the Father of all that gives light '. I know that there are some people who are, as it were, wisely ignorant of the gifts they have received from the Lord, for fear that they may become puffed up with pride and fall into the snare of the devil if they pay any attention to them. But, for myself, I think it is a good thing to know what I have received from the Lord, so that I may also know what I lack; and, with the Apostle, I think it my duty to recognize what God has bestowed upon me so that I may know what to pray and sigh for. A man who has received a gift and yet does not know what sort of gift it is stands in the twofold danger of being both ungrateful for what he has received and careless in guarding it. How can a man return thanks for a gift if he does not know he has received it? Or how can he keep carefully what he has received, if he is not aware of what it is that he has received? May the Lord save me from the disgraceful

---

[1] *Latores enim præsentium fratres nostri nuntiaverunt nobis* . . . Eales: ' My brethren, the bearers of *your* letter, reported to me . . . ' (Italics ours.)

ingratitude of that people about whom it was said: 'They had forgotten all his mercies, all those wonderful deeds of his they had
witnessed'. Even men of the world hold that no one should ever
forget a kindness. It is therefore important that we should know how
to guard what we have received, and that the grace of God should not
be without fruit in our lives; but, so that his grace may abide always
with us, we should never cease to give thanks for it to the Lord our God.
I think it might be useful to add that we should approach by three steps
the acquisition of salvation and grace: humility, faith, and fear. It is
to the humble man that grace is given, it is with faith that he receives it,
and it is with fear that he guards it. If we would rise to grace without
taking these three steps, it is to be feared that we should hear those
words: 'Thou hast nothing wherein to draw, and the well is deep'.
If we would draw the water of wisdom we need the cord which is the
Lord's gift;[1] and this is humility on the lips, in the heart, and in our
lives: 'A triple cord is not easily broken'. Let our faith be like a
water jar, only let it be a big one, so that we may collect much grace
with it. Let fear be the cover of the jar, so that the water of wisdom
may not become contaminated with the filth of vainglory, for it is
written: 'Nothing escapes defilement except what is covered with a
lid or wrapped up'. Your love of reading, which is so great that you
devour not only the books of great men but even my own trifles, has
moved me to write this letter, so that you may know what pleasure
you have given me from the same persons who told me of your
goodness.

THE ABBOT OF ESPINA

In a letter to St. Bernard (Benedictine Edition, 373), the Abbot of Espina, a monastery
in the diocese of Palencia, complains that the burden of supporting his house is beyond
his strength, and he deplores the loss of a certain Brother Nivard (possibly the brother
of St. Bernard), who had apparently been recalled to Clairvaux or sent elsewhere
by St. Bernard.

LETTER 418

TO IDA, COUNTESS OF NEVERS

To his dear daughter in Christ, the Countess of Nevers, greetings and
prayers from Brother Bernard, styled Abbot of Clairvaux.

THE venerable Abbot of Vézelay complains that you and your
vassals are preventing merchants and others from coming to
Vézelay when they want to. This is a thing that the Count William
of happy memory and his son absolutely disavowed in the presence of

---

[1] *Sit ergo ad hauriendam aquam sapientiæ* funiculus hæreditatis? (Roman ours.) Eales comments
on the word *hæreditatis*: 'Surely we ought to read *humilitatis*, as in the next sentence'. And he
translates accordingly. He may be right but it is not impossible that the saint had in mind those
words from the Vulgate: *Pars autem Domini, populus ejus, Jacob* funiculus hæreditatis ejus',
which Knox translates: 'One was the Lord's treasured possession, his own people; and it was
Jacob he had marked out for his own domain', and the Douay: 'But the Lord's portion is his people:
Jacob the lot of his inheritance'. *Deut.* 32.9.

the Bishop of Auxerre and myself, as something quite wrong and unjust. So I advise and warn you to cease from doing it in the future. I fear that if you should begin to act in this way you would do great harm to yourself in the world and to your husband where he is now, and this is what I do not want. Therefore take my advice and for the future desist from this malevolence.

LETTER 419

TO LEONIUS, ABBOT OF ST. BERTIN

To his dear and venerable lord Leonius and to the whole community of St. Bertin, the truth-giving Spirit for whom the world can find no room, from Bernard, styled Abbot of Clairvaux.

I RECEIVED your letter indicating your wish and request, dearest brothers. I shall always remember the services you have rendered myself and my brethren so generously, cheerfully, and serenely. But what if I am found not unforgetful but ungrateful? Will memory alone excuse me and not rather more sharply accuse me? But I know how to show myself grateful to my friends as well as mindful of them. If I have not the means to repay you for all that you have given me, the Lord (I speak as one less wise) will do so for me. Being only a poor and needy man I have to be liberal at the expense of another. He who searches deeply the hidden corners of men's hearts knows how well I love and honour your community and the beauty of God's house in your midst. I am not afraid to say that I love those who love me. But this is not greatly to my credit as the very heathen do as much. That I should love those who love me is no matter for praise, it would be a wretched thing not to do so and I would be a wretch if I did not do it. I loved you even before you earned my affection by your kindness, so why should I not do so now? I would be guilty of something worse than injustice if I did not esteem those who have bestowed benefits on me when they are entitled to my esteem whether they have done so or not. And so I shall always love you in the Lord, and with all the love of which I am capable I shall try to serve you in him whose servants you are, and honour you in Christ whose members you are.

2. But so that the sacrifice I offer you may be reasonable and the honour I pay you well considered, I must be prudent and cautious for ' dearly the kingly heart loves justice '. Therefore concerning that matter about which you wrote to me I answer that I dare not and you ought not to hinder a man who would do good. For how should we answer the Apostle when he says: ' Do not stifle the Spirit '? It would not be safe for you to stifle what you could not light again if you tried. And where does that other saying come in: ' Everyone

has his own vocation, in which he has been called'? Thomas has been called. It was not I who called him, but he ' who can raise up the dead to life and send his call to that which has no being, as if it already were '. This thing has come about, not by men nor through men, but by God. It is not man who has done it, but God who works on the hearts of men that he may incline them to his will. I say that this is the Lord's doing and therefore it ought to be not only wonderful in our eyes, but also unalterable. What is man that he should presume to counsel the Lord and his Spirit? He who seeks his lost sheep knows what he is seeking and where to seek it. And he knows too from whence to call him and where to place him so that he may not be lost again. But do not try to pull down again a man whom God has set up, and do not try to trip up a man whom God is helping to climb.

3. Now let us see what force there is in your objection that Thomas was offered by his parents. Consider carefully which has greater force and reason: what is done for a man, without his knowledge, by another; or what he does of himself and with full deliberation and knowledge. Yet it was not he that did it but God, who went to meet him with his grace when he was still unwilling so that he should become willing, and who supported him so that he should not be willing in vain. I maintain that the vow of his parents remains intact and that their offering, so far from having been rendered void, has been made richer. For the offering they made still holds and is still being offered to God unto whom it was first made, but what was first offered only by the parents is now being offered by the son as well. On this matter I have no command to give you, but this is my advice: The word has gone forth from the Lord, therefore do not impede the course of God's grace, do not suppress the first fruits of a good will, for what has been done in him is the work of the Holy Spirit. Do not close your eyes to the fact that you are inflicting an injury on us who have never hurt you by trying to entice away the brethren God has sent you. Thomas knows if he has broken the vow of which he has made me the witness; and so too does anyone, whoever he may be, who pushes him to do this, and he must know that I shall come up and face them on the day of the Lord. In the meantime it were better for him, for you, and for us, that we should preserve in unity the bonds of peace.

LETTER 420

TO ALVISUS, BISHOP OF ARRAS

To his venerable father and friend Alvisus, by the grace of God Bishop of Arras, the greetings and, for what they are worth, the prayers of Brother Bernard, styled Abbot of Clairvaux.

Y OU petition me on behalf of the church of St. Bertin which you love and which I have loved from the first. Nevertheless with regard to the request of the abbot of that monastery, I could have wished that you had considered more carefully what sort of thing it is that he is, I do not say doing, but even asking. I have no doubt at all that you would have then opposed him in the matter, because you would have seen that he was failing in his duty not only to his friends but also to the man whose soul he is seeking, and even in his duty towards God himself by trying to thwart his purpose. How, my lord and father, has he been able to induce you to make such a request of your friend? God is calling Thomas, he is calling him ' to leave his country behind him, his kinsfolk, his father's house, and to come away into a strange land which he will show him '. Who am I to set myself up against the Spirit of God, and hinder him when he calls his own sheep by name and goes ahead of them himself so that they shall follow no other but himself? Thomas has chosen to be poor, and are you asking me to send him back to live at his ease in riches?

2. I have no doubt at all that monks can save their souls at St. Bertin, but only those whom God has called there, for ' everyone has his own vocation, in which he has been called; and he should keep it '. But I know well enough where those words are written: ' No one who looks behind him, when once he has put his hand to the plough, is fitted for the kingdom of God '. So I would never wish to beguile my dear son Thomas, and his soul which God has entrusted to me, away from what he has undertaken. I am rather astonished that you should have been so misled in your judgement of the situation to ask such a thing of me. And I, because (as you know) I presume on your affection, might answer you in the words of our Lord to the sons of Zebedee: ' You know not what it is you ask ', if I did not think that this would be presuming too much on your charity and deferring too little to your episcopal authority.

3. Act after your accustomed manner and fulfil the obligations of your office by manfully assisting these chosen souls of Christ, so that they may not be undeserving of his love or hesitant in following his call. Act, I say, as the friend of the Bridegroom, who stands by and listens to him and rejoices at hearing his voice. And, as it is your habit to help others, help these souls, not merely by refusing to stifle the Spirit of God in them, but by proving yourself its faithful assistant. Of one thing you may be quite sure and it is that they will never deviate from their course by my advice or with my acquiescence. I know that I should be sinning myself and be making them to sin, were I to advise or permit any other course. They must pay the vows that lips have uttered, and take great care whom they believe of those who say: ' See, here is Christ, or, see he is there '. They will have to answer to me before the tribunal of Christ concerning their vow of which I am the witness.

LETTER 421

TO LEONIUS, ABBOT OF ST. BERTIN

To his very dear friend Leonius, the venerable Abbot of St. Bertin, greetings in him who sent deliverance to Israel, from Brother Bernard, styled Abbot of Clairvaux.

YOUR charity, which reveals itself on the slightest opportunity, makes it quite clear that my confidence in you is not misplaced. I am most grateful for your kindly services to my brethren who live near you.[1] What you do for them you do for me, indeed I am more pleased by what you do for them than by what you do for me personally. I beg you to continue to take care of them, for they are so far from me that I cannot help them as I should. I beg you, of your goodness, to take my place towards them, so that you may be their father and they your sons. If the time should ever come when I could repay your charity then you would not have to take my gratitude on faith, for your eyes would bear witness to it.

LETTER 422

TO THE MONKS OF ST. BERTIN

To the whole community of St. Bertin that they may serve the Lord with gladness, from Brother Bernard, styled Abbot of Clairvaux.

I AM stirred by your goodness to express my gratitude and satisfy the demands of affection. A kindness should never be forgotten, and so it would not be right for me ever to forget the gratitude I owe you for your kindness to my brethren, or rather to myself. Whatever is bestowed on my own is mine; whatever is given to my sons is given to me. Those to whom I have given my confidence are no strangers to me: I know you love us, not merely in word, but in very deed. The proof of your love and favour rests, not on words, but on deeds, deeds all the more pleasing to God and welcome to men for coming solely from your own good-will and not from any merits on the part of the recipients. For this I offer my thanks to all of you. By your kindness you have placed us all, both my brethren and myself, in your debt, if we should ever be sufficient or have sufficient to repay you. Let it not seem to you a small thing to have pleased men for you have also pleased God, inasmuch as he has said that whatever we do for the least of his brethren we do for him. And how much more is this true of you who have given, not merely to one of his brethren, but to many? I am a poor man and cannot make much return for your kindness, but the Lord will repay you for me. He will repay you who rewards all

---

[1] The abbey of Clairmarais, founded from Clairvaux, April 26th, 1140.

good men who meet his poor with abundant blessings. For past favours I thank you, and for the future I beg you not to grow weary in doing good. The time will come when, from the good seed you have sown, you will reap a rich harvest of peace and glory. May God grant the same to all of us!

LETTER 423

TO THE SAME

To his very dear friends in Christ, the whole community of St. Bertin, the greetings and prayers of Brother Bernard, styled Abbot of Clairvaux.

THUS, dearest brothers, thus may you always act. A forward disciple is the pride of his master. Anyone who does not advance in the school of Christ is not worthy of his teaching, especially when we are so placed that if we do not advance we must inevitably fall back. Let no one say: I have had enough. I shall stay as I am. It is good enough for me to remain the same as I was yesterday and the day before. Anyone who thinks like this pauses on the way and stands still on that ladder where the patriarch saw no one but those who were going up or coming down. Therefore I say: 'He who thinks he stands firmly should beware a fall'. Hard and narrow is the way, and the many mansions are not here, but in the house of the Father. Anyone who claims to dwell in Christ must needs live and move as he lived and moved. For Jesus, the Gospels tell us, 'advanced in wisdom with the years, and in favour both with God and man'. So he did not stand still, on the contrary 'he exulted like some great runner who sees the track before him'. And we too, if we are wise, will run in his footsteps, allured by the fragrance of his perfumes. If we are sluggards and allow him to draw away from us, we will only find the road more difficult and dangerous, and we will not be refreshed by his fragrance or sure of his way.

2. 'Run, then, for victory', my brothers. And you will do this if, 'forgetting what you have left behind, intent on what lies before you', you never flatter yourselves that you have reached the goal, if you 'kiss the rod; do not brave the Lord's anger, and go astray from the sure path'. 'Eat of this fruit', says Wisdom, 'and you will yet hunger for more; drink of this wine, and your thirst for it is still unquenched', so that the sluggard, who surely deserves to be 'pelted with dung from the midden', may know that his poor appetite comes not from satiety but from starvation of 'this fruit'.

3. Because 'everything helps to secure the good of those who love God', we should be stirred by the example of worldly men. Who has ever known an ambitious man content with his position and not covetous of yet further honours? In the same way the eyes of the

curious man are never satisfied with seeing nor are his ears ever filled with hearing.   Does not the insatiable desire of the avaricious man, who lives for pleasures or pursues the flattery of others, rebuke our own tepid and remiss lives?   We should blush to be found less desirous of spiritual goods.   The soul lately turned to God should blush to seek righteousness with less fervour than it had formerly pursued evil.   The inducement is very different: ' Sin offers death for wages; God offers us eternal life as a free gift '.   We should be ashamed to be less ardent in the quest of life than we were in the quest of death, less zealous in the acquisition of the pledge of life than we were in earning the wages of sin.   For, so that we should be without any excuse, the faster we run in the way of life, the easier it is; the more we undertake of our Saviour's light burden, the easier it becomes to carry.   Is not a bird all the more buoyant for the very quantity of its feathers?   Pluck them off, and it will be weighed down by its body.   Even thus is it with the rule, the sweet yoke, the light burden of Christ: the more fully we submit ourselves to it, the more we are lifted up by it; the more we try to avoid it, the heavier we find it.   The rule of silence seems to some burdensome, but the Prophet found it strengthening rather than burdensome, and said: ' In silence and in hope shall our strength be '.   ' In silence ', he says, and ' in hope ', because ' it is good to await in silence the salvation of God '.   Present consolations enervate the soul, but the hope of those to come strengthens it.

4. You have done well to add something to your first rule of silence because, on the witness of the Prophet, it is ' the service of justice '.   You have also done well to keep yourselves more untainted by the world, for this is to offer service pure and unblemished in the sight of God.   A little leaven is enough to leaven the whole lump, dying flies spoil the sweetness of the ointment.   What sense is there in spoiling, not to say endangering, the fruit of so much bodily and spiritual toil and effort for the sake of some contemptible consolation which might more truly be called desolation?   How greatly do trifles of this sort, mere wisps of smoke, hinder the sweetness of interior consolation, the graces of divine visitation!   Especially we monks, whose life, whether we wish it or not, is one of toil, are clearly unhappy beyond other men if we sacrifice so much for so little.   What folly, rather what madness for us, who have left so much, to cling to so little at so great a cost!   If we have scorned the world, renounced the affection of our parents, shut ourselves up in monastic prisons, and chosen not to do our own will but to submit ourselves to other men, how very careful we should be not to lose the fruit of all this through folly.

5. Arise then, dear brothers, arise and see that you persevere in what you have begun and make more of it than ever, so that the fruit of your righteousness may increase from day to day.   ' He who sows

sparingly will reap sparingly; he who sows freely will reap freely too.' No doubt but that a small increase of seed brings no small increase in the harvest. When I heard with joy and delight of your progress, I thought it well to write these things to you, my brothers, so as to encourage you to undertake and embrace with becoming fervour holy observances for the salvation of your souls, for you know ' it is the cheerful giver God loves '. May Christ have you in his safe keeping, praying, as you are, for us.

LETTER 424

TO ESKIL, ARCHBISHOP OF LUND

Eskil was one of St. Bernard's most devoted admirers, and the admiration was mutual. We are told that when Eskil, at great trouble and expense, came to Clairvaux with the express purpose of meeting the man of God, the monks were no less edified by the bishop than the bishop was edified by the monks. He wished ardently to join the community but was not able to satisfy this wish until the end of his life.

To his most loving father and lord Eskil, by the grace of God Archbishop of Lund, greetings in the Lord, from Brother Bernard, styled Abbot of Clairvaux.

Your letter and greetings, or rather your expressions of affection, were most welcome because of the special love you and I have for each other. Your troubles are, for this reason, my own; I do not have to make them so. I cannot but grieve for your grief, dear father, or hear of your worries and troubles but with worry and trouble. Whatever provokes you touches me and wrings my heart, and whatever oppresses you weighs on me too. I believe I owe you and you owe me all the favour and affection that absent friends can bestow on one another. I am undaunted, but I am not untruthful: it is your condescension that makes me bold. How, but for this, could I ever dare to presume to much? How, otherwise, could a small person like myself ever dare to hope for so much from a great man like you? I cannot repay you for your affection, but I have one, whose mercy endures for ever, who will repay for me. I speak of the Lord in whom and for whom you love me with such devotion and bind me to you with such affection. Blessed be your holy angel who put this in your heart, and blessed be God who disposed you to it. I am proud of the privilege of your affection, and I have been much refreshed from the riches of your heart by our most dear brother, your son William. I am refreshed by your messenger, by your letter, and by all who pass from you to me or by way of me.

2. Would that I had the power from on high to say all this to you

17

and not write it, so that I might open my heart to you by word of mouth rather than by the written word. Certainly the living word is more welcome than the written word, and the tongue more eloquent than the pen; for the eyes of the speaker lend credence to his words, and the expression of the face conveys affection better than the pen.[1] But, being absent from you, this is beyond my power and so I must satisfy myself with the second best alternative of a letter. I saw your messenger with great pleasure, and I have done all I could to further your business with the Pope. About that secret wish that burns in your heart,[2] the bearer of this letter, your William, will tell you what I think; your William, I say, and especially yours in the heart of Christ. Attend to what he says on this matter as you would to myself. My daily cares are calling me, a crowd of visitors oblige me to break off this letter before I have finished. But although all this may make my letter brief, it cannot lessen my affection. It can control my actions but not my heart. This is all yours to command as you wish for as long as I am alive, my very dear friend worthy of all honour and respect.

LETTER 425

TO THE ABBESS OF FAVERNEY

FROM Bernard, styled Abbot of Clairvaux, to A—, Abbess of Faverney, the title of modesty and virtue.

THESE good brothers, who came to me for spiritual counsel, have given me not a little pleasure by telling me of your excellent zeal in restoring the property over which, by the grace of God, you preside. But I advise and beg you to take as much trouble in reforming manners as you do in repairing buildings. It is most important that you should give your best attention not only to the convent but also to the ' Maison-Dieu ' hospice which these brothers serve under your guidance, so that it may be protected from the oppression and rapacity of your agents and vassals. I understand that, on the evil advice of these men, you have taken away the property with which your predecessors had endowed this place, and I beg you to return it. For just as it is your business to suppress or correct the misdeeds of others, so it is your duty to increase and multiply, not merely to preserve firm and unshaken, what has been done well. It seems that a priest who is living in the house still keeps his possessions outside being obliged by you either to give them up or leave the house. Farewell, and, believe me, I am ready and willing to serve you in every way I can for the sake of the good I have heard about you.

[1] St. Bernard was a Burgundian.
[2] Eskil's desire to enter Clairvaux.

LETTER 426

TO RUDOLPH, THE PATRIARCH OF ANTIOCH

To his lord and most reverend father Rudolph, by the grace of God Patriarch of Antioch, whatever the devotion of a poor man and the prayers of a sinner can achieve, from Brother Bernard, Abbot of Clairvaux.

IT is not in presumption but in confidence that I, a mere nobody, address myself to your Highness, for I am doing so at the suggestion of Brother Hatto and at the bidding of charity. Having thus briefly but nonetheless sincerely offered you my respects and greetings, I implore Almighty God that he whom he has deemed worthy of the see of Peter he may also judge to be worthy of Peter's crown. But, as you know very well, ' the athlete will win no crown, if he does not observe the rules of the contest '. Hence the blessed Apostle, when he wished to say that he looked forward to the prize that awaited him, explained first that he had fought the good fight. And if it is true that man's life on earth is nothing but a campaign, what sort of life is that of a bishop who has two battles to fight, for himself namely and for those committed to his care? The fight is against the wanton flesh, the wicked world, and those ' malign influences in an order higher than ours '. And who is capable of this? It is a three-stranded cord difficult to break. These are the three bands of robbers that came down from Chaldea to drive away the flocks of Job, the flesh, that is, with all its passions and impulses. ' Let God bestir himself now, and rout his enemies '; and it is important that he should bestir himself for he has told us: ' Without me you have no power to do anything '. And what can we do with him? ' Nothing is beyond my powers, thanks to the strength God gives me.' Do you too, my father, take strength from him and be stout of heart. Gird yourself, stand to battle, and fight hard for the flock committed to your care, the whole of which you will have to hand back to him who entrusted it to you. And fight for yourself too, for you will have to render an account of yourself. Keep an eye upon yourself in your high station, lest you fall and are all the more broken for having fallen from such a great height. Hold your high station without being high-minded, for, in the words of the Apostle, ' thou hast no reason for pride but rather for fear '. For the sensible man a high station is an occasion more for fear than for pride. A bishopric brings honour but it also brings fear. It is not the high station but the high-mind that is to blame. Who can keep a lowly mind in a high station, save the man who always fears a fall? The fear of a fall represses the haughtiness born of dominion. Let us always behave towards others as we would wish others to behave towards ourselves. We all want the deference of our subjects, and I

could wish that we were equally ready to defer to our superiors.
' One balance for getting and one for giving, one yard-wand for selling
and one for buying, the Lord will not endure.' Therefore the Lord
will not endure us unless we show the same weight and measure to
our superiors that we exact from our subjects. I cannot admire
enough the humble faith and careful answer of the centurion when
he said to our Saviour: ' I too know what it is to obey authority'.
What a truly wise and humble soul was his! Before explaining that
he was in charge of soldiers he repressed any boastfulness by admitting
that he himself was subject to others, in fact he mentions his own
subjection first, because it was more important for him to be subject
to others than to have others subject to himself. He made this clear
by the very order of his words, and by the way he arranged his petition
he indicated clearly the excellent dispositions of his mind. I did intend
to follow this up further, to develop it at greater length, but diffidence
forbids. It will be time enough to write more with greater assurance
when I know that you are pleased with the little that I have already said.
Finally I beg that the knights of God in the temple of Jerusalem may
experience in their persons the favour with which I am told you
regard me, so that for love of me you may welcome them even more
warmly than hitherto. By doing this you will render yourself more
pleasing to God and more acceptable to men.

LETTER 427

TO PETER, ARCHBISHOP OF LYONS

*This was Peter, the archbishop who was involved in the dispute over the
election to the vacant see of Langres.*

To the Archbishop of Lyons, Legate of the Apostolic See, that he may
' study his behaviour not only in the Lord's sight, but in the sight of
men ', from Bernard, Abbot of Clairvaux.

IT would be a matter of great grief to me were you to lose the
fragrance of the fair reputation which you have had hitherto in the
garden of the Church. As the stately cedar of Lebanon, so have you
grown in the Church of God, a man gracious, praiseworthy, and
loved by all. You have achieved great things amongst us, and we
are expecting things even greater from you. In the meantime keep
what you have got: do not allow your fair reputation to see corruption. The value of a good name is beyond all riches. What have you
done to the Abbot of Ainay?[1] He has already been judged,
condemned, and deposed. He has lost the place and office of an abbot.
And all this very quickly, ' in a moment, in the twinkling of an eye ',

A Benedictine abbey in Lyons.

like the resurrection of the dead! I speak with confidence because my great love for you leaves no room for fear. Yet what wrong has that man done? What evil has he done, that man whom all the Church praises? I know what I am saying when I tell you that he is well spoken of by his own people and by outsiders. Moreover, since it is still unknown whether he is at fault, and it seems that he has not evaded canonical examination, he ought either to be still holding his position or to have been deposed by a canonical judgement. You have condemned a man who has not admitted anything, whose guilt is by no means apparent, and who is not accused by his own people. You tell me his case broke down when it was being heard, because he could not produce the witnesses which you mentioned in a letter to him. Well and good, but this was because they did not appear for him but were appearing on the other side. It was as if they had been told: Either you will plead against yourselves or he will be deposed. I maintain that he could not have had those persons as witnesses, but he might have had others whose testimony would have been no less trustworthy. But let us look at the case from the other side. Granted that he is the defendant: half-way through the hearing both his defence and the case collapsed. But what about that clause: ' A faulty case may be remedied by an appeal '? And even if you did not wish to hear his appeal, yet nevertheless he ought to have been brought before him to whom he had appealed. And it is most unbecoming that heedless words and rash judgements should fall from your lips. I say that it does not at all become a prince of the Church to speak hasty words, especially in public. You will offend many people by your action against this man, and many will be very grieved at his prosecution. I will be frank with you. Several persons are asking me to write on his behalf to the Apostolic See, and they are people whose requests it would not be safe to ignore. But how can I do this without first coming to you, my lord and dear father? So I come to you with words of peace, as to one whose honour I have always had at heart; and I beg you to withdraw that most inopportune sentence and restore the man to his former position until his case has been examined with greater care. I write to you as your servant, and I do so for your own sake. I would wish to appear before God and men as your supporter, not your opponent.

LETTER 428

TO RICUIN, BISHOP OF TOUL

To the venerable Ricuin, by the grace of God Bishop of Toul, health and peace, from Brother Bernard, styled Abbot of Clairvaux, and the small flock entrusted to his care.

I GIVE thanks to the Author of salvation that I am deemed worthy to be saluted by you. Nevertheless I was as much cast down by your command as I was uplifted by your salutation; but yet, grievous as it was, I have done what you commanded.[1] Before both God and yourself, on the witness of the venerable Brother William himself, I declare in my excuse that I did not know the man was your subject when I received him. If it is the fault of anyone that he was received in this way, it is his and not mine. After this sincere and frank satisfaction of mine, I deserve your favour and blessing. Farewell.

P.S.—It is my wish for you, most holy and reverend father, that you may finish a life as full of years as of virtues with a peaceful death.

LETTER 429

TO ODO, THE ABBOT OF MARMOUTIER, NEAR TOURS

To his most reverend father and lord Odo, by the grace of God Abbot of Marmoutier, and to all his holy community united in Christ, that they may always live the life of the spirit and fervently seek the glory of God, from Hugh of Pontigny and Bernard of Clairvaux.

WE are prompted by charity to write to you for your own good because, although we are separated from each other by a great distance, we are united in spirit. The sweet fragrance of your wide-spread reputation for holiness easily brings souls into harmony with your brotherhood. But we are grieved that, from yesterday and the day before, the great tranquillity between us has been rather troubled. For your fair reputation has suddenly become clouded by the winds of evil rumour and we have been covered with confusion at the report we have heard of behaviour both unlike you and out of keeping with your good name. We greatly fear that both your good name and the pride we take in it are even now in jeopardy, unless the report which has spread so swiftly should be dispersed by more favourable tidings. And so, inspired by brotherly love, we propose to do what we can to warn you by letter of the swift retribution which winged rumour, spreading day by day, never fails to bring down upon our evil deeds. We are astonished that certain of you (God forbid that we should suspect all), deceived by their simplicity or blinded by their greed, should be so careless of their good name as to prefer the minute revenues of one altar to their world-wide renown for sanctity. It is not fitting, not at all fitting, that you should prefer any temporal gain whatsoever to the fair reputation you have earned by your holy way of life for so many years, in fact from the very first. Perhaps you will say that you have harmed no one, that you are only claiming what is due to you, and that you are prepared, if anyone

---

[1] Evidently a command to send back the subject of the bishop whom the saint had received at Clairvaux.

should dispute your title, to submit the matter to arbitration. Well and good. But what if another should answer you: 'It is a defect in you, at the best of times, that you should have quarrels among you at all. How is it that you do not prefer to put up with wrong, prefer to suffer loss?' What if another should read: 'If a man strikes thee on the cheek, offer him the other cheek too; if a man would take away thy cloak, do not grudge him thy coat along with it'?

2. We might bring up these and like texts against you if we did not prefer to correct rather than shame you. But we do say: it is safer for a Christian, and especially for a monk, to possess a little in peace than a lot with dispute.[1] Thus you sing in your office: 'Innocence, little endowed, has the better of the wicked in their abundance'. Why are you quarrelling about the revenues of an altar with the sons of Levi, that is to say with the clergy? The clergy live by the altar because it is their duty to serve the altar. But we monks, on the other hand, are obliged by our profession and by the example of our fathers to live by our own toil, and not from the sanctuary of God. Moreover the altar, about which there is this quarrel, is served only by the clergy, and yet you wish to share with them the benefice without sharing the duties. Paul cries out against you on behalf of the clergy, in fact Moses before him, 'Thou shalt not muzzle the ox that treads on thy threshing floor'; and 'Who would plant a vineyard, and not live on its fruits, or tend a flock, and not live on the milk which the flock yields'? But we look on the matter from the other side, and ask how can you, monks, be so brazen as to claim either wine from the vines you have not planted, or milk from the flock you have not tended? Assuredly if you wish to do this, you must baptize the newly born, bury the dead, visit the sick, join in holy matrimony those to be married, instruct the ignorant, correct the erring, excommunicate the proud, absolve the fallen, reconcile the repentant: and thus monks will be opening their mouths in the midst of the Church when it is their duty to dwell apart and keep silent. But in this way perhaps the servant will prove himself worthy of his hire. It is a vicious practice to reap where we have not sown, to gather what another has scattered, and it is also harmful.

3. Yet let us grant that you are entitled to the revenue from this altar by gift of the bishop, and that it cannot be considered wrong for you to have it because you have been canonically invested with it. But what about the pact you made, what are you going to do about that? Unless we are mistaken, you will not deny that, on the protests and complaints of the canons, you finally consented to put your case into the hands of the Bishop of Chartres and Count Theobald, and both you and your opponents agreed to uphold whatever they should

---

[1] Doubtless very good advice, but the Cistercians themselves were embroiled in violent disputes over tithes with the monks of Cluny.

decide would be the best way of finishing the quarrel. This was a very good and well-advised thing to do. The chosen arbitrators were men in whose justice and friendship you could have every confidence. There can therefore be no doubt that these good men and your friends would be completely honest in whatever course of action they might agree on as most likely to restore the peace. Why then do you not uphold their decision according to the terms of your pact? Do you accuse them of not having acted honestly because the exchange does not seem to be fair since you lose by it? So it might certainly seem, but only to men who are seeking their own interests, who value coins more than friends, money more than justice, and property more than charity. If you had been worldly men, and so men loved by the world, this attitude would not have seemed surprising or unusual. But now, so it seems, the children of light and peace prefer darkness to light and temporal gain to peace. These are the men deplored by the Prophet in his lamentation: 'They that were brought up in scarlet, now clutch at the dung-hill'.

4. Naturally, they say, we do not wish to keep an agreement in which we are the losers. But what if the other side should seem to be the losers? Oh then, of course, the agreement would be regarded as perfectly fair and right! Nevertheless this ought to have been fore-seen before the pact was made. Where there is no obligation, there can be no violation of obligations. But now the pact, by its obliga-tions, is concerned, not with the convenience of anyone, but with its terms. What have you to say to this, in opposing it? While you pretend to be seeking counsel, you betray yourselves as disturbers of the peace, shifters, and deceivers. Either denounce the pact or keep it. Why? You do not deny that there was a meeting, but you complain that you have been circumvented, and you blame the bishop for not being honest with you, but for having deceived you with craft and cunning, and led you on to making this pact which you now regret. You can say this, but it would be surprising if anyone believed you; even surprising if you believed it yourself. Not at all, you say: but nothing should stand which has been done without consulting us, that is without the consent of our chapter. Cannot what the abbot decides, after consulting the seniors, be allowed to stand unless all the community agree to it? Have you forgotten or are you ignoring what your Rule says on the matter? It commands that the community should be summoned to council whenever there is anything important to be decided, and that each monk should humbly give his advice, without presuming stubbornly to defend his opinion; but that the abbot, when he has heard what each monk has to say, shall do whatever he thinks best, and that all shall submit to his decision.[1] If therefore the Rule declares that the abbot's authority

Rule St. of Benedict, Chap. 3.

in the ordering of the monastery shall be unquestioned, it is evident
that you are acting as disobedient and rebel monks in attempting to
undermine the agreement made by your abbot, unless of course ' he
was only exchanging forms of speech ', and is using you in secret to
demolish what he has set up in public, thereby acting as a deceiver
himself. May we never have to believe such a thing of him, even the
suspicion of such a thing in so excellent a man is very bad. We know
that certain of you have scruples in the matter, men who are more just
than it behoves them, men who are seeking difficulties where there are
none, and that they think that such exchanges between one church and
another savour of simony. But we consider that those who are
curiously inquiring into this matter have been sufficiently answered by
learned and orthodox men; if not, it is not difficult even now to reply
to them, on the authority of the canons, that it is permissible to make
changes in the goods of the Church for the advantage of the churches.
We say this against those who are for ever interfering in what does not
concern them, and always ready to stir up trouble.

LETTER 430

TO ABBOT GUY AND THE BRETHREN OF MONTIER-RAMEY

*This letter concerns the Office in honour of St. Victor which the Abbot of
Clairvaux composed at the request of the community of Montier-Ramey. It
is of interest because it contains St. Bernard's views on liturgical worship.
The Office is published amongst the works of St. Bernard.*

To the venerable Guy, Abbot of Montier-Ramey, and the holy
brethren of his community, that they may serve the Lord in holiness,
from Bernard their servant.

You, my dear Abbot Guy, and your brethren are asking me to
compose for you something which can be solemnly recited or sung
by you on the feast of St. Victor whose relics repose in your midst.
I hesitate, but you press me; I try to excuse myself, but you urge me
on. You will take no refusal, and you ignore my only too well
justified diffidence. You add the requests of others to your own, as
if anyone would be more likely to persuade me than you. But even
you must understand that in a matter like this, it is not your affection
for me that you should consider, but the sort of position I hold in the
Church. The sublime nature of the task you have set demands that
you should require the services, not of a friend, but of someone learned
and worthy: of a man whose great authority, holy life, mature
style, would imbue his work and accord better with the holiness
of it.

2. Shall the writings of one so insignificant amongst the Christian

18

peoples as myself be read aloud in the churches? What capacity or what eloquence do I possess that from me, of all people, joyous and pleasing prayers and hymns should be required? Shall I begin anew to praise upon earth one who is deemed praiseworthy and praised in heaven itself? To try and add to the praises sung in heaven were a depredation rather than an augmentation. Not that men should deny their praises to those who are glorified by the angels, but in their festivals anything that savours of novelty or frivolity would be out of place. Such occasions require something venerable and beyond question orthodox, something redolent with holy gravity that would edify the people. But if you want to hear something new, and if the occasion demands it, then let something be chosen that would both please and profit the hearers by the dignity of its diction and the authority of the author. Furthermore, the sense of the words should be unmistakable, and they should shine with truth, tell of righteousness, incite to humility, and inculcate justice; they should bring truth to the minds of the hearers, devotion to their affections, the Cross to their vices, and discipline to their senses. If there is to be singing, the melody should be grave and not flippant or uncouth. It should be sweet but not frivolous; it should both enchant the ears and move the heart; it should lighten sad hearts and soften angry passions; and it should never obscure but enhance the sense of the words. Not a little spiritual profit is lost when minds are distracted from the sense of the words by the frivolity of the melody, when more is conveyed by the modulations of the voice than by the variations of the meaning.

3. This is what should be heard in churches and the sort of man the composer should be. Am I such a person, or is what I have composed like this? In the words of the Lord, I have bestirred myself to give you what I could out of my poverty, at your entreaties, at your persistence; if not because of your friendship, at any rate because of your importunity. I have given, not what you wanted, but what I could, according to my powers if not according to your desires. I have written two sermons on the life of the saint in my own words but based upon the ancient accounts you sent me. I have tried to avoid obscure brevity on one hand and wearisome prolixity on the other. As regards the singing, I have composed a hymn, but I have kept the sense clear at the expense of the metre. I have arranged twelve responsories with twenty-seven antiphons in their places, and I have added one responsory which I have assigned to first vespers, likewise two short ones to be sung, according to your custom, one at Lauds and one at Vespers on the day itself. And for all this I demand payment, I am after a reward. I have done my best and, whether you are pleased with it or not, you must reward me with your prayers.

LETTER 431

TO LELBERT, ABBOT OF ST. MICHAEL

To his father and friend Lelbert, Abbot of St. Michael, the affection due to him, from Brother Bernard, the unprofitable servant of the servants of God at Clairvaux.

THIS son of yours is returning to you, having, on my advice, given up his pilgrimage, although he had undertaken it with your permission. When I understood that he had taken the road through instability, and that you had acquiesced because of his importunity, I scolded him severely, as he deserved, and persuaded him to return. As far as I can judge he is truly sorry for his instability and impudence, and he promises future amendment, rightly deeming it better for a monk, however guilty, to do penance in his monastery than to wander about the countryside. It is the vocation of a monk to seek not the earthly but the heavenly Jerusalem, and he will do this not by setting out on his feet but by progressing in his dispositions. I beg you, my father, not to take ill his return to you even though you have your suspicions of his life. Rather rejoice that your son who was dead has come to life again; who was lost, is found.

LETTER 432

TO THE ABBOT OF LIESSIES

To the venerable father of Liessies and his sons, that they may ' serve the Lord, rejoicing in his presence, but with awe in their hearts ', from Brother Bernard, the unprofitable servant of the servants of God at Clairvaux.

I AM sending back to you Brother Robert, praying for him and with him, first that you may give him a kinder reception than is usual in the case of returned fugitives. The cause of his departure was different, and so the punishment should not be the same. Next, I pray that he may be removed from the grange where, so he says, he was kept for a long time, in spite of his protests, at grave danger to his soul, and transferred to another place where he can live more securely and more advantageously. Otherwise, as far as I can read his heart, I fear that you may lose him for good.

I have heard that the lord abbot is seriously ailing. Inform us with all speed, I pray you, whether he still lives or is dead, so that we may either rejoice that his life is spared, although it be but mortal; or grieve at his death, although it be for him the entry into life; or, as I confess is more likely, learn of either event with a mixture of joy and sorrow. If he should still live, we will sympathize with him on the postponement of his entry into life, but rejoice for our own sakes that he is still preserved for us; or if he be dead, we will rejoice for his sake that he should have obtained his reward, but grieve for our own sakes over the loss of so valued a friend.

LETTER 433

TO ABBOT BALDWIN OF CHÂTILLON

I KNOW that you are fond of me from the fact that you fear for me. But be of good heart, for what you feared has not happened to me. The matter has been carefully looked into, as you advised, and it has been found that the man who told you those things was speaking from spite. Of one of two things you may be quite sure: either the man spoke from ill-will or on grounds of mere suspicion. Without any doubt ' all his spite will recoil on himself and all his violence will fall on his own head '. He is guilty of the very thing he is trying to fasten on another.

LETTER 434

TO BALDWIN, BISHOP OF NOYON

This letter is remarkable for its quiet humour. Evidently, as we can gather from the end of the letter, this was considered a characteristic of the saint. It is to be regretted that so many of his letters have perished, and that these were, most probably, his personal familiar letters.

To the lord Baldwin, Bishop of Noyon, something better than he deserves, from Brother Bernard, styled Abbot of Clairvaux.

I AM sending you the small boy who is bringing this letter to eat your bread, that I may find out how mean you are from the sort of welcome you give him. But you have no cause for tears or lamentations, he has a small stomach and will be content with little. I shall be grateful if he returns wiser rather than stouter. The tone of this letter will have to serve as my seal because it is not to hand, neither is your Godfrey.

LETTER 435

TO HENRY, THE ARCHDEACON

This Henry was the brother of Louis the Younger, King of France. When the following letter was written, he was Archdeacon of Orleans.

To his dear friend Archdeacon Henry, greetings and prayers from Bernard, styled Abbot of Clairvaux.

I WILL answer your question briefly, but without prejudice to the opinions of those wiser than myself. You tell me that a child, in danger of death, was taken from its mother's womb and baptized by a layman using, instead of the common form, the words: 'I baptize you in the name of God, and of the holy and true Cross'. You ask whether the child has been baptized at all; or, rather, whether it must still be baptized if it lives. For my part, I believe that the child has been baptized, and that the words used were powerless to impair the truth of the man's faith or the piety of his intention. Not to mention that by the name of God he expressed the one substance of the Trinity, I say that by the words he added, 'of the holy and true Cross', he clearly commemorated the Lord's passion; unless perhaps we think that the Apostle taught the contrary when he said: 'If anyone boasts, let him make his boast in the Lord', but he boasted in the substance of the Cross itself as much as in the grace of the crucified when he said: 'God forbid that I should boast of anything, except the Cross of our Lord Jesus Christ'. Nor, when we baptize according to the general law of the Church, do we understand anything else but the Trinity by the formula: 'In the name of the Father, and of the Son, and of the Holy Ghost'. Moreover when we honour the Cross, we honour the Crucified. We read in the Acts of the Apostles that some were baptized not only 'in the name of the Father, and of the Son, and of the Holy Ghost', but also in the name of the Lord Jesus Christ.

2. You go on to enquire concerning the layman who baptized whether he has sinned, or whether it would be permissible for the form he used to be copied by others. But it does not at all follow that, if the action of the man seems to be excused by his simplicity so that there would be no sin or no great sin, anyone who wished could, without sin, rashly introduce a new way of baptizing contrary to the form of the Church. Even if someone should maintain that the man had sinned, yet I do not believe that his sin would be great enough to prejudice the salvation either of himself or of the child he baptized. He did not act from contempt of the ecclesiastical form, but seems to have burst forth into these words in the haste of his devotion and faith.[1]

LETTER 436

TO ALBERT, A SOLITARY

To Albert, a solitary, that he may fight the good fight, from Brother Bernard of Clairvaux.

YOU ask of me some sort of rule of fasting for yourself in your cell, and whether you may have my permission to hold conversations with women which you remember I had forbidden to you but which,

---

[1] . . . sed ex devotione quadam festinantis fidei in hanc vocem erupisse videtur.

you write, you cannot avoid on account of your poverty.   I do not now claim any authority over you.   I did not command you, but I advised you always to eat only once a day;   on no account to hold conversations with women, or to permit their visits;   to keep yourself by the work of your hands;   and much else which it would be too long to repeat.   If you perceive that you are not able thus to support yourself, then you should not have begun what you could not finish. I believe that my advice to you was safe.   You are not obliged to follow it by any command of mine, but neither will you change it by my advice.

LETTER 437

TO G—, ABBOT

To the lord G—, whatever he could wish for himself, from Brother Bernard.

KNOW that Brother G—, from the moment that he arrived here from La Chreste,[1] where he had been receiving treatment, has been able to follow the life in everything without faltering, as one of the stronger brethren.   He has not been allowed any food beyond what everyone receives, and he has always been present at the vigils with the others.   If, in future, he should act differently with you, he should not be countenanced.   You can be sure that what ails him is not his body but his soul.

LETTER 438

TO THE ABBOT OF ST. NICOLAS

To his most dear friend and brother, the Abbot of St. Nicolas, a spirit of piety, from Brother Bernard of Clairvaux.

THE enemy of Christ, the devil, has acted according to his habit by leading astray a Christian;   and I also, to whom he happened to come, have tried to act as far as I could according to my habit by reclaiming the straying soul.   It remains for you to do what you can by receiving him back now that he is reclaimed.   And so we can all hope that God will fulfil his part by rendering to each according to his deeds.

LETTER 439

TO ODO, ABBOT OF BEAULIEU

To his brother and friend Odo, Abbot of the Clerks Regular of Beaulieu, greetings from Brother Bernard, the unworthy steward of the monastery of Clairvaux.

---

[1] La Chreste (Crista Alba), a Cistercian house founded from Morimond in 1121.

IT is neither good nor honourable for you to hold on to the savings of this poor man (if indeed you are doing so), which, so he says, he gave you to keep for him. He came to me with his lamentations because he had heard of the special and intimate friendship between us. And I, presuming on the friendship, ask you, with all due respect, why you have not chosen to sell the chalice off the altar so as to keep the man quiet, if you have not got an ox or a horse to sell so that he might receive back what belongs to him. Have some respect for your good name, for the good name of your house, for this holy season of Lent which is on us, and return without delay this man's savings which you are keeping back without excuse, before the matter should become so widely known that it could not be settled without greater embarrassment.

LETTER 440

TO THE ABBOT OF TROYES

To his friend and fellow-servant Lord W., Abbot of the Canons Regular at Troyes, greetings in the Lord, from Brother Bernard, the unprofitable servant of the church of Clairvaux.

I HAVE persuaded this cleric, who desires to leave the world and remain with us, to come instead to you, because I fear that the hardness of our life would break him. I therefore commend him to you as one well known to all of us here, excellently behaved, and highly cultured; in fine, as a servant of God whom I believe will be, by God's grace, a great comfort to you. I am very fond of him and am sending him to you as much for your sake as for his, since I would gladly keep him here on account of his virtuous life, but for the fact that, delicate and unused to manual work as he is, I fear to receive him. Farewell.

LETTER 441

TO RORGO OF ABBEVILLE

To his illustrious and well-loved friend Rorgo of Abbeville, greetings and prayers from Bernard, styled Abbot of Clairvaux.

I HAVE been told that you wish very much for an opportunity of seeing and talking to me, because, in the goodness of your heart, you believe me to be one of the servants of God. And I say to you that because of your humility, and the good report I have heard of your noble life, I too would be delighted to meet you. But although this human affection in us is something good and praiseworthy, it is not perfect. For what we desire is merely the sight of each other, a fleeting bodily thing which we possess in common with the animals. We would do better to sigh for that most joyful sight of an ever-lasting fellowship, and strive by good works to arrive at it. I beg you, of your goodness, to give as an alms to my dear friend the Abbot of Alchi that land in the parish of Curren of which he has spoken to you. It is an uncultivated wilderness that has been useless to you and to your predecessors until now, but if you bestow it as an alms on the church of Alchi your own soul, and the souls of your predecessors and heirs, will be benefited before God by your good deed.

LETTER 442

TO GILDUIN, ABBOT OF ST. VICTOR

To his reverend fathers, lords, and dear friends, Gilduin, by God's grace the venerable Abbot of St. Victor, and all his holy community, the greetings and, for what they are worth, the prayers of Brother Bernard, styled Abbot of Clairvaux.

I MUST needs ask for much because much is asked of me; and I cannot spare my friends, for some of my friends do not spare me. My father and friend, the Lord Bishop of Lucca, has commended to me the venerable Peter Lombard, asking me to see that he is provided for by my friends during the short time that he is spending in France for the sake of study; which I did so as long as he was at Rheims. Now that he is staying in Paris I commend him to your care because I feel that I can ask more of you. I beg you to provide him with his keep for the short time that remains until his departure on the Nativity of the blessed Virgin Mary.

LETTER 443

TO T—, A YOUNG MAN WHO HAD PROMISED HIMSELF TO THE MONASTIC LIFE

To his very dear son T—, that he may go forth to meet the Bridegroom and his bride, from Bernard, Abbot of Clairvaux.

To use terms familiar to you: man is a rational and mortal animal. The one we are by the grace of the Creator, the other as a consequence of sin. By our reason we share in the nobility of the angels, by our mortality in the weakness of animals. Both the fear of death and the dignity of reason should stir and raise us up to seek God. ' Go not back on thy word, there lies all my hope.' I seek the fruit of your promise, the time to pluck it is at hand. Do not tremble with fear, when you have no cause to fear. To serve the Lord with joy is no burden but an honour. You can permit yourself no respite: nothing is more certain than death, nothing less sure than the hour of death. What shall I say of your tender years? The unripe fruit oft falls to tempest or the hand of man. What of your natural beauty, your comely form? 'Trust not too much to beauty, fair boy: the pale privet withers, the purple hyacinth falls.'[1] Go forth, go forth with Joseph from the house of Pharao, and turn your back upon the glory of the world. Go forth from your country and your kinsmen, 'forget, henceforth, thy own nation, and the house of thy father; thy beauty, now, is all for the king's delight'. You will not find the child Jesus among relations and friends. Go forth from your home to meet him for, because of you, he has left his father's house: 'His going out has been from the ends of heaven'. The woman who cried out to him, 'Have pity on me, Lord, thou son of David', deserved to find him by leaving her country. And he, with 'lips overflowing with gracious utterance', quickly answered: 'Woman, for this great faith of thine, let thy will be granted'.

2. Satan can turn out Satan; but the Spirit of Truth, can it act against itself? I believe it was the Spirit of Truth that told me of your conversion by your lips. See, therefore, that you turn not aside either to the right or to the left, but come straight to Clairvaux. I have written briefly and in confidence, and I am sending the letter by my dear son, your friend Gerard. Don't put forward any excuses. If you still have your heart set on study, if you still wish to learn and be under a master, the Master himself is here and calls you, the Master in whom all the treasures of wisdom are stored. He it is who teaches man all that man knows, who makes the lips of infants vocal; and when he opens no man may shut, when he closes no man may open.

LETTER 444

TO ABBOT RAINALD

This may have been Rainald the first Abbot of Foigny, a daughter house of Clairvaux founded in 1121.

To the Lord Abbot Rainald, whatever spiritual grace he may wish for himself, from Brother Bernard.

I ADMIRE your prudence in fearing to upset a monk for the sake of a novice; I admire even more your humility in bearing so patiently the great injury that has been done you; but I immeasurably prefer your charity in refusing to allow the bruised reed to be broken, and in sending him to me for advice. You have shown a prudent humility and a humble prudence in sparing the monk who has injured you, yet in such a way as not to fail in your duty towards a novice who is unsettled. I am sending him back to you strengthened in purpose and, I think, ready to correct everything of which he has been told.

1 Virgil, *Ec.* 2, 17. *Leguntur*—literally: 'are plucked'.

Mindful of your well tried kindness, I advise you and, if necessary, implore you to receive him back so that he may, if possible, turn that aforesaid brother, to whom I have sent an imploring letter, from his first decision.

LETTER 445

TO ALARD, THE MONK

This appears to be the 'imploring letter' which the saint mentions at the end of his letter to Abbot Rainald.

To his dear son Alard, the paternal affection of Brother Bernard.

BROTHER Adamarus complains that you are behaving very disagreeably towards him: that not only was he expelled from the house at your instigation but also that, owing to your obstruction, he cannot be received back. I might have believed that you were acting from a good zeal, but when I call to mind that obstinacy of yours with which, as you know, you so often in friendly confidence reproach yourself, I begin to fear that your zeal may not be very well informed. For, to quote the words of the Rule, it is exceedingly presumptuous for anyone to strike or excommunicate, let alone expel, any of the brethren, especially during the absence of the abbot and without his knowledge.[1] It would be more in keeping with your humility to behave towards others as you would wish them to behave towards yourself. Indeed it ought to be more conducive towards your perfection to act like the Apostle when he says: 'With the weak, I have behaved myself like one who is weak, to win the weak'; and again: 'If a man is found guilty of some fault, you, who are spiritually minded, ought to show a spirit of gentleness in correcting him'. You tell me it was the prior who turned him out. I know this; but it was you who persuaded him and did everything you could to induce him to do so. And now, so I hear, when the prior himself, moved by pity, wishes to recall him, you persist in your obduracy and will not permit him to correct the action he ill-advisedly allowed himself to be forced into taking. Whence, I ask you, such overweening self-assurance on your part that when everyone else would have pity on the man, and the abbot himself is willing, you alone stand out implacable? Have you ever read those words: 'The merciless will be judged mercilessly'? Or have you forgotten that 'award shall be made to you as you have made award'? Or do you scorn the reward of mercy that is promised to the merciful?

2. But, you tell me, I do not know what good reasons there were for his expulsion. I am not interested, and do not greatly care whether there were good reasons or not. What I complain about, what I

[1] *Rule of St. Benedict*, Ch. 7.

protest against, what astonishes me, is that the man by his humble satisfaction, by his urgent prayers, by his patient waiting, by his promises of amendment, has not deserved to receive from you that ' assurance of good will ' the Apostle advises and, in the words of our Master, to be tried again in all patience.[1] Certainly if he were unjustly expelled, it would be just to receive him back; if he were justly expelled, it would be merciful. Whatever the reason for his expulsion, you would be well advised, either as an act of mercy or as an act of justice, to receive him back so that he does not turn away from the just and merciful God. I ask you, dearest son, to grant at any rate in answer to my prayers, which he has sought for so long, what he has been unable to obtain from you by his own.

LETTER 446

TO SOMEONE WHO BROKE HIS WORD

ALTHOUGH you care not for yourself, yet I do not cease to care for you since I am fond of you and grieve over you. Because I am fond of you I grieve over you; because I grieve over you, I think of you. But how sad and unhappy are my thoughts! I wonder what is preventing you from coming as you promised. I cannot believe that you would break your word, so solemnly given, except for some very compelling reason, for I gather that you are a faithful and tolerably truthful young man. And I am not deceived in my opinion; it is indeed something grave and compelling that is keeping you back. The same thing that overcame David the mighty, the same thing that deceived Solomon the wise. What can I say to you? In the words of the Prophet, I say, ' A man falls but to rise, errs but to retrieve his path '. I have much that is important to say to you, too much for a letter. But this much I do say: If there lives in you the faintest spark of your old love for me; if you have any hope at all of eventually escaping from your wretched captivity; if you do not wish that confidence in the prayers and friendship of this community, which I am told you have even while living as you are, to be utterly empty and false, come at once to Clairvaux . . . that is if you are free and sufficiently master of yourself to dare to leave, even for a short time, the bloodstained monster which daily devours both your substance and your soul. Otherwise know you that from now on you are cut off from the fellowship of our brotherhood, and will never again be able, except in vain, to flatter yourself on your friendship with good men, because, by refusing to take their advice, you will prove yourself unworthy of their fellowship. But if you do not loiter but come at once, you can be sure that before you leave you will be, by God's mercy, freed of the deadly thraldom that now grips you.

[1] *Ibid.*, Ch. 58.

LETTER 447

TO AN UNKNOWN PERSON

THE biting letter which, after your fashion, you have lately written to me, shows the wound in your own heart.   At first I thought you were not serious but only teasing me, as is your habit, but a monk who chanced to arrive here from your parts soon dispersed the clouds of that foolish opinion of mine.   For, while knowing nothing of the letter save what he heard from me, he explained it in quite another manner but, without knowing it, quite truthfully; so that I cannot now have any doubt that you really suspect me of distributing the alms of the Count of Champagne[1] without any friendly consideration for my absent friends.   And this you endure because you believe that the affair was my responsibility.   But whoever thinks that the count manages either himself or his estate by my advice, cannot, I feel sure, know very well either the count or myself.   And this has been proved, since I was not able to obtain anything for some monasteries and especially for the bishop concerning whom, so as not to mention openly yourself, you have so bitterly taunted me, although I was certainly quite importunate and impudent enough in begging for them. The count distributed his goods as he wished and to whom he wished. Some of his benefactions were made under my eyes but not under my influence, the greater part of them were made without my seeing them and without my grudging them.   Perhaps I could have squeezed something out of him for myself, had I so wished.   But I thank God that, under his inspiration, I refused what he offered.   I think you should believe what I have now told you about myself rather than the rumours you hear about me.   So far as I can see no occasion remains for you to judge either the bishop or myself more unworthy than usual of those benefactions you are accustomed to make and which you do not think we deserve.   But you must know that I am ready to bear with complete equanimity the loss of what I am not considered worthy of receiving.

LETTER 448

TO THE ABBOT OF ARROUAISE

To his dear brother, Abbot G— of Arrouaise, the greetings of Brother Bernard.

WHEN Brother Dodo had consulted me in my simplicity, he took away with him the following advice or, rather, decision.   As he could not give any sound reason for wanting to change his place and Order, there did not seem any justification for allowing him to do so.   As for that vow which he said he made before he entered, since

[1] Count Theobald.

it is clear that it was only in thought, or at least in word, and no more than that, it should on no account be preferred to what he has certainly, although later, bound himself by word, by careful thought, by habit, and by profession, especially as this vow he made, and which seems to be the chief source of his scruples, was for something less strict and less regular. And so I do not think it would be safe for you, who will have to render an account of his soul to Christ, to yield to his wishes in this matter, since it is written: ' Feet that stray into the snare the Lord will punish, as he punishes wrong-doers '. Receive him kindly therefore, and watch over him carefully, for he is your responsibility and, unless I am mistaken, he is ready to follow your precept and advice.

LETTER 449

TO HUGH, ARCHBISHOP OF ROUEN

To his lord and dear father Hugh, by the grace of God Archbishop of Rouen, greetings and whatever his prayers can avail with God, from Brother Bernard, styled Abbot of Clairvaux.

I WISH you to know and I bear certain testimony that the lord Philip, Bishop of Bayeux, has granted, at my petition, to your sons our brothers of Savigny, in my presence and, at the same time, in the presence of the reverend father the lord Henry, now Archbishop of York, the lord Guy, Abbot of Cherlieu, and other brothers of ours, the ploughland situated before the grange of Écurey. Wherefore I beg and earnestly implore you, friend most dear to me in the Lord, to provide with fatherly care and affection that they shall not be molested in future on that land. Should they, either now or at any future date, suffer any abuse or violence with regard to that ploughland, I beg you to stand out like a rampart for the protection of your house, and to uphold its rights in the matter, so that it may possess the property unmolested, since this is the truth, the certain truth, that I have written to you.

LETTER 450

TO PETER, ABBOT OF CELLES

To Peter, by God's grace the venerable Abbot of Celles, greetings and whatever his prayers can avail with God, from Brother Bernard, styled Abbot of Clairvaux.

I CONCEDE and confirm to you and your house the forge situated at Troyes, which was the property of our house at Mores. Because my brethren are not able to take the revenues from it, they give it over by the hand of us, who built it, to you and to your house in freehold.   This we ratify and confirm with our seal.

Witnessed by the brethren of our house: Peter, the prior.

Jocelin, the sub-prior.

Stephen, the dean.

Walcher and Rainaud, the cellarers.

Fromund, the builder of it.

Given in the year of our Lord 1152.

LETTER 451

TO NICHOLAS, BISHOP OF CAMBRAI

To his venerable lord and most dear father Nicholas, Bishop of Cambrai, that he may ' study his behaviour not only in the Lord's sight, but also in the sight of men ', from Bernard, styled Abbot of Clairvaux.

I SEEK new evidence from you of your old friendship for me, not to remove any doubts but to confirm it.   For I am sure that you are fond of me, but as your affection . . . [MS. defective].

LETTER 452

TO MAR AND HIS WIFE

BERNARD, Abbot of Clairvaux, to his dear friends Mar and his wife, that they may love each other, but not so as to prefer their mutual love to the love of Christ.

IT is very certain that sooner or later you will lose whatever possessions you have, unless you send them on ahead to heaven by the hands of the poor.   Come, dearest friends, lay up treasure in heaven where moth cannot corrupt, where thieves will not break in and steal, and where the leader himself cannot take anything from you.[1] You have not to look far for those who will bear thither your treasure, for they who will faithfully do so are at your door, not one but many. God has multiplied their miseries at this time so as to give you an opportunity of laying up treasure in a place of endless joy and inviolable security.   Do you, for your part, recommend the same course to T—, to my brother and your good nephew, to W—, who has married your granddaughter, and to any others whom you know would listen; and I hope that especially those who are in the house of God may have the blessing of a visit from you quite soon.

---

[1] *ubi dux ipse nobis nihil vobis possit auferre.*   The Latin as it stands seems corrupt.

LETTER 453

TO A CERTAIN ABBOT

EVERYTHING he could wish for himself, from Bernard, Abbot of Clairvaux.

I AM fully aware that the brevity and aridity of my letters displeases you. My many affairs render me brief; my stony heart, arid. Pardon me I beg you, for my daily troubles are forcing me once more to put your indulgence to the proof. To come to the point. This young man from your part of the world has come to us for the good of his soul, passing you over for some reason I cannot imagine. As you know, I cannot receive him here, and so I have persuaded him to return to you for I believe that, if you cared to take him in, he would not be without use to you; and I hope and pray you will.

LETTER 454

TO A CERTAIN BISHOP

THAT he may always do the will of God, from Bernard, Abbot of Clairvaux.

ARE you satisfied that the poor church of St. Martin, more for lack of friends than for want of justice, should lose the relief of her poverty which has been granted to her by God's mercy? Otherwise, if you do not think the claim is just, it would be greatly to her advantage were she to cease from her unjustified complaints. I wish you would have the kindness to look into the matter and see that it is settled either peacefully or through justice, that is either by agreement or in the courts.

LETTER 455

TO A FRIEND

THE reason why I have not come as you asked is one so grave that, although as yet you know nothing of it, you will not be able to help feeling sorry when you do. With my whole heart I beg you to pray Almighty God about the matter. As for the affair we were going to arrange with the legate, you must do what you can in the matter alone.

LETTER 456

TO A CERTAIN JUDGE

I HAVE hitherto had such confidence in you that I have always felt I could leave in your hands the matters which concern our interests. I am therefore astonished that you should be so apathetic in the affairs of the abbey of Fontenay which I have so often begged you to visit and which, after God, I entrusted to your care. I have heard that you have not given a decision yet in the suits you have undertaken on behalf of the abbey. I shall continue to complain to you so long as you continue to delay in this matter and so long as you do not take the trouble to visit and console the brethren as you used to do.

LETTER 457

TO A FRIEND

THAT everywhere and in all things he may please God, from Bernard, Abbot of Clairvaux.

I COMMEND to your charity the bearer. He is dear to me on account of his piety, and he wants your support in some business he has with the count. Let him see by the help you give him how great is my influence with you, and how much the count is influenced by the respect he has for you.

LETTER 458

TO A FRIEND

I KNOW you always like to hear what I have to tell you. Thanks be to God who has prospered all my doings! A great work and a weary journey have just been successfully and happily accomplished. I have left my brethren joyful and in peace, well provided for and with many friends, pleasing enough, I should say, to both God and man. I could hardly have brought Brother G— back with me without offending the brethren and the bishop. After the harvest, which is now in progress, if you still have need of him, you shall have him.

LETTER 459

TO AN UNKNOWN PERSON

MY Lord Bishop of Avellino has done me a great favour, I confess, by reassuring and gladdening me with news of your good health, after having given me much desired and welcome information of himself. Nevertheless I would sooner have heard of your spiritual welfare for, in the words of the bishop, I indeed love your body, but I love more your soul. Just as I do not love my own body except for the sake of my soul, so too is my love for you; according to that command: 'Thou shalt love thy neighbour as thyself'. Therefore I prefer your soul to your body, just as I prefer my soul to my body. Take away the soul and what is left of the body, except what can be said of every human body: 'Dust thou art, and to dust thou shalt return'? The soul still lives after it has been released from the body, unless it is so loaded with sin that, when the body returns to the earth from which it was taken, the soul cannot, in the words of Scripture, 'return to God who gave it'. It is not right to love equally what moves and what is moved, what rules and what is ruled, what is of the earth earthy and what has come from above signed with the image of a higher nature. Alas, how many there are who value this grass of the field and the evil-smelling fruit thereof, which is the flesh and the goods of the flesh, not only equally with, but even more than the soul which has been created capable of everlasting happiness! You know better than this, but I grieve that you have not yet begun to live according to your knowledge. I could wish that you would 'thy own self befriend, doing God's will with endurance'. Why do you still keep the company of men with whose outlook you have no sympathy? You must either change your way of life, or ignore your own convictions. But you would do better to act according to what you have already accepted with your reason and embraced with your heart. A wise man does not scorn the advice of Wisdom: 'How is a man the better for it, if he gains the whole world at the cost of losing his own soul?' What does the knowledge of the truth advantage you, if you still cling to vanity in your life? Go off, I beg you, and depart from the company of 'alien foes who make treacherous promises, and lift their right hands to perjury'. 'Happy men call such a people as this', but do you cry out, more with the experience of the Prophet than in the words of the Prophet: 'Is not the people happy, that has the Lord for its God?' They delight in the world who are to perish with the world, but do you 'fix thy longing on the Lord, and he will give thee what thy heart desires'. Do you cling only to the Lord, so as to be able to say with the Prophet: 'The Lord is good to the soul that seeketh him'. If he is good to those that seek him, how much more so is he to those that find him!

LETTER 460

TO A CERTAIN PRIOR

THE prayers of Bernard, Abbot of Clairvaux.

I FOUND the young man who is bringing you this letter awaiting me at Châlons. When he saw me he asked me with great diffidence and simplicity to receive him into our Order and make a monk of him.

He explained that Thomas of Marla, whose shield-bearer he had been, wished to make him a knight in the service of the world, but that he preferred the service of Christ, and for this reason sought refuge with us. Consult some of your brethren and, if they should approve and you see fit, receive him and put him to the test. I have to inform you that I have secured, not by my prayers but by those of the lady Beatrice, the permission of the bishop to spend the winter near you, not at Clairvaux, but on the land of Dementin. In the meantime stir up the slothful, restrain the reckless, and comfort the fainthearted; be all things to all men and make the virtues of all your own.

LETTER 461

TO A BENEDICTINE ABBOT

THAT he may prize peace and charity.

THESE young men have good wills but not the physical strength necessary for our Order; I am therefore sending them on to you. If they continue as I have found them to be, then I am sure they will be useful to you. Take them and test them for yourself, and see whether or not I am mistaken in them. But do not be in any hurry to profess them, until you have assured yourself of their worth.

LETTER 462

TO A FRIEND

I HAVE done what you wanted. It was no concern of mine, except that it was your wish that I should do it. For how do your lands, pleasures, and relations concern me? I have always known that this man, on behalf of whom you persuaded me to intercede with the duke's lady, has been intent on evil and far removed from good, since his early youth; and so I cannot but believe that this misfortune has befallen him even more by the judgement of God than from the greed of the duchess. Although he is a sinner, I have never seen him on any pilgrimage; although he is rich, I have never heard of him giving alms; although he has for long been a steward, I have never heard of him protecting the orphan and widow. And now he continues to exalt himself above his station and above his capacity. You must know that hardly ever, if ever, can any advantage come to him from the company of noblemen. For, without considering his modest station in life, he only thinks of marrying his sons and daughters to them. But I wish and greatly desire that what, for your sake, I gladly undertook to ask for, may turn out well for him.

LETTER 463

TO A CERTAIN ABBOT

I BEG you by the mercy of God and for the sake of our common affection to receive back kindly Brother L—. He is anxious to return and he promises to amend his ways. I also beg that he may be accorded a more lenient and gentle reception than is usual in the case of returned runaways, so that he shall know that it was to his advantage to have commended himself to you through me and to have fortified himself with my intercession.

LETTER 464

TO A FRIEND

WHATEVER he wishes for himself, from Bernard, Abbot of Clairvaux.

I TOO have for long been anxious over the anxiety from which, I gathered from your letter, you were suffering. I could not but realize, when I considered the state I was in when you last left me, how much you would be worrying. But up to the present I have lacked a messenger by whom, when my body began to recover through God's mercy, I could set your mind too at ease. Now you can take heart because, although 'the Lord has chastened me, chastened me indeed, he has not doomed me to die'. On the First Sunday of Advent I was able for the first time to approach the altar of God for the reception of the sacrament, without anyone helping me; and I have written this letter with my own hand. From these two signs you will be able to gather how much better I am, by the goodness of God, in both body and mind. I would be glad to see you, if it could be arranged conveniently and without any bother.

LETTER 465

TO AN UNKNOWN PERSON

I COMMEND to you the Abbot of Farfa, Cardinal of the Apostolic See, and a man noble alike in birth and in life, that you may receive him with honour and good grace. He comes from the person of the Pope to the court of the king who has summoned him, and he has matters to discuss with him in secret concerning the affairs of the kingdom and the Church. Receive him courteously, for he is a man of good-will and, in his person, honour the two great princes of the world from whom he has come and to whom he is bound, the Pope and the Emperor. It were audacious on my part, being a person of no consequence, to venture to recommend such a man to you; but his humility in asking me to do so leaves no opportunity for my modesty to refuse. And so if I seem to have behaved foolishly in acting thus, it is his humility that has driven me to do so.

LETTER 466

TO A FRIEND

WHAT he wishes for himself, from Bernard, styled Abbot of Clairvaux.

You have composed a useful and, so far as I can see, quite orthodox work; yet I have a mind to read it through once more in your presence, if I should live to do so, and to discuss each point with you. Then if we should chance to find anything that needs altering, it could either be deleted altogether or re-written, so that it would need no further alteration. You can rejoice with me for, although the Lord 'has chastened me, chastened me indeed, he has not doomed me to die'. The axe was already at the root of the unfruitful tree, so that I was even then beginning to fear that it would be cut down; but I was restored by the prayers of my friends. By promising to dig and dung it around with their dear tears and prayers, they obtained for me a reprieve from the all-merciful Husbandman.

LETTER 467

TO BROTHERS —

You know who it is that said, ' Blessed are the merciful for they shall obtain mercy'; and, ' Blessed is the man who takes thought for the poor and the destitute', and again, in the book of holy Job, ' Thou shalt visit thy fair lands, and nought shall go amiss'. My reason for quoting to you these few texts out of so many of the same nature in the Scriptures is that the poor and destitute are in greater need than usual at this time of famine.[1] And so if you have any mercy at all in your heart, any capacity at all for compassion, now is your opportunity to show it. However wretched and disreputable they may appear, they are still your flesh and blood, and it is only right that they should be made to feel that you do not regard them otherwise than as this; that they should be made to feel this, if not by your gifts then at any rate by your kind thoughts and words. For instance, you should instruct your chaplain to excite and exhort the people, both privately and in public, to relieve their needs.

[1] This may have been the famine in 1146.

LETTER 468

TO AN UNKNOWN PERSON

How could anyone admire enough the warmth of your charity? And because it is not right that anyone should be allowed to remain in anxiety any longer than it is necessary, we bear witness to you that if our Stephen, who is also yours, should crown the good beginning that he has made with a worthy end, if he should endeavour to complete his sacrifice by offering the tail with the head of his victim, he will bring forth the acceptable fruit of penance.

LETTER 469

TO ARNOLD OF CHARTRES, ABBOT OF BONNEVAL

I HAVE received your charitable gift in the spirit of charity, if not of pleasure. What room can there be in me for pleasure when suffering claims me completely for her own? The only sort of pleasure I have is in eating nothing. So that suffering may never be absent from me, even sleep has left me. Weakness of stomach is the whole of my trouble. I take a little liquid food frequently during the day and night, so as to keep up my strength, but I cannot take anything solid. This little that I do take causes me great suffering, but I fear that it might be worse if I took nothing at all. If I sometimes take a little more than usual, it is only with the greatest discomfort. My feet and legs are swollen as though I had dropsy. But in the midst of all this, so as to conceal nothing from an anxious friend, according to the inward man (I speak as one without knowledge of such things) I have a ready spirit in a weak body. Pray our Saviour, who wills not the death of a sinner, that he will not put off my timely departure, but that he may watch over me in my passing. Support, I beg you, with your prayers a poor wretch destitute of all virtue, so that the enemy who lies in wait for me may find no place where he can grip me with his teeth and wound me. I have written this with my own hand so that when you see the familiar writing you may recognize how well I love you. But I would have preferred to have answered one of your letters than to have been the one to write first.

CHRONOLOGY OF EVENTS
IN THE LIFE OF
BERNARD OF CLAIRVAUX

1090/91	Birth of Bernard to Aleth and Tescelin the Red at Fontaine-les-Dijon
c. 1098–1108	Education with the canons of St Vorles at Châtillon-sur-Seine
1113	Entrance into the 'New Monastery' at Cîteaux
1115	Founding of the monastery at Clairvaux under Bernard's direction
1118–1119	Composition of *On the Steps of Humility and Pride*
1121	Condemnation of Abelard at the Council of Soissons
1123	First Lateran Council
1121–1125	Composition of *Apologia*
1129	Council of Troyes
1130s	Increased involvement in ecclesiastical affairs outside the monastery, especially in support of Innocent II's claims to the papacy against Anacletus. Composition of *On the Necessity of Loving God*
1135	Council of Pisa
1139	Second Lateran Council affirming Innocent II as pope
1139	Archbishopric of Rheims offered to Bernard and refused
1140	Controversy with Abelard and his condemnation at the Council of Sens
1141–1143	Dispute over the election of the archbishop of York
1145	Bernard Paganelli, monk of Clairvaux, named Pope Eugene III
	Journey to Aquitaine and Languedoc to preach against heresy
1146	Preaching of the Second Crusade at Vézelay on Easter Sunday
	Journey to Germany and meeting with Conrad III
1147	Departure of the Second Crusade
	Attendance at the Council of Etampes and the Diet of Frankfurt
1148	Council of Rheims and condemnation of Gilbert de la Porrée

1152	Council of Beaugency; dispute over the see of Auxerre
1153	Journey to Lorraine in the spring
	Death on 20 August
1163	First request for canonizing Bernard, not acted upon by Pope Alexander III
1174	Canonization of Saint Bernard

The dates given above are based on chronologies given by: Jacques Berlioz, *Saint Bernard en Bourgogne. Lieux et mémoires.* Couchey-Dijon: Editions du Bien Public, 1990; Adriaan Bredero, *Bernard of Clairvaux: between Cult and History*, Grand Rapids, Mich., W. B. Eerdmans, 1996; Christopher Holdsworth, 'The Early Writings of Bernard of Clairvaux', *Cîteaux: commentarii cistercienses* 45 (1994): 58–60; Guy Lobrichon, *Bernard de Clairvaux. Histoire, mentalités, spiritualité*, SC 380, Paris, 1992, pp. 32–41. A. Bredero proposes 1091 as the date for Bernard's birth. For dates of specific letters, consult the chart on pages 000–000.

SELECTED BIBLIOGRAPHY

The bibliography below includes primarily works published since 1990, emphasizing writings in English. A few items published just before 1990 are listed, as are some essential works in other languages.

Arabeyre, Patrick, Jacques Berlioz, and Philippe Poirrier, eds. *Vies et légendes de Saint Bernard de Clairvaux. Création, diffusion, réception (XIIe–XXe Siècles).* Actes des Rencontres de Dijon, 7–8 juin 1991). Brecht and Saint-Nicolas-les-Cîteaux: *Commentarii Cistercienses*, 1993. English abstracts of these important articles are provided on pages 403–9.

Bok, Nico den. 'Human and Divine Freedom in the Theology of Bernard of Clairvaux: A Systematic Analysis.' *Bijdragen* 54 (1993): 271–95.

Bredero, Adriaan Hendrik. *Bernard of Clairvaux: between Cult and History.* Grand Rapids, Mich.: W. B. Eerdmans, 1996.

Bredero, Adriaan Hendrik. 'Der Brief des heiligen Bernhards auf dem Sterbebett; ein authentische Fälschung', in *Fälschungen im mittelalter*, MGH Schriften B 33V,V, 201–24.

Bredero, Adriaan Hendrik. 'St Bernard and the Historians', in M. Basil Pennington, ed., *Saint Bernard of Clairvaux*, CS 28. Kalamazoo: Cistercian Publications, 1977. pp. 27–62.

Brummer, Vincent. 'God and the Union of Love.' *Bijdragen* 52 (1991): 254–72.

Casey, Michael. *Athirst for God. Spiritual Desire in Bernard of Clairvaux's Sermons on the Song of Songs.* CS 77. Kalamazoo, Mich.: Cistercian Publications, 1988.

Casey, Michael. 'Bernard of Clairvaux: the Man behind the Image.' *Pacifica* 3 (1990): 269–87.

Constable, Giles. *The Reformation of the Twelfth Century.* Cambridge/New York: Cambridge University Press, 1996.

Constable, Giles. *Letters and Letter Collections*, Typologie des sources du moyen âge occidental 17. Turnhout, 1976.

Farkasfalvy, Dennis. 'Bernard the Theologian: Forty Years of Research.' *Communio* 17 (1990): 580–94.

Farkasfalvy, Dennis. 'The Authenticity of Saint Bernard's Letter from his Deathbed.' *Analecta Cisterciensia* 34 (1987): 263–8.

Gilson, Etienne., trans. Alfred Howard Campbell Downes. *The Mystical Theology of Saint Bernard.* Lectures delivered in 1933 at University College of Wales [Aberystwith.] 'Appendices: Around St. Bernard, men and movements'. p. [153]–214.: Curiositas – Abelard – Berenger the scholastic – St. Bernard and courtly love – Notes on William of Saint-Thierry. Includes indexes. Reprint. With a new introduction by Jean Leclercq. CS 120. Kalamazoo: Cistercian Publications, 1990.

Gervers, Michael, ed. *The Second Crusade and the Cistercians.* New York: St Martin's Press, 1992.
[Editor's preface; G. Constable, Introduction; Y. Katzir, 'The Second Crusade and the redefinition of *ecclesia, christianitas* and papal coercive power'; K. Guth, 'The Pomeranian missionary journeys of Otto I of Bamberg and the Crusade movement of the eleventh to twelfth centuries'; of J. Brundage, 'St Bernard and the jurists'; H. Kahl, 'Crusade eschatology as seen by St Bernard in the years 1146 to 1148'; A. Grabois, '*Militia* and *malitia*: the Bernardine vision of chivalry'; M. L. Bulst-Thiele, 'The influence of St Bernard of Clairvaux on the formation of the Order of the Knights Templar'; M. Switten, 'Singing the Second Crusade'; J. Rowe, 'The origins of the Second Crusade: Pope Eugenius III, Bernard of Clairvaux and Louis VII of France'; G. Ferzoco, 'The origin of the Second Crusade'; J. Riley-Smith, 'Family traditions and participation in the Second Crusade'; T. Evergates, 'Louis VII and the counts of Champagne'; M. Hoch, 'The Crusaders' strategy against Fatimid Ascalon and the 'Ascalon project' of the Second Crusade'; B. Bolton, 'The Cistercians and the aftermath of the Second Crusade'; A. Derbes, 'The frescoes of Schwarzrheindorf, Arnold of Wied and the Second Crusade'; M. Gervers, 'Donations to the Hospitallers in England in the wake of the Second Crusade'; P. Edbury, 'Looking back on the Second Crusade: some late twelfth-century English perspectives'; J. Folda, 'Reflections on art in Crusader Jerusalem about the time of the Second Crusade: c 1140–c 1150'; D. Pringle, 'Cistercian houses in the Kingdom of Jerusalem'; J. Richard, 'The Cistercians in Cyprus'.]

Heinzer, F. 'Zwei unbekannte Briefe Bernhards von Clairvaux in einer

Handschrift der Zisterzienserinnenabtei Lichtental.' *Scriptorium* 41 (1987): 97–105.

Hendrix, Guido. *Conspectus Bibliographicus Sancti Bernardi Ultimi Patrum*, 1989–1993. 2. ed. augm. Recherches de théologie ancienne et médiévale. Supplementa vol. 2. Leuven: Peeters, 1995.

Holdsworth, Christopher. 'Bernard chimera of his age?', in Robert G. Benson and Eric W. Naylor, ed., *Essays in Honor of Edward B. King*, Sewanee, Tenn., 1991.

Holdsworth, Christopher. 'Sanctity and Secularity in Bernard of Clairvaux.' *Dutch Review of Church History* 75.2 (1995): 149–64.

Holdsworth, Christopher. 'The Early Writings of Bernard of Clairvaux.' *Cîteaux: commentarii cistercienses* 45 (1994): 21–61.

Kereszty, Roch A. 'The significance of St Bernard's thought for contemporary theology.' *Communio* 18 (1991): 574–89.

Kienzle, Beverly Mayne. 'Tending the Lord's Vineyard: Cistercians, Rhetoric and Heresy, 1143–1229. Part I: Bernard of Clairvaux, the 1143 Sermons and the 1145 Preaching Mission.' *Heresis* 25 (1995): 29–61.

Krahmer, Shawn Madison. 'Interpreting the Letters of Bernard of Clairvaux to Ermengarde, countess of Brittany: The Twelfth-century context and the Language of Friendship.' *Cistercian Studies Quarterly* 27 (1992): 217–50.

Leclercq, Jean. *A Second Look at Bernard of Clairvaux*. CS 105. Kalamazoo, Mich.: Cistercian Publications, 1990.

Leclercq, Jean. 'L'écrivain, Bernard de Clairvaux', in *Bernard de Clairvaux. Histoire, mentalités, spiritualité*. Colloque de Lyon-Cîteaux-Dijon. (Sources chrétiennes no. 380). Paris: Cerf, 1992. pp. 529–56. This volume contains other very valuable articles.

Leclercq, J. 'Lettres de S. Bernard: histoire ou littérature?', *Studi Medioevali* 12 (1971): 1–73; rpt. in *Recueil d'etudes sur saint Bernard et ses écrits*, IV. Rome, 1987. pp. 125–225.

Leclercq, Jean. *The Love of Learning and the Desire for God*, trans Catharine Misrahi. New York: Fordham University Press, 1988.

McGuire, Brian Patrick. *The Difficult Saint: Bernard of Clairvaux and his Tradition.* CS 126. Kalamazoo, Mich.: Cistercian Publications, 1991.

McGuire, Brian Patrick. *Friendship & Community: the Monastic Experience, 350–1250.* CS 95. Kalamazoo, Mich.: Cistercian Publications, 1988.

Newman, Martha G. *The Boundaries of Charity. Cistercian Culture and Ecclesiastical Reform,* 1098–1180. Stanford, Calif.: Stanford University Press, 1996.

Paulsell, William O. 'Bernard of Clairvaux and Church Renewal.' *Lexington Theological Quarterly* 26 (1991): 1–12.

Pranger, Marinus B. 'Mystical tropology in Bernard of Clairvaux.' *Bijdragen* 52 (1991): 428–35.

Pranger, M. B. *Bernard of Clairvaux and the Shape of Monastic Thought: Broken Dreams.* Brill's studies in intellectual history, v. 56. Leiden/New York: E. J. Brill, 1994.

Renna, Thomas. 'Bernard of Clairvaux and the Temple of Solomon', in Bachrach, Bernard S., David Nicholas, eds. *Law, Custom, and the Social Fabric in Medieval Europe. Essays in Honor of Bryce Lyon.* Studies in Medieval Culture 28. Kalamazoo, Mich.: Medieval Institute Publications, Western Michigan University, 1990. pp. 73–88.

Rudolph, Conrad. *The 'Things of Greater Importance'. Bernard of Clairvaux's Apologia and the Medieval Attitude toward Art.* Philadelphia: University of Pennsylvania Press, 1990.

Saint-Germain, Christian. 'The Intimate and its Metaphors: Two Love Letters from Saint Bernard to Ermengarde.' *Cistercian Studies Quarterly* 27 (1992): 209–16.

Schurb, Ken. 'A case study of spirituality in Bernard of Clairvaux.' *Concordia Journal* 16 (1990): 352–62.

Smith, R.U. 'Arnold of Bonneval, Bernard of Clairvaux, and Bernard's Epistle 310.' *AC* 49 (1993): 272–318.

Sommerfeldt, John R. *The Spiritual Teachings of Bernard of Clairvaux: an Intellectual History of the Early Cistercian Order.* CS 125. Kalamazoo, Mich.: Cistercian Publications, 1991.

Sommerfeldt, John R., ed. *Bernardus Magister: Papers Presented at the Nonacentenary Celebration of the Birth of Saint Bernard of Clairvaux*. Kalamazoo, Michigan, sponsored by the Institute of Cistercian Studies, Western Michigan University, 10–13 May 1990. CS 135. Spencer, MA: Cistercian Publications/Saint-Nicolas-les-Cîteaux, France: Commentarii Cistercienses, 1992.
[Introduction; J. Leclercq, 'Toward a sociological interpretation of the various Saint Bernards'; P. Phillips, 'The presence – and absence – of Bernard of Clairvaux in the twelfth-century chronicles'; M. Casey, 'Towards a methodology for the *Vita prima*: translating the first life into biography'; J. Sommerfeldt, 'Bernard as contemplative'; B. Pranger, 'The concept of death in Bernard's Sermons *On the Song of Songs*'; L. Anderson, 'The rhetorical epistemology in Saint Bernard's *Super Cantica*;'; E. Stiegman, 'A tradition of aesthetics in Saint Bernard'; B. Kienzle, '*Verbum Dei et verba Bernardi*: the function of language in Bernard's Second Sermon for Peter and Paul'; D. Farkasfalvy, 'The use of Paul by Bernard as illustrated by Saint Bernard's interpretation of Philippians 3:13'; F. Kline, 'Saint Bernard and the Rule of Saint Benedict: an introduction'; T. Davis, ' A further study of the *Brevis commentatio*'; M. Dutton, 'The face and feet of God: the humanity of Christ in Bernard of Clairvaux and Aelred of Rievaulx'; E. Connor, 'Saint Bernard's three steps of truth and Saint Aelred of Rievaulx's three loves'; M. Clinton, 'Bernard of Clairvaux and Gilbert of Hoyland on the Song of Songs 3:1–4'; D. Bell, '*Certitudo fidei*: faith, reason, and authority in the writings of Baldwin of Forde'; E. Oxenham, '"Under the apple tree": a comparative exegesis of the Song of Songs 2:3 in the sermons of Bernard of Clairvaux and John of Ford'; F. Swietek, 'The role of Bernard of Clairvaux in the union of Savigny with Cîteaux: a reconsideration'; C. Berman, 'The development of Cistercian economic practice during the lifetime of Bernard of Clairvaux: the historical perspective and Innocent II's 1132 privilege'; A. Bredero, 'Saint Bernard in his relations with Peter the Venerable'; H. Feiss, '*Bernardus scholasticus*: the correspondence of Bernard of Clairvaux and Hugh of Saint Victor on baptism'; C. Waddell, 'The Clairvaux Saint Bernard office: ikon of a saint'; B. McGinn, '*Alter Moyses*: the role of Bernard of Clairvaux in the thought of Joachim of Fiore'; M. Jordan, 'Thomas Aquinas on Bernard and the life of contemplation'; W. Frank, '*Sine proprio*: on liberty and Christ, a juxtaposition of Bernard of Clairvaux and John Duns Scotus'; J. France, 'From Bernard to Bridget: Cistercian contribution to a unique Scandinavian monastic body'; R. DiLorenzo, 'Dante's Saint Bernard and the theology of liberty in the *Commedia*; 'F. Posset', *Divus Bernhardus*: Saint Bernard as spiritual and theological mentor of the reformer Martin Luther'; A. Lane, 'Bernard

of Clairvaux: a forerunner of John Calvin?'; A. Krailsheimer, 'Bernard and Rancé'; C. Friedlander, 'Saint Bernard and the Trappists in the nineteenth and twentieth centuries'; M. Pennington, 'Like father, like son: Bernard of Clairvaux and Thomas Merton'.]

Sommerfeldt, John R. 'Bernard of Clairvaux's Abbot: Both Daniel and Noah,' in Francis R. Swietek, John R. Sommerfeldt, eds. *Studiosorum Speculum: Studies in Honor of Louis J. Lekai, O. Cist.* CS 141. Kalamazoo, Mich.: Cistercian Publications, 1993. pp. 355–62.

Teubner-Schoebel, Sabine. *Bernhard von Clairvaux als Vermittler an der Kurie: eine Auswertung seiner Briefsammlung.* Studien und Dokumente zur Gallia Pontificia, Etudes et documents pour servir à une Gallia Pontificia 3. Bonn: Bouvier, 1993.

Waddell, Chrysogonus. 'The Reform of the Liturgy from a Renaissance Perspective', in Benson, Robert L., Giles Constable, Carol Lanham, eds. *Renaissance and Renewal in the Twelfth Century* (Conference Papers Honoring Charles H Haskins). Cambridge, Mass, 1977. Cambridge, Mass: Harvard Univ Press, 1982. Medieval Academy of America. pp. 88–109.

Word and Spirit. A Monastic Review, 12. *St. Bernard of Clairvaux* (1090–1153). Petersham, Mass.: St. Bede's Publications, 1990.
[Bernardo Olivera, Help in reading St. Bernard'; Michael Casey, 'Bernard of Clairvaux and the Assumption'; John R. Sommerfeldt, 'The monk and monastic life in the thought of Bernard of Clairvaux'; Eoin de Bhaldraithe, 'St. Bernard, Thomas Merton, and Catholic teaching on peace'; Jean Leclercq, 'From the tender heart of Christ to his glorified body'; Glenn W. Olsen, 'Recovering the Homeland'; M. Basil Pennington, 'Advice to a pope'; Bernard Bonowitz, 'Custody of the heart in the *Sermons on diverse subjects;*' Marion Rissetto, 'Fish for the pond'; Robert O'Brien, 'St. Bernard's use of sacred scripture'; Hugh McCaffery, 'Transformation through petition'; M. Colman O'Dell, 'St. Bernard: fire-bearer'.]

Numerical Index

sigla:
C = Cistercian edition (Jean Leclercq and Henri-Marie Rochais, *Sancti Bernardi Opera*, vii–viii, *Epistolae* (Rome, Editiones Cistercienses, 1974, 1977).
J = Bruno Scott James.

C	J	C	J
1	1	29	30
2	2	30	31
3	3	31	32
4	4	32	33
5	6	33	34
6	7	34	35
7	8	35	36
8	9	36	37
9	10	37	39
10	11	38	40
11	12	39	41
12	13	40	42
13	14	41	43
14	15	42	–
15	16	43	47
16	17	44	48
17	18	45	–
18	19	46	49
19	20	47	50
20	21	48	51
21	22	49	52
22	23	50	53
23	24	51	54
24	25	52	55
25	26	53	56
26	27	54	57
27	28	55	58
28	29	56	59

C	J		C	J
57	60		98	98
58	61		99	99
59	62		100	100
60	63		101	102
61	64		102	103
62	65		103	104
63	66		104	105
64	67		105	106
65	68		106	107
66	69		107	109
67	70		108	110
68	71		109	111
69	72		110	112
70	73		111	113
71	74		112	114
72	75		113	116
73	76		114	117
74	77		115	118
75	78		116	119
76	79		117	120
77	–		118	121
78	80		119	123
79	81		120	124
80	82		121	125
81	83		122	–
82	84		123	126
83	85		124	127
84	86		125	128
84bis	–		126	129
85	87		127	–
86	88		128	130
87	90		129	131
88	91		130	132
89	92		131	140
90	93		132	134
91	94		133	138
92	95		134	135
93	96		135	136
94	168		136	149
95	170		137	139
96	171		138	141
97	97		139	142

C	J		C	J
140	143		182	224
141	150		183	226
142	151		184	227
143	144		185	228
144	146		186	229
145	145		187	237
146	152		188	238
147	147		189	239
148	153		190	–
149	154		191	–
150	155		192	240
151	157		193	241
152	158		194	–
153	159		195	250
154	160		196	251
155	161		197	253
156	162		198	254
157	163		199	255
158	164		200	256
159	–		201	259
160	–		202	260
161	165		203	262
162	166		204	270
163	167		205	271
164	179		206	272
165	180		207	276
166	181		208	277
167	182		209	278
168	183		210	280
169	185		211	281
170	186		212	282
171	211		213	283
172	–		214	284
173	212		215	285
174	215		216	294
175	216		217	295
176	–		218	292
177	–		219	293
178	218		220	296
179	220		221	297
180	221		222	298
181	223		223	299

C	J		C	J
224	300		266	411
225	301		267	307
226	302		268	338
227	303		269	339
228	305		270	340
229	–		271	341
230	219		272	342
231	310		273	343
232	311		274	344
233	312		275	346
234	313		276	345
235	202		277	349
236	203		278	350
237	315		279	351
238	205		280	347
239	206		281	352
240	207		282	348
241	317		283	353
242	318		284	354
243	319		285	412
244	320		286	413
245	321		287	414
246	322		288	410
247	323		289	274
248	324		290	355
249	325		291	356
250	326		292	357
251	327		293	358
252	208		294	359
253	328		295	360
254	329		296	361
255	133		297	362
256	399		298	363
257	330		299	364
258	331		300	365
259	332		301	366
260	333		302	368
261	334		303	369
262	335		304	370
263	336		305	371
264	–		306	373
265	306		307	372

C	J	C	J
308	397	350	288
309	337	351	289
310	469	352	–
311	374	353	199
312	375	354	273
313	169	355	275
314	137	356	384
315	376	357	385
316	377	358	304
317	148	359	5
318	209	360	200
319	175	361	389
320	173	362	316
321	174	363	– (391)
322	378	364	398
323	222	365	393
324	379	366	390
325	380	367	415
326	–	368	416
327	236	369	402
328	381	370	403
329	382	371	401
330	242	372	417
331	243	373	–
332	244	374	386
333	245	375	418
334	246	376	405
335	247	377	404
336	248	378	406
337	–	379	407
338	249	380	408
339	286	381	409
340	258	382	419
341	383	383	421
342	387	384	422
343	–	385	423
344	–	386	–
345	388	387	308
346	187	388	–
347	188	389	309
348	252	390	424
349	287	391	425

C	J		C	J
392	426		434	266
393	217		435	290
394	427		436	291
395	420		437	267
396	428		438	268
397	429		439	269
398	430		440	459
399	431		441	460
400	432		442	461
401	433		443	462
402	434		444	–
403	435		445	463
404	436		446	464
405	437		447	279
406	438		448	465
407	439		449	210
408	440		450	466
409	441		451	467
410	442		452	–
411	108		453	–
412	443		454	468
413	444		455	367
414	445		456	–
415	446		457	394
416	447		458	392
417	448		459	395
418	449		460	–
419	450		461	–
420	451		462	–
421	452		463	–
422	453		464	–
423	454		465	–
424	455		466	–
425	456		467	–
426	457		468	–
427	263		469	–
428	–		470	–
429	458		471	–
430	–		472	–
431	156		473	–
432	264		474	–
433	265		475	–

C	J		C	J
476	–		517	44
477	–		518	45
488	–		519	172
489	–		520	204
490	–		521	400
491	–		522	–
492	–		523	177
493	–		524	257
494	–		525	189
495	–		526	190
496	230		527	191
497	46		528	192
498	261		529	193
499	225		530	194
500	235		531	195
501	184		532	196
502	213		533	197
503	–		534	198
504	214		535	201
505	115		536	–
506	89		537	–
507	176		538	–
508	314		539	–
509	234		540	–
510	178		541	–
511	122		542	–
512	101		543	–
513	233		544	396
514	38		545	–
515	231		546	–
516	232		547	–

TABLE OF LETTERS, RECIPIENTS AND DATES

sigla:

J = James
C = Cistercian edition (Leclercq-Rochais)[1]
Date = from Gastaldelli edition
★ = the date of this letter differs, even slightly, in the Cistercian edition

J	RECIPIENT	C	DATE
1	Robert	1	1125
2	Fulk	2	1120★
3	Eaucourt, Canons of	3	1120★
4	Arnold, Abbot	4	1124 (December)★
5	To Pope Calixtus	359	December 1124–January 1125
6	Adam	5	1124 (December)
7	Bruno of Cologne	6	1124 (December)★
8	Adam	7	1125 (February)★
9	Bruno, Abp.-elect of Cologne	8	1131
10	The same, now Abp. of Cologne	9	1132
11	The same	10	1132–1137
12	Guy, Prior of Grande Chartreuse	11	1116★
13	The same	12	1133 (first months)
14	Pope Honorius	13	1126 (June-July)★
15	The same	14	1128–1129
16	Haimeric, Chancellor	15	1127
17	Peter, Cardinal Priest	16	1128
18	Peter, Cardinal Deacon	17	1126 (May)★
19	The same	18	1126 (summer)
20	The same	19	1126 (October)★
21	Haimeric, Chancellor	20	1126–1128
22	Matthew, Legate	21	end 1127– beginning 1128★
23	Humbold, Abp. of Lyons	22	1126–1128

J	RECIPIENT	C	DATE
53	The same	50	1129 (May)★
54	Haimeric, Chancellor	51	1129 (May)★
55	The same	52	1128
56	The same	53	–★
57	The same	54	1136
58	Geoffrey, Bp. of Chartres	55	1127
59	The same	56	1124
60	The same	57	1127
61	Ebal, Bp. of Châlons	58	1124–1126★
62	Guilencus, Bp. of Langres	59	1126
63	The same	60	1125–1126★
64	Ricuin, Bp. of Toul	61	before February 1124★
65	Henry, Bp. of Verdun	62	before 1129
66	The same	63	1129★
67	Alexander, Bp. of Lincoln	64	1129
68	Alvisus, Abbot	65	1129–1131★
69	Geoffrey, Abbot	66	1129–1131★
70	Monks of Flay	67	1125–1126★
71	The same	68	1125–1126★
72	Guy, Abbot	69	–★
73	The same	70	1128-1133
74	A monk	71	1127
75	Rainald, Abbot	72	1121–1122★
76	The same	73	1122–1123
77	The same	74	1125–1131
78	Artald, Abbot	75	1127★
79	Abbot of Canons of St. Pierremont	76	–
–	Hugh of St. Victor: Treatise on Precept and Dispensation	77	1127-1128
80	Suger, Abbot	78	1127
81	Luke, Abbot	79	1135–1148★
82	Guy, Abbot	80	before 1132
83	Gerard, Abbot	81	1130
84	Abbot of St. John of Chartres	82	1128★
85	Simon, Abbot	83	shortly after 1121
86	The same	84	1125★
–	William, Abbot	84bis	1125★
87	William, Abbot	85	1125
88	The same	86	1125★
89	The same (?)	506	–★
90	Oger, Canon	87	1140★
91	The same	88	1125 (summer)★

J	RECIPIENT	C	DATE
165	Pope Innocent	161	1134 (?)★
166	Haimeric, Chancellor	162	1133 (end of August)★
167	John of Crema, Cardinal	163	1133 (?)
168	Geoffrey, Abbot	94	1133
169	Geoffrey, Abbot	313	1133 (fall)
170	Thurstan, Abp. of York	95	1133 (fall)
171	Richard, Abbot	96	1133 (fall)
172	David, King of Scotland	519	1136★
173	Alexander, Prior	320	1143 (October)★
174	Henry Murdac	321	1143 (October)
175	Thurstan, Abp. of York	319	1139★
176	Monks of Grace-Dieu	507	1135★
177	Ailred, Abbot	523	1142★
178	Albero, Abp. of Trèves	510	1144★
179	Pope Innocent	164	1138 (June–October)★
180	Falk, the Dean	165	1138 (June–October)★
181	Pope Innocent	166	1138 (June–October)★
182	The same	167	1138 (June–October)★
183	Bishops and Cardinals in Curia	168	1138 (June–October)★
184	Umbald, Cardinal Deacon	501	1138 (after June)
185	Pope Innocent	169	1138 (June–October)★
186	Louis the Younger, King of France	170	1139 (first months)★
187	Pope Innocent	346	1142★
188	The same	347	1142★
189	Gerard, Cardinal Priest	525	1142 (first months)★
190	Guy of Castello	526	1142 (first months)★
191	Cardinal Alberic	527	1142 (first months)★
192	Cardinal Stephen	528	1142 (first months)★
193	Unknown person	529	1142 (first months)★
194	A Lady of Rank	530	1142 (first months)★
195	Henry de Blois, Bp. of Winchester	531	1143 (after March)★
196	Robert, Bp. of Hereford	532	1143 (after March)★
197	Stephen, King of England	533	1143 (March–September)★
198	Mathilda, Queen of England	534	1143 (March–September)★
199	William, Abbot	353	1142 (first months)★
200	The same	360	1144 (June–November)★
201	Abbots of Rievaulx and Fountains	535	1143 (around mid-year)
202	Celestine, Pope	235	1143 (shortly after September 26)★

J	RECIPIENT	C	DATE
203	Roman Curia	236	1143 (shortly after September 26)★
204	Pope Lucius	520	1144 (March–June)★
205	Pope Eugenius	238	1145 (March)★
206	The same	239	1145 (March)★
207	The same	240	1145 (March–November)★
208	The same	252	1146 (February 21)–1147 (May 3)★
209	Pope Innocent	318	1139–1140★
210	King of France	449	1139–1140★
211	Pope Innocent	171	1139 (after May)★
–	To the same from Godfrey de la Roche	172	1139 (after May)★
212	Falk, Abp.-elect of Lyons	173	1139 (after May)★
213	Pope Innocent	502	1139
214	Luke, Cardinal	504	1139
215	Canons of Lyons	174	1139 (after May)★
216	Patriarch of Jerusalem	175	1130★
–	To Pope Innocent from Albero, Abp.	176	1135–1136★
–	To the same from the same	177	1135 (March)★
217	William, Patriarch of Jerusalem	393	1138★
218	Pope Innocent	178	1135 (March)★
219	Bishops of Ostia, Tusculum, and Palestrina	230	1142 (June)–1143 (September)★
220	Pope Innocent	179	1140 (December)★
221	The same	180	1140 (December)★
222	The same	323	1140 (shortly before December 20)★
223	Haimeric, Chancellor	181	1136★
224	Henry, Abp. of Sens	182	1136–1139
225	Conrad, King of the Romans	499	–
226	The same	183	1139 (after July 25)★
227	Pope Innocent	184	1140
228	Eustace	185	1138
229	Simon	186	around 1140
230	William, Count of Nevers	496	1147 (after February 18)★
231	The same	515	1147
232	J., Count of Nevers	516	–★
233	Ebal, Count of Flore	513	1131 (February–March)

J	RECIPIENT	C	DATE
234	Berald, Abbot	509	1127–1129*
235	Buggo, Bp. of Worms	500	shortly after 1145*
236	William, Abbot	327	1139 (Lent)*
237	To summon the Bishops of the Archdiocese of Sens	187	1140 (before June 2)
238	The Bishops and Cardinals in Curia	188	1140 (before June 2)
239	Pope Innocent	189	1140 (shortly after June 2)*
–	Treatise on the Errors of Abelard	190	1139-1140*
–	Pope Innocent from the Abp. of Rheims	191	1140 (shortly after June 2)*
240	Guy of Castello	192	1140 (June)*
241	Ivo, Cardinal	193	1140 (June)*
242	Pope Innocent	330	1140 (June)*
243	Stephen, Cardinal	331	1140 (June)*
244	G—, Cardinal	332	1140 (June)*
245	Gregory, Cardinal	333	1140 (June)*
246	Guy of Pisa	334	1140 (June)*
247	A Cardinal Priest	335	1140 (June)*
248	An Abbot	336	1140 (June)*
–	To Pope Innocent from the Bishops of France	337	1140 (June)*
249	Haimeric, Chancellor	338	1140 (June)*
–	Rescript of Pope Innocent	194	July 16, 1140*
250	Bp. of Constance	195	1142
251	Guy, Cardinal	196	1143*
252	Pope Innocent	348	1141*
253	Peter, Dean	197	1141
254	Pope Innocent	198	1141
255	The same	199	1141
256	Ulger, Bp. of Angers	200	1142 (spring)*
257	The same	524	–
258	Pope Innocent	340	1143 (around mid-year)
259	Baldwin, Abbot	201	1137*
260	Clergy of Sens	202	1142 (January–March)*
261	Atto, Bp. of Troyes	498	–
262	The same	203	1140
263	The same	427	1138-1146 (?)*
–	An Abbot (same as C 425)	428	–

J	RECIPIENT	C	DATE
264	Pope Innocent	432	1138 –1143
265	The same	433	1138 –1143
266	The same	434	1138 –1143
267	The same	437	1138 –1143
268	The same	438	1138 –1143
269	The same	439	1138–1143
270	Abbot of St. Aubin	204	1140
271	Bishop of Rochester	205	1142
272	Queen of Jerusalem	206	–
273	The same	354	1143–1144
274	The same	289	1153
275	The same	355	1141*
276	Roger, King of Sicily	207	1140 (circa)*
277	The same	208	1140 (circa)*
278	The same	209	1140 (circa)*
279	Amedeus, Abbot	447	1140*
280	Pope Innocent	210	1140*
281	The same	211	1141 (November December)*
282	The same	212	1143*
283	The same	213	1139
284	The same	214	1140
285	The same	215	1140
286	The same	339	1141–1142*
287	The same	349	–*
288	The same	350	before 1143*
289	The same	351	1143 (first months)*
–	Privilege granted by Pope Innocent	352	1142 (first months)
290	Pope Innocent	435	1138 -1143
291	The same	436	1138 -1143
292	The same	218	1143
293	Bishops in Curia	219	1143
294	Pope Innocent	216	1142 (before June)*
295	The same	217	1143
296	Louis, King of France	220	1143
297	The same	221	1143
298	Jocelin, Bp., and Suger, Abbot	222	1143 (September)*
299	Jocelin, Bp. of Soissons	223	1143 (September)*
300	Stephen of Palestrina	224	1143 (September–October)*
301	Jocelin, Bp. of Soissons	225	1144 (March–April)*

J	RECIPIENT	C	DATE
372	Hugh, Cardinal	307	1150*
373	The same	306	1150 (?)
374	Haimeric, Chancellor	311	1125*
375	Raynald, Abp. of Rheims	312	1124 (?)*
376	Matilda, Queen of England	315	after 1135*
377	Henry, Abp., and Haimeric, Chancellor	316	1135
378	Hugh, novice	322	1138
379	Robert, Abbot	324	1138*
380	The same	325	1138–1153
—	To St. Bernard from Abbot William and Bp. Geoffrey	326	1139 (before Easter)
381	The Roman Pontiff	328	1145 (March–November)*
382	Bp. of Limoges	329	1146
383	Malachy, Abp. of Ireland	341	1140
384	The same	356	1141*
385	The same	357	1142*
386	The brethren in Ireland	374	1148 (shortly after November 3)
387	Jocelin, Bp. of Soisson	342	1141 (January 26 –May 18)*
—	From Abbot Bernard of Italy to Pope Innocent	343	1140
—	From the same to St. Bernard	344	1140
388	The brethren of St. Anastasius	345	1141–1145*
389	Theobald, Abp.	361	1150 –1152*
—	The Archbishops, Bishops, and all the clergy and people of Eastern France and Bavaria	363	1146 (August–September)
390	Hildegarde, Abbess	366	1147*
391	The English People (parallel to M 363)	(363)	1146 (August–September)*
392	Wladislaus, Duke	458	1147 (shortly after February 13)*
393	Henry, Abp. of Mainz	365	1146 (August–September)*
394	All the Faithful	457	1147 (after March 13)*
395	G— de Stoph	459	1147 (shortly after January)*
396	His Brother Abbots	544	1146–1147*
397	Alphonsus, King of Portugal	308	apocryphal letter

J	RECIPIENT	C	DATE
398	Peter the Venerable	364	1150 (March–April)★
399	Pope Eugenius	256	1150 (May–June)★
400	Peter the Venerable	521	1150 (May–June)★
401	Suger, Abbot	371	1146 (around mid-year)★
402	The same	369	1148 (August–September)★
403	The same	370	1148 (last months)★
404	The same	377	1149 (shortly before May 8)★
405	The same	376	1149 (first three months)★
406	The same	378	1149
407	The same	379	1149
408	The same	380	1150 (April)★
409	The same	381	1143 (shortly before September 14)★
410	Andrew, his uncle	288	1153
411	Suger, Abbot	266	1150 (December)★
412	Pope Eugenius	285	1152★
413	The same	286	1152★
414	Hugh, Bp. of Ostia	287	1152★
415	G—, Chancellor	367	1147★
416	Guy Moricot, Cardinal	368	1147
417	Peter, Bp. of Palencia	372	1146–1147
–	From the Abbot of Espina to St. Bernard	373	–
418	Ida, Countess of Nevers	375	1148 (March–April)★
419	Leonius, Abbot and community	382	1138–1145★
420	Alvisus, Bp. of Arras	395	1138–1145★
421	Leonius, Abbot	383	1140–1145★
422	The monks of St. Bertin	384	1140–1145★
423	The same	385	1139 (around mid-year)★
–	From John of Casamare to St. Bernard	386	1149
424	Eskil, Abp. of Lund	390	1152
425	Abbess of Faverney	391	1132★
426	Rudolph, Patriarch of Antioch	392	1138★
427	Peter, Abp. of Lyons	394	1136★
428	Ricuin, Bp. of Toul	396	before February 1124★
429	Odo, Abbot	397	1124–1137

J	RECIPIENT	C	DATE
430	Guy, Abbot	398	after 1137★
431	Lelbert, Abbot	399	1122 (?)★
432	Abbot of Liessies	400	1124–1147 (?)★
433	Baldwin, Abbot	401	before 1146★
434	Baldwin, Bp. of Noyon	402	1148–1153
435	Henry, Archdeacon	403	1142–1146★
436	Albert, a solitary	404	–
437	G—, Abbot	405	1140–1144 (?)★
438	Abbot of St. Nicholas	406	1123 or 1124 (after September 9)★
439	Odo, Abbot	407	1140–1146
440	Abbot of Troyes	408	–★
441	Rorgo of Abbeville	409	–★
442	Gilduin, Abbot	410	1136★
443	T—, a young man	412	shortly before 1138★
444	Rainald, Abbot	413	1121–1131
445	Alard, monk	414	–
446	Someone who broke his word	415	–
447	Unknown person	416	–
448	Abbot of Arrouaise	417	before 1147★
449	Hugh, Abp. of Rouen	418	1153
450	Peter, Abbot	419	1152
451	Nicholas, Bp. of Cambrai	420	–
452	Mar and his wife	421	–★
453	An Abbot	422	1121–1131★
454	A Bishop	423	–
455	A friend	424	–
456	A judge	425	–
457	A friend	426	–
458	A friend	429	–
–	A friend (same as C 377)	430	–
459	Unknown person	440	–
460	A Prior	441	1116–1117★
461	A Benedictine Abbot	442	–
462	A friend	443	–
–	An Abbot (same as C 448)	444	–
463	An Abbot	445	–
464	A friend	446	1152 (December)★
465	Unknown person	448	1144★
466	A friend	450	1152 (December)★
467	To Brothers —	451	–★
–	An abbot (same as C 88)	452	–

J	RECIPIENT	C	DATE
–	Unknown person (same as C 444)	453	–
468	Unknown person	454	1125*
spurious	Raymund	456	not by Bernard
469	Arnold of Chartres	310	1153

[1]*Sancti Bernardi Opera*, 8 volumes. Edited by J. Leclercq, H.M. Rochais, C.H. Talbot, Rome: Editiones Cistercienses, 1957–1977.

INDEX

(References are to James's letter numbers, not pages. Identification of persons mentioned in the letters is sometimes tentative, due to insufficient information. I = James's introduction. NI = Kienzle's new introduction.)